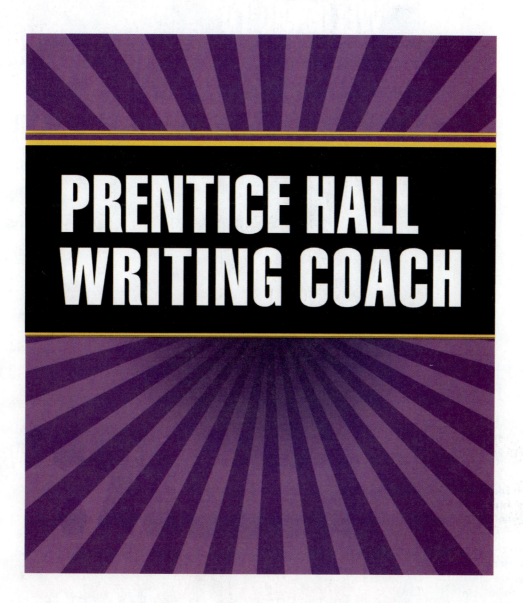

PEARSON

Upper Saddle River, New Jersey
Boston, Massachusetts
Chandler, Arizona
Glenview, Illinois

WRITING COACH

WELCOME TO Writing COACH

Seven Great Reasons to Learn to Write Well

Acknowledgments appear on page R58, which constitute an extension of this copyright page.

Copyright © 2012 Pearson Education, Inc., or its affiliates. All Rights Reserved. Printed in the United States of America. This publication is protected by copyright, and permission should be obtained from the publisher prior to any prohibited reproduction, storage in a retrieval system, or transmission in any form or by any means, electronic, mechanical, photocopying, recording, or likewise. For information regarding permissions, write to Pearson Curriculum Group Rights & Permissions, One Lake Street, Upper Saddle River, New Jersey 07458.

Pearson, Prentice Hall, and Pearson Prentice Hall are trademarks, in the U.S. and/or other countries, of Pearson Education, Inc., or its affiliates.

PEARSON

0-13-253144-5
978-0-13-253144-3
9 10 V063 14 13

1 Writing is hard, but hard is **rewarding**.

2 Writing helps you **sort things out**.

3 Writing helps you **persuade** others.

4 Writing makes you a **better reader**.

5 Writing makes you **smarter**.

6 Writing helps you get into and through **college**.

7 Writing **prepares you** for the world of work.

AUTHORS

The contributing authors guided the direction and philosophy of *Prentice Hall Writing Coach*. Working with the development team, they helped to build the pedagogical integrity of the program and to ensure its relevance for today's teachers and students.

Program Authors

Jeff Anderson

Jeff Anderson has worked with struggling writers and readers for almost 20 years. His works integrate grammar and editing instruction into the processes of reading and writing. Anderson has written articles in NCTE's *Voices from the Middle, English Journal*, and *Educational Leadership*. Anderson won the NCTE Paul and Kate Farmer Award for his *English Journal* article on teaching grammar in context. He has published two books, *Mechanically Inclined: Building Grammar, Usage, and Style into Writer's Workshop* and *Everyday Editing: Inviting Students to Develop Skill and Craft in Writer's Workshop* as well as a DVD, *The Craft of Grammar*.

Grammar gives me a powerful lens through which to look at my writing. It gives me the freedom to say things exactly the way I want to say them.

Kelly Gallagher

Kelly Gallagher is a full-time English teacher at Magnolia High School in Anaheim, California. He is the former co-director of the South Basin Writing Project at California State University, Long Beach. Gallagher is the author of *Reading Reasons: Motivational Mini-Lessons for the Middle and High School, Deeper Reading: Comprehending Challenging Texts 4–12, Teaching Adolescent Writers,* and *Readicide*. He is also featured in the video series, *Building Adolescent Readers*. With a focus on adolescent literacy, Gallagher provides training to educators on a local, national and international level. Gallagher was awarded the Secondary Award of Classroom Excellence from the California Association of Teachers of English—the state's top English teacher honor.

The best swimmers swim the most; the best writers write the most. There's only one way to become a good writer: write!

Contributing Authors

Evelyn Arroyo

Evelyn Arroyo is the author of **A+RISE,** Research-based Instructional Strategies for ELLs (English Language Learners). Her work focuses on closing the achievement gap for minority students and English language learners. Through her publications and presentations, Arroyo provides advice, encouragement, and practical success strategies to help teachers reach their ELL students.

Your rich, colorful cultural life experiences are unique and can easily be painted through words. These experiences define who you are today, and writing is one way to begin capturing your history. Become a risk-taker and fall in love with yourself through your own words.

When you're learning a new language, writing in that language takes effort. The effort pays off big time, though. Writing helps us generate ideas, solve problems, figure out how the language works, and, above all, allows us to express ourselves.

Jim Cummins, Ph.D.

Jim Cummins is a Professor in the Modern Language Centre at the University of Toronto. A well-known educator, lecturer, and author, Cummins focuses his research on bilingual education and the academic achievement of culturally diverse students. He is the author of numerous publications, including **Negotiating Identities: Education for Empowerment in a Diverse Society.**

Grant Wiggins, Ed.D.

Grant Wiggins is the President of Authentic Education. He earned his Ed.D. from Harvard University. Grant consults with schools, districts, and state education departments; organizes conferences and workshops; and develops resources on curricular change. He is the co-author, with Jay McTighe, of **Understanding By Design,** the award-winning text published by ASCD.

I hated writing as a student—and my grades showed it. I grew up to be a writer, though. What changed? I began to think I had something to say. That's ultimately why you write: to find out what you are really thinking, really feeling, really believing.

Concepts of grammar can sharpen your reading, communication, and even your reasoning, so I have championed its practice in my classes and in my businesses. Even adults are quick to recognize that a refresher in grammar makes them keener—and more marketable.

Gary Forlini

Gary Forlini is managing partner of the School Growth initiative **Brinkman—Forlini—Williams,** which trains school administrators and teachers in Classroom Instruction and Management. His recent works include the book **Help Teachers Engage Students** and the data system **ObserverTab** for district administrators, **Class Acts: Every Teacher's Guide To Activate Learning**, and the initiative's workshop **Grammar for Teachers**.

CONTENTS IN BRIEF
WRITING

WRITING GAME PLAN

1. **You, the Writer**
2. **Types of Writing**
3. **The Writing Process**
4. **Sentences, Paragraphs, and Compositions**

Writing without grammar only goes so far. Grammar and writing work together. To write well, grammar skills give me great tools.

CORE WRITING CHAPTERS

5. **Nonfiction Narration**
   Autobiographical Narrative
   Class Yearbook
   Radio Script
   Writing for Assessment

6. **Fiction Narration**
   Mystery Short Story
   Film Teaser
   Script for a Radio Play
   Writing for Assessment

7. **Poetry and Description**
   Sonnet or Free Verse Poem
   Advertisement Based on a Poem
   Descriptive Essay
   Writing for Assessment

8. **Exposition**
   Compare-and-Contrast Essay
   TV Talk Show Script
   Advice Column
   Writing for Assessment

9. **Persuasion**
   Op-Ed Piece
   Op-Ed Message in a Public Service Announcement
   Letter to the Editor
   Writing for Assessment

10. **Response to Literature**
    Response to Literature Essay
    Dialogue Between Literary Characters
    Script
    Writing for Assessment

11. **Research**
    Informational Research Report
    Infomercial
    Script for an Interview
    Writing for Assessment

12. **Workplace Writing**
    Instructions
    Memo
    Business Letter
    Research Report for a Community Service Day
    Multimedia Project Plan
    Writing for Assessment

www.phwritingcoach.com

 Interactive Writing Coach™

 Interactive Graphic Organizer

 Interactive Model

  Online Journal

Resources

 Video

GRAMMAR

GRAMMAR GAME PLAN

20 Major Grammatical Errors and How to Fix Them

> Grammar without writing is only a collection of rules, but when these rules are put into action as I write, the puzzle comes together.

CORE GRAMMAR CHAPTERS

GRAMMAR
- 13 The Parts of Speech
- 14 Basic Sentence Parts
- 15 Phrases and Clauses
- 16 Effective Sentences

USAGE
- 17 Verb Usage
- 18 Pronoun Usage
- 19 Agreement
- 20 Using Modifiers
- 21 Miscellaneous Problems in Usage

MECHANICS
- 22 Capitalization
- 23 Punctuation

STUDENT RESOURCES
Handbooks
Glossaries

- Grammar Tutorials
- Grammar Practice
- Grammar Games

www.phwritingcoach.com

Writing Coach: How to Use This Program

This program is organized into two distinct sections: one for WRITING and one for GRAMMAR.

In the **WRITING** section, you'll learn strategies, traits, and skills that will help you become a better writer.

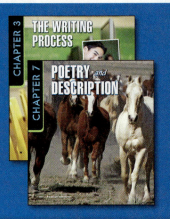

In the **GRAMMAR** section, you'll learn the rules and conventions of grammar, usage, and mechanics.

What DIGITAL writing and grammar resources are available?

The Writing Coach Online boxes will indicate opportunities to use online tools.

In **Writing,** use the **Interactive Writing Coach™** in two ways to get personalized guidance and support for your writing.
- Paragraph Feedback and
- Essay Scorer

Interactive Writing Coach™
- Choosing from the Topic Bank gives you access to the Interactive Writing Coach™.
- Submit your writing and receive instant personalized feedback and guidance as you draft, revise, and edit your writing.

Grammar Tutorials
Brush up on your grammar skills with these animated videos.

Grammar Practice
Practice your grammar skills with Writing Coach Online.

Grammar Games
Test your knowledge of grammar in this fast-paced interactive video game.

In **Grammar,** view grammar tutorials, practice your grammar skills, and play grammar video games.

What will you find in the WRITING section?

Writing Genre

Each chapter introduces a different **writing genre.**

Learn about the key characteristics of the **genre** before you start writing.

Focus on a single form of the genre with the **Feature Assignment**.

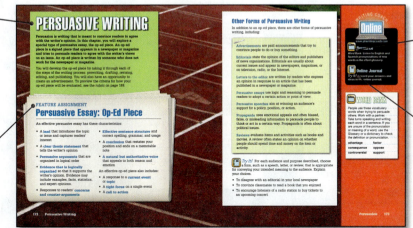

Writing Coach Online
- View the **Word Bank** words in the eText glossary, and hear them pronounced in both English and Spanish.
- Use your **Online Journal** to record your answers and ideas as you respond to *Try It!* activities.

Mentor Text and Student Model

The **Mentor Text** and **Student Model** provide examples of the genre featured in each chapter.

Use the **Mentor Text** to see how a professional crafted a piece of writing.

Review the **Student Model** as a guide for composing your own piece.

Writing Coach Online
- Use the **Interactive Model** to mark the text with Reader's and Writer's Response Symbols.
- Listen to an audio recording of the **Mentor Text** or **Student Model**.

ix

Topic Bank **PREWRITING**

The **Topic Bank** provides prompts for the **Feature Assignment.**

Choose from a bank of topics, or follow steps to find an idea of your own.

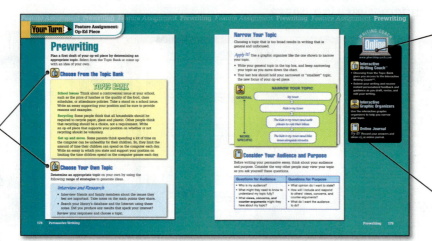

Writing Coach Online
- As you narrow your topic, get the right type of support! You'll find three different forms of graphic organizers—one model, one with step-by-step guidance, and one that is blank for you to complete.
- Use **Try It!** ideas to practice new skills. Use **Apply It!** activities as you work on your own writing.

Outline for Success **DRAFTING**

Whether you are working on your essay drafts online or with a pen and paper, an **Outline for Success** can get you started.

Consult this **outline** for a quick visual specific to the writing task assigned in each chapter.

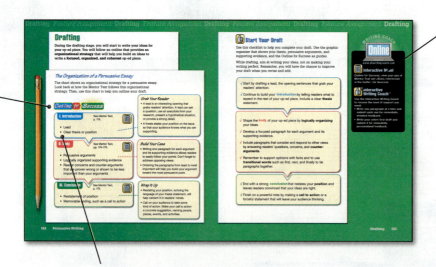

Writing Coach Online
- Start with just a paragraph and build up to your essay draft, or if you are ready, go straight to submitting your essay. The choice is yours!

Follow the bulleted suggestions for each part of your draft, and you'll be on your way to success.

Revision RADaR — REVISING

You can use the **Revision RADaR** strategy as a guide for making changes to improve your draft.

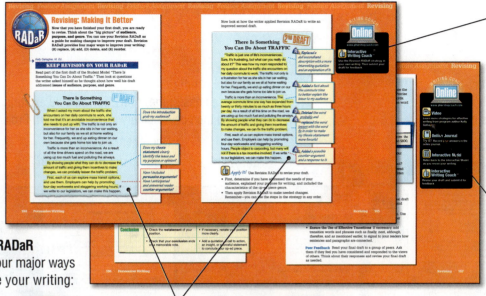

Revision RADaR provides four major ways to improve your writing:
- **R**eplace
- **A**dd
- **D**elete
- **R**eorder

Check out these example drafts to see how to apply **Revision RADaR**.

Writing Coach Online
- With **Interactive Writing Coach™**, submit your paragraphs and essays multiple times. View your progress in your online writing portfolio. Feel confident that your work is ready to be shared in peer review or teacher conferencing.
- View **videos** with strategies for writing from program author **Kelly Gallagher**.

What Do You Notice? — EDITING | PUBLISHING

In the editing stage, **What Do You Notice?** and **Mentor Text** help you zoom in on powerful sentences.

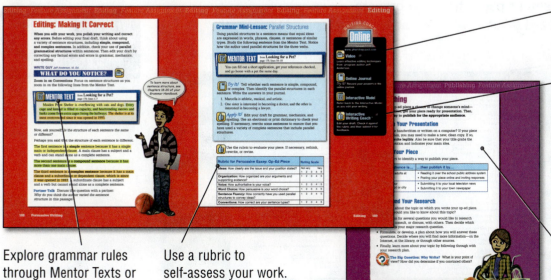

Explore grammar rules through Mentor Texts or Student Models.

Use a rubric to self-assess your work.

Find the best way to share your writing with others.

Writing Coach Online
- View **videos** with strategies for writing from program author **Jeff Anderson**.
- Submit your essay for feedback and a score.

xi

How do end-of-chapter features help you apply what you've learned?

21st Century Learning

In **Make Your Writing Count** and **Writing for Media** you will work on innovative assignments that involve the 21st Century life and career skills you'll need for communicating successfully.

Make Your Writing Count
Work collaboratively on project-based assignments and share what you have learned with others. Projects include:

- Debates
- TV Talk Shows
- News Reports

Writing for Media
Complete an assignment on your own by exploring media forms, and then developing your own content. Projects include:

- Blogs
- Storyboards
- Documentary Scripts
- Multimedia Presentations

Test Prep

The **Writing for Assessment** pages help you prepare for important standardized tests.

SAT/PSAT PREP ACT Notice these icons that emphasize the types of writing you'll find on high-stakes tests.

Use **The ABCDs of On-Demand Writing** for a quick, memorable strategy for success.

Writing Coach Online
Submit your essay for feedback and a score.

What will you find in the GRAMMAR section?

Grammar Game Plan

The **Find It/Fix It** reference guide helps you fix the **20** most common errors in student writing.

Study each of the 20 common errors and their corrections, which are clearly explained on each page.

Follow cross-references to more instruction in the grammar chapters.

Review the **Check It** features for strategies to help you avoid these errors.

Grammar Chapters

Each grammar chapter begins with a **What Do You Notice?** feature and **Mentor Text**.

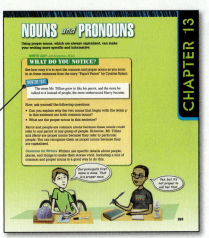

Use the **Mentor Text** to help you zoom in on powerful sentences. It showcases the correct use of written language conventions.

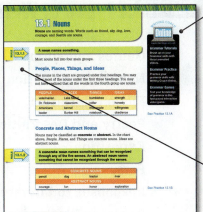

Writing Coach Online
The **Writing Coach Online** digital experience for Grammar helps you focus on just the lessons and practice you need.

Use the grammar section as a quick reference handbook. Each **grammar rule** is highlighted and numbered.

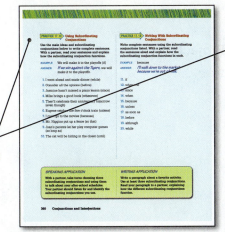

Try **Practice** pages and **Test Warm-Ups** to help you check your progress.

xiii

WRITING

WRITING GAME PLAN

CHAPTER 1 You, the Writer — 2

Why Do You Write? 2
What Do You Write? 3
Where Can You Find Ideas? 3
How Can You Keep Track of Ideas? 4
How Can You Get Started? 5
How Do You Work With Others? 6
Where Can You Keep Your Finished Work? 7
Reflect on Your Writing 7

CHAPTER 2 Types of Writing — 8

Genres and Forms 8
Nonfiction Narration 9
Fiction Narration 11
Poetry and Description 13
Exposition 15
Persuasion 18
Responses to Literature 20
Research Writing 21
Workplace Writing 22
Writing for Media 24
Creating Multimedia Projects 25
Reflect on Your Writing 25

CHAPTER 3 The Writing Process 26

Writing Traits	26
Rubrics and How To Use Them	28
What Is the Writing Process?	30
Why Use the Writing Process?	31
Prewriting	32
Drafting	35
Revising	36
Editing	42
Publishing	46

CHAPTER 4 Sentences, Paragraphs, and Compositions 48

Writing Strong Sentences	49
Writing Strong Paragraphs	50
Composing Your Piece	53
Rhetorical and Literary Devices	54
Using Writing Traits To Develop an Effective Composition	56
Using Interactive Writing Coach	60
Interactive Writing Coach and the Writing Process	61
Paragraph Feedback With Interactive Writing Coach	62
Essay Scoring With Interactive Writing Coach	63

WRITING COACH Online
www.phwritingcoach.com

All content available online
- Interactive Writing Coach™
- Interactive Graphic Organizer
- Interactive Models
- Online Journal
- Resources
- Video

WRITING

CHAPTER 5 Nonfiction Narration ... 64

Feature Assignment: Autobiographical Narrative

Mentor Text: Autobiographical Narrative
"The Trip to Beautiful" by Mary Schmich ... 68

Student Model: Autobiographical Narrative
"Team Player" by Kalim Hunt ... 70

Prewriting ... 72
Topic Bank

Drafting ... 76
The Organization of a Nonfiction Narrative

Revising Making It Better ... 78
Focus on Craft: Sentence Variety

Editing Making It Correct ... 82
What Do You Notice?
Grammar Mini-Lesson: Commas and Clauses

Publishing ... 84
Reflect on Your Writing

21st Century Learning Make Your Writing Count ... 85
Assignment: Celebrate Your Experiences in a Class Yearbook

Writing for Media ... 86
Assignment: Create a Radio Script

Writing for Assessment ... 88
Assignment: Narrative Nonfiction
More Prompts for Practice
More Strategies for Writing for Assessment

Connect to the Big Questions

- **What do you think?**
  What makes conflict interesting?

- **Why write?**
  What should we put in and leave out to be accurate and honest?

CHAPTER 6 Fiction Narration 90

Feature Assignment: Mystery

Mentor Text: Mystery
"The Mystery of the Golden Locket" by Mary Larimer **94**

Student Model: Mystery
"A Rough Night" by Jack McKee **98**

Prewriting **100**
Topic Bank

Drafting **104**
The Organization of a Short Story

Revising   Making It Better **106**
Focus on Craft: Style

Editing   Making It Correct **110**
What Do You Notice?
Grammar Mini-Lesson: Commas in Relative Clauses

Publishing **112**
Reflect on Your Writing

21st Century Learning Make Your Writing Count **113**
Assignment: "Coming Soon…": Planning a Film Teaser

Writing for Media **114**
Assignment: Create a Script for a Radio Play

Writing for Assessment **116**
Assignment: Short Story
More Prompts for Practice
Spiral Review: Narrative

Connect to the Big Questions

- **What do you think?**
  What challenges should we attempt?

- **Why write?**
  What can fiction do better than nonfiction?

WRITING COACH Online
www.phwritingcoach.com

All content available online
- Interactive Writing Coach™
- Interactive Graphic Organizer
- Interactive Models
- Online Journal
- Resources
- Video

Contents   xvii

WRITING

CHAPTER 7 Poetry and Description ... 118

Feature Assignment: Sonnet and Free Verse Poem

Mentor Text: Sonnet and Free Verse Poem
- "Acquainted with the Night" by Robert Frost ... **122**
- "Things" by Lisel Mueller ... **123**

Student Model: Sonnet and Free Verse Poem
- "Paradise" by Tiffany Trevino ... **124**
- "The Cafeteria" by Tiffany Trevino ... **125**

Prewriting ... **126**
Topic Bank

Drafting ... **130**
Drafting a Free Verse Poem or Ballad

Revising Making It Better ... **132**
Focus on Craft: Figurative Language

Editing Making It Correct ... **136**
What Do You Notice?
Grammar Mini-Lesson: Spelling Verbals

Publishing ... **138**
Reflect on Your Writing

21st Century Learning Make Your Writing Count ... **139**
Assignment: Sell It With Poetry

Writing for Media ... **140**
Assignment: Create a Descriptive Essay

Writing for Assessment ... **142**
Assignment: Poetry
More Prompts for Practice
Spiral Review: Narrative

Connect to the Big Questions

- **What do you think?**
  Which words are the most powerful?

- **Why write?**
  How do we best convey feelings through words on a page?

CHAPTER 8 Exposition — 144

Feature Assignment: Compare-and-Contrast Essay

Mentor Text: Analytical Essay
"Where Have Ladybugs Gone?" by Mary Esch **148**

Student Model: Compare-and-Contrast Essay
"Playing Video Games and Board Games: Different Ways to Have Fun"
by Ryan Bradshaw **150**

Prewriting **152**
Topic Bank

Drafting **156**
The Organization of a Compare-and-Contrast Essay

Revising   Making It Better **158**
Focus on Craft: Subtlety of Meaning

Editing   Making It Correct **162**
What Do You Notice?
Grammar Mini-Lesson: Subjunctive Mood

Publishing **164**
Extend Your Research

21st Century Learning Make Your Writing Count **165**
Assignment: Compare and Contrast in a TV Talk Show Script

Writing for Media **166**
Assignment: Create an Advice Column

Writing for Assessment **168**
Assignment: Expository Writing
More Prompts for Practice
Spiral Review: Poetry

Connect to the Big Questions

- **What do you think?**
  What should we celebrate?

- **Why write?**
  What should we tell and what should we describe to make information clear?

WRITING COACH Online
www.phwritingcoach.com

All content available online
- Interactive Writing Coach™
- Interactive Graphic Organizer
- Interactive Models
- Online Journal
- Resources
- Video

WRITING

CHAPTER 9 Persuasion 170

Feature Assignment: Op-Ed Piece

Mentor Text: Op-Ed Piece
"Local BMX Riders Need Our Support"
by Shari McElroy 174

Student Model: Op-Ed Piece
"A Little More Life in Our School"
by Luis Soto 176

Prewriting 178
Topic Bank

Drafting 182
Organization of an Argumentative Essay

Revising — Making It Better 184
Focus on Craft: Style

Editing — Making It Correct 188
What Do You Notice?
Grammar Mini-Lesson: Voice in Complex Tenses

Publishing 190
Extend Your Research

21st Century Learning Make Your Writing Count 191
Assignment: Express an Op-Ed Message in a Public Service Announcement

Writing for Media 192
Assignment: Create a Letter to the Editor

Writing for Assessment 194
Assignment: Persuasive Writing
More Prompts for Practice
Spiral Review: Expository

Connect to the Big Questions

- **What do you think?**
  What best shows someone is ready for more responsibility?

- **Why write?**
  What is your point of view? How will you know if you've convinced others?

CHAPTER 10 Response to Literature — 196

Feature Assignment: Response to Literature Essay

Mentor Text: Response to Literature Essay
"Horror in 'The Monkey's Paw'" by Tamra B. Orr 200

Student Model: Response to Literature Essay
"Good Things in Small Packages'" by Jaymie Dunham 202

Prewriting 204
Topic Bank

Drafting 208
The Organization of an Interpretive Response

Revising Making It Better 210
Focus on Craft: Word Choice

Editing Making It Correct 214
What Do You Notice?
Grammar Mini-Lesson: Quotation Marks

Publishing 216
Extend Your Research

21st Century Learning Make Your Writing Count 217
Assignment: Stage a Dialogue Between Literary Characters

Writing for Media 218
Assignment: Create a Script

Writing for Assessment 220
Assignment: Interpretative Response
More Prompts for Practice
Spiral Review: Persuasive

Connect to the Big Questions

- **What do you think?**
  What most determines our responses to literature?

- **Why write?**
  What should you write about to make others interested in a text?

WRITING COACH Online
www.phwritingcoach.com

All content available online
- Interactive Writing Coach™
- Interactive Graphic Organizer
- Interactive Models
- Online Journal
- Resources
- Video

Contents xxi

WRITING

CHAPTER 11 Research Writing 222

Feature Assignment: Informational Research Report

Student Model: Informational Research Report
"The Building of the Great Brooklyn Bridge" by Jorge Gutierrez 226

Prewriting 230
- Topic Bank
- Make a Research Plan
- Checklist for Evaluating Sources
- Collect and Organize Your Data
- Avoid Plagiarism
- Document Your Sources
- Critique Your Research Process

Drafting 238
- The Organization of an Informational Research Report
- Provide and Document Evidence
- Use Graphics and Illustrations

Revising Making It Better 242
- Focus on Craft: Varying Sentences

Editing Making It Correct 246
- What Do You Notice?
- Grammar Mini-Lesson: Punctuation

Publishing 248
- Reflect on Your Writing

21st Century Learning Make Your Writing Count 249
Assignment: Develop an Infomercial

Writing for Media 250
Assignment: Create a Script for an Interview

Writing for Assessment 254
Assignment: Research Plan
- More Prompts for Practice
- Spiral Review: Narrative
- Spiral Review: Response to Literature

Connect to the Big Questions

- **What do you think?**
  When does research change lives?

- **Why write?**
  Do you understand a subject well enough to write about it? How will you find out what the facts are?

CHAPTER 12 Workplace Writing 256

Feature Assignments: Instructions, Memo, Business Letter

Prewriting › Drafting › Revising › Editing › Publishing

Instructions

Student Model
"How to Take a Phone Message" by Terrence Jackson **258**

Memo

Student Model
"Memo" by Jessica Ruiz **260**

Business Letter

Student Model
Business Letter by Erik Schindler **262**

 **Make Your Writing Count** **264**
Assignment: Present a Research Report for Community Service Day

Writing for Media **266**
Assignment: Create a Multimedia Project Plan

Writing for Assessment **268**
Assignment: Procedural Text
  More Prompts for Practice
    Spiral Review: Research

Connect to the Big Questions

- **What do you think?**
  When is careful listening most critical to success in the workplace?

- **Why write?**
  What do daily workplace communications require of format, content, and style?

www.phwritingcoach.com

All content available online
- Interactive Writing Coach™
- Interactive Graphic Organizer
- Interactive Models
- Online Journal
- Resources
- Video

GRAMMAR GAME PLAN

Find It/Fix It
The 20 Errors

1. Using the Wrong Word 273
2. Missing Comma After Introductory Element 274
3. Incomplete or Missing Documentation 275
4. Vague Pronoun Reference 276
5. Spelling Error 277
6. Punctuation Error With a Quotation 278
7. Unnecessary Comma 279
8. Unnecessary or Missing Capitalization 280
9. Missing Word 281
10. Faulty Sentence Structure 282
11. Missing Comma With a Nonessential Element 283
12. Unnecessary Shift in Verb Tense 284
13. Missing Comma in a Compound Sentence 285
14. Unnecessary or Missing Apostrophe 286
15. Run-on Sentence 287
16. Comma Splice 288
17. Lack of Pronoun-Antecedent Agreement 289
18. Poorly Integrated Quotation 290
19. Unnecessary or Missing Hyphen 291
20. Sentence Fragment 292

GRAMMAR

CHAPTER 13 The Parts of Speech 293

What Do You Notice? 293

13.1 Nouns and Pronouns 294
Nouns 294
Pronouns 298
Test Warm-Up 304

13.2 Verbs 308
Action Verbs and Linking Verbs 308
Transitive and Intransitive Verbs 312
Verb Phrases 313

13.3 Adjectives and Adverbs 315
Adjectives 315
Adverbs 321

13.4 Prepositions, Conjunctions, and Interjections 325
Prepositions and Prepositional Phrases 325
Conjunctions 328
Interjections 330

13.5 Words as Different Parts of Speech 332
Identifying Parts of Speech 332

CHAPTER 14 Basic Sentence Parts 335

What Do You Notice? 335

14.1 Subjects and Predicates 336
Simple Subjects and Predicates 337
Fragments 339

14.2 Hard-to-Find Subjects 343
Subjects in Declarative Sentences Beginning With *Here* or *There* 343
Subjects in Interrogative Sentences 344
Subjects in Imperative Sentences 345
Subjects in Exclamatory Sentences 345

14.3 Complements 347
Direct Objects 347
Indirect Objects 349
Object Complements 350
Subject Complements 350
Test Warm-Up 354

CHAPTER 15 Phrases and Clauses — 355

What Do You Notice? 355

15.1 Phrases — **356**
- Prepositional Phrases 356
- Appositives and Appositive Phrases 360
- Verbal Phrases 364

15.2 Clauses — **375**
- Independent and Subordinate Clauses 375
- Adjectival Clauses 376
- Restrictive Relative Clauses and Nonrestrictive Relative Clauses 378
- **Test Warm-Up** 382
- Adverbial Clauses 384
- Noun Clauses 387

15.3 The Four Structures of Sentences — **392**

Cumulative Review **395**

CHAPTER 16 Effective Sentences — 397

What Do You Notice? 397

16.1 The Four Functions of a Sentence — **398**

16.2 Sentence Combining — **400**

16.3 Varying Sentences — **404**
- Varying Sentence Length 404
- Varying Sentence Beginnings 405
- Using Inverted Word Order 405

16.4 Avoid Fragments and Run-ons — **407**
- Recognizing Fragments 407
- Avoiding Run-on Sentences 410

16.5 Misplaced and Dangling Modifiers — **412**
- Recognizing Misplaced Modifiers 412
- Recognizing Dangling Modifiers 412

16.6 Faulty Parallelism — **415**
- Recognizing the Correct Use of Parallelism 415
- Correcting Faulty Parallelism 415
- Correcting Faulty Parallelism in a Series 416
- Correcting Faulty Parallelism in Comparisons 417

WRITING COACH Online
www.phwritingcoach.com
All content available online
- Grammar Tutorials
- Grammar Practice
- Grammar Games

GRAMMAR

16.7 Faulty Coordination 418
Recognizing Faulty Coordination 418
Correcting Faulty Coordination 419
Test Warm-Up 422

USAGE

CHAPTER 17 Verb Usage   423

What Do You Notice? 423

17.1 Verb Tenses 424
The Six Verb Tenses 424
The Four Principal Parts of Verbs.................. 427
Regular and Irregular Verbs 429
Verb Conjugation 435

17.2 The Correct Use of Tenses 438
Present, Past, and Future Tense 438
Sequence of Tenses 446
Simultaneous Events 449
Sequential Events 449
Modifiers That Help Clarify Tense 453

17.3 The Subjunctive Mood 455
Using the Subjunctive Mood 455
Auxiliary Verbs That Express the Subjunctive Mood .. 456
Test Warm-Up 459

17.4 Voice 460
Active and Passive Voice or Tense 460
Using Active and Passive Voice 462

CHAPTER 18 Pronoun Usage — 465

What Do You Notice? 465

18.1 Case 466
  The Three Cases 466
  The Nominative Case in Pronouns 467
  The Objective Case 470
  The Possessive Case 471
  Test Warm-Up 474

18.2 Special Problems With Pronouns 475
  Using *Who* and *Whom* Correctly 475
  Pronouns in Elliptical Clauses 477

CHAPTER 19 Agreement — 479

What Do You Notice? 479

19.1 Subject–Verb Agreement 480
  Number in Nouns, Pronouns, and Verbs 480
  Singular and Plural Subjects 482
  Compound Subjects 485
  Confusing Subjects 488
  Test Warm-Up 494

19.2 Pronoun–Antecedent Agreement 495
  Agreement Between Personal Pronouns and Antecedents 495
  Agreement With Indefinite Pronouns 499
  Agreement With Reflexive Pronouns 500

19.3 Special Problems With Pronoun Agreement 502
  Vague Pronoun References 502
  Ambiguous Pronoun References 504
  Avoiding Distant Pronoun References 505

Contents   xxvii

GRAMMAR

CHAPTER 20 Using Modifiers — 507

What Do You Notice? 507

20.1 Degrees of Comparison 508
Recognizing Degrees of Comparison 508
Regular Forms 508
Irregular Forms 509

20.2 Making Clear Comparisons 513
Using Comparative and Superlative Degrees 513
Test Warm-Up 516
Using Logical Comparisons 517
Avoiding Comparisons With Absolute Modifiers 519

CHAPTER 21 Miscellaneous Problems in Usage — 521

What Do You Notice? 521

21.1 Negative Sentences 522
Recognizing Double Negatives 522
Forming Negative Sentences Correctly 523
Using Negatives to Create Understatement 524
Test Warm-Up 527

21.2 Common Usage Problems 528

Cumulative Review 543

MECHANICS

CHAPTER 22 Capitalization — 545

What Do You Notice? 545

22.1 Capitalization in Sentences 546
Using Capitals for First Words 546
Using Capitals With Quotations 547
Test Warm-Up 550

22.2 Proper Nouns 551
Using Capitals for Proper Nouns 551
Using Capitals for Proper Adjectives 556

22.3 Other Uses of Capitals 559
Using Capitals in Letters 559
Using Capitals for Titles 559

CHAPTER 23 Punctuation — 565

What Do You Notice? 565

23.1 End Marks 566
Using Periods 566
Other Uses of Periods 566
Using Question Marks 568
Using Exclamation Marks 569

All content available online
- Grammar Tutorials
- Grammar Practice
- Grammar Games

Contents   xxix

GRAMMAR

23.2 Commas ... 571
Using Commas With Compound Sentences ... 571
Avoiding Comma Splices ... 572
Using Commas in a Series ... 573
Using Commas Between Adjectives ... 574
Using Commas After Introductory Material ... 576
Using Commas With Parenthetical Expressions ... 577
Using Commas With Nonessential Expressions ... 578
Test Warm-Up ... 581
Using Commas With Dates, Geographical Names, and Titles ... 582
Using Commas in Numbers ... 583
Using Commas With Addresses and in Letters ... 585
Using Commas in Elliptical Sentences ... 585
Using Commas With Direct Quotations ... 586
Using Commas for Clarity ... 586
Misuses of Commas ... 587

23.3 Semicolons and Colons ... 589
Using Semicolons to Join Independent Clauses ... 589
Using Semicolons to Avoid Confusion ... 590
Using Colons ... 592

23.4 Quotation Marks, Underlining, and Italics ... 595
Using Quotation Marks With Quotations ... 595
Using Direct Quotations With Introductory, Concluding, and Interrupting Expressions ... 595
Quotation Marks With Other Punctuation Marks ... 597
Using Single Quotation Marks for Quotations Within Quotations ... 598
Punctuating Explanatory Material Within Quotes ... 598
Using Quotation Marks for Dialogue ... 600
Using Quotation Marks in Titles ... 601
Using Underlining and Italics in Titles and Other Special Words ... 602
Using Quotation Marks to Indicate Sarcasm or Irony ... 604

23.5 Hyphens ... 607
Using Hyphens in Numbers ... 607
Using Hyphens With Prefixes and Suffixes ... 608
Using Hyphens With Compound Words ... 608
Using Hyphens for Clarity ... 609
Using Hyphens at the Ends of Lines ... 611
Using Hyphens Correctly to Divide Words ... 611

23.6 Apostrophes	**614**
Using Apostrophes to Form Possessive Nouns	614
Using Apostrophes With Pronouns	616
Using Apostrophes to Form Contractions	617
Using Apostrophes to Create Special Plurals	618
23.7 Parentheses and Brackets	**620**
Parentheses	620
Brackets	622
23.8 Ellipses, Dashes, and Slashes	**624**
Using the Ellipsis	624
Dashes	625
Slashes	626
Cumulative Review	**629**

STUDENT RESOURCES

Writing in the Content Areas	**R2**
Writing for Media	**R6**
Writing for the Workplace	**R12**
Note Cards	R12
Meeting Agenda	R13
Business Letter	R14
Friendly Letter	R15
MLA Style for Listing Sources	**R16**
Commonly Misspelled Words	**R17**
English Glossary	**R18**
Spanish Glossary	**R21**
Graphic Organizer Handbook	**R24**
Listening and Speaking Handbook	**R28**
Index	**R32**
Index of Authors and Titles	**R57**
Acknowledgments	**R58**

xxxi

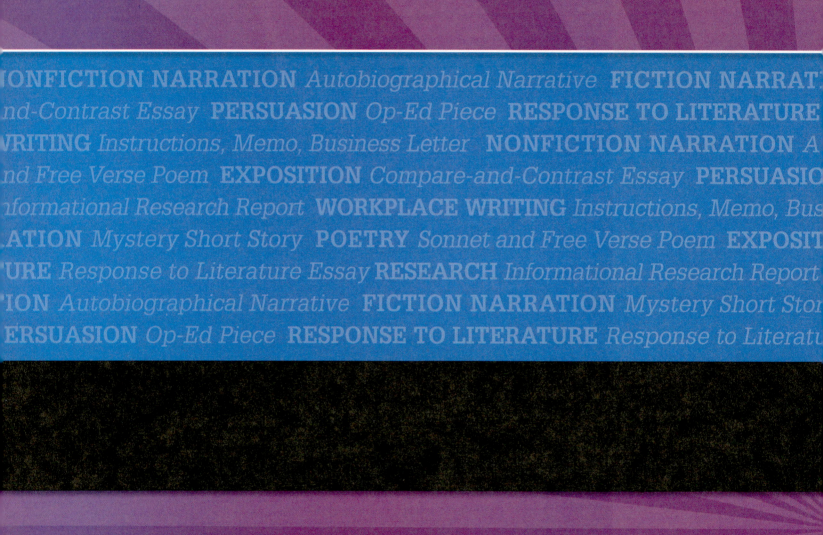

CHAPTER 1

YOU, THE WRITER

Why Do You Write?

Writing well is one of the most important life skills you can develop. Being a good writer can help you achieve success in school and beyond. Most likely, you write for many reasons. You write:

To Share

You probably often write to **share** your experiences with others. Writing can be an easy way to **reach out** to people and connect with them.

To Persuade People

Writing can also be an effective way to **persuade** people to consider your opinions. For example, you may find it's easier to convince someone of your point of view when you've effectively organized your thoughts in an essay or a letter.

To Inform

Another reason to write is to **inform.** Perhaps you want to tell an audience how you built your computer network or how you finally got your e-mail to function properly.

To Enjoy

Personal fullfillment is another important motivation for writing, since writing enables you **to express** your thoughts and feelings. In addition, writing can also help you recall an event, or let you escape from everyday life.

Fortunately, writing well is a skill you can learn and one that you can continue to improve and polish. This program will help you improve your writing skills and give you useful information about the many types of writing.

What Do You Write?

Writing is already an important part of your everyday life. Each day is full of opportunities to write, allowing you to capture, express, think through, and share your thoughts and feelings, and demonstrate what you know. Here are some ways you might write.

- Recording thoughts in a journal
- Texting friends or posting on social networking sites
- E-mailing thank-you notes to relatives
- Creating lists of things to do or things you like
- Writing research reports, nonfiction accounts, fiction stories, and essays in school

How Can You Find Ideas?

The good news is that ideas are all around you. You just need to be aware of the rich resources that are available.

By Observing

Observing is a good way to start to find ideas. Did you see anything interesting on your way to school? Was there something unusual about the video game you played last night?

By Reading

Reading is another useful option—look through newspaper articles and editorials, magazines, blogs, and Web sites. Perhaps you read something that surprised you or really made you feel concerned. Those are exactly the subjects that can lead to the ideas you want to write about.

By Watching

Watching is another way to get ideas—watch online videos or television programs, for example.

WRITING COACH Online

www.phwritingcoach.com

Online Journal

Try It! Record your notes, answers, and ideas in the online journal. You can also record and save your answers and ideas on pop-up sticky notes in the eText.

" Writer to Writer "

I write when I want to be heard or connect. Writing lets me be a vital part of my community and reach outside it as well. All the while, I get to be me—my unique self.

—Jeff Anderson

You, the Writer 3

How Can You Keep Track of Ideas?

You may sometimes think of great writing ideas in the middle of the night or on the way to math class. These strategies can help you remember those ideas.

Start an Idea Notebook or a Digital Idea File

Reserving a small **notebook** to record ideas can be very valuable. Just writing the essence of an idea, as it comes to you, can later help you develop a topic or essay. A **digital idea file** is exactly the same thing—but it's recorded on your computer, cell phone, or other electronic device.

Keep a Personal Journal

Many people find that keeping a **journal** of their thoughts is helpful. Then, when it's time to select an idea, they can flip through their journal and pick up on the best gems they wrote—sometimes from long ago.

Maintain a Learning Log

A **learning log** is just what it sounds like—a place to record information you have learned, which could be anything from methods of solving equations to computer shortcuts. Writing about something in a learning log might later inspire you to conduct further research on the same topic.

Free Write

Some individuals find that if they just let go and write whatever comes to mind, they eventually produce excellent ideas. **Free writing** requires being relaxed and unstructured. This kind of writing does not require complete sentences, correct spelling, or proper grammar. Whatever ends up on the paper or on the computer screen is fine. Later, the writer can go back and tease out the best ideas.

How Can You Get Started?

Every writer is different, so it makes sense that all writers should try out techniques that might work well for them. Regardless of your personal writing style, these suggestions should help you get started.

Get Comfortable

It's important to find and create an environment that encourages your writing process. Choose a spot where interruptions will be minimal and where you'll find it easy to concentrate. Some writers prefer a quiet library. Others prefer to work in a room with music playing softly on their computer.

Have Your Materials Ready

Before starting to write, gather all the background materials you need to get started, including your notes, free writing, reader's journal, and portfolio. Make sure you also have writing tools, such as a pen and paper or a computer.

Spend Time Wisely

Budgeting your available writing time is a wise strategy. Depending on your writing goal, you may want to sketch out your time on a calendar, estimating how long to devote to each stage of the writing process. Then, you can assign deadlines to each part. If you find a particular stage takes longer than you estimated, simply adjust your schedule to ensure that you finish on time.

SUNDAY	MONDAY	TUESDAY	WEDNESDAY	THURSDAY	FRIDAY	SATURDAY
		1 Start Research	2 Finish Research	3 Write Outline	4	5
6	7	8 Finish First Draft	9 Finish Revising	10 Finish Proofreading	11	12
13	14 DUE DATE	15	16	17	18	19
20	21	22	23	24	25	26
27	28	29	30	31		

How Do You Work With Others?

If you think of writing as a solitary activity, think again. Working with others can be a key part of the writing process.

Brainstorming

Brainstorming works when everyone in a group feels free to suggest ideas, whether they seem commonplace or brilliant.

Cooperative Writing

Cooperative writing is a process in which each member of a group concentrates on a different part of an assignment. Then, the group members come together to discuss their ideas and write drafts.

Peer Feedback

Peer feedback comes from classmates who have read your writing and offered suggestions for improvements. When commenting on a classmate's work, it's important to provide constructive, or helpful, criticism.

21st Century Learning

Collaborate and Discuss

In **collaborative writing,** each group member takes an assigned role on a writing project. A collaborative group may decide on such possible roles as leader, facilitator, recorder, and listener. The roles may change as the group discusses and works through the writing process. The goal, however, is to work and rework the writing until all members feel they have produced the best result.

Possible Roles in a Collaborative Writing Project

LEADER — Initiates the discussion by clearly expressing group goals and moderates discussions

FACILITATOR — Works to move the discussion forward and clarify ideas

COMPROMISER — Works to find practical solutions to differences of opinion

LISTENER — Actively listens and serves to recall details that were discussed

Using Technology

Technology allows collaboration to occur in ways that were previously unthinkable.

- By working together on the Internet, students around the world have infinite opportunities to collaborate online on a wide range of projects.
- Collaboration can range from projects that foster community cooperation, such as how to improve debates during local elections, to those that increase global awareness, such as focusing on how to encourage more recycling.
- Being able to log in and to contribute to media, such as journals, blogs, and social networks, allows you to connect globally, express your views in writing, and join a world-wide conversation.

Where Can You Keep Your Finished Work?

A **portfolio,** or growing collection of your work, is valuable for many reasons. It can serve as a research bank of ideas and as a record of how your writing is improving. You can create a portfolio on a computer or in a folder or notebook. You'll learn more about managing a portfolio in chapter 3.

A **Reader's Journal,** in which you record quotes and ideas from your reading, can also be used to store original ideas. Your journal can be housed on a computer or in a notebook.

Reflect on Your Writing

Analyzing, making inferences, and drawing conclusions about how you find ideas can help you become a better, more effective writer. Find out more about how you write by asking yourself questions like these:

- Which strategies have I found most effective for finding good ideas for writing?
- What pieces of writing represent my best work and my weakest work? What do the pieces in each group have in common?

With a partner, talk about your collaborative writing experiences. Be sure to share your responses to such questions as these: What project did you work on as a collaborative effort? What did you learn that you might not have discovered if you were developing a writing project by yourself?

CHAPTER 2
TYPES of WRITING

Genres and Forms

Genres are types, or categories, of writing.

- Each genre has a specific **purpose,** or goal. For example, the purpose of persuasive writing is to convince readers to agree with the writer's point of view.
- Each genre has specific **characteristics.** Short stories, for example, have characters, a setting, and a plot.

In this chapter, you will be introduced to several genres: nonfiction narratives, fiction narratives, poetry and descriptive writing, expository writing, persuasive writing, responses to literature, and workplace writing.

Forms are subcategories of genres that contain all the characteristics of the genre plus some unique characteristics of their own. For example, a mystery is a form of short story. In addition to plot, characters, and setting, it has a mystery to be solved.

Selecting Genres

In some writing situations, you may need to select the correct genre for conveying your intended meaning.

- To **entertain,** you may choose to write a short story or a humorous essay.
- To **describe** an emotion, writing a poem may be best.
- To **persuade** someone to your point of view, you may want to write a persuasive essay or editorial.

Each genre has unique strengths and weaknesses, and your specific goals will help you decide which is best.

Nonfiction Narration

Nonfiction narratives are any kind of literary text that tells a story about real people, events, and ideas. This genre of writing can take a number of different forms but includes well-developed conflict and resolution, interesting and believable characters, and a range of literary strategies, such as dialogue and suspense. Examples include Lynne Cox's "Swimming to Antarctica" and Pat Mora's "The Leader in the Mirror."

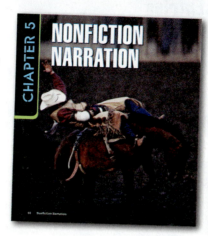

Personal Narratives

Personal narratives tell true stories about events in a writer's life. These types of writing are also called **autobiographical essays.** The stories may tell about an experience or relationship that is important to the writer, who is the main character. They have a clearly defined focus and communicate the reasons for actions and consequences.

Biographical Narratives

In a **biographical narrative,** the writer shares facts about someone else's life. The writer may describe an important period, experience, or relationship in that other person's life, but presents the information from his or her own perspective.

Blogs

Blogs are online journals that may include autobiographical narratives, reflections, opinions, and other types of comments. They may also reflect genres other than nonfiction such as expository writing, and they may include other media, such as photos, music, or video.

www.phwritingcoach.com

 Online Journal

Try It! Record your notes, answers, and ideas in the online journal. You can also record and save your answers and ideas on pop-up sticky notes in the eText.

Diary and Journal Entries

Writers record their personal thoughts, feelings, and experiences in **diaries** or **journals.** Writers sometimes keep diaries and journals for many years and then analyze how they reacted to various events over time.

Eyewitness Accounts

Eyewitness accounts are nonfiction writing that focus on historical or other important events. The writer is the narrator and shares his or her thoughts about the event. However, the writer is not the main focus of the writing.

Memoirs

Memoirs usually focus on meaningful scenes from writers' lives. These scenes often reflect on moments of a significant decision or personal discovery. For example, many modern U.S. presidents have written memoirs after they have left office. These memoirs help the public gain a better understanding of the decisions they made while in office.

Reflective Essays

Reflective essays present personal experiences, either events that happened to the writers themselves or that they learned about from others. They generally focus on sharing observations and insights they had while thinking about those experiences. Reflective essays often appear as features in magazines and newspapers.

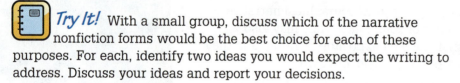 *Try It!* With a small group, discuss which of the narrative nonfiction forms would be the best choice for each of these purposes. For each, identify two ideas you would expect the writing to address. Discuss your ideas and report your decisions.

- To tell about seeing a championship kite-flying tournament
- To write about one of the first astronauts to walk in space
- To record personal thoughts about a favorite teacher

Fiction Narration

Fiction narratives are literary texts that tell a story about imagined people, events, and ideas. They contain elements such as characters, a setting, a sequence of events, and often, a theme. As with nonfiction narratives, this genre can take many different forms, but most forms include well-developed **conflict** and **resolution.** They also include **interesting and believable elements** and a range of **literary strategies,** such as dialogue and suspense. Examples include Anton Chekhov's "A Problem" or Ray Bradbury's "There Will Come Soft Rains."

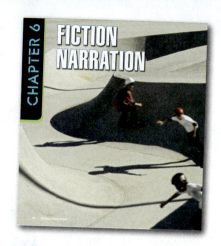

Realistic Fiction

Realistic fiction portrays invented characters and events in everyday situations that most readers would find familiar. Although characters may be imaginary, writers sometimes use real individuals in their own lives as a basis for the fictional ones. Because the focus is on everyday life, realistic fiction often presents problems that many people face and solutions they devise to solve them.

Fantasy Stories

Fantasy stories stretch the imagination and take readers to unreal worlds. Animals may talk, people may fly, or characters may have superhuman powers. Good fantasy stories have the elements of narrative fiction and manage to keep the fantastic elements believable.

Historical Fiction

Historical fiction is about imaginary people living in real places and times in history. Usually, the main characters are fictional people who know and interact with famous people and participate in important historical events.

Mystery Stories

Mystery stories present unexplained or strange events that characters try to solve. These stories are popular, probably because they are often packed full of suspense and surprises. Some characters in mystery stories, such as Sherlock Holmes, have become so famous that many people think of them as real people.

Myths and Legends

Myths and **legends** are traditional stories, told in cultures around the world. They were created to explain natural events that people could not otherwise explain or understand. They may, for example, tell about the origin of fire or thunder. Many myths and legends include gods, goddesses, and heroes who perform superhuman actions.

Science Fiction

Science fiction stories tell about real and imagined developments in science and technology and their effects on the way people think and live. Space travel, robots, and life in the future are popular topics in science fiction.

Tall Tales

You can tell a **tall tale** from other story types because it tells about larger-than-life characters in realistic settings. These characters can perform amazing acts of strength and bravery. One very famous hero of tall tales is Pecos Bill, who could ride just about anything—even a tornado!

Try It! Think about what you've read about narrative fiction and narrative nonfiction genres. Then, discuss in a group which **genre** would be best if you were planning a first draft and had these purposes in mind. **Select the correct genre** for conveying your intended meaning to your audiences. Then, identify two or three ideas that you would expect to include in a first draft. Be sure to explain your choices.

- To tell about a Texas rancher who can lasso lightning
- To share a true story about a famous person
- To tell the story of your most exciting day at school

Poetry and Description

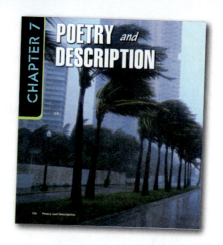

Poetry and other kinds of descriptive literature express ideas and feelings about real or imagined people, events, and ideas. They use rhythm, rhyme, precise language, and sensory details—words that appeal to the senses—to create vivid images. In addition, they use figurative language—writing that means something beyond what the words actually say—to express ideas in new, fresh, and interesting ways.

Structural elements, such as line length and stanzas, also help the poet express ideas and set a mood. Some examples of poetry include Robert Frost's "Mowing" and Dylan Thomas's "Do Not Go Gentle Into That Good Night."

Ballad

A **ballad** is a form of lyric poetry that expresses the poet's emotions toward someone or something. Ballads rhyme, and some have refrains that repeat after each stanza, which makes them easy to translate into songs.

In many places, traditional folk ballads were passed down as oral poems or songs and then later written. Some ballads tell about cultural heroes. Other ballads tell sad stories or make fun of certain events.

Free Verse

Free verse is poetry that has no regular rhyme, rhythm, or form. Instead, a free verse poem captures the patterns of natural speech. The poet writes in whatever form seems to fit the ideas best. A free verse poem can have almost anything as its subject.

> **" Writer to Writer "**
>
> Writing fiction and poetry sharpens your creativity—a skill valued by universities and employers.
>
> —Kelly Gallagher

Think about an example of fiction that you've especially enjoyed reading. Then, choose a partner and report your choices to each other. Be sure to explain what made the fiction piece so enjoyable, interesting, or exciting.

Prose Poem

A **prose poem** shares many of the features of other poetry, since it has rhythm, repetition, and vivid imagery. However, it is different from other poetry in one important way: it takes the form of prose or non-verse writing. Therefore, a prose poem may look like a short story on a page.

Sonnet

The **sonnet** is a form of rhyming lyric poetry with set rules. It is 14 lines long and usually follows a rhythm scheme called iambic pentameter. Each line has ten syllables and every other syllable is accented.

Haiku

Haiku is a form of non-rhyming poetry that was first developed in Japan hundreds of years ago. Many poets who write haiku in English write the poems in three lines. The first line has seven syllables, the second line has five syllables, and the third line has seven syllables. Haiku poets often write about nature and use vivid visual images.

Other Descriptive Writing

Descriptive writing includes descriptive essays, travel writing, and definition essays.

- **Descriptive essays** often use words that involve the senses to create a clear picture of a subject. For example, a descriptive essay about a freshly grilled hamburger might use adjectives such as *juicy*, *spicy*, *steamy*, *fragrant*, *hot*, and *glistening* to paint a word picture.
- A **travel essay** uses sensory words to describe a place.
- A **definition essay** can draw on a writer's emotional experience to describe something abstract, like friendship or happiness.

  The qualities of description can also be used in other types of writing. For example, a short story can be more realistic or compelling when it includes strong description.

Try It! Now that you've learned more about poetry and description, discuss which specific **genre** would be best for each of these purposes. **Select the correct genre** for conveying your intended meaning to your audiences. Then, identify two or three types of information that you would want to include in a first draft. Be ready to explain your thinking.

- To tell about a trip to a beach in Mexico
- To describe a drop of rain
- To tell the story of a character who lives in the wilderness

Exposition

Exposition is writing that seeks to communicate ideas and information to specific audiences and for specific purposes. It relies on facts to inform or explain.

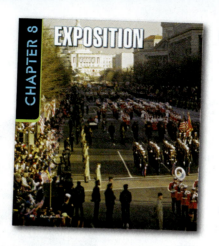

- Effective expository writing reflects an organization that is well planned—with effective introductory paragraphs, body paragraphs, and concluding paragraphs.
- In addition, good expository writing uses a variety of sentence structures and rhetorical devices—deliberate uses of language for specific effects.

Examples of expository writing include Ann Douglas's' "Feel the City's Pulse? It's Be-Bop, Man!" and Kelcey Rieger's "All That Jazz."

Analytical Essay

An **analytical essay** explores a topic by supplying relevant information in the form of facts, examples, reasons, and valid inferences to support the writer's claims.

- An **introductory paragraph** presents a thesis statement, the main point to be developed.
- The **body of the essay** provides facts about the topic, using a variety of sentence structures and transitions to help the writing flow.
- The **concluding paragraph** sums up ideas, helping readers understand why the topic is important.

Compare-and-Contrast Essay

A **compare-and-contrast** essay explores similarities and differences between two or more things for a specific purpose. As with other expository essays, the compare-and-contrast essay offers clear, factual details about the subject.

Cause-and-Effect Essay

A **cause-and-effect essay** traces the results of an event or describes the reasons an event happened. It is clearly organized and gives precise examples that support the relationship between the cause and effect.

> **" Writer to Writer "**
>
> Expository forms can shape my thinking and help my writing gel. I find the expository patterns clarifying my thoughts and filling in gaps that I may have otherwise missed.
>
> —Jeff Anderson

Choose a different partner this time. Discuss a poem that you've read in class. Share your thoughts about the poem and describe what made the piece successful.

Classification Essay

In a **classification essay,** a writer organizes a subject into categories and explains the category into which an item falls.

- An effective classification essay **sorts** its subjects—things or ideas—into several categories.
- It then offers **examples** that fall into each category. For example, a classification essay about video games might discuss three types of video games—action, adventure, and arcade.
- The essay might conclude with a statement about how the items classified are different or about how they are similar.

Problem-Solution Essay

A **problem-solution essay** presents a problem and then offers solutions to that problem. This type of essay may contain opinions, like a persuasive essay, but it is meant to explain rather than persuade.

- An effective problem-solution essay presents a clear statement of the problem, including a summary of its causes and effects.
- Then, it proposes at least one realistic solution and uses facts, statistics, or expert testimony to support the solution.
- The essay should be clearly organized, so that the relationship between the problem and the solution is obvious.

Pro-Con Essay

A **pro-con essay** examines arguments for and against an idea or topic.

- It has a topic that has two sides or points of view. For example, you might choose the following as a topic: Is it right to keep animals in zoos?
- Then, you would develop an essay that tells why it's good to keep animals in zoos, as well as why it's harmful to keep animals in zoos.
- It's important to be sure to give a clear analysis of the topic.

Newspaper and Magazine Articles

Newspaper and **magazine articles** offer information about news and events. They are typically factual and do not include the writer's opinions. They often provide an analysis of events and give readers background information on a topic. Some articles may also reflect genres other than the analytical essay, such as an editorial that aims to persuade.

Internet Articles

v on the **Internet** can supply relevant information about a topic.

- They are often like newspaper or magazine articles but may include shorter sentences and paragraphs. In addition, they include more visuals, such as charts and bulleted lists. They may also reflect genres other than analytical essays.
- It's always wise to consider the source when reading Internet articles because only the most reputable sources should be trusted to present correct facts.

On-Demand Writing

Because essay questions often appear on school tests, knowing how to write to **test prompts**, especially under time limits, is an important skill.

Test prompts provide a clear topic with directions about what should be addressed. The effective response to an essay demonstrates not only an understanding of academic content but also good writing skills.

Try It! Think about what you've learned about expository writing and consider the other genres you've discussed. Then, discuss in a group which **genre** would be best if you were planning a first draft with these purposes in mind. **Select the correct genre** for conveying your intended meaning to your audiences. Then, identify two or three key ideas that you would want to include in a first draft. Be sure to explain your choices.

- To weigh the benefits of two kinds of pets
- To imagine what life would be like on the moon

Partner Talk

Share your experiences with writing expository essays with a partner. Talk about strategies that worked well for you, as well as those that weren't as successful. Be sure to include your analysis of why certain strategies worked better than others.

Persuasion

Persuasive writing aims to influence the attitudes or actions of a specific audience on specific issues. A strong persuasive text is logically organized and clearly describes the issue. It also provides precise and relevant evidence that supports a clear thesis statement. Persuasive writing may contain diagrams, graphs, or charts. These visuals can help to convince the reader. Examples include *The Los Angeles Times's* "For the Primary Ballot" and "Watch This Space in '08."

Persuasive Essays or Argumentative Essays

A **persuasive essay** or **argumentative essay** uses logic and reasoning to persuade readers to adopt a certain point of view or to take action. A strong persuasive essay starts with a clear thesis statement and provides supporting arguments based on evidence. It also anticipates readers' counter-arguments and responds to them as well.

Persuasive Speeches

Persuasive speeches are presented aloud and aim to win an audience's support for a policy, position, or action. These speeches often appeal to emotion and reason to convince an audience. Speakers sometimes change their script in order to address each specific audience's concerns.

Editorials

Editorials, which appear in newspapers, in magazines, or on television, radio, or the Internet, state the opinion of the editors and publishers of news organizations. Editorials usually present an opinion about a current issue, starting with a clear thesis statement and then offering strong supporting evidence.

Op-Ed Pieces

An **op-ed, or opposite-editorial, piece** is an essay that tries to convince the readers of a publication to agree with the writer's views on an issue. The writer may not work for the publication and is often an expert on the issue or has an interesting point of view. The writer is identified so that people can judge his or her qualifications.

Letters to the Editor

Readers write **letters to editors** at print and Internet publications to express opinions in response to previously published articles. A good letter to the editor gives an accurate and honest representation of the writer's views.

Reviews

Reviews evaluate items and activities, such as books, movies, plays, and music, from the writer's point of view. A review often states opinions on the quality of an item or activity and supports those opinions with examples, facts, and other evidence.

Advertisements

Advertisements in all media—from print to online sites to highway billboards—are paid announcements that try to convince people to buy something or do something. Good advertisements use a hook to grab your attention and support their claims. They contain vivid, persuasive language and multimedia techniques, such as music, to appeal to a specific audience.

Propaganda

Propaganda uses emotional appeals and often biased, false, or misleading information to persuade people to think or act in a certain way. Propaganda may tap into people's strongest emotions by generating fear or attacking their ideas of loyalty or patriotism. Because propaganda appears to be objective, it is wise to be aware of the ways it can manipulate people's opinions and actions.

Try It! Think about what you have learned about exposition, description, and persuasion. Form a group to discuss and draw conclusions about which **genres** would be best if you were planning a first draft with each of these intentions in mind. **Select the correct genre** for conveying your intended meaning to your audiences. Then, identify two or three types of information that you would want to include in a first draft.

- To explain how an event happened
- To describe a beautiful landscape
- To encourage teens to buy teeth-whitening toothpaste

Partner Talk

Share your experiences with various types of persuasive texts with a partner. Talk about the types of persuasive texts that you think are most effective, honest, and fair. Be sure to explain your thinking.

Responses to Literature

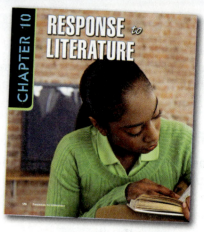

Responses to literature analyze and interpret an author's work. They use clear **thesis statements** and **evidence from the text using embedded quotations to support the writer's ideas.** They also evaluate how well authors have accomplished their goals. Effective responses to literature extend beyond literal analysis to evaluate and discuss how and why the text is effective or not effective.

Critical Reviews

Critical reviews evaluate books, plays, poetry, and other literary works. Reviews present the writer's opinions and support them with specific examples. The responses may analyze the aesthetic effects of an author's use of language in addition to responding to the content of the writing.

Compare-and-Contrast Essays

Compare-and-contrast essays explore similarities and differences between two or more works of literature. These essays provide relevant evidence to support the writer's opinions.

Letters to Authors

Readers write **letters to authors** to share their feelings and thoughts about a work of literature directly.

Blog Comments

Blog comments on an author's Web site or book retailer pages let readers share their ideas about a work. Readers express their opinions and give interpretations of what an author's work means.

 *Try It!* As a group, decide which **genre** would be most appropriate if you were planning a first draft for each of these purposes. **Select the correct genre** for conveying your intended meaning to your audiences. Then, identify two or three key questions that you would want to answer in a first draft.

- To tell an author why you think her book is excellent
- To write an opinion about a newspaper article
- To imagine how a certain landform came to be

Partner Talk

Interview your partner about his or her experiences writing interpretative responses. Be sure to ask questions such as these:

- How did you support your opinion of the author's work?
- How did you choose evidence, such as quotes, to support your analysis or opinion?

Research Writing

Research writing is based on factual information from outside sources. Research reports organize and present ideas and information to achieve a particular purpose and reach a specific audience. They present evidence in support of a clear thesis statement.

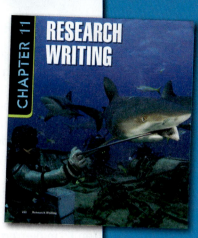

Research Reports and Documented Essays

Research reports and **documented essays** present information and analysis about a topic that the writer has studied. Start with a clear thesis statement. Research reports often include graphics and illustrations to clarify concepts. Documented essays are less formal research writings that show the source of every fact, quote, or borrowed idea in parentheses.

Experiment Journals and Lab Reports

Experiment journals and **lab reports** focus on the purposes, procedures, and results of a lab experiment. They often follow a strict format that includes dates and specific observation notes.

Statistical Analysis Reports

A **statistical analysis report** presents numerical data. Writers of this type of report must explain how they gathered their information, analyze their data, tell what significance the findings may have, and explain how these findings support their thesis statement.

Annotated Bibliographies

An **annotated bibliography** lists the research sources a writer used. It includes the title, author, publication date, publisher, and brief notes that describe and evaluate the source.

Try It! Discuss which kinds of reports you might write if you were planning a first draft for these purposes. **Select the correct form** for conveying your intended meaning to your audiences. Then, identify two or three key questions that you would want to answer in a first draft. Explain your choices.

- To accompany a project you plan to enter in a science fair
- To write about a poll taken to predict the results of a local election

Share with a partner the kinds of research writing you've done in school. Explain which projects you've enjoyed and why.

Workplace Writing

Workplace writing is writing done on the job or as part of a job, often in an office setting. It usually communicates details about a particular job or work project. This type of writing features organized and accurately conveyed information and should include reader-friendly formatting techniques, such as clearly defined sections and enough blank space for easy reading.

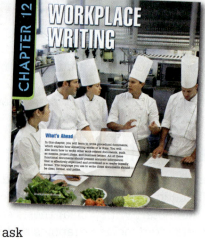

Business Letters and Friendly Letters

A **business letter** is a formal letter written to, from, or within a business. It can be written to make requests or to express concerns or approval. For example, you might write to a company to ask about job opportunities. Business letters follow a specific format that includes an address, date, formal greeting, and closing.

In contrast, a **friendly letter** is a form of correspondence written to communicate between family, friends, or acquaintances. For example, you might write a thank-you note for a gift.

Memos

Memos are short documents usually written from one member of an organization to another or to a group. They are an important means of communicating information within an organization.

E-mails

E-mail is an abbreviation for "electronic mail" and is a form of electronic memo. Because it can be transmitted quickly allowing for instant long-distance communication, e-mail is a very common form of communication that uses a computer and software to send messages.

Forms

Forms are types of workplace writing that ask for specific information to be completed in a particular format. Examples include applications, emergency contact information forms, and tax forms.

22 Types of Writing

Instructions

Instructions are used to explain how to complete a task or procedure. They provide clear, step-by-step guidelines. For example, recipes and user manuals are forms of instructions.

Project Plans

Project plans are short documents usually written from one member of an organization to another. They outline a project's goals and objectives and may include specific details about how certain steps of a project should be achieved.

Résumés

A **résumé** is an overview of a person's experience and qualifications for a job. This document lists a person's job skills and work history. Résumés can also feature information about a person's education.

College Applications

College applications are documents that ask for personal information and details about someone's educational background. College administrators use this information to decide whether or not to accept a student.

Job Applications

Job applications are similar to résumés in that they require a person to list work experience and educational background. Most employers will require a completed job application as part of the hiring process.

Partner Talk

Share with a partner your experience with workplace and procedural writing. For example, have you ever written instructions, created a résumé, or completed a job application? What do you find are particular challenges with this type of writing?

Try It! As a group, discuss which form of workplace writing would be best for each of these purposes. Select the correct form for conveying your intended meaning to your audiences. Identify two or three types of information you would expect to include in a first draft.

- To inform the company that made your cell phone that it does not work properly
- To give information about your qualifications for a job search
- To create a plan for your group assignment in science class

Writing for Media

The world of communication has changed significantly in recent years. In addition to writing for print media such as magazines and books, writers also write for a variety of other **media**, in forms such as:

- Scripts for screenplays, video games, and documentaries
- Storyboards for graphic novels and advertisements
- Packaging for every kind of product
- Web sites and blogs

Scripts

Scripts are written for various media, such as documentaries, theater productions, speeches, and audio programs. Movies, television shows, and video games also have scripts.

- A good script focuses on a clearly expressed or implied **theme** and has a specific **purpose**.
- It also contains interesting details, which contribute to a definite **mood or tone**.
- A good script also includes a clear **setting**, **dialogue**, and well-developed **action**.

Blogs

Blogs address just about every purpose and interest. For example, there are blogs about local issues, pets, or food.

Advertisements

Advertisements are designed to persuade someone to buy a product or service. Advertisements use images, words, and music to support their message. Writers write the content of advertisements. In addition, they may help create music and design the sound and the images in the ad.

Creating Multimedia Projects

A **multimedia project** or presentation uses sound, video, and other media to convey a point or entertain an audience. No matter what type of project you choose as your own multimedia project, it is important to follow these steps:

- Decide on the project's **purpose** and your target **audience**.
- Choose **media** that will effectively convey your **message**.
- **Plan** your presentation. Will you work alone or with a partner or group? If you work with others, how you will assign the tasks?
- What **equipment** will you need? Will you produce artwork, record audio, and take photographs? Should you produce a storyboard to show the sequence of details in your presentation? Be sure to allow enough time to produce the text and all the other elements in your project.
- Keep the **writing process** in mind. There should be working and reworking along the way.
- **Assess** the progress of the project as you work. Ask questions, such as: Does my project incorporate appropriate writing genres? Will the presentation interest my audience? Have I kept my purpose in mind?
- **Rehearse!** Before presenting your project, be sure to do several "practice runs" to weed out and correct any errors.
- Keep an electronic record of your presentation for future reference.
- After your presentation, have others assess the project. Their critique will help you to do an even better job next time!

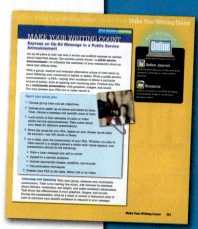

Partner Talk

Share with a partner your experience with writing for media or multimedia projects. Have you created a Web site or contributed to one? Have you had to complete multimedia projects for a class assignment or for a personal project on which you worked? Talk about how writing for media presents different challenges from more traditional writing and how you have dealt with those challenges.

Reflect on Your Writing

Learning more about the different types of writing can help you focus on the characteristics of each type so you can keep improving your own writing. Think about what you've learned in Chapter 2 as you answer these questions:

- What type of writing most interests you?
- What type of writing do you think is most useful? Why?

THE WRITING PROCESS

Writing Traits

Good writing has specific qualities, or traits. In this chapter you will learn about these traits and how to use rubrics to evaluate your writing in terms of them. You will also learn how to address them during the writing process.

Ideas

The best writing is built from strong ideas. It shows original thinking and provides readers with interesting, significant information. It also sends a strong message or presents a clear "angle" or point of view on a subject. In good writing, ideas are well developed, or explained and supported with examples and other details.

Organization

A well-organized paper has an obvious plan. Ideas move from sentence to sentence and paragraph to paragraph in a logical way. For example, events in a story often appear in chronological order, the order in which they occurred. Some expository writing presents ideas in order of importance. Descriptive writing may use a spatial organization, describing something from top to bottom or left to right.

Voice

Voice is the combination of word choice and personal writing style that makes your writing unique. It shows your personality or "take" on a story. Voice connects a reader to the writer. While the content of your writing is critical, effective writing features a strong voice.

Word Choice

To best achieve your purpose in writing, choose words carefully. When you choose precise words, you choose words that express your exact meaning. When you choose vivid words, you choose words that create pictures for readers, words that describe how a subject looks, sounds, smells, and so on. You may also use figures of speech (direct or indirect comparisons of unlike things) to create memorable images of your subject.

Sentence Fluency

Sentence fluency refers to the rhythm and flow of writing. Keep the rhythm of your writing fresh by varying sentence patterns, and create flow by choosing sentence structures that match your meaning. For example, you might show the connection between two ideas by joining them in one longer sentence, or you might create emphasis by breaking off a series of long sentences with one short sentence.

Conventions

By following the rules of spelling, capitalization, punctuation, grammar, and usage, you help readers understand your ideas.

Overview of Writing Traits	
Ideas	• Significant ideas and informative details • Thorough development of ideas • Unique perspective or strong message
Organization	• Obvious plan • Clear sequence • Strong transitions
Voice	• Effective word choice expressing personality or perspective • Attention to style
Word Choice	• Precise, not vague, words • Vivid, not dull, words • Word choices suited to audience and purpose
Sentency Fluency	• Varied sentence beginnings, lengths, and structures • Smooth sentence rhythms used to support meaning
Conventions	• Proper spelling and capitalization • Correct punctuation, grammar, usage, and sentence structure

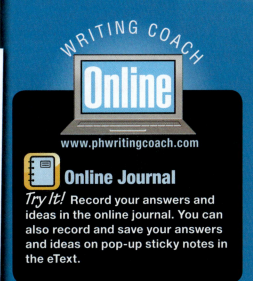

WRITING COACH Online
www.phwritingcoach.com

Online Journal

Try It! Record your answers and ideas in the online journal. You can also record and save your answers and ideas on pop-up sticky notes in the eText.

" Writer to Writer "

Good writing is a symphony of traits—all coming together to make the paper sing.

—Kelly Gallagher

Writing Traits

Rubrics and How to Use Them

You can use rubrics to evaluate your writing. A rubric allows you to score your writing on a scale for each trait. You will use a six-point rubric like this to help evaluate your writing in chapters 5–12.

Writing Traits	Rating Scale
Ideas: How interesting, significant, or original are the ideas you present? How well do you develop, or explain, support, and extend, ideas?	Not very Very 1 2 3 4 5 6
Organization: How logically is your piece organized? How much sense do your transitions, or movements from idea to idea, make?	1 2 3 4 5 6
Voice: How authentic and original is your voice?	1 2 3 4 5 6
Word Choice: How precise and vivid are the words you use? How well does your word choice help achieve your purpose?	1 2 3 4 5 6
Sentence Fluency: How well do your sentences flow? How strong and varied is the rhythm they create?	1 2 3 4 5 6
Conventions: How correct is your punctuation? Your capitalization? Your spelling?	1 2 3 4 5 6

Each trait to be assessed appears in the first column. The rating scale appears in the second column. The higher your score for a trait, the better your writing exhibits that trait.

Using a Rubric on Your Own

A rubric can be a big help in assessing your writing while it is still in process. Imagine you are about to start writing a piece of narrative fiction. You consult a rubric, which reminds you that narrative fiction should have characters, a setting, and a conflict and resolution. As you write, you try to incorporate and develop each element. After drafting, you might check the rubric again to make sure you are on track. For example, after reviewing the rubric again, you might decide that you have not developed the conflict or its resolution well. You would then go back and revise to improve your writing and get a better score.

Narrative Fiction Elements	Rating Scale
	Not very Very
Interesting characters	1 2 3 4 5 6
Believable setting	1 2 3 4 5 6
Literary strategies	1 2 3 4 5 6
Well-developed conflict	1 2 3 4 5 6
Well-developed resolution	1 2 3 4 5 6

Try It! If you checked your story against the rubric and rated yourself mostly 1s and 2s, what actions might you want to take?

Using a Rubric With a Partner

In some cases, building your own rubric can help you ensure that your writing will meet your expectations. For example, if your class has an assignment to write a poem, you and a partner might decide to construct a rubric to check one another's work. A rubric like the one shown here can help point out whether you should make any changes. Extra lines allow room for you to add other criteria.

Poetry Elements	Rating Scale
	Not very Very
Good sensory details	1 2 3 4 5 6
Colorful adjectives	1 2 3 4 5 6
	1 2 3 4 5 6
	1 2 3 4 5 6
	1 2 3 4 5 6

Try It! What other elements might you add to the rubric?

Using a Rubric in a Group

It is also helpful to use a rubric in a group. That way you can get input on your writing from many people at the same time. If the group members' ratings of your piece are similar, you will probably have an easy time deciding whether to make changes. If the responses vary significantly, you might want to discuss the results with the group. Then, analyze what led to the differing opinions and make careful judgments about what changes you will make.

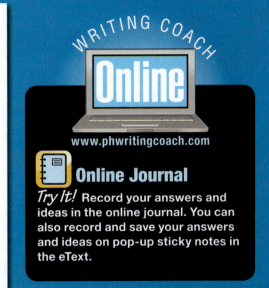

WRITING COACH Online
www.phwritingcoach.com

Online Journal
Try It! Record your answers and ideas in the online journal. You can also record and save your answers and ideas on pop-up sticky notes in the eText.

What Is the Writing Process?

The five steps in the writing process are prewriting, drafting, revising, editing, and publishing. Writing is a process because your idea goes through a series of changes or stages before the product is finished.

Study the diagram to see how moving through the writing process can work. Remember, you can go back to a stage in the process. It does not always have to occur in order.

Why Use the Writing Process?

Writing involves careful thinking, which means you will make changes as you write. Even professional writers don't just write their thoughts and call it a finished work of art. They use a process. For example, some writers keep going back to the revising stage many times, while others feel they can do the revision in just one step. It is up to each writer to develop the style that works best to produce the best results.

You might find that the writing process works best for you when you keep these tips in mind:

- Remember that the five steps in the writing process are equally important.
- Think about your audience as you plan your paper and develop your writing.
- Make sure you remember your topic and stick to your specific purpose as you write.
- Give your writing some time to "rest." Sometimes it can be good to work on a piece, walk away, and look at it later, with a fresh eye and mind.

The following pages will describe in more detail how to use each stage of the writing process to improve your writing.

WRITING COACH Online
www.phwritingcoach.com

Online Journal
Try It! Record your answers and ideas in the online journal. You can also record and save your answers and ideas on pop-up sticky notes in the eText.

" Writer to Writer "
Writing process gives us the freedom to write like mad, tinker like an engineer, evaluate like a judge—playing different roles at different stages. Most importantly it gives us the freedom to get our words out of our heads and into the world.

—Jeff Anderson

What Is the Writing Process? 31

Prewriting

Prewriting
Drafting
Revising
Editing
Publishing

No matter what kind of writing you do, planning during the prewriting stage is crucial. During prewriting, you determine the topic of your writing, its purpose, and its specific audience. Then, you narrow the topic and gather details.

Determining the Purpose and Audience

What Is Your Purpose?
To be sure your writing communicates your ideas clearly, it is important to clarify why you are writing. Consider what you want your audience to take away from your writing. You may want to entertain them, or you may want to warn them about something. Even when you write an entry in a private journal, you're writing for an audience—you!

Who Is Your Audience?
Think about the people who will read your work and consider what they may already know about your topic. Being able to identify this group and their needs will let you be sure you are providing the right level of information.

Choosing a Topic

Here are just a few of the many techniques you can use to determine an appropriate topic.

- **Brainstorm**
  You can brainstorm by yourself, with a partner, or with a group. Just jot down ideas as they arise, and don't rule out anything. When brainstorming in a group, one person's idea often "piggy-backs" on another.

- **Make a Mind Map**
  A mind map is a quick drawing you sketch as ideas come to you. The mind map can take any form. The important thing is to write quick notes as they come to you and then to draw lines to connect relationships among the ideas.

- **Interview**
  A fun way to find a writing topic is to conduct an interview. You might start by writing interview questions for yourself or someone else. Questions that start with *what*, *when*, *why*, *how*, and *who* are most effective. For example, you might ask, "When was the last time you laughed really hard?" "What made you laugh?" Then, conduct the interview and discover the answers.

- **Review Resources and Discuss Ideas**
  You can review resources, such as books, magazines, newspapers, and digital articles, to get ideas. Discussing your initial ideas with a partner can spark even more ideas.

Narrowing Your Topic

Once you have settled on a topic idea you really like, it may seem too broad to tackle. How can you narrow your topic?

- **Use Graphic Organizers**
  A graphic organizer can help narrow a topic that's too broad. For example, you might choose "Animals" as a topic. You might make your topics smaller and smaller until you narrow the topic to "The Habitat of Emperor Penguins."

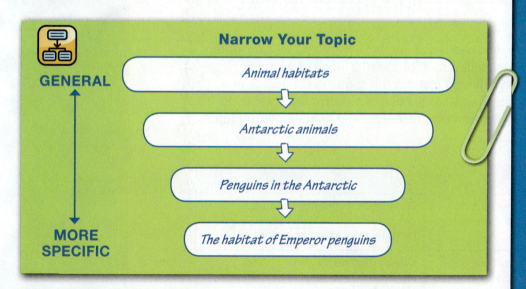

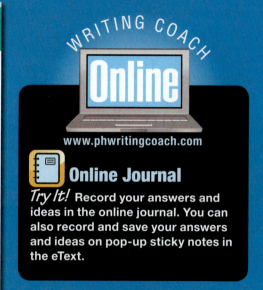

Online Journal

Try It! Record your answers and ideas in the online journal. You can also record and save your answers and ideas on pop-up sticky notes in the eText.

" Writer to Writer "

Put something down. Anything. Then, magic will happen.

—Jeff Anderson

Prewriting (continued)

- **Use Resource Materials**
  The resource materials you use to find information can also help you narrow a broad topic. Look up your subject online in an encyclopedia or newspaper archive. Scan the resources as you look for specific subtopics to pursue.

Gather Details

After you decide on a topic, you will want to explore and develop your ideas. You might start by looking through online resources again, talking with people who are knowledgeable about your topic, and writing everything you already know about the topic. It will be helpful to gather a variety of details. Look at these types:

- Facts
- Statistics
- Personal observations
- Expert opinions
- Examples
- Descriptions
- Quotations
- Opposing viewpoints

After you have narrowed your topic and gathered details, you will begin to plan your piece. During this part of prewriting, you will develop your essay's thesis or controlling idea—its main point or purpose. If you are writing a fiction or nonfiction story, you will outline the events of the story.

As you plan your piece, you can use a graphic organizer. Specific kinds of graphic organizers can help structure specific kinds of writing. For example, a plot map can help plot out the sequence of events in a mystery story. A pro-con chart like this one can clarify the reasons for and against an idea. It presents arguments for and against adding funds to a school music program.

Pro	Con
Adding funds to the school music budget would allow more students to learn to play instruments.	Giving more money to the music department would mean other programs would get less money.
Research shows that music helps the brain become more flexible.	Other programs, such as sports, are important in keeping students physically healthy.
Band members could stop selling gift-wrap materials at holiday time.	The school board has already approved the current budget allocations.

Drafting

No matter what kind of writing you do, planning during the prewriting stage is crucial. During prewriting, you determine the topic of your writing, its purpose, and its specific audience. Then, you narrow the topic and gather details.

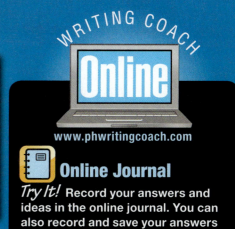

The Introduction

Most genres should have a strong introduction that immediately grabs the reader's attention and includes the thesis. Even stories and poems need a "hook" to grab interest.

Try It! Which of these first sentences are strong openers? Read these examples of first sentences. Decide which ones are most interesting to you. Explain why they grab your attention. Then, explain why the others are weak.

- Have you ever wondered what it would be like to wake up one morning to find you're someone else?
- There are many ways to paint a room.
- Yogi Berra, the famous baseball star, said, "You got to be careful if you don't know where you're going, because you might not get there."
- Autumn is a beautiful season.
- On Sunday, we went to the store.
- When I woke up that morning, I had no idea that it would be the best day of my life.

The Body

The body of a paper develops the main idea and details that elaborate on and support the thesis. As you tell your story or build an argument these details may include interesting facts, examples, statistics, anecdotes or stories, quotations, personal feelings, and sensory descriptions.

The Conclusion

The conclusion typically restates the thesis and summarizes the most important concepts of a paper.

Revising: Making It Better

No one gets every single thing right in a first draft. In fact, most people require more than two drafts to achieve their best writing and thinking. When you have finished your first draft, you're ready to revise.

Revising means "re-seeing." In revising, you look again to see if you can find ways to improve style, word choice, figurative language, sentence variety, and subtlety of meaning. As always, check how well you've addressed the issues of purpose, audience, and genre. Carefully analyze what you'd want to change and then go ahead and do it. Here are some helpful hints on starting the revision stage of the writing process.

Take a Break

Do not begin to revise immediately after you finish a draft. Take some time away from your paper. Get a glass of water, take a walk, or listen to some music. You may even want to wait a day to look at what you've written. When you come back, you will be better able to assess the strengths and weaknesses of your work.

Put Yourself in the Place of the Reader

Take off your writer's hat and put on your reader's hat. Do your best to pretend that you're reading someone else's work and see how it looks to that other person. Look for ideas that might be confusing and consider the questions that a reader might have. By reading the piece with an objective eye, you may find items you'd want to fix and improve.

Read Aloud to Yourself

It may feel strange to read aloud to yourself, but it can be an effective technique. It allows you to hear the flow of words, find errors, and hear where you might improve the work by smoothing out transitions between paragraphs or sections. Of course, if you're more comfortable reading your work aloud to someone else, that works, too.

Share Your Work to Get Feedback

Your friends or family members can help you by reading and reacting to your writing. Ask them whether you've clearly expressed your ideas. Encourage them to tell you which parts were most and least interesting and why. Try to find out if they have any questions about your topic that were not answered. Then, evaluate their input and decide what will make your writing better.

Use a Rubric

A rubric might be just what you need to pinpoint weaknesses in your work. You may want to think about the core parts of the work and rate them on a scale. If you come up short, you'll have a better idea about the kinds of things to improve. You might also use a rubric to invite peer review and input.

21st Century Learning

Collaborate and Discuss

When presenting and sharing drafts in the revision stage with a small group, it may be wise to set some ground rules. That way, the group is more likely to help each other analyze their work and make thoughtful changes that result in true improvements.

Here are some suggestions for reviewing drafts as a group:

- Cover the names on papers the group will review to keep the work anonymous.
- Print out copies for everyone in the group.
- Show respect for all group members and their writing.
- Be sure all critiques include positive comments.
- While it is fine to suggest ways to improve the work, present comments in a positive, helpful way. No insults are allowed!
- Plan for a second reading with additional input after the writer has followed selected suggestions.

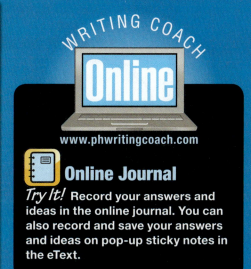

www.phwritingcoach.com

Online Journal

Try It! Record your answers and ideas in the online journal. You can also record and save your answers and ideas on pop-up sticky notes in the eText.

After a group revision session, talk with a partner to analyze each other's feeling on how the session went. Discuss such issues as these: Did the group adhere to the ground rules? What suggestions could you and your partner make to improve the next session?

Revision RADaR

The Revision RADaR strategy, which you will use throughout this book, is an effective tool in helping you conduct a focused revision of your work.

You can use your Revision RADaR to revise your writing. The letters **R**, **A**, **D**, and **R** will help you remember to **r**eplace, **a**dd, **d**elete, and **r**eorder.

To understand more about the Revision RADaR strategy, study the following chart.

R	A	D and	R
Replace . . .	**Add . . .**	**Delete . . .**	**Reorder . . .**
• Words that are not specific • Words that are overused • Sentences that are unclear	• New information • Descriptive adjectives and adverbs • Rhetorical or literary devices	• Unrelated ideas • Sentences that sound good, but do not make sense • Repeated words or phrases • Unnecessary details	• So most important points are last • To make better sense or to flow better • So details support main ideas

R Replace

You can strengthen a text by replacing words that are not specific, words that are overused, and sentences that are unclear. Take a look at this before and after model.

BEFORE
As I ran to the finish line, my heart was beating.

AFTER
As I sprinted to the finish line, my heart was pounding in my chest.

Apply It! How did the writer replace the overused verb *ran*? What other replacements do you see? How did they improve the text?

Add

You can add new information, descriptive adjectives and adverbs, and rhetorical or literary devices to make your piece more powerful. Study this before and after model.

BEFORE
Shadows made the night seem scary.
AFTER
Ominous shadows made the dark night seem even more sinister.

Apply It! **How did the second sentence make you feel, compared with the first? Explain.**

 Delete

Sometimes taking words out of a text can improve clarity. Analyze this before and after model.

BEFORE
The candidates talked about the issues, and many of the issues were issues that had been on voters' minds.
AFTER
The candidates talked about the issues, many of which had been on voters' minds.

Apply It! **Describe the revision you see. How did taking out unnecessary repetition of the word *issues* help the sentence flow more naturally?**

 Reorder

When you reorder, you can make sentences flow more logically. Look at this example.

BEFORE
Put the sunflower seeds over the strawberries, which are on top of the pineapple in a bowl. You'll have a delicious fruit salad!
AFTER
To make a delicious fruit salad, cut pineapple into a bowl. Add strawberries and then sprinkle a few sunflower seeds over the top.

Apply It! **Which of the models flows more logically? Why?**

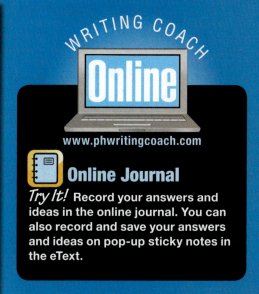

Online Journal

Try It! Record your answers and ideas in the online journal. You can also record and save your answers and ideas on pop-up sticky notes in the eText.

"Writer to Writer"

Anyone can write a first draft, but revision is where the paper comes to life.

—Kelly Gallagher

USING TECHNOLOGY

Most word processing programs have a built-in thesaurus tool. You can use the thesaurus to find descriptive words that can often substitute for weaker, overused words.

Revision RADaR (continued)

Read the first draft of the Student Model—a review of the book *Technology Drives Me Wild!* Think about how you might use your Revision RADaR to improve the text in a second draft.

Kelly Gallagher, M. Ed.

KEEP REVISION ON YOUR RADAR

Technology Book Drives Reviewer Wild

As a technology fan, I always look for new books about the latest in technology, as soon as they come out. So, when I bought *Technology Drives Me Wild!* by James Frank, after reading other books by Mr. Frank, I had high hopes this would be another winner that would improve my life. Those high hopes were not met by reading this disappointing book.

This book, which dashed my high hopes of learning some new stuff, has many mistakes. One error is that computers were not invented in the early 1800s. Did Thomas Jefferson use a computer when he was president? I don't think so.

The one good thing about *Technology Drives Me Wild!* is the fact that it is a very short book. That way, you won't waste too much time, if you decide not to take my advice and read this boring book after all.

It would have helped to show more pictures when explaining how computer chips work. Besides that, the text is boring and there are no diagrams or photos to keep the text from being boring. In addition, the boring text is very wordy and many of the explanations are unclear and impossible to understand. Also, the photograph of Mr. Frank on the book jacket is out of focus.

Here's a summary of my recommendation about this book: don't read it! Use your time to find better information about technology in other sources.

*Does my **introduction** grab reader interest?*

*Are my **word choices** varied?*

After writing the first draft, the student used Revision RADaR and asked questions like these:

- What could I **replace**?
- What could I **add**?
- What words might I **delete**?
- Should I **reorder** anything?

The student writer created this second draft after using Revision RADaR.

Technology Book Drives Reviewer Wild

2ND DRAFT

==There's no doubt about it. I find the expansion of technology fascinating.== I'm always anxious to read the latest developments and to consider how they might enhance my own life. Having read James Frank's previous excellent books on technology, I rushed out to buy his latest—*Technology Drives Me Wild!* Unfortunately, this book turned out to be a be grave disappointment.

I'd hoped to glean new information and a fresh understanding of improvements in global positioning systems, netbooks, and cell phones from the book. What I discovered instead was a substandard account, fraught with errors. For example, I am quite certain that while some people may have dreamed of computers in the 1800s, I doubt any actually existed. Mr. Frank should have checked his facts.

==Perhaps additional diagrams, photographs, and other visuals would have helped clarify the weak explanations of how, for example, computer chips work. The addition of lively text would have also helped.==

It's fortunate that *Technology Drives Me Wild!* is a short book. That way, even if you pick it up in error, you will not have wasted much of your valuable time.

R — Replaced opening with more engaging sentences

D — Deleted repetitive words
A — Added details about what would improve the text

Writing Coach Online
www.phwritingcoach.com

Online Journal

Try It! Record your answers and ideas in the online journal. You can also record and save your answers and ideas on pop-up sticky notes in the eText.

Partner Talk

Work with a partner to write as many substitutions for the verb *walk* as possible. Remember to consider the different ways people walk. For example, how does a young child walk? How does a successful team captain walk? How might a very elderly person walk? Discuss the value of using more specific words in your writing.

Try It! What other words did the writer replace? Add? Delete? Reorder?

Editing: Making It Correct

Editing is the process of checking the accuracy of facts and correcting errors in spelling, grammar, usage, and mechanics. Using a checklist like the one shown here can help ensure you've done a thorough job of editing.

Prewriting
Drafting
Revising
Editing
Publishing

Editing Checklist

Task	Ask Yourself
Check your facts and spelling	❏ Have I checked that my facts are correct? ❏ Have I used spell check or a dictionary to check any words I'm not sure are spelled correctly?
Check your grammar	❏ Have I written any run-on sentences? ❏ Have I used the correct verbs and verb tenses? ❏ Do my pronouns match their antecedents, or nouns they replace?
Check your usage	❏ Have I used the correct form of irregular verbs? ❏ Have I used object pronouns, such as *me*, *him*, *her*, *us*, and *them* only after verbs or prepositions? ❏ Have I used subject pronouns, such as *I*, *he*, *she*, *we*, and *they* correctly—usually as subjects?
Check for proper use of mechanics	❏ Have I used correct punctuation? ❏ Does each sentence have the correct end mark? ❏ Have I used apostrophes in nouns but not in pronouns to show possession? ❏ Have I used quotation marks around words from another source? ❏ Have I used correct capitalization? ❏ Does each sentence begin with a capital letter? ❏ Do the names of specific people and places begin with a capital letter?

Using Proofreading Marks

Professional editors use a set of proofreading marks to indicate changes in a text. Here is a chart of some of the more common proofreading marks.

Proofreader's Marks	
(b.f.)	boldface
⌐	break text / start new line
(caps)	capital letter
⌒	close up
ℓ	delete
∧/	insert word
︵/	insert comma
=/	insert hyphen
+/	insert letter
⊙/	insert period
(ital)	italic type
(stet)	let stand as is
(l.f.)	lightface
(l.c.)	lower case letter
⌐	move left
⌐	move right
¶	new paragraph
(rom)	roman type
	run text up
(sp)	spell out whole word
	transpose

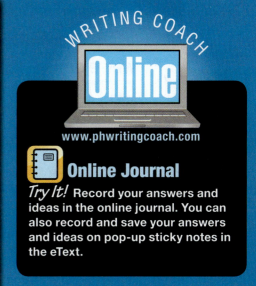

Online Journal

Try It! Record your answers and ideas in the online journal. You can also record and save your answers and ideas on pop-up sticky notes in the eText.

www.phwritingcoach.com

USING TECHNOLOGY

Many word processing programs have automatic spelling and grammar checks. While these tools can be helpful, be sure to pay attention to any suggestions they offer. That's because sometimes inappropriate substitutes are inserted automatically!

Editing: Making It Correct (continued)

WRITE GUY Jeff Anderson, M. Ed.

WHAT DO YOU NOTICE?

Using an editing checklist is a great way to check for correct grammar. However, using a checklist is not enough to make your writing grammatically correct. A checklist tells you what to look for, but not how to correct mistakes you find. To do that, you need to develop and apply your knowledge of grammar.

Looking closely at good writing is one way to expand your grammar know-how. The *What Do You Notice?* feature that appears throughout this book will help you zoom in on passages that use grammar correctly and effectively.

As you read this passage, from "One Dog's Feelings," zoom in on the sentences in the passage.

> *Bo clearly shows when he is angry. He gnashes his teeth, growls, and sometimes even spits! On the other hand, Bo, who can simultaneously chew on two pairs of shoes, is usually content. When he's happy, he simply smiles.*

Now, ask yourself: *What do you notice about the sentences in this passage?*

Maybe you noticed that the writer uses sentences of varying lengths and with different structures. Or perhaps you noticed that the writer varies the way sentences begin.

After asking a question that draws your attention to the grammar in the passage, the *What Do You Notice?* feature provides information on a particular grammar topic. For example, following the passage and question, you might read about simple and complex sentences, which are both used in the passage.

The *What Do You Notice?* feature will show you how grammar works in actual writing. It will help you learn how to make your writing correct.

What Do You Notice?

One Dog's Feelings

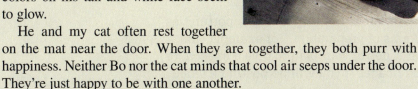

Some people wonder if animals feel and show emotions. However, I am absolutely positive that dogs experience a full range of emotions. I owe this knowledge to my dog, Bo.

Bo clearly shows when he is angry. He gnashes his teeth, growls, and sometimes even spits! On the other hand, Bo, who can simultaneously chew on two pairs of shoes, is usually content. When he's happy, he simply smiles. The colors on his tan and white face seem to glow.

He and my cat often rest together on the mat near the door. When they are together, they both purr with happiness. Neither Bo nor the cat minds that cool air seeps under the door. They're just happy to be with one another.

If my brothers or I want to play fetch, Bo is always up for a game. We often throw a ball into the woods, where it sometimes gets buried under leaves and sticks. Bo always rushes for the ball. And running back to us with the stick in his mouth is obviously his great joy. As for the sticks, few are ever left unfound.

When I leave for school in the morning, Bo whimpers—an obvious sign of sadness. That makes me feel miserable. However, the big payoff comes when I return home. Then Bo jumps up on the door, his tail wagging enthusiastically with excitement. Everybody wants to be loved like that!

Try It! Read "One Dog's Feelings." Then, write a response to each question in your journal.

1. What do you notice about the pronouns (*he, they, one, another*) in the third paragraph?
2. How does the writer use transitions, such as the word *however*, to connect ideas in the last paragraph?

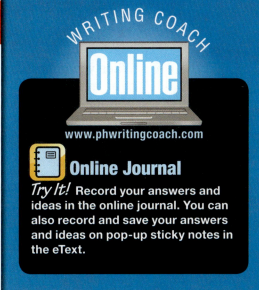

WRITING COACH Online
www.phwritingcoach.com

Online Journal

Try It! Record your answers and ideas in the online journal. You can also record and save your answers and ideas on pop-up sticky notes in the eText.

" Writer to Writer "

If I wonder how to write any kind of writing, I look at models—well-written examples of the kind of writing I want to do. Models are the greatest how-to lesson I have ever discovered.

—Jeff Anderson

Publishing

When you publish, you produce a final copy of your work and present it to an audience. When publishing you'll need to decide which form will best reach your audience, exhibit your ideas, show your creativity, and accomplish your main purpose.

To start assessing the optimal way to publish your work, you might ask yourself these questions:

- What do I hope to accomplish by sharing my work with others?
- Should I publish in print form? Give an oral presentation? Publish in print form and give an oral presentation?
- Should I publish online, in traditional print, or both?
- What specific forms are available to choose from?

The answers to most of these questions will most likely link to your purpose for writing and your audience. Some choices seem obvious. For example, if you've written a piece to contribute to a blog, you'll definitely want to send it electronically.

Each publishing form will present different challenges and opportunities and each will demand different forms of preparation. For example, you may need to prepare presentation slides of your plan to give a speech, or you may want to select music and images if you will be posting a video podcast online.

Ways to Publish

There are many ways to publish your writing. This chart shows some of several opportunities you can pursue to publish your work.

Genre	Publishing Opportunities	
Narration: Nonfiction	• Blogs • Book manuscript • Audio recording	• Private diary or journal entries • Electronic slide show
Narration: Fiction	• Book manuscript • Film	• Audio recording • Oral reading to a group
Poetry and Description	• Bound collection • Visual display	• Audio recording • Oral reading to a group
Exposition and Persuasion	• Print or online article • Web site • Slide show • Visual display	• Film • Audio recording • Oral reading or speech
Response to Literature	• Print or online letters • Visual displays	• Blogs • Slide show
Research Writing	• Traditional paper • Print and online experiment journals	• Multimedia presentation

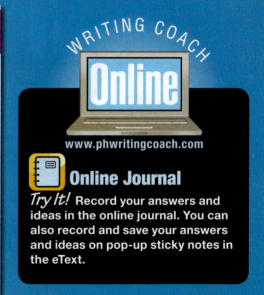

Online Journal

Try It! Record your answers and ideas in the online journal. You can also record and save your answers and ideas on pop-up sticky notes in the eText.

Discuss the chart on this page with a partner. If there are ways to publish that neither of you has ever tried, talk about how you might go about experimenting with those forms.

Reflect on Your Writing

Think about what you learned in Chapter 3 as you answer these questions:

- What did you learn about the writing process?
- What steps in the writing process do you already use in your writing?
- Which stage do you think is the most fun? Which one may be most challenging for you? Explain.

CHAPTER 4

SENTENCES, PARAGRAPHS, *and* COMPOSITIONS

Good writers know that strong sentences and paragraphs help to construct effective compositions. Chapter 4 will help you use these building blocks to structure and style excellent writing. It will also present ways to use rhetorical and literary devices and online tools to strengthen your writing.

The Building Blocks: Sentences and Paragraphs

A **sentence** is a group of words with two main parts: a subject and a predicate. Together, these parts express a complete thought.

A **paragraph** is built from a group of sentences that share a common idea and work together to express that idea clearly. The start of a new paragraph has visual clues—either an indent of several spaces in the first line or an extra line of space above it.

In a good piece of writing, each paragraph supports, develops, or explains the main idea of the whole work. Of course, the traits of effective writing—ideas, organization, voice, word choice, sentence fluency, and conventions—appear in each paragraph as well.

Writing Strong Sentences

To write strong paragraphs, you need strong sentences. While it may be your habit to write using a single style of sentences, adding variety will help make your writing more interesting. Combining sentences, using compound elements, forming compound sentences, and using subordination all may help you make your sentences stronger, clearer, or more varied.

Combine Sentences

Putting information from one sentence into another can make a more powerful sentence.

BEFORE
Video games can be effective educational tools. They can help teach many subjects.

AFTER
Video games, which can help teach many subjects, can be effective educational tools.

Use Compound Elements

You can form compound subjects, verbs, or objects to help the flow.

BEFORE
Students can play video games on their laptops. Students can also play video games on their cell phones.

AFTER
Students can play video games on their laptops and cell phones.

Form Compound Sentences

You can combine two sentences into a compound sentence.

BEFORE
Video games can motivate students to learn. They must have educational value.

AFTER
Video games can motivate students to learn, but they must have educational value.

Use Subordination

Combine two related sentences by rewriting the less important one as a subordinate clause.

BEFORE
Video games can take time away from exercise. That can be unhealthy.

AFTER
Video games can take time away from exercise, which can be unhealthy.

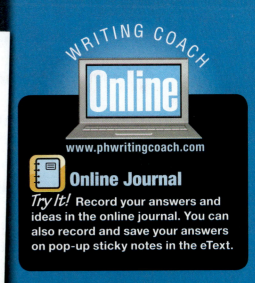

WRITING COACH Online
www.phwritingcoach.com

Online Journal
Try It! Record your answers and ideas in the online journal. You can also record and save your answers on pop-up sticky notes in the eText.

LEARN MORE
For more on sentence combining see Chapter 16.

Writing Strong Paragraphs

If all the sentences in a paragraph reflect the main idea and work together to express that idea clearly, the result will be a strong paragraph.

Express Your Main Idea With a Clear Topic Sentence

A **topic sentence** summarizes the main idea of a paragraph. It may appear at the beginning, middle, or end of a paragraph. It may even be unstated. When the topic sentence comes at the beginning of a paragraph, it introduces the main idea and leads the reader naturally to the sentences that follow it. When it appears at the end of a paragraph, it can draw a conclusion or summarize what came before it. If the topic sentence is unstated, the rest of the paragraph must be very clearly developed, so the reader can understand the main idea from the other sentences.

Think about the topic sentence as you read this paragraph.

> Without a doubt, hiking must be the best sport in the world. Hiking is good exercise and makes me feel totally free. When I'm out on the trail, I can think more clearly than anywhere else. Even solving problems that seemed totally unsolvable at home becomes possible. I also use all of my senses when I hike. I hear birds singing, I notice strange plants, and I feel the soft underbrush beneath my boots. Sometimes I even think I can smell and taste the fresh air.

 Try It! Look back at the sample paragraph to answer these questions.

1. What is the topic sentence?
2. Does the topic sentence introduce the main idea or draw a final conclusion? Explain.
3. What makes this topic sentence strong?

Sentences, Paragraphs, and Compositions

Write Effective Supporting Sentences

A clear topic sentence is a good start, but it needs to be accompanied by good details that support the paragraph's main idea. Your supporting sentences might tell interesting facts, describe events, or give examples. In addition, the supporting sentences should also provide a smooth transition, so that the paragraph reads clearly and logically.

Think about the topic sentences and supporting details as you read this paragraph.

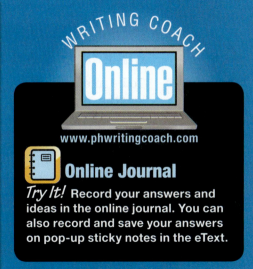

www.phwritingcoach.com

Online Journal

Try It! Record your answers and ideas in the online journal. You can also record and save your answers on pop-up sticky notes in the eText.

> What was life like before cell phones? It's barely imaginable! People were tied to land lines and could make and take calls only in homes, offices, or on pay phones. If there were an emergency, there could be unavoidable delays as people searched for an available phone. If they wanted to chat with friends, they usually had to wait until they got home. How ever did they live without being able to text? Some people send text messages to their friends about 50 times a day. What a different world it was way back then.

 Try It! Look at the paragraph and answer these questions.

1. What is the topic sentence of the paragraph?
2. Do you think it's an effective topic sentence? Why or why not?
3. What supporting details does the writer provide?
4. If you were the writer, what other supporting details might you add to strengthen the paragraph?
5. Which sentence in the paragraph breaks up the flow of ideas and does not provide a smooth transition to the next sentence?

Writing Strong Paragraphs

Include a Variety of Sentence Lengths, Structures, and Beginnings

To be interesting, a paragraph should include sentences of different lengths, types, and beginnings. Similarly, if every sentence has the same structure—for example, article, adjective, noun, verb—the paragraph may sound boring or dry.

Work with a partner to take another look at the writing sample on this page. Talk about what you think the writer did well. Then, discuss what might make the paragraph even stronger.

21st Century Learning

Collaborate and Discuss

With a group, study this writing sample.

> The scene was tense as Carlos stepped to the plate. Looking confident, he took a few practice swings. Then he stopped and stared straight at the pitcher. The first pitch zoomed over home plate at about 90 miles an hour—right past Carlos. Strike one! The second pitch was high and outside. Ball one! Next Carlos took a deep breath; it was obvious he meant business now. He stared down the pitcher and raised his bat. Crack! Carlos hit that ball right over the fence behind second base and the game was over. It was a 4-2 victory for the home team, thanks to Carlos!

Discuss these questions about the paragraph.

1. What is the topic sentence? How does it draw in the reader?
2. What details support the topic sentence?
3. Point out some examples of varying sentence lengths and beginnings.
4. What examples can you find of sentences with a variety of sentence structures?
5. Which words help the transitions and flow of the paragraph?

Composing Your Piece

You've learned that the building blocks of writing are strong sentences and paragraphs. Now it's time to use those building blocks to construct an effective composition. While the types of writing vary from short poems to long essays and research papers, most types have a definite structure with clearly defined parts.

The Parts of a Composition

Writers put together and arrange sentences and paragraphs to develop ideas in the clearest way possible in a composition. Some types of writing, such as poetry and advertisements, follow unique rules and may not have sentences and paragraphs that follow a standard structure. However, as you learned in Chapter 3, most compositions have three main sections: an introduction, a body, and a conclusion.

I. Introduction

The introduction of a composition introduces the focus of the composition, usually in a thesis statement. The introduction should engage the reader's interest, with such elements as a question, an unusual fact, or a surprising scene.

II. Body

Just as supporting statements develop the ideas of a topic sentence, the body of a composition develops the thesis statement and main idea. It provides details that help expand on the thesis statement. The paragraphs in the body are arranged in a logical order.

III. Conclusion

As the word implies, the conclusion of a composition concludes or ends a piece of writing. A good way to ensure the reader will remember your thesis statement is to restate it or summarize it in the conclusion. When restating the thesis, it's usually most effective to recast it in other words. Quotations and recommendations are other ways to conclude a composition with memorable impact. The conclusion should provide a parting insight or reinforce the importance of the main idea.

> **" Writer to Writer "**
>
> Strong, varied sentences and unified paragraphs are the building blocks of effective writing.
>
> —Kelly Gallagher

Rhetorical and Literary Devices

Like any builders, good writers have a set of tools, or devices, at their fingertips to make their writing interesting, engaging, and effective. Writers can use the rhetorical devices of language and their effects to strengthen the power of their style. This section presents some tools you can store in your own writing toolbox to develop effective compositions.

Sound Devices

Sound devices, which create a musical or emotional effect, are most often used in poetry. The most common sound devices include these:

- **Alliteration** is the repetition of consonant sounds at the beginning of words that are close to one another.

    Example: Bees buzzed by both bouquets.

- **Assonance** is the repetition of vowel sounds in words that are close to one another.

    Example: My kite flew high into the sky.

- **Consonance** is the repetition of consonants within or at the end of words.

    Example: Each coach teaches touch football after lunch.

Structural Devices

Structural devices determine the way a piece of writing is organized. Rhyme and meter are most often used to structure poetry, as are stanzas and many other structural devices.

- **Rhyme** is the repetition of sounds at the ends of words. Certain poetry forms have specific rhyme schemes.
- **Meter** is the rhythmical pattern of a poem, determined by the stressed syllables in a line.
- **Visual elements**, such as stanzas, line breaks, line length, fonts, readability, and white space, help determine how a piece of writing is read and interpreted. These elements can also affect the emotional response to a piece.

Sentences, Paragraphs, and Compositions

Other Major Devices

You can use these devices in many forms of writing. They help writers express ideas clearly and engage their readers.

Device	Example
Figurative language is writing that means something beyond what the words actually say. Common forms of figurative language include these: • A **simile** compares two things using the words *like* or *as*. • A **metaphor** compares two things by mentioning one thing as if it is something else. It does not use *like* or *as*. • **Personification** gives human characteristics to a non-human object.	*The fallen autumn leaves were like colorful jewels.* *Her smile was a beacon of good cheer.* *Shadows crawled over the sand just before dusk.*
Hyperbole is exaggeration used for effect.	*The elephant was as big as a house.*
Irony is a contradiction between what happens and what is expected.	*In a famous story, a wife cuts her hair to buy her husband a watch fob, and he sells his watch to buy her a brush.*
Paradox is a statement that contains elements that seem contradictory but could be true.	*George Orwell said, "Ignorance is strength."*
An **oxymoron** is word or phrase that seems to contradict itself.	*I had jumbo shrimp for dinner.*
Symbolism is an object that stands for something else.	*An owl is often used as a symbol for wisdom.*
An **allegory** is a narrative that has a meaning other than what literally appears.	*Some say that his sci-fi story is actually an allegory for the effects of war.*
Repetition (or tautology) occurs when content is repeated, sometimes needlessly—for effect.	*The forest was dense, dense and dark as coal.*

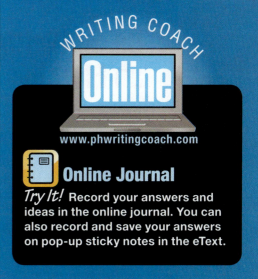

Online Journal

Try It! Record your answers and ideas in the online journal. You can also record and save your answers on pop-up sticky notes in the eText.

USING TECHNOLOGY

Most word processing programs have a built-in thesaurus tool. You can use the thesaurus to find descriptive words that can often substitute for weaker, overused words.

There are many online tools that can help you strengthen your writing. For example, you can search for examples of figurative language and sound devices. Then you can model your own writing after the samples. Just be sure that you don't plagiarize or copy the written work of others.

Using Writing Traits to Develop an Effective Composition

You read about rubrics and traits in Chapter 3. Now it's time to look at how they function in good writing.

Ideas

In an excellent piece of writing, the information presented is significant, the message or perspective is strong, and the ideas are original. As you read the sample, think about the ideas it presents and how it develops them.

Leaves of Three

Leaves of three. Let them be! It's an old rhyme that warns against the dangers of poison ivy—a plant with three waxy-looking leaves. If you've ever had a poison ivy rash, you know that the itching and pain it can cause are nothing to sneeze at. You may not know that the rash is caused by a colorless oil called urushiol or that not all people are allergic to this substance. However, those who are allergic never forget its effects.

Contracting the rash is, unfortunately, all too easy. Perhaps you've been outside, pulling up weeds on a sunny weekend. Because of the way poison ivy leaves bend down, you might not have even noticed them. Then it might have taken 12 to 48 hours before you felt a sharp itch and saw the telltale red blisters caused by even a brief brush with the plant.

What can you do for the discomfort of poison ivy? Applying ice helps some people. Others need anti-itch medication, especially if the reaction is intense or covers a large area. However, the best idea is to keep that old rhyme in mind and to be careful not to let those leaves of three ever come close to thee!

 Try It! Think about ideas in the sample as you respond to these prompts.

1. List two details that help readers relate to the topic.
2. List two significant pieces of information the writer includes.
3. List two details that clearly convey the writer's perspective.

Using Writing Traits: Sentences, Paragraphs, and Compositions

Organization

A well-organized composition flows easily from sentence to sentence and paragraph to paragraph. It smoothly progresses from one idea to the next, indicating the connections between ideas with transitions. The paper also avoids needless repetition.

Think about organization as you reread "Leaves of Three" on page 56.

 Try It! Answer the questions about the writing sample on page 56.

1. Identify the transition the writer uses to move from the ideas in the first paragraph to the ideas in the second.
2. List three details in the third paragraph. Explain how each detail supports the first sentence in the paragraph.
3. Identify the topic of each paragraph, and explain whether the topics are presented in logical order.

Voice

Voice is the individual "sound" of a writer's writing, reflecting the writer's personality and perspective. A well-written piece has a distinctive voice that expresses the writer's individuality.

Read the writing sample. Think about voice as you read.

> What is it like to know a person who looks exactly like you? As identical twins, my brother, Ben, and I can tell you that it's totally great. There are many reasons why.
>
> First, it's great to have a special non-verbal communication with another person. Sometimes it's even scary. Take this morning. Ben and I never dress alike, since we like to show that we're individuals. So, each of us got dressed in our own room and then skipped down the stairs for breakfast. You guessed it! We'd chosen exactly the same clothes—right down to our striped socks.
>
> Second, we can have fun fooling people by pretending to be each other. It's great fun to see Dad's expression when he finds he's treated the wrong twin to a reward.

 Try It! Consider the writer's voice as you answer these questions.

1. Describe the writer's tone—his attitude toward his subject.
2. Which words and phrases create a voice in this sample? Explain.

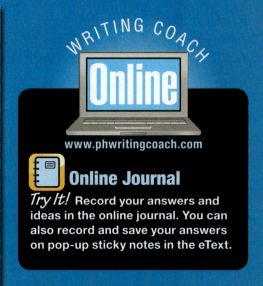

www.phwritingcoach.com

Online Journal

Try It! Record your answers and ideas in the online journal. You can also record and save your answers on pop-up sticky notes in the eText.

Analyze the composition about poison ivy on page 56 with a partner. Discuss how well it might score for the traits of ideas and organization—from ineffective (1), to somewhat effective (2), to fairly effective (3), to effective (4), to highly effective in parts (5), to highly effective throughout (6).

Word Choice

By choosing words with precision, and by using vivid words to create images, good writers give their writing energy and help readers understand their exact meaning.

Think about the writer's word choice as you read these two drafts:

Sally and Alice ran until they reached a place to make a turn. They headed off to the left, where the flowers were pretty and smelled nice.

Sally and Alice jogged at a steady pace on the dirt path along the lake until they reached a fork in the trail. Without breaking stride, the two turned in unison and headed left, bound by their silent understanding that left was best—left, where the cream-and-gold honeysuckle blossoms, drooping with fragrance, filled the air with a drowsy sweetness.

 Try It! Answer the question about the two drafts.

1. List two vague or imprecise words in the first draft.
2. Explain which words in the second draft replace the words you listed. What do the words in the second draft help you understand?

Sentence Fluency

When you read the best writing aloud, you will find that the sentences flow smoothly; they do not sound choppy or awkward. The meaning and the rhythm of the sentences work together. To create and control rhythm in writing, good writers use a variety of sentence structures and patterns. Think about the rhythm of the sentences as you read this draft:

Since I first joined the student council in the ninth grade, I have been a tireless advocate for many important student causes. My experience makes me a good candidate for president of the council; my advocacy makes me a great one. No one else matches my record.

 Try It! Answer the question about the sample.

Describe the rhythm created by the sentences. How does the writer emphasize the final sentence?

Conventions

If a piece of writing reflects a good command of spelling, capitalization, punctuation, grammar, usage, and sentence structure, it is much more likely to communicate clearly to readers.

Pay attention to spelling, capitalization, punctuation, grammar, usage, and sentence structure in the following first draft.

Super-Hero III Doesn't Fly

If you're among the thousands who have been waiting for the latest installment of the popular Super-Hero movie series, you'are in for a big disappointment. This sequel misses the boat—literally.

Me and my companion couldn't believe it! At the very beginning of the movie, as usual, our "hero" runs for the ship on his quest to capture the evil warlord. However, this time he misreads, the schedule and it took off for asia without his assistant and he.

Now, read this section of the reviewer's second draft.

Super-Hero III Doesn't Fly

If you're among the thousands who have been waiting for the latest installment of the popular Super-Hero movie series, you're in for a big disappointment. This sequel misses the boat—literally.

My companion and I couldn't believe it! At the very beginning of the movie, as usual, our "hero" runs for the ship on his quest to capture the evil warlord. However, this time he misreads the schedule, and the ship takes off for Asia without his assistant and him.

Try It! Answer these questions about both drafts.

1. What errors in convention did the writer correct in the second draft?
2. Why is the last sentence easier to read in the second draft?

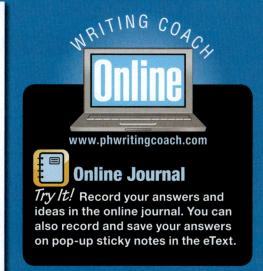

Online Journal

Try It! Record your answers and ideas in the online journal. You can also record and save your answers on pop-up sticky notes in the eText.

Work with a partner to make sure you both found every error the move reviewer corrected in the second draft.

Using Interactive Writing Coach

As you learned in Chapter 3, you can use rubrics and your Revision RADaR to check how well your paragraphs and essays read. With Writing Coach, you also have another tool available to evaluate your work: the Interactive Writing Coach.

The Interactive Writing Coach is a program that you can use anywhere that you have Internet access. Interactive Writing Coach functions like your own personal writing tutor. It gives you personalized feedback on your work.

The Interactive Writing Coach has two parts: **Paragraph Feedback** and **Essay Scorer**.

- Paragraph Feedback gives you feedback on individual paragraphs as you write. It looks at the structure of sentences and paragraphs and gives you information about specific details, such as sentence variety and length.

- Essay Scorer looks at your whole essay and gives you a score and feedback on your entire piece of writing. It will tell you how well your essay reflects the traits of good writing.

This chart shows just a few questions that Paragraph Feedback and Essay Scorer will answer about your writing. The following pages explain Paragraph Feedback and Essay Scorer in more detail.

Sentences	• Are sentences varied in length? • Do sentences have varied beginnings? • Which sentences have too many ideas? • Are adjectives clear and precise? • Is the sentence grammatically correct? • Is all spelling correct in the sentence?
Paragraphs	• Does the paragraph support its topic? • Does the paragraph use transitions? • Does the paragraph contain the right amount of ideas and information?
Compositions	• Does the essay reflect characteristics of the genre? • Does it demonstrate the traits of good writing? • Is the main idea clear? • Is the main idea well supported? • Is the essay cohesive—does it hold together?

Interactive Writing Coach and the Writing Process

You can begin to use Essay Scorer during the drafting section of the writing process. It is best to complete a full draft of your essay before submitting to Essay Scorer. (While you are drafting individual paragraphs, you may want to use Paragraph Feedback.) Keep in mind, however, that your draft does not need to be perfect or polished before you submit to Essay Scorer. You will be able to use feedback from Essay Scorer to revise your draft many times. This chart shows how you might use the Interactive Writing Coach and incorporate Essay Scorer into your writing process.

Paragraph Feedback With Interactive Writing Coach

The Paragraph Feedback assesses the ideas and topic support for each paragraph you write. You can enter your work into Paragraph Feedback one paragraph at a time. This makes it easy to work on individual paragraphs and get new feedback as you revise each one. Here are some things that Paragraph Feedback will be able to tell you.

Overall Paragraph Support	• Does the paragraph support the main idea? • Which sentences do not support the main idea?
Transitions	• Which sentences contain transition words? • Which words are transition words?
Ideas	• How well are ideas presented? • Which sentences have too many ideas?
Sentence Length and Variety	• Which sentences are short, medium, and long? • Which sentences could be longer or shorter for better sense or variety? • Are sentences varied?
Sentence Beginnings	• How do sentences begin? • Are sentence beginnings varied?
Sentence Structure	• Are sentence structures varied? • Are there too many sentences with similar structures?
Vague Adjectives	• Are any adjectives vague or unclear? • Where are adjectives in sentences and paragraphs?
Language Variety	• Are words repeated? • Where are repeated words located? • How can word choice be improved?

Essay Scoring With Interactive Writing Coach

Essay Scorer assesses your essay. It looks at the essay as a whole, and it also evaluates individual paragraphs, sentences, and words. Essay Scorer will help you evaluate the following traits.

Ideas	• Are the ideas original? Is a clear message or unique perspective presented? • Is the main idea clearly stated? • Is the main idea supported by informative details?
Organization	• Is the organization logical? • Is the introduction clear? Is the conclusion clear? • What transitions are used, and are they effective?
Voice	• Does the writer create a unique voice, expressing his or her personality or perspective? • Does the tone match the topic, audience, and purpose?
Word Choice	• Are precise words used? • Are vivid words used? • Do the word choices suit the purpose and audience?
Sentence Fluency	• Are sentence beginnings, lengths, and structures varied? • Do the sentences flow smoothly?
Conventions	• Is spelling correct? • Is capitalization used properly? • Is all punctuation (ending, internal, apostrophes) accurate? • Do subjects and verbs agree? • Are pronouns used correctly? • Are adjectives and adverbs used correctly? • Are plurals formed correctly? • Are commonly confused words used correctly?

Whenever you see the Interactive Writing Coach icon you can go to Writing Coach Online and submit your writing, either paragraph by paragraph or as a complete draft, for personalized feedback and scoring.

WRITING COACH Online
www.phwritingcoach.com

Interactive Writing Coach™

Interactive Writing Coach provides support and guidance to help you improve your writing skills.
- Select a topic to write about from the Topic Bank.
- Use the interactive graphic organizers to narrow your topic.
- Go to Writing Coach Online and submit your work, paragraph by paragraph or as a complete draft.
- Receive immediate, personalized feedback as you write, revise, and edit your work.

CHAPTER 5
NONFICTION NARRATION

What Do You Remember?

What interesting events have happened in your life? What makes these events special?

To tell a story about an event, you will need to remember details of the experience. Using vivid details to describe your memories will make them more interesting to others.

Try It! Think about an interesting event in your life. What story could you tell about it? Consider these questions as you participate in an extended discussion with a partner. Take turns expressing your ideas and feelings.

- What happened?
- Where were you?
- Who was there?
- What did you see, smell, touch, and feel?

Review the list you made, and then think about how you would include these details when telling someone about the recent event. Tell your story to a partner. As you listen to your partner's memory, see if you can answer the questions listed above.

What's Ahead

In this chapter, you will review two strong examples of an autobiographical narrative: a Mentor Text and a Student Model. Then, using the examples as guidance, you will write an autobiographical narrative of your own.

www.phwritingcoach.com

Online Journal

Try It! Record your answers and ideas in the online journal.

You can also record and save your answers and ideas on pop-up sticky notes in the eText.

Connect to the Big Questions

Discuss these questions with your partner:

1 What do you think? What makes conflict interesting?

2 Why Write? What should we put in and leave out to be accurate and honest?

NARRATIVE NONFICTION

Narrative nonfiction is writing that tells a true-life story. In this chapter, you will explore a special type of narrative nonfiction: the autobiographical narrative. An autobiographical narrative allows you to present a true story about *your* life, from *your* perspective. By sharing a personal experience, you can give readers some insights into who you are—and perhaps into who they are, too!

You will develop your autobiographical narrative by taking it through each of the steps of the writing process: prewriting, drafting, revising, editing, and publishing. You will also have an opportunity to write a short radio script. To preview the criteria for how your autobiographical narrative will be evaluated, see the rubric on page 83.

FEATURE ASSIGNMENT

Nonfiction Narrative: Autobiographical Narrative

An effective narrative nonfiction essay has these characteristics:

- An **engaging story** that holds readers' attention
- A **well-developed conflict,** or problem to be solved, that shows why a situation created a problem
- A **resolution,** the outcome of the conflict, that shows how the problem was solved
- **A range of literary strategies and devices,** such as dialogue and suspense, that can make your narrative stand out and enhance the plot
- A specific **mood,** or emotion, that the writing conveys
- A unique **tone,** or attitude toward the subject
- **Sensory details**—details that appeal to the five senses of taste, touch, sight, sound, and smell that build the description in the writing
- **Effective sentence structure** and correct spelling, grammar, and usage

An autobiographical narrative also includes:

- Specific **details** about your personal experiences
- Strong **characterization** of real people, or your characters, by showing their thoughts, feelings, and actions
- A **theme,** or main idea, about a life lesson you learned through this experience

66 Narrative Nonfiction

Other Forms of Narrative Nonfiction

In addition to an autobiographical narrative, there are other forms of narrative nonfiction, including:

Biographical narratives are stories that share facts about someone else's life.

Blogs, or comments that writers share in online forums, may include autobiographical narratives (brief or extended), reflections, opinions, and other types of comments. Blogs often invite responses; they usually are not considered a "permanent" form of writing.

Diary entries, which are highly personal, include experiences, thoughts, and feelings—but the audience is private, unless writers choose to share the entries.

Narrative essays use one or more autobiographical narratives to illustrate or otherwise support a point that the writer wishes to make.

Memoirs contain a writer's reflections on an important person or event from his or her own life. Book-length memoirs by famous people often make popular reading.

Reflective essays present personal experiences (either events that happened to the writers themselves or that they learned about from others), but they focus more on sharing the observations and insights that writers had later, while thinking about those experiences. Magazines and newspapers often feature reflective essays.

Try It! For each audience and purpose described, choose a form, such as a memoir, diary entry, or blog, that is appropriate for conveying your intended meaning to multiple audiences. Explain your choices.

- To tell a relative how you reached an important decision
- To remind yourself, in the future, about what happened today during a class visit to the Science Museum
- To recount your softball team's victory to online friends

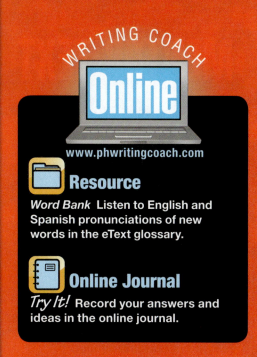

WRITING COACH Online
www.phwritingcoach.com

Resource
Word Bank Listen to English and Spanish pronunciations of new words in the eText glossary.

Online Journal
Try It! Record your answers and ideas in the online journal.

WORD BANK

People often use these basic and content-based vocabulary words when they talk about narrative nonfiction. Work with a partner. Take turns saying and writing each word in a sentence. If you are unsure of the meaning or pronunciation of a word, use the Glossary or a dictionary to check the definition or pronunciation.

appreciate	realize
capable	sense
chaos	theme

Nonfiction Narration 67

MENTOR TEXT — Autobiographical Narrative

Learn From Experience

 After reading the autobiographical narrative on pages 68–69, read the numbered notes in the margins to learn how the author presented her ideas.

Answer the *Try It!* questions online or in your notebook.

❶ The introduction develops the **conflict,** or problem, that the mother faces. She would like to go to Paris but has difficulty walking.

Try It! How does describing the conflict in the introduction help build interest in reading more?

❷ Dialogue helps create **interesting and believable characters** and further develops the narrative.

Try It! From the dialogue, what do you think the mother is like? How do the mother and daughter solve the mother's problem?

❸ The author uses **sensory details** to describe the benefits of traveling in a wheelchair.

Try It! What details does the author use to describe the other fliers? To which of the five senses do these details appeal?

Extension Find another example of an autobiographical narrative, and compare it with this one.

The Trip to Beautiful

by Mary Schmich

❶ My mother needed to go to Paris before she died. She had never talked of it that way—Paris as a stamp on her passport to the afterlife—but every now and then when one of my siblings and I talked about the years each of us had spent living in France, she would muse, "I'd love to go to Paris someday."

As my mother got older, the idea bubbled up more and more; in other words, as it grew less and less likely that she could physically make the trip. By her mid-70s, she was leaning on a cane for simple jaunts from her front door to the mailbox. I couldn't imagine how she'd make it through the Charles de Gaulle airport. . . .

Paris? In her physical condition, it might as well be the moon. Then I had a thought.

❷ "Mama, how do you feel about a wheelchair?"

At the time, talking to my mother about a wheelchair felt to me like asking about her casket. I had met elderly people who would rather shut themselves inside their homes for good than be seen outside it in a wheelchair. A wheelchair to them was at best a hassle, at worst a humiliation, infantilization, the defeat of the will to walk.

"A wheelchair?" my mother said. "That's a wonderful idea." And so we went to France.

The wheelchair, as it turned out, was a ticket to the express lane and respect.

❸ At customs, the wheelchair attendant whisked us past the parade of rumpled, yawning fliers. At the taxi stand, we were waved to the head of the line.

At the Musee d'Orsay, the grand railroad station turned museum, we checked out a wheelchair in the cloakroom and were granted access to the paintings before they opened to the mob.

South of Paris, in the Loire Valley, we used one of the wheelchairs supplied by the chateau of Chenonceau and rolled merrily through the long tiled corridors, across the River Cher,

68 Narrative Nonfiction

out into the gardens of the kings and queens.

"This is how to get the royal treatment," my mother said. "Get a wheelchair."

We couldn't get and didn't want a wheelchair everywhere. In the streets of Paris, as long as she could lean on a cane or someone's arm, my mother could walk a few blocks. In truth, she walked farther than she did at home. Beauty is therapy.

One day we drove north to Mont St. Michel, the Gothic abbey that rises like a dream on a cone of rock in the middle of a bay. I told my mother I was going to hike the 900 or so steps to the top while she sat in a cafe. I was sorry she couldn't come, but there were no elevators, no cars, no wheelchairs.

❹ "Maybe I'll walk just a little ways," she said.

Slowly, we climbed the first few stairs. She held my arm with one hand, the stone banister of the ramparts with the other. We stopped to rest, the bay glittering below.

"Just a few more," she said. Another stair, then two, four, 10. She had to sit down.

And then—I still don't know how this happened—she decided to crawl. And somehow, a few hundred steps later, she was at the top.

If I were a certain kind of person, I would call what happened that day a miracle, that a white-haired woman, stooped by time and tired bones, made it, on her feet and hands and knees, to the top of one of the wonders of the world.

❺ My mother's 86 now. A few months ago someone knocked her down and broke her hip. She uses a wheelchair in the grocery store and a walker just to get from the bathroom to the bed. One of my brothers had been promising for several years to take her to Scotland, her ancestral home, but all the miracles and wheelchairs in the world won't make that happen.

There comes a time in most lives when travel truly is impossible. But that time may not be as soon as you imagine. If you can, give your parents the gift of travel. It will be a gift to yourself.

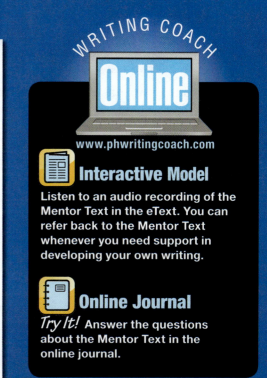

❹ The **character** of the mother is further developed in this passage. Her behavior helps reveal what she is like.

Try It! How would you describe the mother? Give reasons for your answer.

❺ In the **resolution,** or final outcome of the conflict, the daughter shares an insight she gained from her mother's experiences and makes a suggestion.

Try It! Why is the resolution a logical way to end the narrative? What insights did you gain by reading the autobiographical narrative?

STUDENT MODEL   Autobiographical Narrative

With a small group, take turns reading the Student Model aloud. As you read, practice newly acquired vocabulary by correctly producing the word's sound. Also note how the writing interweaves personal examples and ideas with factual information to present a perspective and describe a situation or event.

Use a Reader's Eye

Now, reread the Student Model. On your copy of the Student Model, use the Reader's Response Symbols to react to what you read.

Reader's Response Symbols

+ I like where this is going.

− This isn't clear to me.

? What will happen next?

! Wow! That is really cool/weird/interesting!

Review the Student Model with a partner. Discuss the elements of plot you find in the narrative. Take notes to describe and explain the specific details of the plot line.

Team PLAYER

by Kalim Hunt

"Are you kidding?" I scowled, jabbing my finger at the bulletin board. A new notice, tacked in a corner, listed the students who would appear on our local TV's *Student Scholars* quiz show. My name was there, too—but as an alternate.

"What's up, Kalim?" asked Amani, my cousin.

"I should be on the team," I complained. "I'm pulling straight A's."

Amani looked hard at the list. "I imagine that they are, too," she commented. "Besides, I don't know if a sophomore has ever been on the team."

"Yes," Mrs. Jacobs, the team's coach, explained after school, "we look at seniors and juniors first, and those four met our qualifications. Your grades are terrific, Kalim, so you'll probably be a front-runner next year. In the meantime, you can help us prepare. Can we count on you?"

Figuring that the school needed me, I nodded. In early practices, I served as emcee, but then Mrs. Jacobs put me on the "opposing team." That's when I really started to have fun—analyzing each question, searching my memory, and signaling my answer before the other team did. I soon lost not only my sweaty palms while playing but also my frustration about not being on the "real" team. Still, when Mrs. Jacobs invited me to the taping downtown, I wasn't sure that I could hide my earlier disappointment, but Mom and Amani encouraged me to go.

When I walked into the studio, Mrs. Jacobs rushed over. "Lindsey Carmichael's mother just

1

called. Lindsey came home with a fever. It looks like the flu—so, Kalim, you're taking her place!"

Before I knew it, I was seated with the rest of the Hamilton High team, facing the team from Riverview Academy. The emcee stepped to the podium, the cameras rolled, and the game was on!

All that practice paid off: I signaled first on six questions and answered them all correctly, helping our team to a 25–21 win and a shot at the championship later that season.

"Lindsey will be playing by then," I said to Mrs. Jacobs, "but it was great to play on the team, even for an hour!"

"Kalim," Mrs. Jacobs smiled, "even if you're not on camera, you're a great team player!"

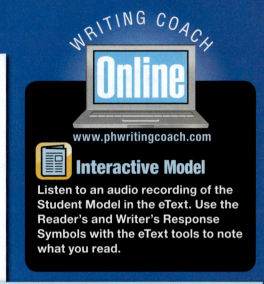

www.phwritingcoach.com

Interactive Model

Listen to an audio recording of the Student Model in the eText. Use the Reader's and Writer's Response Symbols with the eText tools to note what you read.

Use a Writer's Eye

Now, evaluate the narrative as a writer. On your copy of the Student Model, use the Writer's Response Symbols to react to what you read. Identify places where the student writer uses characteristics of an effective autobiographical narrative.

Writer's Response Symbols

E.S. Engaging story

W.D. Clear, well-developed conflict and resolution

B.C. Believable characters

S.D. Specific and vivid details

Your Turn — Feature Assignment: Autobiographical Narrative

Prewriting

Plan a first draft of your autobiographical narrative by **determining an appropriate topic**.

Choose from the Topic Bank or come up with a topic of your own.

 ## Choose From the Topic Bank

TOPIC BANK

Surprise! Recall a time when you were truly surprised. Write a brief anecdote in which you tell the story of the situation and describe your actions.

A Second Look Sometimes events occur that make us see someone we thought we knew in a different way. Think about a time or an event that led you to a new respect or admiration for someone in your life. Write an autobiographical narrative that describes this time or event and explains how your feelings toward this person changed.

Time for a Change Recall a time of change in your life. Maybe it was a time when you changed schools, moved to a new home, or added a new member to your family. Write an autobiographical narrative that describes this time of change and explains how that change affected you.

 ## Choose Your Own Topic

To **determine an appropriate topic** on your own, use the following **range of strategies** to generate ideas.

Interview and Reflect

- Interview friends or relatives, asking them to recall a story about you; then tell that story from your perspective. Jot down ideas that may present good writing topics.
- If you blog, reflect upon some recent posts. Where might you find the online seed of an autobiographical narrative?

Review your responses and choose a topic.

Narrow Your Topic

If your topic is too broad, readers may not identify with you, so narrow your focus as you begin to plan an engaging story.

Apply It! Use a graphic organizer like the one shown to narrow your topic.

- Record your general topic—your broadest story idea—in the top box and then narrow that topic as you move down the chart.
- The bottom box should hold your narrowest story idea, the new focus of your autobiographical narrative.

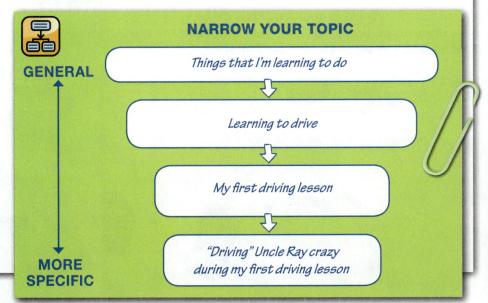

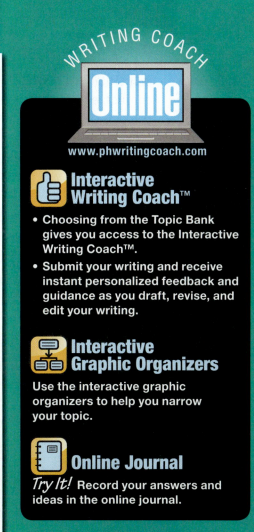

WRITING COACH Online
www.phwritingcoach.com

Interactive Writing Coach™
- Choosing from the Topic Bank gives you access to the Interactive Writing Coach™.
- Submit your writing and receive instant personalized feedback and guidance as you draft, revise, and edit your writing.

Interactive Graphic Organizers
Use the interactive graphic organizers to help you narrow your topic.

Online Journal
Try It! Record your answers and ideas in the online journal.

Consider Multiple Audiences and Purposes

Before writing, think about your audiences and purposes. Consider how your writing will convey your intended meaning to multiple audiences. Consider the ways others will see events as you ask yourself these questions.

Questions for Audience	Questions for Purpose
• Who are my audiences? • Why will the topic of my narrative engage each audience's interest? • What might each audience want to know about me—and why?	• What is my purpose? Do I want to be humorous, thought-provoking, serious, or something else? • As I develop my purpose, how much about myself do I want to share with each audience?

Record your answers in your writing journal.

Prewriting 73

Plan Your Piece

You will use a graphic organizer like the one shown to develop your conflict, establish details, and determine a resolution. When it is complete, you will be ready to write your first draft.

Develop Your Conflict Think about the major obstacle, or struggle, you had to overcome. How did the problem grow or change? What were the different ways you tried to deal with it? Think about the events that led to the moment you faced the problem, the climax, and what the outcome was.

Map Out Your Plot Events Plan the plot events of your narrative. By choosing to describe only those events that directly relate to the conflict, you will be able to structure your ideas and write a sustained narrative.

DEVELOP YOUR PLOT EVENTS

Theme
Learning can be difficult, but it's worth the reward.

Setting
The parking lot and streets around the Cliffside Library

Characters
Me, Uncle Ray, _____, _____

Mood
Nervous excitement

Rising Action
On Sunday afternoon, he drove me to the parking lot of the Cliffside Library.

Climax
I pulled onto busy Central Avenue without going into a panic!

Falling Action

Problem
When Uncle Ray offered to teach me to drive, I was thrilled!

Resolution

74 Narrative Nonfiction

Gather Details

Autobiographical writers usually build upon the story elements of character, setting, and plot by using literary strategies and devices. Dialogue, suspense, and sensory details—details that appeal to the five senses—can enhance the plot and establish a definite mood or tone. These are examples of devices that can provide more narrative detail:

- **Dialogue:** *Uncle Ray cleared his throat. "Anita," he said, looking me in the eye, "You're old enough to answer an important question: Would you like me to teach you to drive?"*
  "Yes!" I sputtered, dropping my fork. "When can we start?" (builds a mood of excitement)

- **Sensory Details:** *The dark cloudy sky and wet gray air couldn't dampen my anticipation as Uncle Ray pulled into Cliffside Library's parking lot that afternoon. I giggled as we got out and changed places. The steering wheel felt smooth and ready beneath my hands.* (helps the readers to feel as if they are there as events are happening and enhances the mood)

- **Suspense:** *I tried to turn a corner—and almost drove onto someone's lawn! Suddenly, driving wasn't as easy as it looked! I shut off the engine, looked away from Uncle Ray, and wondered if I could find the courage to start the car again.* (establishes a serious mood and tone)

Try It! Read the Student Model excerpt and decide how the author develops the mood and tone in this autobiographical narrative.

STUDENT MODEL from **Team Player** pages 70–71; lines 29–32

> When I walked into the studio, Mrs. Jacobs rushed over. "Lindsey Carmichael's mother just called. Lindsey came home with a fever. It looks like the flu—so, Kalim, you're taking her place!"

 Apply It! Review the elements that narrative writers often use. Decide how your details will make those elements clear.

- Choose details that will create an **engaging story.** Use a variety of **literary strategies** and **devices** to enhance your **plot.**
- Use **sensory details** to define the **mood** and **tone.**
- Add these details to your graphic organizer so that you create a well-developed **conflict** and **resolution.**

WRITING COACH Online
www.phwritingcoach.com

Interactive Graphic Organizers
Use the interactive graphic organizers to help you create a plan for your writing.

Interactive Model
Refer back to the Interactive Model in the eText as you plan your writing.

Prewriting 75

Drafting

During the drafting stage, you will start to write your ideas for your autobiographical narrative. You will follow an outline that provides an organizational strategy that will help you write a focused and organized autobiographical narrative.

The Organization of a Nonfiction Narrative

The chart shows an organizational strategy for a nonfiction narrative. Look back at how the Mentor Text follows this organizational strategy. Then, use this chart to help you outline your draft.

I. Beginning See Mentor Text, p. 68.

- Engaging opening
- Setting, problem, and character

II. Middle See Mentor Text, pp. 68-69.

- Well-developed conflict
- Literary devices and strategies that enhance the plot
- Sensory details to set the mood or tone

III. End See Mentor Text, p. 69.

- Resolution that ends the conflict
- Satisfying conclusion that reflects the theme

Grab Your Reader

- An engaging opening will catch your readers' attention by starting with a question or some dialogue to draw them into your narrative.
- Using specific details will realistically establish the setting, yourself as the main character, and the conflict.

Develop Your Plot

- Presenting plot events in chronological order helps build the intensity of the conflict and show why it presented a problem for you.
- Literary devices, such as dialogue, make characters true to life and help connect readers to the story.
- Sensory details help readers to see and feel the story. You can use them to set a particular mood.

Wrap It Up

- A resolution shows how the problem was solved or how events ended it, and reminds readers of the beginning of your narrative.
- A narrative's conclusion reflects on how the event affected you, ties readers back to the theme, and ends the narrative in a satisfying way.

Narrative Nonfiction

 **Start Your Draft**

Use the checklist to help complete your draft. Use the Plot Structure Map and the Outline for Success as guides to show the plot details that develop your conflict and resolution.

While drafting, aim at writing your ideas, not on making your writing perfect. Remember, because you are developing your draft in an open-ended situation, you will have the chance to improve your draft when you revise and edit.

√ Start by drafting an attention-getting **opening** paragraph.

√ Continue your **beginning** with details that introduce yourself and the setting and that hint at the **conflict** that will drive the narrative.

√ Use plot events to build the **middle** of your autobiographical narrative. Present a series of events that develop the conflict by showing how the **problem** grows or changes and how you or others respond.

√ To streamline your writing, limit the number of **events** you present.

√ Pay attention to your use of language. Use a range of **literary strategies** and devices, such as dialogue and suspense, to enhance your plot and move the action forward.

√ Use **rhetorical devices** like hyperbole—exaggeration—to establish your particular writing style and to convey a specific meaning subtly.

√ Create a defined mood or tone by providing specific, **sensory details** about the characters, setting, and action. To review, **tone** is the attitude you convey in your writing. **Mood** is the emotion your writing generates with your readers.

√ At the **end** of your narrative, provide the **resolution**—how the conflict in your true story worked out—in a satisfying way.

√ Fully **develop** the resolution by discussing how the events of your narrative affected you or your life.

Interactive Model

Outline for Success View pop-ups of Mentor Text selections referenced in the Outline for Success.

 **Interactive Writing Coach™**

Use the Interactive Writing Coach to receive the level of support you need:
- Write one paragraph at a time and submit each one for immediate, detailed feedback.
- Write your entire first draft and submit it for immediate, personalized feedback.

Drafting 77

Revising: Making It Better

Now that you have finished your first draft, you are ready to revise. Think about the "big picture" of **audience, purpose, and genre.** You can use Revision RADaR as a guide for making changes to improve your draft. Revision RADaR provides four major ways to improve your writing: **(R) replace, (A) add, (D) delete,** and **(R) reorder.**

Kelly Gallagher, M. Ed.

KEEP REVISION ON YOUR RADaR

Read part of the first draft of the Student Model "Team Player." Then, look at questions the writer asked himself as he thought about how well his draft **addressed issues of audience, purpose, and genre.**

from Team Player

"What's up, Kalim?" asked Amani, my cousin.

"I should be on the team," I said. "I'm a good student."

Amani looked hard at the list. "I imagine that they are, too," she commented. "Besides, I don't know if a sophomore has ever been on the team."

"Yes," Mrs. Jacobs, the team's coach, explained after school, "we look at seniors and juniors first, and those four met our qualifications. Your grades are terrific, Kalim, so you'll probably be a front-runner next year. In the meantime, may we count on you? You can help us prepare."

Figuring that the school needed me, I nodded. In early practices, I served as emcee, but then Mrs. Jacobs put me on the "opposing team." That's when I really started to have fun at the practices. I soon lost not only my nervousness but also my frustration about not being on the "real" team. Still, when Mrs. Jacobs invited me to the taping downtown, I wasn't sure about it, but Mom and Amani encouraged me to go.

> *I want my audience to identify with me and my story. Are my readers able to do that?*

> *A clear conflict is critical to this genre. Do these parts of the narrative make the conflict clear?*

> *My purpose in these two sentences is to show my change of thinking, but is that purpose clear enough?*

78 Narrative Nonfiction

Now, look at how the writer applied Revision RADaR to write an improved second draft.

from Team PLAYER — 2ND DRAFT

"What's up, Kalim?" asked Amani, my cousin.

"I should be on the team," I complained. "I'm pulling straight A's."

Amani looked hard at the list. "I imagine that they are, too," she commented. "Besides, I don't know if a sophomore has ever been on the team."

"Yes," Mrs. Jacobs, the team's coach, explained after school, "we look at seniors and juniors first, and those four met our qualifications. Your grades are terrific, Kalim, so you'll probably be a front-runner next year. In the meantime, you can help us prepare. May we count on you?"

Figuring that the school needed me, I nodded. In early practices, I served as emcee, but then Mrs. Jacobs put me on the "opposing team." That's when I really started to have fun—analyzing each question, searching my memory, and signaling my answer before the other team did. I soon lost not only my nervousness while playing but also my frustration about not being on the "real" team. Still, when Mrs. Jacobs invited me to the taping downtown, I wasn't sure that I could hide my earlier disappointment, but Mom and Amani encouraged me to go.

R — Replaced dull language with specific details to make the story more vivid

R — Reordered words and sentences to make the conflict pop in the question

D — Deleted a detail that I don't need, "at the practices," and **A** added more supporting details

R — Replaced simple language with more specific language to strengthen the sense of conflict

WRITING COACH Online
www.phwritingcoach.com

Interactive Writing Coach™
Use the Revision RADaR strategy in your own writing. Then submit your paragraph or draft for feedback.

 Apply It! Use your Revision RADaR to revise your draft.

- First, determine if you have made a connection with your audience, used plot events and details to express your purpose, and included the characteristics of the narrative nonfiction genre.
- Then, apply Revision RADaR to make needed changes. Remember—you can use the steps in the strategy in any order.

Revising 79

Look at the Big Picture

Use the chart to evaluate how well each section of your autobiographical narrative addresses **purpose, audience, and genre.** When necessary, use the suggestions in the chart to revise your narrative.

Section	Evaluate	Revise
Beginning	• Decide whether your opening is **engaging,** encouraging your audience to read on.	• Add a question, a bit of dialogue, or some other detail that stirs readers' curiosity.
	• Consider how well you convey your purpose and check your overall **subtlety of meaning.** Readers should sense why you're writing, even if you are subtle in presenting your underlying theme.	• Sum up the point of your narrative; then, decide whether you want to state that sentence or use plot events and details to hint at its idea.
Middle	• Review the narrative's plot. Do you have a well-developed **conflict?**	• Reorder events to ensure chronological order. Make changes to show, rather than tell, the conflict.
	• Do **transitions** connect events that show how the problem involves you?	• Add transitions where needed to convey meaning.
	• Underline details that show your real-life characters in action in one or more settings. Do **sensory details** make the characters and settings interesting and believable? Do they set a certain mood or tone?	• To help readers identify with your characters and settings and to establish a particular mood or tone, add descriptive details that help readers imagine the setting.
	• Look at the middle as a whole and evaluate your use of a range of **literary strategies** and devices to hold readers' interest.	• Experiment with figurative language to develop the conflict and build the suspense in your narrative.
End	• Check for **a resolution**—one that is well-developed and clearly reveals the conflict's outcome.	• Add or revise details to show how the problem was solved or how events ended it. Show how you were affected by this resolution.
	• Decide whether your **closing** is satisfying.	• Add dialogue or some other detail that connects with readers and leaves a lasting impression.

Focus on Craft: Sentence Variety

Effective writers use a mix of sentence types, lengths, and structures to hold readers' interest. A narrative consisting of short statements will seem choppy and dull. On the other hand, using too many long, complicated sentences will make writing tedious and difficult to follow. So, include both long and short sentences, complicated and simple sentences, and sentences that do more than just make statements.

Think about sentence variety as you read these sentences from the Student Model.

STUDENT MODEL from **Team Player** page 70; lines 12–17

> "Yes," Mrs. Jacobs, the team's coach, explained after school, "we look at seniors and juniors first, and those four met our qualifications. Your grades are terrific, Kalim, so you'll probably be a front-runner next year. In the meantime, you can help us prepare. Can we count on you?"

 Try It! Now, ask yourself these questions:

- How has the writer used sentence variety in this paragraph? What makes each sentence distinctive?
- Would the final sentence be better if it were longer, and if it were a statement instead of a question? Explain.

 ## Fine-Tune Your Draft

Apply It! Use the revision suggestions to prepare your final draft after rethinking how well questions of purpose, audience, and genre have been addressed.

- **Ensure Sentence Variety** Raise the interest level by using long and short sentences, as well as various sentence types and structures.
- **Ensure Subtlety of Meaning** Don't tell readers everything—instead, encourage them to make inferences and judgments about characters, setting, and action.

Peer or Family Feedback Read your final draft to a group of peers or your family. Ask if you have created a story that is interesting to read. Think about their responses and revise your final draft as needed.

www.phwritingcoach.com

Video
Learn more strategies for effective writing from program author Kelly Gallagher.

 ### Online Journal
Try It! Record your answers in the online journal.

 ### Interactive Model
Refer back to the Interactive Model as you revise your writing.

 ### Interactive Writing Coach™
Revise your draft and submit it for feedback.

Editing: Making It Correct

When you edit, you check spelling and correct mistakes in grammar, punctuation, and capitalization.

Before editing your final draft, think about using a variety of sentence structures, including **compound, complex, and compound-complex sentences**. Also keep in mind the rules for punctuating clauses with commas. Then, correct errors in **grammar, mechanics, and spelling**.

WRITE GUY *Jeff Anderson, M. Ed.*

Zoom in on Conventions Focus on sentence structure as you zoom in on these sentences from the Student Model.

> **STUDENT MODEL** from **Team Player**
> page 70; lines 18–30
>
> In early practices, I served as emcee, but then Mrs. Jacobs put me on the "opposing team."… Still, when Mrs. Jacobs invited me to the taping downtown, I wasn't sure that I could hide my earlier disappointment, but Mom and Amani encouraged me to go.
>
> When I walked into the studio, Mrs. Jacobs rushed over.

To learn more about sentence structures, see Chapter 14 of your Grammar Handbook.

Now, ask yourself: *Is the structure of each sentence the same or different?*

Perhaps you said that the sentences vary in structure.

The first sentence is a **compound** sentence because it has more than one main or independent clause. A main clause has a subject and a verb and can stand alone as a complete sentence. In most compound sentences, the clauses are joined by a comma and a coordinating conjunction, such as *and, or,* and *but*.

The third sentence is a **complex** sentence because it has a main clause and a subordinate clause, which is *When I walked into the studio*. A subordinate clause has a subject and a verb but cannot stand alone as a complete sentence.

The second sentence is a **compound-complex** sentence. It has two main clauses and one subordinate clause, which is *when Mrs. Jacobs invited me to the taping downtown*.

Partner Talk Discuss these questions with a partner: *What effect does each sentence structure have on the reader? What effect does the sentence variety have on the passage as a whole?*

82 Narrative Nonfiction

Grammar Mini-Lesson: Commas and Clauses

In complex and compound-complex sentences, use a **comma** to set off a subordinate clause that precedes a main clause. In compound and compound-complex sentences, use either a comma and a conjunction or a semicolon between main clauses. In the passage, notice how the author uses commas to **punctuate clauses**.

from **The Trip to Beautiful**
page 69; lines 39–40

In the streets of Paris, as long as she could lean on a cane or someone's arm, my mother could walk a few blocks.

Try It! Place commas where needed to correctly punctuate the clauses in each sentence. Then, identify the structure of each sentence. Write the answers in your journal.

1. When I go to a restaurant I try to eat healthy foods.
2. The sky darkened and we heard a rumble of thunder.
3. Even though she was tired Lisa went to the party but she left early.

Apply It! Edit your draft for grammar, mechanics, **capitalization and spelling**. If necessary, rewrite some sentences to ensure that you have used **a variety of correctly structured sentences**. Make sure that you used correct comma placement with clauses.

To learn more, see Chapter 23.

www.phwritingcoach.com

 Video
Learn effective editing techniques from program author Jeff Anderson.

 Online Journal
Try It! Record your answers in the online journal.

 Interactive Model
Refer back to the Interactive Model as you edit your writing.

 Interactive Writing Coach™
Edit your draft. Check it against the rubric and then submit it for feedback.

 Use the rubric to evaluate your piece. If necessary, rethink, rewrite, or revise.

Rubric for Narrative Nonfiction: Autobiographical Narrative	Rating Scale
Ideas: How well do you narrate a single, important event?	Not very Very 1 2 3 4 5 6
Organization: How clearly organized is your sequence of events?	1 2 3 4 5 6
Voice: How authentic and engaging is your voice?	1 2 3 4 5 6
Word Choice: How effectively do you use sensory details to show characters and setting?	1 2 3 4 5 6
Sentence Fluency: How well have you used sentence variety to raise the interest level?	1 2 3 4 5 6
Conventions: How correctly have you used commas with subordinate clauses?	1 2 3 4 5 6

Publishing

Give readers something special to think about by publishing your autobiographical narrative. First, get your narrative ready for presentation; then, choose a way to **publish it for appropriate audiences.**

Wrap Up Your Presentation

Is your narrative handwritten or written on a computer? If it is handwritten, you may need to make a new, clean copy. If so, be sure to **write legibly.** Also be sure to add a title that grabs the reader's attention and indicates the topic of your narrative.

Publish Your Piece

Use the chart to identify ways to publish your autobiographical essay.

If your audience is…	…then publish it by…
Classmates and teachers at school	• Presenting it in the form of a skit • Posting it to your class Web site, if available • Submitting it to the school newspaper
People outside of your school	• Sharing it (perhaps via email or a Web site) with those who had a role in the narrative • Submitting it to an online or print magazine for teens, perhaps with a photograph that helps tell the story and supports your submission

 Reflect on Your Writing

Now that you are done with your autobiographical narrative, read it over and use your writing journal to answer these questions. Use specific details to describe and explain your reflections. Increase the specificity of your details based on the type of information requested.

- What do you think are the best parts of your narrative? Why?
- Are any parts weak? If so, what goals will you set for your next writing assignment?
- What makes narrative nonfiction a valuable genre? Explain.

 The Big Question: Why Write? What did you decide to put in or leave out to be accurate and honest?

Manage Your Portfolio You may wish to include your published autobiographical narrative in your writing portfolio. If so, consider what this narrative reveals about your writing and your growth as a writer.

21st Century Learning

MAKE YOUR WRITING COUNT

Celebrate Your Experiences in a Class Yearbook

An autobiographical narrative provides readers with a window into the writer's life. Learn more about your classmates' lives by creating a **class yearbook**.

As a group, create pages for a printed yearbook or a yearbook Web site that reveals something about each group member's experiences at school, as well as his or her unique family and cultural traditions. Include each student's narrative, as well as photos, art, and quotations.

Here's your action plan.

1. Choose roles, such as interviewer, artist, editor, and—if you are creating a Web site—Webmaster.

2. Review your peers' narratives. Then, interview each other for more details. Ask each other about topics such as favorite classes, hobbies, and so on.

3. Work together to create a two-page spread or Web page for each group member. One side of the spread might contain the personal narrative. The other might include:
   - A photo or illustration of the student
   - The student's interview responses
   - Graphic icons that symbolize ideas or activities important to the student

4. Meet with other groups and bind all the yearbook pages into one class yearbook, or plan an online presentation.

5. Share your yearbooks with the class.

Listening and Speaking Present your yearbook as a group. If you created a Web site—or if you scanned your yearbook pages into presentation software—use projection equipment if available. Then, as you show the yearbook, explain your group's process for creating each page. As a class, discuss the merits and drawbacks of each process.

www.phwritingcoach.com

 Online Journal

Reflect on Your Writing Record your answers and ideas in the online journal.

Resource

Link to resources on 21st Century Learning for help in creating a group project.

Script for a Radio Show

There are many types of **radio shows,** or programs providing audio without video support. Some feature music and others feature talk. Many radio shows have themes, or main ideas or focus points, such as sports or politics. Sometimes this theme is explicit, or clearly stated. Other times, the theme is implicit, or only implied.

With the rise in new technologies, even more people are creating their own "listen in" programs, accessible as webcasts or podcasts. Whatever the method of delivery, a well-planned radio show usually involves a **script.** The script includes notes about what the host of the program will say, what segments will be part of each episode, how long each segment will run, and what music or sound effects will be used.

Try It! Read this part of a radio script and imagine hearing it presented. Then, answer these questions, recording your answers in your journal.

1. What is the **topic** of this particular episode? What do you think its **purpose** and **theme** might be?
2. Is the theme **explicitly** or **implicitly stated**?
3. How would you describe the **mood** and **tone** of the program? What details contribute to that mood or tone?
4. What sound effects do you see in the script? What other **audio elements** might you expect to hear as the program continues?

Extension Find another example of a radio show script, and compare it with this one.

THE COLLINSVILLE CHRONICLES

Episode 14 (20:00 minutes)

(Theme music up and fade)

SHARLA: This is Sharla Evans, and welcome to Episode 14 of "The Collinsville Chronicles," our weekly look at what makes our student body tick. Today's topic is "A Brush with Greatness." Today, a few students are going to share the stories of their personal "close encounters" with celebrities! First up is Kevin Washington—welcome, Kevin!

(Prerecorded applause)

KEVIN: Hi, Sharla.

SHARLA: I don't want to give anything away to our listeners, Kevin, so why don't you just tell us your story, in your own words?

(KEVIN'S segment—4:45 minutes. Background music: Marching band/"football" music)

KEVIN: I guess my story starts last year, when the Longhorns were having such a great season. I wanted to get tickets to a game, but couldn't afford to go. And then I had this idea. . . .

SHARLA: And what idea was that, Kevin?

KEVIN: I wrote a letter to the Longhorns' quarterback, explaining that I was a huge fan and asking if there was any way I could get tickets.

SHARLA: And he sent you tickets?

KEVIN: He *called* me! I had put my number in my letter. He called to tell me that he loved hearing from his fans and told me he was sending me tickets. He also said he wanted to meet me after the game. It was awesome!

86 **Narrative Nonfiction**

Create a Radio Script

Follow these steps to create a 5-minute radio script for an episode of your choice. To plan your script, review the graphic organizers on R24–R27 and choose one that suits your needs.

Prewriting
- List possible topics for your episode. Consider the types of stories you might like to tell.
- Narrow your list by considering your purpose and your target audience. What topic might appeal the most to them, and why?
- Once you choose a topic, identify the segments that your episode will need, including the host's introduction, comments, and conclusion.
- Plan audio elements, such as possible music and sound effects.

Drafting
- Create an outline to organize the segments in a way that makes sense.
- Draft your script and identify the placement of each audio element.
- Keep your purpose, audience, and explicit or implicit theme in mind—this will help you focus on what to include in your draft.

Revising and Editing
- Review your draft to ensure that your script moves clearly from segment to segment and that the various audio elements are appropriate and appealing.
- Make sure that the host's words have a purpose and that they set the overall mood or tone of the program.
- Decide if each segment is the right length, and think about whether each includes enough detail for listeners to get the main idea.
- Check that spelling, grammar, and mechanics are correct.

Publishing
- Prepare to present your episode to some members of your target audience. You may use traditional audio recording, rehearsing to be sure you have the timing and pacing right. Add sound effects as the script dictates.
- You may want to enhance the audio file and add images to play it as a webcast, podcast, or multimedia slide show. In that case, include graphics, text, and images that will appeal to your specific audience. As you select images, be sure they support the point of view and tone that your work conveys.
- Invite feedback and ideas for future episodes.

www.phwritingcoach.com

 Online Journal

Try It! Record your answers in the online journal.

 Interactive Graphic Organizers

Choose from a variety of graphic organizers to plan and develop your project.

Before you start drafting, explain your program to a partner. Use specific details to describe and explain your ideas. Increase the specificity of your details based on the type of information you are delivering. Then, ask for feedback. What does your partner think about the purpose and mood or tone of the program? What ideas for the audio elements of the program does your partner have?

Writing for Assessment

Many standardized tests include a prompt that asks you to write a narrative nonfiction essay. Respond using the characteristics of your autobiographical narrative. (See page 66.)

 Try It! Read the **narrative nonfiction** prompt and the information on format and academic vocabulary; then use the ABCDs of On-Demand Writing to help you plan and write your essay.

Format
The prompt directs you to write a *narrative nonfiction essay*. Be sure to include a beginning that introduces yourself as the main character, a middle driven by a conflict, and an end that presents a resolution in a satisfying way.

Narrative Prompt
While you can learn lessons from books and academic classes, you also can learn lessons from life. Write a narrative nonfiction essay about a life lesson that has been meaningful to you. Use the narrative's conflict and resolution to show how you were affected and what you learned.

Academic Vocabulary
Remember that a *conflict* is a problem to be solved or a clash to be settled. A *resolution* is the outcome of that conflict.

The ABCDs of On-Demand Writing

Use the following ABCDs to help you respond to the prompt.

Before you write your draft:

Attack the prompt [1 MINUTE]

- Circle or highlight important verbs in the prompt. Draw a line from the verb to what it refers to.
- Rewrite the prompt in your own words.

Brainstorm possible answers [4 MINUTES]

- Create a graphic organizer to generate ideas.
- Use one for each part of the prompt if necessary.

Choose the order of your response [1 MINUTE]

- Think about the best way to organize your ideas.
- Number your ideas in the order you will write about them. Cross out ideas you will not be using.

After you write your draft:

Detect errors before turning in the draft [1 MINUTE]

- Carefully reread your writing.
- Make sure that your response makes sense and is complete.
- Look for spelling, punctuation, and grammar errors.

More Prompts for Practice

Apply It! Respond to Prompts 1 and 2 in open-ended or timed situations by writing **narrative nonfiction** essays that present **an engaging story**. As you write, be sure to:

- Identify an appropriate audience for your intended **purpose**
- Use a plot map to **organize** your ideas
- Give your narrative a well-developed **conflict** and **resolution**
- Include appropriate **transitions** to connect ideas and convey meaning
- Use **sensory details** to define the mood and tone
- Include appropriate **rhetorical devices**, such as figurative language, and **literary strategies and devices** to enhance the plot

Prompt 1 Think of a childhood memory that comes back to you over and over again. Write a narrative nonfiction essay that shares the story behind that memory and shows why it still is meaningful to you today.

Prompt 2 Who are some of the older people who are part of your life? Perhaps you have a special bond with a grandparent or an elderly neighbor. In a narrative nonfiction essay, recount an event that the two of you shared. Through your story, show the importance of that relationship.

More Strategies for Writing for Assessment

- Consider several possible topics and quickly list details that you might use in your response. Then, choose the topic for which you have the strongest ideas.
- If you do not understand any words in the prompt, use context clues to help you determine the meaning of any unfamiliar words.
- Be sure to follow the ABCDs of writing to a prompt. Planning is an important part of writing. Don't just start writing right away.
- Make sure to reread your piece after you have completed it. This will give you time to find and correct errors. If you are in a timed situation, be sure to leave enough time for this step.

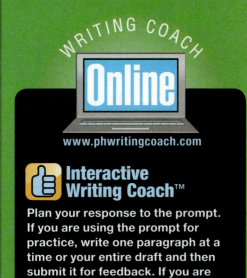

Interactive Writing Coach™

Plan your response to the prompt. If you are using the prompt for practice, write one paragraph at a time or your entire draft and then submit it for feedback. If you are using the prompt as a timed test, write your entire draft and then submit it for feedback.

Remember ABCD

Attack the prompt

Brainstorm possible answers

Choose the order of your response

Detect errors before turning in the draft

CHAPTER 6
FICTION NARRATION

What's the Story?

What is happening in the photo? What do you think will happen next? What story can you tell about it?

Many stories have realistic settings. Believable details about setting, such as a description of the skate park, help get the reader interested and add to the story. Conflict is also important. Conflict is a challenge or problem the main character faces.

Try It! Think about the events of the day at the skate park. What led up to this moment?

Consider these questions as you participate in an extended discussion with a partner. Make a few notes then take turns expressing your ideas and feelings.

- Who are the skateboarders?
- How do they know each other?
- What is about to happen?
- What is the conflict or challenge?

Review your notes. Use your notes to tell a story about the skateboarders. Be sure to use believable details and descriptions.

What's Ahead

In this chapter, you will review two strong examples of a short story: a Mentor Text and a Student Model. Then, using the examples as guidance, you will write a fiction story of your own.

www.phwritingcoach.com

 Online Journal

Try It! Record your answers and ideas in the online journal.

You can also record and save your answers and ideas on pop-up sticky notes in the eText.

 **Connect to the Big Questions**

Discuss these questions with your partner:

1 What do you think? What challenges should we attempt?

2 Why Write? What can fiction do better than nonfiction?

SHORT STORY

A short story is a brief work of fiction that presents characters in a conflict that is first developed and then resolved. In this chapter, you will explore a special type of literary text called a mystery story. A mystery story is a type of short story—a made-up story often less than twenty pages long. It focuses on unexplained or strange events that one of the characters tries to solve. These stories are often full of suspense and surprises.

You will develop the mystery story by taking it through each of the steps of the writing process: prewriting, drafting, revising, editing, and publishing. You will also have an opportunity to create a script for a radio play that is a mystery. To preview the criteria for how your mystery story will be evaluated, see the rubric on page 111.

FEATURE ASSIGNMENT
Short Story: Mystery

An effective and imaginative short story has these characteristics:

- **An engaging story** that grabs and keeps your reader's interest
- **A well-developed conflict** with action related to the main problem and a **resolution** that shows how the problem is solved
- **Interesting and believable characters** including a main character who struggles to resolve the conflict
- A **range of literary strategies and devices,** such as dialogue and suspense, **to enhance the plot,** or make it more interesting
- **Sensory details** related to sight, sound, touch, taste, and smell **that define the mood**—the emotion or feeling the story gives the reader—**or tone**—the writer's attitude toward the subject
- **Details** that establish a particular setting
- **Effective sentence structure** and correct spelling, grammar, and usage

An effective mystery story also includes:

- A **conflict** that focuses on a mystery or crime to be solved
- A **resolution** that shows what happens after the mystery is solved

Other Forms of Short Stories

In addition to mystery, there are other forms of short stories, including:

Fantasy stories stretch the imagination and take readers to unreal worlds. Animals may talk, people may fly, or characters may have superhuman powers.

Historical fiction tells about imaginary people living in real places and times in history. Typically, the main characters are fictional people who know and interact with famous people in history and participate in important historical events.

Myths and legends are traditional stories that different cultures have told to explain natural events, human nature, or the origins of things. Often handed down orally, they can include gods and goddesses from ancient times and heroes who perform superhuman acts.

Realistic fiction portrays invented characters and events in everyday-life situations that most readers would find familiar.

Science fiction stories focus on real or imagined developments in science and technology and how they affect the way people think and live. Space travel, aliens, and life in the future are popular topics for science fiction.

Tall tales are about larger-than-life characters in realistic settings. Typically, tall tales explain how the main character solves a problem or reaches a goal by doing something wild and fantastic that normal people could never do.

Try It! For each audience and purpose described, choose a story form, such as a fantasy story, mystery, or realistic fiction, that is appropriate for conveying your intended meaning to the audience. Explain your choices.

- To make adults laugh by describing how a character did something outlandish
- To help teenagers with a problem by showing how a fictional teen deals with a similar problem
- To show readers what life was like in Ancient Greece

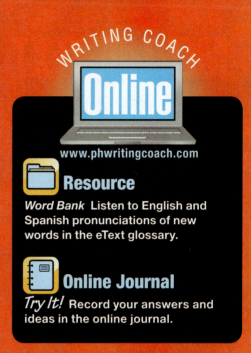

WRITING COACH Online
www.phwritingcoach.com

Resource
Word Bank Listen to English and Spanish pronunciations of new words in the eText glossary.

Online Journal
Try It! Record your answers and ideas in the online journal.

WORD BANK

People often use these vocabulary words when they talk about short story writing. Work with a partner. Take turns using each word in a sentence. If you are unsure of the meaning of a word, use the Glossary or a dictionary to check the definition.

conflict	resolution
detective	suspect
mysterious	suspense

Fiction Narration 93

MENTOR TEXT — Mystery

Learn From Experience

 Read the mystery on pages 94–97. As you read, takes notes to develop your understanding of basic sight and English vocabulary. Then, read the numbered notes in the margins to learn about how the author presented her ideas.

Answer the *Try It!* questions online or in your notebook.

---

❶ Through the use of **details**, the author creates a particular **setting**.

Try It! Which details establish the place and the time period of the story? What do these details tell you about life in that particular historical period?

❷ The author uses **sensory details** to help define the **mood** in different parts of the story.

Try It! To which of the five senses do the details in this passage appeal? How do these details help to define the mood in this part of the story?

❸ Through the use of **dialogue** and **details**, the author creates interesting, believable **characters**.

Try It! Which details describe the characters? How does the author use dialogue to further the characterizations of Gabe and Rusty?

Extension Find another example of a mystery story, and compare it with this one.

The Mystery of the Golden Locket

by Mary Larimer

❶ Unlike other gold prospectors, Rusty Beckett kept to himself. The way he figured, a man on his own had a better chance of getting rich if he didn't have to share. So when the Rush inspired most prospectors to settle in Coloma Valley after the first discovery, Rusty headed downriver. His destination was an outpost known as Sandy Mills. The mill had not been operational for decades, and Rusty bet that meant the gold had settled. It was there. And he would find it.

Rusty set up camp miles away from Main Street, under a great black oak. His campsite was protected by a stand of ponderosa pines. **❷** On his first morning in Sandy Mills, Rusty woke to the sharp scent of fresh evergreen. Although he was excited to be on his way, he boiled rich coffee and fried some bacon to have with his cornbread before heading out.

Although he was hoping to go unnoticed, it was not to be. Rusty's route to the north branch of the river took him right by a small group of prospectors headed south. **❸** A bearded old man trudged along at the head of the group, gold pan in hand. He stopped when he saw Rusty.

"You're not heading to the north branch of the river," he said. It was a statement, not a question.

"I reckon to," Rusty answered.

The group following the old man paused, eyebrows raised. One man tipped his hat back and looked Rusty up and down.

"You new to these parts?" he asked.

Rusty's silence was his assent.

"Gabe Danielson," the man in the hat said, extending his hand. Rusty shook it.

"You don't want to prospect north of the fork," Gabe said. "There's a swift current up that neck of the river. It's too dangerous for panning. Come on this way. You're welcome to join us, and we'll show you the south fork of the river."

Rusty smiled. That was a good one, a warning to keep the new prospectors away from the gold. These miners mistook his youth for inexperience.

"Is that right? A swift current?" He perused the group of men standing before him. "Well then it's a good thing I know how to swim."

And with that, Rusty continued on his way to the north fork, where he could pan for gold alone.

❹ Later that day, the midday sun beat down on Rusty's head. The cool river water swirled around his boots but did nothing to alleviate the heat of the day. Sweat dripped from Rusty's face. He dropped his pan into the water for a moment to splash his face, bringing cool water to his lips.

As he lowered his hands, Rusty saw the glint of gold. There it was! Rusty skimmed the river water with his pan, bringing the gold nugget to the surface. A wide smile spread across his face as he said a silent word of gratitude for the hunch that had sent him north.

Rusty's smile soon turned to a frown, however. This was gold, all right, but not a gold nugget. It was a locket of some sort, gold on a leather rope. Rusty cradled the locket in his hand as he waded back to the river's edge.

The little locket snapped open easily, and Rusty peered inside. A curl of dark brown hair fluttered to the ground. Rusty picked up the lock of hair and stared at it in wonder. *This must've been very dear to someone...,* he thought.

Rusty found no gold nuggets that first day. But as he walked back to his campsite at sunset, he carried gold in the front pocket of his shirt.

❺ That night, Rusty had trouble sleeping. He tossed and turned, as the wind through the great oak echoed like a voice in his head. *My conscience,* Rusty thought. He lit his lantern and fished out the locket.

Gazing at the beautiful hair, Rusty knew what he had to do—find the rightful owner of the locket. But how? Who could this possibly belong to? It was clearly quite old. How would Rusty find its true owner?

The next morning, Rusty went to the local saloon on Main Street for his coffee. Gabe and the other men sat around a table nearby. Rusty nodded at them. "Join you?" he asked.

"Certainly," Gabe replied. A chair was pulled out, and the group shifted around the table.

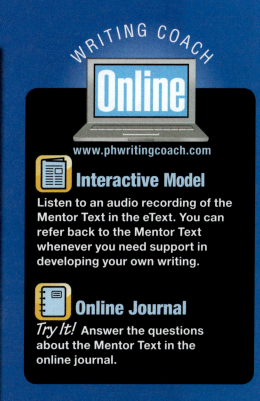

Interactive Model
Listen to an audio recording of the Mentor Text in the eText. You can refer back to the Mentor Text whenever you need support in developing your own writing.

Online Journal
Try It! Answer the questions about the Mentor Text in the online journal.

❹ The author uses additional **sensory details** in this passage to help the reader feel as if he or she were actually there.

Try It! To which of the five senses do these details appeal? How would your reading experience be different if the text just said, "Rusty was hot"?

❺ The **conflict** of the mystery is fully revealed here.

Try It! What is the mystery that Rusty has to solve?

6 The **suspense** in this passage moves the plot forward and keeps readers interested in the mystery.

Try It! How does the author build suspense in this passage?

7 In this passage, the author uses details to describe the **setting.**

Try It! What do the details in this passage tell you about the setting? How does the historical setting affect the story?

75　　The bearded old man clapped Rusty on the back. "Don't believe we met yesterday, but I'm Sully." John Sullivan. Been mining these here parts 'round 40 years now. So forgive me if I overstep myself, but you don't look like you're much accustomed to sleeping rough, son."

80　　Rusty didn't realize his sleepless night was so obviously written on his face. But he could have guessed. He hadn't gotten a wink after deciding to solve the mystery of the golden locket, so the bags beneath his eyes gave him away.

　　"You manage to get any gold out of the north fork yesterday?" 85　Gabe asked.

　　"I did," Rusty replied, "but not the kind I'd hoped for."

　　Rusty pulled the locket from under his shirt. He held it up to the men, and it swung like a pendulum from the long, leather string.

　　"I found this locket. And I've a mind to return it to its rightful 90　owner, if I can find that person."

6　"You'll have a long time looking," Sully said. Gabe frowned, head down.

　　"What exactly do you mean?" Rusty asked.

　　"Let's go boys!" Sully announced. And with that, the group 95　of men stood and marched out of the saloon.

　　Gabe paused, just before leaving the table. "A word?" he said to Rusty, "Put that locket back where you found it. There's nothing but misery in that story."

　　The reaction of the men only made Rusty more curious about 100　the locket's owner. Nothing but misery? What could Gabe have meant? Rusty didn't want to bring bad memories back to anyone, but he did want to see if he could find the person who had owned the locket—or someone who knew her.

7　Rusty wandered aimlessly through the small town, letting 105　his feet lead the way. The saloon, a lodging house, a tack shop—it was the shortest Main Street he had ever seen. In the distance, a bell tolled.

　　It wasn't long before Rusty found himself walking up the steps of an old schoolhouse. He had a mind to talk to the 110　schoolteacher, to see if she knew anything about lost objects and solving mysteries.

　　Rusty walked into the schoolroom just as the students were running outside to play. When he turned the corner into the main room, Rusty stopped in his tracks. There, behind the teacher's 115　desk, was a woman with dark, curly hair . . . just like the lock of hair from the locket.

❽ "Can I help you?" she asked.

"I hope so," Rusty said. He held out the locket in the palm of his hand. "I'm trying to find the owner of this locket. Is it yours, by any chance?"

The woman took a quick breath, and put her hand to her throat. "Where did you find that?"

"I was at the north fork yesterday," Rusty replied. "I was panning and—"

"You went to the north fork of the river?" the woman asked. Rusty was surprised by her tone.

"I'm sorry," she said. "It's just that no one dares to go there anymore, since the first settlers to the area came through." The schoolteacher took the locket gently from Rusty's hand.

❾ "I believe this is my grandmother's hair," she said. "My mother told me about this locket, but I thought it was lost forever."

"What happened to the first settlers?" Rusty asked.

"There was a terrible fever," the teacher replied. "Hardly anyone survived. My mother was one of the only children who made it. She wore this locket as a child, but later she couldn't find it. She never forgave herself for losing it."

"But how could it have ended up in the river?" Rusty asked.

The schoolteacher looked up at Rusty and smiled. "That will always be a mystery, won't it?"

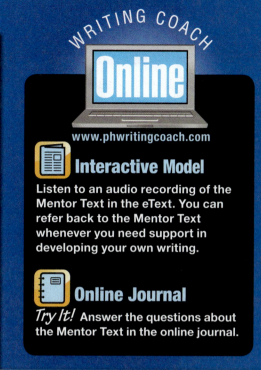

WRITING COACH Online

www.phwritingcoach.com

Interactive Model

Listen to an audio recording of the Mentor Text in the eText. You can refer back to the Mentor Text whenever you need support in developing your own writing.

Online Journal

Try It! Answer the questions about the Mentor Text in the online journal.

❽ This exchange of **dialogue** is an important device the author uses to serve a specific purpose in this story.

Try It! How does this dialogue move the plot forward? Is there any other way Rusty could have resolved the mystery without having this conversation?

❾ In the **resolution** of the story, the mystery is solved and loose ends are tied up.

Try It! Summarize in your own words the answer to the mystery of the locket. What hint of further mystery is revealed in the final lines?

STUDENT MODEL — Mystery

With a small group, take turns reading this Student Model aloud. Watch for the crime or mystery and how it is solved.

Use a Reader's Eye

Now, reread the Student Model. On your copy of the Student Model, use the Reader's Response Symbols to react to what you read.

Reader's Response Symbols

+ This is a good description.
− This isn't clear to me.
! This is really cool/weird/interesting.
? What will happen next?

Participate in an extended discussion with a partner. Express your opinions and share your responses to the Student Model. Discuss how the author created a sense of suspense and used sensory details to develop the mood in the Student Model.

A Rough Night
by Jack McKee

Babysitting is never without its moments, and this night was especially rough. After the kids got to sleep, a huge thunderstorm rolled in, pounding the house with wind and rain. Tree branches rustled like rattling bones. Then things got *very* creepy.

With a flash and a bang, the lights went out. It was pitch dark all along the street. I collected candles and sat down at the kitchen table to read a newspaper. Patch, the family dog, curled up on my feet. "Patch," I asked nervously, "are you protecting me or do you need protection?"

Candlelight flickered, throwing spooky shadows against the kitchen walls. In the dim glow, I read an article about an unsolved crime in our city. The police hadn't found the suspects yet….

Suddenly, I heard a sad, low moan outside the window. A chill swept down my back. The dog growled menacingly. There was another low moan. Patch growled again in warning. With my heart pounding, I peered out the window to see what—or who—was there. I could only see bushes tossing in the wind.

Grabbing the candles, I moved to the living room. Patch slinked along, close on my heels. Our shadows cast ghostly images on the walls as we passed. I had just settled in and was starting to relax, when I heard that sound again, but now it was outside the living room window. It was following me!

The moan grew into a yowl. I shrank away from the window and whispered hoarsely, "Patch, go see what's going on." He obeyed and started to bark in true watchdog style.

1

I was deciding where to hide with the kids when Patch's bark changed to one of excitement, and his tail swished in welcome. Reluctantly, I looked out the window in the door. Nobody was there. Then I heard a clear "meow" from outside. I gathered my courage and opened the front door a crack. In slipped a very wet cat. A huge wave of relief—and embarrassment—flooded over me. I couldn't believe that a cat had scared me so badly! She seemed to belong at the house because she was letting Patch lick her dry.

Immediately, car lights swept across the front window. In another minute, the kids' parents walked through the door. They explained that they'd recently brought the cat home from a shelter. However, she'd disappeared two days ago, and they thought she was gone for good. They were happy she was back. And I was happy that she was just a cat, instead of something much worse!

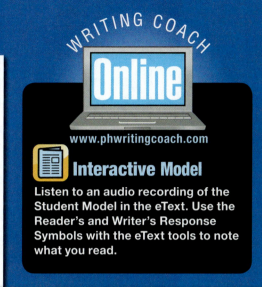

Interactive Model

Listen to an audio recording of the Student Model in the eText. Use the Reader's and Writer's Response Symbols with the eText tools to note what you read.

Use a Writer's Eye

Now, evaluate the piece as a writer. On your copy of the Student Model, use the Writer's Response Symbols to react to what you read. Identify places where the student writer uses characteristics of an effective mystery story.

Writer's Response Symbols

R.D.   Realistic and believable dialogue

S.D.   Viivid sensory details

W.C.   Well-developed, interesting characters

E.S.   Engaging story

Feature Assignment: Mystery Story

Prewriting

Plan a first draft of your mystery story by **determining an appropriate topic**. You can select from the Topic Bank or come up with an idea of your own.

Choose from the Topic Bank

TOPIC BANK

Something's Missing What happens when something important turns up missing? Write a mystery story about an important article that gets lost, only to be found later in a surprising way.

Lost Memory Write about a main character who suffers from short-term memory loss. What has he or she forgotten? An event? A secret? The mystery gets solved when the character's memory is restored.

The Stranger in Town What happens when a mysterious stranger moves to a small town? From where has the person come? What changes happen in the town? How do the townspeople react? Write a mystery to answer these questions.

Choose Your Own Topic

Determine an appropriate topic on your own by using the following **range of strategies** to generate ideas.

Interview and Background Reading

- Interview classmates and family about mysteries that have been especially intriguing to them. Note some topics that appeal to you.
- Think about mystery stories you have read. What were they about? What made them memorable? Jot down some key ideas that these stories suggest to you.
- Flip through mystery anthologies at your library, or look up mystery stories online. Note titles or topics that interest you.

Review your responses and choose a topic.

Narrow Your Topic

If the topic for your mystery is too broad, you may end up with a complex plot that is confusing for your readers to follow.

Apply It! Use a graphic organizer like the one shown to narrow your topic.

- Write the main topic of your mystery in the top box.
- Move down the chart, narrowing your topic to help focus your plot.
- Your last box should hold the main focus of your story.

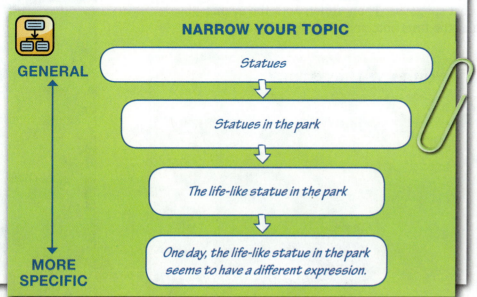

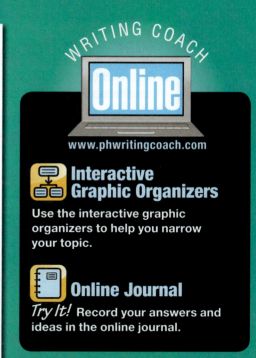

Interactive Graphic Organizers
Use the interactive graphic organizers to help you narrow your topic.

Online Journal
Try It! Record your answers and ideas in the online journal.

Consider Multiple Audiences and Purposes

Before writing, think about your audiences and purposes. Consider how your writing will convey the intended meaning to multiple audiences—classmates, teachers, and perhaps a wider set of readers. Consider the views of the others as you ask yourself these questions.

Questions for Audience	Questions for Purpose
• Who is my audience? • What kinds of story lines will my audience find engaging? • What background information will my audience need to understand my mystery story?	• Why am I writing the story? To puzzle my audience? To make them feel scared? Something else? • How will I develop my mystery? What devices can I use to enhance my plot?

Record your answers in your writing journal.

Plan Your Piece

You will use the graphic organizer to develop a conflict, characters, and a resolution. When it is complete, you will be ready to write your first draft.

Develop the Story Line Review your notes and determine your controlling idea and the overall story line, including a well-developed conflict and resolution.

Structure Ideas in a Sustained Way Use a graphic organizer to chart events from introducing the conflict through complications, to the climax, or point of greatest suspense. Then, finish with the events resulting from the climax and the final outcome of all the events.

DEVELOP YOUR MYSTERY STORY

Theme
Trust in what you see

Setting
A small town park

Characters
Marco, a 10-year-old boy! _____, _____

Mood
unease

Rising Action
Marco thinks the expression on the statue's face changed last spring, and again this fall.

Climax
One winter night, Marco thinks the statue winks at him.

Falling Action
_____

Resolution
_____

Conflict/Mystery
Marco thinks a lifelike statue in the town park changes from time to time.

102 Short Story

Gather Details

To engage the audience, develop interesting characters and a believable setting. Include sensory details, which define the mood—the sense the story develops in the reader. You can also use these details to project a tone—the author's attitude toward story events. Look at these examples.

- **Sight:** *In the amber haze, a shady figure moved.*
- **Smell:** *The old clothes gave off a musty smell.*
- **Sound:** *The windows rattled, as if frightened.*
- **Taste:** *Fear left a sour a taste in my mouth.*
- **Touch:** *I felt something sharp against my back.*

Writers also use a variety of **literary strategies and devices** to enhance the style and tone of a story.

- **Dialogue:** *"Everyone knows that statues are made of stone," Mike said. "But I'm telling you the truth," Marco replied.*
- **Suspense:** *Marco tiptoed closer to the statue. Would it dare to wink at him again?*

Try It! Read the Student Model excerpt and identify which kinds of details the author uses to make the story engaging.

STUDENT MODEL from A Rough Night
page 98; lines 6–11

> With a flash and a bang, the lights went out. It was pitch dark all along the street. I collected candles and sat down at the kitchen table to read a newspaper. Patch, the family dog, curled up on my feet. "Patch," I asked nervously, "are you protecting me or do you need protection?"

 Apply It! Review the types of details a short story writer can use. Then write at least one detail for each section of your story.

- Include details that develop the **conflict and resolution** and help make the **characters interesting and believable**. Also identify **literary strategies and devices** you could use to enhance the plot and **sensory details** that could help you to define the mood or tone of the story.
- Then, add these details to your graphic organizer. Be sure to include details that fit in with the action to help build suspense.

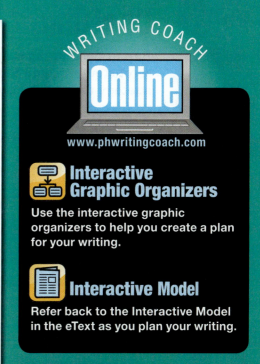

WRITING COACH Online
www.phwritingcoach.com

Interactive Graphic Organizers
Use the interactive graphic organizers to help you create a plan for your writing.

Interactive Model
Refer back to the Interactive Model in the eText as you plan your writing.

Prewriting 103

Drafting

During the drafting stage, you will start to write your ideas for your short story. You will follow an outline that provides an organizational strategy that will help you write an engaging mystery story.

The Organization of a Short Story

The chart shows an organizational strategy for a short story. Look back at how the Mentor Text follows this organizational strategy. Then, use this chart to help you outline your draft.

Beginning — See Mentor Text, p. 94.
- Setting and characters
- Conflict or problem

Middle — See Mentor Text, pp. 95–97.
- Plot with well-developed conflict
- Events and actions linked to the conflict
- Climax when the suspense is at its highest point

End — See Mentor Text, p. 97.
- A well-developed resolution to the mystery
- Characters' reactions to outcome
- Change in mood or tone due to outcome

Set the Scene
- The setting and characters of a story engage readers and set the story's tone.
- The conflict or problem to be solved should be introduced early in the story to interest the reader.

Build Suspense
- The plot should slowly unfold. The conflict often shows several events that involve the main character learning about or dealing with the problem.
- These events and actions often include subtle clues about the resolution.
- At the climax, readers should be wondering how the mystery will be solved. Use dialogue, sound devices, and other literary strategies and devices to enhance the plot by heightening the readers' experience. A red herring, or false clue, is a common mystery device.

Wrap It Up
- A well-developed resolution explains the mystery or solves the problem.
- The characters must react in a way that is consistent with what the reader knows about them.
- The mood or tone may change at the end depending on how the mystery is solved.

Start Your Draft

To complete your draft, follow each step in the process. Use the graphic organizer that shows the Beginning, Middle, and End, as well as the Outline for Success on the opposite page as guides.

While drafting, aim at writing your ideas down, not on making your writing perfect. Remember, you will have the chance to improve your draft when you revise and edit.

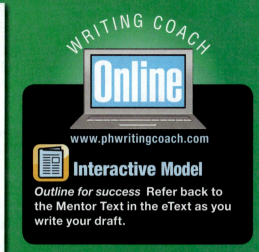

Interactive Model
Outline for success Refer back to the Mentor Text in the eText as you write your draft.

- √ Start with the opening of your mystery story. Describe the setting and create interesting, believable **characters** by using specific details that tell about their thoughts and actions.
- √ Continue the **beginning** by hinting at the **conflict** or mystery to come.

- √ Create a well-developed **conflict** and build suspense in the **middle** of your story. Use other literary strategies and devices to enhance the plot and keep readers interested.
- √ Use rhetorical devices such as transitions to connect the chain of events and to convey meaning.
- √ Include **sensory details** to set the mood or tone and show how the characters feel. Use sensory details to create a specific atmosphere such as spooky, threatening, or puzzling.
- √ Keep the **action** focused on the conflict. Describe events in time order, with each event building in intensity to the climax.

- √ In the **end** of the story, create a well-developed **resolution**—how the conflict works out. As appropriate, include additional details to explain how the mystery was solved.
- √ Build your **denouement**—the final outcome—by showing how the characters and mood change after the climax. Wrap up any unanswered questions or details.

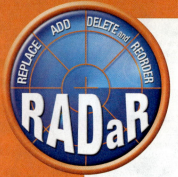

Revising: Making It Better

Now that you have finished your first draft, you are ready to revise. Think about the "big picture" of **audience, purpose, and genre**. You can use the Revision RADaR strategy as a guide for making changes to improve your draft. Revision RADaR provides four major ways to improve your writing: (R) replace, (A) add, (D) delete, and (R) reorder.

Kelly Gallagher, M. Ed.

KEEP REVISION ON YOUR RADaR

Read part of the first draft of the Student Model "A Rough Night." Then look at questions the writer asked himself as he thought about how well this draft addressed issues of audience, purpose, and genre.

A Rough Night

One night I was babysitting. After the kids got to sleep we had a big thunderstorm with lots of wind and rain. Tree branches scratched against the house. It was pretty scary.

With a flash and a bang, the lights went out. It was pitch dark all along the street. I figured that lightning must have struck a power line somewhere. I collected candles and sat down at the kitchen table to read a newspaper. Patch, the family dog, curled up on my feet. In the dim glow of the candlelight, I read the newspaper.

Candlelight flickered, throwing spooky shadows against the kitchen walls. In the dim glow, I read an article about an unsolved crime in our city. The police hadn't found the suspects yet. . . .

Suddenly, I heard a sad, low moan outside the window. The dog growled menacingly. There was another low moan. Patch growled again in warning. A chill swept down my back. With my heart pounding, I peered out the window to see what—or who—was there.

*Does my **opening** grab my audience? Is the style appealing?*

*Do my descriptions suit my **purpose** and help to develop the **conflict**?*

*Am I using events and **specific details** that develop the conflict and define the mood?*

106 Short Story

Now, look at how the writer applied Revision RADaR to write an improved second draft.

A Rough Night — 2ND DRAFT

Babysitting is never without its moments, and this night was especially rough. After the kids got to sleep, a huge thunderstorm rolled in, pounding the house with wind and rain. Tree branches rustled like rattling bones. Then things got *very* creepy.

With a flash and a bang, the lights went out. It was pitch dark all along the street. I collected candles and sat down at the kitchen table to read a newspaper. Patch, the family dog, curled up on my feet. "Patch," I asked nervously, "are you protecting me or do you need protection?"

Candlelight flickered, throwing spooky shadows against the kitchen walls. In the dim glow, I read an article about an unsolved crime in our city. The police hadn't found the suspects yet....

Suddenly, I heard a sad, low moan outside the window. A chill swept down my back. The dog growled menacingly. There was another low moan. Patch growled again in warning. With my heart pounding, I peered out the window to see what—or who—was there. I could only see bushes tossing in the wind.

R — Replaced dull sentences with figurative language and sensory details to get readers' attention

D — Deleted a sentence that didn't fit with the mood

A — Added dialogue as a literary device to enhance the plot and intensify the mood

R — Reordered sentences to emphasize the tension

WRITING COACH Online
www.phwritingcoach.com
Video Learn more strategies for effective writing from program author Kelly Gallagher.

Apply It! Use your Revision RADaR to revise your draft.

- First, determine if you have engaged your audience, met your writing purpose, and included all the characteristics of the short story genre.
- Then apply the Revision RADaR strategy to make needed changes. Pay close attention to the plot and stylistic elements of your story. Make revisions as necessary. Remember: you can use the Revision RADaR steps in any order.

Look at the Big Picture

Use the chart and your analytical skills to evaluate how well each section of your mystery story addresses **purpose, audience, and genre**. When necessary, use the suggestions in the chart to revise your short story.

Section	Evaluate	Revise
Beginning	• Check the **opening**. Will it grab readers' attention and make them want to read more?	• Use sensory details and other techniques to define an appropriate mood, such as threatening, curious, or weird.
	• Introduce the **setting** and characters.	• Add specific details to describe where the action takes place and to create interesting, believable characters.
	• Introduce the **conflict** or mystery to be solved.	• Experiment with literary strategies and devices, such as suspense, to draw your readers into the story and enhance the plot.
Middle	• Check that the action is well-paced and the **plot** is clear to engage your readers and to create a well-developed conflict.	• Show events in time order leading up to the climax. Use transitions to convey meaning and connect the chain of events.
	• Underline details that develop the conflict and build **suspense**. Number them in order up to the climax.	• Reorder details as necessary to better build suspense. Delete or replace details that don't contribute to building the story.
End	• Make sure that your **resolution** ties up all loose ends of the story.	• To create a well-developed resolution, answer questions such as *What happened then? What did the characters do after the mystery was solved?*
	• Make sure you described the **results** of solving the mystery.	• Show how the mood and characters changed after the mystery was solved.

Focus on Craft: Style

A writer's **style** comes from the kinds of words and sentences the writer chooses to use, as well as the details he or she chooses to include in a work. Writing style sets the tone or mood of a piece, conveys subtleties of meaning, and engages readers. Notice the difference in style between these sentences and the meaning each conveys: *I don't like to go outside when it's cold. /When it's cold, I like to stay inside, snuggled up on my couch with a good book and a cup of cocoa.*

Think about style as you read the following sentences from the Student Model.

> **STUDENT MODEL** from **A Rough Night**
> page 98; lines 2–5
>
> After the kids got to sleep, a huge thunderstorm rolled in, pounding the house with wind and rain. Tree branches rustled like rattling bones. Then things got *very* creepy.

Try It! Now, ask yourself these questions. Record your answers in your journal.

- How does the writer's choice of words affect the meaning in this passage?
- In the second sentence, how does the simile comparing trees to bones add to the mood? How would the mood be affected if the second sentence were written like this: *Tree branches swayed in the wind*?
- Is the last sentence specific or vague? How does it hint at what is to come?

Fine-Tune Your Draft

Apply It! Use the revision suggestions to prepare your final draft **after rethinking how well questions of purpose, audience, and genre have been addressed**.

- **Improve Style** Choose vivid, specific words and a variety of sentence structures that best express your meaning.
- **Improve Figurative Language and Subtlety of Meaning** Review your language choices to make sure they convey the shades of meaning you intend. Use similes and metaphors, which draw a comparison between two usually unrelated things, to enhance your subtlety of meaning. (See pages 54–55.)

Peer Feedback Read your final draft to a group of peers. Ask if your story is **engaging and has a well-developed conflict and resolution**. Think about their responses and revise your final draft as needed.

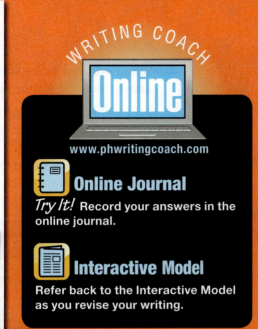

WRITING COACH

www.phwritingcoach.com

Online Journal
Try It! Record your answers in the online journal.

Interactive Model
Refer back to the Interactive Model as you revise your writing.

Editing: Making It Correct

When editing, make sure your sentences are complete, your commas are in place, and your verbs are in the right tense.

Think about using **relative clauses** to help you tell your story. Relative clauses are subordinate clauses that modify nouns in a sentence. Make sure to determine whether the clauses are **restrictive or nonrestrictive** in order to **place commas correctly**. Then, edit your final draft for errors in **grammar, mechanics, and spelling**.

WRITE GUY Jeff Anderson, M. Ed.

WHAT DO YOU NOTICE?

To learn more about clauses, see Chapter 15 of your Grammar Handbook.

Zoom in on Conventions Focus on relative clauses as you zoom in on these lines from the Mentor Text.

> **MENTOR TEXT** from **The Mystery of the Golden Locket** pages 95–96; lines 48–50, 101–103
>
> A wide smile spread across his face as he said a silent word of gratitude for the hunch that had sent him north.... Rusty didn't want to bring bad memories back to anyone, but he did want to see if he could find the person who had owned the locket...

Now, ask yourself: *Is the information in each highlighted section within the Mentor Text important to the meaning of the sentences?*

Perhaps you said that both highlighted sections, or clauses, are essential to the meanings of the sentences.

Both clauses in the model are **relative clauses**. A relative clause is introduced by a relative pronoun (e.g., *who, whom, that, which, whose*) and cannot stand alone.

- A **restrictive relative clause** gives information that is essential to the meaning of the sentence. In both of the example sentences, the relative clauses are essential in understanding the sentences. Without the clauses, the reader would not know which "hunch" or which "person" to which the author was referring.

- **Nonrestrictive relative clauses** give extra information that is not needed to understand the sentence. For example: *The girl, who had brown hair, was the fastest runner on the team.* The reader does not need to know the girl's hair color to understand the sentence.

Partner Talk Discuss this question with a partner: *How do the relative clauses add meaning to the sentences?*

110 Short Story

Grammar Mini-Lesson:
Commas in Relative Clauses

Restrictive relative clauses add essential information to a sentence, so they should not be set off with **commas**. In contrast, **nonrestrictive relative clauses** add extra information, so they should be set off with commas. Notice how the Mentor Text author did not use commas for the restrictive clause beginning with the relative pronoun *who*.

MENTOR TEXT from **The Mystery of the Golden Locket**
page 97; lines 134–135

> My mother was one of the only children who made it.

To learn more, see Chapter 23.

Try It! Identify the restrictive and nonrestrictive relative clauses in each sentence. Then use commas to set off the nonrestrictive relative clause. Write your answers in your journal.

1. The bright light that shown through the window suddenly flickered out.
2. Briana who was seventeen took a step backward and reached for the phone.

Apply It! Edit your draft for grammar, mechanics, and spelling. Consider revising sentences to add restrictive and nonrestrictive relative clauses. Use commas to identify nonrestrictive clauses.

Use the rubric to evaluate your piece. If necessary, rethink, rewrite, or revise.

Rubric for Short Story: Mystery	Rating Scale
Ideas: How well do you narrate a story with a clear conflict and resolution?	Not very Very 1 2 3 4 5 6
Organization: How clearly organized is the sequence of events?	1 2 3 4 5 6
Voice: How authentic and engaging is your voice?	1 2 3 4 5 6
Word Choice: How effective is your word choice in creating the tone and style of your mystery?	1 2 3 4 5 6
Sentence Fluency: How well have you used transitions when moving from idea to idea?	1 2 3 4 5 6
Conventions: How correct are your commas with relative clauses?	1 2 3 4 5 6

WRITING COACH

www.phwritingcoach.com

Video
Learn effective editing techniques from program author Jeff Anderson.

Online Journal
Try It! Record your answers in the online journal.

Interactive Model
Refer back to the Interactive Model as you edit your writing.

Publishing

Publish your mystery story to let others enjoy it. First, get the story ready to present. Then choose a way to **publish your work for appropriate audiences**.

Wrap Up Your Presentation

If your story is written on a computer, be sure to choose a font, or type style, that is legible, or easy to read. Fonts that look like handwriting or old-fashioned type may be appealing, but they are difficult to read.

Publish Your Piece

Use this chart to identify a way to publish your written work.

If your audience is…	…then publish it by…
A club for mystery fans of all ages at a community center	• Recording it as a 1940s-style radio program, adding music and sound effects to enhance the story, and making it available as a podcast • Producing it as a video with a narrator, background music, and sound effects, and posting it online
Students and teachers at your school	• Adding graphics to turn it into a graphic novel • Including it in a Web-based anthology

 ## Reflect on Your Writing

Now that you are done with your mystery story, read it over and use your writing journal to answer the following questions:

- Do you feel that you built up enough suspense in the first part of your story? If not, how could you make different word choices to build suspense in future stories?
- What part of the story do you feel is the strongest? Why do you think so?
- How can you use the skills you learned in writing your mystery story to help you write other stories?

 The Big Question: Why Write? What can fiction do better than non-fiction?

Manage Your Portfolio You may wish to include your published mystery story in your writing portfolio. If so, consider what this piece reveals about your writing and your growth as a writer.

21st Century Learning

MAKE YOUR WRITING COUNT

"Coming Soon...": Planning a Film Teaser

Mystery writers rely on suspense to keep their readers interested. Use the mystery writer's tools to plan a **teaser** for a film version of a story.

Like a movie trailer, a teaser is a video advertisement for a movie. It appears well before a film is finished, and runs under one minute in length. Your teaser should be a **multimedia presentation,** a presentation that incorporates text, images, graphics, and sound. Present your teaser using these print-based or electronic suggestions.

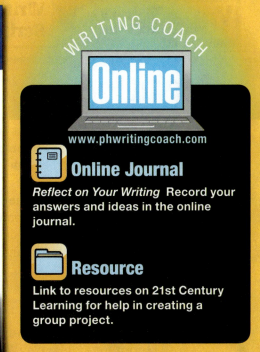

Here's your action plan.

1. Choose roles, such as artist, writer, and editor.
2. As a group, review your peers' mystery stories and choose one.
3. Learn by looking online for teasers. Notice the tools teasers use to reflect a distinct point of view and appeal to a specific audience. Most teasers employ a three-act structure:
   - The first act establishes the characters, setting, and conflict.
   - The second ends in a climactic scene.
   - The third features a montage, or collection of scenes, and music.
4. Create a storyboard—a visual outline that presents chronological sketches of the scenes. Under each sketch, write the dialogue or narration and notes about music and sound effects. Include the film title in the first or last sketch.
5. Plan to share your final storyboard with the class by providing them with individual copies or projecting it as a slideshow.

Listening and Speaking With your group, present your storyboard to the class. Show your storyboard using slideshow software with added sound files, or act it out using costumes, props, and music.

WRITING COACH

Online

www.phwritingcoach.com

Online Journal
Reflect on Your Writing Record your answers and ideas in the online journal.

Resource
Link to resources on 21st Century Learning for help in creating a group project.

Your Turn — Writing for Media: Script

Script

A **script** is a form of writing that is intended to be performed by actors for an audience. Scripts are commonly written for stage plays or radio plays, which are designed to entertain audiences. Some scripts directly state an **explicit theme,** and other merely suggest an **implicit** one through the actions and dialogue they present. A script shows the speaking lines for each character and stage directions telling actors how to speak. Scripts also provide detailed descriptions of the setting, characters, and background sound effects. These details contribute to a definitive **mood or tone.**

Try It! Study the example of a **script** for a radio play. Then answer these questions. Record your answers in your journal.

1. At what **audience** is this script most likely aimed?
2. Is the story **engaging**? Explain why or why not.
3. What is the **conflict** of this script?
4. What is the **theme** of this script?
5. How would you describe the **mood, or** the feeling the script conveys? Which **details** best define the mood?
6. Which **character** is most interesting to you? Why?
7. How do the **stage directions** in italic type help you to understand the scene?

Extension Find another example of a script and compare it with this one.

RADIO PLAY: The Sinking Sailboat

[Scene: a family's home. MOTHER, FATHER, and SISTER are in the living room. BROTHER is offstage in the bathroom tub.]

BROTHER. *[Whining. Splashing.]* Ma! My sailboat is still sinking!

MOTHER. *[Complaining.]* He's still whining about that sailboat!

SISTER. *[Sensibly.]* What's wrong with it? It floated fine last week.

FATHER. *[Resigned.]* Beats me.

SISTER. Yeah, that was just before Uncle Frank's visit. Remember how he spent hours leaning over the tub sailing that boat?

[Sound of television news report in the background.]

FATHER. *[Chuckles.]* Old Uncle Frank did seem to enjoy that!

MOTHER. *[Accusing.]* Your Uncle Frank has always been childish!

FATHER. *[Surprised.]* My Uncle Frank? I thought he was your Uncle!

SISTER. Hey, Look! *[Volume goes up on TV program.]*

TV NEWS ANNOUNCER. ...announced they've caught "Fingers Franklin," the prime suspect in the jewelry store robbery two weeks ago. Franklin, shown here,...*[Fades.]*

MOTHER. That's him!

BROTHER. *[Enters the room.]* This boat won't work!

[Sound of plastic crashing against the wall as BROTHER throws boat.]

FATHER. *[Calmly.]* Now, there's no need to throw things, son.

SISTER. *[Interrupts, excited.]* Look! What's that?

MOTHER. Gold! Diamonds! Rubies!

FATHER. It's Uncle Frank's heist! He hid it in the bath toy!

SISTER. *[Quietly, walking away.]* I'm calling the police.

114 **Short Story**

Create a Script for a Radio Play

Follow these steps to create your own script for a radio play based on a mystery story. To plan your script, review the graphic organizers on pages R24–R27 and choose one that suits your needs.

Prewriting
- Identify and narrow a topic for your radio play, and then determine your purpose and target audiences. For instance, you might decide to intrigue adults and children with the mystery of a lost civilization.
- Invent a detailed, interesting setting and colorful, engaging characters.
- Identify a theme and the conflict and resolution. State your theme explicity in your script, or use details to make it implicit.
- Outline the beginning, middle, and end of your script.

Drafting
- Draft an opening that grabs your audience with interesting dialogue, a startling event, or other literary strategy or device. Introduce your characters and setting.
- Develop the conflict with events and actions and use details to convey your theme through the beginning, middle, and end. Be sure to write your draft in script form.
- Develop a definitive mood or tone with specific, sensory details.

Revising and Editing
- Review your draft to make sure events are organized logically. Make sure the conflict and resolution are clear.
- Check that spelling, grammar, and mechanics are correct.

Publishing
- Read through your script with classmates, and then produce the radio play with sound effects. If technology allows, create an audio recording of the play.
- Turn your radio script into a film script. Add graphics, images, and sound that will help convey your distinctive point of view and appeal to a specific audience. Use a video recorder to film your script.

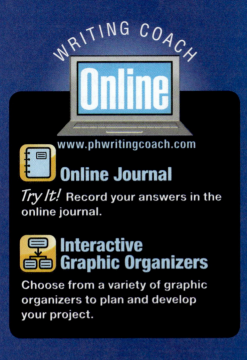

Before you start drafting, describe your script to a partner. Ask for your partner's opinions about your plan. For example, does your story convey a theme? Monitor your partner's spoken language by asking follow-up questions to confirm your understanding.

Writing for Media

Writing for Assessment

Some prompts ask you to write a short story. Use the prompts here to practice. Your responses should include the same characteristics as your mystery story. See page 92 to review these characteristics.

Try It! To begin, read the **short story** prompt and the information on format and academic vocabulary. Use the ABCDs of On-Demand Writing to help you plan and write your essay.

Format
The prompt directs you to write a *short story*. Start by introducing the characters. Then develop the conflict and resolution. End by showing how the mystery is solved.

Short Story Prompt
Write a short story about a mysterious new student at your school. Show how one character learns the new student's secret. Use sensory details to define the mood.

Academic Vocabulary
Remember that *sensory* details appeal to the five senses: sight, sound, smell, touch, and taste. The *mood* of a story is the emotion or feeling it conveys.

The ABCDs of On-Demand Writing

Use the following ABCDs to help you respond to the prompt.

Before you write your draft:

Attack the prompt [1 MINUTE]

- Circle or highlight important verbs in the prompt. Draw a line from the verb to what it refers to.
- Rewrite the prompt in your own words.

Brainstorm possible answers [4 MINUTES]

- Create a graphic organizer to generate ideas.
- Use one for each part of the prompt if necessary.

Choose the order of your response [1 MINUTE]

- Think about the best way to organize your ideas.
- Number your ideas in the order you will write about them. Cross out ideas you will not be using.

After you write your draft:

Detect errors before turning in the draft [1 MINUTE]

- Carefully reread your writing.
- Make sure that your response makes sense and is complete.
- Look for spelling, punctuation, and grammar errors.

More Prompts for Practice

Apply It! Respond to Prompts 1 and 2 by writing engaging mystery **stories** that sustain the reader's interest.

- Identify an appropriate audience.
- Establish a focused topic.
- Develop the **conflict** with logical and well-paced action.
- Use **sensory details** to define the mood or tone.
- Develop interesting, believable **characters.**
- Use **literary strategies and devices** to enhance your style and tone.
- Include a well-developed **resolution** that ties up any loose ends and explains the mystery.

Prompt 1 Write a mystery story about a character who finds a briefcase filled with thousands of dollars and sets out to discover its owner. Develop an engaging story with a clear plot. Include a specific setting and interesting, believable characters.

Prompt 2 Write a short story about a series of strange items (such as people's socks or a certain kind of food) that mysteriously go missing in a neighborhood. Create a setting that is specific and believable, and develop an engaging story line with a well-developed conflict and resolution.

Spiral Review: Narrative Respond to Prompt 3 by writing a **nonfiction narrative** essay. Make sure your short story reflects all of the characteristics described on page 66, including: a well-developed **conflict and resolution**, a range of **literary strategies and devices**, and **sensory details** that define the mood or tone. Remember that a nonfiction narrative essay is just like a short story, but the people, places, and events are all real.

Prompt 3 We all deal with conflict on a daily basis, from deciding who will get the best seat on the bus to deciding which movie to see with a group of friends. Some conflicts, though, are more significant. Write an essay about a conflict you've experienced and how you handled the situation.

WRITING COACH Online
www.phwritingcoach.com

Interactive Writing Coach™

Plan your response to the prompt. If you are using the prompt for practice, write one paragraph at a time or your entire draft and then submit it for feedback. If you are using the prompt as a timed test, write your entire draft and then submit it for feedback.

Remember ABCD

- **A**ttack the prompt
- **B**rainstorm possible answers
- **C**hoose the order of your response
- **D**etect errors before turning in the draft

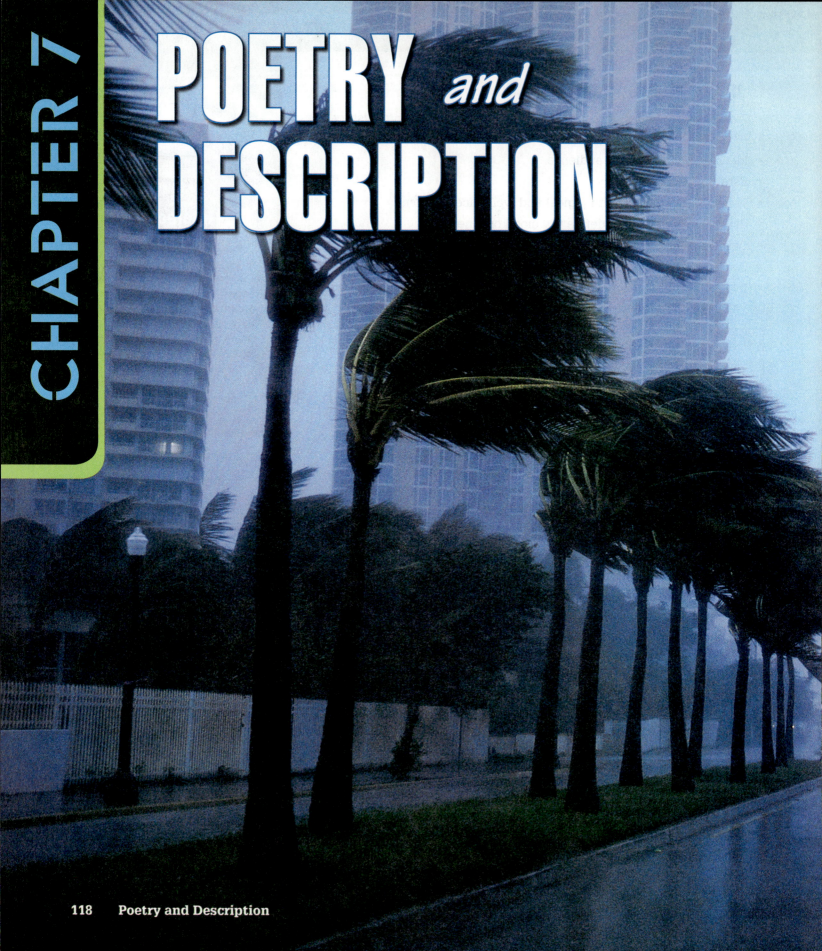

CHAPTER 7

POETRY and DESCRIPTION

What Do You See?

People see different things when they look at something. Some people may look at this photograph and see a hurricane. Others might see the power of nature or danger. Still others might see the contrast between nature and civilization.

People use different words to describe what they see. Words can be a powerful way to capture the beauty or danger of nature.

Try It! Take a few minutes to list what you see in the photograph of the hurricane. Consider these questions as you participate in an extended discussion with a partner. Take turns expressing your ideas and feelings.

- What do you actually see?
- What emotions does this photograph make you feel?
- What would you feel if you were actually outside in this storm?

Review the list you made. Use your list to describe to a partner what you see in this photograph. Think about how you would use these words to make a poem.

What's Ahead

In this chapter, you will review some strong examples of poems: Mentor Texts and Student Models. Then, using the examples as guidance, you will write a poem of your own.

www.phwritingcoach.com

Online Journal

Try It! Record your answers and ideas in the online journal.

You can also record and save your answers and ideas on pop-up sticky notes in the eText.

Connect to the Big Questions

Discuss these questions with your partner:

1 What do you think? Which words are the most powerful?

2 Why Write? How do we best convey feeling through words on a page?

POETRY AND DESCRIPTION

In this chapter, you will focus on writing a poem. Poetry is a form of writing that uses imaginative language, rhythm, and sometimes rhyme to communicate ideas and feelings. To make every word count, a poet carefully chooses language that is vivid, precise, and often musical, or pleasing to hear. An especially important part of poetry—and most other kinds of writing—is description. Descriptive details create imagery that helps readers picture what something looks like or imagine its smell, sound, texture, or taste.

You will develop a poem by taking it through each of the steps of the writing process: prewriting, drafting, revising, editing, and publishing. To preview the criteria for how your poem will be evaluated, see the rubric on page 137. You will also have an opportunity to apply the elements of descriptive writing to another form of writing—a descriptive essay.

FEATURE ASSIGNMENT

Poem

An effective poem has these characteristics (see page 129):

- A clear **topic, theme,** or **controlling idea**
- **Structural elements,** such as rhyme and meter
- **Figurative language,** such as similes and metaphors
- **Sensory details** that allow the reader to see, smell, hear, taste, and feel what the poet describes.
- **Sound devices** that create a musical or emotional effect

An English **sonnet** also has these characteristics:

- A **rhyme scheme** that usually follows the pattern *abab cdcd efef gg*
- A specific **meter,** usually in iambic pentameter, in which each line has five stressed syllables that alternate with unstressed syllables
- 14 lines in four **stanzas**—three stanzas of four lines and one stanza of two lines

A **free-verse poem** also has these characteristics:

- Text written to mimic the speech patterns of **natural speech**
- No specific rhyme pattern
- No specific meter
- No specific length

Forms of Poetry and Description

There are many forms of poetry and description, including:

Ballads are poems that tell a story and are usually meant to be sung. Ballads often contain repetition and have a simple, regular rhyme pattern and meter, or "beat."

Descriptive essays use imagery and vivid details to help readers imagine a person, place, thing, or event. Like all essays, they are made up of an introduction, body, and conclusion.

Free verse is poetry that imitates the rhythms of everyday speech. Freed of set rhythm and rhyme patterns, free verse uses figurative language and sound devices to convey ideas and feelings.

Haiku are three-line poems that originated in Japan. In a haiku, the first and last lines consist of five syllables, and the middle line consists of seven syllables. Classic haiku are usually about nature.

Lyric poems express a speaker's feelings about a particular person, place, thing, or event. Unlike ballads, lyric poems usually do not tell a story.

Prose poems look like prose, or regular text you might find in a story or essay, but use poetic techniques to create a memorable description of a person, place, thing, or event.

Sonnets are 14-line poems written in a regular meter and pattern of rhyme. One kind of sonnet—the English sonnet—consists of three four-line stanzas and a final couplet, or two rhyming lines. In each stanza, alternating lines rhyme.

Try It! For each audience and purpose described, choose a form, such as a sonnet, haiku, or free verse poem, that is appropriate for conveying your intended meaning to the audience. Explain your choices.

- To freely express your feelings about something in your life that made you happy, such as reaching a goal
- To help friends picture the beauty of a bird, using only a few words
- To express your love of someone using set rhyme patterns and a regular meter

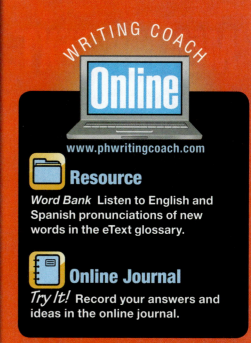

WRITING COACH Online

www.phwritingcoach.com

Resource
Word Bank Listen to English and Spanish pronunciations of new words in the eText glossary.

Online Journal
Try It! Record your answers and ideas in the online journal.

WORD BANK

People often use these basic and content-based vocabulary words when they talk about poetry writing. Work with a partner. Take turns saying each word aloud. Then, write one sentence using each word. If you are unsure of the meaning of a word, use the Glossary or a dictionary to check the definition.

meter	rhythm
repetition	senses
rhyme	stanza

MENTOR TEXT — Sonnet and Free Verse Poem

Learn From Experience

 After reading the poems on pages 122–123, read the numbered notes in the margins to learn how the poets presented their ideas.

 Answer the *Try It!* questions online or in your notebook.

❶ Sonnets follow a strict rhyme pattern. Rhyming words are **sound devices** that create a **musical effect**.

Try It! Which words rhyme in the first four lines of the sonnet? Which words rhyme in the rest of the poem? How do the rhymes help organize the poem?

❷ The simple **diction**, or choice of words, creates a definite **mood** and **impression**.

Try It! What impression or feeling do you get from the words in this section? Which words are most important in making that impression on you?

❸ The poet uses **figurative language** to help readers picture the night. The **personification** in these lines adds to the overall effect of the poem.

Try It! Which object is given a human quality? What is the effect of personifying this object?

Extension Find other examples of poems, and compare them with these.

Acquainted with the Night

by Robert Frost

❶ I have been one acquainted with the night.
I have walked out in rain—and back in rain.
I have outwalked the furthest city light.

I have looked down the saddest city lane.
5   I have passed by the watchman on his beat
And dropped my eyes, unwilling to explain.

❷ I have stood still and stopped the sound of feet
When far away an interrupted cry
Came over houses from another street,

10   But not to call me back or say good-by;
And further still at an unearthly height
❸ One luminary clock against the sky

Proclaimed the time was neither wrong nor right.
I have been one acquainted with the night.

Things

by Lisel Mueller

❹ What happened is, we grew lonely
living among the things,
so we gave the clock a face,
the chair a back,
the table four stout legs
which will never suffer fatigue.

We fitted our shoes with tongues
as smooth as our own
and hung tongues inside bells
so we could listen
to their emotional language,

and because we loved graceful profiles
the pitcher received a lip,
the bottle a long, slender neck.

❺ Even what was beyond us
was recast in our image;
we gave the country a heart,
the storm an eye,
the cave a mouth
so we could pass into safety.

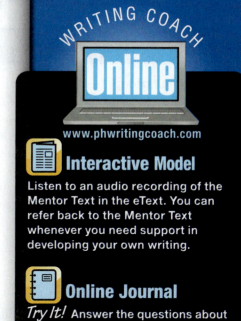

WRITING COACH

www.phwritingcoach.com

Interactive Model
Listen to an audio recording of the Mentor Text in the eText. You can refer back to the Mentor Text whenever you need support in developing your own writing.

Online Journal
Try It! Answer the questions about the Mentor Text in the online journal.

❹ These lines point out some everyday **metaphors**—comparisons between dissimilar things that are alike in some striking way.

Try It! How are a human face and the front of a clock similar? What other comparisons between human body parts and objects are made?

❺ The last lines add to the list of things named after human body parts, further developing the **theme**, or controlling idea, of the poem.

Try It! What do you think is the theme of the poem? Why?

Mentor Text 123

STUDENT MODEL — Sonnet and Free Verse Poem

With a small group, take turns reading each of the Student Models aloud. As you read, practice newly acquired vocabulary by correctly producing the word's sound. Also note the structures and elements of the poems. You may want to take a look at the Poet's Toolbox on page 129. Ask yourself how the poetic language shapes your understanding of the poems.

Use a Reader's Eye

Now, reread the Student Models. On your copies of the Student Models, use the Reader's Response Symbols to react to what you read.

Reader's Response Symbols
- **+** I can picture this.
- **−** This image could be stronger.
- **?** I wonder what this means.
- **!** This is cool!

Discuss your opinions and feelings about the Student Models with a partner. How do your opinions and feelings about the poems differ?

Paradise

A Sonnet by Tiffany Trevino

Sun turns the waves to jewels and warms my cheeks
Sand slips between my toes and dusts my hands
Gulls caw while fish swim by in silver streaks
Clouds gently float in white, weightless bands

5 My lips relax into a smile miles wide
A joyful sound comes bubbling from my throat
I spread my towel and lie at the ocean's side
The waves lap up my cares; my mind can float

Then racing, jumping, leaping through the spray
10 I plunge into a bed of deepest blue
Birds wheel, waves crash, while lazy palms sway
The heartbeat of the sea is all that's true

Happiness is nothing but clean, white sand
And truth is just saltwater in my hand

124   Poetry and Description

The Cafeteria

A Free-Verse Poem by Tiffany Trevino

Green slime slinking, stinking by
Could that be meat?
Cauliflower, I think, brown as dead grass
Corn, I'm sure, pebble hard
5 Now what is that?!
Chunky, gloopy, soupy
Dessert or potatoes, take your pick
Tomorrow, my lunch box will be packed

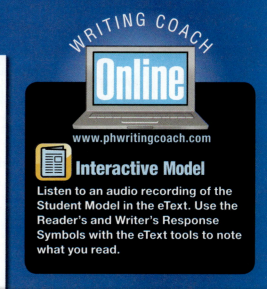

Interactive Model

Listen to an audio recording of the Student Model in the eText. Use the Reader's and Writer's Response Symbols with the eText tools to note what you read.

 Use a Writer's Eye

Now, evaluate each piece as a writer. On your copies of the Student Models, use the Writer's Response Symbols to react to what you read. Identify places where the student writers use characteristics of an effective sonnet or free verse poem.

Writer's Response Symbols	
R.R.	Rhythm or rhyme fits the poem's form
S.D.	Effective use of sound devices
F.L.	Figurative language conveys a mood
I.D.	Imagery and details appeal to the senses

Your Turn — Feature Assignment: Free Verse Poem or Sonnet

Prewriting

Plan a first draft of your poem by deciding which form of poem you want to write—a sonnet, free-verse poem, or other form—and then **by determining an appropriate topic.** Select a topic from the Topic Bank or come up with an idea of your own.

Choose From the Topic Bank

TOPIC BANK

V.I.P. Write a poem honoring someone you admire or find interesting. Be sure to clearly explain the qualities that make the person so admirable. Be specific and detailed.

Object of Attention Write a poem about either an element of nature or a human-made object you find intriguing. Offer a detailed description of your subject, including sensory details to help the reader connect with your ideas.

Ideal Subject Write a poem about an abstract ideal, such as freedom or beauty. Experiment with the literary technique of symbolism to represent your subject and show why the subject is important. (See page 129.)

Choose Your Own Topic

Determine an appropriate topic on your own by using the following **range of strategies** to generate ideas.

Brainstorm, Discuss, and Read

- With a partner, brainstorm for a list of people, places, or things in nature; events; or "favorites" that you might choose as a topic.
- Discuss your list with your partner. Delete topics that are not interesting to you. Star topics that you find interesting.
- Skim poetry collections or poetry found in a literature book to see examples of poetry topics. Make a list of topics and choose one that interests you.

Review your responses and choose a topic.

Narrow Your Topic

Because poems are relatively short, they cannot cover broad topics very well. Narrow your topic so you can thoroughly describe it.

Apply It! Use a graphic organizer like the one shown to narrow your topic.

- Write your general topic in the top box, and keep narrowing your topic as you move down the chart.
- Your last box should contain your narrowest or "smallest" topic, the new focus of your poem.

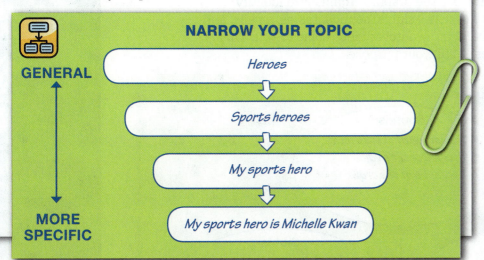

NARROW YOUR TOPIC

GENERAL → Heroes → Sports heroes → My sports hero → My sports hero is Michelle Kwan ← MORE SPECIFIC

WRITING COACH Online
www.phwritingcoach.com

Interactive Graphic Organizers
Use the interactive graphic organizers to help you narrow your topic.

Online Journal
Try It! Record your answers and ideas in the online journal.

Consider Multiple Audiences and Purposes

Before writing, think about your audiences and purposes. Consider how others may see things as you ask yourself these questions.

Questions for Audience	Questions for Purpose
• Who will read this poem? My teacher? Other students? Members of my family? A friend? • What information will my readers need to know to understand my poem? • Which form of poetry is the best choice to convey the meaning to my reader?	• Why am I writing this poem? Do I want to make my reader laugh? Do I want my reader to feel how I feel? Do I want my reader to have a different reaction, such as sadness or anger? • Which poetic techniques will help me achieve my purpose in writing?

Record your answers in your writing journal.

Prewriting 127

Plan Your Piece

You will use a graphic organizer like the one shown to organize your poem and **structure ideas in a consistent or sustained way.** When it is complete, you will be ready to write your first draft.

Develop a Topic, Theme, or Controlling Idea To focus your poem, write a clear statement of your topic, theme, or controlling idea. Name the most important idea or feeling you want to communicate. Add your statement to the center of your graphic organizer.

Develop Ideas and Details Use the graphic organizer to identify ideas, feelings, and sensory details—sights, sounds, tastes, smells, and touch—related to your topic. Write whatever ideas come to you. Then, underline the ones that best fulfill your purpose.

Develop Your Ideas

Sounds
- The scrape of skates on ice
- The announcer's voice
- The gasps of the crowd

Smells and Tastes
- Hot chocolate
- Popcorn
- Damp wool

Sights
- Kwan twirling in the air
- Kwan gliding over the ice
- Kwan's shiny costume

Topic, Theme, Controlling Idea

Figure skater Michelle Kwan is my sports hero.

Touch
- My hands raw and stinging from clapping so hard
- The scratch of my wool muffler at my throat
- My cold nose

Emotions and Feelings
- Excited
- Amazed
- Inspired

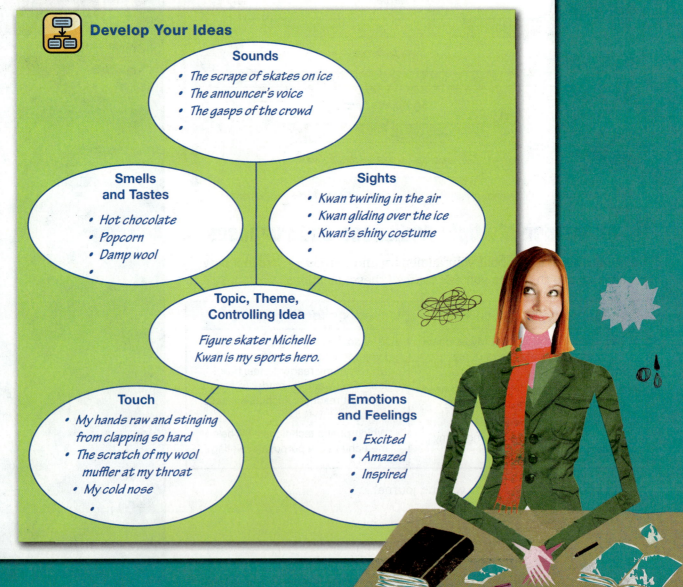

Poet's Toolbox

Writers use a variety of poetic techniques to make their ideas vivid and clear. These techniques help describe emotions, feelings, and ideas. Here are some techniques you might use in your poem.

Figurative Language is writing that means something beyond what the words actually say.	
Simile: comparison using *like* or *as*	*Kwan glided across the ice like a swan.*
Metaphor: comparison made by saying that one thing is something else	*The blades of her skates were knives cutting thin lines in the ice.*
Personification: human characteristics applied to non-human objects	*The skater's scarf danced around her neck.*
Symbols add depth and insight to poetry.	
An object that stands for something else	*A heavy gym bag might symbolize the difficult pressures put on skaters.*
Sound Devices create a musical or emotional effect.	
Alliteration: repetition of consonant sounds at the beginning of nearby words	*Her **s**ilver **s**kates **s**lid in **s**ilent **s**wirls.*
Assonance: repetition of vowel sounds in nearby words	*She r**a**ced gr**a**cefully **a**way.*
Consonance: repetition of consonants in the middle or at the end of words	*She cli**ck**ed her s**k**ates, gave a ki**ck**, and landed in the ni**ck** of time.*
Structural Elements help build the framework for poetic language.	
Rhyme: repetition of sounds at the ends of lines of poetry	*"The great skater **Kwan** Glides on ice like a **swan**."*
Meter: rhythmical pattern of a poem. It is determined by stressed syllables in a line. Some forms of poetry have specific patterns of stressed syllables.	*Her **sil**ver **skates** cut **cir**cles **in** the **ice**.* (Stressed syllables in poetry are marked with a ´, while unstressed syllables are marked with a ˘.)
Graphic Elements position the words on a page.	
Arrangement of words on a page	capital letters, line spacing, and line breaks

 Apply It! Review the ideas, feelings, and sensory details in the graphic organizer you created.

- First, confirm the poetic **form** you will develop.
- Then, decide what **techniques** from the Poet's Toolbox you would like to use in your poem. Keep in mind that some poetic techniques are used in specific forms.

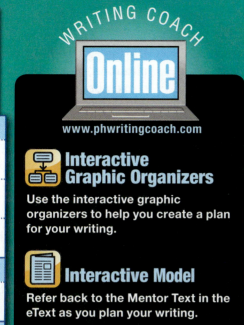

WRITING COACH Online
www.phwritingcoach.com

Interactive Graphic Organizers
Use the interactive graphic organizers to help you create a plan for your writing.

Interactive Model
Refer back to the Mentor Text in the eText as you plan your writing.

Drafting

During the drafting stage of an open-ended, or untimed, writing situation, you will start to write your ideas for your sonnet, free verse poem, or other form of poetry. You will build on the ideas you developed in prewriting and structure them carefully, choosing an organizational strategy that is appropriate for the poem form you chose.

Drafting a Free Verse Poem or Sonnet

Each poetic form has specific characteristics. You will write your poem using these characteristics, the techniques from the Poet's Toolbox, and the ideas, feelings, and sensory details you developed in your graphic organizer.

These charts show the characteristics of each form. Review the characteristics. Then answer the questions in the right column as you draft your poem.

Free Verse Characteristics	Questions to Answer While Drafting
• Varied number of lines • Varied number of stanzas, if stanzas are used • No meter used; follows natural patterns of speech • No rhyme pattern used • Poetic techniques may be used • Feelings or emotions conveyed • Vivid descriptions	• How long do I want my poem to be? **Tip:** You don't have to decide the *exact* number of stanzas and lines. • What sound devices will I use? • What poetic techniques or other devices will I use? • What feelings or emotions will I express? • How will I make my descriptions vivid?

English Sonnet Characteristics	Questions to Answer While Drafting
• 14 lines • Written in iambic pentameter, with five stressed syllables per line • Three stanzas with four lines and one stanza with two lines • Rhyme scheme is *abab cdcd efef gg* • Final two lines are a twist on or clarification of the first 12 lines • Poetic techniques used • Feelings or emotions conveyed • Vivid descriptions	• What do I want to describe or express in each stanza? • Do my lines follow iambic pentameter? **Tip:** Read aloud as you write to confirm beat and meter. Use a dictionary to determine how specific words are divided into syllables. • What words will I rhyme in each stanza? **Tip:** Consult a rhyming dictionary and thesaurus. • What sound devices will I use? • What poetic techniques or other devices will I use? • What feelings or emotions will I express? • How will I make my descriptions vivid?

 **Start Your Draft**

Writing poetry is different than creating most other genres. The process is more open. Use the graphic organizer that shows your topic, ideas, and sensory details, and the Poet's Toolbox as guides, but be open to experimenting with your draft.

While developing your poem, aim at writing your ideas, not on making your writing perfect. Remember, you will have the chance to improve your poem when you revise and edit.

Interactive Model
Refer back to the Mentor Text in the eText as you write your draft.

Before You Write

√ Choose the **poetic form** you want to use, either free-verse or a sonnet.

√ Review the **characteristics** of your poetic form that are listed in Drafting a Free Verse Poem or Sonnet. Make sure you use these characteristics when you write your draft.

√ Think of an image, figurative language, or other **poetic technique** to start your poem that will attract your readers' attention.

While You Write

√ State or imply the theme, topic, or controlling idea. This idea does not have to be apparent in each line, but needs to be expressed clearly in the poem as a whole.

√ Make sure to fully describe the **elements** of your poem's topic. Make your readers feel as if they are there, feeling what you feel and experiencing what you are experiencing. Include sensory details to achieve a specific, detailed description.

√ Include your ideas from prewriting. If a feeling, emotion, **sensory detail,** or other idea does not seem to work, you may decide not to keep it in your poem.

√ Use **poetic techniques** to support your ideas. Refer to the Poet's Toolbox if you need ideas for which techniques to use. If you experiment with a technique that does not seem to work, try another.

√ As you draft, pay attention to the sounds and the **rhythm** of the language you use.

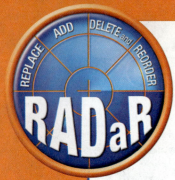

Revising: Making It Better

Now that you have finished your first draft, you are ready to revise. Think about the "big picture" of **audience, purpose, and genre**. You can use Revision RADaR as a guide for making changes to improve your draft. Revision RADaR provides four major ways to improve your writing: (R) replace, (A) add, (D) delete, and (R) reorder.

Kelly Gallagher, M. Ed.

KEEP REVISION ON YOUR RADAR

Read part of the first draft of the Student Model "Paradise." Then look at questions the writer asked herself as she thought about how well her draft **addressed issues of audience, purpose, and genre.**

Paradise

Sun sparkles on the waves and warms my cheeks
Sand moves between my toes and dusts my hands
Birds caw while fish swim by in silver streaks
Clouds gently float in pretty, fluffy bands

My lips relax into a smile miles wide
A joyful sound comes bubbling from my throat
I spread my towel and lie at the ocean's side
The waves lap at the shore; I want to float

Does this line use strong imagery to help my audience picture what I am describing?

Are my word choices in this line interesting and engaging? Do the lines hint at my theme?

Does this line clearly develop my theme or controlling idea?

132 Poetry and Description

Now, look at how the writer applied Revision RADaR to write an improved second draft.

Paradise
2ND DRAFT

Sun turns the waves to jewels and warms my cheeks
Sand slips between my toes and dusts my hands
Gulls caw while fish swim by in silver streaks
Clouds gently float in white, weightless bands

My lips relax into a smile miles wide
A joyful sound comes bubbling from my throat
I spread my towel and lie at the ocean's side
The waves lap up my cares; my mind can float

A — Added sensory details (*jewels*, *slips*) to improve imagery, and used alliteration (*Sand slips*) to create a musical sound

D R — Deleted dull, flat words (*birds*, *pretty*, *fluffy*) and replaced them with engaging descriptive words and language (*weightless*) that introduce the theme of being relieved of heavy, daily pressures

R — Replaced language that did not clearly express my theme of the relaxation I feel at the beach with more precise language

WRITING COACH
Online
www.phwritingcoach.com

Video
Learn more strategies for effective writing from program author Kelly Gallagher.

Apply It! Now, revise your draft after rethinking how well you have addressed questions of **purpose, audience, and genre.**

- First, determine whether you have included a **variety of poetic techniques.** Decide whether you have included all the characteristics of your poetic form—a sonnet, free verse poem, or other form you have chosen.
- Then, apply your Revision RADaR to make needed changes. Focus especially on revising your **word choices** to create the best impact on your audience. Remember—you can use the steps in any order.

Look at the Big Picture

Use the chart and your analytical skills to evaluate how well each section of your poem **addresses purpose, audience, and genre.** When necessary, use the suggestions in the chart to revise your poem.

	Evaluate	Revise
Topic and Sensory Details	• Make sure your controlling idea or **theme** is clear in the poem.	• Think about the most important idea or feeling you want to convey. If needed, add a statement of theme.
	• Check that the **sensory details** you have chosen support the controlling idea or theme.	• Replace sensory details that do not support the controlling idea with new details that help paint a clearer picture.
Structural Devices	• Ensure that your poem uses all of the elements of the **poetic form** you chose.	• Review the characteristics of free verse poems and sonnets in Drafting a Free Verse Poem or Sonnet. If necessary, revise to add or delete elements for that particular form.
	If you are writing a sonnet: • Check that the meter and **rhyme scheme** work. • Confirm that your stanzas are the right length.	• Use a rhyming dictionary to substitute rhymes. • Add or delete lines and replace and reorder words to improve the rhyme and meter.
	If you are writing a free verse poem: • Check that your line length suits your purpose. • Be sure your **language** reflects the patterns of natural speech.	• Combine or shorten lines to better achieve your goals. • Revise your word choice to more precisely convey your ideas.
Poetic Techniques	• Make sure your **figurative language** and word choices help convey your meaning and purpose to your audience.	• Substitute figurative language, vivid words, and sensory details for dull or vague words.
	• Read aloud to check that your **sound devices** are effective and achieve the sound you intended.	• Use a dictionary or thesaurus to find words to create better assonance or alliteration.

Focus on Craft: Figurative Language

Figurative language, such as similes and metaphors, helps readers see everyday things in a new and interesting way. Carefully crafted figurative language can also help convey the mood of a poem. For example, note the difference between darkness "as comforting as a warm blanket" and darkness "like the inside of a coffin." Think about figurative language as you read these lines from the Student Model.

STUDENT MODEL from **Paradise**
page 124; lines 9–14

> Then racing, jumping, leaping through the spray
> I plunge into a bed of deepest blue
> Birds wheel, waves crash, while lazy palms sway
> The heartbeat of the sea is all that's true
>
> Happiness is nothing but clean, white sand
> And truth is just saltwater in my hand

Try It! Now, ask yourself these questions:

- What two things are being compared in each of the last two lines?
- How would your feelings about the ocean change if the lines described "a dark abyss of inky blue" instead of "a bed of deepest blue"?

Fine-Tune Your Draft

Apply It! Use the revision suggestions to prepare your final draft after rethinking how well questions of purpose, audience, and genre have been addressed.

- **Improve Figurative Language** Substitute fresh figurative language for flat or dull words and phrases that do not help convey your meaning or contribute to the poem's mood.
- **Improve Word Choice** Use a dictionary or thesaurus to choose the best words to convey your meaning.
- **Include Transitions** Add transition words, such as *then*, *now*, and *so*, to help your readers see how ideas, lines, and stanzas are connected.

Teacher Feedback Read your poem aloud to your teacher. Ask for advice and feedback about the poetic form and poetic techniques you have chosen. Think about the feedback and revise your final draft as needed.

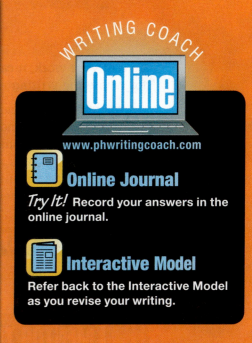

Online Journal
Try It! Record your answers in the online journal.

Interactive Model
Refer back to the Interactive Model as you revise your writing.

Editing: Making It Correct

To edit your work, it can be helpful to read your draft aloud to listen for where the writing needs correction.

As you review your grammar, pay particular attention to your use of **verbals,** such as gerunds, infinitives, and participles. A verbal is a verb form that functions as another part of speech. Also, double check your spelling of words with suffixes, especially those ending with *-ing*. Then edit your final draft for any errors in **grammar, mechanics, capitalization, and spelling**. Use a dictionary to check your spelling.

WRITE GUY *Jeff Anderson, M. Ed.*

WHAT DO YOU NOTICE?

Zoom in on Conventions Focus on verbals as you zoom in on the Mentor Text.

> **MENTOR TEXT** from **Acquainted with the Night**
> page 122; lines 1, 5–6
>
> I have been one acquainted with the night....
> I have passed by the watchman on his beat
> And dropped my eyes, unwilling to explain.

To learn more about verbals, see Chapter 15 of your Grammar Handbook.

Now, ask yourself: *Which words in these lines are verbs acting as other parts of speech?*

Perhaps you said that the words *acquainted* and *to explain* are verbs used here as other parts of speech.

Verbals are forms of a verb that function as another part of speech. A **participle** is a verbal that functions as an adjective. Participles can end in *-ing* or *-ed*, or have an irregular ending, such as *-t* or *-en*. The participle *acquainted* modifies the pronoun *I*.

An **infinitive** is a verbal that functions as a noun, adjective, or adverb. The word *to* usually appears before a verb in the infinitive form. The infinitive *to explain* acts as an adjective with *unwilling* to modify the pronoun *I*.

A **gerund** is a verb form that ends in *-ing* and acts as a noun. For example: *Racing* is one of his favorite activities.

Partner Talk Discuss this question with a partner: *How do verbals add meaning to the passage?*

Grammar Mini-Lesson: Spelling Verbals

Many verbals are formed by adding a suffix to the end of another word.

- When a suffix is added to a word that ends in one consonant, double the last letter *(jog, jogged)*.
- When a suffix is added to a word ending in two or more consonants, do not double the last letter *(jump, jumping)*.
- When a word ends in a silent *e*, the *e* may be dropped *(race, racing)*.
- When adding *-ed* to a word ending in *y*, change the *y* to an *i (vary, varied)*.
- When adding *-ing* to a word ending in *y*, keep the *y (study, studying)*. Notice the spelling of the participles in the Student Model.

To learn more, see Chapter 15.

STUDENT MODEL from **Paradise** page 124; lines 9–10

Then racing, jumping, leaping through the spray
I plunge into a bed of deepest blue

 Try It! Put the verbs in parentheses in their correct verbal form. Write the answers in your journal.

1. (Blow) wildly, the wind carried away the (fall) leaves.
2. Still (shiver), Kayla returned to her (interrupt) conversation.

Apply It! Edit your draft for **grammar, mechanics, and spelling.** Make sure you use verbals correctly. Check spellings with a dictionary.

www.phwritingcoach.com

Video
Learn effective editing techniques from program author Jeff Anderson.

Online Journal
Try It! Record your answers in the online journal.

Interactive Model
Refer back to the Interactive Model as you edit your writing.

Use the rubric to evaluate your piece. If necessary, rethink, rewrite, or revise.

Rubric for Poetry: Sonnet or Free Verse Poem	Rating Scale
Ideas: How well is the poem's subject or controlling idea defined and developed?	Not very Very 1 2 3 4 5 6
Organization: How organized are your ideas?	1 2 3 4 5 6
Voice: How effectively do you use figurative language and poetic techniques to create a unique voice?	1 2 3 4 5 6
Word Choice: How well do the specific words you have chosen convey your meaning?	1 2 3 4 5 6
Sentence Fluency: How naturally does your writing flow?	1 2 3 4 5 6
Conventions: How correct is your use of verbals?	1 2 3 4 5 6

Publishing

Share your feelings, experiences, and insights with others by publishing your poem. First, prepare your poem for presentation. Then, choose a way to **publish your poem for appropriate audiences**.

Wrap Up Your Presentation

Is your poem handwritten or written on a computer? If your poem is handwritten, you may need to make a new, clean copy. If so, be sure to **write legibly**. Also be sure to add a title that grabs the reader's attention and indicates your topic.

Publish Your Piece

Use the following chart to identify ways to publish your poem.

If your audience is…	…then publish it by…
A small group of close friends	• Reading it aloud at a gathering • Recording it with background music and visual images as a podcast and sending it to your friends • Posting it on a social networking site
Teachers and students at your school	• Submitting it to your school's literary magazine • Displaying it on a poster for a library poetry display • Posting it on your school's Web site

Reflect on Your Writing

Now that you are done with your poem, read it over and use your writing journal to answer these questions. Use specific details to describe and explain your reflections. Increase the specificity of your details based on the type of information requested.

- Are you happy with your final poem? Why or why not?
- Which parts of the poem do you think could be stronger? How can you make your writing stronger in your next writing assignment?
- How does writing a poem help you appreciate the work of other poets? Explain.

 The Big Question: Why Write? How do we best convey feeling through words on a page?

Manage Your Portfolio You may wish to include your published poem in your writing portfolio. If so, consider what this piece reveals about your writing and your growth as a writer.

Poetry and Description

21st Century Learning

MAKE YOUR WRITING COUNT

Sell It With Poetry

Many poems have a frankly admiring point of view. The language of poetry can be used to honor an inspiring figure, such as Abraham Lincoln, and to celebrate simple objects, such as bread. It can also be used to sell dish soap, blue jeans, and cars.

Create an **advertisement** to "sell" the subject of one of your group's poems. Present a **multimedia presentation** with graphics, images, and sound that conveys a distinctive point of view and appeals to a specific audience, or market. You can compose your ad online, using Web authoring tools, or you can present it live, blending your various media.

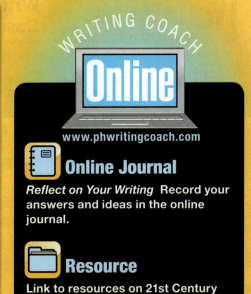

www.phwritingcoach.com

Online Journal
Reflect on Your Writing Record your answers and ideas in the online journal.

Resource
Link to resources on 21st Century Learning for help in creating a group project.

Here's your action plan.

1. Choose group roles and set objectives.
2. Identify a poem from your group that celebrates something. Whatever that poem celebrates will become the product. Identify your product's target market—to whom do you want to "sell" it?
3. Revise as necessary to convert the poem into appealing ad copy or a jingle (an advertisement's song).
4. Build a multimedia ad around your product, including:
   - The product's name
   - Ad copy or a jingle, which you will recite aloud or record as a sound element
   - A logo or icon that symbolizes the product and a slogan. Your slogan can come from a line or phrase in the poem.
5. Look online for models of ads that combine these elements.
6. Present your multimedia ad to the class, either by projecting the Web ad on a large screen or performing the presentation live.

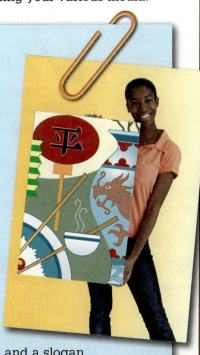

Listening and Speaking If you are planning a live presentation of your various media, rehearse to ensure the sound, images, text, and graphics interact effectively. As a class, discuss how persuasively each group's ad addressed its target market.

Writing for Media: Descriptive Essay

Descriptive Essay

A **descriptive essay** describes a person, place, or thing in vivid detail so the reader can visualize the topic of the essay. Descriptive essays express the opinions and feelings of the writer.

Blogs, travel guides, and Web sites often use descriptive essays to persuade readers to visit a specific place or try a new product. When you understand that descriptive essays are subjective, you can make better decisions about visiting a place or buying a new product.

Try It! Study the text in the sample travel Web site. Then, answer these questions. Record your answers in your journal.

1. What **place** is described?
2. What is the **purpose** of this essay?
3. A descriptive essay describes a place in so much detail that a reader can visualize being there. What words or phrases helped you create an **image** in your mind?
4. What is the **main idea** of this descriptive essay?
5. To what **audience** would this essay appeal?
6. In what other types of **publications** might you see an essay like this one?

Extension Find another example of a descriptive essay, and compare it with this one.

A Beach Town Worth Seeing

I have found paradise! I recently vacationed in Playa Del Carmen, Mexico. The minute I arrived in this seaside town, I was captivated by the colors, sounds, and textures.

The white sand beach instantly drew me to the shore, where I couldn't wait to take off my shoes and sink my bare feet into the warm, soft sand.

Everywhere I looked, I was rewarded with a rainbow of colors. The sea was as blue as a sapphire. Red and hot pink flowers posed in front of orange and yellow walls, and ladies strolled by in dresses of vivid printed cloth.

The people of Playa del Carmen were as beautiful as the scenery. Everywhere I went, smiles blossomed to greet me. I spent a whole day just sitting next to an elderly man and listening as he played his guitar. At dinner, I went to Rosita's, where the owner herself cooked for me as though I were part of her family. Welcome to paradise!

Create a Descriptive Essay

Follow these steps to create your own descriptive essay about a person, place, or thing that is important to you. When you finish your draft, you can use it to build a multimedia presentation. To plan your essay, review the graphic organizers on pages R24–R27 and choose one that suits your needs.

Prewriting
- Identify a place, person, or thing to describe.
- Identify your possible audiences. Anticipate each audience's views.
- List details that appeal to sight, sound, smell, texture, and taste.
- State your feelings about the place, person, or thing.

Drafting
- Use imagery and vivid details to appeal to the senses and help readers visualize the person, place, or thing being described. You will want your readers to feel as if they are actually there, experiencing the person, place, or thing firsthand.
- Include sound devices, such as alliteration, that create a musical or emotional effect. Consider using examples of figurative language to convey a mood of happiness or excitement or some other type of mood.
- Be sure to clearly express your feelings about the person, place, or thing that is your poem's focus.

Revising and Editing
- Review your draft to ensure that the topic is clear and fully described.
- Make sure your feelings about the person, event, idea, or place are clearly expressed.
- Delete material that is not necessary to the meaning of your essay.
- Check that spelling, grammar, and mechanics are correct.

Publishing
- Use your essay to help you develop a multimedia presentation. Include graphics, images, and sound to show your distinctive point of view to your audience—your classmates.
- Give your presentation to the class.

WRITING COACH Online
www.phwritingcoach.com

Online Journal
Try It! Record your answers in the online journal.

Interactive Graphic Organizers
Choose from a variety of graphic organizers to plan and develop your project.

Partner Talk

Before you start drafting, describe your essay to a partner. Use specific details to describe and explain your ideas. Increase the specificity of your details based on the type of information you are delivering. Then, ask for feedback about your plan. For example, Can your partner visualize the topic?

Writing for Assessment

Writing a good poem can take a lot of practice. You can use these prompts to do just that—practice writing poems. Your responses should include the same characteristics as your sonnet or free verse poem. Look back at page 120 to review these characteristics.

Try It! To begin, read the prompt and the information on format and academic vocabulary. Then, use the ABCDs of On-Demand Writing to help you plan and write your **poem**.

Format
The prompt directs you to write a *poem*. Develop your topic, theme, or controlling idea by deciding on ideas and sensory details you would like to use in your poem. Make sure the format of your poem includes the characteristics for the particular poetic form you chose.

Poetry Prompt
Think about a painting or work of art you have seen in a museum, art gallery, or in a book. Then, write a poem about that work of art. Use a variety of poetic techniques and choose from a range of poetic forms.

Academic Vocabulary
Remember that *poetic techniques*, such as figurative language, sensory details, and sound devices, are the tools poets use to convey their ideas. When you write a poem, you use a specific *poetic form*, such as the sonnet, lyric poem, ballad, haiku, or free verse.

 ## The ABCDs of On-Demand Writing

Use the following ABCDs to help you respond to the prompt.

Before you write your draft:

Attack the prompt [1 MINUTE]

- Circle or highlight important verbs in the prompt. Draw a line from the verb to what it refers to.
- Rewrite the prompt in your own words.

Brainstorm possible answers [4 MINUTES]

- Create a graphic organizer to generate ideas.
- Use one for each part of the prompt if necessary.

Choose the order of your response [1 MINUTE]

- Think about the best way to organize your ideas.
- Number your ideas in the order you will write about them. Cross out ideas you will not be using.

After you write your draft:

Detect errors before turning in the draft [1 MINUTE]

- Carefully reread your writing.
- Make sure that your response makes sense and is complete.
- Look for spelling, punctuation, and grammar errors.

More Prompts for Practice

Apply It! Respond to Prompt 1 by writing a **poem** that **uses a variety of poetic techniques**. As you write, be sure to:

- Identify multiple audiences
- Choose from a variety of **poetic forms**
- Establish a clear topic, **theme**, or controlling idea
- Use **poetic techniques** to develop ideas

Prompt 1 You may not think that sports and poetry go together, but many poets have written about sports. Write a poem about your favorite sport. Choose a poetic form that best conveys your meaning to your audience. Communicate your enthusiasm with fresh, descriptive language.

Spiral Review: Narrative Respond to Prompt 2 by writing an **autobiographical narrative**. Make sure your story reflects all of the characteristics described on page 66. Your narrative should:

- Develop an engaging story with a well-developed **conflict** that establishes a problem to be solved
- Present interesting and believable **characters**
- Use a range of **literary strategies and devices** to enhance the plot
- Include **sensory details** that define the mood and tone
- Finish with a well-developed **resolution** that wraps up the conflict

Prompt 2 Think about the idea of a grand adventure! Write an autobiographical narrative about something interesting or exciting that happened on a trip with your family. The trip could be a vacation or something as simple as a trip to the grocery store.

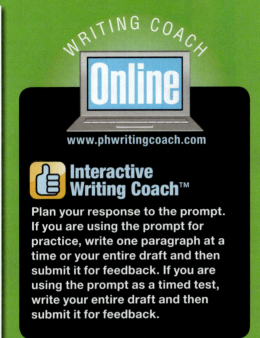

WRITING COACH Online
www.phwritingcoach.com

Interactive Writing Coach™

Plan your response to the prompt. If you are using the prompt for practice, write one paragraph at a time or your entire draft and then submit it for feedback. If you are using the prompt as a timed test, write your entire draft and then submit it for feedback.

Remember ABCD

- **A**ttack the prompt
- **B**rainstorm possible answers
- **C**hoose the order of your response
- **D**etect errors before turning in the draft

CHAPTER 8
EXPOSITION

How Can You Explain This?

What do you know about parades and the people who march in them? What information and ideas could you share with others?

Information can be presented many ways. For example, you can compare two things, you can discuss causes and effects, or you can present a problem and a solution.

Try It! Imagine that you wanted to compare two different groups marching in this parade. How would you explain each group?

Consider these questions as you participate in an extended discussion with a partner. Take turns expressing your ideas and feelings.

- What details would you use to explain how and why each group is dressed as they are?
- What similarities do the two groups have?
- What differences do the two groups have?

Review the ideas you wrote. Tell your partner your comparison.

What's Ahead

In this chapter, you will review two strong examples of an analytical essay: a Mentor Text and a Student Model. Then, using the examples as guides, you will write an analytical essay in the compare-and-contrast form.

www.phwritingcoach.com

Online Journal

Try It! Record your answers and ideas in the online journal.

You can also record and save your answers and ideas on pop-up sticky notes in the eText.

Connect to the Big Questions

Discuss these questions with your partner:

1 What do you think? What should we celebrate?

2 Why Write? What should we tell and what should we describe to make information clear?

145

ANALYTICAL ESSAY

An analytical essay is a type of expository essay that examines the details of a topic in order to better understand the topic. In this chapter, you will learn to write a type of analytical essay known as a compare-and-contrast essay. In a compare-and-contrast essay, the writer explores details that show the similarities and differences between two or more subjects. A compare-and-contrast essay may contain opinions, like a persuasive essay, but its purpose is to explain rather than persuade.

You will develop your compare-and-contrast essay by taking it through each of the steps of the writing process: prewriting, drafting, revising, editing, and publishing. You will also have an opportunity to write an advice column. To preview the criteria for how your compare-and-contrast essay will be evaluated, see the rubric on page 163.

FEATURE ASSIGNMENT

Analytical Essay: Compare-and-Contrast Essay

An effective analytical essay has these characteristics:

- Effective **introductory** and **concluding paragraphs**
- A **controlling idea** or **thesis**
- An **organizing structure** appropriate to the **purpose, audience,** and **context**
- A **variety of sentence structures** and **rhetorical devices,** such as analogies and rhetorical questions, that help express ideas effectively
- Smooth **transitions** between paragraphs and ideas
- **Relevant evidence** and **well-chosen details** in the form of facts, examples, reasons, and valid inferences to support ideas
- **Distinctions about the value of specific evidence** used to support the thesis, such as phrases like *most importantly* to signal key evidence
- **Effective sentence structure** and correct **spelling, grammar,** and **usage**

A compare-and-contrast essay also includes:

- A **thesis** that identifies the two or more things, people, places, or ideas to be compared and contrasted
- A clear **analysis** of similarities and differences

Other Forms of Analytical Essays

In addition to compare-and-contrast essays, there are other forms of analytical essays, including:

Cause-and-effect essays trace the results of an event or the reasons an event happened.

Classification essays organize a subject into categories or explain the category into which an item falls.

Newspaper and magazine articles that are printed or published on the Internet supply relevant information about a particular topic by analyzing the topic's elements. They may also reflect genres other than analytical essays (for example, persuasive writing or narrative nonfiction writing).

Problem-solution essays explore a particular problem and present one or more possible solutions to it.

Pro-con essays examine the arguments for and against a particular action or decision.

 Try It! For each audience and purpose described, choose a form, such as a pro-con essay, cause-and-effect essay, or problem-solution essay, that is appropriate for conveying your intended meaning to the audience. Explain your choices.

- To explain the results of an experiment to students in your science class
- To inform community members about the increase of litter in your town and to suggest ways to decrease littering
- To present students with the benefits and drawbacks of voting for a particular candidate in a student government election

www.phwritingcoach.com

Resource
Word Bank Listen to English and Spanish pronunciations of new words in the eText glossary.

Online Journal
Try It! Record your answers and ideas in the online journal.

People often use these vocabulary words when they talk about expository writing. Work with a partner. Take turns using each word in a sentence. If you are unsure of the meaning of a word, first look at its root word or affixes, word parts placed at the beginning or end of a root word. Prefixes, such as *re-* and *un-*, are affixes that are added at the beginning of words. Suffixes, such as *-ly* and *-ment*, are added to the end of words. Knowing the meaning of common affixes can help you determine the meaning of unknown words. If you are still unsure of a word's meaning, use the Glossary or a dictionary to check the definition.

analysis	conversely
comparison	inference
context	method

Exposition 147

MENTOR TEXT — Analytical Essay

Learn From Experience

 After reading the analytical essay on pages 148–149, read the numbered notes in the margins to learn about how the author presented her ideas. Later you will read a Student Model, which shares these characteristics and also has the characteristics of a compare-and-contrast essay.

Answer the *Try It!* questions online or in your notebook.

---

❶ The essay has two one-sentence **introductory paragraphs.** In just two sentences, the author grabs readers' attention and states the **controlling idea,** identifying the topic to be analyzed.

Try It! Write a sentence stating the controlling idea in your own words.

❷ The essay goes into more depth about the problem, and the author includes **relevant facts, reasons, and inferences** to support the analysis.

Try It! In your opinion, how believable is the inference, or "educated guess," about the reason for the ladybugs' decline? Explain.

❸ The **organizing structure** of this section is to describe a series of events in a process.

Try It! Why is the organizing structure appropriate for this section?

Extension Find another example of an analytical essay, and compare it with this one.

Where Have Ladybugs Gone?

by Mary Esch

❶ The number of native ladybugs is dwindling fast. John Losey wants to do something about that.

Losey, an entomologist at Cornell University, launched the "Lost Ladybug Project" last year to try to figure out why once-common native ladybug species have all but disappeared across the country. The project, funded by the National Science Foundation, recruits citizen scientists—especially children—to search for ladybugs and send photos of them to Losey and his colleagues via their Web site at www.lostladybug.org.

❷ Of particular interest: the nine-spotted, two-spotted and transverse ladybugs—three native species that have declined dramatically in the last decade, possibly because of the release of non-native species to control crop pests.

"Between 1999 and last year, when we started the program, less than 10 individuals of the nine-spot were collected anywhere in the country," Losey says. "That used to be the most dominant species across the U.S. and Canada."

Hundreds of participants across the United States and Canada have sent in thousands of photos since the project launched. Some of the photos were of native species. Most, though, showed the multicolored Asian ladybug and the European seven-spotted ladybug, which were introduced for agricultural pest control and have become widespread as the dominant species.

❸ The big breakthrough came in June, when 6-year-old Alyson Yates and her mom, Kate, started sending in photos of nine-spotted ladybugs from their rural backyard in Lakeview, Ore., in the sagebrush desert east of the Cascades.

"It was really an amazing find," Losey says. "Usually, someone just finds one or two. Alyson and Kate sent in a couple one day, a few more three days later, a couple more a few days after that. It became apparent they had a population out there."

So Losey and a colleague flew out with their collecting nets and came back with 13 nine-spotted and more than 30 transverse ladybugs.

"Aly was thrilled that people would come all the way from New York to go collecting in our yard," says Kate Yates, who got involved in the project when her daughter saw an ad in the National Wildlife Federation's Ranger Rick magazine for kids. "She just had a wonderful time looking for ladybugs. And we were ecstatic when we found some of the nine-spots they were looking for."

The researchers got an overnight shipment of 13 more nine-spots from Illinois. Sheena Beaverson, 40, of Champaign, sent in more than 200 ladybug photos while she was staying in Boulder, Colo., for a month.

❹ Seeking ladybugs was a lot like looking for seashells on the beach, says Beaverson, who works for the Illinois State Geological Survey. "At first, you look at every single one; later on, you start looking for something rare or something special."

❹ At Cornell, the beetles have been busily reproducing inside gossamer net cages lined up in Losey's lab, gorging on juicy green pea aphids raised for them on fava bean plants in the university greenhouse.

❺ Losey plans to conduct a number of studies with the captive populations in hopes of learning why they declined in the wild.

"The leading theory is that the decline had something to do with ladybugs that were imported," Losey says. "That's mostly based on the timing of the decline, which coincides with the introduction of the seven-spot. It does do a lot of good in pest control. The question is whether it just replaced the existing ladybugs or added to the diversity."

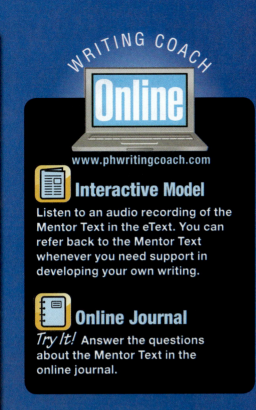

❹ The author uses **rhetorical devices,** including figurative language and sensory details, to describe aspects of the research.

Try It! Choose one of the highlighted passages in these paragraphs. Identify the rhetorical device and explain what it contributes to the essay.

❺ Rather than wrapping up the topic, the **conclusion** looks forward to the next steps in figuring out the ladybugs' decline.

Try It! Why is this an effective way to conclude this analytical essay? What other types of conclusions have you seen in other essays you have read? How does this conclusion differ from those?

STUDENT MODEL   Compare-and-Contrast Essay

With a small group, take turns reading this Student Model aloud. Ask yourself if the writer clearly expresses the similarities and differences in the essay.

 ## Use a Reader's Eye

Now, reread the Student Model. On your copy of the Student Model, use the Reader's Response Symbols to react to what you read.

Reader's Response Symbols

+ **Aha! This makes sense to me.**

− **This isn't clear to me.**

? **I have a question about this.**

! **Wow! That is cool/weird/ interesting.**

Participate in an extended discussion with a partner. Express your opinions and share your responses to the Student Model. Focus on the author's purpose and the main idea of the essay. Discuss what the author expresses explicitly and what he only suggests implicitly. When your partner is finished speaking, summarize his or her thoughts aloud.

Playing Video Games and Board Games: Different Ways to Have Fun

by Ryan Bradshaw

"Ryan!"—I think I hear my dad calling my name, but I don't really notice because I'm racing a sports car around a track at 200 miles per hour. Okay, so I'm not really racing a car, but the loud sounds, bright graphics, and realistic feel of the controller on my video game make it seem like I am. Board games, on the other hand, are not nearly as interactive, but I still enjoy playing them from time to time. In this essay, I will discuss these and other differences and similarities between playing a video game and playing a board game.

One contrast is that playing a video game is more exciting than playing a board game. At times, a board game gets boring, like when you're waiting for another person to take their turn. In most video games, players don't have to take turns, and the action is non-stop. Video games appeal to my senses of sight, hearing, and touch, which really helps me get "lost" in that other world. Board games, on the other hand, aren't as exciting to the senses.

Playing video games and board games affects your body differently, too. In most video games, the player performs the same motion repeatedly. You may have to press a button over and over again. If you play too long, your hands, arms, or neck can become sore. On the other hand, most board games require a variety of movements. In one turn, a player might

150   Analytical Essay

have to roll a dice, move a game piece, and draw a card. Players also have "rest" time between turns.

Are playing a board game and playing a video game at all similar? Yes, because both types of game play are social—you play them with other people. Many people assume that video games are always played alone, but I often play video games with a group of friends. I wish my computer were fast enough to play against online gamers, too. More importantly, a 2008 study by the American Gamers' Association found that 76 percent of teens play with others at least some of the time.

Like many teens, I prefer that my gaming occur on a video game system. Playing a video game is like zooming down the road in a fast car, while playing a board game is like riding in a slow car, looking out the window—it's still enjoyable, but it's not thrilling. Although these activities are quite different, they are both good ways to have fun with family and friends.

WRITING COACH Online

www.phwritingcoach.com

Interactive Model

Listen to an audio recording of the Student Model in the eText. Use the Reader's and Writer's Response Symbols with the eText tools to note what you read.

Use a Writer's Eye

Now evaluate the piece as a writer. On your copy of the Student Model, use the Writer's Response Symbols to react to what you read. Identify places where the student writer uses characteristics of an effective compare-and-contrast essay.

Writer's Response Symbols	
C.T.	Clearly stated thesis
I.C.	Effective introduction and conclusion
R.D.	Good use of rhetorical devices
S.E.	Effective supporting evidence

Your Turn — Feature Assignment: Compare-and-Contrast Essay

Prewriting

Plan a first draft of your compare-and-contrast essay by determining an appropriate topic. Choose from the Topic Bank or come up with a topic of your own.

 ## Choose From the Topic Bank

TOPIC BANK

Smart Shopper Select two competing products that you would consider buying. Write a compare-and-contrast essay in which you focus on the merits and shortcomings of these two products. Include a recommendation about which one is a better product or better value.

Past and Present Time can make a big difference. For example, even though both involve space travel, the moon landing in 1969 was different from a trip to the International Space Station that might take place today. Write an essay in which you compare and contrast these two events.

Middle School vs. High School For many students, life changed when they moved from middle school to high school. They may have to deal with different schedules, classes, and amounts of homework. Think about how your middle school experience is similar to and different from your high school experience. Write a compare-and-contrast essay explaining the differences and similarities between middle school and high school.

 ## Choose Your Own Topic

Determine an appropriate topic on your own by using the following **range of strategies** to generate ideas.

Observe, Discuss, and Research

- Be on the lookout for occasions when you compare and contrast in daily life. For example, you might compare and contrast two movies when you are trying to decide which one to see.
- Skim newspapers or magazines, noting topics that are related yet have some differences, too. Discuss the topics' similarities and differences in class.

Review your responses and choose a topic.

152 Analytical Essay

Narrow Your Topic

If the topic of your compare-and-contrast essay is too broad, your writing will be vague and unmemorable. Narrowing your topic lets you present a convincing analysis of the most important similarities and differences.

Apply It! Use a graphic organizer like the one shown to narrow your topic to two related things, ideas, people, or places.

- Write your general topic in the top box, and keep narrowing as you move down the chart.
- Your last two boxes should hold your two narrowest subjects, which will form the basis of your thesis statement.

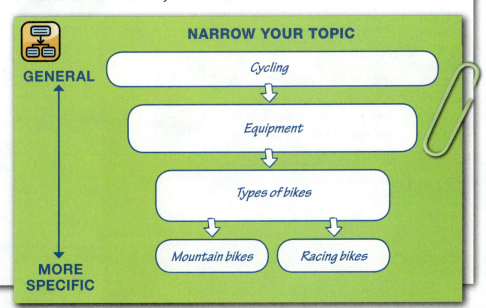

www.phwritingcoach.com

Interactive Writing Coach™

- Choosing from the Topic Bank gives you access to the Interactive Writing Coach.
- Submit your writing and receive instant personalized feedback and guidance as you draft, revise, and edit your writing.

Interactive Graphic Organizers

Use the interactive graphic organizers to help you narrow your topic.

Online Journal

Try It! Record your answers and ideas in the online journal.

Consider Multiple Audiences and Purposes

Before writing, think about your audiences and purposes. Consider the views of others as you ask yourself these questions.

Questions for Audience	Questions for Purpose
• Who are my various audiences? • How familiar are the audiences with this topic? • What questions might my audiences have about this topic?	• How will I explain my purpose in a clear thesis to create an effective introduction? • How might I organize my essay's structure to make the similarities and differences in my topic clear to my audiences?

Record your answers in your writing journal.

Prewriting 153

Plan Your Essay

You will use the graphic organizer to state your thesis, organize your points of comparison and contrast, and identify details. To write an analytical essay of sufficient length, determine what you need to say, and the level of detail you will require.

Develop a Clear Thesis Evaluate your preliminary ideas and information to help you develop a clear thesis that states the subjects of your essay and sets up a comparison and contrast.

Develop Your Points of Comparison or Contrast Evaluate the similarities and differences in your subjects, and decide which seem the strongest. On your graphic organizer, add notes that clearly list the points of comparison and contrast you plan to include. This will help to structure your ideas so that they build on one another in a sustained way.

DEVELOP YOUR POINTS OF COMPARISON AND CONTRAST

Clear Thesis That States the Topic	*Although they look similar at first glance, there are many differences between mountain bikes and racing bikes.*
First Point of Comparison/ Contrast	*Frames*
Details	
Second Point of Comparison/ Contrast	*Wheels*
Details	
Third Point of Comparison/ Contrast	*Gears*
Details	

154 Analytical Essay

Gather Details

To provide support for comparisons and contrasts, writers use many types of details. Look at these examples:

- **Fact:** *A racing bike can weigh as little as 15 pounds, while a mountain bike can weigh as much as 45 pounds.*
- **Personal Observation:** *When coasting downhill on my racing bike, I gain a lot more speed than I do when I coast my mountain bike downhill.*
- **Valid Inference:** *Racing bikes have thinner, lighter frames than mountain bikes, so racing bikes are easily damaged when ridden off-road.*
- **Logical Reasoning:** *The straight handlebars on a mountain bike let cyclists sit more upright, which helps them ride more safely.*

Try It! Read the Student Model excerpt. Then identify and take notes about which kinds of details the author used to support his ideas.

STUDENT MODEL from **Playing Video Games and Board Games: Different Ways to Have Fun** page 151; lines 31–38

> Many people assume that video games are always played alone, but I often play video games with a group of friends… More importantly, a 2008 study by the American Gamers' Association found that 76 percent of teens play with others at least some of the time.

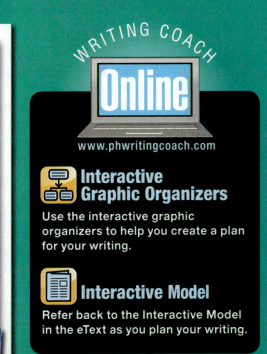

Apply It! Review the types of support an analytical essay can use. Think about examples of each type that you might include to develop ideas in the draft of your compare-and-contrast essay.

- Think about details that you can use to create an **effective introduction** that grabs your reader's attention and clearly states your **thesis**.
- For each point of comparison or contrast, list **relevant evidence and well-chosen details** to support your analysis. Relevant details are the most important and most closely related to each point.
- On your graphic organizer, note **distinctions**, or important points, **about the relative value of specific data, facts, and ideas.** When determining the relative value, think about how important it is for the audience to know the information and how well it supports your thesis statement.
- Use a **variety of sentence structures,** including some long sentences and some short sentences, in your notes for inclusion in your writing to make it interesting and engaging.

Prewriting 155

Drafting

During the drafting stage, you will start to write your ideas for your compare-and-contrast essay. You will follow an outline that provides an organizational strategy that will help you write a focused, organized, and coherent compare-and-contrast essay.

The Organization of a Compare-and-Contrast Essay

The chart provides an organizing structure for an analytical essay. Look back at how the Mentor Text follows this organizational strategy. Then, use this chart to help you outline your draft.

I. Introduction See Mentor Text, p. 148.

- An explanation of the topic
- Clear thesis statement

Start Strong
- An effective introduction, such as a question, an anecdote, or a strong detail about your topic, captures the reader's interest.
- A clear thesis states what you are comparing and contrasting.

II. Body See Mentor Text, pp. 148–149.

- Points of comparison and contrast
- Logical organization of points

Point-by-Point
- Point 1: Topic A and B
- Point 2: Topic A and B
- Point 3: Topic A and B

Block Organization
- Topic A: Points 1, 2, and 3
- Topic B: Points 1, 2, and 3

Compare and Contrast
- In a point-by-point format, you are comparing and contrasting one point at a time. Point-by-point is used when you have several points of comparison.
- In block organization, all the points about the first subject are made before the second subject is discussed. Block organization works best if you have only one or two points of comparison.
- Make sure your essay is of sufficient length—it should be long enough to convey your comparison well.

III. Conclusion See Mentor Text, p. 149.

- Summary of key points
- A satisfying conclusion

Create a Lasting Impression
- An effective conclusion restates the most important similarities and differences.
- A new detail that supports your overall conclusion about the topic makes your conclusion memorable.

156 Analytical Essay

👍 Start Your Draft

Use the checklist to help you complete your draft. Use the graphic organizer with your thesis and points for comparison and contrast, and the Outline for Success as guides.

Before drafting, express your opinions and ideas aloud with a partner. Then, draft in an open-ended, or untimed, situation. Your goal is to get your ideas down, not to make your writing perfect. Remember, you will have the chance to improve your draft when you revise and edit.

- √ Draft the attention-grabbing **opening sentences** of your **introduction** and then present your thesis statement to build an effective introductory paragraph.

- √ Shape the **body** of your compare-and-contrast essay. Think carefully about your audience, purpose, and context when choosing your **organizing structure**.

- √ Choose point-by-point or block organization based on the number of comparisons you will be discussing. Use **transitions** between paragraphs to smoothly connect ideas and clearly convey your meaning.

- √ Support each main point with **relevant evidence** and well-chosen details. Each detail should clearly support your thesis statement.

- √ Make distinctions about the **relative value** of specific data, facts, and ideas to your thesis by using phrases such as *most importantly*. Include only the information that best supports your thesis.

- √ Remember to use a variety of **sentence structures,** including compound, complex, and compound-complex, to create a pleasing rhythm for the reader. Use phrases or clauses to add detail and make your writing more interesting.

- √ End with an effective **conclusion** that restates your **main points.**

- √ Use **rhetorical devices** such as alliteration—using several words with the same beginning sound—to liven up your writing, and rhetorical questions to help convey your meaning and leave your reader thinking.

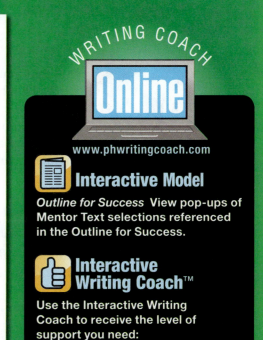

WRITING COACH Online
www.phwritingcoach.com

Interactive Model
Outline for Success View pop-ups of Mentor Text selections referenced in the Outline for Success.

👍 Interactive Writing Coach™
Use the Interactive Writing Coach to receive the level of support you need:
- Write one paragraph at a time and submit each one for immediate, detailed feedback.
- Write your entire first draft and submit it for immediate, personalized feedback.

Revising: Making It Better

Now that you have finished your first draft, you are ready to revise. Think about the "big picture" of **audience, purpose,** and **genre**. You can use the Revision RADaR strategy as a guide for making changes to improve your draft. Revision RADaR provides four major ways to improve your writing: (R) replace, (A) add, (D) delete, and (R) reorder.

Kelly Gallagher, M. Ed.

KEEP REVISION ON YOUR RADAR

Read part of the first draft of the Student Model "Playing Video Games and Board Games: Different Ways to Have Fun." Then look at questions the writer asked himself as he thought about how well his draft **addressed issues of audience, purpose, and genre.**

Playing Video Games and Board Games: Different Ways to Have Fun

I love to play video games, especially ones about car racing. Although I'm not really racing a car around a track, the loud sounds, bright graphics, and realistic feel of the controller on my video game make it seem like I am. I enjoy playing video games with my friends and brother, but my parents prefer board games to video games. Board games, on the other hand, are not nearly as interactive, but I still enjoy playing them from time to time.

As I have described, playing a video game is exciting. Playing a board game is less exciting. On family game night, we gather around a table instead of a computer. There are always times when a board game gets boring, like when you are waiting for another person to take their turn. In most video games, play goes quickly, and you hardly notice that time is passing.

*Have I written an **effective introduction** that grabs my audience?*

*Have I developed a **thesis** that clearly states what I am comparing and contrasting?*

*Can I make my **organizing structure** clearer for my purpose?*

*Have I included **relevant evidence** to support my point?*

158 Analytical Essay

Now look at how the writer applied Revision RADaR to write an improved second draft.

Playing Video Games and Board Games: Different Ways to Have Fun

2ND DRAFT

"Ryan!"—I think I hear my dad calling my name, but I don't really notice because I'm racing a sports car around a track at 200 miles per hour. Okay, so I'm not really racing a car, but the loud sounds, bright graphics, and realistic feel of the controller on my video game make it seem like I am. Board games, on the other hand, are not nearly as interactive, but I still enjoy playing them from time to time. In this essay, I will discuss these and other differences and similarities between playing a video game and playing a board game.

One contrast is that playing a video game is more exciting than playing a board game. At times, a board game gets boring, like when you're waiting for another person to take their turn. In most video games, players don't have to take turns, and the action is non-stop. Video games appeal to my senses of sight, hearing, and touch, which really helps me get "lost" in that other world. Board games, on the other hand, aren't as exciting to the senses.

A Added a more personal anecdote to make the introduction more interesting

A Added a thesis that clearly states the subjects being compared and contrasted

A Added a topic sentence with the word <u>contrast</u> to make the purpose of this paragraph clear

D Deleted a sentence that didn't support the thesis and
R replaced weak details with specific ones that more strongly support my point

 Apply It! Use your Revision RADaR to revise your draft.

- Include all the appropriate characteristics of the analytical essay genre and use a **variety of sentence structures.**
- Make sure that your **purpose** is clear and that you have considered your audience's needs and responses.
- Improve clarity of meaning by adding **transition words and phrases** between paragraphs.
- Use **rhetorical devices,** such as analogies, to reinforce your ideas and make your writing interesting.
- Then apply the Revision RADaR strategy to make needed changes. Remember—you can use the steps in the strategy in any order.

Look at the Big Picture

Use the chart and your analytical skills to evaluate how well each section of your compare-and-contrast essay addresses **purpose**, **audience**, and **genre**. When necessary, use the suggestions in the chart to revise your piece.

Section	Evaluate	Revise
Introduction	• Be sure that your **opening sentences** draw the reader in to your discussion.	• Make your introduction more effective by adding a question, an anecdote, or a strong detail.
	• Make sure your **thesis** clearly identifies your purpose and what you are going to compare and contrast.	• Write a thesis that clearly answers the question: "What people, places, things, or ideas am I comparing and contrasting?"
Body	• Check that you clearly identify both **similarities and differences** between your subjects.	• For similarities, add transitions such as *like, both,* and *too,* and for differences, add words such as *however, instead,* and *whereas.*
	• Check that you have considered audience, purpose, and context in developing an **organizing structure**.	• Reorder your points from weakest to strongest.
	• Logically organize your points of comparison and contrast. Use **transitions** to connect ideas.	• Keep paragraphs about similarities together, and paragraphs about differences together.
	• Underline **details** that support your points. Draw a line from each detail to the point it supports.	• Reorder details that are not close to the ideas they support. Add additional relevant evidence and well-chosen details if a comparison or contrast point isn't clear.
	• Make distinctions about the **relative value** of specific data, facts, and ideas that support the thesis statement.	• Add phrases that clarify value, such as *more importantly* or *equally important.* Delete information that does not support the main points.
Conclusion	• Check that you have restated your **main points**.	• Rewrite to sum up all your main points and only your main points.
	• Make sure that you have summed up your **conclusions** about your subjects.	• Add a sentence expressing how similar and/or different your subjects are overall.
	• Make sure that your **closing sentences** will stay with the reader.	• Add rhetorical devices, such as analogies, to make the conclusion more effective and memorable.

Focus on Craft: Subtlety of Meaning

With **subtlety of meaning,** your tone, word choice, and writing style combine to create exactly the meaning and feeling you want your audience to understand. In these examples, notice how the sentence acquires more strength and precision as it is revised:

1. There were colorful leaves on the sidewalk, which was broken.
2. The colorful fall leaves covered the broken sidewalk.
3. The scarlet and gold leaves protected the sidewalk's cracked cement.

STUDENT MODEL from **Playing Video Games and Board Games: Different Ways to Have Fun** page 151; lines 39–42

> Playing a video game is like zooming down the road in a fast car, while playing a board game is like riding in a slow car, looking out the window—it's still enjoyable, but it's not thrilling.

Try It! Now, ask yourself these questions:

- Which words add to the mood or feeling in these sentences?
- Would the sentence be more or less effective if it were written more simply? For example: *Playing a board game is still enjoyable, but it's not as thrilling as playing a video game.* Explain.

Fine-Tune Your Draft

Apply It! Use these revision suggestions to prepare your final draft **after rethinking how well questions of audience, purpose, and genre have been addressed.**

- **Improve Subtlety of Meaning** Make your writing more precise by using language that is specific, detailed, and packed to convey emotion.
- **Improve Style and Word Choice** A print or online thesaurus can suggest more effective synonyms to improve your word choice. In addition, use a variety of sentence structures to help create an effective style.
- **Choose Effective Transitions** Use transitions like *in contrast* and *similarly* to clarify the relationships between ideas and paragraphs.

Teacher Feedback After submitting your final draft for review, revise your writing in response to your teacher's feedback.

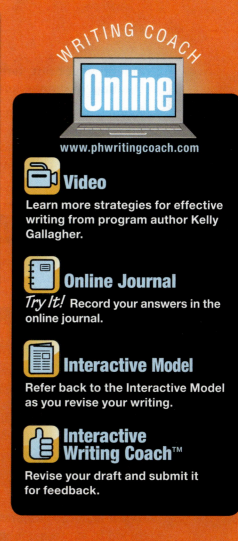

Editing: Making It Correct

To edit your draft, reread your work, sentence by sentence. Check the spelling, grammar, and punctuation in each sentence.

Before editing your final draft, think about how verb moods can express an action or condition. For example, the **subjunctive mood** expresses doubts, wishes, and possibilities. Then edit your final draft for any errors in **grammar, mechanics, and spelling**.

WRITE GUY Jeff Anderson, M. Ed.

Zoom in on Conventions Focus on the verbs as you zoom in on this sentence from the Student Model.

> **STUDENT MODEL** from *Playing Video Games and Board Games: Different Ways to Have Fun,* page 151; lines 38–39
>
> Like many teens, I prefer that my gaming occur on a video game system.

To learn more about subjunctive mood, see Chapter 17 in your Grammar Handbook.

Now, ask yourself: *Which verb expresses the action that the author wishes would happen?*

Perhaps you said that the verb *occur* expresses the author's wish.

You also may have noticed that *occur* does not end in *-s*, even though the subject *gaming* is a singular subject. This is because the verb *occur* is in the **subjunctive mood**. Writers use the subjunctive mood to express doubts, wishes, and possibilities. In the Student Model, the verb *prefer* lets you know that the author is stating a preference or wish.

You can also use the subjunctive mood in clauses beginning with *if* or *that* when the situation they describe is unlikely to occur. For example:

I would go outside if it were not raining.

The subjunctive mood can also be used in clauses beginning with *that* to express a demand or proposal. For example:

Janice demanded that Ramesh leave early that morning.

The council proposed that the bill pass by voice vote.

Partner Talk Discuss this question with a partner: *Which writing forms are most likely to use the subjunctive mood?*

Grammar Mini-Lesson: Subjunctive Mood

To learn more, see Chapter 17.

The **subjunctive mood** is most noticeable in a verb's third-person singular form. For the verb *be*, in the indicative mood we say "he/she/it *is*" (present tense) or "he/she/it *was*" (past tense). However, correct verb forms in the subjunctive mood are "he/she/it *be*" (present tense) and "he/she/it *were*" (past tense). Notice the verb forms in these example sentences: "I demand that she be present" and "If she were absent, I'd be upset."

Regular verbs in the subjunctive mood drop the *-s/-es* ending in the third-person singular form. For example, the verb *fall* in the third-person singular is usually "he/she/it *falls*," but in the subjunctive mood it is "he/she/it *fall*." Notice how the Student Model uses the subjunctive mood.

STUDENT MODEL from **Playing Video Games and Board Games: Different Ways to Have Fun,** page 151; lines 33–35

I wish my computer were fast enough to play against online players, too.

Try It! For each sentence, identify which verb is in the subjunctive mood and whether the sentence expresses a doubt, wish, or possibility. Write the answers in your journal.

1. The teacher desires that each student read 20 pages a week.
2. If Sam were friends with Jon, the two could study together.

Apply It! Edit your draft for grammar, mechanics, capitalization, and spelling. Check that you used the subjunctive mood to express doubts, wishes, and possibilities.

Use the rubric to evaluate your piece. If necessary, rethink, rewrite, or revise.

Rubric for Analytical Essay: Compare-and-Contrast Essay	Rating Scale
Ideas: How clearly are the comparisons and contrasts developed?	Not very Very 1 2 3 4 5 6
Organization: How well are your ideas organized?	1 2 3 4 5 6
Voice: How well have you engaged your reader?	1 2 3 4 5 6
Word Choice: How effective is your word choice in conveying your specific meaning?	1 2 3 4 5 6
Sentence Fluency: How well do you use transitions to create sentence fluency?	1 2 3 4 5 6
Conventions: How well have you used the subjunctive mood?	1 2 3 4 5 6

WRITING COACH Online

www.phwritingcoach.com

Video
Learn effective editing techniques from program author Jeff Anderson.

Online Journal
Try It! Record your answers in the online journal.

Interactive Model
Refer back to the Interactive Model as you edit your writing.

Interactive Writing Coach™
Edit your draft. Check it against the rubric and then submit it for feedback.

Publishing

If you want to let readers compare and contrast their ideas with yours, get your essay ready for presentation. Then, choose a way to **publish it for the appropriate audiences.**

Wrap Up Your Presentation

Before you publish your essay, you may need to make a new, clean copy. Add images to help readers see what you are comparing and contrasting, and include a title for your essay that grabs the reader's attention and indicates your essay's topic.

Publish Your Piece

Use the chart to identify a way to share your ideas with the world.

If your audience is…	…then publish it by…
Classmates and others at your school	• Submitting it to the school newspaper or school Web site
Your local community	• Submitting it to a local newspaper or posting it on a community Web site • Reading and discussing it on local public-access TV
The larger community	• Posting it on a social networking Web site and inviting responses • Entering it in a regional or national essay contest

 ## Extend Your Research

Think more about the topic on which you wrote your compare-and-contrast essay. What else would you like to know about this topic?

- Brainstorm for several questions you would like to research and then consult, or discuss, with others.

- Formulate, or develop, a plan about how you will answer these questions. Decide where you will find more information—on the Internet, at the library, or through other sources.

- Finally, learn more about your topic by following through with your research plan.

 The Big Question: Why Write? What should we tell and what should we describe to make information clear?

21st Century Learning

MAKE YOUR WRITING COUNT

Compare and Contrast in a TV Talk Show Script

Compare-and-contrast essays explain how things are similar or different. Compare and contrast trends in this year's pop culture with last year's.

In groups, write a **script** for a TV talk show comparing two examples of popular culture, such as fashion, music, or film, from this year and last year. Use it as the basis of a **multimedia presentation** that conveys distinctive points of view. For example, you might be biased toward this year's trends or nostalgic about last year's. Keep your audience—your school's student body—in mind as you develop your presentation.

Here's your action plan.

1. Choose roles, such as co-hosts, guests, and director.
2. Review your peers' compare-and-contrast essays for ideas as well as effective compare-contrast structure.
3. Go online to find year-in-review lists to help you identify a topic. In a group discussion, compare and contrast elements of one element of popular culture this year versus a year ago.
4. View online talk shows for ideas about staging and recording the presentation.
5. Write the script, which should:
   - State explicitly and directly or implicitly through suggestions the overall theme or purpose of the show
   - Deliver two distinct points of view, either via guests or two co-hosts
   - Incorporate multiple media elements, such as sound or film clips, photos, and other graphics
6. Rehearse and present your talk show.

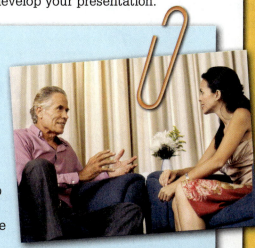

Listening and Speaking Rehearse the script with your group. First, discuss how the media elements should be incorporated with the dialogue of the co-hosts and guests to achieve a particular mood or tone. Then, read the script aloud. Accept feedback about content and delivery, making adjustments accordingly.

WRITING COACH Online

www.phwritingcoach.com

Online Journal
Extend Your Research Record your answers and ideas in the online journal.

Resource
Link to resources on 21st Century Learning for help in creating a group project.

Writing for Media: Advice Column

Advice Column

An **advice column** is a print or online column in which someone knowledgeable about a topic answers questions about it. General-interest newspapers and magazines often have several such columns, with topics ranging from health to gardening to personal concerns, such as relationships or manners. Readers usually send in letters or e-mails to ask questions about problems they have, and the columnist writes and publishes solutions to some of these problems. In the columnist's responses, he or she may compare and contrast different approaches to dealing with the writers' problems.

Try It! Study this sample advice column. Then, answer these questions. Record your answers in your journal.

1. What **credentials,** or proof of expertise, does Sylvia have to be the writer of this column?
2. What **solutions** does Sylvia suggest to Shy in Chicago? Which solution does Sylvia think would be better for the reader?
3. What **solutions** does Sylvia suggest to Brat's Brother in Boise, and how are the solutions different?
4. How would you describe Sylvia's **tone?** What words and phrases communicate this?
5. What interests would the **audience** for this column have? How does the column appeal to those interests?

Extension Find another example of an advice column, and compare it with this one.

Ask Sylvia

Dear Sylvia, I just started at a new school that is much larger than my old school. I'm rather shy, and I find it difficult to talk to people. I would like to make new friends, but I'm not sure how. What's the best way to make new friends?
—Shy in Chicago

Dear Shy: It can be difficult making new friends, but it's not impossible. Here are a couple options. First, look around—who else seems to need a friend? There are probably other new students at your school who are going through exactly the same thing as you. It will take some courage, but go up to the person, smile, and introduce yourself. Another great way to meet people is to get involved! Join the band, a club, or sports team—anything that interests you. As part of a group, you'll automatically have things in common and find it easier to talk to people.

Dear Sylvia, My little brother is constantly following me around—his goal usually is to annoy me or get me in trouble. My parents tell me to ignore him, but I want him to stop. What can I do?
—Brat's Brother in Boise

Dear Brother: Asking your parents for help might make your brother's behavior worse. A better solution would be to spend some time with your brother. If you give him a little attention every week, he should stop trying to get your attention in the wrong way.

Sylvia Semple was a school guidance counselor for 20 years. You can e-mail Sylvia at the newspaper.

Short Assignment

Create an Advice Column

Follow these steps to create your own advice column. To plan your column, review the graphic organizers on pages R24—R27 and choose one that suits your needs.

Prewriting

- Identify a topic for the column. It might be a sport or a game you play, a hobby you enjoy, or something else you know about or do regularly. Your knowledge makes you an "expert."
- Devise a catchy name for the column that indicates its topic.
- Think of two problems that someone might have with an issue related to your topic. Invent names for the two writers asking about these problems.
- Think of two or more solutions to each of these problems. Note facts, examples, and reasons that you can use to compare and contrast your solutions.

Drafting

- Write a column using question-and-answer format as its organizing structure.
- Put your title at the top.
- Write two short letters, each about one of the problems. Identify the problem and ask advice about it in the form of a question. Use informal language, and sign each letter with the name you chose.
- Write a brief response—a miniature analytical essay—to each letter, comparing two possible solutions to the problem. Include facts, examples, and reasons as support.

Revising and Editing

- Make sure that questions and answers are clearly stated with smooth transitions that show the relationships between ideas.
- Be sure that the advice achieves an upbeat tone and uses correct terminology that shows knowledge of the topic.

Publishing

Pool your column with classmates' columns to create an advice print or Web page to share with others. If you are producing a Web page, post it on your school's Web site.

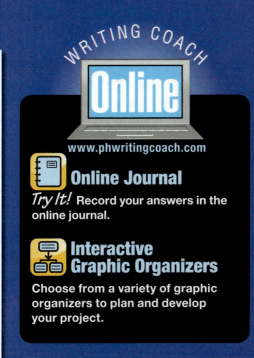

WRITING COACH Online
www.phwritingcoach.com

Online Journal
Try It! Record your answers in the online journal.

Interactive Graphic Organizers
Choose from a variety of graphic organizers to plan and develop your project.

Share information about your advice column with a partner. Ask how your partner would answer the questions in your column, and take notes on his or her responses. Monitor your partner's spoken language by asking follow-up questions to confirm your understanding.

Writing for Media

Writing for Assessment

Many standardized tests include a prompt that asks you to write an expository or analytical essay. You can use the prompts on these pages to practice. Your responses should include most of the same characteristics as your compare-and-contrast essay. Look back at page 146 to review these characteristics.

 Try It! To begin, read the **analytical essay** prompt and the information on format and academic vocabulary. Then write an essay by following the instructions shown in the ABCDs of On-Demand Writing.

Format
The prompt directs you to write an *analytical essay*. Include a clear thesis, details to support your main ideas, and a conclusion that sums up your key ideas.

Analytical Prompt
Write an analytical essay that compares and contrasts your current home town with a city or town you have visited. Describe the similarities and differences of the two places.

Academic Vocabulary
Remember that *similarities* are elements that are alike; *differences* are elements that are not alike.

The ABCDs of On-Demand Writing

Use the following ABCDs to help you respond to the prompt.

Before you write your draft:

Attack the prompt [1 MINUTE]

- Circle or highlight important verbs in the prompt. Draw a line from the verb to what it refers to.
- Rewrite the prompt in your own words.

Brainstorm possible answers [4 MINUTES]

- Create a graphic organizer to generate ideas.
- Use one for each part of the prompt if necessary.

Choose the order of your response [1 MINUTE]

- Think about the best way to organize your ideas.
- Number your ideas in the order you will write about them. Cross out ideas you will not be using.

After you write your draft:

Detect errors before turning in the draft [1 MINUTE]

- Carefully reread your writing.
- Make sure that your response makes sense and is complete.
- Look for spelling, punctuation, and grammar errors.

More Prompts for Practice

Apply It! Respond to Prompts 1 and 2 in open-ended or timed situations by writing **expositoy** or **analytical essays**. As you write, be sure to:

- Grab reader attention with an effective **introductory paragraph**
- State your **thesis**, or controlling idea
- Provide relevant **evidence** and well-chosen details to help you write an essay of sufficient length
- Make distinctions about the **relative value** of supporting data, facts, and ideas
- Use a variety of **sentence structures** and include **rhetorical devices**, such as analogies, to convey meaning and make your writing interesting
- Choose an **organizing structure** appropriate to your audience, purpose, and context
- Use **transitions** to clarify relationships between paragraphs
- Create a memorable end with an effective **concluding paragraph**

Prompt 1 Think about how different clothing and behavior is appropriate for different types of events. For example, you wouldn't dress or act the same at the movies as you would at the opera. Write an essay that compares and contrasts how one would behave and dress for a formal event with how one would behave and dress for a sports event.

Prompt 2 Most people—adults and students—have busy lives, but the responsibilities and activities in people's lives can differ based on age. Write an essay that compares and contrasts your responsibilities and activities with those of a parent or guardian. Be sure to provide strong supporting evidence.

Spiral Review: Poetry Respond to Prompt 3 by writing a **poem**. Make sure your poem reflects all the characteristics listed on page 120. Choose a specific **poetic form** to use and include a variety of **poetic techniques**, such as sensory details and sound devices.

Prompt 3 Think about someone you know who has a pet. How does that person feel about his or her pet? Write a poem about a pet you know.

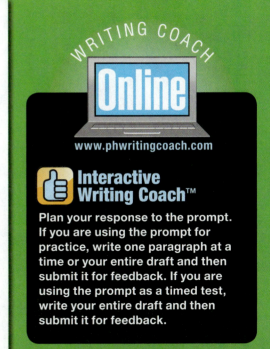

Interactive Writing Coach™

Plan your response to the prompt. If you are using the prompt for practice, write one paragraph at a time or your entire draft and then submit it for feedback. If you are using the prompt as a timed test, write your entire draft and then submit it for feedback.

Remember ABCD

- **A**ttack the prompt
- **B**rainstorm possible answers
- **C**hoose the order of your response
- **D**etect errors before turning in the draft

What Do You Think?

Teenage driving is a topic on which most people have an opinion. Some people think teenagers should be allowed to drive at the age of 16. Others think teens shouldn't be allowed to drive until they are 18 or older.

You probably have an opinion on this topic. You may want to convince someone to share your opinion or you may want to justify your ideas. In order to persuade someone to share your opinion, you must use facts and details to support your point of view.

Try It! List reasons why you think teens should be allowed to drive at 16 or why you think teens shouldn't drive until they are 18.

Consider these questions as you participate in an extended discussion with a partner. Take turns expressing your ideas and feelings.

- Why should teens be allowed to drive at 16?
- What are the drawbacks of teens driving at 16?
- How does being two years older make a difference?
- Is there a compromise solution?

Review the list you made. Choose a position on the issue by deciding which side to take. Write a sentence that states which position, or side, you will take. Then, find a partner and take turns talking about your ideas and positions.

What's Ahead

In this chapter, you will review two strong examples of an argumentative essay: a Mentor Text and a Student Model. Then, using the examples as guidance, you will write an argumentative essay of your own.

Online Journal

Try It! Record your answers and ideas in the online journal.

You can also record and save your answers and ideas on pop-up sticky notes in the eText.

Connect to the Big Questions

Discuss these questions with your partner:

1 What do you think? What best shows someone is ready for more responsibility?

2 Why Write? What is your point of view? How will you know if you've convinced others?

ARGUMENTATIVE ESSAY

An argumentative essay is a type of writing that presents a writer's idea or position and then provides evidence to support or prove it. In this chapter, you will explore a particular kind of argumentative essay, the op-ed piece. An op-ed piece is a signed piece that tries to persuade readers of a newspaper or magazine to agree with the writer's views about an issue that may be in opposition to others' views. An op-ed piece is written by someone who does not work for the newspaper or magazine.

You will develop the op-ed piece by taking it through each of the steps of the writing process: prewriting, drafting, revising, editing, and publishing. You will also have an opportunity to write a letter to an editor of a newspaper, magazine, or blog to state your views about an issue that matters to you. To preview the criteria for how your op-ed piece will be evaluated, see the rubric on page 189.

FEATURE ASSIGNMENT

Argumentative Essay: Op-ed Piece

An effective argumentative essay has these characteristics:

- A **clear description of the issue**
- A **clear thesis statement** that uses logical reasons to support the writer's opinions
- **Logical and relevant evidence** that supports the thesis
- Consideration of a **whole range of information and views**, or many different ways of looking at a topic, with **accurate and honest representation of these views**
- **Counter-arguments** based on evidence to anticipate and address objections
- An **organizing structure** that is appropriate to the persuasive purpose, audience, and context
- **A range of appropriate appeals,** such as case studies, descriptions, and examples, with an **analysis of the relative value** of each piece of information provided, which means to identify which data, facts, or ideas are more important than the others
- **Vivid, persuasive language** to appeal to the audience
- **Effective sentence structure** and correct spelling, grammar, and usage

An effective op-ed piece also includes:

- A response to a **current event** or topic
- A tight **focus** on a single issue
- A **call to action**

Other Forms of Argumentative Essays

In addition to the op-ed piece, there are other forms of argumentative essays, including:

Advertisements are paid announcements that try to convince people to buy a company's goods or services. They can be written, spoken, or performed.

Editorials are written by a member of the editorial staff of a magazine, newspaper, or other news source, stating that publication's position on a certain issue. They are usually about current events.

Letters to the editor are written by a reader of a magazine or newspaper in response to a statement or position in the publication.

Persuasive essays use logic and reasoning, as well as some emotional appeals, to persuade the reader of the value of an opinion or a position.

Persuasive speeches aim at winning an audience's support of an opinion or position. Such speeches are often given during political campaigns.

Propaganda uses emotional appeals and often biased or misleading information to gain support, usually for a political cause or government.

Reviews evaluate items and activities, such as products, movies, and books. A review often states an opinion on whether people should spend time or money on the item or activity.

Try It! For each audience and purpose described, select a correct form, such as an advertisement, speech, or letter to the editor, for conveying intended meaning to multiple audiences. Explain your choices.

- To convince parents and students that they should support the girls' basketball team
- To persuade voters and city council members of the need for more street lights
- To disagree with a newspaper's stand in favor of a teen curfew

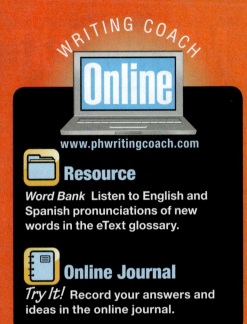

WRITING COACH Online
www.phwritingcoach.com

Resource
Word Bank Listen to English and Spanish pronunciations of new words in the eText glossary.

Online Journal
Try It! Record your answers and ideas in the online journal.

WORD BANK

People often use these basic and content-based vocabulary words when they talk about persuasive writing. Work with a partner. Take turns saying and writing each word in a sentence. If you are unsure of the meaning of a word, use the Glossary or a dictionary to check the definition.

appeal	consider
argue	oppose
benefits	urge

Persuasion

MENTOR TEXT — Op-Ed Piece

Learn From Experience

 Read the op-ed piece on pages 174–175. As you read, take notes to develop your understanding of basic sight and English vocabulary. Then, read the numbered notes in the margins to learn about how the author presented her ideas.

Answer the *Try It!* questions online or in your notebook.

---

❶ The introduction includes a clear **thesis statement and uses a range of appropriate appeals** to reach the audience, such as rhetorical questions, facts, and counter-arguments.

Try It! What is the thesis statement, or main message, of this op-ed piece? How do the appeals support the thesis statement?

❷ The purpose of an op-ed piece is to persuade, so the body paragraphs include **vivid, persuasive language** to appeal to the audience.

Try It! Who might the audience be for this op-ed piece? What specific language in this paragraph is crafted to persuade that audience?

❸ A good op-ed writer anticipates **objections** and addresses those objections with **counter-arguments** supported by clear evidence.

Try It! What objection does the writer anticipate in this paragraph? What example of evidence supports her counter-argument?

Extension Find another example of an op-ed piece, and compare it with this one.

Local BMX Riders Need Our Support

by Shari McElroy

❶ There has been controversy in our community about the construction of a BMX bike track, but building a BMX track is truly the best thing the community can do for local riders. Was there controversy around the new swimming pool constructed at our local park? Was there controversy when community funds were used to resurface the runners' track at the community center? "But those facilities were for legitimate sports," people have said. BMX, however, *is* a legitimate sport. Sure, it started out as a bunch of kids riding bikes around in the 1970s, emulating their favorite motocross riders. But it has since grown into both a popular pastime and a legitimate sport. Even professional athletes now train to compete internationally in BMX riding. With that in mind, there are many good reasons why our community should build a BMX bike track.

First of all, the bike track would promote physical activity for young people. **❷** A study by the Center for Disease Control discovered that the childhood obesity rate for kids ages 12 to 19 has increased in recent years to 17.6%! Because obesity can lead to health risks later in life, our community should support all types of physical activity for local kids, whether it's swimming, running, dancing, or BMX biking. The benefits of physical activity are well documented, so we ought to do everything we can to encourage our young citizens to get active and stay physically fit. These health benefits alone are well worth the cost of building a BMX bike track in our community.

❸ While some agree that physical fitness is a good cause to support, they also believe that BMX bike riding is too dangerous and "extreme" a sport. However, building a community bike track would promote safe and responsible riding. Here's how: Every rider who used the track would be required to pass a safety course and earn a permit to use the track. Rules for safety would be clearly posted, and all

174 Argumentative Essay

riders would be required to follow those rules and wear protective gear. Rule-breakers and dangerous riders would lose privileges until they complied with the community rules and regulations.

Finally, the people in the community would be brought together by the building of a BMX track. Adult volunteers would supervise riders on the track. This would ensure that riders stayed safe and obeyed the rules, but it would also draw community members together for recreation. A fun activity like BMX riding could bond young and older community members in a common goal: enjoying and promoting safe riding. This would add great value to our community.

❹ And speaking of value, there are some opponents to this plan who say our community can't afford it. Their arguments, however, aren't valid. According to local construction company owner Mike Durain, the primary building supplies needed to construct a legitimate BMX bike track are scrap lumber and dirt. Those are the least costly supplies of any recreation facility our community has ever endeavored to build! In addition, Durain said, "To keep costs down, my company will supply free labor to build the track because it has supported the community for many years."

I say our community can't afford *not* to build a BMX bike track. Without a community track, kids find or make their own tracks. These tracks could be more dangerous than an official community trail and could result in injury. They are likely to be unsupervised, with no rules or regulations. Riders could end up trespassing on private property without even realizing it. If that happens, BMX biking becomes a major inconvenience for some citizens. Is that the type of activity our community wants to promote?

❺ Our community promotes safe, fun physical activity for all its citizens. We do this through the many parks and recreation sites that exist now. It's time to add a community BMX bike track to the list. It would be a safe, supervised track where riders can have a great time staying physically fit while bringing our community closer together. Let's build that track!

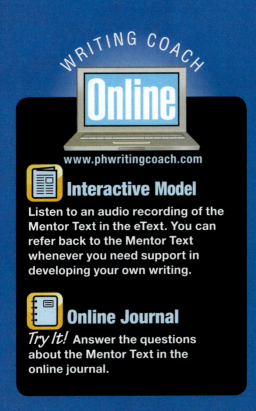

Interactive Model
Listen to an audio recording of the Mentor Text in the eText. You can refer back to the Mentor Text whenever you need support in developing your own writing.

Online Journal
Try It! Answer the questions about the Mentor Text in the online journal.

❹ The author piece uses **precise and relevant evidence** to support her opinion.

Try It! What are two examples of types of evidence the author uses in this paragraph to support her ideas?

❺ The op-ed piece's **organizational structure** is logical, including an introduction and conclusion that provide a **clear description of the issue.**

Try It! How does the conclusion restate the issue presented in the introduction? After you read the conclusion, were you convinced that the author's opinion is correct? Why or why not?

STUDENT MODEL Op-Ed Piece

With a small group, take turns reading the Student Model aloud. As you read, practice newly acquired vocabulary by correctly producing the words' sounds. Also ask yourself if you find the writer's arguments convincing.

Use a Reader's Eye

Now, reread the Student Model. On your copy of the Student Model, use the Reader's Response Symbols to react to what you read.

Reader's Response Symbols

+ I strongly agree with this.
− I strongly disagree with this.
? I have a question about this.
! Wow! That is cool/weird/interesting.

Express your opinions and share your responses to the Student Model with a partner. Take notes on your partner's responses. Then, compare your responses and discuss why you responded differently to certain ideas.

A Little More Life in Our School

by Luis Soto

"Normally, I don't like to get dirty," said one tenth-grade student. "But this is different." The "difference" was making a community garden at school. I suggest that creating a vegetable garden would be a great project for our school.

For one thing, kids who grow vegetables will probably eat more vegetables. When you pull a bunch of green stuff out of the ground and there's a carrot at the end of it, that carrot seems completely different from those little orange logs at the supermarket.

That's only one of the benefits of a school garden. The National Gardening Association (NGA) recently studied 216 school gardens. Its report shows that the schools used the gardens to teach 12 different subjects, from science to art to history. Also, students who gardened took more interest in the environment and had more community spirit and self-confidence. Their attitude toward school changed for the better, too.

I know that some people have a problem with the idea of digging up part of the school lawn. I understand what they are saying, but I would argue that grass is not the best use of our resources anyway. It takes so much water and fertilizer and mowing to keep it up that digging up a small area for a garden would be an improvement.

Other people have said that we can't afford to make a garden, but I disagree. Seeds do not cost much, and classes can start plants from the seeds inside in the spring. More importantly, the NGA and other organizations offer financial help for school gardens.

I know that gardens are a lot of work. We would need volunteers to weed and water, run things, and keep track of schedules, but I think students would get excited about the garden and be proud of their work. One of the teachers in the NGA report said about her school, "Becoming a garden captain is an honor and a privilege, with many students competing for the right to be on the gardening team."

I asked Ms. Greene, who runs the cafeteria, about using the vegetables, and she said the staff would be happy to use them if students will eat them. I think they will, but if they don't, the community food pantry would love to have fresh vegetables.

So let's all sign a petition asking the principal to consider a school garden. Remembering that we are part of nature and getting closer to the earth would be good for all of us.

Use a Writer's Eye

Now evaluate the piece as a writer. On your copy of the Student Model, use the Writer's Response Symbols to react to what you read. Identify places where the student writer uses characteristics of an effective op-ed piece.

Writer's Response Symbols

C.T. Clearly stated thesis

P.A. Strong persuasive arguments

S.E. Effective, credible supporting evidence

C.A. Good responses to readers' counter-arguments

 **Feature Assignment: Op-Ed Piece**

Prewriting

Plan a first draft of your op-ed piece by **determining an appropriate topic**. You can select from the Topic Bank or come up with an idea of your own.

 ## Choose From the Topic Bank

TOPIC BANK

Dress Codes High schools, restaurants, work places, and the military all use dress codes. Think about the reasons for instituting dress codes and why they might be enforced in each case. Then, select one example of the use of dress codes. Write an essay in which you argue the benefits or drawbacks of a dress code in that situation.

Technology Many people believe that training and experience in computer use are critical for the success of all students in high school now, perhaps more important than anything else they will learn. Take a position on that issue and write an op-ed piece explaining that position.

Driving Age There is evidence that teenage drivers have more accidents and more traffic fatalities than adult drivers. Write an op-ed piece in which you are for or against changing the driving age to 21.

 ## Choose Your Own Topic

Determine an appropriate topic on your own by using **the following range of strategies** to generate ideas.

Brainstorming and Questioning

- Give yourself five minutes to make a list of any topics that come to mind.
- Read what you have written and circle topics that seem interesting to you.
- Talk your list over with a classmate. Ask questions about the topics you have circled. Then, look at research sources in the library or online to try to answer those questions. When you find a topic of interest, choose that one and pursue it, keeping a careful record of your sources.

Review your responses and choose a topic.

Narrow Your Topic

If you choose a topic that is too broad, you will have a hard time trying to research it.

Apply It! Use a graphic organizer like the one shown to narrow your topic and develop your thesis.

- Write your general topic in the top box, and keep narrowing your topic as you move down the chart.
- Your last box should hold your narrowest or "smallest" topic, the new focus of your op-ed piece.

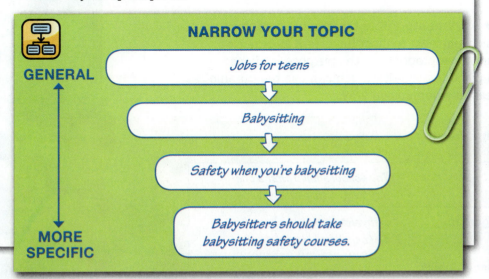

 ## Consider Multiple Audiences and Purposes

Before writing, think about your potential audiences, or readers, and the purposes you have for writing. Consider a range of information and views on your topic as you ask yourself these questions.

Questions for Audience	Questions for Purpose
• Who besides my teacher will read my op-ed piece? • What background information do I need to provide to help my audience understand my topic? • What might be the views, concerns, and counter-arguments of people who disagree with me?	• What is my purpose for writing? • What is my viewpoint about my topic? • What do I want my audience to think or do?

Record your answers in your writing journal.

Interactive Writing Coach™

- Choosing from the Topic Bank gives you access to the Interactive Writing Coach™.
- Submit your writing and receive instant personalized feedback and guidance as you draft, revise, and edit your writing.

 Interactive Graphic Organizers

Use the interactive graphic organizers to help you narrow your topic.

 Online Journal

Try It! Record your answers and ideas in the online journal.

Plan Your Piece

You will use the graphic organizer to state your thesis, organize your arguments, and identify details. When it is complete, you will be ready to write your first draft.

Develop a Clear Thesis To clearly present your position to the appropriate audience, review your notes and develop a clear **thesis** or controlling idea. In one sentence, state a position. This should be based on logical reasons that you will be able to support with precise and relevant **evidence**. Add your thesis statement to a graphic organizer like the one shown.

Logically Organize Your Arguments Fill in the graphic organizer to organize your arguments from least to most important in order to create an **organizing structure** appropriate to the purpose, audience, and context of your op-ed piece. As you draft, you can use the graphic organizer to **structure ideas in a persuasive way.**

Develop Your Persuasive Arguments

Clear Thesis	*The school should offer a one-day babysitting safety class.*
First Persuasive Argument	*Babysitters need to know how to keep little kids safe.*
Supporting Evidence/Details	
Second Persuasive Argument	*Babysitters need to know how to keep themselves safe.*
Supporting Evidence/Details	
Counter-arguments	*It's not the school's job to train students to be babysitters.*
Response to Counter-arguments	

Argumentative Essay

Gather Details

To provide supporting evidence for your arguments, you will use specific data, facts, and ideas that add value to your position. Use a range of appropriate **appeals**, from strong facts to interesting quotations. Look at these examples:

- **Facts:** *Children 14 and under account for one-third of all fall-related visits to hospital emergency rooms.*
- **Logical Reasoning:** *Whoever is caring for a child needs to deal with household dangers. A babysitter is the caretaker for a child. A babysitter needs to learn how to deal with dangers.*
- **Expert Opinions:** *Our fire chief strongly recommends that babysitters take a training course.*
- **Quotations:** *Babysitter Diane Ruiz says, "I like knowing just what to do when I'm babysitting."*

As you gather details, keep careful track of all your sources. **Evaluate** the relevance, quality, sufficiency, and depth of your ideas and information. You also need to **consider** a whole range of information and views on the topic and give an **accurate** and **honest** representation of those views. For example, some people might agree with you about the problem you present, but not about your solution. Part of your preparation involves anticipating and addressing objections to your position and presenting **counter-arguments** based on solid evidence.

Try It! Read the Student Model and identify the types of details that the author used to support his point.

STUDENT MODEL from *A Little More Life in Our School* page 176; lines 11–15

The National Gardening Association (NGA) recently studied 216 school gardens. Its report shows that the schools used the gardens to teach 12 different subjects, from science to art to history.

 *Apply It!* Review the types of support a persuasive writer can use. Then, identify at least one detail for each of your arguments.

- Review your details and determine the importance of each piece of data, each fact, and each idea. Whenever possible, use **quotations**.
- Complete your graphic organizer by matching details to the right argument so that your evidence is **logically organized** to support your viewpoint.

WRITING COACH Online
www.phwritingcoach.com

Interactive Graphic Organizers
Use the interactive graphic organizers to help you create a plan for your writing.

Interactive Model
Refer back to the Interactive Model in the eText as you plan your writing.

Drafting

During the drafting stage, you will start to write your ideas for your op-ed piece. Creating an outline will help you **structure your ideas in a persuasive way.** Be sure to choose an **organizational structure** that is appropriate to your purpose, audience, and context.

The Organization of an Argumentative Essay

The chart shows an organizational strategy for an argumentative essay. Look back at how the Mentor Text follows this organizational strategy. Then, use this chart to help you outline and structure your draft in a persuasive way.

Outline for Success

I. Introduction — See Mentor Text, p. 174.

- Lead
- Clear thesis or position

Grab Your Reader
- A good introduction grabs the reader's attention. You might ask a question, use an anecdote (or personal story), or use a startling fact.
- A thesis statement clearly presents the writer's purpose and position on the issue.

II. Body — See Mentor Text, pp. 174–175.

- Logical reasons
- Logical, precise, and relevant evidence
- Objections and counter-arguments

Build Your Case
- Only one argument is usually discussed in each paragraph.
- The facts, statistics, and quotations used to support each argument must come from many different and trustworthy sources.
- All evidence must clearly relate to the topic and directly support the writer's ideas.
- There are several ways to view an issue. These other views are called objections or counter-arguments.

III. Conclusion — See Mentor Text, p. 175.

- Restatement of position
- Memorable ending, such as a call to action

Wrap It Up
- The conclusion briefly restates the writer's position, using strong, persuasive language.
- A strong conclusion tells readers what the writer wants them to do or think.

 ## Start Your Draft

Use the checklist to help you complete your draft. Use the graphic organizer that shows your thesis, persuasive arguments, supporting evidence, and the Outline for Success as guides.

While drafting, aim at writing your ideas, not on making your writing perfect. Remember, you will have the chance to improve your draft when you revise and edit.

√ Start by drafting a **lead,** or the opening sentences that grab your readers' attention.

√ Continue to build your **introduction** by telling readers what to expect in the rest of your op-ed piece. Include your **thesis statement,** or point of view on the issue.

√ Shape the **body** of your op-ed piece. **Organize** your body by developing a focused paragraph for each argument and its supporting evidence.

√ Make sure that your **supporting evidence** is logical, relevant, and precise, and that it includes a range of appropriate appeals, including facts, anecdotes, case studies, and so on.

√ Evaluate the relevance, quality, sufficiency, and depth of your ideas to be sure that you are using the best arguments and evidence and the ones that are most relevant to your topic and point of view. Also evaluate the **relative value** of specific evidence by pointing out which data, facts, or ideas are more important than others.

√ Be sure that you have considered the whole range of information and views on your topic, and that you have represented them honestly and **accurately.**

√ Think about people whose views differ from yours and anticipate the kinds of objections they might have to your arguments. Include evidence-based **counter-arguments** to address those possible objections. Use facts and details to explain why these objections are not valid and why readers should agree with your position instead.

√ End with a strong **conclusion** that restates your position and makes a **call to action.**

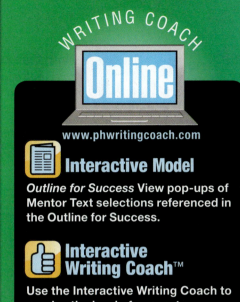

Interactive Model

Outline for Success View pop-ups of Mentor Text selections referenced in the Outline for Success.

Interactive Writing Coach™

Use the Interactive Writing Coach to receive the level of support you need:
- Write one paragraph at a time and submit each one for immediate, detailed feedback.
- Write your entire first draft and submit it for immediate, personalized feedback.

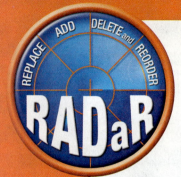

Revising: Making It Better

Now that you have finished your first draft, you are ready to revise. Think about the "big picture" of **audience, purpose, and genre.** You can use your Revision RADaR as a guide for making changes to improve your draft. Revision RADaR provides four major ways to improve your writing: (R) replace, (A) add, (D) delete, and (R) reorder.

▸ *Kelly Gallagher, M. Ed.*

KEEP REVISION ON YOUR RADaR

Read part of the first draft of the Student Model "A Little More Life in Our School." Then look at questions the writer asked himself as he thought about how well his draft addressed his **audience, purpose, and genre.**

A Little More Life in Our School

I know that some people have a problem with the idea of digging up part of the school lawn. I understand what they are saying, but I would argue that grass is not the best use of our resources anyway. It takes so much water and fertilizer and mowing to keep up that digging up a small area for a garden would be an improvement. Other people have said that we can't afford to make a garden, but I disagree.

I know that gardens are a lot of work. We would need volunteers to weed and water, run things, and keep track of schedules, but I think students would get excited about the garden and be proud of their work. One of the teachers in the NGA report said that the students in her school really liked to work in the garden.

I'm sure we could find a use for the vegetables. A garden would be a good thing for the school. Remembering that we are part of nature and getting closer to the earth would be good for all of us.

I've brought up a good objection to a school garden. Did I give a good counter-argument too?

My source tells what she actually said. Would inserting that quotation make my appeal more persuasive and interesting to readers?

Have I really done my research? Can I provide more precise evidence?

Have I made a strong call to action?

184 Argumentative Essay

Now look at how the writer applied his Revision RADaR to write an improved second draft.

A Little More Life in Our School

Other people have said that we can't afford to make a garden, but I disagree. Seeds do not cost much, and classes can start plants from the seeds inside in the spring. More importantly, the NGA and other organizations offer financial help for school gardens.

A — Added facts to support my counter-argument

I know that gardens are a lot of work. We would need volunteers to weed and water, run things, and keep track of schedules, but I think students would get excited about the garden and be proud of their work. One of the teachers in the NGA report said about her school, "Becoming a garden captain is an honor and a privilege, with many students competing for the right to be on the gardening team."

R — Replaced a less interesting paraphrase with a quotation

I asked Ms. Greene, who runs the cafeteria, about using the vegetables, and she said the staff would be happy to use them if students will eat them. I think they will, but if they don't, the community food pantry would love to have fresh vegetables.

A — Added carefully researched evidence

So let's all sign a petition asking the principal to consider a school garden. Remembering that we are part of nature and getting closer to the earth would be good for all of us.

D — Deleted a general statement and added a call to action

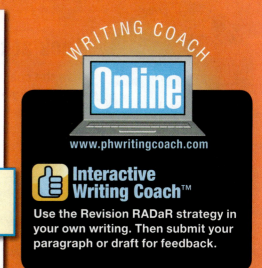

WRITING COACH

www.phwritingcoach.com

Interactive Writing Coach™

Use the Revision RADaR strategy in your own writing. Then submit your paragraph or draft for feedback.

 Apply It! Use your Revision RADaR to revise your draft.

- First, rethink how well you have addressed questions of **purpose**, and **audience**. Then determine whether or not you have included all the **genre** characteristics of an op-ed piece.
- Then apply your Revision RADaR to make needed changes. Remember—you can use the steps in Revision RADaR in any order.

Look at the Big Picture

Use the chart and your analytical skills to evaluate how well each section of your op-ed piece addresses **purpose**, **audience**, and **genre**. When necessary, use the suggestions in the chart to refine key ideas, organize them more logically, and draw the reader to the author's purpose.

Section	Evaluate	Revise
Introduction	• Check the **lead.** Will it grab readers' attention and make them want to read more?	• Make your lead more interesting by adding a question, anecdote, quotation, or strong detail.
	• Make sure the **thesis** clearly identifies the issue and states your position on it.	• To clearly identify the issue or state your opinion forcefully, turn the thesis statement into a question, and answer the question by stating your opinion.
Body	• Check that you have **organized** your persuasive arguments in a logical way that is appropriate for the genre, is clear for your readers, and supports the purpose and context.	• Reorder arguments to build toward your main point. Present your second strongest argument first, the weaker arguments in the middle, and save the strongest argument for last.
	• Check that supporting evidence is **precise** and includes facts for which you have reliable sources.	• Include a range of information and evidence. Add facts where needed to strengthen your arguments and back up your opinion.
	• Make sure that your evidence is **relevant,** convincing, and varied.	• Analyze the value of your data, facts, and ideas. Delete those that do not add value to your argument. Add different types of arguments to include an interesting range of appeals.
	• Review reader concerns and **counter-arguments.** Determine if you have considered a range of views and addressed each objection through your own counter-arguments.	• Answer each of your anticipated readers' concerns and counter-arguments. Be fair—honestly and accurately represent others' views.
Conclusion	• Check the **restatement** of your position.	• If necessary, restate your position more clearly.
	• Check that your **conclusion** ends on a memorable note.	• Add a quotation, a call to action, or a forceful statement. Your goal is to influence the attitudes or actions of your specific audience on your specific issue.

Focus on Craft: Style

Style is the unique way an author uses language. **Diction**, the words an author uses, and **tone**, an author's attitude toward something, are important elements of style. Style choices can affect whether or not an audience connects with an author and finds him or her reliable. For example, it is important to balance formal and informal language. A style that is too formal or too informal may keep an audience from reading on.

Think about style as you read the following sentence from the Student Model.

STUDENT MODEL from **A Little More Life in Our School** page 176; lines 7–10

When you pull a bunch of green stuff out of the ground and there's a carrot at the end of it, that carrot seems completely different from those little orange logs at the supermarket.

 Try It! Now, ask yourself these questions. Record your answers in your journal.

- Does the style help you connect with the author's point of view? Explain.
- Would the sentence be more or less powerful if the author said "those small carrots that come in a plastic bag and do not actually look much like carrots"? Why?

www.phwritingcoach.com

 Video
Learn more strategies for effective writing from program author Kelly Gallagher.

 Online Journal
Try It! Record your answers in the online journal.

 Interactive Model
Refer back to the Interactive Model as you revise your writing.

 **Interactive Writing Coach™**
Revise your draft and submit it for feedback.

Fine-Tune Your Draft

Apply It! Use the revision suggestions to revise your draft after **rethinking how well questions of purpose, audience, and genre have been addressed**.

- **Improve Style** Check your diction and tone to find the right level of formality. Adapt your language as needed to make corrections.
- **Improve Figurative Language** Look for places to make your writing stronger by using a simile or metaphor.
- **Improve Subtlety of Meaning** Use exact adjectives and adverbs to clarify meaning and make your writing sharper and more precise.

Peer Feedback Read your final draft to a group of peers. Ask if your ideas and evidence are convincing and organized logically. Think about your peers' feedback and revise your final draft as needed.

Editing: Making It Correct

To edit your work, read your draft carefully to correct errors in spelling and grammar. It can be helpful to read your draft aloud to listen for where the writing needs correction.

Before editing your final draft, consider using **more complex active and passive tenses** to add clarity and variety to your writing. If the subject of a verb performs the action, the verb is in the **active voice**; if the subject receives the action, the verb is in the **passive voice**. As you focus on grammar, also pay attention to your use of **complex tenses**, or those that include helping verbs. Then edit your final draft for any errors in **grammar, mechanics, and spelling**.

WRITE GUY Jeff Anderson, M. Ed.
WHAT DO YOU NOTICE?

To learn more about active and passive voice, see Chapter 17 of your Grammar Handbook.

Zoom in on Conventions Focus on the author's use of active and passive voice as you zoom in on this passage from the Mentor Text.

> **MENTOR TEXT** from **Local BMX Riders Need Our Support** page 175; lines 39–41
>
> Finally, the people in the community would be brought together by the building of a BMX track. Adult volunteers would supervise riders on the track.

Now, ask yourself: *Which highlighted verb is in the active voice? Which is in the passive voice?*

When the **passive voice** is used, the subject receives the action of the verb. In the first sentence, the subject *people* receives the action of the verb. The passive voice is constructed by adding a form of *be* to the past participle of a verb *would be brought*. In the first sentence, the passive voice is used to shift emphasis when the agent performing the action is unimportant. This technique can be used for persuasive purposes.

A verb is active if its subject performs the action. In the second sentence, the subject *volunteers* performs the action of the verb *would supervise*. In general, active voice is preferred because it is more direct and persuasive.

Partner Talk Discuss this question with a partner: *What effect does the author's use of active and passive voice have on the reader?*

188 Argumentative Essay

Grammar Mini-Lesson: Voice in Complex Tenses

Active and passive voice can be used with **complex verb tenses**. For example, the active voice of the present perfect (*has/have* + past participle), past perfect (*had* + past participle), and future perfect (*will have* + past participle) tenses use helping verbs along with the main verb.

These tenses can be changed from the active to the passive voice by adding a form of the verb *be* as a helping verb right before the past participle of the main verb, which for regular verbs ends in *-ed*. Notice how the Mentor Text uses the active voice of the present perfect tense.

> To learn more, see Chapter 17.

MENTOR TEXT from **Local BMX Riders Need Our Support** page 175; lines 54–57

"To keep costs down, my company will supply free labor to build the track because it <u>has supported</u> the community for many years."

 *Try It!* Change each sentence from the active voice to the passive voice, keeping the same **complex tense**. Write the answers in your journal.

1. The school has purchased a new piece of sports equipment.
2. Most of the passengers had boarded the ship.

Apply It! Edit your draft for **grammar, mechanics, and spelling errors**. Use a dictionary to check your spelling. When you used the passive voice, did you have a good reason for using it? If not, change those verbs to the active voice. Try to incorporate complex tenses.

 Use the rubric to evaluate your piece. If necessary, rethink, rewrite, or revise.

WRITING COACH

Online
www.phwritingcoach.com

 Video
Learn effective editing techniques from program author Jeff Anderson.

 Online Journal
Try It! Record your answers in the online journal.

 Interactive Model
Refer back to the Interactive Model as you edit your writing.

 Interactive Writing Coach™
Edit your draft. Check it against the rubric and then submit it for feedback.

Rubric for Argumentative Essay: Op-Ed Piece	Rating Scale
Ideas: How clearly are the issue and your position stated?	Not very Very 1 2 3 4 5 6
Organization: How organized are your arguments and supporting evidence?	1 2 3 4 5 6
Voice: How authoritative and persuasive is your voice?	1 2 3 4 5 6
Word Choice: How persuasive is the language you have used?	1 2 3 4 5 6
Sentence Fluency: How well have you used transitions to convey meaning?	1 2 3 4 5 6
Conventions: How effective is your use of active and passive voice?	1 2 3 4 5 6

Publishing

Give your op-ed piece a chance to change someone's mind—publish it! First, get your piece ready for presentation. Then, choose a way to **publish it for the appropriate audiences**.

Wrap Up Your Presentation

Is your piece handwritten or written on a computer? If your piece is handwritten, you may need to make a new, clean copy. If so, be sure to **write legibly**. Also be sure to add a title that grabs the reader's attention and indicates your piece's topic.

Publish Your Piece

Use the chart to identify a way to publish your piece.

If your audience is...	...then publish it by...
Students or adults at school	• Submitting it to your school newspaper • Reading it at a school assembly • Posting your piece on your school Web site and inviting others to comment on it
People in your neighborhood or city	• Submitting it to your local television news station • Submitting it to a town or neighborhood magazine • Posting your piece online in a blog

 ## Extend Your Research

Think more about the topic on which you wrote your op-ed piece. What else would you like to know about this topic?

- Brainstorm for several questions you would like to research and then consult, or discuss, with others. Then, decide which question is your major research question.

- Formulate, or develop, a plan about how you will answer these questions. Decide where you will find more information—on the Internet, at the library, or through other sources.

- Finally, learn more about your topic by following through with your research plan.

 The Big Question: Why Write? What is your point of view? How will you know if you've convinced others?

Argumentative Essay

21st Century Learning

MAKE YOUR WRITING COUNT

Express an Op-Ed Message in a Public Service Announcement

An op-ed piece is only one way a writer can publicly express an opinion about important issues. Use another public forum—a **public service announcement**—to influence the members of your community about an issue that affects them.

With a group, analyze and evaluate alternative points of view about an issue affecting your community's health or safety. Write a public service announcement—a PSA—urging your audience to follow a particular course of action, such as spaying and neutering pets. Produce your PSA as a **multimedia presentation** with graphics, images, and sound. You may present your PSA live or video-record it.

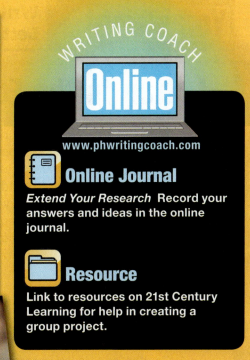

WRITING COACH Online
www.phwritingcoach.com

Online Journal
Extend Your Research Record your answers and ideas in the online journal.

Resource
Link to resources on 21st Century Learning for help in creating a group project.

Here's your action plan.

1. Choose group roles and set objectives.
2. Discuss your peers' op-ed pieces and select an issue. Then, choose a message and specific point of view.
3. Look online to find examples of radio or video public service announcements. Take notes about your ideas for effective presentations.
4. Write the script for your PSA, based on your chosen op-ed piece. Be succinct—use 100 words or fewer.
5. As a team, plan the presentation of your PSA. Whether you plan to video-record it or simply present a script with visual support, your presentation should do the following:
   - State a clear message and call to action
   - Appeal to a specific audience
   - Include appropriate images, graphics, and sounds
   - Use persuasive techniques
6. Present your PSA to the class, either live or on video.

Listening and Speaking With your group, rehearse your multimedia presentation. Take turns reading the script. Ask listeners for feedback about delivery, vocabulary, and length, and make necessary adjustments. Talk about the effectiveness of your graphics, images, and sounds. During the presentation, work as a team to convey a distinctive point of view to convince your specific audience to respond to your message.

Your Turn — Writing for Media: Letter to the Editor

21st Century Learning

Letter to the Editor

A **letter to the editor** is written by a reader of a magazine or newspaper in response to a statement or position that was published in it. Sometimes, the reader praises the position. Often, however, a reader writes a letter to the editor in order to oppose or disagree with the position. People also write a very similar kind of response on some blog sites. A good letter to the editor cites the article to which it is a response, restates the original position, and then gives logical reasons for opposing it.

 Try It! Read the letter to the editor on this page. Then, answer the questions. Record your answers in your journal.

1. To what is this letter **responding**?
2. How does the letter restate the **position** of the original article?
3. Letter writers often express respect for and an understanding of the original writer's points before they state their **objections**. How does this writer do that?
4. What is the writer's **main objection** to the school garden? Is it clearly stated and supported with **evidence**?
5. What **alternative** does the writer suggest?
6. Does this writer **persuade** you that the idea of a school garden should be dropped? Why or why not?

Extension Find another example of a letter to the editor, and compare it with this one.

Wednesday, February 20   14

To: The Editor

Re: "A Little More Life in Our School"

You recently published an interesting op-ed piece that proposed that our local high school create a garden. Ordinarily, I would be the last person to oppose a gardening effort. I love gardens. However, I have to speak out against this plan.

I have been working for two years to get music education back into the high school. It would be great if we could have both a garden and a music program, but the budget won't stretch that far. Reports at the last school board meeting made that clear.

Music education does many of the things that working in a garden would do, including character building, developing work skills, and promoting teamwork. However, studies have shown that music education also has great benefits in brain development. Recent studies even show that students who study the arts do better on their SATs.

Let's try for a garden next year or the year after. For now, we need music!

Sonia Wozniak

Create a Letter to the Editor

Follow these steps to create your own letter to the editor. To plan your letter to the editor, review the graphic organizers on pages R24–R27 and choose one that suits your needs.

Prewriting
- Identify an audience for your letter.
- Reread your op-ed piece, looking at it from the opposite perspective—the perspective of someone who does not agree with the opinions in your op-ed piece.
- Look for an objection that the person you are imagining might have to what you have written. This is your thesis.
- Look for evidence supporting that objection.
- Include a variety of evidence, such as studies or anecdotes, to support your new point of view.

Drafting
- At the top of your letter, reference the title of your op-ed piece.
- State a thesis based on logical reasons that clearly shows your objection to the position of the original piece.
- Give logical and relevant evidence for your objection.

Revising and Editing
- Review your draft to ensure that your thesis is clearly focused.
- Make sure that you have logically developed your ideas in well-organized paragraphs, structured your ideas in a persuasive way, and used language that advances the letter's purpose.
- Check that spelling, grammar, and mechanics are correct.

Publishing
- Make a clean draft of your letter and trade letters with a partner.
- Read each other's op-ed pieces and letters to the editor.
- Decide which one is more persuasive and talk to each other about why.

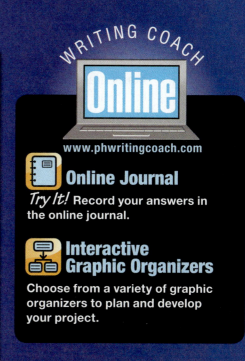

WRITING COACH Online
www.phwritingcoach.com

Online Journal
Try It! Record your answers in the online journal.

Interactive Graphic Organizers
Choose from a variety of graphic organizers to plan and develop your project.

Discuss your op-ed piece with a partner. Describe the objection that you make in your letter to the editor. Use specific details to describe and explain your ideas. Increase the specificity of your details based on the type of information you are delivering.

Writing for Assessment

SAT/PSAT PREP ACT

Many standardized tests include writing prompts. Use the prompts on these pages to practice. Your responses should include the same characteristics as your op-ed piece. (See page 172.)

 Try It! Read the prompt and the information on format and academic vocabulary. Then write an **argumentative essay** using the ABCDs of On-Demand Writing.

Format
The prompt directs you to write an *op-ed piece*. Be sure to include an introduction, body paragraphs with solid ideas and evidence, and a conclusion that reinforces your opinion.

Argumentative Prompt
Write an op-ed piece to persuade shoppers to use reusable bags, as opposed to using the plastic bags provided by stores. Be sure to clearly state your position and to support your position with evidence.

Academic Vocabulary
Remember that your *position* tells the reader how you feel about your topic. Your *evidence* is information that supports your position. Evidence includes facts, quotations, and other information.

The ABCDs of On-Demand Writing

Use the following ABCDs to help you respond to the prompt.

Before you write your draft:

A ttack the prompt [1 MINUTE]

- Circle or highlight important verbs in the prompt. Draw a line from the verb to what it refers to.
- Rewrite the prompt in your own words.

B rainstorm possible answers [4 MINUTES]

- Create a graphic organizer to generate ideas.
- Use one for each part of the prompt if necessary.

C hoose the order of your response [1 MINUTE]

- Think about the best way to organize your ideas.
- Number your ideas in the order you will write about them. Cross out ideas you will not be using.

After you write your draft:

D etect errors before turning in the draft [1 MINUTE]

- Carefully reread your writing.
- Make sure that your response makes sense and is complete.
- Look for spelling, punctuation, and grammar errors.

194 Argumentative Essay

More Prompts for Practice

Apply It! Respond to Prompt 1 by writing an **op-ed piece** to influence the attitudes or actions of a specific audience on a specific issue. As you write, be sure to:

- Identify an appropriate audience
- Establish a **clear thesis** or position based on logical reasons and supported by logical and relevant **evidence**
- Create an **organizing structure** appropriate to your purpose, audience, and context
- Analyze the **relative value** of specific data, facts, and ideas by including phrases such as *most importantly*
- Consider the whole range of information and views and give an honest and accurate **representation** of those views
- Give **counter-arguments** to anticipate and address objections
- Use a range of appropriate **appeals**, or arguments

Prompt 1 The town council has announced a writing contest about the importance of being involved in the community. Write an op-ed piece to persuade teens to become volunteers or mentors.

Spiral Review: Expository Respond to Prompt 2 by writing a problem-solution **analytical essay.** Make sure your essay reflects all the characteristics listed on page 146, including:

- Effective **introductory and concluding paragraphs**
- A variety of **sentence structures, rhetorical devices, and transitions** between paragraphs
- Relevant **evidence** and well-chosen **details**
- A controlling idea or **thesis**
- An **organizing structure** appropriate to purpose, audience, and context
- Distinctions about the **relative value** of specific data, facts, and ideas that support the thesis statement

Prompt 2 Think about a pollution problem in your area or in another place somewhere in the world. Write a problem-solution essay that clearly explains the problem and offers possible solutions for it.

Interactive Writing Coach™

Plan your response to the prompt. If you are using the prompt for practice, write one paragraph at a time or your entire draft and then submit it for feedback. If you are using the prompt as a timed test, write your entire draft and then submit it for feedback.

Remember ABCD

Attack the prompt

Brainstorm possible answers

Choose the order of your response

Detect errors before turning in the draft

CHAPTER 10
RESPONSE to LITERATURE

www.phwritingcoach.com

What Do You Think?

Authors have purposes for writing. Some authors write to inform. Some write to entertain. Others write to persuade.

Part of being an active reader is analyzing the author's purpose. You think about the author's purpose and use details to show how the author achieves that purpose.

Try It! Think about your favorite book. What do you think the author was trying to communicate by writing this book? Consider these questions as you participate in an extended discussion with a partner. Take turns expressing your ideas and feelings.

 **Online Journal**

Try It! Record your answers and ideas in the online journal.

You can also record and save your answers and ideas on pop-up sticky notes in the eText.

- How did you feel when reading this book?
- How did the author achieve his purpose?
- Do you think the author did a good job achieving his or her purpose? Why or why not?

What's Ahead

In this chapter, you will review two strong examples of an interpretative response essay: a Mentor Text and a Student Model. Then, using the examples as guides, you will write an interpretative response essay of your own.

 Connect to the Big Questions

Discuss these questions with your partner:

1 What do you think? What most determines our responses to literature?

2 Why write? What should you write about to make others interested in a text?

INTERPRETATIVE RESPONSE

When you write an interpretative response, you analyze an author's work and explain your reactions to it. You share your thoughts and feelings about what you have read and discuss what the work communicated to you. You also examine how the author's writing style added to the work. In this chapter, you will explore a special kind of interpretative response, the response to literature essay.

You will develop your response to literature essay by taking it through each of the steps of the writing process: prewriting, drafting, revising, editing, and publishing. You will also have an opportunity to write a script for a stage play. To preview the criteria for how your response to literature essay will be evaluated, see the rubric on page 215.

FEATURE ASSIGNMENT

Interpretative Response: Response to Literature Essay

An effective interpretative response has these characteristics:

- A clear **thesis statement** that expresses the main idea of the writer's response to the author's work
- An in-depth **analysis** that goes beyond a summary and literal analysis to provide insight about how or why the work is effective
- **Evidence** from the text, including **embedded quotations**—quotations set into the text of your essay—and specific examples, to support the analysis
- Analysis of the **author's style,** including a discussion of the **aesthetic** **effects** and **stylistic devices** that make the language powerful
- The use of writing skills used in an **analytical essay**
- **Effective sentence structure** and correct spelling, grammar, and usage

A response to literature essay also includes:

- Valid **inferences,** or interpretations, about what the work means
- Analysis of plot, characters, and setting and how these elements relate to theme

Other Forms of Interpretative Response

In addition to a response to literature essay, there are other forms of interpretative responses, including:

Blog comments on an author's Web site share readers' ideas about an author's work. Readers express their opinions and give their interpretations of what an author's work means.

Comparison essays explore similarities and differences between two or more works of literature. For example, a comparison essay may compare how main characters in two different stories handle a similar problem.

Critical reviews evaluate books, plays, poetry, and other literary works. They appear in newspapers and magazines, on television and radio, and on the Internet. These kinds of interpretative works present the writer's opinions and support them with specific examples.

Letters to an author give you the chance to respond personally to a piece of literature. In a letter, you can ask questions, make requests, and express your reactions and your ideas about the characters, theme, style, and other elements of the literature.

Try It! For each audience and purpose described, choose a form, such as a blog or critical review, that is appropriate for conveying your intended meaning to the audience. Explain your choices.

- To demonstrate the similarities between two poems
- To learn more about a novel and to express your reaction to an author's point of view
- To convince your classmates to read a particular book

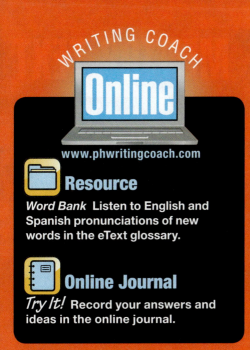

WRITING COACH Online

www.phwritingcoach.com

Resource
Word Bank Listen to English and Spanish pronunciations of new words in the eText glossary.

Online Journal
Try It! Record your answers and ideas in the online journal.

WORD BANK

People often use these vocabulary words when talking about interpretative response writing. Work with a partner. Take turns using each word in a sentence. If you are unsure of the meaning of a word, use the Glossary or a dictionary to check the definition.

adequate	device
analysis	style
context	symbol

A root word is the most basic part of a word. An affix is a word part that is added to the beginning of a word, as a prefix, or at the end of a word, as a suffix. Prefixes and suffixes change the meaning of the root word in some way. Think about how the words below are related to the words above.

adequacy	analyze
stylistic	symbolize

Response to Literature

MENTOR TEXT: Response to Literature Essay

Learn From Experience

 Read the response to literature essay on pages 200–201. As you read, take notes to develop your understanding of basic sight and English vocabulary. Then, read the numbered notes in the margins to learn about how the author presented her ideas.

Answer the *Try It!* questions online or in your notebook.

---

❶ The introduction has a clearly stated **thesis**. It also grabs **the readers' interest** because it mentions contemporary authors' names.

Try It! What is the thesis of this essay? What comparison is the author making between King and Koontz and Jacobs?

❷ The author describes plot **details** and gives **evidence** from the text in the form of a quotation to help the reader quickly connect to the characters.

Try It! How do the details about the characters support the author's thesis?

❸ The author analyzes the **aesthetic effects** of Jacobs's use of foreshadowing.

Try It! What evidence from the text does the author use to support her ideas about Jacobs's use of foreshadowing?

Extension Find another example of a response to literature essay, and compare it with this one.

Horror in "The Monkey's Paw"

by Tamra Orr

❶ Although Stephen King and Dean Koontz may be the current leaders in horror fiction, they may well have learned a few lessons from W.W. Jacobs. His short story "The Monkey's Paw" is full of many of the techniques that give readers the shivers today—as well as when he wrote it more than a century ago. From the element of foreshadowing to the theme that fate should never be tampered with, this story keeps the readers holding their breath to see what will happen next.

The story begins, as many do, with a detailed exposition, in which the reader is given a number of background details. These details set the stage for the events that are going to unfold. Each one of the details plays a role in what is to come and provides clues for the careful reader on what direction the plot is sure to go. The family's discussion of money problems certainly foreshadows their first wish. Their reference to their remote location intensifies the fear that is awaiting them.

❷ The characters of Mr. and Mrs. White, along with their son Herbert, seem the picture of a close, happy family enjoying a quiet evening at home. The arrival of Sergeant Major Morris changes everything. He is not at ease from the beginning. Jacobs gives many clues to Morris's state of mind, stating that the character spoke solemnly and slowly: "His tones were so grave that a hush fell upon the group." Morris's ominous story about the holy man, his belief in fate, and the monkey's paw that grants wishes causes him more discomfort in the telling. He lets his enrapt audience know that the last person who owned the paw used his last wish to ask for death. **❸** When Mr. White asks for the paw, Morris attempts to toss it in the fire. Then, he delivers a warning when he says, "If you keep it, don't blame me for what happens." This is another example of the foreshadowing Jacobs uses throughout the story to indicate what will eventually occur. Other instances include the faces that Herbert sees in the fire and the reference to "something horrible squatting up on the

200 Interpretative Response

wardrobe watching you." These lines all help to heighten the sense that something terrible will happen.

This short story could easily be the basis for the familiar adage, "Be careful what you wish for," because that is certainly the truth for the innocent White family. Unknowingly, they tempt fate and pay the heaviest possible price for it. Their first wish is granted, but at a cost they could not have imagined even in their nightmares. The conditions under which Herbert is killed—mangled in factory machinery—are hideous.

After the loss of her son Herbert, grief turns to madness for Mrs. White. She finds herself seeking the exact source of her pain as a possible solution. When it appears her wish has actually been granted, her husband cannot abide the idea of what his son might be now and what might walk through the front door once the bolt is drawn. Desperately, he uses his third wish to return his son to the grave. Jacobs emphasizes the awful moment with Mrs. White's ❹ "long loud wail of disappointment and misery." Sharing in her pain, but hoping that he has saved her from something far worse, Mr. White goes to his wife. Together they face the deserted road in front of their house. They are united in their loss and their punishment for attempting to take fate into their own hands.

❺ The dire consequences of interfering with fate are evident throughout this short story. Jacobs combines the theme with a sprinkle of clues and blends it with characters that the reader quickly learns to like and understand. The combination creates a timeless story that modern horror authors might well have learned from and incorporated into their own stories. As Jacobs made clear, be careful what you wish for—because you just might get it.

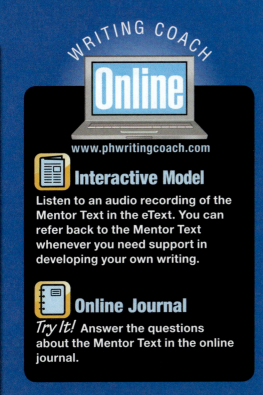

Interactive Model

Listen to an audio recording of the Mentor Text in the eText. You can refer back to the Mentor Text whenever you need support in developing your own writing.

Online Journal

Try It! Answer the questions about the Mentor Text in the online journal.

❹ Throughout the essay, the author uses evidence from the text, such as **embedded quotations** like this one, to support her ideas.

Try It! Why are quotations from literature strong evidence in a response to literature essay?

❺ The author connects the **conclusion** of the essay to the **introduction** by linking back to the idea of past and present horror fiction writers.

Try It! How does the connection between past and present writers change how you see this story? How are the historical periods and cultural contexts of those writers similar? How are they different?

STUDENT MODEL
Response to Literature Essay

With a small group, take turns reading this Student Model aloud. Ask yourself whether the writer has presented and defended her perspective. Then, decide if you agree with the author's interpretation of the text.

Use a Reader's Eye

Now, reread the Student Model. On your copy of the Student Model, use the Reader's Response Symbols to react to what you read.

Reader's Response Symbols

+ I agree with this point.
− This isn't clear to me.
? I have a question about this.
! Well said!

Participate in an extended discussion with a partner. Express your opinions and share your responses to the Student Model. Look at the supporting evidence together. Discuss the specific ways the writer supports her ideas.

Good Things in Small Packages

by Jaymie Dunham

"The Open Window" by Saki made me think of the saying "Good things come in small packages." Though the story is very short, Saki puts some very good things in it. Two of these "good things" are the narrative's point of view and irony.

The plot of the story seems simple. A man named Framton Nuttel goes to the country to rest. He has a problem with his nerves, and his sister has arranged for him to visit the Sappletons. At the Sappletons' house, Framton meets Vera, Mrs. Sappleton's niece. Mrs. Sappleton is busy when he first arrives, so Vera keeps Framton company.

During this meeting, the narrator focuses on Framton's thoughts and feelings. It is clear that Framton doesn't like being with complete strangers, because the narrator says that he wonders "whether these formal visits on a succession of total strangers would do much towards helping the nerve cure which he was supposed to be undergoing." All the narrator says about Vera is that she is fifteen and "self-possessed." It's important that readers don't know much about Vera, because that sets up the irony at the end.

Vera tells Framton about a tragedy that had happened three years before. Her aunt's husband and brothers went hunting, got trapped in a bog, and died. Vera says, "Poor aunt always thinks that they will come back some day, and the little brown spaniel that was lost with them, and walk in at that window just as they used to do." At this point, Vera seems like a nice person who feels sorry for her aunt, but that's only because the narrator never tells us what Vera is thinking.

After Mrs. Sappleton meets Framton, she looks out the window and says, "Here they are at last!"

1

35 Framton looks, sees three men and a dog walking toward the house, and runs away terrified, thinking they're ghosts. When Mrs. Sappleton acts surprised, Vera explains that Framton was probably afraid of the dog. She says Framton told her he was once attacked
40 by a pack of wild dogs. Actually, Framton never said any such thing, and this is where the irony comes in. Readers realize that Vera lied to Framton about her aunt's so-called tragedy to scare Framton. Ironically, he came to the country to find peace but found
45 terror instead.

By focusing on Framton's point of view, Saki establishes a sense of irony and sets up readers for a surprise ending. Though I didn't see it coming, the ending made the story more interesting for me. Saki's
50 ability to fit a lot into a little space makes "The Open Window" more than just another short story.

Writing Coach Online

www.phwritingcoach.com

Interactive Model

Listen to an audio recording of the Student Model in the eText. Use the Reader's and Writer's Response Symbols with the eText tools to note what you read.

Use a Writer's Eye

Now, evaluate the piece as a writer. On your copy of the Student Model, use the Writer's Response Symbols to react to what you read. Identify places where the student writer uses characteristics of an effective response to literature essay.

Writer's Response Symbols

C.T.	Clearly stated thesis
I.A.	In-depth analysis
S.E.	Effective supporting evidence
E.Q.	Effective quotations

Feature Assignment: Response to Literature Essay

Prewriting

Plan a first draft by **determining an appropriate topic.** Choose from the Topic Bank or come up with a topic of your own.

Choose From the Topic Bank

Brave Characters Characters in literature often display intense courage when they face a difficult or dangerous situation. Choose a character from a work of literature you have recently read. Summarize the situation in which the character demonstrates bravery and explain how the character's courage helped resolve the problem he or she faced.

Motives and Emotions Characters may act for reasons that are both stated and unstated. Think about the motives of a character in a story. Choose a character from a work of literature you have read. Write a response to literature essay explaining how the motives of this character created a problem.

Response to a Mentor Text Read "A Trip to Beautiful" by Mary Schmich on page 68. Consider the purpose of setting in this story. Write a response to literature essay that explains why the setting is so important.

Choose Your Own Topic

Determine an appropriate topic on your own by using the following **range of strategies** to generate ideas.

Reviewing and Discussing

- Review class notes and journals to help you recall literature you have read and the characters and ideas you found interesting. Take notes on ideas that interest you.
- Discuss favorite authors with your classmates. Why did these authors make an impression on you?

Review your responses and choose a topic.

Narrow Your Topic

Narrowing your topic will help you to write a response that extends beyond a summary and literal analysis of the work. Narrow your topic to find an insight to develop.

Apply It! Use a graphic organizer like the one shown to narrow your topic.

- Write your general topic in the top box, and keep narrowing your topic as you move down the chart.
- Your last box should hold your narrowest or "smallest" topic, the new focus of your response to literature essay. The topic should not simply tell what happens in the text, but provide your ideas about the text.

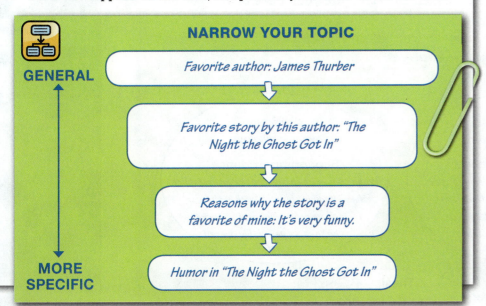

NARROW YOUR TOPIC

GENERAL → Favorite author: James Thurber
↓
Favorite story by this author: "The Night the Ghost Got In"
↓
Reasons why the story is a favorite of mine: It's very funny.
↓
MORE SPECIFIC → Humor in "The Night the Ghost Got In"

WRITING COACH Online
www.phwritingcoach.com

Interactive Writing Coach™
- Choosing from the Topic Bank gives you access to the Interactive Writing Coach™.
- Submit your writing and receive instant personalized feedback and guidance as you draft, revise, and edit your writing.

Interactive Graphic Organizers
Use the interactive graphic organizers to help you narrow your topic.

Online Journal
Try It! Record your answers and ideas in the online journal.

Consider Multiple Audiences and Purposes

Before writing, think about your audiences and purposes. Consider how your writing will convey the intended meaning to these audiences. Consider how others will view the selection as you ask yourself these questions.

Questions for Audience	Questions for Purpose
• Who will read my essay? My teacher? My classmates?	• What do I want my audience to understand about the work?
• What do they already know about the short story on which I'm writing?	• What personal responses to the work do I want to share?
• What new information should I give to help my audience understand my ideas?	• How do I want my audience to respond to my thoughts on this work?

Record your answers in your writing journal.

Prewriting 205

Plan Your Piece

You will use a graphic organizer like the one shown to state your thesis and to identify and organize your evidence. When it is complete, you will be ready to write your first draft.

Develop a Clear Thesis Plan your response to the literature by **developing a thesis statement** that clearly expresses your ideas. Add your thesis to a graphic organizer like the one shown.

Logically Organize Your Supporting Evidence Use a graphic organizer to organize evidence from the literature. Your evidence should include quotations, examples, and other specific details. Later, you can use the graphic organizer to plan and **structure your ideas in a sustained way.**

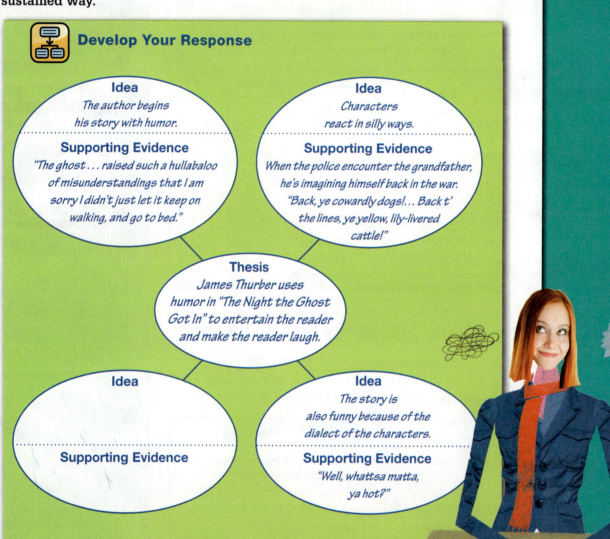

Develop Your Response

Idea
The author begins his story with humor.

Supporting Evidence
"The ghost ... raised such a hullabaloo of misunderstandings that I am sorry I didn't just let it keep on walking, and go to bed."

Idea
Characters react in silly ways.

Supporting Evidence
When the police encounter the grandfather, he's imagining himself back in the war. "Back, ye cowardly dogs!... Back t' the lines, ye yellow, lily-livered cattle!"

Thesis
James Thurber uses humor in "The Night the Ghost Got In" to entertain the reader and make the reader laugh.

Idea

Supporting Evidence

Idea
The story is also funny because of the dialect of the characters.

Supporting Evidence
"Well, whattsa matta, ya hot?"

Interpretative Response

Gather Details

To support their opinions in a response to literature essay, writers use various kinds of evidence. Look at these examples:

- **Quotations:** *"What is it?" he asked me. "It's an old zither our guinea pig used to sleep on," I said.*
- **Examples:** *It's hilarious when the police open all the drawers and pull clothes from hooks and make a real mess of the house when they're looking for intruders.*
- **Descriptive Details:** *Mom has to get the neighbors' attention so they'll call the police. Thurber describes it this way: "She flung up a window of her bedroom . . . picked up a shoe, and whammed it through a pane of glass across the narrow space that separated the two houses."*
- **Personal Observations:** *What makes the story so original is the dialect and the specific details that really help me visualize the action.*
- **Related Information:** *Thurber is a cartoonist as well as a humorous writer. His sketches of the story help readers visualize events.*

Try It! Read the Student Model excerpt and identify the evidence that the author uses to support her ideas.

> **STUDENT MODEL** from **Good Things in Small Packages** page 202; lines 13–19
>
> During this meeting, the narrator focuses on Framton's thoughts and feelings. It is clear that Framton doesn't like being with complete strangers, because the narrator says that he wonders "whether these formal visits on a succession of total strangers would do much towards helping the nerve cure which he was supposed to be undergoing."

Apply It! Review the types of supporting evidence that can be used in a response to literature essay. Then identify and write one piece of evidence of each type.

- Review your evidence to make certain that it truly supports your response. It must be relevant and well-chosen—so that it supports your response. Use the writing skills of analytical essays. (See page 146.)
- Be sure some of your evidence from the text includes **embedded quotations.** These are quotations set into the text of your essay.
- Identify details that will take you beyond a summary and literal analysis and help you to analyze the author's style. Be ready to address the author's use of stylistic and rhetorical devices, such as dialect and humor, and their **aesthetic effects** on the work.
- Add the evidence to your graphic organizer.

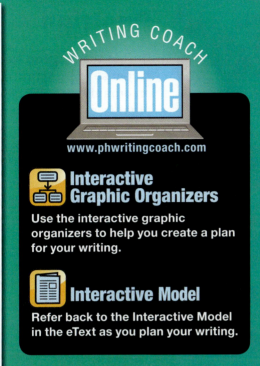

WRITING COACH Online
www.phwritingcoach.com

Interactive Graphic Organizers
Use the interactive graphic organizers to help you create a plan for your writing.

Interactive Model
Refer back to the Interactive Model in the eText as you plan your writing.

Drafting

During the drafting stage, you will start to write your ideas for your response to literature essay. You will follow an outline that provides an organizational strategy that will help you write a focused, organized, and coherent response to literature essay.

The Organization of an Interpretative Response

The chart shows an organizational strategy for an interpretative response. Look back at how the Mentor Text follows this organizational strategy. Then, use this chart to help you outline your draft.

I. Introduction — See Mentor Text, p. 200.

- Interesting opening statements
- Name of work and author
- Clear thesis

Grab Your Reader

- An interesting opening that makes a statement or asks a question will grab readers' attention. Use a question or a powerful statement.
- The title and author of the literature are always noted in the introduction.
- The thesis states the main idea of your response to the work.

II. Body — See Mentor Text, pp. 200–201.

- In-depth analysis and interpretation
- Supporting evidence and details
- Logical organization

Develop Your Ideas

- An in-depth analysis and interpretation of the text goes beyond simply restating and summarizing the major events of the text. Rather, you should focus on the work's artistic effect or interpreting the meanings of different story elements.
- Supportive evidence that is provided in detail, such as by including quotations from the text, goes far to prove your points.
- A logically organized response helps your readers follow your argument. Order sentences and paragraphs so that they flow in a way that makes sense.

III. Conclusion — See Mentor Text, p. 201.

- Restatement of thesis, or main points
- Explanation of the significance of those points to the writer, such as what the writer has learned

Wrap It Up

- Restating your thesis reminds readers of your main point.
- Explaining the significance of your main point will leave your reader with a clear understanding of your ideas.

 **Start Your Draft**

Use the checklist to help you complete your draft. Use the graphic organizer that shows your thesis and supporting evidence, and the Outline for Success as guides.

While drafting, aim at writing your ideas, not on making your writing perfect. Remember, because you are drafting in an open-ended situation, you will have the chance to improve your draft when you revise and edit.

- √ Start with a strong opening. Use **rhetorical devices,** such as a rhetorical question or an analogy, to convey meaning and create a powerful opening.
- √ Identify the **literary work** and the author about which you're writing.
- √ Continue to create an effective **introduction** by presenting a clear thesis statement.

- √ Use the **body** of your essay to develop your ideas. Write a **response** that extends beyond a summary and literal analysis.
- √ Support your ideas with specific and relevant **evidence** from the text. **Include** embedded quotations to help support your ideas.
- √ In addition to writing about the context of the selection, work to analyze the author's style. Discuss the **aesthetic effects** of the author's use of language. Address the author's use of stylistic and rhetorical devices. Be sure to point out where the author uses artistic effects, such as irony and point of view, or devices, such as analogies, rhetorical questions, and metaphors and similes—which compare two usually unrelated things.
- √ Response to literature is a unique type of analytical essay—you should effectively support your analysis. Organize your paragraphs and structure your ideas in a **logical order** and use the writing skills of analytical essay. (See page 146.)

- √ To create an effective **conclusion**, restate or paraphrase your **thesis.**
- √ End with a memorable **final statement** that clearly expresses your reaction to the literature.

www.phwritingcoach.com

Interactive Model

Outline for Success View pop-ups of Mentor Text selections referenced in the Outline for Success.

 **Interactive Writing Coach**™

Use the Interactive Writing Coach to receive the level of support you need:
- Write one paragraph at a time and submit each one for immediate, detailed feedback.
- Write your entire first draft and submit it for immediate, personalized feedback.

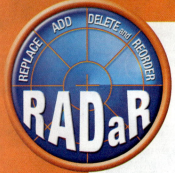

Revising: Making It Better

Now that you have finished your first draft, you are ready to revise. Think about the "big picture" of **audience, purpose, and genre.** You can use Revision RADaR as a guide for making changes to improve your draft. Revision RADaR provides four major ways to improve your writing: (R) replace, (A) add, (D) delete, and (R) reorder.

Kelly Gallagher, M. Ed.

KEEP REVISION ON YOUR RADaR

Read part of the first draft of the Student Model "Good Things in Small Packages." Then look at questions the writer asked herself as she thought about how well her draft **addressed issues of audience, purpose, and genre.**

Good Things in Small Packages

Vera tells Framton about a tragedy that had happened three years before. Her aunt's husband and brothers went hunting, got trapped in a bog, and died. She explains that her aunt keeps thinking they'll all come back some day, and walk through the window. At this point, Vera seems like a nice person who feels sorry for her aunt, but that's only because the narrator never tells what Vera is thinking.

After Mrs. Sappleton meets Framton, she looks out the window and says, "Here they are at last!" Framton runs away, scared. He had looked out the window and had seen three men and a dog walking toward the house. When Mrs. Sappleton acts surprised, Vera explains that Framton was probably afraid of the dog. She says Framton told her he was once attacked by a pack of wild dogs. Actually, Framton never said any such thing, and this is where the irony comes in. Readers realize that Vera lied to Framton about her aunt's so-called tragedy to scare Framton.

> *Have I included enough **evidence** and **specific examples** from the text?*

> *Have I used **precise word choices**? Are my details **logically organized**?*

> *Is this **in-depth analysis**?*

210 Interpretative Response

Now, look at how the writer applied Revision RADaR to write an improved second draft.

Good Things in Small Packages

2ND DRAFT

Vera tells Framton about a tragedy that had happened three years before. Her aunt's husband and brothers went hunting, got trapped in a bog, and died. Vera says, "Poor aunt always thinks that they will come back some day, and the little brown spaniel that was lost with them, and walk in at that window just as they used to do." At this point, Vera seems like a nice person who feels sorry for her aunt, but that's only because the narrator never tells what Vera is thinking.

After Mrs. Sappleton meets Framton, she looks out the window and says, "Here they are at last!" Framton looks, sees three men and a dog walking toward the house, and runs away terrified, thinking they're ghosts. When Mrs. Sappleton acts surprised, Vera explains that Framton was probably afraid of the dog. She says Framton told her he was once attacked by a pack of wild dogs. Actually, Framton never said any such thing, and this is where the irony comes in. Readers realize that Vera lied to Framton about her aunt's so-called tragedy to scare Framton. Ironically, he came to the country to find peace but found terror instead.

R Replaced description from the text with an embedded quotation

R Replaced scared with the more precise word terrified to better explain how the character felt

R Rearranged ideas for a more logical flow

A Added a sentence to more fully analyze the story elements

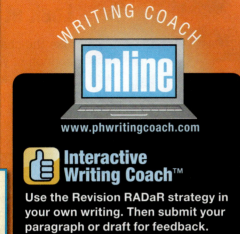

Interactive Writing Coach™

Use the Revision RADaR strategy in your own writing. Then submit your paragraph or draft for feedback.

Apply It! Use Revision RADaR to revise your draft.

- First, ask yourself: Have I addressed the needs of my audience, made clear my purpose for writing, and included the characteristics of the interpretative response genre?
- Then, ensure that you have created an analysis that extends beyond a summary and literal analysis. Confirm that you have provided evidence from the text using embedded quotations. Review your word choices to make sure they are precise.
- Use your Revision RADaR to make needed changes. Remember—you can use the steps in the strategy in any order.

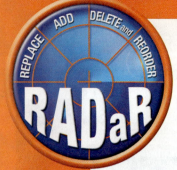

Look at the Big Picture

Use the chart and your analytical skills to evaluate how well each section of your response to literature essay addresses **purpose, audience, and genre.** When necessary, use the suggestions in the chart to revise your essay.

Section	Evaluate	Revise
Introduction	• Check the opening. It should grab readers' attention and make them want to read on.	• Make your opening more interesting by writing a strong first sentence or asking a question.
	• Make sure the **thesis** is clearly stated and exactly expresses the main idea of your response.	• Reread your essay, keeping your thesis in mind. Did you make points that are not covered in the thesis? Revise it so that it covers your main points.
Body	• Make sure that you have supported your thesis and each idea with relevant **evidence** and well-chosen details from the text, including embedded quotations.	• Skim the story to find relevant examples, details, and quotations to support your ideas. Add them as necessary. Review the other writing skills of an analytical essay. (See page 146.)
	• Make sure your **analysis** goes beyond summarizing and literal analysis.	• Don't just tell what happens; also tell why it happens and interpret what it means.
	• Check that you have a logical organizing structure and convey meaning using **transitions.**	• Arrange ideas so that they flow logically.
	• Make sure you have analyzed the **aesthetic effects** of the author's use of stylistic or rhetorical devices.	• Identify something you think the author did well, such as creating powerful imagery. Then analyze how that affects the reader's experience of the story.
Conclusion	• Check the restatement of your thesis. Confirm that the body of your essay supports your thesis.	• Reword your conclusion to reflect the ideas you have presented.
	• Check that your **conclusion** leaves readers with a clear understanding of your ideas.	• Add a final statement that provides insight and sums up what you think about the work or why it is meaningful to you.

Focus on Craft: Word Choice

Making precise **word choices** is essential to accurately conveying your meaning in a response to literature essay. For example, compare the vague and precise meanings of the words in these pairs: *quickly/abruptly, caused/provoked, deep/enduring.* While revising, look for ways to be more precise.

Think about precise word choices as you read these sentences from the Student Model.

 **STUDENT MODEL** from **Good Things in Small Packages** page 203; lines 34–38

> Framton looks, sees three men and a dog walking toward the house, and runs away terrified, thinking they're ghosts. When Mrs. Sappleton acts surprised, Vera explains that Framton was probably afraid of the dog.

 Try It! Now, ask yourself these questions:

- How does the word *terrified* make Framton's emotions clear?
- How would the sentence's effect be different if the sentence were written this way: *Framton looks, sees three men and a dog walking toward the house, and runs away scared, thinking they're ghosts*?

 **Fine-Tune Your Draft**

Apply It! Use the revision suggestions to prepare your final draft after rethinking how well questions of purpose, audience, and genre have been addressed.

- **Improve Word Choice** To help your readers see your point, use precise or more descriptive language in place of vague words.
- **Improve Style** Use rhetorical devices, such as rhetorical questions and analogies, to make your writing more interesting to your reader.
- **Use a Variety of Sentence Structures** To be sure your essay has a mix of sentences lengths, avoid presenting paragraphs made up only of short sentences.

Teacher Feedback Share your final draft with your teacher. Ask if your interpretative response discusses the **aesthetic affects of the work** and supplies ample evidence. Listen carefully to your teacher's responses and revise your final draft as needed.

www.phwritingcoach.com

Video Learn more strategies for effective writing from program author Kelly Gallagher.

 Online Journal *Try It!* Record your answers in the online journal.

Interactive Model Refer back to the Interactive Model as you revise your writing.

 Interactive Writing Coach™ Revise your draft and submit it for feedback.

Revising 213

Editing: Making It Correct

Editing your draft means polishing your work and correcting errors. You may want to read through your work several times, looking for different errors and issues each time.

As you edit your final draft, pay particular attention to the conventions of **capitalization**. Capital letters are important to helping your readers understand the meaning of your essay. Also look at your use of **quotation marks** to indicate sarcasm or irony. Then, edit your final draft for any errors in **grammar, mechanics, and spelling**.

WRITE GUY Jeff Anderson, M. Ed.

WHAT DO YOU NOTICE?

To learn more about capitalization, see Chapter 22 of your Grammar Handbook.

Zoom In on Conventions Focus on capitalization as you zoom in on these lines from the Mentor Text.

 from **Horror in "The Monkey's Paw"**
page 200; lines 1–5, 19–10

> Although Stephen King and Dean Koontz may be the current leaders in horror fiction, they may well have learned a few lessons from W.W. Jacobs. His short story, "The Monkey's Paw" is full of many techniques that give readers the shivers today… The arrival of Sergeant Major Morris changes everything.

Now, ask yourself: *Which words in the text did the writer capitalize?*

Perhaps you said that the writer capitalized the beginnings of sentences and the names of particular things. Proper nouns name specific examples of people, places, things, or ideas. They are always capitalized.

Proper nouns such as *Stephen King, Dean Koontz, W.W. Jacobs* and *Morris* are all capitalized because they are people's names. *Seargent Morris is* capitalized because it is a professional title associated with a name.

The first word and key words in the titles of books, poems, stories, and other works of art are always capitalized. Prepositions and articles (*a, an, the*) are not capitalized unless they are the first or last word in a title or contain four or more letters.

Partner Talk Discuss this question with a partner: *How does correct capitalization make this passage easier to understand?*

214 **Interpretative Response**

Grammar Mini-Lesson: Quotation Marks

To learn more, see Chapter 23.

Quotation marks are used to set off direct quotations, dialogue, and certain types of titles, such as short stories. They may also be used to indicate **sarcasm or irony.** Using words to express something other than their literal meaning is considered irony. Sarcasm is often a remark made using ironic language. Notice how quotation marks set off a phrase in the Student Model. Although the words are a direct quote, the Student Model author also notes that there is some irony in the way the original author used the phrase.

STUDENT MODEL from *Good Things in Small Packages* page 202; lines 19–22

All the narrator says about Vera is that she is fifteen and "self-possessed." It's important that readers don't know much about Vera, because that sets up the irony at the end.

 Try It! Write one or two sentences using irony or sarcasm. Be sure to use quotation marks to indicate the sarcasm or irony. Write the sentence(s) in your journal.

 Apply It! Edit your draft for grammar, mechanics, and spelling. Use a dictionary to check your spelling. Be sure to check your use of quotation marks to indicate sarcasm or irony.

 **WRITING COACH Online**
www.phwritingcoach.com

 Video
Learn effective editing techniques from program author Jeff Anderson.

 Online Journal
Try It! Record your answers in the online journal.

 Interactive Model
Refer back to the Interactive Model as you edit your writing.

 Interactive Writing Coach™
Edit your draft. Check it against the rubric and then submit it for feedback.

Use the rubric to evaluate your piece. If necessary, rethink, rewrite, or revise.

Rubric for Interpretative Response: Response to Literature Essay	Rating Scale
Ideas: How well does your response present a focused statement and analysis of the work?	Not very Very 1 2 3 4 5 6
Organization: How clearly organized is your analysis?	1 2 3 4 5 6
Voice: How well have you engaged the reader and sustained his or her interest?	1 2 3 4 5 6
Word Choice: How precisely do your word choices accurately reflect your purpose?	1 2 3 4 5 6
Sentence Fluency: How well have you varied sentence structure and length?	1 2 3 4 5 6
Conventions: How correct is your use of punctuation, quotation marks, and capitalization?	1 2 3 4 5 6

Publishing

Share the feelings and thoughts expressed in your response to literature—publish it! First, get your piece ready for presentation. Then, choose a way to **publish it for the appropriate audiences**.

Wrap Up Your Presentation

Whether or not you wrote your essay by hand or using a computer, be sure to add page numbers to each page of your essay. This will help readers stay organized while they read your essay. Also be sure to add a title to your essay that grabs your readers' attention and indicates the topic.

Publish Your Piece

Use the chart to identify a way to publish your response to literature essay.

If your audience is…	…then publish it by…
Students or adults at your school	• Submitting it to your school newspaper • Posting it on your school's Web site
People outside your school community	• Posting it on your blog • Submitting it to an online literary magazine • Presenting a class anthology of essays

 ## Extend Your Research

Think more about the topic on which you wrote your response to literature essay. What else would you like to know about this topic? As you write, use specific details to describe and explain your ideas. Increase the specificity of your details based on the type of information you are recording.

- Brainstorm for several questions you would like to research and then consult, or discuss, with others. Then, decide which question is your major research question.
- Formulate, or develop, a research plan about how you will answer these questions. Decide where you will find more information—on the Internet, at the library, or through other sources.
- Learn more about your topic by following through with your plan.

Manage Your Portfolio You may wish to include your published response to literature essay in your writing portfolio. If so, consider what this essay reveals about your writing and your growth as a writer.

 The Big Question: Why Write? What should you write about to make others interested in a text?

216 **Interpretative Response**

21st Century Learning

MAKE YOUR WRITING COUNT

Stage a Dialogue Between Literary Characters

Response to literature essays examine the elements of a story, book, or play. Help your classmates deepen their understanding of stories by holding a **dialogue** among literary characters about an issue relevant to both the characters and your peers.

With a group, analyze the points of view of major characters in selected stories. Then, plan a dialogue among characters, conveying the themes and tone associated with each one. Perform your dialogue live for the class, and if possible, make an audio recording or podcast for listening later.

www.phwritingcoach.com

Online Journal

Extend Your Research Record your answers and ideas in the online journal.

Resource

Link to resources on 21st Century Learning for help in creating a group project.

Here's your action plan.

1. As a group, review your peers' essays and assign characters to each group member. The characters may be from different stories.

2. Analyze the themes and concerns associated with your characters. Then, choose a dialogue topic to which both your characters and your classmates will relate.

3. Look for online literary criticism that tells you more about the characters you have chosen. Take notes for the dialogue.

4. Plan your dialogue. While "in character," you should:
   - Reflect your character's general attitude
   - Express your character's point of view on the dialogue topic
   - Present details about your character based on the story

Listening and Speaking As a group, rehearse your conversation. Work as a team to convey the characters and their points of view. Along with words and tone, use gestures and expressions to convey each character's point of view. Listeners should be attentive and offer constructive feedback. During the live presentation of your dialogue, remember to incorporate your peers' feedback.

Script

A **script** is the written version of words spoken in a play, a movie, a television show, or a commercial. As in other written works, the **theme** of a script can be either suggested **implicitly** or directly and **explicitly** stated. Because scripts are delivered orally, they are usually written in dialogue format. Sometimes scripts include special directions, often called *stage directions*, that give the speakers extra information about how to speak or move.

Try It! Study the script based on a scene from "The Night the Ghost Got In" by James Thurber. Then, answer the questions. Record your answers in your journal.

1. What is the **theme** of this script? Is it implicit or explicit?
2. What **details,** or specific words or events, in the story convey the mood or tone—the overall emotion—of the story?
3. Identify two examples of **stage directions** for movement. How are they indicated?
4. Which information is an example of a direction that instructs the speaker about the **emotion** he or she should show?
5. In Thurber's original story, the main character and narrator isn't named. The author of this **script** gave the character a name: Charlie. Why do you think the author did this?

Extension Find another example of a script, and compare it with this one.

(Setting: In Charlie's house at night. It is very dark. His mother and brother, Herman, are asleep. Charlie has just finished his bath when he hears odd noises coming from downstairs.)

CHARLIE: *(startled)* What was that? *(He opens the bathroom door and peers down the stairs.)*

(The sounds of heavy, running, footsteps are heard.)

CHARLIE: *(mumbling to himself)* But…but…there's no one there! How can there be footsteps? *(surprised and scared)* Oh… Oh! A ghost!

(Charlie runs down the hallway to his brother's room.)

CHARLIE: Herman!

HERMAN: *(screams, from being startled awake)*

CHARLIE: It's just me, Herman. Wake up! There's a ghost downstairs.

HERMAN: *(terrified)* What?!

(The sounds of the footsteps are louder.)

MOM: *(Walks in sleepily, rubbing her eyes)* What's going on boys? Is that Grandpa downstairs?

CHARLIE: No way, Mom. It's a ghost!

(The footsteps are even louder, and moving faster.)

MOM: Burglars! We have to call the police! But the phone's downstairs. Mr. Bodwin from next door will have to call for us.

CHARLIE: But Mom—

(Mom picks up one of Herman's shoes, opens a window, and throws the shoe out. The sound of breaking glass is heard.)

MR. BODWIN: *(unseen, angry voice)* You're nuts! I'm calling the police!

MOM: Good! Do it quickly. We have burglars in our house!

Create a Script

Follow these steps to adapt a story and create your own script for a stage play. To plan your script, review the graphic organizers on pages R24–R27 and choose one that suits your needs.

Prewriting
- Identify a short story, novel, or other literary work to transform into a script for a stage play. You might consider using the literary work that was the subject of your response to literature essay.
- Determine the explicit or implicit theme and mood your script will have, based on the theme of the short story.
- Decide which details you will use from the short story to establish the mood in your script, and how you will present those details. For example, will you present those details as stage directions or dialogue?
- Identify any dialogue from the story that can be used in your script.
- Identify descriptive writing that can be converted into dialogue.

Drafting
- First, write stage directions that create a sense of setting for the script. Put these directions at the start of your script.
- Add any usable dialogue from the short story to your script, making some adjustments to make sure the dialogue will be understood.
- Next, rewrite some descriptive writing into a dialogue format.
- Include stage directions to give the speakers extra information about movement and emotion in the scene.

Revising and Editing
- Review your draft to ensure that the events are ordered logically and that the dialogue of your script communicates the story.
- Read the dialogue aloud to make sure it will sound natural when spoken. Revise the dialogue as necessary and remove any dialogue that does not advance the plot.
- Check spelling, grammar, and mechanics.

Publishing
- With your classmates, act out the movie script.
- If technology allows, make a video recording of the performance. Be sure to include graphics, images, and sound. Think of ways you can creatively use these elements to replace some of the dialogue.

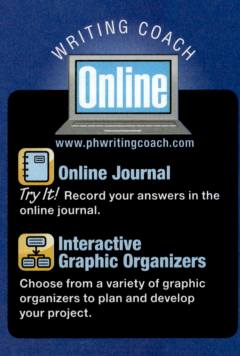

WRITING COACH Online
www.phwritingcoach.com

Online Journal
Try It! Record your answers in the online journal.

Interactive Graphic Organizers
Choose from a variety of graphic organizers to plan and develop your project.

Partner Talk

Before you start drafting, describe your planned script to a partner, and ask for feedback on your idea. Monitor your partner's spoken language by asking follow up questions to confirm your understanding.

Writing for Media

Writing for Assessment

You may see a prompt that asks you to write an essay in which you respond to, analyze, or interpret literature. You can use the prompts on these pages to practice. Your responses should include the same characteristics as your response to literature essay. Look back at page 198 to review these characteristics.

Try It! To begin, read the **interpretative** prompt and the information on format and academic vocabulary. Use the ABCDs of On-Demand Writing to help you plan and write your essay.

Format
The prompt directs you to write an *interpretative response*. Your introduction should include a clear thesis statement. The body should state your ideas and give supporting evidence. The conclusion should reinforce your thesis.

Critical Review Prompt
Write an **interpretative response** that is a critical review of a short story, book, or poem you have read. Analyze and evaluate the work. Support your **analysis** and **judgment** with specific details, such as examples from the work. [30 minutes]

Academic Vocabulary
Remember that in an *analysis* of a story, book, or poem, you study the elements of the work. Your *judgment* is your opinion of how well these elements work.

The ABCDs of On-Demand Writing

Use the following ABCDs to help you respond to the prompt.

Before you write your draft:

Attack the prompt [1 MINUTE]

- Circle or highlight important verbs in the prompt. Draw a line from the verb to what it refers to.
- Rewrite the prompt in your own words.

Brainstorm possible answers [4 MINUTES]

- Create a graphic organizer to generate ideas.
- Use one for each part of the prompt if necessary.

Choose the order of your response [1 MINUTE]

- Think about the best way to organize your ideas.
- Number your ideas in the order you will write about them. Cross out ideas you will not be using.

After you write your draft:

Detect errors before turning in the draft [1 MINUTE]

- Carefully reread your writing.
- Make sure that your response makes sense and is complete.
- Look for spelling, punctuation, and grammar errors.

220 **Interpretative Response**

More Prompts for Practice

Try It! Respond to Prompt 1 in an open-ended or timed situation by writing an **interpretative response** essay. As you write, be sure to:

- Express the main idea of your response in a **thesis statement**
- Go **beyond summary and literal analysis**
- Include supporting **evidence from** the text
- Analyze the **aesthetic effects** of the author's use of stylistic or rhetorical devices
- Address the **writing skills for an analytical essay** (See page 146.)
- Convey meaning by using **transitions** and **rhetorical devices**

Prompt 1 Authors have created some fascinating characters in fiction and described interesting real people in expository texts. Choose two people or characters from two different selections you have read. Write an interpretative response essay that compares and contrasts the characters. Support your ideas with evidence from the fiction or nonfiction texts.

Spiral Review: Persuasive Respond to Prompt 2 by writing a **persuasive essay**. Make sure your persuasive essay reflects all of the characteristics described on page 172, including:

- A **clear thesis** or position based on logical reasons supported by precise and relevant evidence
- Consideration of the whole range of information and views on the topic, and an accurate and honest **representation** of these views
- **Counter-arguments** based on evidence to anticipate and address objections
- An **organizing structure** appropriate to purpose, audience, and context
- An analysis of the **relative value** of specific data, facts, and ideas
- A **range of appropriate appeals**

Prompt 2 Many automobile makers are offering cars that help to conserve energy, but many consumers would rather buy cars that use gasoline. Write an essay to persuade your parents about your opinion—whether to buy an electric or hybrid car or a car that uses only gasoline for fuel.

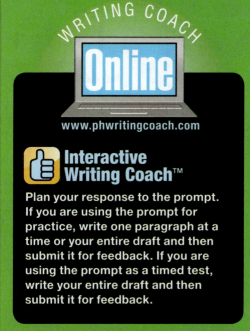

Interactive Writing Coach™

Plan your response to the prompt. If you are using the prompt for practice, write one paragraph at a time or your entire draft and then submit it for feedback. If you are using the prompt as a timed test, write your entire draft and then submit it for feedback.

Remember ABCD

Attack the prompt
Brainstorm possible answers
Choose the order of your response
Detect errors before turning in the draft

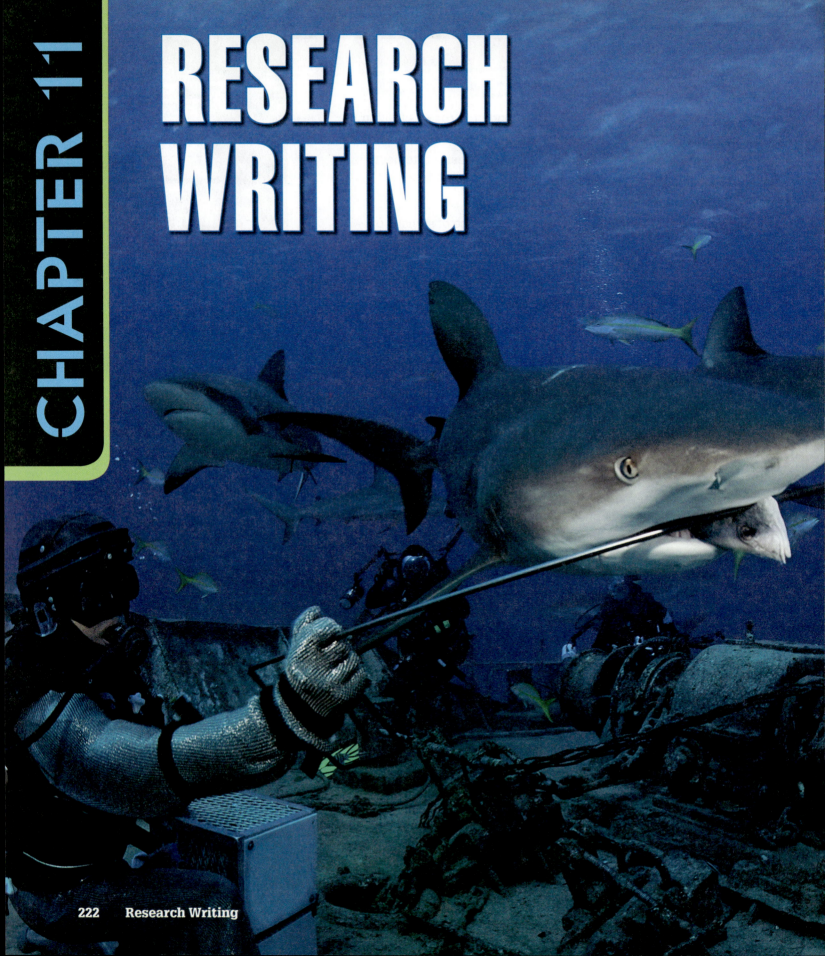

What Do You Want To Know?

How do people find out more information about interesting topics? They do research to gather, organize, and present information.

One of the first steps of research writing is to identify a topic that interests you and then formulate open-ended research questions. Open-ended research questions ask what you want to find out about the topic. For example, if you want to find out more about working with sharks, you would first decide what you want to know about it.

Try It! Take a few minutes to list some things you want to know about these divers and sharks. Consider these questions as you participate in an extended discussion with a partner. Take turns expressing your ideas.

- What are the divers doing?
- What can we learn about sharks?
- How can we learn more about sharks?
- What have scientists learned by researching sharks?

Review your list of questions with your partner. Compare lists to determine which ideas overlap or how you might build off each other's ideas. Then, discuss where you would go to research answers to your questions.

What's Ahead

In this chapter, you will review a strong example of an informational research report. Then, using the example as guidance, you will develop your own research plan and write your own informational research report.

WRITING COACH
Online
www.phwritingcoach.com

Online Journal

Try It! Record your answers and ideas in the online journal.

You can also record and save your answers and ideas on pop-up sticky notes in the eText.

Connect to the Big Questions

Discuss these questions with your partner:

1. **What do you think?** When does research change lives?

2. **Why write?** Do you understand a subject well enough to write about it? How will you find out what the facts are?

RESEARCH WRITING

Research writing is a way to gather information from various sources, and then evaluate, organize, and synthesize that information into a report for others to read. In this chapter, you will write an informational research report that conveys what you have learned about a topic that interests you. Before you write, you will search for information about your topic in different kinds of sources. You will evaluate the information you find, choose the best facts and details for your report, and organize your ideas so that you can clearly communicate them to your audience.

You will develop your informational research report by taking it through each of the steps of the writing process: prewriting, drafting, revising, editing, and publishing. You will also have an opportunity to use your informational research report in an oral or multimedia presentation that uses photos, charts, graphs, and other visuals and sound to share what you have learned and to convey a distinctive point of view. To preview the criteria for how your research report will be evaluated, see the rubric on page 247.

FEATURE ASSIGNMENT

Research Writing: Informational Research Report

An effective informational research report has these characteristics:

- A specific **thesis statement** that states the report's main ideas
- **Evidence,** such as facts and the opinions of experts, to support the thesis
- An **analysis** of the topic that is organized in a **logical progression,** or order, with a clearly stated **point of view**
- **Graphics** and **illustrations** that help explain important ideas when appropriate
- Proper **documentation of sources** to show where the author found information
- Correct **formatting,** or presentation, of written materials according to a style manual
- **Effective sentence structure** and correct spelling, grammar, and usage

Other Forms of Research Writing

In addition to an informational research report, there are other forms of research writing, including:

Biographical profiles present specific information about the life and work of a real person, living or dead. The subject may be well-known or someone familiar to the writer.

Documentaries are filmed reports that focus on a particular topic or issue. These multimedia presentations use spoken and written text, as well as photographs, videos, music, and other sound effects.

Experiment journals record detailed notes about the purpose, materials, procedures, results, and conclusions of a scientific experiment.

Health reports present up-to-date information, statistics, and research about a specific disease or health-related issue.

Historical reports give in-depth information about a past circumstance or event. An historical report focuses on a limited subject and may discuss causes and effects.

Trend analyses present information, data, and conclusions about a current development or tendency, such as current events, opinions, styles, or cultural and technological developments.

Try It! For each research report described, brainstorm for possible topics with other students. Then, consult with one another to decide on and formulate a major research question to address each major research topic.

- A trend analysis of social networking Web sites
- A biographical profile of a favorite author or artist
- A documentary about the history of your community

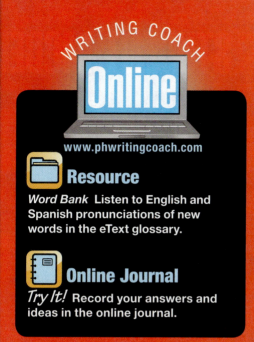

WRITING COACH Online
www.phwritingcoach.com

Resource
Word Bank Listen to English and Spanish pronunciations of new words in the eText glossary.

Online Journal
Try It! Record your answers and ideas in the online journal.

WORD BANK

People use these basic and content-based words when they talk about writing that reports information. Work with a partner. Take turns saying and writing each word in a sentence. If you are unsure of the meaning of a word, use the Glossary or a dictionary to check the definition.

accuracy	logical
analysis	standard
document	summarize

Informational Research Report

STUDENT MODEL | Informational Research Report

Use a Reader's Eye

Read the Student Model on pages 226–229. On your copy of the Student Model, use the Reader's Response Symbols to react to what you read.

Reader's Response Symbols

✓ OK. I understand this. It's very clearly explained.

? I don't follow what the writer is saying here.

+ I think the writer needs more details here.

– This information doesn't seem relevant.

! Wow! That is cool/weird/interesting.

Learn From Experience

Read the numbered notes in the margins as you reread the Student Model to learn how the writer presented ideas.

Answer the *Try It!* questions online or in your notebook.

---

① The writer uses **proper formatting** for his paper. Note the heads and pagination.

② The **parenthetical citation** reveals the writer's source of information. It refers to a source on the Works Cited list at the end of the report.

③ The **thesis statement** clearly states the writer's main idea or reason for the research and how it will be supported by evidence.

Try It! In the thesis statement, the writer uses the adjectives *fascinating* and *great*. How do these adjectives reveal his point of view?

---

① Gutierrez 1

① Jorge Gutierrez
Ms. L. Applegate
American History
21 February 2010

① The Building of the Great Brooklyn Bridge

To get to Manhattan from Brooklyn, everyone has to cross the East River. Today there are subways, a tunnel, and several bridges, but until 1883 there were only boats. There was talk of a bridge in 1800, but nothing happened until John A. Roebling, a German-
5 born engineer, bridge builder, and manufacturer of wire cable, submitted a detailed plan for a bridge over the East River. Roebling had already built three suspension bridges in Niagara, Pittsburgh, and Cincinnati. In 1867, the New York State Legislature approved his proposal and appointed him chief engineer for the Brooklyn
10 Suspension Bridge **②** (Johnson and Leon 44). **③** Historical data will be used to show the fascinating story of how the great Brooklyn

Figure 1. The Brooklyn Bridge; photo courtesy of Library of Congress.

Gutierrez 2

Bridge was built despite many obstacles and why the bridge is a monument to architectural advancement.

The Brooklyn Bridge has been called the Eighth Wonder of the World (Burns). It is 1.13 miles long, and its two stone towers (in 1883 the tallest buildings in America) rise 276½ feet above the river (Johnson 45). Fourteen thousand miles of galvanized steel wire bound into four huge cables support the bridge ("Sunshine and Shadow") reinforced by cables strung diagonally (see figure 1). The bridge took 14 years to build and cost 15.1 million dollars, more than twice its budget (Johnson and Leon 50).

In 1964, it was named a National Historic Landmark because it was one of "the world's first wire cable suspension bridges" and "established a number of engineering precedents in bridge-building" (National). When it opened in May 1853, it was the world's largest suspension bridge and the first bridge made from steel cables. It had other "firsts" too: a pedestrian walkway and tracks for special trains. Roebling designed it to be "six times as strong as it need be" (McCullough 28, 33).

John A. Roebling died in July 1869, before construction began. His foot was crushed by a ferry when he was searching for a site for the bridge. His toes were amputated, but he survived. He would die of lockjaw 16 days later. His son, Colonel Washington Roebling, who had built bridges for the Union Army, took over as chief engineer.

Construction began with the two great towers. For each tower, a huge wooden box called a caisson (pronounced key-suhn) was gradually sunk to the bottom of the river. The air inside the caissons was pressurized so workers could breathe as they dug the river's bottom and the muck was dredged to the surface. Great stones piled on top gradually sank the caissons—to bedrock on the Brooklyn side, 44½ feet below the surface; and to the river bottom (78½ feet) on the New York side (McCullough 520). Filled with concrete, each sunken caisson became the foundation of a tower (see figure 2 on page 228).

The workers were mostly German and Irish immigrants, doing

STUDENT MODEL
Informational Research Report (continued)

Gutierrez 3

6 The writer has inserted a **graphic**, a diagram he created based on information from multiple sources. It helps explain the difficult and complicated work of building the two towers.

Try It! In your own words, explain what the diagram shows. What additional information does it provide that text cannot?

7 In this paragraph, the **topic sentence** reveals the writer's **point of view**. Which three words suggest his **point of view**?

Try It! What type of information does the writer include to support the paragraph's topic sentence?

8 Notice the **formatting style** for indenting and setting off a direct quotation that is four lines or longer.

9 The concluding paragraph restates the writer's **point of view** and adds a final thought about the greatness of the Brooklyn Bridge.

10 The Works Cited list provides proper **documentation** by listing publication information for each source used to write the report. The **formatting** of the list follows the MLA style manual.

Try It! Study the Works Cited list on page 229. Why is it helpful to readers to list sources in alphabetical order? Why might readers want to know what types of resources—print, Web, and so on—were used?

Extension Locate one of the sources from the Works Cited page, and write a brief synopsis of it in your own words.

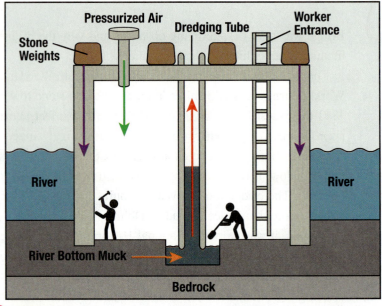

6 Figure 2. Diagram of a cassion, based on information from McCullough (520); *Harper's Weekly*, v.14, 17 Dec. 1870, p. 812, print; courtesy Library of Congress.

dangerous work for $2.00 a day. Twenty to thirty died building the bridge (Feuerstein). At least three died of caisson disease, or the bends, caused by nitrogen bubbles in the bloodstream. Workers
50   in the pressurized caissons had to decompress (get their bodies used to air pressure above ground) slowly in a series of airlock rooms. Even the leader, Washington Roebling, was paralyzed by caisson disease in 1872. From then on, he supervised construction by telescope from his bedroom window. His wife Emily delivered
55   instructions to his assistants.

   The bridge was plagued with other disasters. In 1870, a caisson fire caused great damage (Johnson and Leon 46). McCullough reports that a week after the bridge opened a woman screamed, the crowd panicked, and 12 people died in a stampede (500). To dispel
60   the rumor that the bridge wasn't strong enough for the weight of its traffic, P. T. Barnum led a parade of 21 elephants across the bridge. **7** The beauty and genius of the Brooklyn Bridge have been celebrated in poems, songs, paintings, photographs, and movies.

Gutierrez 4

Before writing his own book about the Brooklyn Bridge, the historian David McCullough was the narrator of a film about the bridge. In the film, McCullough likens the bridge to the Grand Canyon, "all the more exciting because it's manmade" (Burns). To Brooklyn artist Peter Ketchum, the bridge has special meaning:

> At least once a month to clear my soul, I amble across the bridge, feeling suspended in time and space: carefree and a very tiny speck in the universe when measured against the span of the bridge, the vastness of the East River and the sky scraping buildings on both sides. (Ketchum)

In his preface, McCullough says that the "Great Bridge," as he calls it, is "a reminder of what noble work we are capable of. It was superbly built. It was built to last, and so it does, along with its extraordinary story" (11). To all those who know it well, the Brooklyn Bridge is truly a work of genius and a beautiful manmade wonder.

Works Cited

Burns, Kenneth Lauren, dir. *America: Brooklyn Bridge*. PBS. WNET/Thirteen, New York, 24 May 1982. Television.

Feuerstein, Gary. "Brooklyn Bridge: Facts, History, and Information." *Brooklyn Bridge Website*. N.p., 19 May 1998. Web. 4 Feb. 2010.

Johnson, Stephen, and Roberto T. Leon. *Encyclopedia of Bridges and Tunnels*. New York: Checkmark Books, 2002. Print.

Ketchum, Peter. Message to the author. 7 Feb. 2010. E-mail.

McCullough, David. *The Great Bridge: The Epic Story of the Building of the Brooklyn Bridge*. New York: Simon & Schuster, 1972, 2001. Print.

National Historic Landmarks Program. "Brooklyn Bridge" *National Parks Service*. U.S. Dept. of Interior, n.d. Web. 4 Feb. 2010.

"Sunshine and Shadow." *American Experience: New York: A Documentary Film*. Writ. Ric Burns and James Sanders. Dir. Ric Burns. PBS Home Video, 2003. DVD.

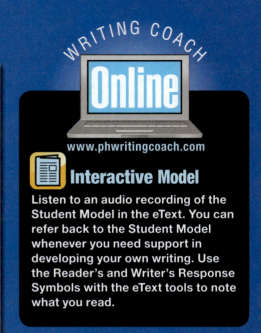

Interactive Model

Listen to an audio recording of the Student Model in the eText. You can refer back to the Student Model whenever you need support in developing your own writing. Use the Reader's and Writer's Response Symbols with the eText tools to note what you read.

Use a Writer's Eye

Now go back to the beginning of the Student Model and evaluate the piece as a writer. On your copy of the Student Model, use the Writer's Response Symbols to react to what you read. Identify places where the student writer uses characteristics of an effective informational research report.

Writer's Response Symbols

T.S.	Clear thesis statement
S.E.	Supporting evidence
R.G.	Relevant graphic
D.S.	Proper documentation of sources

Your Turn — Feature Assignment: Informational Research Report

Prewriting

Begin to plan a first draft of your research report by determining an appropriate topic. You can select from the Topic Bank or come up with an idea of your own. Choose a topic that is **complex and multi-faceted.**

 Choose From the Topic Bank

TOPIC BANK

A Natural Tourist Spot Discuss a unique natural occurrence that attracts ecotourism to a region, such as the Great Barrier Reef, the Galapagos Islands, or the Florida Everglades. What is the special ecology or geology of the area? Why do people visit the region?

Innovation: How It Changes History Explain the contributions and impact of a significant scientist or inventor. For example, how has the work of Thomas Edison impacted society? Where would medicine be today without the work of Marie Curie?

Media Is Everywhere Explore the influence of media in different parts of the world. What kinds of media are widely available? What role does media play in day-to-day life?

 Choose Your Own Topic

Determine an appropriate topic of your own by using the following **range of strategies** to generate ideas.

Brainstorm and Browse

- **Consult** with a partner to **brainstorm** for a list of topics that interest you. **Decide upon a topic,** and **formulate open-ended research questions** about your topic. Circle key words in your questions.
- Use your key words and phrases to browse your library's research resources. Note what sparks your curiosity and may make a good research topic.
- Search the Internet, using the same key words and phrases. Work with your partner to decide which aspect of the topic provides results that interest you the most.
- Review your work and choose a topic.

Formulate Your Research Question

A broad, general topic is almost impossible to research well and cover thoroughly. Plan to do some preliminary research in order to narrow your topic and then formulate your research question.

Apply It! Use a printed or online graphic organizer like the one shown to narrow your topic.

- Write your general topic in the top box, and keep narrowing your topic with research questions as you move down the chart.
- Your last box should hold your narrowest or "smallest" research question. This will be the focus of your informational research report.

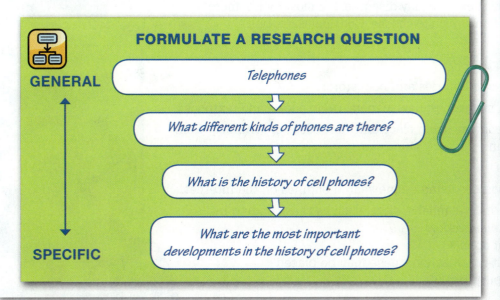

Consider Multiple Audiences and Purposes

Before researching for your informational research report, think about your audiences and purposes. **Consider the views of others** as you ask yourself these questions.

Questions About Audiences	Questions About Purposes
• Who are my audiences: My teacher? My classmates? Someone else? • What do my audiences already know about my topic? What will interest my audiences? • What technical terms will I need to explain to my audiences?	• What is my point of view, or attitude, toward my topic? • What is my purpose: To inform? To astonish? To arouse curiosity? Something else? • How do I want my audiences to respond to my report?

Record your answers in your writing journal.

www.phwritingcoach.com

Interactive Writing Coach™

- Choosing from the Topic Bank gives you access to the Interactive Writing Coach™.
- Submit your writing paragraph by paragraph and receive detailed feedback and guidance as you draft, revise, and edit your writing.

Interactive Graphic Organizers

Use the interactive graphic organizers to help you narrow your topic.

Online Journal

Record your answers and ideas in the online journal.

Make a Research Plan

Once you have written your major research question, you are ready to make a research plan. As part of your plan, you will create a timeline for finishing your report. You also will find and evaluate sources of information.

Find Authoritative, Objective Sources As you **compile data** and search for information, determine the full range of relevant resources which address your question. Locate and explore sources that are **authoritative**—written or edited by experts on your topic. Your sources should also be **objective** and unbiased, or fair. The best sources will be up-to-date and complete, **identifying major issues and debates** relevant to your topic, including points about which experts may disagree. For most topics, there are a variety of resources from which to choose. Consider these tips:

Print Resources
- Find print resources in libraries and bookstores.
- Use encyclopedias, magazines, newspapers, trade books, and textbooks.
- Search for print resources using electronic databases or with help from a reference librarian.

Electronic Resources
- Find electronic resources using online search engines on the Internet.
- Choose only authoritative, reliable sites, such as those ending in:
    - .edu (educational institution)
    - .gov (government agency)
    - .org (not-for-profit organization; these may be biased toward specific purposes)
- If you are not sure that a site is reliable and unbiased, do not use it.

Interviews With Experts
- Ask questions of an expert on your topic.
- Set up a short in-person, e-mail, or telephone interview.
- Record the interview and take good notes.

Multimedia Resources
- Watch movies about your topic.
- Listen to podcasts or seminars related to the topic.
- Search for relevant photos, diagrams, charts, and graphs.

Evaluate Your Sources Do not assume that all sources of information on your topic are useful, good, or trustworthy. Use the checklist on page 233 to evaluate sources of information you find. The more questions that you can answer with a yes, the more likely you should use the source.

Checklist for Evaluating Sources

Does the source of information:

☐ Contain **relevant** information that answers your research question?
☐ Provide **facts** and not just **subjective opinions** unsupported by facts?
☐ Give **valid** facts and details that you can understand?
☐ Tell all sides of a story, including opposing viewpoints, so that it is **objective** and **unbiased**?
☐ Provide **authoritative, reliable, accurate,** and **valid** information written or compiled by experts?
☐ Have a recent **publication date,** indicating it is up-to-date?

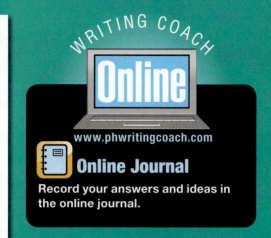

Online Journal
Record your answers and ideas in the online journal.

Distinguish Between Types of Sources As you research, you will discover two kinds of sources: primary sources and secondary sources. Your teacher may require that you use both kinds of sources in your report.

- A **primary source** is an original text or **text itself** without any interpretation by another person. For example, the U.S. Constitution and a letter from Abigail Adams to her husband John are primary texts.

- A **secondary source** comments on or interprets a primary source. Textbooks, encyclopedia articles, newspaper and magazine articles, books about history and science are all secondary sources. If you find conflicting information in secondary sources (for example, accounts of a Civil War battle), try to find a primary source (such as an eyewitness report or letter). Remember that a secondary source gives the writer's interpretation of a primary source or an event.

Apply It! Devise a **research plan** and timeline for finishing your informational report, and list at least four sources of information that you plan to use.

- Work with your teacher to determine the dates by which you need to finish your research, thesis statement, draft, and your final report.
- Make sure your topic is complex and multi-faceted. As you compile data from authoritative sources be sure to examine any **major issues** or **debates.**
- Organize and synthesize the data from all your sources and create needed **charts, graphs, or forms** to best share main ideas.
- For each source you plan to use, give full publication information.
- Show that you have evaluated whether each source is authoritative and objective by using the Checklist for Evaluating Sources.

Modify Your Plan At every stage of research writing, **critique** your research **plan** and be prepared to **modify,** or change, your research question. For instance, you may not find enough sources, or you may find too much information. If so, **refocus,** or change the emphasis of, your topic.

Prewriting 233

Collect and Organize Your Data

For your informational research report, you will need to use **multiple sources** of information. Notes will help you remember and keep track of your sources and information. Different forms of systematic note-taking include handwritten notes on note cards, typed notes in an electronic document, and a learning log summarizing what you know and still need to know about your topic.

Keep Track of Multiple Sources You can create a card for each source and give each its own number. Write the full publishing information (author, title, city of publication, publisher, copyright date). The example shown is from the Student Model. It matches MLA style used in the Works Cited on page 229.

Take Notes When you take notes from a source, follow these guidelines.

- Write only **relevant** facts and details that directly relate to your research question.
- Group notes under a **heading** that sums up a main idea. These headings will help you organize information and access it later.
- Use your own words to **paraphrase** and **summarize** the author's ideas.
- If you find a quotation you might want to use, copy it carefully. Enclose the exact words in very large quotation marks so you'll remember that it is a direct quotation.

Source 1

McCullough, David. <u>The Great Bridge.</u> New York: Simon & Schuster, 1972, 2001. Print.

Notes From Source 3

<u>Brooklyn Bridge—National Historic Landmark</u>
(Web site run by National Park Service)

- Named Jan. 29, 1964
- One of first suspension bridges in world using wire cable
- "Established a number of engineering precedents in bridge-building"

Apply It! Take notes on information that is relevant to your research and topic. Effectively **organize the information** from different sources on note cards. **Paraphrase and summarize** the researched information in your own words. If you want to quote, copy the original **quotation,** using quotation marks. Be sure to **accurately cite sources** using a standard format, such as MLA style.

Avoid Plagiarism

Plagiarism is using someone else's words or ideas without acknowledging the source of the information. Plagiarism is a serious error that has severe consequences. Do not plagiarize. Teachers know when a paper you turn in isn't yours. They know your "voice."

Careful Note-taking Matters Sometimes, plagiarism occurs unintentionally because students do not take good notes. For example, this note card follows the wording in the original source too closely and does not include a full citation.

Online Journal
Record your answers and ideas in the online journal.

As a result, caisson workers died horrible, painful deaths when they failed to decompress properly to allow the safe dissipation of the nitrogen bubbles pushed into their tissues. At least 20 men died during construction of the bridge, but only a handful fell victim to caisson disease as nitrogen bubbles expanded uncontrollably inside their bodies.

Original Source

Notes From Source 2
Caisson workers
Men died painful, horrible deaths if they didn't decompress correctly—allow safe dissipation of nitrogen bubbles.

At least 20 men died while bridge was being built; only a handful were victims of caisson disease = nitrogen bubbles expanded inside their bodies.

p. 46, Encyclopedia

Plagiarized Notes

Review taking notes with a partner. Explain why each of these is essential:
- A source card for each source
- A source card number on each note card
- Your own words to paraphrase or summarize ideas
- Large quotation marks for direct quotations

Use these strategies to avoid plagiarism.
- **Be Brief** Use phrases, abbreviations, and symbols in your notes. Don't write whole sentences.
- **Paraphrase** Restate an idea in your own words. Think about what you've read, and write it as you might explain it to another person.
- **Summarize** In your own words, sum up an important passage. Your summary should be shorter than the original passage.
- **Direct Quotations** Identify the source and enclose exact words in quotation marks. (See page 247.)

Try It! Look at the Notes From Source 2 in the example. Highlight the parts that are plagiarizing the original source. Then, take your own notes based on the orginal source. Be sure to avoid plagiarizing the content.

Prewriting 235

Document Your Sources

In your report, you must accurately **cite** all **researched information according to a standard format.** In other words, you have to use a standard style to indicate where you found your information. The only exception to this requirement is facts that are common knowledge, such as the fact that the Brooklyn Bridge connects Manhattan and Brooklyn.

Works Cited The Works Cited page at the end of your report is an alphabetical list of all the sources you actually used to write your report. Your teacher will require you to follow a standard format shown in a style manual, such as that of the Modern Language Association (MLA) or American Psychological Association (APA). Your teacher will tell you which standard format style to use.

Look at the example citations shown. Use these and the MLA Style for Listing Sources on page R16 as a guide for writing your citations. Pay attention to formatting including, italics, abbreviations, and punctuation.

Book

Author's last name, author's first name followed by the author's middle name or initial (if given). *Full title of book.* City where book was published: Name of publisher, date of publication. Medium of publication.

McCullough, David. *The Great Bridge.* New York: Simon & Schuster, 1972, 2001. Print.

Magazine Article

Author's last name, author's first name followed by the author's middle name or initial (if given). "Title of article." *Title of magazine.* Date of magazine issue: page(s) article appears on; use a plus (+) after first page number if pages are not consecutive. Medium of publication.

Birdsall, Blair. "The Brooklyn Bridge at 100." *Technology Review.* April 1983: 60. Print.

Web Page

Author's last name, author's first name followed by author's middle name or initial OR name of editor or compiler (if given). "Name of page." *Name of site.* Publisher or N.p. if not known, date page was posted or n.d. if not known. Medium of publication. Date on which you accessed the page.

Feuerstein, Gary. "Brooklyn Bridge: Facts, History, and Information." *Brooklyn Bridge Web site.* N.p., 19 May 1998. Web. 4 Dec. 2010.

Parenthetical Citations A parenthetical citation is a quick reference to a source listed on the Works Cited page. These citations give the author's last name or a book or article title and the page number on which the information is located. Look at the Student Model.

> **STUDENT MODEL** from **"The Building of the Great Brooklyn Bridge"** page 226, lines 8–10
>
> In 1867, the New York State Legislature approved his proposal and appointed him chief engineer for the Brooklyn Suspension Bridge (Johnson and Leon 44).

If the author or source is mentioned in the sentence, only the page number is given in parentheses.

> McCullough reports that a week after the bridge opened a woman screamed, the crowd panicked, and 12 people died in a stampede (500).

If no author's name is given, use only the first words of the title.

> More than 5,000 workers built the bridge ("Sunshine and Shadow").

Try It! Use MLA style to create a short Works Cited page based on the sources described.

- A book by David J. Brown titled *Bridges: Three Thousand Years of Defying Nature*. It was published in 2005 by Firefly Books in New York.
- An article on p. 46 of the June 30, 2003 issue of *U.S. News & World Report* titled "High and Mighty (Brooklyn Bridge)." No author is given.
- A Web page "Roebling and the Brooklyn Bridge" from the Library of Congress American Memory project. The page was accessed Dec. 26, 2009. No date or publisher was given.

Critique Your Research Process

At every step in the research process, be prepared to modify or change your research plan. If you can't find enough information to write your thesis statement, try rewording your research question. Don't get bogged down in the research step. Stick to your timeline. You're ready to wrap up the prewriting part of your research paper and start drafting your paper.

Apply It! Write an entry on your Works Cited for every source you have consulted for your informational research report. To format and document your entries accurately, use MLA style or the style your teacher requires. After confirming that you have researched enough information to begin writing your draft, write a clear thesis statement for your research report in your writing journal.

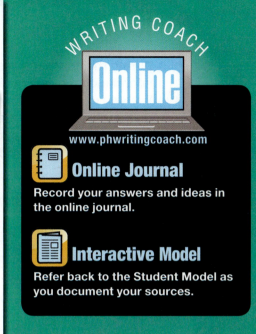

WRITING COACH Online
www.phwritingcoach.com

Online Journal
Record your answers and ideas in the online journal.

Interactive Model
Refer back to the Student Model as you document your sources.

Partner Talk
Participate in an extended discussion with a partner. Discuss research sources. Express your opinions and ideas. Where have you looked for information on your topic? What sources do you like? What hasn't been reliable? How have you been keeping track of them?

Drafting

During the drafting stage, you will start to write your ideas for your informational research report. You will write a **clear thesis statement**. You will follow an outline that provides an **organizational strategy** that will help you write a **focused, organized, and coherent** research report. As you write your draft or prepare your notes for an oral presentation, remember to keep your audience in mind.

The Organization of an Informational Research Report

The chart shows an organizational strategy for a research report. Look back at how the Student Model follows this same strategy. Then, create a detailed outline for your informational research report. Use the outline template shown on page R26 to develop your outline. Also refer to the Outline for Success as you work.

I. Introduction
See Student Model, p. 226.

- Attention-grabbing introduction
- Clear thesis statement

Introduce Your Thesis Statement
- A **clear thesis statement** is often the last sentence in the introduction and answers the research question.
- A story, question, quotation, or intriguing fact will grab the reader's attention.

II. Body
See Student Model, pp. 227-229.

- Synthesis of facts and ideas from multiple sources
- Logical progression of ideas
- Evidence to support the thesis statement
- Graphics and illustrations to explain concepts

Support Your Thesis Statement
- This is where the writer **synthesizes** information from your various notes.
- The headings on your notes help you to group similar ideas and arrange them in a logical order.
- Each paragraph states a major idea and supports it with evidence, such as facts, statistics, examples, and quotations.
- Photos, charts, diagrams, or other visuals help convey complicated information.

III. Conclusion
See Student Model, p. 229.

- Summary of findings and final conclusions
- Definite ending that adds a final thought or conclusion

Add a Final Thought
- A conclusion pulls all the details together, reminding readers of the importance of the thesis.
- The final paragraph reveals or restates the writer's point of view about the topic.
- The reader may be asked to do something as a follow-up to the report.

Start Your Draft

Use the checklist below to help complete your draft. Use your specific thesis statement; your detailed outline that lists your supporting evidence, logical progression of ideas, graphics, and illustrations; and the Outline for Success as guides.

While drafting, aim at writing your ideas, not on making your writing perfect. Remember, you will have the chance to improve your draft when you revise and edit.

- √ Start your **introduction** with attention-getting sentences.
- √ End this part of your draft with a clearly worded **thesis statement** based on your research question. Your thesis should be the roadmap for your report.

- √ Draft the **body** one paragraph at a time. Organize and present your ideas to suit the purpose of your research and the needs of your specific audience. For each paragraph, draft a topic sentence that states the paragraph's **main idea.**
- √ Choose the strongest **supporting evidence** (facts, quotations, examples) for each main idea.
- √ Each paragraph should use marshalled evidence—information you have collected and organized—to support the thesis statement and any other related claims your report is making.
- √ Provide an **analysis of the evidence** that builds on your ideas in a logical progression and states a clear point of view.

- √ Draft a **conclusion** that sums up, restates, and adds a final thought.

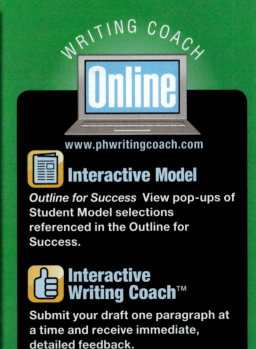

WRITING COACH Online
www.phwritingcoach.com

Interactive Model
Outline for Success View pop-ups of Student Model selections referenced in the Outline for Success.

Interactive Writing Coach™
Submit your draft one paragraph at a time and receive immediate, detailed feedback.

Provide and Document Evidence

While you are drafting, you will provide **evidence** to support your thesis and related claims. Your claims are an important part of your analysis of your topic. They are your opinions or understanding of information connected to your thesis, stated from your **point of view**. Be careful to differentiate between your opinions and those of other people. **Document** the words and ideas of other people when you provide evidence.

Give Facts and Statistics A **fact** is a statement that can be proven true. **Statistics** are facts stated in numbers. Facts and statistics are convincing when they come from authoritative and up-to-date sources. Document facts and statistics that are not common knowledge or that could not be found in most sources about a topic.

Give Examples An example makes an abstract or complicated idea easier to understand. You do not need to document examples from your own experiences or observations. You do, however, need to document examples from other sources as shown in the excerpt from the Student Model.

STUDENT MODEL from **"The Building of the Great Brooklyn Bridge"** page 227, lines 20–21

The bridge took 14 years to build and cost 15.1 million dollars, more than twice its budget (Johnson and Leon 50).

Quote Authorities A **direct quotation** from an expert not only provides convincing evidence, but also adds interest and variety to an informational research report. Make sure the quotation fits smoothly into your paragraph and use your own words to identify the speaker.

- Only quote if you must use an expert's exact words.
- Don't quote if paraphrasing is just as clear.
- Separate and inset a quote of four lines or more.
- Always indicate who said or wrote the quotation and explain why that person is an expert.
- Be sure to punctuate quotations correctly. (See page 247.)
- Follow quotations with a proper parenthetical citation.

Try It! Use the Notes From Source 5 to write a paragraph that supports this thesis: *John A. Roebling's Brooklyn Bridge is a work of genius built to last.* Your paragraph should include facts, examples, a quotation, and a citation.

Notes From Source 5

- Many designers thought the suspension bridge was the only way to span distances required for crossings such as New York's East River.
- Roebling drew his conservative plans for the Brooklyn Bridge with a record span of 1,600 feet.
- Designers without Roebling's intuitive sense for stability were increasing span lengths.
- Many suspension bridges in the United Kingdom and the United States had been destroyed by wind.
- Roebling recognized the value of a single cable mass, while others called for large cables composed of several small ones laid side by side. Roebling's cables were a single, compact bundle. —from "The Brooklyn Bridge at 100" by Blair Birdsall

Use Graphics and Illustrations

Now is the time to decide how you can use graphics as well as words. While you are preparing your draft, think about how you can create graphics such as diagrams and charts to help your audience understand the analysis, ideas, and related claims in your report. Remember to label your visuals with a figure or table number, caption, and source citations for the data. Use caution when copying an existing graphic because you will need permission from the copyright holder if you publish your work for use outside school.

- **Photographs** Photographs help your audience visualize your topic. Be sure to acknowledge the source and write a caption, or brief explanation of what each photo shows.
- **Charts, Graphs, and Tables** Create a chart, table, or graph to provide information in a more visual or organized way. Give each a title that tells what it shows. If you include more than one, number them in chronological order. Include a complete citation for the source of information you used to create the chart, table, or graph. Put it below after the word *Source* and a colon.

Table 1. Children Who Speak a Language Other Than English at Home by Region: 2007
[In thousands (10,918 represents 10,918,000), except percent. For children 5 to 17 years old.]

Characteristic	U.S.	Northeast	Midwest	South	West
Children who speak another language at home	10,918	1,853	1,339	3,443	4,28
Percent of children 5 to 17 years old	20.5	20.3	11.4	17.6	33.6
Speak Spanish	7,872	1,005	804	2,735	3,328

Table 1. Source: U.S. Census Bureau, 2007 American Community Survey; Table B16003 "Age by Language at Home for the Population 5 Years and Over" using American Factfinder; (accessed 28 December 2009).

- **Diagrams** A diagram efficiently explains a process or shows the parts of an object and their functions.
- **Maps** If you are writing about a specific place, a map will be helpful to your reader. You may draw a map yourself (such as a map of your neighborhood) or find one online. Add a legend and a compass to your map, as well as labels, a caption, source, and a figure number.

Apply It! Think of two graphics that would improve your informational research report. What would each graphic explain? How would you search for these graphics? Find or create both graphics, and insert them in your report. Remember to write titles or captions as needed. Use a style manual to format graphics and to **document and acknowledge sources**. Use **peer, teacher, or family feedback** to check that the quality of your created and researched visuals is appropriate for your report.

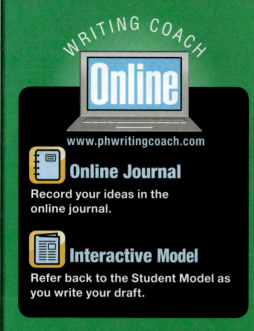

Online Journal
Record your ideas in the online journal.

Interactive Model
Refer back to the Student Model as you write your draft.

Think of two graphics that you plan to include in your report. With a partner, evaluate each graphic's usefulness and the reliability, validity, and accuracy of the source.

Revising: Making It Better

Now that you have finished your draft, you are ready to revise. Think about the "big picture" of **audience, purpose, and genre**. You can use the Revision RADaR strategy as a guide for making changes to improve your draft. Revision RADaR provides four major ways to improve your writing: (R) replace, (A) add, (D) delete, and (R) reorder.

Kelly Gallagher, M. Ed.

KEEP REVISION ON YOUR RADaR

Read part of the first draft of the Student Model "The Building of the Great Brooklyn Bridge." Then, look at questions the writer asked himself as he thought about how well his draft addressed issues of audience, purpose, and genre.

from The Building of the Great Brooklyn Bridge

…This report explores the fascinating story of the building of the Brooklyn Bridge.

Fourteen thousand miles of wire support the bridge (New York), reinforced by cables strung diagonally. The Brooklyn Bridge has been called the Eighth Wonder of the World. There were Seven Wonders of the Ancient World, which included the Egyptian pyramids and the hanging gardens of Babylon. The Brooklyn Bridge is 1.13 miles long and has two stone towers. The bridge took 14 years to build and cost 15.1 million dollars, more than twice its budget.

In 1964, it was named a National Historic Landmark because it was one of the world's first wire cable suspension bridges and established a number of engineering precedents in bridge-building. When it opened, it was the world's largest suspension bridge and the first bridge made from steel cables. It had other "firsts" too: a pedestrian walkway and tracks for special trains. Roebling designed it to be "six times as strong as it need be."

*Is there enough **evidence** to support my **thesis statement**? Have I presented my ideas **clearly** and in a **logical order**? Is all of the information **relevant** to my thesis statement?*

*Have I explained why the Brooklyn Bridge is so special? Do I need to add more facts or **define terms**?*

*Have I **documented** my sources according to a style manual?*

Now, look at how the writer applied Revision RADaR to write an improved second draft.

from The Building of the Great Brooklyn Bridge
2ND DRAFT

... Historical data will be used to show the fascinating story of how the great Brooklyn Bridge was built despite many obstacles and why the bridge is a monument of architectural achievement.

The Brooklyn Bridge has been called the Eighth Wonder of the World (Burns). It is 1.13 miles long, and its two stone towers (in 1883 the tallest buildings in America) rise 276½ feet above the river (Johnson 45). Fourteen thousand miles of galvanized steel wire bound into four huge cables support the bridge ("Sunshine and Shadow"), reinforced by cables strung diagonally (see figure 1). The bridge took 14 years to build and cost 15.1 million dollars, more than twice its budget (Johnson and Leon 50).

In 1964, it was named a National Historic Landmark because it was one of "the world's first wire cable suspension bridges" and "established a number of engineering precedents in bridge-building" (National). When it opened in May 1853, it was the world's largest suspension bridge and the first bridge made from steel cables. It had other "firsts" too: a pedestrian walkway and tracks for special trains. Roebling designed it to be "six times as strong as it need be" (McCullough 28, 33).

R *Reordered sentences in a logical order, placing topic sentence at the beginning of the paragraph*
D *Deleted sentence about the seven Wonders of the Ancient World—not relevant to this report*

R *Replaced vague, general term wire with specific, accurate term galvanized steel.*

A *Added more facts and details about the bridge and Figure 1, a photograph of the bridge*

A *Added quotation marks and parenthetical citation for direct quotation and proper documentation of sources throughout the report*

www.phwritingcoach.com

Video
Learn more strategies for effective writing from program author Kelly Gallagher.

Interactive Writing Coach™
Use the Revision RADaR strategy in your own writing. Then, submit your draft paragraph by paragraph for feedback.

 Apply It! Use your Revision RADaR to revise your draft.

- First, make sure you have addressed the needs of your audience and explained your ideas clearly to meet your purpose. Check that you have included all the characteristics of an informational research report.
- Then, apply Revision RADaR to make needed changes. Remember, you can use the steps in the strategy in any order.

Revising 243

Look at the Big Picture

Use the chart and your analytical skills to evaluate how well each section of your informational research report addresses **purpose, audience, and genre.** When necessary, use the suggestions in the chart to revise your piece.

Section	Evaluate	Revise
Introduction	• Does the **opening paragraph** grab your reader's attention? It should make the reader want to find out more about your research question.	• Begin with a quotation, question, comparison, or anecdote to build interest and make clear your point of view
	• Have you written a **clear thesis statement** that indicates the major ideas in your report?	• Clarify your thesis statement to be sure it answers your research question and identifies the key points of your report.
Body	• Does each body paragraph clearly develop one **major idea?**	• Add a topic sentence to each paragraph. Use marshalled evidence to support the thesis and any related claims.
	• Check that you use **graphics and illustrations** to help explain complex ideas.	• Review the research and look for data that can best be shared visually. Then, correctly format it for the report.
	• Are the information and your analysis **logically organized and presented,** and do they progress in a way that the audience can understand? Have you addressed your **audiences** and **purposes**?	• Reorder sentences and paragraphs as needed for a logical progression of ideas and information. Add transitions—as words, phrases, or even sentences or paragraphs—to guide your audience through your analysis.
	• Are all quotations and facts that are not common knowledge **cited, documented,** and **formatted** according to a style manual?	• Review your note and source cards to confirm the source of each quotation and add a parenthetical citation, following the standard format specified in a style manual. Set off extended quotes.
Conclusion	• Does your concluding paragraph reveal or restate your **point of view** about your topic?	• Add a statement of what you learned and how you feel about what you learned.
	• Does your research report end in an interesting way and leave the reader with a **final thought**?	• Add a quotation or an anecdote that brings your report to a definite end and helps your reader understand your purpose.
Works Cited/ Bibliography	• Does your list of **documented sources** follow the format and style shown in a style manual?	• Use a style manual to properly document all sources you used in your paper on the Works Cited page or bibliography.

Focus on Craft: Varying Sentences

English sentences are very flexible. They can be short or long, they can start off in different ways, and they can vary in structure—simple, compound, complex, or compound-complex. If all of the sentences in your report have the same length, beginning, and structure, your readers may lose interest in your report. Make a conscious effort to vary the **length, beginning,** and **sentence structure** of sentences within each paragraph.

Think about sentence variety as you read these sentences from the Student Model. How would this paragraph sound if all the sentences were alike?

from **"The Building of the Great Brooklyn Bridge"**
page 228; lines 56–61

> The bridge was plagued with other disasters. In 1870, a caisson fire caused great damage (Johnson and Leon 46). McCullough reports that a week after the bridge opened a woman screamed, the crowd panicked, and 12 people died in a stampede (500). To dispel the rumor that the bridge wasn't strong enough for the weight of its traffic, P. T. Barnum led a parade of 21 elephants across the bridge.

 Try It! Now, analyze each sentence in this paragraph. Ask yourself these questions and record your answers in your journal.

- How many of the sentences are short? How many are long?
- How does each of the four sentences begin? Identify the beginning.
- Analyze the structure of each sentence. What different types of sentence structure has the writer used in this paragraph?

 Fine-Tune Your Draft

Apply It! Use these revision suggestions to prepare your final draft.

- **Improve Sentence Variety** Read each paragraph aloud—one paragraph at a time. The sentences should fit together smoothly. If they sound repetitive, vary the sentence beginnings. Vary structure by combining short sentences into compound or complex sentences.
- **Improve Word Choice** Focus on the key words that communicate essential information related to your topic.

Teacher and Family Feedback Share your draft with your teacher or a family member. Carefully review the comments on your draft, and revise your final draft as needed.

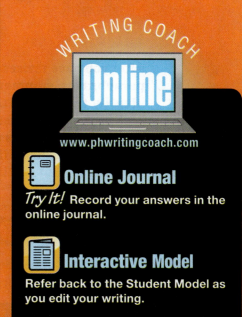

www.phwritingcoach.com

Online Journal
Try It! Record your answers in the online journal.

Interactive Model
Refer back to the Student Model as you edit your writing.

Interactive Writing Coach™
Revise your draft and submit it paragraph by paragraph for feedback.

Editing: Making It Correct

After you have revised your paper, check again to make sure that all **paraphrases, summaries,** and quotations are accurate and that you **identify** their **sources.** Then, edit your draft using a **style manual,** such as the one published by the **Modern Language Association,** to **document sources** and to **format the materials,** including quotations. Finally, edit your final draft for errors in **grammar, mechanics, and spelling.**

WRITE GUY *Jeff Anderson, M. Ed.*

WHAT DO YOU NOTICE?

Zoom in on Conventions Focus on quotations as you zoom in on these lines from the Student Model.

> **STUDENT MODEL** from **"The Building of the Great Brooklyn Bridge"**
> page 229; lines 64–67
>
> Before writing his own book about the Brooklyn Bridge, the historian David McCullough was the narrator of a film about the bridge. In the film, McCullough likens the bridge to the Grand Canyon, "all the more exciting because it's manmade" (Burns).

To learn more about integrating quotations, see Grammar Game Plan Error 18, page 290.

Now, ask yourself this question: *How has the writer made sure you know who spoke the quotation and where he spoke it?*

Perhaps you noted that the writer used these helpful techniques to surround the quote.

- An introductory phrase prepares the reader for a statement about the bridge.
- Parts of the first sentence and the subject of the next sentence—right after the introductory phrase—identify *who* spoke the quoted words.
- The writer uses proper **parenthetical documentation** to identify the source in which he found the words spoken by McCullough.

Partner Talk Discuss this question with a partner: *Why might the writer have both paraphrased McCullough ("likens . . . Canyon") and quoted him in the same sentence? Is the sentence smooth or awkward? Monitor your partner's spoken language by asking follow-up questions to confirm your understanding.*

246 Research Writing

Grammar Mini-Lesson: Punctuation

Punctuating Quotations With Citations Quotations follow specific punctuation rules. Study these sentences from the Student Model. Notice how the writer punctuated the quotation and information about its source in the excerpt from the Student Model.

To learn more, see Chapter 23.

STUDENT MODEL from **"The Building of the Great Brooklyn Bridge"** page 227; lines 28–29

Roebling designed it to be "six times as strong as it need be" (McCullough 28, 33).

Try It! Are these sentences with quotations and source information punctuated correctly? Write your answers in your journal.

1. Crossing the bridge to Manhattan is "like walking onto a stage set." (Kurash)
2. Ken Burns said "To me, the building of the Brooklyn Bridge is still one of the most dramatic stories in all of American history" ("About the Film").

Apply It! Edit your draft for grammar, mechanics, and spelling. Use a style manual to check your formatting and documentation of sources. If necessary, rewrite sentences so that quotations and citations are integrated properly. Also punctuate quotations and identify sources correctly.

Use the rubric to **evaluate your piece and research process**. If necessary, rethink, rewrite, or revise.

www.phwritingcoach.com

 Video
Learn effective editing techniques from program author Jeff Anderson.

 Online Journal
Try It! Record your answers in the online journal.

 Interactive Model
Refer back to the Student Model as you edit your writing.

 Interactive Writing Coach™
Edit your draft and check it against the rubric. Submit it paragraph by paragraph for feedback.

Rubric for Informational Research Report	Rating Scale
Ideas: How clearly have you expressed and developed your thesis statement?	Not very Very 1 2 3 4 5 6
Organization: How logical is the progression of your ideas?	1 2 3 4 5 6
Voice: How clearly have you expressed your point of view?	1 2 3 4 5 6
Word Choice: How well have you used precise language to develop your supporting evidence?	1 2 3 4 5 6
Sentence Fluency: How well have you used sentence variety in your report?	1 2 3 4 5 6
Conventions: How correct is the formatting of sources that you used?	1 2 3 4 5 6

Publishing

The final step in the writing process is **publishing**—sharing your research report with an **audience**. You have worked long and hard to complete your report on time. Now find a way to share what you have learned.

Wrap Up Your Presentation

Your teacher may require a word-processed final report. Follow the guidelines provided—give your report a title, and create a cover sheet, table of contents, and a Works Cited list.

Publish Your Piece

You may be publishing a written report or presenting your report as an oral or **multimedia presentation**.

If your audience is...	...then publish it by...
Students or adults at school	• Displaying your written report in the school library or media center • Presenting your research at an assembly or to another class (for example, a science class or a history class, depending on your topic)
A group or club with a special interest in your topic	• Presenting an oral or multimedia report at a club meeting and answering questions about your research • Posting your report online and inviting comments

 Reflect on Your Writing

Now that you are done with your informational research report, read it over and use your writing journal to answer these questions.

- Which parts of your research report are the strongest? Which parts, if any, do you think still need improvement?
- What are the most important things you learned about doing research?
- What will you do differently the next time you are assigned a research report? Why?

 The Big Question: Why Write? Do you understand a subject well enough to write about it? How did you find out what the facts were?

Manage Your Portfolio You may wish to include your published informational research report in your writing portfolio. If so, consider what this piece reveals about your writing and your growth as a writer.

21st Century Learning

MAKE YOUR WRITING COUNT

Develop an Infomercial

To prepare a research report, you must evaluate information and decide if it is credible. Use your evaluation skills to produce an **infomercial** that informs your classmates about a product or service related to one of your research reports.

An infomercial is an extended TV commercial that promotes a service or product by providing information about how it works. Infomercials show demonstrations and testimonials, or positive comments by people familiar with the product. With your group, produce a **multimedia presentation** with graphics, images, and sound based on an infomercial script. You may present the infomercial live or video-record it.

Here's your action plan.

1. Choose roles, such as writer, image and sound researcher and, if filming, director, actor, and camera operator.

2. Review your research reports to identify interesting services or products you can promote. Select and evaluate one. Is it a good product or service? Will it appeal to a specific audience?

3. View an online infomercial to see how to incorporate demonstrations and testimonials in your script. Locate appropriate visuals, graphics, and sounds.

4. Work together to write a script that will:
   - Identify and promote a product or service using persuasive language that communicates a definite point of view
   - Target a specific audience. Then, provide this group information about the uses and benefits of the product or service
   - Use script formatting to indicate speaking
   - Include notes about stage directions, visuals, and sound

5. Rehearse your presentation. Then, record and assemble your video, if you wish to present one.

Listening and Speaking Hold a group discussion about how to present your script or video to the class. Then, practice your presentation, tying in graphics, music, and other sounds. Listeners should provide feedback, and presenters should adjust their delivery to best influence and persuade the audience. During your presentation, work as a team to promote your product or service, provide information, and engage your audience.

WRITING COACH Online
www.phwritingcoach.com

Online Journal
Reflect on Your Writing Record your answers and ideas in the online journal.

Resource
Link to resources on 21st Century Learning for help in creating a group project.

Your Turn — Writing for Media: Script for an Interview

Script for an Interview

Suppose you could interview an eyewitness to an event or a situation you wrote about in your informational research report. What questions would you ask? In this assignment, you will write a radio or TV **script for a fictional interview** with a person who witnessed or was involved in some aspect of your research topic. You'll write the questions as well as the answers for your fictional interview. If you need more information to write your script, create a research plan and gather information from multiple sources. With a partner, read your script aloud to your classmates.

Try It! Study the excerpt from the interview shown on this page. Then, answer the questions. Write your answers in your journal.

1. What is the **theme** or message of this interview?
2. What would you say is the **tone** of Mr. Sheehan's replies? What details reveal that attitude?
3. Some interviewers may be **objective** and avoid showing a personal opinion. Others are **subjective**, presenting their biases and feelings. How can you tell? Do you think Jorge, the interviewer, is objective or subjective? How can you tell? Are Sheehan's replies objective or subjective? Explain.
4. If you were writing **stage directions** for the script, how would you identify each speaker's tone of voice for each speech? Does each speaker's tone change or remain the same throughout the interview? Explain.
5. Think of three more **questions** you'd like to ask Mr. Sheehan about building the Brooklyn Bridge. Where would you look for answers to these questions?

Excerpt From Interview With Joseph Sheehan, Brooklyn Bridge Worker

May 24, 1880

Jorge: Tell me something about what your work is like.

Sheehan: I've worked on the bridge for almost four years—ever since the New York tower was finished in July 1876. My job is to work with a team attaching the suspenders, which are wire ropes, to the four gigantic cables that hang from the two towers. After we hang the suspenders and the deck beams from the cables, we'll attach the diagonal wire ropes. I climb and balance high up in the air, but that doesn't bother me because I'm used to working the rigging on the ships I've sailed on.

Jorge: Did you work underground, too?

Sheehan: No. Some of my friends worked in the two caissons, digging in the dark and the muck for years. I tried it, but I couldn't stand being confined deep under the river, and that was dangerous work, too. You know, the workers used to be paid just $2.00 a day, but after they went on strike in May 1872, the pay went up to $2.75 a day. Soon after that, one of my friends, William Reardon, died from what they call caisson disease, just like that. He came up from underground too fast, they say. He couldn't walk at all and kept throwing up. They took him to hospital, but he died the next day.

Jorge: What's it like to work so high above the river?

Sheehan: It's grand. We are higher up in the sky than anybody's ever been before. I can see the whole city. Passengers on the ferries cheer and wave at us, but of course we can't wave back. We have important work to do.

Script for an Interview

Follow these steps to create your own **script** for a fictional interview. To plan your script, review the graphic organizers on pages R24–R27 and choose one that suits your needs.

Prewriting

- Think of real or fictional people related in some way to your research report. Choose one whom you would like to interview.
- **Brainstorm** for a list of open-ended questions you want to ask that person. Choose five questions to research and use in your interview.
- Identify the audience for your interview. Are you writing to inform your audience, or do you have a different purpose?
- Formulate a **research plan** to answer these five questions. You may already have compiled information from **multiple sources** as you did research for your informational research report. You may need to find additional facts and details to answer these new **research questions**.
- Determine the types of resources you will need to consult. Locate and explore the full range of relevant sources that address your research questions.
- For every source you consider using, evaluate whether it is **authoritative, reliable, valid, and accurate**. Is each source objective? Be sure to examine any **major issues** or **debates** related to your topic.
- To systematically record the information you gather, take notes on note cards, on the computer, or in a learning log. Make a source card to document each source, using a standard format for citations. As you take notes, use your own words to paraphrase or summarize information. Enclose direct quotations in quotation marks.
- Organize the data you've collected from all your sources to help you see big ideas. You may need to **clarify** your **research question** after you evaluate and synthesize the information you have researched.
- **Plan graphics, forms,** or **illustrations** to add to your script. Be sure to record source information for any graphics you intend to use.

Notes From Source 1

<u>Deaths from caisson disease</u>
- Englishman named Reardon
- 5/17/1872 Extreme pain and couldn't walk after shift in caisson; next morning died in hospital
- 5/18/1872 Roebling stopped caisson work on NY tower @ 78 ½ ft. below E. River; not on bedrock pp. 293-294

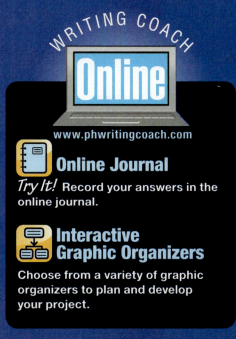

Online Journal
Try It! Record your answers in the online journal.

Interactive Graphic Organizers
Choose from a variety of graphic organizers to plan and develop your project.

Partner Talk
Ask a partner to critique your research plan. Does your partner have interview questions you haven't thought about asking? Modify your research questions to refocus your research plan.

Your Turn: Script for an Interview (continued)

Drafting

- **Organize** your notes by grouping together all of the information dealing with each interview question. Remember, you are writing both the interview questions and the answers.
- Draft an introductory paragraph with a **thesis statement** about the purpose of the interview and a clear point of view on the topic.
- Identify the **speakers**. Use your name for the interviewer, and devise a name for a fictional character or, if the person being interviewed is based on a real person, use that person's name.
- Write each **interview question** as clearly as you can. You should have at least five questions. Arrange them in a logical order.
- Review the information you have collected. Marshal, or organize, the evidence to draft **answers** to each question. The evidence should support the main idea, or thesis, as well as any related claims within each answer.
- Choose words and details that express the speaker's **analysis** of the subject and point of view. Present the information in a **logical progression** that the audience can easily follow.
- Acknowledge your **sources** as needed in context or in a credits section.

Revising

Use Revision RADaR techniques as you review your draft carefully.

- **Replace** general terms with vivid details and unclear explanations with precise ideas.
- **Add** specific details or missing information to support your argument.
- **Delete** information that does not support your thesis or develop your argument.
- **Reorder** sentences and paragraphs to present ideas clearly and logically.
- Read aloud your script to make sure it reads smoothly. Vary sentence beginnings and lengths.
- Use an **evaluative tool,** such as a rubric or teacher feedback, to check the quality of your researched script.

Editing

Now take the time to check your script of a fictional interview carefully before you read it aloud with a partner. Focus on each sentence and then on each word. Look for these common kinds of errors:

- Errors in subject-verb agreement
- Errors in pronoun usage
- Run-on sentences and sentence fragments
- Spelling and capitalization mistakes
- Omitted punctuation marks
- Problems with proper citations and credits for any graphics and images

Publishing

- With a partner, read aloud your script of a fictional interview to your classmates or to another class. If you have included any graphics or images with your script, be sure to show them at that appropriate point in your performance.
- Print a copy of your script of a fictional interview to share with friends and relatives.
- Search for online forums related to your topic (such as an American history forum or a chemistry forum), and submit your report as a comment.
- Enter your script of a fictional interview in a writing contest related to a particular school subject. Consult with your teacher or librarian to find out about possible contests.
- With your classmates, create an anthology of your scripts of fictional interviews. Print your anthology for classroom display or for your school library.

Extension Find another example of an interview script, and compare it with the one you are developing.

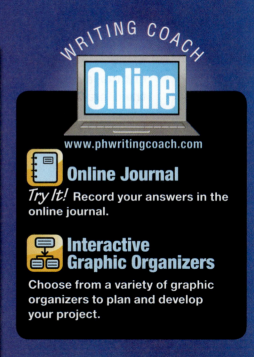

WRITING COACH Online
www.phwritingcoach.com

Online Journal
Try It! Record your answers in the online journal.

Interactive Graphic Organizers
Choose from a variety of graphic organizers to plan and develop your project.

Partner Talk

Before you read aloud your script of a fictional interview, ask a partner to check it carefully. Proofread each other's scripts for errors in grammar, spelling, capitalization, or punctuation.

Writing for Media 253

Writing to a Prompt

Many standardized tests include a prompt that asks you to write or critique a research plan. Use these prompts to practice. Respond using the characteristics of your informational research report. (See page 224.)

 Try It! Work with a partner to read the prompt carefully, and then create a detailed **research plan**. Your plan should include a research topic and question, a list of possible source ideas, the intended audiences, and a timeline of the steps you'll take.

Format
Write your research plan in the form of an outline. List everything you would do in the order that you would do it. You may devise headings like *Sources* and *Timeline* to help organize your response.

Research Plan Prompt
Write a research plan for an informational research report about a person or event related to the Women's Suffrage Movement. First, narrow the topic. Then, tell how you will go about your research. Tell what primary and secondary sources might be useful as well as what print and electronic sources you will explore. [30 minutes]

Academic Vocabulary
In your plan, you may want to plan for a *primary source*, such as an original document or an interview with an expert. Most of your other research can come from *secondary sources*, such as books, Web sites, or encyclopedias.

The ABCDs of On-Demand Writing

Use the following ABCDs to help you respond to the prompt.

Before you write your draft:

Attack the prompt [1 MINUTE]

- Circle or highlight important verbs in the prompt. Draw a line from the verb to what it refers to.
- Rewrite the prompt in your own words.

Brainstorm possible answers [4 MINUTES]

- Create a graphic organizer to generate ideas.
- Use one for each part of the prompt if necessary.

Choose the order of your response [1 MINUTE]

- Think about the best way to organize your ideas.
- Number your ideas in the order you will write about them. Cross out ideas you will not be using.

After you write your draft:

Detect errors before turning in the draft [1 MINUTE]

- Carefully reread your writing.
- Make sure that your response makes sense and is complete.
- Look for spelling, punctuation, and grammar errors.

More Prompts for Practice

Apply It! Work with a partner to **critique the research plans** in Prompt 1. In a written response, make specific suggestions to improve each research plan. Consider these questions:

- Has the **research plan** covered all of the prewriting steps?
- Is there a limited **topic?** Is it appropriate for the audience and purpose?
- Is the writer planning to find enough **sources?** Are the sources varied?
- Does the research plan say anything about **evaluating** sources?

Prompt 1 Jenna is writing a research paper for her world history class. Explain what she did well and what needs improvement.

My Topic: I am writing about government censorship in China.

My Research: I'll interview my aunt, who worked for a year in China, and find all the rest of the information on the Internet.

My Writing: After I do my research, I'll write a draft. Then, I will type a final copy to turn in to my government teacher.

Spiral Review: Narrative If you choose to write a **personal narrative** in response to Prompt 2, make sure your story reflects all of the characteristics described on page 66.

Prompt 2 Think about a time you took an action or made a decision that you were proud of. Write a personal narrative to share this experience. Use specific details to tell about the events leading up to it and explain what your action or decision meant to you.

Spiral Review: Response to Literature If you choose to write a **response to literature**, make sure your response reflects all of the characteristics described on page 198, including:

- **Extends** beyond a summary and literal analysis
- Addresses the **writing skills** for an analytical essay (See page 146.)
- Provides **evidence** from the text using embedded quotations if appropriate
- Analyzes the **aesthetic effects** of the author's use of stylistic or rhetorical devices

Prompt 3 Life's challenges are often at the heart of fiction and nonfiction. Write an interpretative response to an expository or literary text that features a person facing a difficult time. Explain what message the writer conveyed and analyze how the text developed that message.

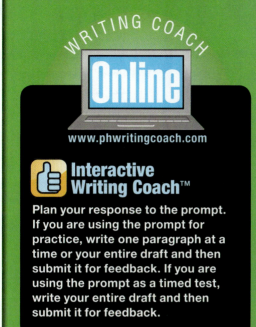

www.phwritingcoach.com

Interactive Writing Coach™

Plan your response to the prompt. If you are using the prompt for practice, write one paragraph at a time or your entire draft and then submit it for feedback. If you are using the prompt as a timed test, write your entire draft and then submit it for feedback.

Remember ABCD

Attack the prompt

Brainstorm possible answers

Choose the order of your response

Detect errors before turning in the draft

CHAPTER 12
WORKPLACE WRITING

What's Ahead

In this chapter, you will learn to write procedural documents, which explain how something works or is done. You will also learn how to write other work-related documents, such as memos, project plans, and business letters. All of these functional documents should present accurate information that is effectively organized and presented in a reader-friendly format. The language you use to write these documents should be clear, formal, and polite.

CHARACTERISTICS OF WRITING

Effective workplace and procedural writing has these characteristics:

- **Information** that is well organized and accurate
- **Reader-friendly formatting techniques,** such as headings and numbered steps
- **Formal, polite** language
- A clearly defined **purpose** and **audience**
- Correct **grammar, punctuation, and spelling** appropriate to the form of writing

Forms of Writing

Forms of workplace writing you will learn in this chapter include:

Business letters are formal correspondence written to, from, or within a business. They can be written for various reasons, including to make requests and to express concerns or approval.

Instructions explain how to complete a task or procedure. These procedural texts are written in a step-by-step format.

Memos are short documents usually written by one member of an organization to another member or group within the same organization. A memo, or memorandum, assumes some background knowledge of the topic.

Project plans usually divide a project into steps or stages and outline what will be accomplished in each stage.

Other forms of workplace writing include:

Business e-mails are an electronic form of correspondence written to, from, or within a business. Because e-mail is sent over the Internet, it is used for informal communication.

 Try It! For each audience and purpose described, select the correct form, such as instructions, a memo, or an e-mail, that is appropriate. Explain your choices, evaluating the different forms of text according to the way each one presents information.

- To tell your parents how to access your school's Web site
- To make a detailed, formal suggestion to your principal about changing the cafeteria's selections

WRITING COACH

www.phwritingcoach.com

Resource
Word Bank Use the eText glossary to learn more about these words.

Online Journal
Try It! Record your answers and ideas in the online journal.

Connect to the Big Questions

Discuss these questions:

1 What do you think? When is careful listening most critical to success in the workplace?

2 Why write? What do daily workplace communications require of format, content, and style?

These vocabulary words are often used with workplace writing. Use the Glossary or a dictionary to check the definitions.

accurate	instructions
consider	procedure

STUDENT MODEL Instructions

Learn From Experience

After reading the instructions on this page, read the numbered notes in the margin to learn about how the writer presented his ideas. As you read, practice newly acquired vocabulary by correctly producing the word's sound.

Try It! Record your answers and ideas in the online journal.

---

❶ The title is a **reader-friendly formatting technique.**

❷ The main idea is stated in a general directive. That is an **organized** way to begin.

❸ **Accurate information** is organized in numbered steps—another **reader-friendly technique.**

❹ The writer anticipates and addresses a question the reader might have: "What do I do if the message is urgent?"

Try It!

- Identify the audience and purpose for these instructions.
- When do you think it would be important to identify the audience for a set of instructions?
- Why is it important when writing instructions to anticipate the audience's questions?
- Why is it important to provide steps in the order they are used?

❶ # How to Take a Phone Message

by Terrence Jackson

❷ Follow this procedure to take a phone message when answering the office phone:

1. Answer the phone in a professional-sounding voice, saying, "Jackson Skateboard Repair, this is (your name)."

2. Use the phone message pad that is always on the desk, and fill in every blank. Include the time and date of the call, the caller's name and phone number, and the reason for the call.

❸
3. When you finish the writing, read back the entire content of the message (including contact information) to the caller and make any corrections.

4. If the message is not urgent, leave it on my desk. I will check for messages when I return to the office.

❹ If the message is urgent, send me a text message (speed dial #5) that includes the caller's name, number, and reason for calling. I will call the office if I need more information.

 **Feature Assignment: Instructions**

Prewriting

- Plan a first draft of your **instructions**. You can select from the Topic Bank or come up with an idea of your own.

> **TOPIC BANK**
>
> **Online Research** Write step-by-step instructions that tell a younger brother, sister, or friend how to do online research.
>
> **Prepare a Meal** Write step-by-step instructions that tell how to prepare a favorite dish, such as hamburgers.

- Think about who will be reading your instructions so that you know how much detail to include. For example, a young person doing research online might need directions for locating a search engine.
- Think about the purpose of your instructions; then, to make this procedural document useful, list steps the audience will need to take to fulfill the purpose.

 ## Drafting

- Use **reader-friendly formatting techniques.** Provide a title that communicates the purpose of the instructions.
- **Organize the information** by writing steps in the order they will need to be followed.
- **Anticipate reader questions** and try to include information that addresses those questions.

 ## Revising and Editing

- Review your draft to ensure you have conveyed all the necessary information and **accurately described the process** and any tools required.
- Rethink your audience and the questions they might have. Then, add any missing steps and take out any unnecessary information.
- Ask for feedback from your peers and teacher. Revise your final draft in response to this feedback.
- Double-check your spelling, grammar, and **style.**

Publishing

Consider posting your instructions online or in another forum where people will find them useful. You might combine your procedural documents with those of others to create a class booklet or online collection.

WRITING COACH Online
www.phwritingcoach.com

 **Interactive Model**
Listen to an audio recording of the Student Model.

 **Online Journal**
Try It! Record your answers and ideas in the online journal.

 **Interactive Writing Coach**
Submit your writing and receive personalized feedback and support as you draft, revise, and edit.

 Video
Learn strategies for effective revising and editing from program authors Jeff Anderson and Kelly Gallagher.

 **Partner Talk**
Read your partner's final draft. If the purpose isn't clear, suggest improvements.

STUDENT MODEL Memo

Learn From Experience

After reading the memo on this page, read the numbered notes in the margin to learn about how the writer presented her ideas.

Try It! Record your answers and ideas in the online journal.

---

1 The traditional memo heading is a **reader-friendly formatting technique.** In just a few words, it tells who wrote the memo, when it was written, and why.

2 This clear main idea follows **accurate background information** about return rates.

3 A clear topic sentence like this one helps **organize information** effectively.

4 In this call to action, the writer **anticipates and addresses possible questions** by stating the action she would like taken. She also provides a time frame for the response.

Try It!
- Outline the memo by writing the purpose of each paragraph.
- Why is a formal memo sometimes used instead of an informal e-mail or a face-to-face conversation?
- How might the reader be affected by reading a formal document?

Extension Inferring from the letter's tone, consider the way a recipient might respond. Use the letter's tone to help you distinguish fact from opinion. Then, write a response from the recipient that summarizes the issue and responds to the original writer's request.

Memo

1 To: Rachel Wilson
From: Jessica Ruiz
Date: November 18, 2010
Subject: Proposed Dog Training

As you know, we have a high return rate on adopted dogs. Last month alone, 22 dogs were returned to our shelter by people who had adopted them. Most dogs are returned because of bad behavior, such as jumping up on people. **2** For this reason, I propose that our dogs receive behaviorial training before adoption.

3 Since dog training is not in our budget, I wonder whether we might get professional dog trainers to volunteer their services. They could train dogs directly, and they could teach staff and volunteers to train dogs. In exchange, we could give the trainers free advertising in the shelter's newsletter.

4 If possible, I would like to meet with you to discuss this idea further. Please let me know whether there is a convenient time that we might meet for a half hour next week.

260 Workplace Writing

 **Feature Assignment: Memo**

Prewriting

- Plan a first draft of your **memo**. You can select from the Topic Bank or come up with an idea of your own.

> **TOPIC BANK**
>
> **Debit Card Account** Write a memo to your parents about why you should be given a debit card.
>
> **Mobile Devices in Hallways** Write a memo to the school district administration about why students should be allowed to use their mobile devices in the school hallways.

- Brainstorm for a list of information that your audience will need to know to understand your memo.
- If you write to school administration, gather information for the memo heading. Make sure you send the memo to somebody who has the administrators authority to act on your request.

 Drafting

- Use **reader-friendly formatting techniques,** including all of the features of formal memos.
- Work-related documents should be concise and formal. **Organize the information** so that it is easy to follow. Begin with the main idea. Then, support it with reasons. End with a call to action.
- **Accurately convey information,** tell where your facts come from, and make sure you have cited them correctly.

 Revising and Editing

Review your draft to ensure that information is presented accurately and concisely. Ask yourself whether the purpose of your memo is clearly identified and whether you have addressed the needs of your audience. **Anticipate reader questions,** and answer them in your writing. Revise the draft to make sure your **word choice** suits your purpose and audience.

Publishing

- Memos are work-related documents. You should print the memo on paper that is suitable for business correspondence.
- Deliver or send the memo to the intended recipient.

www.phwritingcoach.com

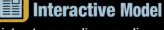 **Interactive Model**

Listen to an audio recording of the Student Model.

 **Online Journal**

Try It! Record your answers and ideas in the online journal.

 **Interactive Writing Coach**

Submit your writing and receive personalized feedback and support as you draft, revise, and edit.

 Video

Learn strategies for effective revising and editing from program authors Jeff Anderson and Kelly Gallagher.

Read your partner's memo, and summarize its contents. Identify opinions and evidence.

Memo 261

STUDENT MODEL Business Letter

Learn From Experience

After reading the business letter on this page, read the numbered notes in the margin to learn about how the writer presented his ideas. As you read, take notes to develop your understanding of basic sight and English vocabulary.

Try It! Record your answers and ideas in the online journal.

---

❶ The writer follows standard business-letter format. First, he lists his name, address, and the date. Then, he lists his recipient's name and address, being careful to ensure that the **information is accurate.**

❷ The writer shows respect by using the councilman's title in the salutation. Notice that the salutation of a business letter is followed by a colon.

❸ The writer **anticipates reader questions** by stating the purpose early in the letter. This shows respect for the councilman and his time.

❹ Clear transitions such as *first* and *second* help **organize information.**

❺ The writer uses a **formal, friendly tone** in the letter.

Try It!
- Why is it important to use formal, polite language in a business letter?
- Why is it important to format a business letter correctly?

Extension Take the role of the recipient of the letter and write a response to the sender.

Erik Schindler
709 N. Tyler St.
Wichita Falls, TX 76301

❶ May 7, 2010

Councilman Merle Jones
445 E. Washington Ave.
Wichita Falls, TX 76306

❷ Dear Councilman Jones:

❸ I am a student at Wichita Falls High School, and I am writing to make a suggestion about how to improve our town's Independence Day celebration. The celebration offers great rides and games for little kids, and it offers the first-rate symphony performance and the melodrama theatre for adults. The problem is that the celebration does not have many activities for teenagers. I have a few ideas for how to involve teenagers in the celebration.

❹ First, there could be some kind of sporting competition, such as flag-football or softball. Second, there could be an art exhibit that includes the work of local teenagers. Perhaps awards could be given to the winners of these events to encourage teens to participate in them.

❺ Since not all teens care for sports or art, perhaps there could be volunteer opportunities, too. Picking up trash or helping people find parking spots might be a way for teenagers to enjoy the day and be productive at the same time.

I hope these suggestions will be useful.

Sincerely yours,

Erik Schindler

Erik Schindler

 **Feature Assignment: Business Letter**

Prewriting

- Plan a first draft of your **business letter**. You can select from the Topic Bank or come up with an idea of your own.

TOPIC BANK

Fund-raising School systems have to operate on a budgeted amount of money each school year. Often, there is not enough money to cover all program costs and many extracurricular programs are cut. Think of a way that your community can help, either by fund raising or by donating the use of public facilities. Then, write a formal letter to the editor of your local newspaper persuading people to help.

Product Improvement Think of a product you use that could be improved. Write a letter to the manufacturer suggesting improvements.

- Think about your purpose and audience. Brainstorm positive things to say in addition to your request, complaint, or suggested action.
- Find the accurate contact information for the letter's recipient.

Drafting

- Use **reader-friendly formatting techniques**.
- Remember that you are drafting a work-related document—one to be read by a busy professional. Be concise. **Organize the information** so that the purpose is clearly stated early in the letter and so that each paragraph has a clear purpose.
- **Accurately convey information,** presenting positives before problems.
- **Anticipate readers' questions** or objections, and address them.

 Revising and Editing

Review your draft to ensure that information is presented accurately and concisely. Ask yourself if your letter fulfills your purpose or addresses your audience properly. Then, revise to improve your **word choice.** If possible, incorporate feedback from your teacher before making a final draft.

Publishing

- Print the letter on paper that is suitable for business correspondence.
- To e-mail it, create a PDF before attaching to your message.

www.phwritingcoach.com

 Interactive Model
Listen to an audio recording of the Student Model.

 Online Journal
Try It! Record your answers and ideas in the online journal.

 Interactive Writing Coach
Submit your writing and receive personalized feedback and support as you draft, revise, and edit.

 Video
Learn strategies for effective revising and editing from program authors Jeff Anderson and Kelly Gallagher.

Work with a partner to edit your letter. Ask for feedback about the tone of your letter. Monitor your partner's spoken language by asking follow-up questions to confirm your understanding.

21st Century Learning

MAKE YOUR WRITING COUNT

Present a Research Report for Community Service Day

Instructions, memos, and business letters help people communicate important information to very specific audiences. These workplace documents may involve the seeds for activities or ideas that will help classmates learn more. Make a **research report** and presentation to share.

With a group, **brainstorm** for several topics drawn from your work in this chapter. Have a discussion with others to **decide upon a topic** that will be helpful to someone trying to make the community a better place. Consider topics such as park cleanup, town maps and brochures for tourists, community celebrations and events, and local charities.

Then, work together to formulate **an open-ended research question** that will help you produce a research report about the topic.

As you develop your report, you may need to **modify research questions** and **evaluate collected information.** Group members should **consult** one another to critique the process as you work. Be prepared to refocus and implement changes as needed. Focus on researching information related to the workplace and helping the community. Remember that a research report should:

- State a specific thesis
- Consider audience and purpose
- Express a clear point of view
- Provide supporting evidence
- Present ideas in a logical way
- Document sources properly

Organize a Community Service Day showing how your research results can be useful to students in your school who wish to improve their community. Share the information you have gathered in a **multimedia presentation that uses** text, images, and sound that will appeal to your audience. You may use posters and other displays or an electronic slide show that uses presentation software.

Workplace Writing

21st Century Learning

Here's your action plan.

1. Research takes time. In a group, make a plan for several group meetings, set objectives, and choose roles for each member.

2. Work together to develop a research plan. Each team member should help gather initial research and take notes. A research plan involves:
   - Collecting and organizing **evidence** to support a clear thesis statement and related claims
   - Identifying any **major issues or debates** related to your topic
   - Checking the authority and objectivity of your sources to determine if they are **reliable, valid, and accurate**
   - Using **feedback** to check the quality of your research

3. Discuss your findings. Evaluate the information you have gathered to check its **relevance** to your topic. Determine which evidence you want to keep or reject. Then, work together to create **a thesis statement** that clearly reflects your purpose and considers your audience.

4. Outline the content of the report. Assign sections of the outline to each group member. You may need to research further before you write a draft based on your notes. During this research stage, be sure to **paraphrase, summarize, quote, and accurately cite sources.**

5. Work together to **compile** data and write a rough draft. As you write, analyze data in a way that allows the audience to follow the **logical progression** of your ideas. Work to clearly reflect your point of view on the topic. Where needed, organize the information from all your sources to create appropriate graphics and forms that help explain the topic. Use the proper style for **documenting sources.**

6. Revise and edit your writing to ensure that the **thesis** is well-supported, the analysis is logical and easy to follow, and that you communicate a clear **point of view**.

7. Finally, consider including **audio support,** such as music, recorded interviews, or sound effects, and video clips in your final presentation.

8. Once you have organized your ideas to suit your audience and purpose, present your report to students, counselors, and teachers.

Listening and Speaking Practice the presentation in front of another group or each other and request feedback to make improvements. On Community Service Day, speak clearly and confidently to your audience. Be prepared for questions that may need to be researched further and answered later.

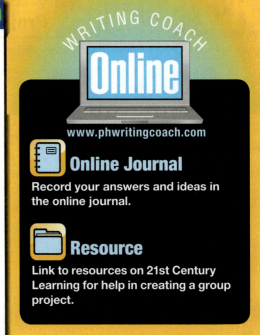

WRITING COACH Online
www.phwritingcoach.com

Online Journal
Record your answers and ideas in the online journal.

Resource
Link to resources on 21st Century Learning for help in creating a group project.

Your Turn — Writing for Media: Project Plan

21st Century Learning

Project Plan

Multimedia presentations are frequently used in schools, in the workplace, at conferences, and online because they are an effective way to present information to a wide audience. Multimedia presentations use a combination of text, images, music, charts, graphics, and animations to allow people to share information on a variety of topics. Slide shows allow the presenter to share only key points in text, supported or elaborated by an oral presentation.

A multimedia presentation is well-suited to sharing a **project plan** because the presenter can pace the information, discussing one point fully before exposing the audience to the next part of the presentation.

Try It! Study the slides on this page. Then answer these questions. Record your answers in your journal.

1. How does the **title slide** help to communicate the purpose of the multimedia presentation?
2. How do the **subtitled phrases** help the reader see the benefits of the proposed club?
3. How do the images used on the slides help show the presenter's **point of view**? How do they appeal to the specific audience?
4. Is the amount of text per slide **reader-friendly**? Explain.
5. What do you think the **presenter** should say as each slide is shown?

Extension Find another example of a project plan and compare it with this one.

Coming Soon
The Stitch in Time Knitting Club
Knitting Generations Together

Freshness In
- Stitch in Time would bring teenagers into the Shady Village Retirement Center to knit with residents.
- The residents would experience improved mood.
- Teenagers would benefit from their helping role.

Wisdom Out
- Stitch in Time gives Shady Village residents the opportunity to teach teens to knit.
- Teens benefit from the opportunity to see life from a different perspective.

Create a Multimedia Project Plan

Follow these steps to create your own work-related document—a **multimedia presentation** of a **project plan**. Review the graphic organizers on pages R24–R27 to select one best suited to your needs.

Prewriting

- Brainstorm for project topics that you would like to propose for your school or another organization.
- Think about how the project would benefit your school or organization.
- Make a detailed list of the steps involved in completing the project.
- Consider the needs of your specific audience. What does your audience already know about the project? What does the audience need to know?

Drafting

- Divide your plan into phases. Organize your information in sequential order.
- Draft a script for the oral presentation. Include an introduction that briefly explains the project and its benefits and a description of each phase of the project.
- Create a slide or poster to accompany each part of your presentation, including the introduction and the phases of the project.
- To ensure you use reader-friendly formatting techniques, each slide should contain only a small amount of text. This will allow your audience to focus on the details of your oral presentation.
- Choose **graphics, images, and sound** that convey your **point of view**, or attitude, about the project. For example, red letters could convey a sense of urgency.

Revising and Editing

As you revise, review each slide to be sure that its content correctly matches each section of your oral presentation. Check that the design of your slides makes them easy to read. Is your point of view coming across? Double-check the accuracy of information on your slides. Anticipate reader questions and answer them. Remember to check your spelling and grammar.

Publishing

- Present your slide show to the class or to another audience.
- Speak clearly and allow time for your audience to ask questions.

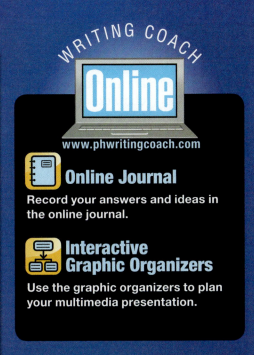

Writing Coach Online
www.phwritingcoach.com

Online Journal
Record your answers and ideas in the online journal.

Interactive Graphic Organizers
Use the graphic organizers to plan your multimedia presentation.

Partner Talk

Before publishing, practice your presentation with a partner. Ask for feedback about the effectiveness of your slides or posters in supporting your oral presentation. Provide the same type of feedback for your partner.

Writing for Assessment

Sometimes a test includes a prompt that asks you to write a procedure for a task. Use these prompts to practice. Responses should include characteristics similar to those used in a set of instructions. Look back at pages 258–259 to review these characteristics.

 Try It! Read the procedural text prompt and the information on the format and academic vocabulary. Use the ABCDs of On-Demand Writing to help you plan and write your procedural text.

Format
The prompt directs you to write a *procedural text*. Describe the purpose of the text in the first section. Be sure to include steps that organize information using reader-friendly formatting techniques. Anticipate your reader's questions and answer them in the text.

Procedural Text Prompt
Your friend wants to add songs to his MP3 player. He needs to have written instructions about how to find and move music files as he gets started. Write a procedural text that anticipates and answers reader questions.

Academic Vocabulary
A procedural text is a kind of text that tells somebody how to perform a task. *Anticipate* means to predict something and deal with it in advance.

The ABCDs of On-Demand Writing

Use the following ABCDs to help you respond to the prompt.

Before you write your draft:

Attack the prompt [1 MINUTE]

- Circle or highlight important verbs in the prompt. Draw a line from the verb to what it refers to.
- Rewrite the prompt in your own words.

Brainstorm possible answers [4 MINUTES]

- Create a graphic organizer to generate ideas.
- Use one for each part of the prompt if necessary.

Choose the order of your response [1 MINUTE]

- Think about the best way to organize your ideas.
- Number your ideas in the order you will write about them. Cross out ideas you will not be using.

After you write your draft:

Detect errors before turning in the draft [1 MINUTE]

- Carefully reread your writing.
- Make sure that your response makes sense and is complete.
- Look for spelling, punctuation, and grammar errors.

More Prompts for Practice

Apply It! Respond to Prompt 1 in a timed or open-ended situation by writing a **procedural text** that **organizes information, accurately conveys information, and includes reader-friendly formatting techniques.** As you write, be sure to follow these steps:

- Consider what your **audience** knows and needs to know about the procedure to best anticipate questions
- Clearly state the **purpose** of the text you are writing
- **Organize information** into steps or paragraphs that have a clear purpose
- **Define** any terms that your audience may not know
- Develop a draft with **transitions** that clearly convey meaning

> **Prompt 1** Your grandmother wants to buy a book online. Write a procedural text that includes stepped-out instructions for finding and purchasing a book of her choice.

Spiral Review: Research Respond to Prompt 2 by writing a **critique of the research process** it describes. Your critique should determine if the research plan:

- Addresses a major topic and **research question**
- Sets up to do research on a complex, **multifaceted topic**
- Contains plans for **compiling data** from reliable sources
- Mentions **organizing information** using graphics and forms
- References using a standard format from an appropriate **style manual**

> **Prompt 2** Gillian wrote this research plan. Write a critique describing what she did well and what needs work.
>
> *My Topic and Question:* I'm interested in the Romany people in the United States. Is there a thriving culture here, as there is in Europe?
>
> *My Research:* I'm going to use any Web sites I can find and a general encyclopedia. I'll take notes in a standard form that I'll create which will have blanks for the title and author of each source.
>
> *My Writing:* I will start writing in two weeks. I will use the MLA Handbook for style as I write.

WRITING COACH Online

www.phwritingcoach.com

Interactive Writing Coach

Plan your response to the prompt. If you are writing the prompt for practice, write one paragraph at a time or your entire draft and submit it for feedback. If you are using the prompt for a timed test, write your entire draft and submit it for feedback.

Remember ABCD

- **A**ttack the prompt
- **B**rainstorm possible answers
- **C**hoose the order of your response
- **D**etect errors before turning in the draft

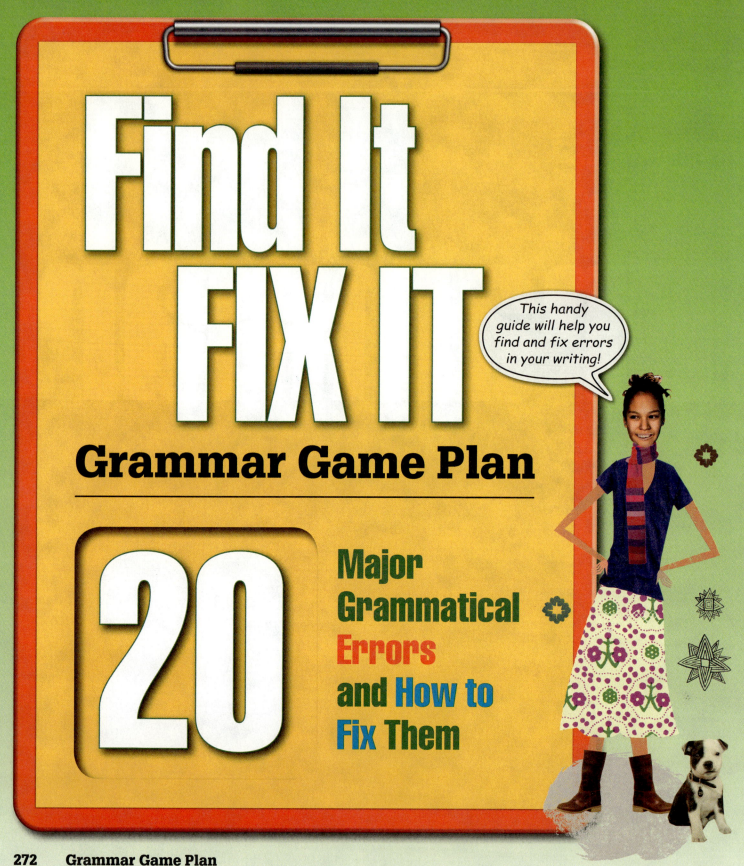

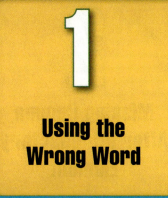

Find It/FIX IT

1

Using the Wrong Word

GAME PLAN Use the right words to add clarity and authority to your writing. Make sure your words say exactly what you mean them to say.

CLARIFY MEANING Do not confuse the meanings of words with similar spellings. Also, words with similar definitions can have important shades of meaning. Check that words you found in a thesaurus are used correctly.

The ~~principle~~ principal read to the students.

The ~~precedent~~ president of the university held a press conference.

Tech Tip

Be your own "spell-checker"! Proofread! Your computer's spell-checker will not identify every misspelling or incorrectly used word.

SPELL-CHECK ERRORS Computer spell-checkers often correct a misspelling with a different, similarly spelled word. Be sure to proofread your work carefully to catch these errors. In each of the following examples, the word with a strikethrough represents an inappropriate spell-checker correction.

I will ~~vend~~ send you a letter shortly.

My younger sister needs ~~blue~~ glue for her school project.

LEARN MORE
- See Chapter 21, Miscellaneous Problems in Usage, pages 528–542
- See Writing Coach Online

Use a current or completed draft of your work to practice using words correctly.

✓ **READ carefully.** Take the time to read your draft closely. For a double-check, have someone else read your work.

✓ **IDENTIFY possible mistakes.** Mark any difficult or commonly misused words in your draft.

✓ **USE a dictionary.** If you are not sure of a word's meaning, consult a dictionary.

Grammar Game Plan 273

Find It/FIX IT

2 Missing Comma After Introductory Element

Tech Tip
Remember to add commas to introductory elements that you cut and paste from different parts of a sentence or paragraph.

LEARN MORE
- See Chapter 23, Punctuation, pages 576–577
- See Writing Coach Online

GAME PLAN Place a comma after the following introductory elements in your work.

WORDS Place a comma after introductory words of direct address, words of permission, and interjections.

James, can you hand me that paper?
No, I can't find it.
Great, I will see you at the movie.

PHRASES Place a comma after introductory prepositional, participial, and infinitive phrases.

At the door, my brother waited.
Running slowly, I finally made it to the finish line.
To play your best, you need to practice.

CLAUSES Introductory adverbial clauses should be followed by a comma.

When the conductor boards the train, it will start moving.

✓ Check It

Use a current or completed draft of your work to practice placing commas after introductory elements.

- ✓ **SCAN your draft.** Look for introductory words, phrases, and clauses.
- ✓ **IDENTIFY missing commas.** Mark sentence starters that might need a comma.
- ✓ **USE your textbook.** Consult the grammar section of your textbook if you are not sure whether or not to use a comma.

Find It/FIX IT

3 Incomplete or Missing Documentation

GAME PLAN Provide complete citations for borrowed words and ideas. Use the citation style (such as MLA) that your teacher recommends.

MISSING CITATIONS Cite sources of direct quotes and statistics. Remember—when in doubt, cite the source.

As Dr. Jackson said, "The species continues to thrive" ∧(Jackson 23).

Williams suggested that its population should double in ten years∧(Williams 42).

INCOMPLETE CITATIONS Make sure your citations include complete source information. This information will vary depending on the source and the citation style, but it may include the author's name, the source's title, and the page number or other location information.

The response claimed the text was "brilliant and exciting" (Lin∧42). (incomplete citation)

Half of all students at Jefferson High School ride the bus (Marshall∧18).

Tech Tip
Be sure to include the citations attached to sentences when you cut and paste text.

LEARN MORE
- See Chapter 11, Research Writing, pages 234–237
- See Writing Coach Online

✓ Check It

Use a current or completed draft of your work to practice documenting your sources.

- ✓ **REVIEW your notes.** Look for introductory words, phrases, and clauses.
- ✓ **USE a style guide.** Check the appropriate format and contents for your citations in the style guide your teacher recommends.

Grammar Game Plan

Find It/FIX IT

4

Vague Pronoun Reference

GAME PLAN Create clear pronoun-antecedent relationships to make your writing more accurate and powerful.

VAGUE IDEA Pronouns such as *which, this, that,* and *these* should refer to a specific idea. Sometimes, changing a pronoun to an adjective that modifies a specific noun can avoid a vague reference.

 Mr. Stevens was named head coach of the varsity soccer team. That ^decision might get the team to the state finals this year.

UNCLEAR USE OF *IT, THEY,* AND *YOU* Be sure that the pronouns *it, they,* and *you* have a clearly stated antecedent. Replacing the personal pronoun with a specific noun can make a sentence clearer.

 The high school is hosting the homecoming football game next Friday. ~~It~~ ^The football game should be well attended.

The directors told the band members ~~that they needed~~ to start practicing for the concert.

When preparing for the driving exam, ~~you~~ ^potential drivers need to practice the rules of the road.

Tech Tip

It is important to proofread your work after you cut and paste text to form new sentences or paragraphs. You may have inserted vague pronoun references while restructuring.

LEARN MORE
- See Chapter 19, Agreement, pages 502–506
- See Writing Coach Online

✓ Check It

Use a current or completed draft of your work to practice identifying vague pronoun references.

- ✓ **READ carefully.** Read your draft slowly to locate pronouns.
- ✓ **IDENTIFY possible errors.** Mark any vague pronoun references.
- ✓ **REVISE your draft.** Rewrite sentences with vague pronoun-antecedent relationships.

Find It/FIX IT

Spelling Error

GAME PLAN Spelling errors can change the meaning of a sentence. Proofread your work after spell-checking to be sure you have used the correct words.

SPELL-CHECK ERRORS Computer spell-checkers often replace misspelled words with others close in spelling but different in meaning. Proofread your work carefully to correct these errors.

> When I drove through the ~~dessert~~ desert with my family, I was surprised to see so many different types of cacti!
>
> The road was ~~sick~~ slick with ice so we had to be careful driving.

HOMOPHONES Words that are pronounced the same but have different spellings and meanings are called homophones. Check that you have used the correct homophones to convey your intended meaning.

> His best friend plays the ~~base~~ bass guitar in the jazz band.
>
> My younger sister likes to read stories about ~~nights~~ knights and dragons.

Tech Tip
Proper nouns are not checked by a computer spell-checker. Proofread to make sure that you have spelled people's names correctly.

LEARN MORE
- See Chapter 21, Miscellaneous Problems in Usage, pages 528–542
- See Writing Coach Online

✓ Check It

Use a current or completed draft of your work to practice spelling words correctly.

- ✓ **READ** carefully. Read your draft word by word looking for spelling errors.
- ✓ **IDENTIFY** possible mistakes. Mark any incorrect words or words that are misspelled.
- ✓ **USE** a dictionary. If you are not certain how to spell a word or think a homophone has been used incorrectly, consult a dictionary.

Grammar Game Plan 277

Find It/FIX IT

6 Punctuation Error With a Quotation

GAME PLAN Quotation marks are used to identify direct quotations. Proper punctuation helps to identify quotations and relate them to your work.

DIRECT AND INDIRECT QUOTATIONS A direct quotation is enclosed in quotation marks. Indirect quotations do not need quotation marks.

The dance teacher said**,** **"**Our newest dance instructor begins teaching tomorrow.**"**

The dance teacher said that a new dance instructor will be teaching tomorrow.

QUOTATION MARKS WITH OTHER PUNCTUATION When commas or periods end a quotation, the punctuation goes inside the quotation marks. Question marks and exclamation marks go either inside or outside the quotation marks, depending on the sentence structure. Colons and semicolons used after quoted material should be placed outside the quotation marks.

"We'll start planting our garden**,**" my mom said.

"I will get to plant my own garden**!**" my sister exclaimed.

Did she say, "You'll get to pick out the flowers to plant"**?**

The gardener said, "The newest flowers are out back"**;** the twins raced to the back of the store to get them.

✓ Check It

Use a current or completed draft of your work to practice punctuating quotations correctly.

- ✓ **READ** carefully. If you used indirect quotations, make sure that they are not set in quotation marks.
- ✓ **MARK** each direct quotation in your work. Is each quotation punctuated correctly?
- ✓ **REVISE** your sentences. Correct all punctuation errors in your quotations.

Tech Tip
If you cut and paste quotations, remember to copy the taglines to make sure you have included all of the correct punctuation marks that accompany direct quotations.

LEARN MORE
- See Chapter 23, Punctuation, pages 595–599
- See Writing Coach Online

Find It/FIX IT

7

Unnecessary Comma

GAME PLAN Before you insert a comma, think about how your ideas relate to one another. Make sure the comma is necessary.

ESSENTIAL ELEMENTS Appositives, participial phrases, and adjectival clauses that are essential to the meaning of a sentence are not set off by commas.

My classmate, Bill, goes to Ms. Leonard's trigonometry review sessions after school on Tuesdays.

The student, helping Ms. Leonard, is in advanced math classes.

The test, that everyone is studying for, is next Friday.

COMPOUND PREDICATE Commas should not break apart a compound predicate.

She studied in New York, and had come from Los Angeles.

The professor taught creative writing, and wrote fictional stories.

✓ Check It

Use a current or completed draft of your work to practice correctly punctuating essential elements.

- ✓ **SCAN** Mentor Texts. Notice how professional writers use commas.
- ✓ **IDENTIFY** essential elements. Did you use commas to indicate these elements?
- ✓ **REVISE** your sentences. Delete any commas that set off essential elements.

Tech Tip

As you restructure sentences by cutting and pasting from different parts of a sentence or paragraph, remember to add or delete commas.

LEARN MORE
- See Chapter 23, Punctuation, pages 578–580, 587–588
- See Writing Coach Online

Grammar Game Plan 279

Find It/FIX IT

8 Unnecessary or Missing Capitalization

Tech Tip
Sometimes word processors will automatically capitalize any word that follows a period, even if the period is part of an abbreviation. Proofread carefully for incorrectly capitalized words.

LEARN MORE
- See Chapter 22, Capitalization, pages 545–564
- See Writing Coach Online

GAME PLAN Follow the rules of capitalization, such as capitalizing proper nouns, the first word of a sentence, and titles of works of art.

PROPER NOUNS Names, geographical locations, and organizations are examples of nouns that should be capitalized.

Benjamin Franklin held many jobs, one of which was a publisher in Philadelphia.

I volunteer at the Red Cross on Tuesdays.

TITLES OF WORKS OF ART The first word and all other key words in the titles of books, poems, stories, plays, paintings, and other works of art are capitalized.

Have you read "The Raven" by Edgar Allan Poe?

She said her favorite childhood book was *Wind in the Willows.*

✓ Check It

Use a current or completed draft of your work to practice correctly capitalizing words.

- ✓ **SCAN** your draft. Look for words that are capitalized.
- ✓ **IDENTIFY** incorrect capitalization. Mark words that might be capitalized incorrectly.
- ✓ **USE** your textbook. Consult the grammar section of your textbook if you are not sure if a word should be capitalized.

Find It/FIX IT

9

Missing Word

GAME PLAN Make sure there are no missing words in a text. This will allow ideas to flow smoothly and will help readers understand the text.

ARTICLES In order to make sure that ideas follow smoothly and sentences are coherent, you must proofread your work. A missing word, even a missing article (*a, an, the*), is enough to confuse a reader.

> The debate team held a short meeting to discuss ^the upcoming invitational.

KEY IDEAS When copying and pasting text, you might miss moving a word in a sentence. If that word is central to the main idea of the sentence, the intended meaning could be lost.

> After the eight cheerleading squads performed, it was clear which would win ^first place.
>
> Nellie knew her team was the ^strongest, so she wasn't surprised when it won.

✓ Check It

Use a current or completed draft of your work to practice proofreading.

- ✓ **READ** carefully. Read your draft word by word to make sure that you did not omit a word.
- ✓ **IDENTIFY** unclear sentences. Mark any sentences you find that do not make sense. Are they unclear because of a missing word?
- ✓ **REVISE** your sentences. Add words to your sentences to make the meaning clear.

Tech Tip

When cutting and pasting sentences, you may accidentally insert the same word twice, one right after the other. While spell-checkers generally highlight duplicate words, proofread to be sure the sentence reads as you intended.

LEARN MORE
- See Editing sections in writing chapters
- See Writing Coach Online

Grammar Game Plan

Find It/FIX IT

10
Faulty Sentence Structure

GAME PLAN Sentences should express complex ideas using consistent tenses and similar structures.

FAULTY PARALLELISM When you express complex ideas, it is important that you use parallel grammatical structures to express ideas in phrases, clauses, or sentences of similar types.

Blake taught his brother to hit, to throw, and ~~catches~~ to catch the ball.

The movie that has good reviews and that opens today is the one I want to see.

FAULTY COORDINATION Ideas that are not of equal importance should not be connected with *and*. Instead, use multiple sentences or turn one idea into a subordinate clause.

After dinner, we went to the movie theater. ~~and the tickets were all sold out and we~~ We did not expect ~~that~~ the tickets to be sold out because the movie did not get good reviews.

I missed my train~~, and~~ even though I left my house early.

✓ Check It

Use a current or corrected draft of your work to practice correctly structuring sentences.

✓ **SCAN** Mentor Texts. Notice how professional writers present complex ideas.

✓ **IDENTIFY** possible mistakes. Mark any sentences that have faulty parallelism or faulty coordination.

✓ **REVISE** your sentences. Rewrite any sentences that do not have correct sentence structure.

Tech Tip
When you cut one part of a sentence and paste it in another, remember to check that the new sentence structure is correct.

LEARN MORE
- See Chapter 16, Effective Sentences, pages 415–421
- See Writing Coach Online

Find It/FIX IT

11
Missing Comma with a Nonessential Element

GAME PLAN Use commas to set off nonessential elements of sentences.

APPOSITIVE If an appositive is not essential to the meaning of a sentence, it should be set off by commas.

Julie's dog, a golden retriever, chased after the tennis ball.

PARTICIPIAL PHRASE A participial phrase not essential to the meaning of a sentence is set off by commas.

The dog, running through the park, brought the ball back to Julie.

ADJECTIVAL CLAUSE Use commas to set off an adjectival clause if it is not essential to the meaning of a sentence.

The dog, whose name is Comet, prefers to fetch tennis balls.

Tech Tip
When you cut part of a sentence and paste it to another, be sure to include the correct punctuation. Proofread these sentences carefully.

LEARN MORE
- See Chapter 23, Punctuation, pages 578–580
- See Writing Coach Online

Check It

Use a current or completed draft of your work to practice using commas correctly with nonessential elements.

- ✓ **SCAN** Mentor Texts. Notice how professional writers use commas to set off nonessential elements.
- ✓ **IDENTIFY** nonessential elements. Did you use commas to indicate these words, phrases, or clauses?
- ✓ **REVISE** your sentences. Use commas to set off nonessential elements.

Grammar Game Plan

Find It/FIX IT

12 Unnecessary Shift in Verb Tense

GAME PLAN Use consistent verb tenses in your work. Shift tenses only to show that one event comes before or after another.

SEQUENCE OF EVENTS Do not shift tenses unnecessarily when showing a sequence of events.

He will ride the bus to school, and then he ~~walks~~ will walk to the library after school.

Mrs. Cummings teaches algebra in the morning and ~~taught~~ teaches geometry in the afternoon.

SUBORDINATE CLAUSE The verb in the subordinate clause should follow logically from the tense of the main verb. The verbs require a shift in tense if one event happens before or after another.

She hopes that she ~~attends~~ will attend her first choice college next year.

Andrew thinks that they ~~saw~~ will see a movie this weekend.

Check It

Use a current or completed draft of your work to practice using consistent tenses.

✓ **SCAN** Mentor Texts. Notice how professional writers use consistent tenses within a sentence.

✓ **IDENTIFY** possible mistakes. Mark any shift in verb tense within a sentence.

✓ **USE** your textbook. Consult the grammar section of your textbook if you are not sure that you have used consistent tenses.

Tech Tip

When you cut text from one section to paste to another, the new sentence may have verbs that are not consistent in tense. Proofread revised sentences to make sure they use consistent tenses.

LEARN MORE
- See Chapter 17, Verb Usage, pages 446–452
- See Writing Coach Online

Find It/FIX IT

13
Missing Comma in a Compound Sentence

GAME PLAN Use a comma before a coordinating conjunction to separate two or more main clauses in a compound sentence.

MAIN CLAUSES Place a comma before a coordinating conjunction (e.g. *and, but, or, nor, yet, so, for*) in a compound sentence.

 She is traveling to China on a nonstop flight, and she is expected to arrive at noon.

BRIEF CLAUSES The main clauses in some compound sentences are brief and do not need a comma if the meaning is clear.

 The plane took off and she fell asleep.

COMPOUND SUBJECTS AND VERBS Commas should *not* be used to separate compound subjects and compound verbs in a sentence.

 The rivers, and lakes are colder than usual for this time of year.

The cat chased after the yarn, and dove under the table.

Tech Tip
Be careful when you create a compound sentence by cutting and pasting from different parts of a sentence or paragraph. Remember to include a comma to separate the main clauses.

LEARN MORE
- See Chapter 23, Punctuation, pages 571–575
- See Writing Coach Online

✓ Check It

Use a current or completed draft of your work to practice using commas in compound sentences.

- ✓ **SCAN** your draft. Look for compound sentences.
- ✓ **IDENTIFY** missing commas. Mark any compound sentences that should be punctuated with a comma.
- ✓ **REVISE** your sentences. Add commas before coordinating conjunctions to separate main clauses.

Grammar Game Plan

Find It/FIX IT

14 Unnecessary or Missing Apostrophe

GAME PLAN Use apostrophes correctly to show possession.

SINGULAR NOUNS To show the possessive case of most singular nouns, add an apostrophe and -s.

 The musical's cast was the best she had seen perform in years.

PLURAL NOUNS Add an apostrophe to show the possessive case for most plural nouns ending in -s or -es. For plural nouns that do not end in -s or -es, add an apostrophe and -s.

 The babies' toys are scattered all around the playroom.

The children's books are piled high on the bookshelves.

POSSESSIVE PRONOUNS Possessive pronouns (e.g., *his, hers, its, our, their*) show possession without the use of an apostrophe. Remember that the word *it's* means "it is" while *its* shows possession.

 His car is at the mechanic because its brake light is out.

✓ Check It

Use a current or completed draft of your work to practice showing possession.

✓ **SCAN** Mentor Texts. Notice when professional writers use apostrophes to indicate possession.

✓ **IDENTIFY** possible mistakes. Mark each apostrophe in your draft. Did you use them correctly to show possession?

✓ **REVISE** your sentences. Make sure to delete any apostrophes you used with possessive pronouns.

Tech Tip
Proofread your draft carefully. Not all computer grammar checkers will point out incorrect uses of apostrophes.

LEARN MORE
- See Chapter 18, Pronoun Usage, pages 471–473
- See Chapter 23, Punctuation, pages 614–619
- See Writing Coach Online

Find It/FIX IT

15 Run-on Sentence

GAME PLAN Use correct punctuation to avoid run-on sentences, which are two or more sentences punctuated as if they were a single sentence.

FUSED SENTENCE A fused sentence contains two or more sentences joined with no punctuation. To correct a fused sentence, place a period (and capitalize the following word) or a semicolon between the main clauses.

A new school superintendent was appointed for our district ~~he~~ . He used to be the high school principal.

Mr. Marshall discussed his goals for the upcoming school year; he was an articulate speaker.

RUN-ON SENTENCE Make sure you place a comma before coordinating conjunctions that join main clauses to avoid run-on sentences.

The new high school principal has a lot of teaching experience, and he makes an effort to get to know the students.

Tech Tip
Remember to proofread your work. Not all grammar checkers identify run-on sentences.

LEARN MORE
- See Chapter 16, Effective Sentences, pages 410–411
- See Writing Coach Online

✓ Check It

Use a current or completed draft of your work to practice correcting run-on sentences.

- ✓ **SCAN** your draft. Look for run-on sentences.
- ✓ **IDENTIFY** missing punctuation. Mark sentences that might need a period or a semicolon to separate main clauses.
- ✓ **REVISE** your sentences. When correcting fused sentences, vary your sentence structure.

Grammar Game Plan 287

Find It/FIX IT

16 Comma Splice

GAME PLAN Use correct punctuation to avoid comma splices. A comma splice happens when two or more complete sentences are joined only with a comma.

PERIOD Replace the comma with a period (and capitalize the following word) to separate two complete thoughts.

 The postal worker delivered the mail two hours late today~~, it~~. It snowed four inches.

SEMICOLON Replace the comma with a semicolon if the ideas are similar.

 It has been raining for the past two days; the weather forecast predicts rain for one more day.

COORDINATING CONJUNCTION A comma splice can be corrected by placing a coordinating conjunction (e.g. *and, or, but, yet, nor*) after the comma.

 I wanted help cooking dinner after I got home from work, and my daughter had already started cooking!

Tech Tip
Some grammar checkers will not catch comma splices. Proofread your work carefully to avoid comma splices.

LEARN MORE
- See Chapter 16, Effective Sentences, pages 410–411
- See Chapter 23, Punctuation, page 572
- See Writing Coach Online

✓ Check It

Use a current or completed draft of your work to practice correcting comma splices.

✓ **READ** carefully. Take time to read your draft carefully. Have someone else read your work for a double-check.

✓ **IDENTIFY** possible mistakes. Mark any comma splices you find.

✓ **REVISE** your sentences. Fix comma splices in different ways to vary your sentence structure.

Find It/FIX IT

17
Lack of Pronoun-Antecedent Agreement

GAME PLAN Check that pronouns agree with their antecedents in number, person, and gender. When the gender is not specified, the pronoun must still agree in number.

GENDER NEUTRAL ANTECEDENTS When gender is not specific, use *his or her* to refer to the singular antecedent.

Each drummer must bring ~~their~~ his or her drumsticks to band practice after school.

OR, NOR, AND When two or more singular antecedents are joined by *or* or *nor*, use a singular personal pronoun. Use a plural personal pronoun when two or more antecedents are joined by *and*.

Neither Ed nor John rode ~~their~~ his bike to school.

Lee and Tom are learning how to program ~~his~~ their computer.

INDEFINITE PRONOUNS A plural indefinite pronoun must agree with a plural personal pronoun. A singular indefinite pronoun must agree with a singular personal pronoun.

Few of the girls remembered that ~~her~~ their team bake sale was today.

One of the coaches supplied all of the treats for ~~their~~ her team's bake sale.

✓ Check It

Use a current or completed draft of your work to practice pronoun-antecedent agreement.

- ✓ **READ** carefully. Take time to read your draft carefully. For a double-check, have someone else read your work.
- ✓ **IDENTIFY** possible mistakes. Mark any pronouns that do not agree with their antecedents in a sentence.
- ✓ **USE** your textbook. Consult the grammar section of your textbook if you are not sure whether your pronouns and antecedents agree.

Tech Tip
When you cut and paste text from one sentence to another, check that the pronouns agree with the antecedent in the new sentence you create.

LEARN MORE
- See Chapter 19, Agreement, pages 495–501
- See Writing Coach Online

Grammar Game Plan

Find It/FIX IT

18

Poorly Integrated Quotation

GAME PLAN Quotations should flow smoothly into the sentences that surround them. Add explanatory information to link quotes to the rest of your work.

QUOTE IN A SENTENCE Prepare the reader for the information contained in the quote by introducing the quote's idea.

The president's biographer ˄discussed the president's life outside the office: "When he had a free moment, he spent it with his family" (72).

Amy˄writes about her feelings toward the book's introduction: "The introduction was informative, yet it lacked creativity."

QUOTE AS A SENTENCE Place an introductory phrase before or after a quotation that stands alone. In most cases, this phrase should identify the quote's author or speaker.

˄According to Beck, "The nation needs a leader in a time of crisis" (Beck 4).

✓ Check It

Use a current or completed draft of your work to practice integrating quotations.

- ✓ **SCAN Mentor Texts.** Notice how professional writers integrate quotations into their work.
- ✓ **IDENTIFY quotes.** Mark each quote in your work. Does each quote flow smoothly with the surrounding sentence?
- ✓ **REVISE your sentences.** Add explanatory information and introductions as needed.

Tech Tip

When you cut a quote from one sentence and paste it in another, remember to revise the surrounding sentence to integrate the quote into the text.

LEARN MORE
- See Chapter 23, Punctuation, pages 595–599
- See Writing Coach Online

Find It/FIX IT

19

Unnecessary or Missing Hyphen

GAME PLAN Use hyphens correctly in your writing, including with compound words and compound adjectives.

COMPOUND WORDS Hyphens can connect two or more words that are used as one compound word. Some compound words do not require a hyphen. Check a current dictionary if you are unsure about hyphenating a word.

My ~~daughterinlaw~~ daughter-in-law was waiting in the ~~drive-way~~ driveway for us to arrive.

The children on the ~~merrygoround~~ merry-go-round looked ~~care-free~~ carefree.

COMPOUND ADJECTIVES A compound adjective that appears before a noun should be hyphenated. Remember, do not hyphenate a compound proper noun acting as an adjective.

The well-known musician was in town performing a concert.

The Native American people cultivated many crops.

Tech Tip

The automatic hyphenation setting in word processors causes words at the end of a line of text to hyphenate automatically. Be sure to turn off this setting when you are writing a standard essay.

LEARN MORE
- See Chapter 23, Punctuation, pages 607–610
- See Writing Coach Online

✓ Check It

Use a current or completed draft of your work to practice hyphenating words.

- ✓ **IDENTIFY** possible errors. Mark any compound adjectives before a noun that are not hyphenated.
- ✓ **REVISE** your sentences. Add a hyphen to words that should be hyphenated.
- ✓ **USE** a dictionary. Consult a dictionary if you are not sure if a word should be hyphenated.

Find It/FIX IT

20 Sentence Fragment

GAME PLAN Use complete sentences when writing. Make sure you have a subject and a complete verb in each and that each sentence expresses a complete thought.

LACKING A SUBJECT OR VERB A complete sentence must have a subject and a verb.

Jamie rushed to get ready for dinner. ~~And~~ ∧She left the house without her purse!

The penguin ∧was diving under water.

SUBORDINATE CLAUSE A subordinate clause cannot stand on its own as a complete sentence because it does not express a complete thought.

Tabitha asked for milk to drink with breakfast~~.~~ ~~Although~~ ∧although she preferred orange juice.

We are all going to the swimming pool after school today~~.~~ ~~Unless~~ ∧unless it starts to rain.

✓ Check It

Use a current or completed draft of your work to practice writing complete sentences.

- ✓ **SCAN** your draft. Look for incomplete sentences.
- ✓ **IDENTIFY** missing words. Mark sentences that have missing subjects or verbs.
- ✓ **REVISE** your sentences. Rewrite any sentences that are missing subjects or verbs or that are subordinate clauses standing on their own.

Tech Tip
Sometimes, when you cut text from a sentence and paste it to another, you may miss cutting the whole sentence. Make sure you have both a subject and a verb in the new sentences.

LEARN MORE
- See Chapter 14, Basic Sentence Parts, pages 339–342
- See Chapter 16, Effective Sentences, pages 407–411
- See Writing Coach Online

Grammar Game Plan

THE PARTS of SPEECH

Use each part of speech to its best advantage to help you craft clear sentences.

WRITE GUY *Jeff Anderson, M.Ed.*

WHAT DO YOU NOTICE?

Track down parts of speech as you zoom in on these sentences from "Swimming to Antarctica: Tales of a Long-Distance Swimmer" by Lynne Cox.

> **MENTOR TEXT**
>
> He and all the crew were watching me intently, their faces filled with tension and concern.
> I put my head down, and something suddenly clicked.

Now, ask yourself the following questions:

- Which nouns are concrete, and which are abstract?
- Which part of speech are the words *intently* and *suddenly*, and what words do they modify?

The concrete nouns, which can be perceived using one of the senses, are *crew*, *faces*, and *head*. *Tension* and *concern* are the abstract nouns; they name concepts that cannot be directly perceived with the senses. The words *intently* and *suddenly* are adverbs. *Intently* modifies the verb *were watching*, and *suddenly* modifies *clicked*.

Grammar for Writers When writers master how to use parts of speech, they have tools for crafting excellent writing. Increase your writing tools by learning why each part of speech is important.

I'd like to see your list of abstract nouns.

Is it okay that the paper it's on is concrete?

CHAPTER 13

13.1 Nouns and Pronouns

Nouns and pronouns make it possible for people to label everything around them.

Nouns

The word *noun* comes from the Latin word *nomen*, which means "name."

> **RULE 13.1.1** A **noun** is the part of speech that names a person, place, thing, or idea.

Nouns that name a *person* or *place* are easy to identify.

PERSON	Uncle Mike, neighbor, girls, Bob, swimmer, Ms. Yang, Captain Smith
PLACE	library, Dallas, garden, city, kitchen, James River, canyon, Oklahoma

The category *thing* includes visible things, ideas, actions, conditions, and qualities.

VISIBLE THINGS	chair, pencil, school, duck, daffodil, fort
IDEAS	independence, democracy, militarism, capitalism, recession, freedom
ACTIONS	work, research, exploration, competition, exercise, labor
CONDITIONS	sadness, illness, excitement, joy, health, happiness
QUALITIES	kindness, patience, ability, compassion, intelligence, drive

WRITING COACH Online
www.phwritingcoach.com

Grammar Tutorials
Brush up on your Grammar skills with these animated videos.

Grammar Practice
Practice your grammar skills with Writing Coach Online.

Grammar Games
Test your knowledge of grammar in this fast-paced interactive video game.

294 The Parts of Speech

Concrete and Abstract Nouns

Nouns can also be grouped as *concrete* or *abstract*. A **concrete noun** names something you can see, touch, taste, hear, or smell. An **abstract noun** names something you cannot perceive through any of your five senses.

CONCRETE NOUNS   person, cannon, road, city, music

ABSTRACT NOUNS   hope, improvement, independence, desperation, cooperation

See Practice 13.1A

Collective Nouns

A **collective noun** names a *group* of people or things. A collective noun looks singular, but its meaning may be singular or plural, depending on how it is used in a sentence.

COLLECTIVE NOUNS			
army	choir	troop	faculty
cast	class	crew	legislature

Do not confuse collective nouns—nouns that name a collection of people or things acting as a unit—with plural nouns.

Compound Nouns

A **compound noun** is a noun made up of two or more words acting as a single unit. Compound nouns may be written as separate words, hyphenated words, or combined words.

COMPOUND NOUNS	
Separate	life preserver coffee table bird dog
Hyphenated	sergeant-at-arms self-rule daughter-in-law
Combined	battlefield dreamland porthole

Check a dictionary if you are not sure how to write a compound noun.

Nouns and Pronouns

Common and Proper Nouns

Any noun may be categorized as either *common* or *proper*.
A **common noun** names any one of a class of people, places, or things. A **proper noun** names a specific person, place, or thing. Proper nouns are capitalized, but common nouns are not. (See Chapter 22 for rules of capitalization.)

COMMON NOUNS	building, writer, nation, month, leader, place, book, war
PROPER NOUNS	Jones, Virginia, *Leaves of Grass*, Revolutionary War, White House, Mark Twain, France, June

A noun of direct address—the name of a person to whom you are directly speaking—is always a proper noun, as is a family title before a name. In the examples below, common nouns are highlighted in yellow, and proper nouns are highlighted in orange.

COMMON NOUNS
My **dad** is a **doctor**.
Our **teacher** is never late for **class**.
My favorite **person** is my **aunt**.

DIRECT ADDRESS
Please, **Grandma**, tell us about your trip.
Dad, can you drop me off?
Alex, please bring your pasta dish when you come to the party.

FAMILY TITLE
Aunt Anne is visiting from **England**.
Grandma doesn't really cook, but she bakes great muffins.
My favorite person is **Aunt Krissy**.

See Practice 13.1B

The Parts of Speech

PRACTICE 13.1A Identifying and Labeling Nouns as Concrete or Abstract

Read each sentence. Then, write the nouns in each sentence, and label them *concrete* or *abstract*.

EXAMPLE Stacy overcame her fears.

ANSWER *Stacy*— concrete
fears— abstract

1. The climbers' main concern was time.
2. Noah was hoping for a major promotion.
3. Thomas often thought about his adolescence.
4. My neighbor shows much compassion for his dog.
5. The sprinter has natural talent and agility.
6. Did the owner expand his business?
7. Success is something that drives Neil.
8. A positive outlook is something that separates Ameera from her co-workers.
9. The fisherman came back with only some seaweed to show for his effort.
10. I gave Terry my advice: search the Internet.

PRACTICE 13.1B Recognizing Kinds of Nouns (Collective, Compound, Proper)

Read each sentence. Then, write whether the underlined nouns are *collective*, *compound*, or *proper*. Answer in the order the words appear.

EXAMPLE Did you lend your suitcase to Louise?

ANSWER *compound, proper*

11. Next semester, our class will be traveling to Utah.
12. Toward the end of the close game, it appeared our team would be the winners.
13. My brother-in-law is moving out of the state.
14. The chef has opened a restaurant called Good Eatin'.
15. The caravan can accommodate many passengers.
16. My cousin, Santos, is a senior at the high school.
17. This book is a biography about a man who spoke for the poor minority.
18. I hope my uncle will visit our family this weekend.
19. We visited a battlefield in Virginia last summer.
20. During this time of year, you can get pecans from Texas.

SPEAKING APPLICATION

With a partner, take turns describing a scene from a movie that you create. The scene must contain three abstract nouns and three concrete nouns. Your partner should listen for and name the specific nouns.

WRITING APPLICATION

Using sentence 11 as your first sentence, write a brief fictional paragraph describing the trip. Be sure to include common, collective, compound, and proper nouns.

Pronouns

Pronouns help writers and speakers avoid awkward repetition of nouns.

> **Pronouns** are words that stand for nouns or for words that take the place of nouns.

Antecedents of Pronouns Pronouns get their meaning from the words they stand for. These words are called **antecedents.**

> **Antecedents** are nouns or words that take the place of nouns to which pronouns refer.

The arrows point from pronouns to their antecedents.

EXAMPLES **Heather** said **she** lost **her** ring at the concert.

When the **Halperns** moved, **they** gave **their** dog to me.

Attending the state seminar is tiring, but **it** is fun!

Antecedents do not always appear before their pronouns, however. Sometimes an antecedent follows its pronoun.

EXAMPLE Because of **its** food, **Houston**, Texas, is my favorite city.

There are several kinds of pronouns. Most of them have specific antecedents, but a few do not.

See Practice 13.1C

298 The Parts of Speech

Personal Pronouns The most common pronouns are the **personal pronouns.**

> **Personal pronouns** refer to the person speaking (first person), the person spoken to (second person), or the person, place, or thing spoken about (third person).

◀ 13.1.4 RULE

PERSONAL PRONOUNS		
	SINGULAR	**PLURAL**
First Person	I, me my, mine	we, us our, ours
Second Person	you your, yours	you your, yours
Third Person	he, him, his she, her, hers it, its	they, them their, theirs

In the first example below, the antecedent of the personal pronoun is the person speaking. In the second, the antecedent of the personal pronoun is the person being spoken to. In the last example, the antecedent of the personal pronoun is the thing spoken about.

FIRST PERSON **My** name is not Heather.

SECOND PERSON When **you** left, **you** forgot **your** phone.

THIRD PERSON The quilt is old, but **its** colors are still bright.

Reflexive and Intensive Pronouns These two types of pronouns look the same, but they function differently in sentences.

> A **reflexive pronoun** ends in *-self* or *-selves* and indicates that someone or something in the sentence acts for or on itself. A reflexive pronoun is essential to the meaning of a sentence.
> An **intensive pronoun** ends in *-self* or *-selves* and simply adds emphasis to a noun or pronoun in the sentence.

◀ 13.1.5 RULE

REFLEXIVE AND INTENSIVE PRONOUNS		
	SINGULAR	PLURAL
First Person	myself	ourselves
Second Person	yourself	yourselves
Third Person	himself, herself, itself	themselves

REFLEXIVE The family prepared **themselves** for the party.

INTENSIVE George McDoogle **himself** built the house.

See Practice 13.1D

Reciprocal Pronouns **Reciprocal pronouns** show a mutual action or relationship.

> **RULE 13.1.6**
> The **reciprocal pronouns** *each other* and *one another* refer to a plural antecedent. They express a mutual action or relationship.

EXAMPLES The two children sprayed water all over **each other**.

The dogs played with **one another**.

See Practice 13.1E
See Practice 13.1F

Demonstrative Pronouns **Demonstrative pronouns** are used to point out one or more nouns.

> **RULE 13.1.7**
> A **demonstrative pronoun** directs attention to a specific person, place, or thing.

There are four demonstrative pronouns.

DEMONSTRATIVE PRONOUNS	
SINGULAR	PLURAL
this, that	these, those

The Parts of Speech

Demonstrative pronouns may come before or after their antecedents.

BEFORE **That** is the **house** I would like to live in.

AFTER I hope to visit **Anita** and **Sonia**. **Those** are my first choices.

One of the demonstrative pronouns, *that*, can also be used as a relative pronoun.

Relative Pronouns

Relative pronouns are used to relate one idea in a sentence to another. There are five relative pronouns.

> A **relative pronoun** introduces an adjective clause and connects it to the word that the clause modifies.

RULE 13.1.8

RELATIVE PRONOUNS				
that	which	who	whom	whose

EXAMPLES We read a **play** **that** contained an account of the couple's story.

The **couple** **who** had written it described their conflicts.

The **storm**, **which** they knew would be strong, was fast approaching.

See Practice 13.1G
See Practice 13.1H

Nouns and Pronouns 301

PRACTICE 13.1C Identifying Pronouns and Antecedents

Read each sentence. Then, identify the pronoun and its antecedent in each sentence. If the sentence has no antecedent, write *none*.

EXAMPLE Steve fell and hurt his foot.
ANSWER *his, Steve*

1. He is nervous about the tryouts.
2. Taylor went to the putting green to practice his skills.
3. Meena had her van towed to the garage.
4. Mark couldn't understand the math problem until Harry wrote it on the board.
5. I will be happy to pay for lunch.
6. My brother sometimes loses his keys.
7. She should ask a teacher for help with the science assignment.
8. Tyra loves advanced science because she gets to dissect frogs.
9. To make an attractive border of roses, plant them close together.
10. After Jeremy painted the portrait, it was hung in the hallway.

PRACTICE 13.1D Identifying Personal, Reflexive, and Intensive Pronouns

Read each sentence. Then, write the pronoun(s) in each sentence and identify it as *personal*, *reflexive*, or *intensive*.

EXAMPLE Do muffins have fruit inside them?
ANSWER *them* — personal

11. My favorite talk show changed its host.
12. A number of my classmates read their essays aloud themselves.
13. He made sure the room was locked himself.
14. Between you and me, I am not sure we are going to make it on time.
15. Colleen and she will be math partners.
16. The waiting children amused themselves by drawing on the chalkboard.
17. The sun itself provides energy.
18. We told ourselves that we were going to win the race.
19. My driving all the way across the country worries my family.
20. The lawyer's clients are they.

SPEAKING APPLICATION

Take turns with a partner. Describe a fun situation you have had with a friend. Use pronouns referring to yourselves whenever possible. Your partner should identify the pronouns and their antecedents.

WRITING APPLICATION

Write a brief paragraph describing a visit to a doctor's office. Use at least one reflexive, intensive, and personal pronoun in your paragraph.

Nouns and Pronouns

PRACTICE 13.1E Identifying Reciprocal Pronouns

Read each sentence. Then, write the reciprocal pronoun in each sentence.

EXAMPLE The groomsmen toasted one another.
ANSWER *one another*

1. They talk to one another about pop culture.
2. The two articles definitely contradict each other.
3. Pam and Howard are completely devoted to each other.
4. We certainly missed each other while on vacation.
5. They all said hello to one another.
6. They met each other at the library.
7. Tyrone, Michael, and Keith help one another with their studies.
8. They made plans to visit one another's families during their break.
9. Lance and Gloria did each other's chores.
10. The candidates had mutual respect for each other after the debate.

PRACTICE 13.1F Writing Sentences With Reciprocal Pronouns

Read each item. Then, write a sentence, using the correct reciprocal pronoun, to summarize each item. Read your sentences to a partner who will tell you if you have used the correct reciprocal pronouns.

EXAMPLE Bob e-mailed Tim. Tim e-mailed Bob.
ANSWER *Bob and Tim e-mailed each other.*

11. Josh rode past Sam. Sam rode past Josh.
12. The brothers wrote to their sisters. The sisters wrote to their brothers.
13. The mayor spoke with the governor. The governor spoke with the mayor.
14. Mr. Wilson waved to Ms. Sanchez. Ms. Sanchez waved to Mr. Wilson.
15. The older runners raced younger runners. The younger runners raced older runners.
16. My aunt helped my uncle paint. My uncle helped my aunt paint.
17. Sandra walked dogs with Lewis. Lewis walked dogs with Sandra.
18. The artists worked with art students. Art students worked with the artists.
19. The brown bears fought the black bears. The black bears fought the brown bears.
20. The cats chased the kittens. The kittens chased the cats.

SPEAKING APPLICATION

Take turns with a partner. Describe an enjoyable weekend you have had. Show that you understand reciprocal pronouns by using some in your response. Your partner should listen for and identify the reciprocal pronouns.

WRITING APPLICATION

Use Practice 13.1F as a model to write three more items. Read your items to a partner. Your partner should say one sentence, using a reciprocal pronoun to summarize each item.

Nouns and Pronouns

Test Warm-Up

DIRECTIONS
Read the introduction and the passage that follows. Then, answer the questions to show that you can use and understand the function of reciprocal pronouns in reading and writing.

Laura wrote this paragraph about her jazz dance class. Read the paragraph and think about the changes you would suggest as a peer editor. When you finish reading, answer the questions that follow.

My Saturday Dance Class

(1) Before our beginner dance class started, we watched a group of advanced dancers perform. (2) Several dancers leaped over one anothers before jumping and spinning high in the air. (3) Their two proud teachers turned and smiled at themselves happily. (4) I looked nervously at my best friend Ellen. (5) My best friend Ellen looked nervously at me. (6) Then, the jazz dancers in our class helped each of the other jazz dancers learn some new steps. (7) Who knows? (8) Maybe one day soon we will soar high in the air, too!

---

1 What change, if any, should be made in sentence 2?

  A Replace *one anothers* with **each others**

  B Replace *one anothers* with **each**

  C Replace *one anothers* with **one another**

  D Make no change

2 What change, if any, should be made in sentence 3?

  F Replace *themselves* with **each other**

  G Replace *themselves* with **each**

  H Replace *themselves* with **one**

  J Make no change

3 What is the most effective way to combine sentences 4 and 5?

  A Ellen and I looked nervous to each other.

  B My best friend Ellen and I looked at one another.

  C Ellen, my best friend, and I looked very nervous together.

  D My best friend Ellen and I looked nervously at each other.

4 What is the most effective way to rewrite the ideas in sentence 6?

  F Then, some dancers helped each other learn some new steps.

  G Then, the jazz dancers helped the dancers in our class learn some steps.

  H Then, all the dancers in our jazz class learned some steps together.

  J Then, the jazz dancers in our class helped one another learn some new steps.

Nouns and Pronouns

PRACTICE 13.1G Writing Demonstrative and Relative Pronouns

Read each sentence. Then, write a demonstrative or relative pronoun to complete each sentence. Label the pronoun *demonstrative* or *relative*.

EXAMPLE ____ star is really bright.

ANSWER *That* — demonstrative

1. The shoes I want are ____ on display.
2. We voted for the candidate ____ was the best speaker.
3. To ____ did you address the letter?
4. ____ is easier to make than that other recipe.
5. This computer, ____ belongs to my brother, doesn't work.
6. Ray wrote the story ____ won first prize.
7. I met the artist ____ paintings hang in the museum.
8. ____ is the best place to plant the rose bush.
9. ____ are my newest suggestions for our school project.
10. Take ____ back to the library before they become overdue.

PRACTICE 13.1H Recognizing Demonstrative and Relative Pronouns

Read each sentence. Then, label the underlined pronoun *demonstrative* or *relative*.

EXAMPLE The book, which was written by a lawyer, was fascinating.

ANSWER relative

11. That was a filling dinner!
12. Last week, my uncle, who is a doctor, saved a patient's life.
13. This and many other questions can be answered by checking online.
14. Tommy is the guy whose answer is correct.
15. The highway that I take to school is under construction.
16. Malia is the baby whom everyone loves to hold.
17. Might these be the earliest films ever recorded?
18. That might be the strangest dress in the show.
19. Of all the shoes on the rack, these appear to be the best-selling pair.
20. Jason's helmet, which is brand new, is guaranteed not to break.

SPEAKING APPLICATION

Take turns with a partner. Using demonstrative and relative pronouns, describe a movie that you've seen. Your partner should listen for and identify the demonstrative and relative pronouns that you use.

WRITING APPLICATION

Write a brief paragraph, describing the room you are in or the items in it. Include two demonstrative and two relative pronouns in your paragraph.

Practice

Interrogative Pronouns
Interrogative pronouns are used to ask questions.

> An **interrogative pronoun** is used to begin a question.

The five interrogative pronouns are *what*, *which*, *who*, *whom*, and *whose*. Sometimes the antecedent of an interrogative pronoun is not known.

EXAMPLE **Who** picked up the puppy?

See Practice 13.1I

Indefinite Pronouns
Indefinite pronouns sometimes lack specific antecedents.

> An **indefinite pronoun** refers to a person, place, or thing that may or may not be specifically named.

INDEFINITE PRONOUNS			
SINGULAR		**PLURAL**	**BOTH**
another	everyone	nothing	both	all
anybody	everything	one	few	any
anyone	little	other	many	more
anything	much	somebody	others	most
each	neither	someone	several	none
either	nobody	something		some
everybody	no one			

Indefinite pronouns sometimes have specific antecedents.

NO SPECIFIC ANTECEDENT **Everyone** has visited New York City.

SPECIFIC ANTECEDENTS **Most** of the **students** read.

Indefinite pronouns can also function as adjectives.

ADJECTIVE **Few** teams are as famous as this one.

See Practice 13.1J

PRACTICE 13.1I Recognizing Interrogative Pronouns

Read each sentence. Then, write the correct interrogative pronoun needed for each sentence.

EXAMPLE   _____ is your favorite movie?
ANSWER   *What*

1. _____ of the houses do you like the best?
2. _____ voice can be heard in the background?
3. _____ gave you the application form to this job?
4. Behind _____ of the walls do you hear the scratching?
5. _____ are you doing after the year is over?
6. Of all the people in the room, _____ can lead you in the right direction?
7. _____ do you think it will take to win the contest?
8. _____ did you think was the best speech?
9. _____ has heard of such horrible behavior?
10. With _____ are you going to the beach?

PRACTICE 13.1J Identifying Indefinite Pronouns

Read each sentence. Then, write the indefinite pronoun or pronouns in each sentence.

EXAMPLE   None of us realized what happened.
ANSWER   *None*

11. Everyone in the stands was cheering loudly.
12. Someone had already collected all the tickets.
13. Though there were plenty of people, none of the guests had much to say.
14. Few of the senators would admit that anything had happened.
15. No one could deny that something specific should be accomplished.
16. Several of my teachers advised me that much remained to be done.
17. Many of my friends have opinions about everything.
18. Does either of the teams seem better than the other?
19. Few people live in areas where there is no electricity.
20. Did you get everything for the party?

SPEAKING APPLICATION

With a partner, take turns interviewing each other as if on a talk show. Use interrogative pronouns in all of your questions.

WRITING APPLICATION

Rewrite sentences 11, 12, and 17, replacing all the nouns and indefinite pronouns. Make sure that the sentences still make sense.

13.2 Verbs

Every complete sentence must have at least one **verb**, which may consist of as many as four words.

WRITING COACH Online
www.phwritingcoach.com

Grammar Tutorials
Brush up on your Grammar skills with these animated videos.

Grammar Practice
Practice your grammar skills with Writing Coach Online.

Grammar Games
Test your knowledge of grammar in this fast-paced interactive video game.

A **verb** is a word or group of words that expresses time while showing an action, a condition, or the fact that something exists.

Action Verbs and Linking Verbs

Action verbs express action. They are used to tell what someone or something does, did, or will do. **Linking verbs** express a condition or show that something exists.

An **action verb** tells what action someone or something is performing.

ACTION VERBS

Tara **learned** about summer sports.

The television **blared** the broadcast of the new show.

We **chose** two artists from Texas.

I **remember** the film about the Alamo.

The action expressed by a verb does not have to be visible. Words expressing mental activities—such as *learn*, *think*, or *decide*—are also considered action verbs.

The person or thing that performs the action is called the *subject* of the verb. In the examples above, *Tara*, *television*, *we*, and *I* are the subjects of *learned*, *blared*, *chose*, and *remember*.

308 The Parts of Speech

> **A linking verb** is a verb that connects its subject with a noun, pronoun, or adjective that identifies or describes the subject.

RULE 13.2.3

LINKING VERBS

The man **is** a famous actor.

The stage floor **seems** polished.

The verb *be* is the most common linking verb.

THE FORMS OF *BE*			
am	am being	can be	have been
are	are being	could be	has been
is	is being	may be	had been
was	was being	might be	could have been
were	were being	must be	may have been
		shall be	might have been
		should be	shall have been
		will be	should have been
		would be	will have been
			would have been

Most often, the forms of *be* that function as linking verbs express the condition of the subject. Occasionally, however, they may merely express existence, usually by showing, with other words, where the subject is located.

EXAMPLE The player **is** on the field.

Other Linking Verbs A few other verbs can also serve as linking verbs.

OTHER LINKING VERBS		
appear	look	sound
become	remain	stay
feel	seem	taste
grow	smell	turn

EXAMPLES

The cut grass **smelled** fresh and clean.

The fans **sound** excited.

The bus driver **stayed** alert.

The conditions on board **remained** dangerous.

The students **grew** nervous.

Some of these verbs may also act as action—not linking—verbs. To determine whether the word is functioning as an action verb or as a linking verb, insert *am*, *are*, or *is* in place of the verb. If the substitute makes sense while connecting two words, then the original verb is a linking verb.

LINKING VERB   The air **felt** warm. (The air **is** warm.)

ACTION VERB   The surfers **felt** the wave crash.

LINKING VERB   The mangos **taste** sweet. (The mangos **are** sweet.)

ACTION VERB   I **taste** the mango.

See Practice 13.2A
See Practice 13.2B

The Parts of Speech

PRACTICE 13.2A Identifying Action and Linking Verbs

Read each sentence. Then, write the action verb in each sentence.

EXAMPLE   They talked about life on Mars.
ANSWER   *talked*

1. The gardener mowed the thick green lawn.
2. The carpenter sawed the pine boards.
3. The waitress looked at the soggy mess.
4. Ana picked the strawberries in the garden.
5. The frog jumped from one lily pad to another.

Read each sentence. Then, write the linking verb(s) in each sentence.

EXAMPLE   Safety should be your first concern.
ANSWER   *should be*

6. Elaine is often late for appointments.
7. That will be a sufficient amount of time.
8. That strawberry tasted sweet.
9. George W. Bush was the forty-third president.
10. That stranger looks suspicious.

PRACTICE 13.2B Distinguishing Between Action and Linking Verbs

Read each sentence. Then, write the verb in each sentence and label it *action* or *linking*.

EXAMPLE   The puppy looks hungry.
ANSWER   *looks* — linking

11. In their garden, they grow tomatoes.
12. Do you feel sick?
13. Our furniture looks new.
14. The boy on horseback sounded the alarm.
15. Pedro tapped the piano keys.
16. Your idea sounds very interesting.
17. She grew fond of her new sister.
18. The car looks unsafe for the road.
19. Taste this salad dressing.
20. The coach praised the players for their effort.

SPEAKING APPLICATION

Take turns with a partner. Tell about a game you played with friends recently. Your partner should listen for and name three action verbs.

WRITING APPLICATION

Use *look*, *feel*, and *taste* in original sentences. First, use the words as action verbs. Then, use the words as linking verbs.

Transitive and Intransitive Verbs

All verbs are either **transitive** or **intransitive**, depending on whether or not they transfer action to another word in a sentence.

> **A transitive verb** directs action toward someone or something named in the same sentence. An **intransitive verb** does not direct action toward anyone or anything named in the same sentence.

The word toward which a transitive verb directs its action is called the *object* of the verb. Intransitive verbs never have objects. You can determine whether a verb has an object by asking *whom* or *what* after the verb.

TRANSITIVE   Cara **read** the book.
(Read what? book)

We **ate** the veggie burger.
(Ate what? veggie burger)

INTRANSITIVE   The choir **practiced** on the stage.
(Practiced what? [no answer])

The teacher **answered** quickly.
(Answered what? [no answer])

> Because linking verbs do not express action, they are always intransitive. Most action verbs can be either transitive or intransitive, depending on the sentence. However, some action verbs can only be transitive, and others can only be intransitive.

TRANSITIVE   I **wrote** a letter from Israel.

INTRANSITIVE   The students **wrote** quickly.

312   **The Parts of Speech**

ALWAYS TRANSITIVE	The Bobcats **rival** the Panthers.
ALWAYS INTRANSITIVE	He **winced** at the sound of the horn.

See Practice 13.2C

Verb Phrases

A verb that has more than one word is a **verb phrase.**

> **A verb phrase** consists of a main verb and one or more helping verbs.

◁ 13.2.6 RULE

Helping verbs are often called auxiliary verbs. One or more helping verbs may precede the main verb in a verb phrase.

VERB PHRASES	I **will be taking** a tour of the city.
	I **should have been watching** the weather report.

All the forms of *be* listed in this chapter can be used as helping verbs. The following verbs can also be helping verbs.

OTHER HELPING VERBS			
do	have	shall	can
does	has	should	could
did	had	will	may
		would	might
			must

A verb phrase is often interrupted by other words in a sentence.

INTERRUPTED VERB PHRASES	I **will** definitely **be taking** a tour of the city next winter.
	Should I **take** a tour of the city next winter?

See Practice 13.2D

Verbs 313

Verbs

PRACTICE 13.2C Distinguishing Between Transitive and Intransitive Verbs

Read each sentence. Then, write the action verb in each sentence, and label it *intransitive* or *transitive*.

EXAMPLE   The harpist plucked the shortest string.

ANSWER   *plucked* — transitive

1. The car moved into the parking space easily.
2. The shop sells beautiful floral centerpieces.
3. Please put those cabbages on the counter.
4. The plane finally arrived after a three-hour delay.
5. The bird cage swung from a golden chain.
6. He shuddered with fright during the scary movie.
7. The dog wagged his tail happily.
8. We made lemonade for the picnic.
9. Steak and potatoes sizzled in the pan.
10. The waves crashed upon the shore.

PRACTICE 13.2D Recognizing Verb Phrases

Read each sentence. Then, write the verb phrase in each sentence.

EXAMPLE   Contact lenses are becoming popular.

ANSWER   *are becoming*

11. The sun will have set by seven o'clock.
12. A dolphin was swimming in the water.
13. My car will be fixed at the service station.
14. The woodcutter has been sawing all day.
15. Paul has acted strangely today.
16. Abigail did tell me about the party.
17. He does ride the bus to school each day.
18. Choi could have offered us his help.
19. Rehearsal should have lasted another hour.
20. I have seen better performances.

SPEAKING APPLICATION

Take turns with a partner. Tell about an important event that has occurred in your life. Your partner should identify both the intransitive and transitive verbs in your sentences.

WRITING APPLICATION

Rewrite sentences 14 and 20, keeping the subject but changing the verb phrases.

13.3 Adjectives and Adverbs

Adjectives and **adverbs** are the two parts of speech known as *modifiers*—that is, they slightly change the meaning of other words by adding description or making them more precise.

Writing Coach Online
www.phwritingcoach.com

Grammar Tutorials
Brush up on your Grammar skills with these animated videos.

Grammar Practice
Practice your grammar skills with Writing Coach Online.

Grammar Games
Test your knowledge of grammar in this fast-paced interactive video game.

Adjectives

An **adjective** clarifies the meaning of a noun or pronoun by providing information about its appearance, location, and so on.

> An **adjective** is a word used to describe a noun or pronoun or to give it a more specific meaning.

RULE 13.3.1

An adjective answers one of four questions about a noun or pronoun: *What kind? Which one? How many? How much?*

EXAMPLES   **oak** tree (What kind of tree?)

that house (Which house?)

12 roses (How many roses?)

extensive snowfall (How much snow?)

When an adjective modifies a noun, it usually precedes the noun. Occasionally, the adjective may follow the noun.

EXAMPLES   The realtor was **tactful** about my concerns.

I considered the realtor **tactful**.

An adjective that modifies a pronoun usually follows it. Sometimes, however, the adjective precedes the pronoun as it does in the example on the next page.

Adjectives and Adverbs   315

AFTER They were **excited** when they heard the news.

BEFORE **Excited** about the upcoming vacation, they began to pack.

More than one adjective may modify a single noun or pronoun.

EXAMPLE We hired a **competent, enthusiastic** coach.

Articles Three common adjectives—*a, an*, and *the*—are known as **articles.** *A* and *an* are called **indefinite articles** because they refer to any one of a class of nouns. *The* refers to a specific noun and, therefore, is called the **definite article.**

INDEFINITE EXAMPLES	DEFINITE EXAMPLES
a daisy	the stem
an orchid	the chair

Remember that *an* is used before a vowel sound; *a* is used before a consonant sound.

EXAMPLES a one-car family (*w* sound)

a unicorn (*y* sound)

an honest president (no *h* sound)

See Practice 13.3A

Nouns Used as Adjectives Words that are usually nouns sometimes act as adjectives. In this case, the noun answers the questions *What kind?* or *Which one?* about another noun.

NOUNS USED AS ADJECTIVES	
flower	flower garden
lawn	lawn chair

See Practice 13.3B

The Parts of Speech

Adjectives and Adverbs

Proper Adjectives Adjectives can also be proper. **Proper adjectives** are proper nouns used as adjectives or adjectives formed from proper nouns. They usually begin with capital letters.

PROPER NOUNS	PROPER ADJECTIVES
Monday	Monday morning
San Francisco	San Francisco streets
Europe	European roses
Rome	Roman hyacinth

Compound Adjectives Adjectives can be compound. Most are hyphenated; others are combined or are separate words.

HYPHENATED   rain-forest plants

water-soluble pigments

COMBINED   airborne pollen

evergreen shrubs

See Practice 13.3C   **SEPARATE**   North American rhododendrons

Pronouns Used as Adjectives Certain pronouns can also function as adjectives. The seven personal pronouns known as either **possessive adjectives** or **possessive pronouns** do double duty in a sentence. They act as pronouns because they have antecedents. They also act as adjectives because they modify nouns by answering *Which one?* The other pronouns become adjectives instead of pronouns when they stand before nouns and answer the question *Which one?*

> A pronoun is used as an adjective if it modifies a noun.

Possessive pronouns, demonstrative pronouns, interrogative pronouns, and indefinite pronouns can all function as adjectives when they modify nouns.

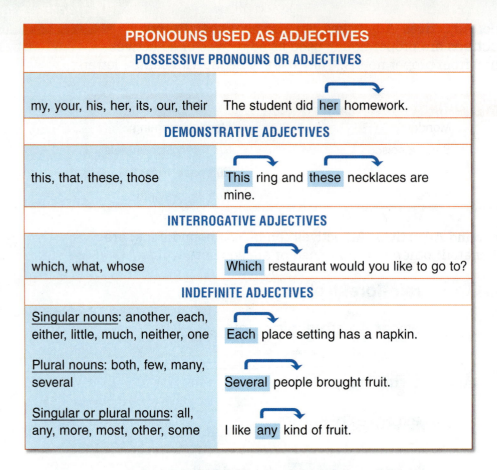

Verb Forms Used as Adjectives Verb forms used as adjectives usually end in *-ing* or *-ed* and are called **participles.**

EXAMPLE   I threw out the **rotting** fruit.

Nouns, pronouns, and verb forms function as adjectives only when they modify other nouns or pronouns. The following examples show how their function in a sentence can change.

	REGULAR FUNCTION	AS AN ADJECTIVE
Noun	The driveway was very slippery.	I slid on the driveway surface.
Pronoun	This was a joyful event.	This event was joyful.
Verb	The snow finally melted!	The melted snow made a puddle.

See Practice 13.3D

318   The Parts of Speech

Adjectives and Adverbs

PRACTICE 13.3A Recognizing Adjectives and Articles

Read each sentence. Then, write the adjective in each sentence.

EXAMPLE   The lonesome howl came from the woods.
ANSWER   *lonesome*

1. There was a major accident on the highway.
2. You have an important medical appointment.
3. There wasn't enough money to pay the bill.
4. A dozen eggs will be enough to make bread.
5. The railing was silvery in the dim shadows.

Read each sentence. Then, write the article(s) in each sentence.

EXAMPLE   The rainy weather turned pleasant.
ANSWER   *The*

6. The timid driver was afraid to drive on the roads.
7. A purple eggplant and a red tomato are in the bowl.
8. An old fence surrounded the vast estate.
9. The bird in the cage is a parrot.
10. The room had dull walls and a dingy rug.

PRACTICE 13.3B Identifying Nouns Used as Adjectives

Read each sentence. Then, write the noun that is used as an adjective in each sentence and the noun that it modifies.

EXAMPLE   Our class is visiting the state capital next week.
ANSWER   *state, capital*

11. We use the good dishes for our holiday meals.
12. Grandma made a peach cobbler.
13. Fernando glanced at the storm clouds.
14. She wished she had worn her leather gloves.
15. She waited at the bus stop.
16. Eve remembered the card that came with her birthday present.
17. My dad hung the curtain rod yesterday.
18. The television station was having a contest.
19. My office chair was broken.
20. Alan showed me how to fix my bicycle chain.

SPEAKING APPLICATION

Take turns with a partner. Tell about your favorite meal. Use different kinds of adjectives. Your partner should name the adjectives and say if they tell what kind or how many.

WRITING APPLICATION

Write three sentences that contain nouns used as adjectives. Then, exchange papers with a partner and underline the nouns used as adjectives.

Adjectives and Adverbs

PRACTICE 13.3C → **Recognizing Proper and Compound Adjectives**

Read each sentence. Then, write the adjective(s) in each sentence, and label each adjective as either *proper* or *compound*.

EXAMPLE   Olivia doesn't like the July heat.
ANSWER   *July* — proper

1. Spencer would like to be an airplane pilot.
2. Celtic music can be heard on the radio.
3. The family enjoys eating in Chinese restaurants.
4. She read another bedtime story to her sister.
5. The concert was held in a downtown park.
6. I know the star of that British science-fiction movie.
7. He tried the Turkish saltwater taffy.
8. The foolishness of their actions was self-evident.
9. We bought a Victorian table for the bedroom.
10. He wore a waterproof Icelandic parka.

PRACTICE 13.3D → **Recognizing Pronouns and Verbs Used as Adjectives**

Read each sentence. Then, write the pronoun or verb used as an adjective in each sentence and the noun that it modifies.

EXAMPLE   Dad replaced the shattered windowpane.
ANSWER   *shattered, windowpane*

11. Their baby kept us awake.
12. We moved the fallen branch from the driveway.
13. The freezing rain was the cause of the icy roads.
14. Many students enjoy doing math work.
15. He flipped the sizzling pancake.
16. The departing passengers checked in at the gate.
17. The milk was spilled by the hurrying waiter.
18. The meeting room will be ready on Tuesday.
19. My solar car is powered by the sun's energy.
20. Each contestant hoped to win the grand prize.

SPEAKING APPLICATION

With a partner, name four adjectives that are proper and compound. Then, take turns using each of them in a sentence.

WRITING APPLICATION

Replace the pronouns or verbs used as adjectives in sentences in Practice 13.3D with other pronouns or verbs.

Adjectives and Adverbs

Adverbs

Adverbs, like adjectives, describe other words or make other words more specific.

> An **adverb** is a word that modifies a verb, an adjective, or another adverb.

When an adverb modifies a verb, it will answer any of the following questions: *Where? When? In what way? To what extent?*

An adverb answers only one question when modifying an adjective or another adverb: *To what extent?* Because it specifies the degree or intensity of the modified adjective or adverb, such an adverb is often called an **intensifier.**

The position of an adverb in relation to the word it modifies can vary in a sentence. If the adverb modifies a verb, it may precede or follow it or even interrupt a verb phrase. Normally, adverbs modifying adjectives and adverbs will immediately precede the words they modify.

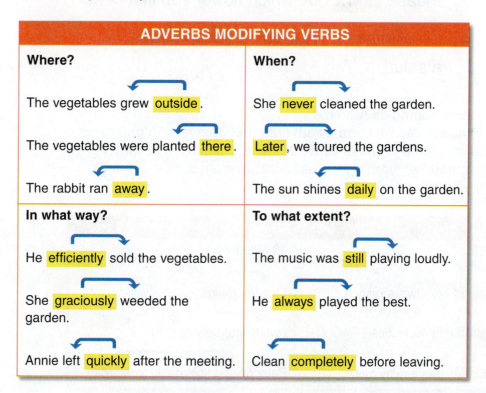

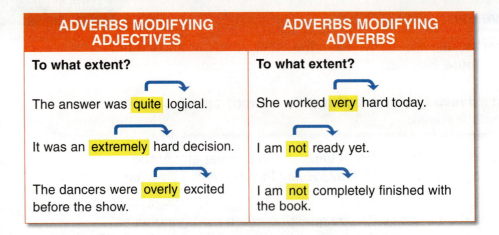

Adverbs as Parts of Verbs Some verbs require an adverb to complete their meaning. Adverbs used this way are considered part of the verb. An adverb functioning as part of a verb does not answer the usual questions for adverbs.

EXAMPLES The car **backed up** into the other car.

Please **point out** which flower you like best.

Carolyn had to **run out** at lunch to get a salad.

See Practice 13.3E

Nouns Functioning as Adverbs
Several nouns can function as adverbs that answer the questions *Where?* or *When?* Some of these words are *home, yesterday, today, tomorrow, mornings, afternoons, evenings, nights, week, month,* and *year.*

NOUNS USED AS ADVERBS	
NOUNS	**AS ADVERBS**
Mornings are always rushed.	I run mornings.
My afternoon looks busy.	I work afternoons.
Yesterday was a rainy day.	Peter finished his book yesterday.

Adjectives and Adverbs

Adverb or Adjective?
Adverbs usually have different forms from adjectives and thus are easily identified. Many adverbs are formed by the addition of *-ly* to an adjective.

ADJECTIVES   The teacher looked **proud**.

Jeff ran through the **open** door.

ADVERBS   The teacher looked at her students **proudly**.

The committee discussed the issue **openly**.

Some adjectives, however, also end in *-ly*. Therefore, you cannot assume that every word ending in *-ly* is an adverb.

ADJECTIVES   a **daily** schedule

an **early** lunch

a **ghostly** noise

hilly terrain

Some adjectives and adverbs share the same form. You can determine the part of speech of such words by checking their function in the sentence. An adverb will modify a verb, adjective, or adverb; an adjective will modify a noun or pronoun.

ADVERB   The class ran **late**.

ADJECTIVE   We enjoy playing in the **late** summer.

ADVERB   The girl walked **straight** through the tunnel.

See Practice 13.3F   **ADJECTIVE**   The road was **straight**.

Adjectives and Adverbs

PRACTICE 13.3E Recognizing Adverbs

Read each sentence. Then, write the adverb or adverbs in each sentence.

EXAMPLE   Ted just recently learned to sail.
ANSWER   *just, recently*

1. Sasha typed quite rapidly.
2. The actors gave a surprisingly good performance.
3. My mom's job suits her very well.
4. He readily accepted the offer.
5. Our hard work and practice made it a truly close contest.
6. Dad leaves for work fairly early.
7. The clothes dried rapidly.
8. Kevin's secret project is very nearly finished.
9. The workers have almost totally rebuilt the home.
10. Alfredo is an exceptionally talented artist.

PRACTICE 13.3F Identifying Adverbs and the Words They Modify

Read each sentence. Then, write the adverb in each sentence and the word it modifies.

EXAMPLE   We are walking home.
ANSWER   *home, walking*

11. The first session of summer camp starts tomorrow.
12. Because she had to leave, Juanita took the test early.
13. We watched to see who would finish first in the contest.
14. Our new neighbors arrived yesterday.
15. I ran fast and tried to warn the others.
16. Dad asked me to go upstairs.
17. Because of the snow, we left later than our friends.
18. My dad works nights.
19. The teacher reminded us that we have only one chance to pass the test.
20. Ping worked hard and was able to finish his project and meet the deadline.

SPEAKING APPLICATION

Take turns with a partner. Tell about something that you enjoy doing. Your partner should name adverbs that you use to describe where, when, in what way, and to what extent you do the activity.

WRITING APPLICATION

Use sentences 13, 16, and 17 as models to write three sentences of your own. Replace the adverbs with other adverbs. Make sure that the sentences still make sense.

13.4 Prepositions, Conjunctions, and Interjections

Prepositions and conjunctions function in sentences as connectors. **Prepositions** express relationships between words or ideas, whereas **conjunctions** join words, groups of words, or even entire sentences. **Interjections** function by themselves and are independent of other words in a sentence.

Grammar Tutorials
Brush up on your Grammar skills with these animated videos.

Grammar Practice
Practice your grammar skills with Writing Coach Online.

Grammar Games
Test your knowledge of grammar in this fast-paced interactive video game.

Prepositions and Prepositional Phrases

Prepositions make it possible to show relationships between words. The relationships may involve, for example, location, direction, time, cause, or possession. A preposition may consist of one word or multiple words. (See the chart on the next page.)

> **A preposition** relates the noun or pronoun that appears with it to another word in the sentence.

RULE 13.4.1

Notice how the prepositions below, highlighted in pink, relate to the words highlighted in yellow.

LOCATION   Vegetables **are grown** around the **world**.

TIME   Some stories **last** for **generations**.

CAUSE   Joe is **late** because of of the **weather**.

> **A prepositional phrase** is a group of words that includes a preposition and a noun or pronoun.

RULE 13.4.2

The noun or pronoun with a preposition is called the **object of the preposition**. Objects may have one or more modifiers. A prepositional phrase may also have more than one object. In the example below, the objects of the prepositions are highlighted in blue, and the prepositions are in pink.

EXAMPLE   Jack and Kara registered for classes on Friday.

Prepositions, Conjunctions, and Interjections   325

PREPOSITIONS

aboard	before	in front of	over
about	behind	in place of	owing to
above	below	in regard to	past
according to	beneath	inside	prior to
across	beside	in spite of	regarding
across from	besides	instead of	round
after	between	into	since
against	beyond	in view of	through
ahead of	but	like	throughout
along	by	near	till
alongside	by means of	nearby	to
along with	concerning	next to	together with
amid	considering	of	toward
among	despite	off	under
apart from	down	on	underneath
around	during	on account of	until
aside from	except	onto	unto
as of	for	on top of	up
as	from	opposite	upon
atop	in	out	with
barring	in addition to	out of	within
because of	in back of	outside	without

See Practice 13.4A

Preposition or Adverb?
Many words may be used either as prepositions or adverbs. Words that can function in either role include *around*, *before*, *behind*, *down*, *in*, *off*, *on*, *out*, *over*, and *up*. If an object accompanies the word, the word is used as a preposition.

PREPOSITION   The novel developed **around** a detailed outline.

ADVERB   My plot originally went **around and around**.

See Practice 13.4B

The Parts of Speech

PRACTICE 13.4A Identifying Prepositions and Prepositional Phrases

Read each sentence. Then, write the prepositional phrase(s) in each sentence and underline the preposition(s).

EXAMPLE I took the kids to the park on Elm Street.

ANSWER *to the park; on Elm Street*

1. According to this poster, the block party starts at noon.
2. There is an empty locker for you next to mine.
3. The teacher announced a contest between the two classes.
4. We need three cups of blueberries for the pie.
5. A city with a warm climate will be perfect for us.
6. Nita likes to ride in the front of the plane.
7. The children peered through the glass door.
8. Our neighbor down the street has a trampoline in his yard.
9. We jumped into the lake with our inflatable raft.
10. The raccoon was hiding underneath the porch.

PRACTICE 13.4B Distinguishing Between Prepositions and Adverbs

Read each sentence. Then, label each underlined word as a *preposition* or an *adverb*.

EXAMPLE The house has a basement storage area and an attic above.

ANSWER *adverb*

11. Before we went inside, we took our boots off.
12. My mom enjoys moving furniture around.
13. We saw fish swimming just below the surface of the water.
14. Let's put our bikes inside the garage tonight.
15. To finish making the batter, mix the nuts evenly throughout.
16. The reporter did not realize that the interview was off the record.
17. Please do not write anything on the lines below the shaded box.
18. Dad had to move the barbeque inside when it started to rain.
19. We built a fence around the yard.
20. The children ride their bikes throughout the neighborhood.

SPEAKING APPLICATION

With a partner, take turns describing the locations of objects in the room. Your partner should listen for and identify the prepositional phrases that you use and the preposition in each phrase.

WRITING APPLICATION

Write a sentence using the word *behind* as a preposition. Then, write a sentence using *behind* as an adverb.

Conjunctions

There are three main kinds of conjunctions: **coordinating, correlative,** and **subordinating.** Sometimes a type of adverb, the **conjunctive adverb,** is also considered a conjunction.

A **conjunction** is a word used to connect other words or groups of words.

Coordinating Conjunctions The seven coordinating conjunctions are used to connect similar parts of speech or groups of words of equal grammatical weight.

EXAMPLES   My mother **and** father ran the club.

Maria left early, **so** I left with her.

Correlative Conjunctions The five paired correlative conjunctions join elements of equal grammatical weight.

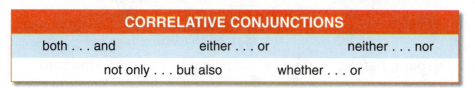

EXAMPLES   She saw **both** whales **and** sharks.

Neither Ricky **nor** Dan came to the meeting.

I don't know **whether** to read the book **or** see the movie.

Subordinating Conjunctions Subordinating conjunctions join two complete ideas by making one of the ideas subordinate to, or dependent upon, the other.

SUBORDINATING CONJUNCTIONS			
after	because	lest	till
although	before	now that	unless
as	even if	provided	until
as if	even though	since	when
as long as	how	so that	whenever
as much as	if	than	where
as soon as	inasmuch as	that	wherever
as though	in order that	though	while

The subordinate idea in a sentence always begins with a subordinating conjunction and makes up what is known as a subordinate clause. A subordinate clause may either follow or precede the main idea in a sentence.

EXAMPLES We protect the rain forest **because** it is important to the environment.

As soon as the firefighters arrived, they began to put the fire out.

Conjunctive Adverbs Conjunctive adverbs act as transitions between complete ideas by indicating comparisons, contrasts, results, and other relationships. The chart below lists the most common conjunctive adverbs.

CONJUNCTIVE ADVERBS		
accordingly	finally	nevertheless
again	furthermore	otherwise
also	however	then
besides	indeed	therefore
consequently	moreover	thus

Punctuation With Conjunctive Adverbs Punctuation is usually required both before and after conjunctive adverbs.

EXAMPLES
The committee was very successful. **Therefore**, they continued to plan with great detail.

Ricky played several sports very well; **however**, his favorite was hockey.

I forgot my ticket; **therefore**, I could not get in.

See Practice 13.4C

Interjections

Interjections express emotion. Unlike most words, they have no grammatical connection to other words in a sentence.

An **interjection** is a word that expresses feeling or emotion and functions independently of a sentence.

Interjections can express a variety of sentiments, such as happiness, fear, anger, pain, surprise, sorrow, exhaustion, or hesitation.

SOME COMMON INTERJECTIONS				
ah	dear	hey	ouch	well
aha	goodness	hurray	psst	whew
alas	gracious	oh	tsk	wow

EXAMPLES
Ouch! That curling iron is very hot.

Wow! That is well done!

Oh! I don't know.

Whew! I thought I'd lost you in the huge shopping mall.

See Practice 13.4D

The Parts of Speech

PRACTICE 13.4C Identifying Different Conjunctions

Read each sentence. Then, write the conjunction in each sentence and label it as *coordinating*, *correlative*, *subordinating*, or *conjunctive adverb*.

EXAMPLE   The movie was not only boring but also long.

ANSWER   *not only ... but also* — correlative

1. We finished cooking dinner before our neighbors arrived.
2. The assignment was difficult yet interesting.
3. The player fell; therefore, the game was stopped briefly.
4. I need both a map and a title to complete my report.
5. Harry bounced a basketball while he waited for the bus.
6. Our new coach is tougher than our old one was.
7. Neither Shawna nor Luke knew the answer.
8. The weather was warm but pleasant on Sunday.
9. The referee was fair; indeed, every call was accurate.
10. We poured water on the fire until it was completely out.

PRACTICE 13.4D Supplying Interjections

Read each sentence. Then, write an interjection that shows the feeling expressed in the sentence.

EXAMPLE   _____, I can't find my coat!

ANSWER   *Oh no*

11. _____! I hurt my arm!
12. _____, the stain did not come out.
13. _____! Did you see that shooting star?
14. _____, I saw you at the game last night.
15. _____, that elephant is huge!
16. _____! I'm afraid of heights.
17. _____, I can't believe I lost again!
18. _____, what will I do now?
19. _____! We won!
20. _____! I need to take a break!

SPEAKING APPLICATION

Take turns with a partner. Tell about something that you did with a friend. Your partner should name conjunctions that you use and tell what kind of conjunction each one is.

WRITING APPLICATION

Write three sentences using interjections.

13.5 Words as Different Parts of Speech

Words are flexible, often serving as one part of speech in one sentence and as another part of speech in another.

Grammar Practice
Practice your grammar skills with Writing Coach Online.

Grammar Games
Test your knowledge of grammar in this fast-paced interactive video game.

Identifying Parts of Speech

To function means "to serve in a particular capacity." The function of a word may change from one sentence to another.

RULE 13.5.1

The way a word is used in a sentence determines its part of speech.

The word *well* has different meaning in the following sentences.

As a Noun	Our well was full.
As a Verb	After arguing with Christopher, tears welled in Amy's eyes.
As an Adjective	Mark did not feel well today.

Nouns, Pronouns, and Verbs A **noun** names a person, place, or thing. A **pronoun** stands for a noun. A **verb** shows action, condition, or existence.

The chart below reviews the definition of each part of speech.

PARTS OF SPEECH	QUESTIONS TO ASK YOURSELF	EXAMPLES
Noun	Does the word name a person, place, or thing?	Our trip to New York City excited George.
Pronoun	Does the word stand for a noun?	They shared some with her.

332 The Parts of Speech

Words as Different Parts of Speech

PARTS OF SPEECH	QUESTIONS TO ASK YOURSELF	EXAMPLES
Verb	Does the word tell what someone or something did? Does the word link one word with another word that identifies or describes it? Does the word show that something exists?	We played soccer. That man was the coach. The coach appeared frazzled. The other team is here.

See Practice 13.5A

The Other Parts of Speech An **adjective** modifies a noun or pronoun. An **adverb** modifies a verb, an adjective, or another adverb. A **preposition** relates a noun or pronoun that appears with it to another word. A **conjunction** connects words or groups of words. An **interjection** expresses emotion.

PARTS OF SPEECH	QUESTIONS TO ASK YOURSELF	EXAMPLES
Adjective	Does the word tell *what kind, which one, how many,* or *how much?*	Those three oranges have an unusual flavor.
Adverb	Does the word tell *where, when, in what way,* or *to what extent?*	Run home. Come now. Speak very quietly. I am thoroughly exhausted.
Preposition	Is the word part of a phrase that includes a noun or pronoun?	Near our house, the bonfire was in full swing.
Conjunction	Does the word connect other words in the sentence or connect clauses?	Both Mom and I will go because they need more help; besides, we will have fun.
Interjection	Does the word express feeling or emotion and function independently of the sentence?	Hey, I want that! Wow! That's great!

See Practice 13.5B

Words as Different Parts of Speech

PRACTICE 13.5A Identifying Nouns, Pronouns, and Verbs

Read each sentence. Then, label the underlined word in each sentence as a *noun*, *pronoun*, or *verb*.

EXAMPLE Jeri is the best writer in our class.

ANSWER *pronoun*

1. I glanced at my watch every five minutes.
2. We will watch the game on TV at eight o'clock.
3. The neighbors are planting a tree in their yard.
4. Belle asked the teacher for her opinion.
5. My mom and dad are both very good cooks.
6. Mom cooks Indian food on the weekends.
7. Ed is coming, and he is wearing a suit and tie!
8. My doctor keeps a record of all my visits.
9. My brother records the songs that he writes.
10. You never know what the future will bring.

PRACTICE 13.5B Recognizing All the Parts of Speech

Read each sentence. Then, write which part of speech the underlined word is in each sentence.

EXAMPLE No one but Dad can help me with this.

ANSWER *preposition*

11. Chris speaks Spanish, but I don't.
12. Let's go outside because the weather is so nice.
13. Hey, what are you doing in the kitchen?
14. I walked home in the rain yesterday, and now I'm sick.
15. Mom took me to the late movie.
16. We arrived late for the start of the game.
17. After the snowstorm, we built a snowman.
18. A band played after the mayor made her speech.
19. I received an early phone call from my friend.
20. Have you chosen a college yet?

SPEAKING APPLICATION

Take turns with a partner. Tell about something that you did earlier today. Your partner should identify the nouns, pronouns, and verbs that you use.

WRITING APPLICATION

Write the part of speech of each word in sentence 18.

BASIC SENTENCE PARTS

CHAPTER 14

Create memorable sentences by pairing interesting subjects and verbs and by using complements for elaboration.

WRITE GUY *Jeff Anderson, M.Ed.*

WHAT DO YOU NOTICE?

Spot different sentence parts as you zoom in on these sentences from the essay "The Spider and the Wasp" by Alexander Petrunkevitch.

> **MENTOR TEXT**
>
> The female produces but a few eggs, one at a time at intervals of two or three days. For each egg the mother must provide one adult tarantula, alive but paralyzed.

Now, ask yourself the following questions:

- What is the verb, and what is the direct object in the first sentence?
- What is the verb, and what is the direct object in the second sentence?

In the first sentence, *produces* is the verb; the direct object is *eggs* because it receives the action of the verb. A direct object is a complement that completes the meaning of an action verb. In the second sentence, the verb is *must provide*, and the direct object is *tarantula*.

Grammar for Writers Writers can use direct objects to bring verbs to life. Try adding interesting and surprising direct objects to your sentences!

Do you think it's better to give or to receive?

Ask some direct objects! They're experts in receiving.

335

14.1 Subjects and Predicates

A **sentence** is a group of words that expresses a complete unit of thought. *The cereal in the bowl* is not a complete unit of thought because you probably wonder what the writer wanted to say about the cereal. *The cereal in the bowl is soggy,* however, does express a complete unit of thought.

RULE 14.1.1

A **sentence** is a group of words that has two main parts: a complete subject and a complete predicate. Together, these parts express a complete thought or paint a complete picture.

The **complete subject** contains a noun, pronoun, or group of words acting as a noun, plus its modifiers. These words tell *whom* or *what* the sentence is about. The **complete predicate** consists of the verb or verb phrase, plus its modifiers. These words tell what the complete subject is or does.

COMPLETE SUBJECTS	COMPLETE PREDICATES
Snakes	slither.
A bell-clanging streetcar	moved through the turn.
Wood or cellulose	makes a delicious meal for a termite.
The candidate's approach to fiscal problems	impressed the voters attending the rally.

Sometimes, part of the predicate precedes the complete subject.

EXAMPLES

At noon, the hive of bees made honey.
  complete   complete subject
                                    predicate

Today my cooking class visited a sushi restaurant.
complete   complete subject
                                       predicate

WRITING COACH Online

www.phwritingcoach.com

Grammar Practice
Practice your grammar skills with Writing Coach Online.

Grammar Games
Test your knowledge of grammar in this fast-paced interactive video game.

See Practice 14.1A

336 Basic Sentence Parts

Simple Subjects and Predicates

The most essential parts of a sentence are the **simple subject** and the **simple predicate.** These words tell you the basics of what you need to know about the topic of the sentence. All of the other words in the sentence give you information about the simple subject and simple predicate.

> The **simple subject** is the essential noun, pronoun, or group of words that acts as a noun in a complete subject. The **simple predicate** is the essential verb or verb phrase in a complete predicate.

Note: When sentences are discussed in this chapter, the term *subject* will refer to a simple subject, and the term *verb* will refer to a simple predicate.

SUBJECTS	VERBS
Small puppies	fit nicely into the box.
Many comedy films	have used stuntmen to hilarious effects.
Bottles of fresh water	were sitting on the table.
A colorful quilt	covered the bed.
The writer's home	explained a lot about his personality.
Studies of wolves	have certainly revealed much about their behavior.

In the last example, the simple subject is *studies,* not *wolves; wolves* is the object of the preposition *of.* Objects of prepositions never function as simple subjects. In this same example, the simple predicate is a verb phrase. In addition, the word *certainly* is not part of the simple predicate because it does not provide essential information.

See Practice 14.1B

Subjects and Predicates

PRACTICE 14.1A Recognizing Complete Subjects and Predicates

Read each sentence. Then, underline the complete subject and double underline the complete predicate.

EXAMPLE The jacket with the hood belongs to me.

ANSWER *The jacket with the hood belongs to me.*

1. Trucks are not permitted on this road.
2. Jean did not have time to stop for lunch.
3. This class demands a lot of reading.
4. Those dark clouds in the sky make me fear an approaching storm.
5. The chef prepared a special meal for us.
6. The first school in our town was a one-room cabin.
7. The library downtown is adding two new floors.
8. Children like to play at the park in the summer.
9. Horseback riding is offered at the camp.
10. We immediately accepted their offer of help.

PRACTICE 14.1B Identifying Simple Subjects and Predicates

Read each sentence. The complete subject is underlined. The rest of the sentence is the complete predicate. Write the simple subject and simple predicate in each sentence.

EXAMPLE An ostrich is a large bird.

ANSWER *ostrich, is*

11. A hat with a wide brim is essential for sun protection.
12. My cousins go to Mexico every year for three weeks.
13. People all around the world enjoy jazz music.
14. In the winter, we skate on the frozen lake.
15. Most birds stay in this area for only part of the year.
16. The basketball team expects to win first place this year.
17. Many autumn leaves turn shades of red and yellow.
18. The mother lion taught her cubs to hunt.
19. A dozen or so bees buzzed around our heads.
20. Ants march in a line back to their nest.

SPEAKING APPLICATION

Take turns with a partner. Tell about something interesting that happened to you. Your partner should tell the complete subject and complete predicate in each of your sentences.

WRITING APPLICATION

Write a paragraph about a favorite place. In each sentence, underline the simple subject and double underline the simple predicate.

Fragments

A **fragment** is a group of words that does not contain either a complete subject or a complete predicate, or both. Fragments are usually not used in formal writing. You can correct a fragment by adding the parts needed to complete the thought.

> A **fragment** is a group of words that lacks a subject or a predicate, or both. It does not express a complete unit of thought.

← 14.1.3 RULE

FRAGMENTS	COMPLETE SENTENCES
the basket of muffins (complete predicate missing)	The basket of muffins was very good. (complete predicate added)
thrive in the woods (complete subject missing)	Bears thrive in the woods. (complete subject added)
from the tree (complete subject and predicate missing)	Bees from the tree swarmed into the house. (subject and complete predicate added)

In conversations, fragments usually do not present a problem because tone of voice, gestures, and facial expressions can add the missing information. A reader, however, cannot ask a writer for clarification.

Fragments are sometimes acceptable in writing that represents speech, such as the dialogue in a play or short story. Fragments are also sometimes acceptable in elliptical sentences.

> An **elliptical sentence** is one in which the missing word or words can be easily understood.

← 14.1.4 RULE

EXAMPLES Until tomorrow.

Why such a happy face?

Please be early!

Locating Subjects and Verbs

To avoid writing a fragment, look for the subject and verb in a sentence. To find the subject, ask, "Which word tells *what* or *whom* this sentence is about?" Once you have the answer (the subject), then ask, "What does the subject do?" or "What is being done to the subject?" This will help you locate the verb.

In some sentences, it's easier to find the verb first. In this case, ask, "Which word states the action or condition in this sentence?" This question should help you locate the verb. Then ask, "*Who* or *what* is involved in the action of the verb?" The resulting word or words will be the subject.

EXAMPLE Kittens often run in the grass.

To find the subject first, ask, "Which word or words tell what or whom this sentence is about?"

ANSWER Kittens (*Kittens* is the subject.)

Then ask, "What do kittens do?"

ANSWER run (*Run* is the verb.)

To find the verb first, ask, "Which word or words state the action or condition in the sentence?"

ANSWER run (*Run* states the action, so it is the verb.)

Then ask, "Who or what runs?"

ANSWER Kittens (*Kittens* is the subject.)

To easily locate the subject and verb, mentally cross out any adjectives, adverbs, and prepositional phrases you see. These words add information, but they are usually less important than the simple subject and verb.

EXAMPLE ~~School~~ **attendance** **should grow** ~~rapidly in the next ten years.~~
           simple subject   verb phrase

340 **Basic Sentence Parts**

Sentences With More Than One Subject or Verb

Some sentences contain a **compound subject** or a **compound verb,** or a subject or verb with more than one part.

> **A compound subject** consists of two or more subjects. These subjects may be joined by a conjunction such as *and* or *or*.

← 14.1.5 RULE

EXAMPLES   The **campers** and **hikers** rappelled against the wall with rope.

Kittens, bunnies, and **puppies** are always running around the yard.

Neither the **puppy** nor the **owner** looked tired.

> **A compound verb** consists of two or more verbs. These verbs may be joined by a conjunction such as *and, but, or,* or *nor*.

← 14.1.6 RULE

EXAMPLES   I neither **saw** the video nor **heard** the song.

Mike **left** work and **ran** to the benefit.

She **complained** and **whined** all day.

Some sentences contain both a compound subject and a compound verb.

EXAMPLES   My **sister** and **mother swatted** at the bees but **hit** the glasses on the table instead.

The **lion** and **hyena** eyed each other, **circled** warily, and then **advanced** toward each other.

See Practice 14.1C
See Practice 14.1D

Subjects and Predicates

Subjects and Predicates

PRACTICE 14.1C Locating Subjects and Verbs

Read each sentence. Then, write the subject and the verb in each sentence. Underline the subject.

EXAMPLE Each of my teammates signed the card.

ANSWER *Each*, signed

1. Many of the children had become restless.
2. Trish and I enjoyed the parade in spite of the large crowd.
3. The sponsors of the show and the audience were thrilled with its content.
4. The scent of night-blooming flowers filled the garden and wafted over the walls.
5. All of the members of the team get a chance to play.
6. You guaranteed your repairs on this car.
7. A few of our neighbors moved away for the winter.
8. A number of farms and homes were flooded by the rains.
9. Who leads the planning committee?
10. The teacher has not graded our tests or read our essays yet.

PRACTICE 14.1D Fixing Sentence Errors

Read each fragment. Then, use each fragment in a sentence.

EXAMPLE will drive us to the store

ANSWER *Dad will drive us to the store.*

11. clapped, cheered, and laughed
12. while she was running for the bus
13. occasional blasts from a car horn
14. fresh bear tracks
15. where palm trees sway in the breeze
16. often windy or stormy
17. sneaking, stalking, and hunting
18. which made me remember that Mom was waiting
19. must have been lost by a fan
20. whomever she chooses

SPEAKING APPLICATION

Take turns with a partner. Tell about your favorite possessions. Your partner should name the subject and verb in each of your sentences.

WRITING APPLICATION

Write your own fragment. Then, use the fragment to write three different sentences.

14.2 Hard-to-Find Subjects

While most sentences have subjects that are easy to find, some present a challenge.

Grammar Practice
Practice your grammar skills with Writing Coach Online.

Grammar Games
Test your knowledge of grammar in this fast-paced interactive video game.

Subjects in Declarative Sentences Beginning With *Here* or *There*

When the word *here* or *there* begins a declarative sentence, it is often mistaken for the subject.

> **Here** and **there** are never the subject of a sentence.

Here and *there* are usually adverbs that modify the verb by pointing out *where* something is located. However, *there* may occasionally begin a sentence simply as an introductory word.

Sentences beginning with *Here* or *There* are often **inverted**. In an inverted sentence, the subject follows the verb. If you rearrange such a sentence in subject–verb order, you can identify the subject more easily.

INVERTED   There **are** the **planes**. (verb–subject order)

REARRANGED   The **planes** **are** there. (subject–verb order)

SENTENCES BEGINNING WITH *HERE* OR *THERE*	SENTENCES REARRANGED IN SUBJECT–VERB ORDER
There **are** the apartment **buildings**.	The apartment **buildings** **are** there.
Here **is** the **ticket** for your movie.	The **ticket** for your movie **is** here.
There **is** **money** in my wallet.	**Money** **is** in my wallet there.

> In some declarative sentences, the subject is placed after the verb in order to give the subject greater emphasis.

Because most sentences are written in subject–verb order, changing that order makes readers stop and think. Inverted sentences often begin with prepositional phrases.

Hard-to-Find Subjects   343

SENTENCES INVERTED FOR EMPHASIS	SENTENCES REARRANGED IN SUBJECT–VERB ORDER
Toward the waiting plane rushed the morning travelers.	The morning travelers rushed toward the waiting plane.
Around the next stop careened the speeding bus.	The speeding bus careened around the next stop.

Subjects in Interrogative Sentences

Some interrogative sentences use subject–verb order. Often, however, the word order of an interrogative sentence is verb–subject.

EXAMPLES   Which store has the best prices?
(subject–verb order)

When are we going?
(verb–subject order)

In interrogative sentences, the subject often follows the verb.

An inverted interrogative sentence can begin with a verb, a helping verb, or one of the following words: *how, what, when, where, which, who, whose,* or *why.* Some interrogative sentences divide the helping verb from the main verb. To help locate the subject, mentally rearrange the sentence into subject–verb order.

INTERROGATIVE SENTENCES	REARRANGED IN SUBJECT–VERB ORDER
Is the Bronx Zoo open this morning?	The Bronx Zoo is open this morning.
Do they own that car?	They do own that car.
Where will the concert be held?	The concert will be held where?

344 Basic Sentence Parts

Hard-to-Find Subjects

Subjects in Imperative Sentences

The subject of an imperative sentence is usually implied rather than specifically stated.

> In imperative sentences, the subject is understood to be *you*.

IMPERATIVE SENTENCES	SENTENCES WITH *YOU* ADDED
First, visit the Magic Kingdom.	First, [you] visit the Magic Kingdom.
After the tour, come back to the hotel.	After the tour, [you] come back to the hotel.
Tara, show me the itinerary.	Tara, [you] show me the itinerary.

In the last example, the name of the person being addressed, *Tara,* is not the subject of the imperative sentence. Instead, the subject is still understood to be *you.*

Subjects in Exclamatory Sentences

In some **exclamatory sentences,** the subject appears before the verb. In others, the verb appears first. To find the subject, rearrange the sentence in subject–verb order.

> In exclamatory sentences, the subject often appears after the verb, or it may be understood.

EXAMPLES   What does she know!
(She does know what.)

Leave now!
(Subject understood: [You] leave now!)

In other exclamatory sentences, both the subject and verb may be unstated.

EXAMPLES   Smoke! ([You watch out for the] smoke!)

See Practice 14.2A
See Practice 14.2B

Bees! ([I see] bees!)

Hard-to-Find Subjects

PRACTICE 14.2A Identifying Hard-to-Find Subjects

Read each sentence. Then, write the subject of each sentence.

EXAMPLE Here is your stepbrother!
ANSWER *stepbrother*

1. Through the doors of the store rushed the eager customers.
2. How will you ever get it all done?
3. Somewhere between bland and hot lies the perfect salsa.
4. There are two accidents on the freeway.
5. Just beyond the pier frolicked several dolphins.
6. Here are your library books.
7. There is the faulty wire.
8. There she was, with no ticket.
9. Here are some ideas for your artwork.
10. There are many possible reasons for the traffic jam.

PRACTICE 14.2B Locating Hard-to-Find Verbs

Read each sentence. Then, write the verb in each sentence.

EXAMPLE Look for the man I told you about.
ANSWER *Look*

11. Can you believe the size of that car?
12. Why would you think such a thing!
13. I see lightning!
14. Before math class, show me your history project.
15. Leave the school grounds, please.
16. Was that a mountain lion?
17. Hey, put that down!
18. Where is your coat?
19. Will you show me the gym?
20. Go outside and play.

SPEAKING APPLICATION

Take turns with a partner. Say sentences that describe someone doing something. Your partner should invert the order of the words in your sentences and then name the subjects.

WRITING APPLICATION

Write three exclamatory sentences. Underline the subject and double underline the verb in each sentence.

14.3 Complements

Some sentences are complete with just a subject and a verb or with a subject, verb, and modifiers: *The crowd cheered.* Other sentences need more information to be complete.

Grammar Tutorials
Brush up on your Grammar skills with these animated videos.

Grammar Practice
Practice your grammar skills with Writing Coach Online.

Grammar Games
Test your knowledge of grammar in this fast-paced interactive video game.

The meaning of many sentences, however, depends on additional words that add information to the subject and verb. For example, although *The satellite continually sends* has a subject and verb, it is an incomplete sentence. To complete the meaning of the predicate—in this case, to tell *what* a satellite sends—a writer must add a **complement.**

> A **complement** is a word or group of words that completes the meaning of the predicate of a sentence.

RULE 14.3.1

There are five kinds of complements in English: **direct objects, indirect objects, object complements, predicate nominatives,** and **predicate adjectives.** The first three occur in sentences that have transitive verbs. The last two are often called **subject complements.** Subject complements are found only with linking verbs. (See Chapter 13 for more information about action and linking verbs.)

Direct Objects

Direct objects are the most common of the five types of complements. They complete the meaning of action verbs by telling *who* or *what* receives the action.

> A **direct object** is a noun, pronoun, or group of words acting as a noun that receives the action of a transitive verb.

RULE 14.3.2

EXAMPLES   I **visited** the Museum of Natural History.
                           direct object

Rain and melting snow **flooded** the gutters.
                                         direct object

Complements   347

Direct Objects and Action Verbs The direct object answers the question *Whom?* or *What?* about the action verb. If you cannot answer the question *Whom?* or *What?* the verb may be intransitive, and there is no direct object in the sentence.

EXAMPLES Hawks **can see** from high in the sky.
(Ask, "Hawks can see *what*?" No answer; the verb is intransitive.)

The satellite **spun** above Earth.
(Ask, "The satellite spun *what*?" No answer; the verb is intransitive.)

See Practice 14.3A

RULE 14.3.3

In some inverted questions, the direct object may appear before the verb. To find the direct object easily, rearrange inverted questions in subject–verb order.

INVERTED QUESTION Which **movies** **did** they **see**?
                        direct object

REARRANGED IN SUBJECT–VERB ORDER **They did see** which **movies**?
                                      direct object

Some sentences have more than one direct object, known as a **compound direct object.** If a sentence contains a compound direct object, asking *Whom?* or *What?* after the action verb will yield two or more answers.

EXAMPLES The bikers **wore** **helmets** and **kneepads**.
              direct object *direct object*

The band **has played** at **stadiums** and **arenas** all over the United States.
direct object *direct object*

In the last example, *United States* is the object of the preposition *over*. The object of a preposition is never a direct object.

See Practice 14.3B

348 **Basic Sentence Parts**

Complements

Indirect Objects

Indirect objects appear only in sentences that contain transitive verbs and direct objects. Indirect objects are common with such verbs as *ask, bring, buy, give, lend, make, show, teach, tell,* and *write*. Some sentences may contain a compound indirect object.

> An **indirect object** is a noun or pronoun that appears with a direct object. It often names the person or thing that something is given to or done for.

EXAMPLES

NASA gave the engineers a course correction.
                              indirect object
direct object

I showed my sister and brother the movie poster.
               compound indirect object
direct object

To locate an indirect object, make sure the sentence contains a direct object. Then, ask one of these questions after the verb and direct object: *To* or *for whom?* or *To* or *for what?*

EXAMPLES

The teacher taught our class poetry.
(The teacher taught poetry *to whom*? ANSWER: our class)

We made our dog a sweater.
(Made a sweater *for what*? ANSWER: our dog)

An indirect object almost always appears between the verb and the direct object. In a sentence with subject–verb order, the indirect object never follows the direct object, nor will it ever be the object of the preposition *to* or *for*.

EXAMPLES

Mike sent the story to me.
         direct   object of
         object preposition

Mike sent me the story.
      indirect direct
      object   object

Mike gave Rick an overview of the book.
       indirect object direct object

See Practice 14.3C

Object Complements

While an indirect object almost always comes *before* a direct object, an **object complement** almost always *follows* a direct object. The object complement completes the meaning of the direct object.

RULE 14.3.5 An **object complement** is an adjective or noun that appears with a direct object and describes or renames it.

A sentence that contains an object complement may seem to have two direct objects. However, object complements occur only with such verbs as *appoint, call, consider, declare, elect, judge, label, make, name, select,* and *think*. The words *to be* are often understood before an object complement.

EXAMPLES

The **organizers** of the auction **declared** **it** (direct object) **successful** (object complement).

The **principal** **declared** **him** (direct object) **valedictorian** (object complement) of the class.

I **consider** **Felix** (direct object) a persuasive **writer** (object complement) and graceful **speaker** (object complement).

Subject Complements

Linking verbs require **subject complements** to complete their meaning.

RULE 14.3.6 A **subject complement** is a noun, pronoun, or adjective that appears with a linking verb and gives more information about the subject.

There are two kinds of subject complements: **predicate nominatives** and **predicate adjectives**.

Complements

Predicate Nominatives

The **predicate nominative** refers to the same person, place, or thing as the subject of the sentence.

> A **predicate nominative** is a noun or pronoun that appears with a linking verb and renames, identifies, or explains the subject. Some sentences may contain a compound predicate nominative.

EXAMPLES

Michael Jones is an agent with the FBI.
                        predicate nominative

The winner will be I.
         predicate nominative

Tara Halpern was a doctor and a former surgeon.
       compound predicate nominative

Predicate Adjectives

A **predicate adjective** is an adjective that appears with a linking verb. It describes the subject in much the same way that an adjective modifies a noun or pronoun. Some sentences may contain a compound predicate adjective.

> A **predicate adjective** is an adjective that appears with a linking verb and describes the subject of the sentence.

EXAMPLES

Your reasoning seems illogical.
             predicate adjective

The runner was fast.
      predicate adjective

The thunder sounded loud and frightening.
          compound predicate adjective

The uniforms are tan and black.
      compound predicate adjective

See Practice 14.3D

PRACTICE 14.3A Identifying Direct Objects

Read each sentence. Then, write the direct object in each sentence. If a sentence does not have a direct object, write *The verb is intransitive*.

EXAMPLE The train left early.
ANSWER *The verb is intransitive.*

1. The artist hung the drawings carefully.
2. The batter slammed the ball against the wall.
3. Our class performed two plays in the festival.
4. My baby sister will sit in her car seat.
5. The hurricane struck the city without warning.
6. We will cut down the sick elm trees today.
7. My friends felt sick this morning.
8. Sam added more fruit to his diet.
9. Cheers and applause greeted the young actors.
10. Lynn waited patiently all day.

PRACTICE 14.3B Rearranging Inverted Questions to Subject-Verb Order

Read each question. Then, write a sentence that rearranges the question to subject-verb order.

EXAMPLE Which target are you aiming at?
ANSWER *You are aiming at which target?*

11. Which story did you write?
12. What assignment are you completing?
13. Which trip are you planning?
14. What computer will you use?
15. Which house did my cousin buy?
16. What bus should we take?
17. Which recipe is Jose preparing?
18. What museum is the group visiting?
19. Which train is the passenger boarding?
20. What gift will you be sending?

SPEAKING APPLICATION

Take turns with a partner. Say sentences that contain direct objects and sentences that contain intransitive verbs. Your partner should identify the direct objects and the sentences that have intransitive verbs.

WRITING APPLICATION

Review the sentences you wrote for Practice 14.3B. For each sentence, write the direct object.

PRACTICE 14.3C Identifying Indirect Objects

Read each sentence. Then, write the indirect object in each sentence.

EXAMPLE I gave the dog a bone.

ANSWER *dog*

1. The teacher gave the students a surprise test.
2. Ray taught his puppy a new trick.
3. The map showed Donna the correct route.
4. Our grandfather told the family a story about his youth.
5. Delores asked the doctor and nurse a question.
6. The storm brought the land some relief from the heat.
7. The happy camper wrote his parents a letter.
8. The bank lent the company money.
9. Dad made Mom a cake for her birthday.
10. The guide bought the tired hikers some water.

PRACTICE 14.3D Locating Object and Subject Complements

Read each sentence. Then, write the complement and label it as an *object complement* or a *subject complement*.

EXAMPLE The play's ending left us sad.

ANSWER *sad* — object complement

11. A man's best friend is his dog.
12. After the storm, we all felt relieved.
13. The fireworks made the evening very festive.
14. We just elected Steve president.
15. Eli became confident during his time away.
16. That movie became an instant hit.
17. The castle's garden is beautiful.
18. The fire chief declared the building unsafe.
19. The constant rain kept us all cranky for days.
20. We decided to call our cockatoo Vinca.

SPEAKING APPLICATION

Take turns with a partner. Say sentences that contain direct objects and indirect objects. Your partner should identify both the direct objects and the indirect objects.

WRITING APPLICATION

Use sentences 11 and 12 in Practice 14.3D as models to write sentences of your own. Underline and label the complement in each sentence.

Complements

Test Warm-Up

DIRECTIONS
Read the introduction and the passage that follows. Then, answer the questions to show that you can use and understand the function of subject complements in reading and writing.

Sam wrote this essay about creating a community garden with his class. Read the paragraph and think about the changes you would suggest as a peer editor. When you finish reading, answer the questions that follow.

Students Help Our Community

(1) Mrs. Gomez represents our district in the city government. (2) She is a well-known architect. (3) She is also known as a city planner. (4) She proposed a simple project to the students. (5) Our tenth grade class would help transform a vacant lot near our high school into a community garden. (6) The design of the garden was well-planned and had clear steps. (7) Today, the garden provides fruit and vegetables for many community members.

---

1 How should sentence 1 be revised to include a predicate nominative?

 A Mrs. Gomez is a city council member for our district.

 B Mrs. Gomez is valued by the people in our district.

 C Mrs. Gomez seems dedicated to improving our district.

 D Mrs. Gomez works hard on behalf of our district.

2 What is the most effective way to combine sentences 2 and 3 to include a compound predicate nominative?

 F In addition to being a well-known architect, she is a city planner.

 G She is a well-known architect; she is also a city planner.

 H She is a well-known architect and city planner.

 J A well-known architect, she is also a city planner.

3 How should sentence 4 be revised to include a predicate adjective?

 A The simple project she proposed had been designed for students.

 B The project she proposed to the students was a simple one.

 C The project she proposed to the students was a simple garden.

 D The project she proposed to the students was simple.

4 What is the most effective way to rewrite the ideas in sentence 6 to include a compound predicate adjective?

 F The garden's design had a good plan and clear steps.

 G The design of the garden was well-planned and clear.

 H The design of the garden had been well-planned, with clear steps.

 J The well-planned design of the garden included clear steps.

PHRASES and CLAUSES

CHAPTER 15

Use phrases and clauses to add interesting detail and description to your sentences.

WRITE GUY Jeff Anderson, M.Ed.

WHAT DO YOU NOTICE?

Focus on phrases as you zoom in on these lines from the poem "Conscientious Objector" by Edna St. Vincent Millay.

MENTOR TEXT

> I shall die, but that is all that I shall do for Death.
>
> I hear him leading his horse out of the stall; I hear the clatter on the barn-floor.

Now, ask yourself the following questions:

- What are the prepositional phrases in these lines?
- How does each prepositional phrase function in the poem: as an adjectival phrase or an adverbial phrase?

The three prepositional phrases in the poem are *for Death, out of the stall*, and *on the barn-floor*. The first two are both adverbial phrases. The phrase *for Death* modifies the verb *do*, and *out of the stall* modifies *leading*. *On the barn-floor* acts as an adjectival phrase that describes the noun *clatter*.

Grammar for Writers Writers are like reporters; they need to answer the questions *What? When? Where, What kind?* or *Which one?* in their writing. Prepositional phrases are keys to the answers.

Do people use prepositional phrases in conversation?

They use them "in conversation" all the time!

15.1 Phrases

When one adjective or adverb cannot convey enough information, a phrase can contribute more detail to a sentence. A **phrase** is a group of words that does not include a subject and verb and cannot stand alone as a sentence.

Grammar Tutorials
Brush up on your Grammar skills with these animated videos.

Grammar Practice
Practice your grammar skills with Writing Coach Online.

Grammar Games
Test your knowledge of grammar in this fast-paced interactive video game.

There are several kinds of phrases, including **prepositional phrases, appositive phrases, participial phrases, gerund phrases,** and **infinitive phrases.**

Prepositional Phrases

A **prepositional phrase** consists of a preposition and a noun or pronoun, called the object of the preposition. *Over their heads, until dark,* and *after the baseball game* are all prepositional phrases. Prepositional phrases often modify other words by functioning as adjectives or adverbs.

Sometimes, a single prepositional phrase may include two or more objects joined by a conjunction.

EXAMPLES   between the **chair** and the **table**
  preposition   object   object

with the **snow** and **hail**
preposition object   object

beside the **night table** and the **bed**
preposition   object   object

See Practice 15.1A

Adjectival Phrases

A prepositional phrase that acts as an adjective is called an **adjectival phrase.**

RULE 15.1.1   An **adjectival phrase** is a prepositional phrase that modifies a noun or pronoun by telling *what kind* or *which one*.

356   **Phrases and Clauses**

ADJECTIVES	ADJECTIVAL PHRASES
A beautiful picture hung in the meeting hall.	A picture **of great beauty** hung in the meeting hall. *(What kind of picture?)*
Anne had a poetry book.	Anne had a book **of poetry**. *(What kind of book?)*

Like one-word adjectives, adjectival phrases can modify subjects, direct objects, indirect objects, or predicate nominatives.

MODIFYING A SUBJECT — The library **across the road** has been an asset.

MODIFYING A DIRECT OBJECT — Let's take a picture **of the Sears Tower**.

MODIFYING AN INDIRECT OBJECT — I gave the people **on the trip** a tour.

MODIFYING A PREDICATE NOMINATIVE — Germany is a country **with many castles**.

A sentence may contain two or more **adjectival phrases.** In some cases, one phrase may modify the preceding phrase. In others, two phrases may modify the same word.

EXAMPLES — We bought tickets **for the trip** **to Florida**.

The statue **of the rearing horse** **in the park** was huge.

Adverbial Phrases

An **adverbial phrase** is a prepositional phrase that modifies a verb, an adjective, or an adverb by pointing out *where, why, when, in what way,* or *to what extent.*

ADVERBS	ADVERBIAL PHRASES
He walked quickly. (Walked *in what way?*)	He walked **with speed**.
I was worried then. (Worried *why?*)	I was worried **by the weather report**.
The plane flew overhead. (Flew *where?*)	The plane flew **over the airport**.

Adverbial phrases can modify verbs, adjectives, or adverbs.

MODIFYING A VERB — The yarn rolled **across the floor**.

MODIFYING AN ADJECTIVE — Amy was happy **beyond question**.

MODIFYING AN ADVERB — She buried the feelings deep **in her mind**.

An adverbial phrase may either follow the word it modifies or be located elsewhere in the sentence. Often, two adverbs in different parts of a sentence can modify the same word.

EXAMPLES

A creek disappeared **during the earthquake**.

During the earthquake, a creek disappeared.

After the play we all met **at the restaurant**.

See Practice 15.1B

358 Phrases and Clauses

PRACTICE 15.1A Identifying Prepositional Phrases

Read each sentence. Write the prepositional phrase or phrases in each sentence and underline the prepositions.

EXAMPLE According to the flyer, the concert begins at dark.

ANSWER *according to the flyer; at dark*

1. The news article announced an agreement between the two countries.
2. Cut one pound of apples into slices.
3. The people at the back of the boat got wet.
4. The wedding guests entered through a breathtaking courtyard.
5. The house down the street has a fountain.
6. We looked into the old house through a broken window.
7. Ted found the toy under the bucket.
8. Sometimes a picture from my childhood will bring back memories.
9. I like stories about other countries.
10. I wish I could return to the lake house.

PRACTICE 15.1B Identifying Adjectival and Adverbial Phrases

Read each sentence. Write the adjectival or adverbial phrases. Then, identify each phrase as either *adjectival* or *adverbial*.

EXAMPLE I often play at the park on Post Street.

ANSWER *at the park* — adverbial
on Post Street — adjectival

11. Mary Cassatt was a leader among American painters.
12. Rosa chose the one with blue stripes.
13. The cavalry will reach the fort by noon.
14. We got our new puppy at an animal shelter.
15. We bought a CD by a punk rock band.
16. She drove for hours in the storm.
17. A flock of gray birds flew overhead.
18. The boat landed on an island near the coast.
19. The library is open on weekends during the day.
20. Here's a gift for you from Uncle Greg.

SPEAKING APPLICATION

Take turns with a partner. Describe the location of an object in the room. Your partner should listen for and identify three prepositions that you use.

WRITING APPLICATION

Use the prepositions in sentences 11, 14, and 18 to write three sentences of your own. Use the same prepositions, but change the other words to create new sentences.

Appositives and Appositive Phrases

The term *appositive* comes from a Latin verb that means "to put near or next to."

Appositives Using **appositives** in your writing is an easy way to give additional meaning to a noun or pronoun.

> An **appositive** is a group of words that identifies, renames, or explains a noun or pronoun.

As the examples below show, appositives usually follow immediately after the words they explain.

EXAMPLES   Mrs. Wilson, **the painter**, donated beautiful paintings.

The school committee, **a group of teachers and parents**, planned the spring dance.

Notice that commas are used in the examples above because these appositives are **nonessential.** In other words, the appositives could be omitted from the sentences without altering the basic meaning of the sentences.

Some appositives, however, are not set off by any punctuation because they are **essential** to the meaning of the sentence.

EXAMPLES   The artist **da Vinci** was also a scientist.
(The appositive is essential because it identifies which specific artist.)

My sister **Kate** is a persuasive speaker.
(The appositive is essential because you might have several sisters.)

Note About Terms: Sometimes, the terms *nonrestrictive* and *restrictive* are used in place of *nonessential* and *essential*.

Phrases and Clauses

Appositive Phrases When an appositive is accompanied by its own modifiers, it is called an **appositive phrase.**

> An **appositive phrase** is a noun or pronoun with modifiers that adds information by identifying, renaming, or explaining a noun or pronoun.

15.1.4 RULE

Appositives and appositive phrases may follow nouns or pronouns used in almost any role within a sentence. The modifiers within an appositive phrase can be adjectives, adjective phrases, or other groups of words functioning as adjectives.

EXAMPLES   Mr. Jane, **my history teacher**, assigned us to watch a documentary.

Bob explained anatomy, **the study of the structure of your body**.

ROLES OF APPOSITIVE PHRASES IN SENTENCES	
Identifying a Subject	William Shakespeare, a famous author, wrote many plays.
Identifying a Direct Object	The chef prepared pitas, a Mediterranean dish.
Identifying an Indirect Object	I brought my sister, a girl of five, a T-shirt from my trip.
Identifying an Object Complement	I chose green, my favorite color, for house shutters.
Identifying a Predicate Nominative	My favorite food is romaine lettuce, an ingredient in a tasty salad.
Identifying the Object of a Preposition	Store the potatoes in the pantry, a cool, dry place.

Phrases 361

Compound Appositives Appositives and appositive phrases can also be compound.

EXAMPLES   The class officers—**president**, **vice-president**, and **secretary**—planned the event.

Some types of shoes, **sandals** and **sneakers**, are on sale this week.

Toby used her favorite colors, **blue**, **green**, and **yellow**, to paint her room.

See Practice 15.1C

Grammar and Style Tip When **appositives** or **appositive phrases** are used to combine sentences, they help to eliminate unnecessary words. One way to streamline your writing is to combine sentences by using an appositive phrase.

TWO SENTENCES	COMBINED SENTENCE
Tel Aviv is located on the Mediterranean Sea. The city is an important Israeli seaport.	Tel Aviv, an important Israeli seaport, is located on the Mediterranean Sea.
The Lion King was performed at the Minskoff Theatre. The musical includes many original songs.	*The Lion King*, a musical performed at the Minskoff Theatre, includes many original songs.
Florida is on the East Coast. It is one of our warmest states.	Florida, one of our warmest states, is on the East Coast.

Read aloud the pairs of sentences in the chart. Notice how the combined sentences, which began as two choppy sentences, include the same information. However, they flow much more smoothly once the information in both sentences is clearly linked.

See Practice 15.1D

Phrases and Clauses

PRACTICE 15.1C Identifying Appositive and Appositive Phrases

Read each sentence. Then, write the appositive or appositive phrase in each sentence.

EXAMPLE We look forward to the main event, tennis.

ANSWER *tennis*

1. Doug's favorite book, The Hobbit, was written by J.R.R. Tolkien.
2. Rachel's hobby, skydiving, is very exciting.
3. Her bad habit, eavesdropping, is very rude.
4. The baby's new skills, walking and waving, seemed to make her very happy.
5. My dog's favorite activity, napping, takes up most of his day.
6. The strangest event, catching a greased pig, was the highlight of the day.
7. The most important task, passing the class, will take a lot of work.
8. The child's chore, cleaning her room, wore her out.
9. Kimber's career goal, teaching, seems a good fit for her.
10. Tony's friend Nico needs a ride to the airport.

PRACTICE 15.1D Using Appositives and Appositive Phrases to Combine Sentences

Read each pair of sentences. Then, combine the sentences using an appositive or an appositive phrase.

EXAMPLE Bart Lukas was a detective. He arrived just in time.

ANSWER *The detective, Bart Lukas, arrived just in time.*

11. Mars is one of the closest planets to Earth. Mars can be seen without a telescope.
12. Misty Alexander is a lawyer. She was the main speaker at the conference.
13. Rubber is an elastic substance. It quickly restores itself to its original size and shape.
14. The North Sea is an arm of the Atlantic Ocean. The North Sea is rich in fish and oil.
15. Imelda is my friend. She loves to knit.
16. Gettysburg is a town in Pennsylvania. An important battle was fought there.
17. Julius is an artist. He owns a gallery.
18. Our old house is on Larchmont Street. That house is my favorite place.
19. My cat is Clive. He loves tuna.
20. Hartford is a bustling city. It is located in Connecticut.

SPEAKING APPLICATION

Take turns saying two sentences about the same subject to a partner. Your partner should combine your sentences, using either an appositive or an appositive phrase.

WRITING APPLICATION

Write a pair of sentences with the same subject. Then, combine the sentences with an appositive or appositive phrase.

Verbal Phrases

When a verb is used as a noun, an adjective, or an adverb, it is called a **verbal**. Although a verbal does not function as a verb, it retains two characteristics of verbs: It can be modified in different ways, and it can have one or more complements. A verbal with modifiers or complements is called a **verbal phrase.**

Participles

Many of the adjectives you use are actually verbals known as **participles.**

> **RULE 15.1.5**
> A **participle** is a form of a verb that can act as an adjective.

The most common kinds of participles are **present participles** and **past participles.** These two participles can be distinguished from one another by their endings. Present participles usually end in *-ing* (*frightening, entertaining*). Past participles usually end in *-ed* (*frightened, entertained*), but many have irregular endings, such as *-t* or *-en* (*burnt, written*).

PRESENT PARTICIPLES	PAST PARTICIPLES
The limping dancer favored her aching foot.	Confused, Joe returned to his interrupted project.

Like other adjectives, participles answer the question *What kind?* or *Which one?* about the nouns or pronouns they modify.

EXAMPLES   Jane's **tearing** eyes betrayed her sadness.
(*What kind* of eyes? Answer: *tearing* eyes)

The **shattered** tiles need to be replaced.
(*Which* tiles? Answer: *shattered* tiles)

Participles may also have a **present perfect** form.

EXAMPLES   **Having decided**, Laura made the call.

Having arrived at his destination, Mark walked off the plane.

364   Phrases and Clauses

Verb or Participle? Because **verbs** often have endings such as *-ing* and *-ed,* you may confuse them with **participles.** If a word ending in *-ed* or *-ing* expresses the action of the sentence, it is a verb or part of a verb phrase. If it describes a noun or pronoun, it is a participle.

> A **verb** shows an action, a condition, or the fact that something exists. A **participle** acting as an adjective modifies a noun or a pronoun.

RULE 15.1.6

ACTING AS VERBS	ACTING AS ADJECTIVES
The dog is growling at the intruder. (What is the dog doing?)	The growling dog attacked the intruder. (Which dog?)
The clown delighted the child. (What did the clown do?)	Delighted, the child clapped for the clown. (What kind of child?)

See Practice 15.1E

Participial Phrases
A participle can be expanded by adding modifiers and complements to form a **participial phrase.**

> A **participial phrase** is a participle modified by an adverb or adverbial phrase or accompanied by a complement. The entire participial phrase acts as an adjective.

RULE 15.1.7

The following examples show different ways that participles may be expanded into phrases.

WITH AN ADVERB
Traveling quickly, we arrived on time.

WITH AN ADVERB PHRASE
Traveling at breakneck speed, we arrived on time.

WITH A COMPLEMENT
Avoiding delays, we arrived on time.

A participial phrase that is nonessential to the basic meaning of a sentence is set off by commas or other forms of punctuation. A participial phrase that is essential is not set off by punctuation.

Phrases 365

NONESSENTIAL PHRASES	ESSENTIAL PHRASES
There is Mark, waiting at the bus stop.	The boy waiting at the bus stop is Mark.
Painted in 1567, the canvas is a masterpiece.	The canvas painted in 1567 is one that needs preservation.

In the first sentence on the left side of the chart above, *waiting at the bus stop* merely adds information about Mark, so it is nonessential. In the sentence on the right, however, the same phrase is essential because many different boys might be in view.

In the second sentence on the left, *Painted in 1567* is an additional description of *canvas*, so it is nonessential. In the sentence on the right, however, the phrase is essential because it identifies the specific canvas that is being discussed.

RULE 15.1.8

Participial phrases can often be used to combine information from two sentences into one.

TWO SENTENCES   We were exhausted by the climb up the mountain. We rested by the side of trail.

COMBINED   **Exhausted by the climb up the mountain**, we rested by the side of the trail.

TWO SENTENCES   We drank coffee. We shared stories about our lives.

COMBINED   **Drinking coffee**, we shared stories about our lives.

Notice how part of the verb in one sentence is changed into a participle in the combined sentence.

See Practice 15.1F

366   **Phrases and Clauses**

PRACTICE 15.1E Identifying Participles

Read each sentence. Show that you understand verbals (participles) by writing whether the underlined word is a *verb* or a *participle*. Use the word in a new sentence. Read your sentences to a partner. Your partner should tell if the word is a verb or a participle.

EXAMPLE They are <u>stopping</u> early today.

ANSWER *verb; The police officer is stopping traffic for the parade.*

1. He gave a <u>moving</u> speech.
2. I was <u>stirring</u> the soup.
3. Barbara put away the <u>laundered</u> shirts.
4. Everyone was <u>singing</u> daily.
5. Do we have any <u>wrapping</u> paper left?
6. The <u>finished</u> artwork was auctioned off.
7. Our summer cabin has <u>running</u> water in the bathroom now.
8. She is <u>shopping</u> for a new coat today.
9. The <u>dreaming</u> student stared out the window.
10. I asked for another <u>formatted</u> disk.

PRACTICE 15.1F Recognizing Participial Phrases

Read each sentence. Write the participial phrase in each sentence. Then, write *E* for *essential* or *N* for *nonessential*.

EXAMPLE One deputy, using a stop watch, timed the car.

ANSWER *using a stop watch* — N

11. Stretching slowly, the cat woke from its nap.
12. The tornado forecasted earlier today did not hit our area.
13. The dress designed by Ellen was already sold.
14. Sitting in the chair, the man tells folktales.
15. Reading the assignment, she took notes carefully.
16. A bowl hollowed out of wood can be valuable.
17. The rabbit hopping along the fence is my pet.
18. The people waiting to see Tiger Woods whistled and clapped.
19. Cheering for the team, we celebrated the victory.
20. Living more than four hundred years ago, Leonardo da Vinci kept journals of his ideas and inventions.

SPEAKING APPLICATION

Tell a partner about movies that you have seen recently. Use participles as you speak. Your partner should write each participle that you use. After you finish speaking, your partner should read aloud each participle, and tell whether it is past or present.

WRITING APPLICATION

Use the participial phrases in sentences 11, 13, and 16 to write three new sentences.

Gerunds

Many nouns that end in *-ing* are actually **verbals** known as **gerunds.** Gerunds are not difficult to recognize: They always end in *-ing,* and they always function as **nouns.**

A **gerund** is a form of a verb that ends in *-ing* and acts as a **noun.**

FUNCTIONS OF GERUNDS	
Subject	Swimming is my favorite activity.
Direct Object	The English people make visiting England a pleasure.
Indirect Object	Mrs. Kay's lecture gave traveling a new perspective.
Predicate Nominative	My mom's favorite activity is cooking.
Object of a Preposition	Their puppy showed signs of extensive training.
Appositive	Anne's profession, teaching, is hard work.

Verb, Participle, or Gerund? Words ending in *-ing* may be parts of verb phrases, participles acting as adjectives, or gerunds.

Words ending in *-ing* that act as **nouns** are called **gerunds.** Unlike verbs ending in *-ing,* gerunds do not have helping verbs. Unlike participles ending in *-ing,* they do not act as adjectives.

VERB	Kim is **sleeping** in her bed.
PARTICIPLE	The **sleeping** girl was very tired.
GERUND	**Sleeping** is very healthful.
VERB	My sister was **crying**, and that upset me.
PARTICIPLE	**Crying**, my sister upset me.
GERUND	My sister's **crying** upset me.

See Practice 15.1G

368 Phrases and Clauses

Gerund Phrases Like participles, gerunds may be joined by other words to make **gerund phrases**.

> A **gerund phrase** consists of a gerund and one or more modifiers or a complement. The entire gerund phrase acts as a noun.

15.1.11 RULE

GERUND PHRASES	
With Adjectives	The baby's constant smiling is adorable.
With an Adverb	Acting quickly is not always a good idea.
With a Prepositional Phrase	Many places in the town prohibit walking dogs on the grass.
With a Direct Object	Rob was incapable of reciting the lines.
With an Indirect and a Direct Object	The English teacher tried giving her students praise.

Note About Gerunds and Possessive Pronouns: Always use the possessive form of a personal pronoun in front of a gerund.

INCORRECT	We never listen to **him** complaining.
CORRECT	We never listen to **his** complaining.
INCORRECT	**Them** refusing to wear seat belts is dangerous.
CORRECT	**Their** refusing to wear seat belts is dangerous.

See Practice 15.1H
See Practice 15.1I

Infinitives

The third kind of verbal is the **infinitive**. Infinitives have many different uses. They can act as nouns, adjectives, or adverbs.

> An **infinitive** is a form of a verb that generally appears with the word *to* in front of it and acts as a noun, an adjective, or an adverb.

Phrases 369

EXAMPLE   The teacher asked the class **to work quietly**.

INFINITIVES USED AS NOUNS	
Subject	To understand history requires reading and studying.
Direct Object	The militia decided to rebel.
Predicate Nominative	The prisoner's only option was to surrender.
Object of a Preposition	I have no goal in life except to dance.
Appositive	You have only one choice, to go.

Unlike gerunds, infinitives can also act as adjectives and adverbs.

INFINITIVES USED AS MODIFIERS	
Adjective	The allies showed a willingness to cooperate.
Adverb	Some animals were unable to fight.

See Practice 15.1J

Prepositional Phrase or Infinitive? Although both **prepositional phrases** and **infinitives** often begin with *to*, you can tell the difference between them by analyzing the words that follow *to*.

> A **prepositional phrase** always ends with a noun or pronoun that acts as the object of the preposition. An **infinitive** always ends with a verb.

PREPOSITIONAL PHRASE	INFINITIVE
The puppy listened to the command.	The obedience instructor's job is to command.
We took the car to the back of the shop.	Make sure to back up your work in case you lose it.

Phrases and Clauses

Note About Infinitives Without *to*: Sometimes infinitives do not include the word *to*. When an infinitive follows one of the eight verbs listed below, the *to* is generally omitted. However, it may be understood.

VERBS THAT PRECEDE INFINITIVES WITHOUT *TO*			
dare	help	make	see
hear	let	please	watch

EXAMPLES He won't dare [to] go without asking.

Please help me [to] leave the package here.

Jon helped Bill [to] complete the project.

Infinitive Phrases Infinitives also can be joined with other words to form phrases.

> An **infinitive phrase** consists of an infinitive and its modifiers, complements, or subject, all acting together as a single part of speech.

RULE 15.1.14

INFINITIVE PHRASES	
With an Adverb	Anne's family likes to eat later.
With an Adverb Phrase	To drive in the snow is not easy.
With a Direct Object	She hated to leave Chicago.

With an Indirect and a Direct Object	They promised to show us the pictures
	                   direct indirect direct
	                   object object object
	 from their wedding.

With a Subject and a Complement	I want her to make her own choices. subject complement

See Practice 15.1K
See Practice 15.1L

PRACTICE 15.1G Writing Gerunds

Read each item. Then, write a sentence using each gerund phrase.

EXAMPLE   cooking (appositive)
ANSWER   *Mary's favorite hobby, cooking, makes us happy.*

1. walking (subject)
2. swimming (indirect object)
3. writing (predicate nominative)
4. gardening (appositive)
5. painting (direct object)
6. burning (object of a preposition)
7. drawing (appositive)
8. editing (predicate nominative)
9. stretching (direct object)
10. worrying (subject)

PRACTICE 15.1H Writing Gerund Phrases

Read each item. Then, write a sentence using the function of each gerund phrase indicated in parentheses. Read your sentences to a partner, who will tell you if your sentences are correct.

EXAMPLE   fishing in the lake (with a prepositional phrase)
ANSWER   *I would like to try fishing in the lake.*

11. descriptive, exciting writing (with adjectives)
12. teaching her dog tricks (with an indirect and a direct object)
13. floating in the lake (with a prepositional phrase)
14. driving slowly (with an adverb)
15. watching the movie (with a direct object)
16. skating rapidly (with an adverb)
17. throwing the ball (with a direct object)
18. telling voters the facts (with an indirect and a direct object)
19. beautiful, clear singing (with adjectives)
20. biking in the park (with a prepositional phrase)

SPEAKING APPLICATION

Take turns with a partner. Choose one of the five functions of gerund phrases. Your partner should write a sentence using a gerund in the function that you've indicated and then read the sentence aloud. Together, discuss if the sentence is correct.

WRITING APPLICATION

Write a sentence for each of the six functions of gerunds. Be sure to mix up the order. Then, read your sentences to a partner. Your partner should identify the function of each gerund in your sentences.

Phrases and Clauses

PRACTICE 15.1I Identifying Gerunds and Gerund Phrases

Read each sentence. Then, write the gerund or gerund phrase, and use it in a new sentence.

EXAMPLE Gardening can be a good pastime.
ANSWER *gardening; Mr. Hale enjoys gardening.*

1. On rainy days, Emma enjoys reading.
2. Losing badly is never fun to experience.
3. I helped out in the office, doing the envelope labeling.
4. Trimming is important to the health of most plants.
5. My mom made volunteering an important part of her life.
6. Quan has shown talent for drawing.
7. Knitting can be enjoyable and profitable.
8. The man's crime was stealing.
9. Exercising regularly can be important for good health.
10. With this machine, cleaning seems easy.

PRACTICE 15.1J Identifying the Function of Infinitives

Read each sentence. Then, write the infinitive and tell if it acts as a *noun*, *adjective*, or *adverb*. Discuss your answers with a partner. Determine if your answers are correct.

EXAMPLE The message was hard to hear.
ANSWER *to hear* — adverb

11. The road was difficult to cross.
12. I have a meal to prepare.
13. The dogs seemed eager to eat.
14. The tired runner decided to quit.
15. She always followed her dream, to dance.
16. TJ volunteered to read the poem aloud.
17. My friend Bob went home to study.
18. The student demonstrated her ability to draw.
19. The store owner decided to close.
20. To worry about the test makes no sense.

SPEAKING APPLICATION

Use gerunds in sentences to tell a partner about your favorite activities. Ask your partner to identify the gerunds as you speak.

WRITING APPLICATION

Write sentences using infinitives that act as a noun, adjective, or adverb. Read your sentences aloud to a partner. Your partner should identify each infinitive and tell how it acts.

Infinitives

PRACTICE 15.1K Identifying Infinitives and Infinitive Phrases

Read each sentence. Then, write each infinitive or infinitive phrase.

EXAMPLE Dad went to buy some meat.
ANSWER *to buy some meat*

1. Is this the right path to take?
2. Hayden wants to walk to school.
3. You should try to listen carefully.
4. Jorge is willing to learn new things.
5. Keri asked me to hand you this book.
6. To rebuild the warehouse that burned down is important.
7. When I am in New York City, I like to shop.
8. Would you like to explain your answer?
9. Your teacher is ready to begin speaking.
10. Charlie likes to write e-mails to his friends.

PRACTICE 15.1L Writing Infinitive Phrases

Read each item. Then, write a sentence for each infinitive phrase using the function indicated in parentheses.

EXAMPLE I asked (with a subject and a complement)
ANSWER *I asked Leila to draw the blinds.*

11. Our coach asked (with a subject and a complement)
12. The swimmer wanted (with a direct object)
13. The campers intend (with an adverb)
14. The dancers wanted (with an indirect and direct object)
15. She tried (with a direct object)
16. (With an adverb phrase) will be fun for the class
17. The musicians offered (with an indirect and direct object)
18. The cook plans (with an adverb)
19. (With an adverb phrase) is not a good idea
20. My teacher taught (with a subject and a complement)

SPEAKING APPLICATION

Use the items in Practice 15.1L to say new sentences to a partner. Your partner should write each of your sentences. Take turns reading the sentences aloud. Discuss whether the sentences use the function indicated in parentheses.

WRITING APPLICATION

Show that you understand the function of verbals (infinitives). Write three sentences that use infinitives and read them to a partner. Ask your partner to identify the infinitives as you speak.

Phrases and Clauses

15.2 Clauses

Every **clause** contains a subject and a verb. However, not every clause can stand by itself as a complete thought.

Grammar Tutorials
Brush up on your Grammar skills with these animated videos.

Grammar Practice
Practice your grammar skills with Writing Coach Online.

Grammar Games
Test your knowledge of grammar in this fast-paced interactive video game.

> A **clause** is a group of words that contains a subject and a verb.

Independent and Subordinate Clauses

The two basic kinds of clauses are **independent** or **main clauses** and **subordinate clauses.**

> An **independent** or **main clause** can stand by itself as a complete sentence.

Every sentence must contain an independent clause. The independent clause can either stand by itself or be connected to other independent or subordinate clauses.

STANDING ALONE
Mr. Holden teaches history.
independent clause

WITH ANOTHER INDEPENDENT CLAUSE
Mr. Holden teaches history, and his sister teaches math.
independent clause — *independent clause*

WITH A SUBORDINATE CLAUSE
Mr. Holden teaches history, while his sister teaches math.
independent clause — *subordinate clause*

When you subordinate something, you give it less importance.

> A **subordinate clause,** although it has a subject and verb, cannot stand by itself as a complete sentence.

Subordinate clauses can appear before or after an independent clause in a sentence or can even split an independent clause.

Clauses • 375

LOCATIONS OF SUBORDINATE CLAUSES	
In the Middle of an Independent Clause	The man to whom I introduced you teaches history.
Preceding an Independent Clause	Unless the snow stops soon, the roads will be closed.
Following an Independent Clause	Hannah asked that she be excused.

See Practice 15.2A

Like phrases, subordinate clauses can function as adjectives, adverbs, or nouns in sentences.

Adjectival Clauses

One way to add description and detail to a sentence is by adding an **adjectival clause.**

> **RULE 15.2.4**
> An **adjectival clause** is a subordinate clause that modifies a noun or pronoun in another clause by telling *what kind* or *which one.*

An adjectival clause usually begins with one of the relative pronouns: *that, which, who, whom,* or *whose.* Sometimes, it begins with a relative adverb, such as *before, since, when, where,* or *why.* Each of these words connects the clause to the word it modifies.

> **RULE 15.2.5**
> An **adjectival clause** often begins with **a relative pronoun** or a **relative adverb** that links the clause to a noun or pronoun in another clause.

The adjectival clauses in the examples on the next page answer the questions *What kind?* and *Which one?* Each modifies the noun in the independent clause that comes right before the adjectival clause. Notice also that the first two clauses begin with relative pronouns and the last one begins with a relative adverb.

Phrases and Clauses

EXAMPLES I finished watching the movie **that you lent me**.

We gave the research, **which we found fascinating**, a second look.

In Holland, we visited the village **where my father was born**.

Adjectival clauses can often be used to combine information from two sentences into one. Using adjectival clauses to combine sentences can indicate the relationship between ideas as well as add detail to a sentence.

TWO SENTENCES	COMBINED SENTENCES
The dancer is a prima ballerina. She is dressed to dance.	The dancer, **who is a prima ballerina**, is dressed to dance.
My sister graduated from college in less than four years. She is in medical school now.	My sister, **who is in medical school now**, graduated from college in less than four years.

Essential and Nonessential Adjectival Clauses Adjectival clauses, like appositives and participial phrases, are set off by punctuation only when they are not essential to the meaning of a sentence. Commas are used to indicate information that is not essential to the meaning of the sentence. When information in an adjectival clause is essential to the sentence, no commas are used.

NONESSENTIAL CLAUSES	ESSENTIAL CLAUSES
One of Shakespeare's best characters is Lady Macbeth, **who is a main character in** *Macbeth*.	The documentary **that everyone must watch by Friday** promises to be very interesting.
Anne James, **who studied hard every night for a year**, won the scholarship.	A student **who prepares faithfully** usually finds getting good grades easy.

See Practice 15.2B
See Practice 15.2C
See Practice 15.2D

Clauses

Restrictive Relative Clauses and Nonrestrictive Relative Clauses

Relative clauses begin with one of the relative pronouns: *who, whose, whom, which, what,* or *that.* When a relative clause serves as an adjective and modifies a noun or pronoun in another clause, it is an adjectival clause.

Relative clauses can be restrictive or nonrestrictive. A relative clause is restrictive, or essential, when the information in the relative clause is important to the meaning of the sentence. A restrictive relative clause begins with *who, whose, whom,* or *that.* No commas are used to set it off.

> **RULE 15.2.6**
> A **restrictive** (or **essential**) **relative clause** contains information that is essential to the meaning of the sentence. Commas are not needed with a restrictive relative clause.

A relative clause is nonrestrictive, or nonessential, when leaving the clause out does not change the intended meaning of the sentence. Introduce a nonrestrictive relative clause with *who, whose, whom,* or *which* and use commas to set it off.

> **RULE 15.2.7**
> A **nonrestrictive** (or **nonessential**) **relative clause** contains information that is not essential to the meaning of the sentence. Use commas to set off a nonrestrictive relative clause.

In general, *that* is the relative pronoun used in restrictive relative clauses, while *which* is the relative pronoun used in nonrestrictive relative clauses.

RESTRICTIVE RELATIVE CLAUSES	NONRESTRICTIVE RELATIVE CLAUSES
The man who dropped his cell phone picked it up.	Ted, who is a teacher, lives next door.
The chair that is made of bamboo is eco-friendly.	The door, which squeaks, will be repaired next week.

See Practice 15.2E
See Practice 15.2F

Phrases and Clauses

PRACTICE 15.2A Identifying Independent and Subordinate Clauses

Read each sentence. Identify the underlined clause in each sentence as either *independent* or *subordinate*.

EXAMPLE <u>Whenever we visit my aunt</u>, we always eat seafood.

ANSWER *subordinate*

1. Marcos bought the coat, <u>although it was really too expensive</u>.
2. Italy is a country <u>that I have always wanted to visit</u>.
3. <u>When Sarah made the honor roll</u>, her father was very proud.
4. <u>I'm a big fan of the Miami Heat</u>, but I like the San Antonio Spurs even better.
5. <u>David is a terrific tennis player</u> because he practices all the time.
6. I left the present on the counter, <u>where you can find it easily</u>.
7. <u>If you want to take a walk</u>, I can go with you.
8. <u>Because of the heat</u>, the room felt uncomfortable.
9. If you want to feel a slight breeze, <u>wave a sheet of paper in front of your face</u>.
10. <u>Although the fire was blazing</u>, we were still cold.

PRACTICE 15.2B Identifying Adjectival Clauses

Read each sentence. Then, write the adjectival clause in each sentence.

EXAMPLE Frank is the person that I met at Ronnie's party.

ANSWER *that I met at Ronnie's party*

11. I can't see where the boat is docked.
12. Max is the one for whom I left the message.
13. Texas is a state that has a large population.
14. Edgar Allen Poe is a poet whose work was once ignored.
15. Marcus is the one who answered all the questions correctly during the game show.
16. I still have some of the money that I earned over the summer.
17. The movie, which is playing now, is scary.
18. This dish has an ingredient that I don't like.
19. Is this the year when the planets will align?
20. Sheila, whose father is a doctor, wants to be a surgeon.

SPEAKING APPLICATION

Take turns with a partner. Say sentences that have independent and subordinate clauses. Your partner should identify the clauses as either independent or subordinate.

WRITING APPLICATION

Show that you understand restrictive relative clauses (essential) and nonrestrictive relative clauses (nonessential) by writing two sentences that use either type of clause. Then, read your sentences to a partner. Ask your partner to identify the clauses as you speak.

PRACTICE 15.2C Writing Independent Clauses

Read each item. Then, write a sentence using each item in an independent clause.

EXAMPLE   the textbook
ANSWER   *The textbook fell to the floor.*

1. the serious student
2. dove into the water
3. the basketball players
4. the well-trained dog
5. rode their bikes
6. all the excited visitors
7. finished the race
8. painted the house
9. many newspaper reporters
10. walked to the bus station

PRACTICE 15.2D Writing Subordinate Clauses

Read each item. Then, write a sentence using each item in a subordinate clause.

EXAMPLE   the howling wind
ANSWER   *The cause of the noise, which is the howling wind, scared my dog.*

11. Until the new library opens
12. that the students like
13. who is the new class president
14. After the snowstorm stopped
15. that the farmer planted
16. whom I e-mailed yesterday
17. Although I missed the train
18. that you know the correct answer
19. When our vacation is over
20. to whom we sent the package

SPEAKING APPLICATION

Take turns with a partner. Read your sentences for Practice 15.2C to each other. Compare your sentences and decide if they are independent clauses.

WRITING APPLICATION

Write a few paragraphs about your favorite holiday. Be sure to include independent clauses and subordinate clauses. Exchange papers with a partner. Your partner should underline the independent clauses and circle the subordinate clauses in your paragraphs.

PRACTICE 15.2E Identifying Restrictive Relative Clauses and Nonrestrictive Relative Clauses

Read each sentence. Then, write each clause and identify it as *restrictive* or *nonrestrictive*. Discuss your answers with a partner. Determine if your answers are correct.

EXAMPLE Venus, which is a planet, can be seen in the sky.

ANSWER *which is a planet* — nonrestrictive

1. The e-mail, which is very long, is important to read.
2. The baseball schedule that we need for the season is still undetermined.
3. Sarah, who is a transfer student, is class president.
4. The athlete who practices every day will win the race.
5. I finished the book that our teacher just assigned.
6. The storm, which the meteorologists warned about, damaged the town.
7. Frank bought the computer that was on sale.
8. The painter who will teach our art class is world famous.
9. My grandmother, whom I just called, is a wonderful writer.
10. I hope the essay that I submitted to the contest wins first prize.

PRACTICE 15.2F Writing Restrictive and Nonrestrictive Relative Clauses

Read each sentence. If the sentence has a restrictive relative clause, rewrite it with a nonrestrictive relative clause. If it has a nonrestrictive relative clause, rewrite it with a restrictive relative clause. Read your sentences to a partner and discuss if they are correct.

EXAMPLE Liz, who is my friend, wrote that song.

ANSWER *The person who wrote that song is my friend Liz.*

11. The movie, which I saw last week, is good.
12. My teacher, who lives nearby, is my advisor.
13. In New York we visited a museum that is new.
14. We followed the trail that led us back to camp.
15. Our family will move to the city where my mother works now.
16. My friend, whose opinion I trust, loves my photographs.
17. The writer whom I most admire agreed to read my poetry.
18. Our class will visit a community center that assists the elderly.
19. The guide, whose name I forgot, will begin the tour.
20. The neighborhood park, which is being repaired, will open soon.

SPEAKING APPLICATION

With a partner, discuss the difference in meaning between the example and answer in Practice 15.2F. Explain the function of the commas in the example.

WRITING APPLICATION

Using restrictive and nonrestrictive relative clauses, write an article about a recent event. Exchange papers with a partner. Your partner should underline any restrictive relative clauses and circle any nonrestrictive relative clauses.

Clauses

Test Warm-Up

DIRECTIONS
Read the introduction and the passage that follows. Then, answer the questions to show that you can use and understand the function of restrictive relative clauses and nonrestrictive relative clauses in reading and writing.

Marsha wrote this paragraph about an organization that trains service dogs. Read the paragraph and think about the changes you would suggest as a peer editor. When you finish reading, answer the questions that follow.

Dogs and People Help Each Other

(1) Freedom Service Dogs which was founded in 1987 helps dogs and people at the same time. (2) This organization trains dogs, that are rescued from animal shelters to help people with disabilities. (3) In early 2009, Freedom Service Dogs shifted its focus to helping those veterans, who were wounded in Iraq and Afghanistan. (4) These service dogs perform many tasks. (5) These tasks include finding keys or pulling wheelchairs for their owners. (6) What wonderful teamwork.

---

1 Which change, if any, should be made in sentence 1?

A Change *which* to *that*

B Add commas before *which* and after *1987*

C Add commas after *which* and after *people*

D Make no change

2 What change, if any, should be made in sentence 2?

F Delete the comma before *that*

G Add a comma after *shelters*

H Delete the infinitive phrase *to help people with disabilities*

J Make no change

3 What change should be made in sentence 3?

A Change *who* to *that*

B Change *who* to *which*

C Change *who* to *whom*

D Delete the comma before *who*

4 What is the most effective way to use a restrictive relative clause to combine sentences 4 and 5?

F These service dogs perform many tasks, which may include finding keys or pulling wheelchairs for their owners.

G For their owners, these service dogs are essential to performing many tasks.

H Finding keys and pulling wheelchairs for their owners are some of the many tasks that these service dogs perform.

J Finding keys and pulling wheelchairs are two of the many tasks where these service dogs perform.

Relative Pronouns **Relative pronouns** help link a subordinate clause to another part of a sentence. They also have a function in the subordinate clause.

> **Relative pronouns** connect adjectival clauses to the words they modify and act as subjects, direct objects, objects of prepositions, or adjectives in the subordinate clauses.

To tell how a relative pronoun is used within a clause, separate the clause from the rest of the sentence, and find the subject and verb in the clause.

FUNCTIONS OF RELATIVE PRONOUNS IN CLAUSES	
As a Subject	A boat that is built correctly is sure to stay afloat. 　　　　subject
As a Direct Object	Jake, whom my sister met at college, is a doctor. 　　　　　direct object (Reworded clause: my sister met *whom* at college)
As an Object of a Preposition	This is the movie about which I heard great reviews. 　　　　　　object of preposition (Reworded clause: I heard great reviews about *which*)
As an Adjective	The star whose actions were in question spoke to the 　　　　　adjective media.

Sometimes in writing and in speech, a relative pronoun is left out of an adjectival clause. However, the missing word, though simply understood, still functions in the sentence.

EXAMPLES　　The novelists [**whom**] we studied were great writers.

　　　　　　　　The ideas [**that**] they suggested were implemented.

See Practice 15.2G

Relative Adverbs Like relative pronouns, **relative adverbs** help link the subordinate clause to another part of a sentence. However, they have only one use within a subordinate clause.

> **RULE 15.2.9** **Relative adverbs** connect adjectival clauses to the words they modify and act as adverbs in the clauses.

EXAMPLE   The patient yearned for the day **when** she'd be out of the hospital.

In the example, the adjectival clause is *when she'd be out of the hospital.* Reword the clause this way to see that *when* functions as an adverb: *she'd be out of the hospital when.*

Adverbial Clauses

Subordinate clauses may also serve as adverbs in sentences. They are introduced by subordinating conjunctions. Like adverbs, **adverbial clauses** modify verbs, adjectives, or other adverbs.

> **RULE 15.2.10** Subordinate **adverbial clauses** modify verbs, adjectives, adverbs, or verbals by telling *where, when, in what way, to what extent, under what condition,* or *why.*

An adverbial clause begins with a subordinating conjunction and contains a subject and a verb, although they are not the main subject and verb in the sentence. In the chart that follows, the adverbial clauses are highlighted in orange. Arrows point to the words they modify.

ADVERBIAL CLAUSES	
Modifying a Verb	Before you visit Germany, you should read a tour book. (Read *when?*)
Modifying an Adjective	Randy seemed successful wherever he was. (Successful *where?*)
Modifying a Gerund	Diving is easy and fun if you have been well taught. (Diving *under what condition?*)

384 Phrases and Clauses

> **Adverbial clauses** begin with **subordinating conjunctions** and contain subjects and verbs.

RULE 15.2.11

EXAMPLE **After** the rain fell, the flowers bloomed.
          subordinating
          conjunction

Recognizing the subordinating conjunctions will help you identify adverbial clauses. The following chart shows some of the most common subordinating conjunctions.

SUBORDINATING CONJUNCTIONS			
after	because	so that	when
although	before	than	whenever
as	even though	though	where
as if	if	unless	wherever
as long as	since	until	while

Whether an adverbial clause appears at the beginning, middle, or end of a sentence can sometimes affect the sentence meaning.

EXAMPLE **Before she graduated**, Tia made plans to study abroad.

Tia made plans to study abroad **before she graduated**.

Like adjectival clauses, adverbial clauses can be used to combine the information from two sentences into one. The combined sentence shows a close relationship between the ideas.

TWO SENTENCES   **It snowed**. They stayed home.

COMBINED   **Because** it snowed, they stayed home.
                subordinating
                conjunction

See Practice 15.2H

Clauses

Clauses

PRACTICE 15.2G Identifying Relative Pronouns and Adjectival Clauses

Read each sentence. Then, write the adjectival clause in each sentence and underline the relative pronoun that introduces the clause.

EXAMPLE   Leslie is the one whose mother is the principal.

ANSWER   *whose mother is the principal*

1. That is the house in which I was born.
2. Janice, who plays the trumpet, joined the school band.
3. The moon is the place where the *Apollo 13* mission was headed.
4. Rob answered the question that the teacher asked.
5. My father works in an office that has a friendly atmosphere.
6. A hurricane develops at a time when a tropical storm picks up wind speed.
7. My mother, whose job is very stressful, worked all weekend.
8. The settlers couldn't understand the reason that it was so difficult to grow crops.
9. My friend whom you liked thought you were nice also.
10. Algebra is a subject about which I know a lot.

PRACTICE 15.2H Recognizing Adverbial Clauses

Read each sentence. Write the adverbial clause in each sentence, and identify the subordinating conjunction.

EXAMPLE   We wanted to stop so that we could grab something to eat.

ANSWER   *so that we could grab something to eat, so that*

11. My dad will worry if we are late.
12. We posted the warning where it would reach the most people.
13. Professor Franklin tutors at the elementary school whenever he has time.
14. After the sauce has simmered, add the basil and thyme.
15. I'm sure Gloria will assist if you ask her.
16. While she was recovering, Rumi read several books a month.
17. Each student was better prepared than the one before was.
18. The mattress was dropped off today, as the salesman had guaranteed.
19. After he gave out homework assignments, Mr. O'Malley started the lesson.
20. Wendell appears excited whenever this topic is debated.

SPEAKING APPLICATION

Take turns with a partner. Describe a book you have read. Your partner should listen for and identify the relative pronouns *that, which, who, whom,* or *whose* in your description.

WRITING APPLICATION

Write sentences using the following adverbial clauses: *while I waited, after the mail was delivered; since I started high school.*

Elliptical Adverbial Clauses Sometimes, words are omitted in adverbial clauses, especially in those clauses that begin with *as* or *than* and are used to express comparisons. Such clauses are said to be *elliptical*.

> **An elliptical clause** is a clause in which the verb or the subject and verb are understood but not actually stated.

15.2.12 RULE

Even though the subject or the verb (or both) may not appear in an elliptical clause, they make the clause express a complete thought.

In the following examples, the understood words appear in brackets. The sentences are alike, except for the words *he* and *him*. In the first sentence, *he* is a subject of the adverbial clause. In the second sentence, *him* functions as a direct object of the adverbial clause.

VERB UNDERSTOOD His sister resembles their father more **than he [does]**.

SUBJECT AND VERB UNDERSTOOD His sister resembles their father more **than [she resembles] him**.

When you read or write elliptical clauses, mentally include the omitted words to clarify the intended meaning.

See Practice 15.2I

Noun Clauses

Subordinate clauses can also act as nouns in sentences.

> **A noun clause** is a subordinate clause that acts as a noun.

15.2.13 RULE

A noun clause acts in almost the same way a one-word noun does in a sentence: It tells what or whom the sentence is about.

RULE 15.2.14 In a sentence, a noun clause may act as a subject, direct object, indirect object, predicate nominative, object of a preposition, or appositive.

EXAMPLES **Whatever you lost** can be found in the house.
              subject

My parents remembered **what I wanted for my graduation**.
                                                direct object

The chart on the next page contains more examples of the functions of noun clauses.

Introductory Words

Noun clauses frequently begin with the words *that, which, who, whom,* or *whose*—the same words that are used to begin adjective clauses. *Whichever, whoever,* or *whomever* may also be used as introductory words in noun clauses. Other noun clauses begin with the words *how, if, what, whatever, where, when, whether,* or *why*.

RULE 15.2.15 **Introductory words** may act as subjects, direct objects, objects of prepositions, adjectives, or adverbs in noun clauses, or they may simply introduce the clauses.

| SOME USES OF INTRODUCTORY WORDS IN NOUN CLAUSES ||
FUNCTIONS IN CLAUSES	EXAMPLES
Adjective	He could not decide **which car** was the best.
Adverb	We want to know **how to get there**.
Subject	I want the recipe from **whoever made that pot pie**!
Direct Object	**Whatever my guidance counselor advised**, I did.
No Function	The doctor determined **that she had broken her leg**.

388   **Phrases and Clauses**

Note that in the following chart the introductory word *that* in the last example has no function except to introduce the clause.

FUNCTIONS OF NOUN CLAUSES IN SENTENCES	
Acting as a Subject	Whoever is last must close the door.
Acting as a Direct Object	Please invite whomever you want to the wedding.
Acting as an Indirect Object	Her attitude gave whoever met her a shock.
Acting as a Predicate Nominative	Our problem is whether we should help or not.
Acting as an Object of a Preposition	Use the car for whatever purpose you choose.
Acting as an Appositive	The country rejected the plea that prisoners be cared for by personal dentists.

Some words that introduce noun clauses also introduce adjectival and adverbial clauses. It is necessary to check the function of the clause in the sentence to determine its type. To check the function, try substituting the words *it, you, fact,* or *thing* for the clause. If the sentence retains its smoothness, you probably replaced a noun clause.

Clauses 389

NOUN CLAUSE   I knew **that she wouldn't be on time**.

SUBSTITUTION   I knew it.

In the following examples, all three subordinating clauses begin with *where,* but only the first is a noun clause because it functions in the sentence as a direct object.

NOUN CLAUSE   Mr. Anderson told the tour group **where they would meet after the show**.
(Told the group *what?*)

ADJECTIVAL CLAUSE   They took the patient to the emergency room, **where they examined him**.
(*Which* room?)

ADVERBIAL CLAUSE   She lives **where the weather is rainy all year**.
(Lives *where?*)

Note About Introductory Words: The introductory word *that* is often omitted from a noun clause. In the following examples, the understood word *that* is in brackets.

EXAMPLES   The security guard suggested **[that] I state my name**.

After his teacher told him he passed, Brian knew **[that] he could do anything**.

We remember **[that] you wanted Japanese food for dinner tonight**.

See Practice 15.2J

PRACTICE 15.2I Identifying Elliptical Adverbial Clauses

Read each sentence. Then, write the adverbial clause in each sentence. For the adverbial clauses that are elliptical, add the understood words in parentheses.

EXAMPLE My sculpture received more praise than his sculpture.

ANSWER *than his sculpture (did)*

1. That building is taller than the Empire State Building.
2. My foot itches more than a bee sting itches.
3. Carrie spoke to Jason longer than to Joe.
4. Nora is as well-spoken as her mother.
5. Carl's explanation is as clear as your explanation.
6. The newly discovered star is as bright as our star.
7. Joanne is as early as you.
8. I can ski faster than Ed.
9. Jill's kite is higher than Mr. William's kite.
10. The baseball is rolling faster than the bowling ball.

PRACTICE 15.2J Recognizing Noun Clauses

Read each sentence. Then, write the noun clause in each sentence and label it *subject, direct object, indirect object, predicate nominative,* or *object of a preposition*.

EXAMPLE We all knew that you would win.

ANSWER *that you would win* — direct object

11. Do you know when the flight departs?
12. The king will give whoever wins a reward.
13. That she was angry was obvious to no one.
14. One concern was which field had better amenities.
15. We ask that you submit your film again.
16. What Francis documented astonished all of us.
17. Roman's main concern was whether he should study or play basketball.
18. Whoever is passionate about film will enjoy this movie.
19. The boss's predicament about how it would be possible to appease both employees demanded much thought.
20. Harold offers advice to whoever is fortunate enough to stand next to him.

SPEAKING APPLICATION

Take turns with a partner. Tell about a vivid dream. Use at least three adverbial clauses. Your partner should listen for and identify the adverbial clauses.

WRITING APPLICATION

Write a paragraph in which you review a film, using three different functions of a noun clause. Underline each noun clause in your paragraph.

15.3 The Four Structures of Sentences

Independent and subordinate clauses are the building blocks of sentences. These clauses can be combined in an endless number of ways to form the four basic sentence structures: **simple, compound, complex,** and **compound-complex.**

A simple sentence contains a single independent or main clause.

Although a simple sentence contains only one main or independent clause, its subject, verb, or both may be compound. A simple sentence may also have modifying phrases and complements. However, it cannot have a subordinate clause.

In the following simple sentences, the subjects are highlighted in yellow, and the verbs are highlighted in orange.

ONE SUBJECT AND VERB	The **rain** **fell**.
COMPOUND SUBJECT	**Dan** and **I** **made** the coffee.
COMPOUND VERB	The **girl** **jumped** and **ran**.
COMPOUND SUBJECT AND VERB	Neither the **teacher** nor the **student** **heard** the alarm or **saw** smoke.

A compound sentence contains two or more main clauses.

The main clauses in a compound sentence can be joined by a comma and a coordinating conjunction *(and, but, for, nor, or, so, yet)* or by a semicolon (;). Like a simple sentence, a compound sentence contains no subordinate clauses.

EXAMPLE   An American **bride** often **carries** flowers at her wedding, and **she** **throws** the flowers at the end.

See Practice 15.3A

392   Phrases and Clauses

The Four Structures of Sentences

> **RULE 15.3.3** A **complex sentence** consists of one independent or main clause and one or more subordinate clauses.

The independent clause in a complex sentence is often called the main clause to distinguish it from the subordinate clause or clauses. The subject and verb in the independent clause are called the subject of the sentence and the main verb. In the examples below, the main clauses are highlighted in blue, and the subordinate clauses are highlighted in pink.

EXAMPLES No one moved when he sang.

The bouquet of flowers that the girl carried didn't have any lilies.

Note on Complex Sentences With Noun Clauses: The subject of the main clause may sometimes be the subordinate clause itself.

EXAMPLE That he wanted to run upset them.

> **RULE 15.3.4** A **compound-complex sentence** consists of two or more independent clauses and one or more subordinate clauses.

In the example below, the independent clauses are highlighted in blue, and the subordinate clauses are highlighted in pink.

EXAMPLE The deck boards splinter when it snows heavily, and we have to repair the wood finish so that the splinters are covered.

See Practice 15.3B

The Four Structures of Sentences

PRACTICE 15.3A **Distinguishing Among the Four Structures of Sentences**

Read each sentence. Then, label each sentence as *simple*, *compound*, *complex*, or *compound-complex*.

EXAMPLE   Joe dove for the ball and missed.
ANSWER   *simple*

1. We had hoped for good news from our teacher but the scores had not been published yet.
2. Teammates and rivals alike worked side by side covering the field.
3. Sandy stood behind the podium, collected herself, and began her speech.
4. The counselors were satisfied, but the campers were not happy with the new rules.
5. Phillip completed his lessons late, so he was not free to come along with us.
6. Mr. Henderson laughed long and hard.
7. The assignment that our teacher gave is challenging.
8. We remained on the side of the road.
9. Some travelers pack well; some prepare halfheartedly; others reject the entire process.
10. I like to cook when people come to visit, and I always make dessert so that there's a nice end to the meal.

PRACTICE 15.3B **Writing the Four Structures of Sentences**

Read the words in each item. Then, use each group of words to write the type of sentence indicated in parentheses. Read your sentences to a partner. Discuss if your sentences are correct.

EXAMPLE   Chad (simple)
ANSWER   *Chad spent his time wisely.*

11. plates, silverware (compound)
12. the winning team (complex)
13. Mr. Witherspoon (simple)
14. actors, audience (compound-complex)
15. thunderstorm (simple)
16. field-hockey players, football players (compound)
17. studying (complex)
18. blue skies, sunshine (compound-complex)
19. Irene, Kylan (compound)
20. laptop (complex)

SPEAKING APPLICATION

Take turns with a partner. Describe your favorite activity. Your partner should listen for and identify simple, compound, complex, and compound-complex sentences in your description.

WRITING APPLICATION

Write a brief paragraph on any topic of your choice, using a variety of correctly structured sentences: simple, compound, complex, and compound-complex.

Cumulative Review Chapters 13–15

PRACTICE 1 ▶ Identifying Nouns

Read the sentences. Label each underlined noun as *concrete* or *abstract*. If the noun is concrete, label it *collective*, *compound*, or *proper*.

1. Jonathan has a <u>passion</u> for photography.
2. Next December I will be traveling to <u>Scotland</u>.
3. Preparing for his trip to <u>Lake Minnetonka</u>, Carl packed a <u>flashlight</u>.
4. It is William's <u>concern</u> for others that makes him special.
5. Gregory meets with his <u>staff</u> every Tuesday.

PRACTICE 2 ▶ Identifying Pronouns

Read the sentences. Then, label each underlined pronoun *reciprocal*, *demonstrative*, *relative*, *interrogative*, or *indefinite*.

1. Harold and Ben shook hands with <u>each other</u>.
2. <u>That</u> is Carla's ticket.
3. The woman <u>who</u> hired me was incredibly courteous.
4. <u>What</u> do you want to do this weekend?
5. <u>All</u> of the seats were occupied at the PTA meeting.

PRACTICE 3 ▶ Classifying Verbs and Verb Phrases

Read the sentences. Then, write the verb or verb phrase in each sentence. Label them as *action verb* or *linking verb*, and *transitive* or *intransitive*.

1. The competitors looked intently at one another before the game.
2. The committee selected a new chairperson to head the science department.
3. Zachary always feels invigorated after taking a walk.
4. Samantha appeared excited at the news of the election.
5. Mr. Hampton greeted the Weatherman family at the door.

PRACTICE 4 ▶ Identifying Adjectives and Adverbs

Read the sentences. Then, label the underlined word as *adverb* or *adjective*. Write the word that is modified.

1. Hanson made a <u>powerful</u> serve to win the match.
2. The charity event attracted many <u>well-known</u> celebrities.
3. Marcus handled the situation <u>rather</u> calmly.
4. After the <u>second</u> lap, Jacqueline had a lead.
5. Gloria was <u>not</u> involved in the argument.

PRACTICE 5 ▶ Using Conjunctions and Interjections

Read the sentences. Then, write the conjunction or interjection. If there is a conjunction in the sentence, label it *coordinating*, *correlative*, or *subordinating*.

1. Hector searched through the couch for change as Fred ordered the pizza.
2. Kenneth's flight was canceled, so he was forced to stay another night.
3. Man! I just can't seem to finish this puzzle.
4. Not only did we catch four big fish, but we also ate them later that night.
5. Both Simon and Christine received scholarships to college.

Continued on next page ▶

Cumulative Review Chapters 13–15

PRACTICE 6 Recognizing Direct and Indirect Objects and Object of a Preposition

Identify the underlined items as a *direct object*, *indirect object*, or *object of a preposition*.

1. Meena rode the train to the museum.
2. Gary gave his girlfriend a necklace.
3. Adrian showed the talent scout a glimpse of his portfolio.
4. The principal praised Rich and Jessica for their perfect attendance.
5. Joshua asked the doorman for directions to the arena.
6. Has Flora shown Luther and Ruth her new dress?
7. Will Kent buy us tickets to the rodeo?
8. Mrs. O'Connor reads her daughter a story every night.
9. The plumber sent me a bill for his services.
10. My uncle Sean gave us tickets to the match.

PRACTICE 7 Identifying Phrases

Write the phrases contained in the following sentences. Identify each phrase as a *prepositional phrase*, *appositive phrase*, *participial phrase*, *gerund phrase*, or *infinitive phrase*.

1. During the weekend, Anya went to the circus.
2. Mark went to the post office to mail his application.
3. Mr. Newsome, my first-grade teacher, wrote me a letter.
4. Studying for the quiz is a good idea.
5. I was completely soaked by the pouring rain.
6. Working hard, the detective solved the case.
7. Coach Landry asked Thomas to join the team.
8. Playing baseball is Sean's favorite activity.
9. Constance Reynolds, our regional supervisor, gave her annual report.
10. Victor Gonzalez, a former professional athlete, took a job coaching collegiate sports.

PRACTICE 8 Recognizing Clauses

Label the underlined clauses in the following sentences *independent* or *subordinate*. Identify any subordinate clause as *adjectival*, *adverbial*, or *noun clause*. Then, label any adjectival clauses *essential* or *nonessential*.

1. Although Trevor could not play ball, he ran out onto the field.
2. My good friend Larry, who lives in Dallas, just graduated from high school.
3. After I left the gym, I ran into Nathan in the parking lot.
4. If you want to sing well, you must practice.
5. Professor Jenkins is impressive for what he knows about ancient history.
6. William's idea that I hire you was a stroke of genius.
7. You take out the garbage while I clean the attic.
8. Frederick, who put on a hat and scarf, set off into the snowstorm.
9. My mom has decided to hire an interior decorator because she wants to brighten the room.
10. Why you forgot me is hard to comprehend.

EFFECTIVE SENTENCES

Use both shorter and longer sentences, including compound and complex sentences, to add variety to your writing.

WRITE GUY *Jeff Anderson, M.Ed.*

WHAT DO YOU NOTICE?

Investigate how ideas are combined as you zoom in on this sentence from "Rama's Initiation," an excerpt from the *Ramayana* by R. K. Narayan.

MENTOR TEXT

> When they meditated on and recited these incantations, the arid atmosphere was transformed for the rest of their passage and they felt as if they were wading through a cool stream with a southern summer breeze blowing in their faces.

Now, ask yourself the following questions:

- How did the author combine ideas in the subordinate clause that begins the sentence?
- How does the author combine the remaining ideas in the sentence?

A compound verb connects ideas in the subordinate clause *when they meditated on and recited these incantations*. Rather than use two clauses, one about meditating and one about reciting, the author uses *and* to combine the ideas. The author then combines two main, or independent, clauses using the conjunction *and*, he includes another subordinate clause, beginning with the subordinating conjunction *as if*, to complete the idea in the second main clause.

Grammar for Writers Writers often combine sentences to make their writing flow smoothly. Add a graceful rhythm to your sentences by looking for different ways to combine ideas.

I have too many short sentences in this paragraph. What's a simple solution?

Simply turn them into complex sentences!

CHAPTER 16

16.1 The Four Functions of a Sentence

Sentences can be classified according to what they do—that is, whether they state ideas, ask questions, give orders, or express strong emotions.

Grammar Practice
Practice your grammar skills with Writing Coach Online.

Grammar Games
Test your knowledge of grammar in this fast-paced interactive video game.

Declarative sentences are used to declare, or state, ideas.

> **RULE 16.1.1** A **declarative sentence** states an idea and ends with a period.

DECLARATIVE   Toronto is a city in Canada.

To *interrogate* means "to ask." An **interrogative sentence** is a question.

> **RULE 16.1.2** An **interrogative sentence** asks a question and ends with a question mark.

INTERROGATIVE   In which countries do gorillas live?

Imperative sentences give commands or directions.

> **RULE 16.1.3** An **imperative sentence** gives an order or a direction and ends with either a period or an exclamation mark.

Most imperative sentences start with a verb. In this type of imperative sentence, the subject is understood to be *you*.

IMPERATIVE   Follow the list exactly.

Exclamatory sentences are used to express emotions.

> **RULE 16.1.4** An **exclamatory sentence** conveys strong emotion and ends with an exclamation mark.

EXCLAMATORY   This is ridiculous!

See Practice 16.1A
See Practice 16.1B

The Four Functions of a Sentence

PRACTICE 16.1A Identifying the Four Types of Sentences

Read each sentence. Then, label each sentence *declarative, interrogative, imperative,* or *exclamatory.*

EXAMPLE   Leave a note if no one is in the office.
ANSWER   *imperative*

1. Have you located the movie you wanted to see?
2. Sign here after you fill out the form.
3. Which of the applicants do you think deserves the job?
4. Skate parks are becoming increasingly popular.
5. Make sure the bolt is screwed on tightly.
6. What a thoughtful thing to do!
7. Walk south on Second Street and then make a right turn.
8. The heat from the oven fills the room.
9. Have you seen Luanne since yesterday?
10. What a mess!

PRACTICE 16.1B Punctuating the Four Types of Sentences

Read each sentence. Then, label each sentence *declarative, interrogative, imperative,* or *exclamatory.* Then, in parentheses, write the correct end mark.

EXAMPLE   Porcupines use sharp quills as a defense against predators
ANSWER   *declarative* (.)

11. What a fantastic night
12. Did you return the movie
13. What a strange looking cat that is
14. Please stop staring at me
15. Tomorrow's function should be interesting
16. Who wrote that novel
17. Now that is what I call a performance
18. During the summer, I plan to read lots of books
19. Be sure to tell your mother that I returned her scarf
20. You can tour the Alamo and see artifacts that date back to the Texas Revolution

SPEAKING APPLICATION

Take turns with a partner. Say sentences that are declarative, interrogative, imperative, and exclamatory. Your partner should identify each type of sentence.

WRITING APPLICATION

Write a paragraph, using any sentence in Practice 16.1B as your topic. Use declarative, imperative, and exclamatory sentences in your paragraph.

16.2 Sentence Combining

Too many short sentences can make your writing choppy and disconnected.

One way to avoid the excessive use of short sentences and to achieve variety is to combine sentences.

RULE 16.2.1 — Sentences can be combined by using a **compound subject**, a **compound verb**, or a **compound object**.

TWO SENTENCES	Kate enjoyed watching the movie. Mike enjoyed watching the movie.
COMPOUND SUBJECT	Kate and Mike enjoyed watching the movie.
TWO SENTENCES	Tara studied hard today. Tara passed the test.
COMPOUND VERB	Tara studied hard today and passed the test.
TWO SENTENCES	Rob saw the band. Rob saw the fans.
COMPOUND OBJECT	Rob saw the band and the fans.

Grammar Tutorials
Brush up on your Grammar skills with these animated videos.

Grammar Practice
Practice your grammar skills with Writing Coach Online.

Grammar Games
Test your knowledge of grammar in this fast-paced interactive video game.

See Practice 16.2A

RULE 16.2.2 — Sentences can be combined by joining two **main** or **independent clauses** to create a **compound sentence**.

Use a compound sentence when combining ideas that are related but independent. To join main clauses, use a comma and a coordinating conjunction (*for, and, but, or, nor, yet,* or *so*) or a semicolon.

EXAMPLE	The lion was looking for prey. It seemed very hungry.
COMPOUND SENTENCE	The lion was looking for prey, and it seemed very hungry.

400 **Effective Sentences**

> **Sentences can be combined by changing one into a subordinate clause to create a complex sentence.** ⬅ **16.2.3 RULE**

To show the relationship between ideas in which one depends on the other, use a **complex sentence.** The subordinating conjunction will help readers understand the relationship. Some common subordinating conjunctions are *after, although, because, if, since, when,* and *while.*

EXAMPLE	We were hungry. It had been a long and active day.
COMBINED WITH A SUBORDINATE CLAUSE	We were hungry **because it had been a long and active day**.

> **Sentences can be combined by changing one of them into a phrase.** ⬅ **16.2.4 RULE**

EXAMPLE	My school plays today. We play the other high school.
COMBINED WITH PREPOSITIONAL PHRASE	My school plays **against the other high school** today.
EXAMPLE	My school will play against the other high school today. They are number one.
COMBINED WITH APPOSITIVE PHRASE	My school will play against the other high school today, **the number one team**.

See Practice 16.2B
See Practice 16.2C

PRACTICE 16.2A Combining Sentences Using Compound Subjects, Verbs, and Objects

Read each set of sentences. Then, write one sentence that combines them.

EXAMPLE Simon doesn't like riding in elevators. Simon doesn't like flying in airplanes.

ANSWER *Simon doesn't like riding in elevators or flying in airplanes.*

1. Skiing is often difficult for beginners. Skiing requires good balance.
2. I like to eat steak. I like to eat potatoes.
3. The book contains pictures of medieval castles. There are pictures of royal armies.
4. Brandon built the bookshelf himself. Brandon built the table himself.
5. Ray went hiking. Ray saw raccoons.
6. She is a talented vocalist. She is the best singer in the choir.
7. Randolph's daughter is a lawyer. Randolph's son is a lawyer.
8. Tony won the race. Tony won a trophy.
9. Clouds covered the sky. A huge flock of birds covered the sky.
10. The magician wanted to go backstage. His assistant wanted to go backstage.

PRACTICE 16.2B Combining Sentences Using Phrases

Read each set of sentences. Then, combine each set by turning one sentence into a phrase that adds detail to the other.

EXAMPLE The howling wind blew through the trees. The trees surrounded our house.

ANSWER *The howling wind blew through the trees that surrounded our house.*

11. Hail fell persistently throughout the city. It fell for an hour.
12. William Tamery was the first captain of the soccer team. He was a major reason for the winning season.
13. Humpback whales communicate with one another. Humpback whales are endangered animals.
14. Doing calisthenics is a great way to stay in shape. Calisthenics is a form of exercise.
15. The Taggert Building was originally a fire station. The Taggert Building is now the town's museum.

SPEAKING APPLICATION

Take turns with a partner. Tell two related sentences. Your partner should combine these sentences into one sentence.

WRITING APPLICATION

Write two related sentences. Then, exchange papers with a partner. Your partner should combine the two sentences into one by turning one sentence into a phrase.

PRACTICE 16.2C **Combining Sentences by Forming Compound or Complex Sentences**

Read each pair of sentences. Then, combine the sentences to form compound or complex sentences using the coordinating or subordinating conjunction indicated in parentheses.

EXAMPLE   Robert and his brother could not spend time together. They wrote letters to each other. (so)

ANSWER   *Robert and his brother could not spend time together, so they wrote letters to each other.*

1. Poetry can express emotions and ideas. Poetry stimulates and entertains the reader. (as)
2. Would you like to go to the zoo? Is reading about animals good enough for now? (or)
3. Giving your new pet plenty of attention takes time. Every moment is worth it. (but)
4. One day, Logan went to a beach. The beach offered all kinds of entertainment. (that)
5. I like horses and dogs. I get along better with cats. (although)
6. The symphony finished its performance. The audience gave it a standing ovation. (and)
7. Bethany finished her test before the rest of the class. She was allowed to go to the library. (so)
8. We had accomplished our goal. We realized there was more work to do. (yet)
9. Steve went into the store. I waited outside. (while)
10. Stanley finished the science project. Leonard added the bibliography. (after)

SPEAKING APPLICATION

Take turns with a partner. Tell about places you would like to visit and explain why. Use at least three compound, complex, or, compound-complex sentences, along with three coordinating or subordinating conjunctions, in your description.

WRITING APPLICATION

Write a paragraph about something you want to accomplish this year. Use at least two compound sentences, one complex sentence, and one compound-complex sentence in your paragraph.

16.3 Varying Sentences

Vary your sentences to develop a rhythm, to achieve an effect, or to emphasize the connections between ideas. There are several ways you can vary your sentences.

Varying Sentence Length

To emphasize a point or surprise a reader, include a short, direct sentence to interrupt the flow of long sentences. Notice the effect of the last sentence in the following paragraph.

EXAMPLE The Jacobites derived their name from *Jacobus,* the Latin name for King James II of England, who was dethroned in 1688 by William of Orange during the Glorious Revolution. Unpopular because of his Catholicism and autocratic ruling style, James fled to France to seek the aid of King Louis XIV. In 1690, James, along with a small body of French troops, landed in Ireland in an attempt to regain his throne. His hopes ended at the Battle of the Boyne.

Some sentences contain only one idea and can't be broken. It may be possible, however, to state the idea in a shorter sentence. Other sentences contain two or more ideas and might be shortened by breaking up the ideas.

LONGER SENTENCE Many of James II's predecessors were able to avoid major economic problems, but James had serious economic problems.

MORE DIRECT Unlike many of his predecessors, James II was unable to avoid major economic problems.

LONGER SENTENCE James tried to work with Parliament to develop a plan of taxation that would be fair and reasonable, but members of Parliament rejected his efforts, and James dissolved the Parliament.

SHORTER SENTENCES James tried to work with Parliament to develop a fair and reasonable taxation plan. However, because members of Parliament rejected his efforts, James dissolved the Parliament.

404 Effective Sentences

Varying Sentence Beginnings

Another way to create sentence variety is to start sentences with different parts of speech.

WAYS TO VARY SENTENCE BEGINNINGS	
Start With a Noun	Cars are difficult to rebuild.
Start With an Adverb	Naturally, cars are difficult to rebuild.
Start With an Adverbial Phrase	Because of their complexity, cars are difficult to rebuild.
Start With a Participial Phrase	Having tried to rebuild several cars, I know how hard it is.
Start With a Prepositional Phrase	For the average person, cars are very difficult to rebuild.
Start With an Infinitive Phrase	To rebuild a classic car was my goal.

See Practice 16.3A

Using Inverted Word Order

You can also vary sentence beginnings by reversing the traditional subject–verb order to create verb–subject order. You can reverse order by starting the sentence with a **participial phrase** or a **prepositional phrase.** You can also move a complement to the beginning of the sentence.

SUBJECT–VERB ORDER

The Browns waited at the traffic light.

The team marched onto the opponent's field.

The cheering of the fans filled the air.

The cheering was deafening.

VERB–SUBJECT ORDER

Waiting at the traffic light were the Browns.
participial phrase

Onto the opponent's field marched the team.
prepositional phrase

Filling the air was the cheering of the fans.
participial phrase

Deafening was the cheering.
predicate adjective

See Practice 16.3B

Varying Sentences 405

Varying Sentences

PRACTICE 16.3A **Revising to Vary Sentence Beginnings**

Read each sentence. Rewrite each sentence to begin with the part of speech or phrase indicated in parentheses. You may need to add a word or phrase.

EXAMPLE I tossed and turned constantly and didn't sleep at all during the night. (participial phrase)

ANSWER *Tossing and turning constantly, I didn't sleep at all during the night.*

1. Oceanographers have worked endlessly to study the sea. (adverb)
2. I lost my concentration when the phone began to ring. (adverb)
3. I asked her to visit. (infinitive phrase)
4. I roasted a turkey. (prepositional phrase)
5. I ate an apple. (participial phrase)
6. I tried to distract my mother. (adverb)
7. I proudly delivered my speech. (infinitive phrase)
8. Trees are homes to birds and other small animals. (prepositional phrase)
9. Fire can spread quickly through a dry forest. (adverbial phrase)
10. Contestants have won lots of prizes. (adverb)

PRACTICE 16.3B **Inverting Sentences to Vary Subject-Verb Order**

Read each sentence. Rewrite each of the following sentences by inverting the subject-verb order to verb-subject order.

EXAMPLE Several tourists stared at the timetable in the train station.

ANSWER *Staring at the timetable in the train station were several tourists.*

11. Burning coals and boiling lava erupted from the mouth of Mount Etna.
12. I seldom walked to the store.
13. The basic requirements for the merit badge are listed here.
14. The mountain loomed above us, jagged and menacing.
15. A horse galloped out of the forest.
16. A family of robins settled in our maple tree.
17. Three dedicated band members practiced for hours in our garage.
18. We were rarely so helpless.
19. We had no sooner left than it began to rain.
20. A gentle stream flows throughout the campgrounds.

SPEAKING APPLICATION

Take turns with a partner. Say sentences aloud. Your partner should revise each sentence to have a different beginning.

WRITING APPLICATION

Write three original sentences about your plans for the future. Then, exchange papers with a partner. Your partner should invert the subject-verb order in your sentences to verb-subject order.

16.4 Avoid Fragments and Run-ons

Hasty writers sometimes omit crucial words, punctuate awkwardly, or leave their thoughts unfinished, causing two common sentence errors: **fragments** and **run-ons**.

Recognizing Fragments

Writing Coach Online
www.phwritingcoach.com

Grammar Practice
Practice your grammar skills with Writing Coach Online.

Grammar Games
Test your knowledge of grammar in this fast-paced interactive video game.

Although some writers use them for stylistic effect, **fragments** are generally considered errors in standard English.

> **Do not capitalize and punctuate phrases, subordinate clauses, or words in a series as if they were complete sentences.**

16.4.1 RULE

Reading your work aloud to listen for natural pauses and stops should help you avoid fragments. Sometimes, you can repair a fragment by connecting it to words that come before or after it.

> **One way to correct a fragment is to connect it to the words in a nearby sentence.**

16.4.2 RULE

PARTICIPIAL FRAGMENT	inspired by the skill of the sensei
ADDED TO A NEARBY SENTENCE	**Inspired by the skill of the sensei**, Rick saw the karate demonstration again.
PREPOSITIONAL FRAGMENT	before his students
ADDED TO A NEARBY SENTENCE	The sensei performed his demonstration **before his students**.
PRONOUN AND PARTICIPIAL FRAGMENT	the one stuffed with vegetables
ADDED TO NEARBY SENTENCE	My favorite sandwich is **the one stuffed with vegetables**.

RULE 16.4.3 — Another way to correct a fragment is to add any sentence part that is needed to make the fragment a complete sentence.

Remember that every complete sentence must have both a subject and a verb and express a complete thought. Check to see that each of your sentences contains all of the parts necessary to be complete.

NOUN FRAGMENT — the group of experienced Boy Scouts

COMPLETED SENTENCES

The group of experienced Boy Scouts [subject] **built** [verb] their campsite here.

We [subject] attentively **watched** [verb] the group of experienced Boy Scouts [direct object].

Notice what missing sentence parts must be added to the following types of phrase fragments to make them complete.

	FRAGMENTS	COMPLETED SENTENCES
Noun Fragment With Participial Phrase	the instructions read by us	The instructions **were** read by us.
Verb Fragment	will be at the meeting today	**I** will be at the meeting today.
Prepositional Fragment	in the pantry closet	**I put the pasta** in the pantry closet.
Participial Fragment	found under the bed	**The sneakers** found under the bed **are mine**.
Gerund Fragment	teaching my children to cook	Teaching my children to cook **is fun**.
Infinitive Fragment	to eat the fresh lasagna	**I expect** to eat the fresh lasagna.

408 Effective Sentences

Avoid Fragments and Run-ons

> You may need to attach a **subordinate clause** to a main clause to correct a fragment.

RULE 16.4.4

A **subordinate clause** contains a subject and a verb but does not express a complete thought and cannot stand alone as a sentence. Link it to a main clause to make the sentence complete.

ADJECTIVAL CLAUSE FRAGMENT which was being displayed outside

COMPLETED SENTENCE I enjoyed visiting the art exhibit, **which was being displayed outside**.

ADVERBIAL CLAUSE FRAGMENT after he painted the new mural

COMPLETED SENTENCE **After he painted the new mural**, he was ready for the exhibit.

NOUN CLAUSE FRAGMENT whatever food is left in the pantry

COMPLETED SENTENCE We will eat **whatever food is left in the pantry**.

Series Fragments A fragment is not always short. A long series of words still needs to have a subject and a verb and express a complete thought. It may be a long fragment masquerading as a sentence.

SERIES FRAGMENT	COMPLETE SENTENCE
after reading Dickens's novel, with its cynical look at poverty and greed, in the style so typical of this writer	After reading Dickens's novel, with it's cynical look at poverty and greed, in the style so typical of this writer, **I was able to prepare an interesting term paper**.

See Practice 16.4A

Avoiding Run-on Sentences

A **run-on** sentence is two or more sentences capitalized and punctuated as if they were a single sentence.

> Use punctuation and conjunctions to correctly join or separate parts of a **run-on** sentence.

There are two kinds of **run-ons: fused sentences**, which are two or more sentences joined with no punctuation, and **comma splices**, which have two or more sentences separated only by commas rather than by commas and conjunctions.

FUSED SENTENCE The team practiced every day they became the best in the state.

COMMA SPLICE The one couple arrived for dinner, the other couple never came.

As with fragments, proofreading or reading your work aloud will help you find run-ons. Once found, they can be corrected by adding punctuation and conjunctions or by rewording the sentences.

FOUR WAYS TO CORRECT RUN-ONS		
	RUN-ON	**CORRECTION**
With End Marks and Capitals	The party was in full swing at the house the people laughed together.	The party was in full swing. At the house, the people laughed together.
With Commas and Conjunctions	The presents needed wrapping we could not locate the tape.	The presents needed wrapping, but we could not locate the tape.
With Semicolons	New York City has many cultures living together, consequently it is called the melting pot.	New York City has many cultures living together; consequently, it is called the melting pot.
By Rewriting	The dog show began late, a judge didn't arrive on time.	The dog show began late because a judge didn't arrive on time.

See Practice 16.4B

410 Effective Sentences

Avoid Fragments and Run-ons

PRACTICE 16.4A Identifying and Correcting Fragments

Read each sentence. If an item contains a fragment, rewrite it to make a complete sentence. If an item contains a complete sentence, write *correct*.

EXAMPLE While she was cooking.

ANSWER *While she was cooking, the phone rang.*

1. Loud music makes studying difficult.
2. Where cattails and reeds grew high.
3. I am sometimes funny, loud, or just silly.
4. Must have been abandoned.
5. He plans to be friendly.
6. After he took the dog to the vet.
7. A gallon of green paint should be enough for this room.
8. When the bell rang, there were students left outside.
9. Concerned about the look of the sky.
10. Because time was running short.

PRACTICE 16.4B Revising to Eliminate Run-on Sentences

Read each sentence. Correct each run-on by correctly joining or separating the sentence parts.

EXAMPLE The beach is pleasant during the week, it is crowded on weekends.

ANSWER *The beach is pleasant during the week. It is crowded on weekends.*

11. The play was good, the cast was only mediocre.
12. Michael wants to become a doctor, he is my brother.
13. You'll love that book, it is a page turner.
14. I applied for a variety of jobs, everyone said I interviewed well.
15. In general, I love to exercise running is the activity that I enjoy most.
16. Catie wrote a poem it was her homework assignment.
17. Patel took driver's education classes, he received his driver's license a few months later.
18. Days turned into years, the years quickly passed.
19. Have you heard the news Marti is moving to Miami.
20. Catherine II was a Russian empress, she was called Catherine the Great.

SPEAKING APPLICATION

Take turns with a partner. Say sentence fragments. Your partner should turn each fragment into a complete sentence.

WRITING APPLICATION

Write three run-on sentences. Then, exchange papers with a partner and correct your partner's run-on sentences.

16.5 Misplaced and Dangling Modifiers

Careful writers put modifiers as close as possible to the words they modify. When modifiers are misplaced or left dangling in a sentence, the result may be illogical or confusing.

Grammar Practice
Practice your grammar skills with Writing Coach Online.

Grammar Games
Test your knowledge of grammar in this fast-paced interactive video game.

Recognizing Misplaced Modifiers

A **misplaced modifier** is placed too far from the modified word and appears to modify the wrong word or words.

> RULE 16.5.1
>
> A **misplaced modifier** seems to modify the wrong word in the sentence.

MISPLACED MODIFIER The girl fell over a hurdle **running on the track**.

CORRECTION The girl **running on the track** fell over a hurdle.

MISPLACED MODIFIER We heard the doorbell ring **while eating dinner**.

CORRECTION **While eating dinner**, we heard the doorbell ring.

Recognizing Dangling Modifiers

With **dangling modifiers,** the word that should be modified is missing from the sentence. Dangling modifiers usually come at the beginning of a sentence and are followed by a comma. The subject being modified should come right after the comma.

> RULE 16.5.2
>
> A **dangling modifier** seems to modify the wrong word or no word at all because the word it should modify has been omitted from the sentence.

See Practice 16.5A

412 Effective Sentences

DANGLING PARTICIPIAL PHRASE	Measuring carefully, each ingredient was placed into the bowl. (Who did the measuring?)
CORRECTED SENTENCE	Measuring carefully, **the cook** placed each ingredient into the bowl.

Dangling participial phrases are corrected by adding missing words and making other needed changes.

Dangling infinitive phrases and elliptical clauses can be corrected in the same way. First, identify the subject of the sentence. Then, make sure each subject is clearly stated. You may also need to change the form of the verb.

DANGLING INFINITIVE PHRASE	To exit the highway, the toll must be paid. (Who is exiting and must pay?)
CORRECTED SENTENCE	To exit the highway, **drivers** must pay the toll.
DANGLING ELLIPTICAL CLAUSE	While lying on the beach, a school of dolphins was spotted. (Who was lying on the beach and spotted the dolphins?)
CORRECTED SENTENCE	While lying on the beach, **we** spotted a school of dolphins.

A dangling adverbial clause may also occur when the antecedent of a pronoun is not clear.

DANGLING ADVERBIAL CLAUSE	When they had been married for fifty years, Sharon and Tom planned a party for their parents. (Who is married for 50 years, Sharon and Tom or their parents?)
CORRECTED SENTENCE	**When their parents had been married for 50 years**, Sharon and Tom planned a party for them.

See Practice 16.5B

Misplaced and Dangling Modifiers

Misplaced and Dangling Modifiers

PRACTICE 16.5A Identifying and Correcting Misplaced Modifiers

Read each sentence. Then, rewrite each sentence, putting the misplaced modifiers closer to the words they should modify. If a sentence is correct, write correct.

EXAMPLE We were happy to find the pizza in the oven that Dad had made.

ANSWER *We were happy to find the pizza that Dad had made in the oven.*

1. The company has a meeting for employees who want to transfer overseas at noon.
2. She wore her new dress to the party with green stripes.
3. Austin drew a picture of a squirrel using computer software.
4. Please send a letter to me about the trip.
5. Clapping and cheering, the astronauts were greeted by the audience.
6. Chandra remembered that she had forgotten the map in the middle of our hike.
7. The dress at the store is on sale.
8. The lost student's book was found in the cloakroom.
9. The boys waded in the creek and waited for a fish to come along with a net.
10. Let us know if you plan to attend the party on the enclosed card.

PRACTICE 16.5B Identifying and Correcting Dangling Modifiers

Read each sentence. Then, rewrite each sentence, correcting any dangling modifiers by supplying missing words or ideas. If a sentence is correct, write correct.

EXAMPLE Having arrived late, a note from the office was needed.

ANSWER *Having arrived late, the girl needed a note from the office.*

11. Paddling along the lake, the scenery was relaxing.
12. To locate the missing hamster, a thorough search will be necessary.
13. Practicing the piano, the kids playing baseball were distracting.
14. Before leaving, turn off the lights.
15. Having given his customer a refund, the matter seemed to be closed.
16. The landscape became lush descending into the valley.
17. While logging in California, gold was discovered.
18. Before she left, Claire kissed her mother.
19. Walking onto the patio, the swimming pool looked inviting.
20. Drinking tea, my spoon fell on the floor.

SPEAKING APPLICATION

Take turns with a partner. Tell about something interesting that you have done. Use modifiers in your sentences. Your partner should name the modifiers and tell whether they are correctly placed.

WRITING APPLICATION

Use sentences 18, 19, and 20 as models to write your own examples of dangling modifiers. Then, rewrite each sentence to correct the dangling modifier.

16.6 Faulty Parallelism

Good writers try to present a series of ideas in similar grammatical structures so the ideas will read smoothly. If one element in a series is not parallel with the others, the result may be jarring or confusing.

Recognizing the Correct Use of Parallelism

To present a series of ideas of equal importance, you should use parallel grammatical structures.

> **Parallelism** involves presenting equal ideas in words, phrases, clauses, or sentences of similar types.

PARALLEL WORDS   The athlete looked **strong**, **fit**, and **agile**.

PARALLEL PHRASES   The greatest feeling I know is **to run a marathon flawlessly** and **to have all my friends watch me enviously**.

PARALLEL CLAUSES   The sneakers **that you recommended** and **that my sister wants** are on sale.

PARALLEL SENTENCES   **It couldn't be**, of course. **It could never, never be**. –Dorothy Parker

Correcting Faulty Parallelism

Faulty parallelism occurs when a writer uses unequal grammatical structures to express related ideas.

> **Correct a sentence containing faulty parallelism by rewriting it so that each parallel idea is expressed in the same grammatical structure.**

Faulty parallelism can involve words, phrases, and clauses in a series or in comparisons.

Nonparallel Words, Phrases, and Clauses in a Series

Always check for parallelism when your writing contains items in a series.

Correcting Faulty Parallelism in a Series

NONPARALLEL STRUCTURES **Scheduling**, **purchasing**, and **management** of inventory are all steps in the retail process.
(gerund, gerund, noun)

CORRECTION **Scheduling**, **purchasing**, and **managing** inventory are all steps in the retail process.
(gerund, gerund, gerund)

NONPARALLEL STRUCTURES I could not wait **to taste the new foods** (infinitive phrase), **to experience the new restaurant** (infinitive phrase), and **visiting the town** (participial phrase).

CORRECTION I could not wait **to taste the new foods** (infinitive phrase), **to experience the new restaurant** (infinitive phrase), and **to visit the town** (infinitive phrase).

NONPARALLEL STRUCTURE Some experts feel **that jogging is not a sport** (noun clause), but **it requires athleticism** (independent clause).

CORRECTION Some experts feel **that jogging is not a sport** (noun clause) but **that it requires athleticism** (noun clause).

Another potential problem involves correlative conjunctions, such as *both ... and* or *not only ... but also*. Though these conjunctions connect two related items, writers sometimes misplace or split the first part of the conjunction. The result is faulty parallelism.

416 Effective Sentences

NONPARALLEL Bill **not only** won the tennis match **but also** the state title.

PARALLEL Bill won **not only** the tennis match **but also** the state title.

Nonparallel Words, Phrases, and Clauses in Comparisons

As the saying goes, you cannot compare apples with oranges. In writing comparisons, you generally should compare a phrase with the same type of phrase and a clause with the same type of clause.

Correcting Faulty Parallelism in Comparisons

NONPARALLEL STRUCTURES Most people prefer **apples** (noun) to **eating celery** (gerund phrase).

CORRECTION Most people prefer **apples** (noun) to **celery** (noun).

NONPARALLEL STRUCTURES I left work **at 12:00 P.M.** (prepositional phrase) rather than **staying at work until 5:00 P.M.** (participial phrase)

CORRECTION I left work **at 12:00 P.M.** (prepositional phrase) rather than **at the usual 5:00 P.M.** (prepositional phrase)

NONPARALLEL STRUCTURES **George** (subject) delights **in rainy days** (prepositional phrase) as much as sunny **days** (subject) delight other **people** (direct object).

CORRECTION **George** (subject) delights **in rainy days** (prepositional phrase) as much as other **people** (subject) delight **in sunny days** (prepositional phrase).

See Practice 16.6A
See Practice 16.6B

Faulty Parallelism

Find It/FIX IT 10 Grammar Game Plan

16.7 Faulty Coordination

When two or more independent clauses of unequal importance are joined by *and*, the result can be faulty **coordination**.

WRITING COACH Online
www.phwritingcoach.com

Grammar Practice
Practice your grammar skills with Writing Coach Online.

Grammar Games
Test your knowledge of grammar in this fast-paced interactive video game.

Recognizing Faulty Coordination

To *coordinate* means to "place side by side in equal rank." Two independent clauses that are joined by the coordinating conjunction *and*, therefore, should have equal rank.

RULE 16.7.1

Use *and* or other coordinating conjunctions only to connect ideas of equal importance.

CORRECT COORDINATION   Blake designed an airplane, **and** Jane built it.

Sometimes, however, writers carelessly use *and* to join main clauses that either should not be joined or should be joined in another way so that the real relationship between the clauses is clear. Faulty coordination puts all the ideas on the same level of importance, even though logically they should not be.

FAULTY COORDINATION   Production of ships accelerated in World War II, **and** ships became a decisive factor in the war.

I didn't do well, **and** the contest was easy.

Walt Whitman was one of our greatest poets, **and** he was from New York.

Occasionally, writers will also string together so many ideas with *and*'s that the reader is left breathless.

STRINGY SENTENCE   The tractor that drove through the field did a few twists and turns, **and** the people on the opposite side turned their necks to watch, **and** everyone laughed.

418 Effective Sentences

Correcting Faulty Coordination

Faulty coordination can be corrected in several ways.

> **One way to correct faulty coordination is to put unrelated ideas into separate sentences.** 16.7.2 RULE

When faulty coordination occurs in a sentence in which the main clauses are not closely related, separate the clauses and omit the coordinating conjunction.

FAULTY COORDINATION Production of ships accelerated in World War II, **and** ships became a decisive factor in the war.

CORRECTION Production of ships increased in World War II. Ships became a decisive factor in the war.

> **You can correct faulty coordination by putting less important ideas into subordinate clauses or phrases.** 16.7.3 RULE

If one main clause is less important than, or subordinate to, the other, turn it into a subordinate clause. You can also reduce a less important idea to a phrase.

FAULTY COORDINATION I didn't do well, **and** the contest was easy.
CORRECTION I didn't do well, **even though** the contest was easy.

FAULTY COORDINATION Walt Whitman was one of our greatest poets, **and** he was from New York.
CORRECTION Walt Whitman, a native of New York, was one of our greatest poets.

Stringy sentences should be broken up and revised using any of the three methods just described. Following is one way that the stringy sentence on the previous page can be revised.

REVISION OF A STRINGY SENTENCE The tractor that drove through the field did a few twists and turns. Turning to watch, the people on the opposite side laughed.

See Practice 16.6C
See Practice 16.6D

Faulty Coordination

PRACTICE 16.6A Revising to Eliminate Faulty Parallelism

Read each sentence. Then, rewrite the sentence to correct any nonparallel structures.

EXAMPLE We enjoy walking on the beach and to collect seashells.

ANSWER *We enjoy walking on the beach and collecting seashells.*

1. The quarterback was criticized for making poor throws and that he was rushing plays.
2. I like painting, but I do not like to draw.
3. The store wants to hire someone who will help clean up and to stock shelves.
4. Seeing the movie was fun, but to write a review of it was challenging.
5. The actor played the role well but a couple of times forgetting his lines.
6. My family likes to ski and snorkeling.
7. To make a profit, we must increase sales or by cutting costs.
8. Everyone likes to receive cards but not sending them.
9. The main duties of a pet sitter are walking, feeding, and to give baths.
10. Eating, sleeping, and to have fun are important to me.

PRACTICE 16.6B Writing Parallelisms in Comparisons

Read each item. Then, rewrite each item and complete the comparisons using correct parallelism.

EXAMPLE Joe cooks stews as well as ____.

ANSWER *Joe cooks stews as well as he cooks casseroles.*

11. Sam wants to camp in the state park as much as ____.
12. I prefer swimming to ____.
13. For the school arts festival the students hope to write plays as much as ____.
14. We followed the trail across the bridge instead of ____.
15. The author wrote not only two new novels ____.
16. I bought the book that I wanted, not the book ____.
17. On a spring day the garden looks sunny rather than ____.
18. Our science project about electricity is different from the one ____.
19. Good dog owners walk their pets, whereas ____.
20. The movie that opened last weekend is much better than the one ____.

SPEAKING APPLICATION

Take turns with a partner. Tell about something you plan to do with your family. Your partner should point out and correct any faulty parallelism in your description.

WRITING APPLICATION

Use Practice 16.6B as a model to write five additional items. Exchange papers with a partner. Your partner should complete each comparison using correct parallelism.

Effective Sentences

Faulty Coordination

PRACTICE 16.6C **Rewriting to Correct Faulty Coordination**

Read each sentence. Then, correct the faulty coordination in each sentence by reducing a less important idea to a phrase or clause.

EXAMPLE   The train ride was fun and it was long.

ANSWER   *The train ride was fun, even though it was long.*

1. The new science lab opened, and it is located near the stairway.
2. That building is a landmark, and it has a simple design.
3. The tree branch is about to fall, and it is swaying in the air.
4. Jess hopes to be a vet, and she studies hard.
5. We always shop at the farmers' market, and we like fresh fruit.
6. Our friends arrive tomorrow, and they are from New York.
7. Sam is working to buy a new computer, and he is always very busy.
8. I promised to walk Lou's dog, and it is very friendly.
9. The video is excellent, and Michelle made it.
10. I couldn't make that recipe, and I didn't have the cookbook.

PRACTICE 16.6D **Revising to Eliminate Faulty Coordination**

Read each sentence. Then, rewrite the sentence to correct the faulty coordination.

EXAMPLE   Mom bought a new car, and it's a small sedan.

ANSWER   *Mom bought a new car, a small sedan.*

11. I added illustrations and I didn't have to.
12. We arrived at the mall, and the doors were about to open.
13. The beaches are wide and white, and they attract thousands of tourists.
14. We set up our campsite, and it has tents and a cooking stove.
15. We had bought everything that we needed, and we headed for our car.
16. I was so excited that I ran out the door, and I didn't eat breakfast.
17. Tripp is buying a new bike, and he sold his old one last week.
18. We hung a bird feeder in a tree, but a squirrel ate the seeds, so we put the feeder on a pole, and now the birds are able to get to the seeds.
19. Jemal waved to me, and he left for school.
20. Your dad was late picking us up, and we got to the class on time.

SPEAKING APPLICATION

Take turns with a partner. Use Practice 16.6C to say similar sentences. Your partner should correct the faulty coordination by reducing a less important idea to a phrase or clause.

WRITING APPLICATION

Use sentence 14 in Practice 16.6D as a model to write a sentence with faulty coordination. Exchange papers with a partner. Your partner should correct the faulty coordination in your sentence.

Practice   421

Faulty Coordination

Test Warm-Up

DIRECTIONS
Read the introduction and the passage that follows. Then, answer the questions to show that you can use and understand the function of faulty parallelism and faulty coordination in reading and writing.

Larry wrote this paragraph about the earliest camera. Read the paragraph and think about the changes you would suggest as a peer editor. When you finish reading, answer the questions that follow.

The Pinhole Camera

(1) The earliest camera was a large dark room with a small hole at one end. (2) It was called a camera obscura. (3) Bright light entered the small hole, a lens or mirror projected it, and producing an upside-down image on the opposite wall. (4) We know that people first used the camera obscura to view solar eclipses and for aiding their drawing. (5) There is a giant Camera Obscura in San Francisco. (6) It is one of 20 in the world.

---

1 What is the most effective way to combine sentences 1 and 2?

A It was large as a room and called a camera obscura, which was the earliest camera.

B The earliest camera, called a camera obscura, was a large dark room with a small hole at one end.

C The camera obscura was a large dark room with a small hole at one end.

D A large dark room with a small hole at one end called a camera obscura.

2 What is the most effective way to rewrite the ideas in sentence 3?

F Light entered the small hole, producing an upside-down image.

G We know that light entered a small hole and produced an image on the wall.

H A lens or mirror produced an upside-down image of the light.

J Through the small hole, bright light entered and was projected by a lens or mirror as an upside-down image.

3 What is the most effective way to rewrite the ideas in sentence 4?

A People first used the camera obscura for viewing and to aid their drawing.

B The camera obscura was used to view and for aiding people's drawing.

C People first used the camera obscura to view solar eclipses and to aid their drawing.

D We know that people first viewed solar eclipses and aided their drawing.

4 What is the most effective way to combine sentences 5 and 6?

F There is one of 20 giant camera obscuras in San Francisco.

G There are 20 giant Camera Obscuras in the world and one in San Francisco.

H There are visit 20 Camera Obscuras, but there is only one in San Francisco.

J In San Francisco, there is a giant Camera Obscura, which is one of 20 in the world.

422   Test Warm-Up

VERB USAGE

Portray events as you intend by using the correct forms of verbs in your writing.

WRITE GUY *Jeff Anderson, M.Ed.*

WHAT DO YOU NOTICE?

Discover the verbs as you zoom in on this sentence from the story "How Much Land Does a Man Need?" by Leo Tolstoy and as translated by Louise and Aylmer Maude.

MENTOR TEXT

"If it were my own land," thought Pahom, "I should be independent, and there wouldn't be all this unpleasantness."

Now, ask yourself the following questions:

- Why does the author use the verb *were* instead of *was* in the subordinate clause, *If it were my own land*?
- What do the auxiliary verbs *should* and *would* tell you about the mood of the sentence?

The author uses *were* instead of *was* to create the subjunctive mood, which is used to express something contrary to what is true. The auxiliary verbs *should* and *would* indicate that the other verbs in the sentence are also in the subjunctive mood. The use of the subjunctive mood helps the author express Pahom's wishes about what would happen *if* he had the land.

Grammar for Writers Verbs help connect and highlight ideas as much as they help express action. Use verbs to convey a mood or state of being in your writing.

I should start my homework...

Watch out. Should can get moody.

CHAPTER 17

423

17.1 Verb Tenses

Besides expressing actions or conditions, verbs have different **tenses** to indicate when the action or condition occurred.

A **tense** is the form of a verb that shows the time of an action or a condition.

The Six Verb Tenses

There are six tenses that indicate when an action or a condition of a verb is, was, or will be in effect. Each of these six tenses has at least two forms.

Each tense has a **basic** and a **progressive** form.

The chart that follows shows examples of the six tenses.

Grammar Tutorials
Brush up on your Grammar skills with these animated videos.

Grammar Practice
Practice your grammar skills with Writing Coach Online.

Grammar Games
Test your knowledge of grammar in this fast-paced interactive video game.

THE BASIC FORMS OF THE SIX TENSES	
Present	Meg skis for a hobby.
Past	She skied every day last year.
Future	She will ski again this year.
Present Perfect	She has skied at many different resorts all over the country.
Past Perfect	She had skied first when she was only three years old.
Future Perfect	She will have skied ten times this season by Presidents Day.
Present	Damon reads mysteries.
Past	He read two mysteries last week.
Future	He will read other kinds of books, too.
Present Perfect	He has read Sherlock Holmes stories.
Past Perfect	He had read Agatha Christie stories.
Future Perfect	He will have read many mystery stories by the end of the year.

See Practice 17.1A

Basic Verb Forms or Tenses

Verb tenses are identified simply by their tense names. The **progressive tenses,** however, are identified by their tense names plus the word *progressive.* Progressive tenses show that an action is or was happening for a period of time.

The chart below shows examples of the six tenses in their progressive form or tense. Note that all of these progressive tenses end in *-ing.* (See the section on verb conjugation later in this chapter for more about the progressive tense.)

THE PROGRESSIVE TENSES	
Present Progressive	Meg is ice skating now.
Past Progressive	She was ice skating yesterday morning.
Future Progressive	She will be ice skating again tomorrow.
Present Perfect Progressive	She has been ice skating since she was a young child.
Past Perfect Progressive	She had been ice skating when she broke her leg.
Future Perfect Progressive	She will have been ice skating for a decade by the end of this year.

The Emphatic Form

There is also a third form or tense, the **emphatic,** which exists only for the present and past tenses. The **present emphatic** is formed with the helping verbs *do* or *does,* depending on the subject. The **past emphatic** is formed with *did.* The purpose of the emphatic tense is to put more emphasis on, or to stress, the action of the verb.

THE EMPHATIC TENSES OF THE PRESENT AND THE PAST	
Present Emphatic	Jeff does play tennis more often than Jimmy. I do read more books than my older brother.
Past Emphatic	Michael and Jake did play guitar in a band. My mom did insist that I finish my homework before I could watch TV.

See Practice 17.1B

Verb Tenses

PRACTICE 17.1A Identifying Verb Tenses

Read each sentence. Then, write the verb or verbs in each sentence and label their tenses (*present, past, future, present perfect, past perfect,* or *future perfect*).

EXAMPLE The athlete jumped over the hurdle and reached the finish line.

ANSWER *jumped* — past; *reached* — past

1. After she had explored the island, the adventurer felt more secure.
2. The movie theater will have closed by the time we arrive.
3. The boy has always loved his dog and cat.
4. During the storm, the children slept.
5. The zoo has stayed open all winter, but the animals hibernate.
6. When the teachers heard about the panel's decision, they were very happy.
7. The actors had walked off the stage and into the audience.
8. *Dogsong* and *Hatchet* are my favorite books.
9. My grandmother answered when I called her cellphone number.
10. If the boy grows to six feet, he will be taller than his father.

PRACTICE 17.1B Recognizing Tenses or Forms of Verbs

Read each sentence. Then, rewrite each sentence, using the verb form shown in parentheses, and underline the verb.

EXAMPLE My father ate lunch at 2:00 P.M. (past emphatic)

ANSWER My father *did eat* lunch at 2:00 P.M.

11. By that time, the flowers will have bloomed for a week. (past perfect progressive)
12. The teacher asked the class for their book reports. (present perfect progressive)
13. I sometimes wish that the day would never end. (present emphatic)
14. The children had been playing outside. (past)
15. Roberto washed his car for three hours! (past progressive)
16. His mother did bake a loaf of bread. (past)
17. Over time, the tree had grown taller than the fence. (future perfect)
18. The guitarist played the difficult tune with ease. (present progressive)
19. The passing trains sure did make a lot of noise. (past perfect progressive)
20. Ming struggled to keep his umbrella from collapsing. (past emphatic)

SPEAKING APPLICATION

Take turns with a partner. Tell about a story that you recently read. Your partner will listen for and identify the different verb tenses that you use.

WRITING APPLICATION

Write a paragraph about a trip that you would like to take. Use at least eight different verb forms or tenses in your paragraph. Then, rewrite the sentences by changing the verb tenses. Underline the verbs you used.

The Four Principal Parts of Verbs

Every verb in the English language has four **principal parts** from which all of the tenses are formed.

> A verb has four principal parts: the **present**, the **present participle**, the **past**, and the **past participle**.

The chart below shows the principal parts of the verbs *walk*, *speak*, and *run*.

THE FOUR PRINCIPAL PARTS			
PRESENT	**PRESENT PARTICIPLE**	**PAST**	**PAST PARTICIPLE**
walk	walking	walked	(have) walked
speak	speaking	spoke	(have) spoken
run	running	ran	(have) run

The first principal part, the present, is used for the basic forms of the present and future tenses, as well as for the emphatic forms or tenses. The present tense is formed by adding an -*s* or -*es* when the subject is *he, she, it,* or a singular noun. The future tense is formed with the helping verb *will*. (*I will walk. Mary will speak. Carl will run.*) The present emphatic is formed with the helping verb *do* or *does*. (*I do walk. Mary does speak. Carl does run.*) The past emphatic is formed with the helping verb *did*. (*I did walk. Mary did speak. Carl did run.*)

The second principal part, the present participle, is used with helping verbs for all of the progressive forms. (*I am walking. Mary is speaking. Carl is running.*)

The third principal part, the past, is used to form the past tense. (*I walked. Mary spoke. Carl ran.*) As in the example *ran*, the past tense of a verb can change its spelling. (See the next section for more information.)

The fourth principal part, the past participle, is used with helping verbs to create the perfect tenses. (*I have walked. Mary had spoken. Carl had run.*)

See Practice 17.1C
See Practice 17.1D

Verb Tenses

PRACTICE 17.1C Recognizing the Four Principal Parts of Verbs

Read each sentence. Then, write the verb or verb phrase in each sentence that contains the principal part in parentheses.

EXAMPLE   The band was playing loudly. (present participle)

ANSWER   *was playing*

1. After their victory, the team celebrated at a restaurant. (past)
2. The teacher was helping students with their homework. (present participle)
3. Since the age of twelve, Gloria has moved quite often. (past participle)
4. I have studied hard in Spanish class, and now I can speak it fluently. (past participle)
5. After reaching the summit, the climber shouted with joy. (present participle)
6. Many birds have chirped loudly since I sat down on this bench. (past participle)
7. The ice melts by spring. (present)
8. The dog is barking because you're bothering him. (present participle)
9. The bride walks down the aisle. (present)
10. The man made his way through the crowd. (past)

PRACTICE 17.1D Identifying the Four Principal Parts of Verbs

Read each set of verbs. Then, for each set, write which principal part or parts (*present, present participle, past, past participle*) are listed.

EXAMPLE   cried, have baked

ANSWER   *past, past participle*

11. boasting, calling
12. twinkled, have winked
13. crunch, munch
14. sneezed, wheezed
15. dozing, sleeping
16. blinked, have settled
17. create, escape
18. edge, wedge
19. promised, have pledged
20. placing, tracing

SPEAKING APPLICATION

Take turns with a partner. Perform a mock radio broadcast about the weather, using many verb tenses in your description. Your partner should listen for and identify the principal parts of the verbs that you use.

WRITING APPLICATION

Use at least three word pairs from Practice 17.1D to write a fictional short story. Underline and label the principal parts of all the verbs you use in your story.

Verb Tenses

Regular and Irregular Verbs

The way the past and past participle forms of a verb are formed determines whether the verb is **regular** or **irregular.**

Regular Verbs The majority of verbs are regular. Regular verbs form their past and past participles according to a predictable pattern.

> **A regular verb** is one for which the past and past participle are formed by adding *-ed* or *-d* to the present form.

RULE 17.1.4

In the chart below, notice that a final consonant is sometimes doubled to form the present participle, the past, and the past participle. A final *e* may also be dropped to form the participle.

PRINCIPAL PARTS OF REGULAR VERBS			
PRESENT	**PRESENT PARTICIPLE**	**PAST**	**PAST PARTICIPLE**
bat	batting	batted	(have) batted
produce	producing	produced	(have) produced
depend	depending	depended	(have) depended

See Practice 17.1E
See Practice 17.1F

Irregular Verbs Although most verbs are regular, many of the most common verbs are irregular. Irregular verbs do not use a predictable pattern to form their past and past participles.

> **An irregular verb** is one whose past and past participle are *not* formed by adding *-ed* or *-d* to the present form.

RULE 17.1.5

Usage Problems Remembering the principal parts of irregular verbs can help you avoid usage problems. One common usage problem is using a principal part that is not standard.

INCORRECT Simon **buyed** new shoes.

CORRECT Simon **bought** new shoes.

A second usage problem is confusing the past and past participle when they have different forms.

Verb Tenses 429

INCORRECT Ben **done** his homework.

CORRECT Ben **did** his homework.

Some common irregular verbs are shown in the charts that follow. Use a dictionary if you are not sure how to form the principal parts of an irregular verb.

IRREGULAR VERBS WITH THE SAME PRESENT, PAST, AND PAST PARTICIPLE			
PRESENT	**PRESENT PARTICIPLE**	**PAST**	**PAST PARTICIPLE**
burst	bursting	burst	(have) burst
cost	costing	cost	(have) cost
cut	cutting	cut	(have) cut
hit	hitting	hit	(have) hit
hurt	hurting	hurt	(have) hurt
let	letting	let	(have) let
put	putting	put	(have) put
set	setting	set	(have) set
shut	shutting	shut	(have) shut
split	splitting	split	(have) split
spread	spreading	spread	(have) spread

Note About *Be:* *Be* is one of the most irregular of all of the verbs. The present participle of *be* is *being*. The past participle is *been*. The present and the past depend on the subject and tense of the verb.

CONJUGATION OF *BE*		
	SINGULAR	**PLURAL**
Present	I **am**. You **are**. He, she, or it **is**.	We **are**. You **are**. They **are**.
Past	I **was**. You **were**. He, she, or it **was**.	We **were**. You **were**. They **were**.
Future	I **will be**. You **will be**. He, she, or it **will be**.	We **will be**. You **will be**. They **will be**.

Verb Usage

Verb Tenses

IRREGULAR VERBS WITH THE SAME PAST AND PAST PARTICIPLE

PRESENT	PRESENT PARTICIPLE	PAST	PAST PARTICIPLE
bring	bringing	brought	(have) brought
build	building	built	(have) built
buy	buying	bought	(have) bought
catch	catching	caught	(have) caught
fight	fighting	fought	(have) fought
find	finding	found	(have) found
get	getting	got	(have) got or (have) gotten
hold	holding	held	(have) held
keep	keeping	kept	(have) kept
lay	laying	laid	(have) laid
lead	leading	led	(have) led
leave	leaving	left	(have) left
lose	losing	lost	(have) lost
pay	paying	paid	(have) paid
say	saying	said	(have) said
sell	selling	sold	(have) sold
send	sending	sent	(have) sent
shine	shining	shone or shined	(have) shone or (have) shined
sit	sitting	sat	(have) sat
sleep	sleeping	slept	(have) slept
spend	spending	spent	(have) spent
stand	standing	stood	(have) stood
stick	sticking	stuck	(have) stuck
sting	stinging	stung	(have) stung
strike	striking	struck	(have) struck
swing	swinging	swung	(have) swung
teach	teaching	taught	(have) taught
win	winning	won	(have) won
wind	winding	wound	(have) wound

Verb Tenses

IRREGULAR VERBS THAT CHANGE IN OTHER WAYS

PRESENT	PRESENT PARTICIPLE	PAST	PAST PARTICIPLE
arise	arising	arose	(have) arisen
become	becoming	became	(have) become
begin	beginning	began	(have) begun
bite	biting	bit	(have) bitten
break	breaking	broke	(have) broken
choose	choosing	chose	(have) chosen
come	coming	came	(have) come
do	doing	did	(have) done
draw	drawing	drew	(have) drawn
drink	drinking	drank	(have) drunk
drive	driving	drove	(have) driven
eat	eating	ate	(have) eaten
fall	falling	fell	(have) fallen
fly	flying	flew	(have) flown
give	giving	gave	(have) given
go	going	went	(have) gone
grow	growing	grew	(have) grown
know	knowing	knew	(have) known
lie	lying	lay	(have) lain
ride	riding	rode	(have) ridden
ring	ringing	rang	(have) rung
rise	rising	rose	(have) risen
run	running	ran	(have) run
see	seeing	saw	(have) seen
sing	singing	sang	(have) sung
sink	sinking	sank	(have) sunk
speak	speaking	spoke	(have) spoken
swim	swimming	swam	(have) swum
take	taking	took	(have) taken
tear	tearing	tore	(have) torn
throw	throwing	threw	(have) thrown
wear	wearing	wore	(have) worn
write	writing	wrote	(have) written

See Practice 17.1G
See Practice 17.1H

Verb Usage

PRACTICE 17.1E Recognizing Principal Parts of Regular Verbs

Read each set of verbs. Then, for each set, write the name of the two principal parts of the verbs that are listed.

EXAMPLE smell, (have) smelled

ANSWER *present, past participle*

1. typing, typed
2. slap, slapped
3. asked, asking
4. assign, assigning
5. calculating, (have) calculated
6. brighten, brightened
7. repair, repairing
8. brushing, (have) brushed
9. pictured, picturing
10. plan, planning

PRACTICE 17.1F Using the Correct Form of Regular Verbs

Read each sentence. Then, write the principal part of the verb in parentheses that best completes each sentence, and identify the principal part used.

EXAMPLE The children are (shout) loudly outside.

ANSWER *shouting* — present participle

11. During her freshman year, Calista (enjoy) college very much.
12. After eating the spicy food, the water (taste) good.
13. Rocking back and forth can (calm) a baby.
14. Once you have (press) the button, the elevator will start to ascend.
15. Stop (push) me; that is against the rules!
16. My uncle has (row) a boat from Michigan to Canada.
17. Please help me while I (try) to decipher this code.
18. I accidentally (toast) the bread too long.
19. Can you (replace) the battery in my watch?
20. The back-up singers have (hum) the national anthem.

SPEAKING APPLICATION

Take turns with a partner. Say all four principal parts of the verbs in Practice 17.1E. Then, choose one verb and use all four principal parts of that verb in four different sentences.

WRITING APPLICATION

Write a newspaper article about your hometown. Use the four principal parts of different regular verbs in your article. Underline and label the principal parts of each verb that you use.

Verb Tenses

PRACTICE 17.1G Recognizing Principal Parts of Irregular Verbs

Read each verb. Then, write the four principal parts of each verb in the following order: present, present participle, past, past participle.

EXAMPLE winning

ANSWER *win, winning, won, (have) won*

1. chosen
2. build
3. slept
4. stood
5. losing
6. kept
7. arisen
8. bit
9. rang
10. sunk

PRACTICE 17.1H Supplying the Correct Form of Irregular Verbs

Read each sentence. Then, rewrite each sentence with the correct main verb form, and write the principal part of the corrected verb. Do not change any helping verbs.

EXAMPLE The astronomer finded a new plant species last week.

ANSWER *The astronomer found a new plant species last week.* — past

11. The pilot has flied around the world hundreds of times.
12. My mother is speak on the phone with her sister.
13. After years of practice, the chess player has winned a major tournament.
14. Joe's sister is frustrated that she has losed her keys again.
15. My cousin rung the doorbell.
16. When the space shuttle took off, my friends standing in amazement.
17. The judge is given the defendant time to speak.
18. Sally's friend worn the same hat every day.
19. When I went to camp, I leaved my stuffed animals at home.
20. David is throw the rope to Ann.

SPEAKING APPLICATION

Take turns with a partner. Give your partner two irregular verbs not used in Practice 17.1G. Your partner should state the four principal parts of each verb.

WRITING APPLICATION

Write a short essay about plans for a camping trip. Use at least ten irregular verbs in your description of what you will pack and what you will do. Underline each irregular verb in your essay.

Verb Conjugation

The **conjugation** of a verb displays all of its different forms.

> **A conjugation is a complete list of the singular and plural forms of a verb in a particular tense.**

17.1.6 RULE

The singular forms of a verb correspond to the singular personal pronouns (*I, you, he, she, it*), and the plural forms correspond to the plural personal pronouns (*we, you, they*).

To conjugate a verb, you need the four principal parts: the present (*see*), the present participle (*seeing*), the past (*saw*), and the past participle (*seen*). You also need various helping verbs, such as *has, have,* or *will.*

Notice that only three principal parts—the present, the past, and the past participle—are used to conjugate all six of the basic forms.

CONGUGATION OF THE BASIC FORMS OF *SEE*			
		SINGULAR	**PLURAL**
Present	First Person Second Person Third Person	I see. You see. He, she, or it sees.	We see. You see. They see.
Past	First Person Second Person Third Person	I saw. You saw. He, she, or it saw.	We saw. You saw. They saw.
Future	First Person Second Person Third Person	I will see. You will see. He, she, or it will see.	We will see. You will see. They will see.
Present Perfect	First Person Second Person Third Person	I have seen. You have seen. He, she, or it has seen.	We have seen. You have seen. They have seen.
Past Perfect	First Person Second Person Third Person	I had seen. You had seen. He, she, or it had seen.	We had seen. You had seen. They had seen.
Future Perfect	First Person Second Person Third Person	I will have seen. You will have seen. He, she, or it will have seen.	We will have seen. You will have seen. They will have seen.

See Practice 17.1I

Conjugating the Progressive Tense With *Be*

As you learned earlier, the **progressive tense** shows an ongoing action or condition. To form the progressive tense, use the present participle form of the verb (the *-ing* form) with a form of the verb *be*.

CONJUGATION OF THE PROGRESSIVE FORMS OF *SEE*		SINGULAR	PLURAL
Present Progressive	First Person Second Person Third Person	I am seeing. You are seeing. He, she, or it is seeing.	We are seeing. You are seeing. They are seeing.
Past Progressive	First Person Second Person Third Person	I was seeing. You were seeing. He, she, or it was seeing.	We were seeing. You were seeing. They were seeing.
Future Progressive	First Person Second Person Third Person	I will be seeing. You will be seeing. He, she, or it will be seeing.	We will be seeing. You will be seeing. They will be seeing.
Present Perfect Progressive	First Person Second Person Third Person	I have been seeing. You have been seeing. He, she, or it has been seeing.	We have been seeing. You have been seeing. They have been seeing.
Past Perfect Progressive	First Person Second Person Third Person	I had been seeing. You had been seeing. He, she, or it had been seeing.	We had been seeing. You had been seeing. They had been seeing.
Future Perfect Progressive	First Person Second Person Third Person	I will have been seeing. You will have been seeing. He, she, or it will have been seeing.	We will have been seeing. You will have been seeing. They will have been seeing.

See Practice 17.1J

Verb Usage

PRACTICE 17.1I Conjugating the Basic Forms of Verbs

Read each word. Then, conjugate each verb using the subject indicated in parentheses. Write the words in the past, present, past perfect, and future perfect.

EXAMPLE see (I)

ANSWER *I saw, I see, I had seen, I will have seen*

1. scare (we)
2. thrive (he)
3. drift (they)
4. sniff (she)
5. buy (you)
6. imagine (I)
7. live (they)
8. sigh (you)
9. pay (we)
10. ride (I)

PRACTICE 17.1J Conjugating the Progressive Forms of Verbs

Read each sentence. Rewrite each sentence, using the progressive forms of the verb that are indicated in parentheses.

EXAMPLE He strikes. (past progressive; present progressive)

ANSWER *He was striking. He is striking.*

11. He blames. (future perfect progressive; future progressive)
12. We think. (past perfect progressive; past progressive)
13. They tease. (past progressive; future progressive)
14. She leads. (future perfect progressive; past perfect progressive)
15. You create. (present progressive; present perfect progressive)
16. They travel. (past perfect progressive; present progressive)
17. I show. (past progressive; future progressive)
18. We form. (present perfect progressive; present progressive)
19. They act. (future progressive; past progressive)
20. You breathe. (future progressive; past perfect progressive)

SPEAKING APPLICATION

Take turns with a partner. Say sentences that use one of the conjugated verb forms from Practice 17.1I. Your partner should listen for and identify each verb and its form.

WRITING APPLICATION

Use progressive verb forms to write a paragraph about your favorite band or music artist. Underline all of the progressive verb forms that you use.

17.2 The Correct Use of Tenses

The basic, progressive, and emphatic forms of the six tenses show time within one of three general categories: **present**, **past**, and **future**. This section will explain how each verb form has a specific use that distinguishes it from the other forms.

Writing Coach Online
www.phwritingcoach.com

Grammar Tutorials
Brush up on your Grammar skills with these animated videos.

Grammar Practice
Practice your grammar skills with Writing Coach Online.

Grammar Games
Test your knowledge of grammar in this fast-paced interactive video game.

Present, Past, and Future Tense

Good usage depends on an understanding of how each form works within its general category of time to express meaning.

Uses of Tense in Present Time

Three different forms can be used to express present time.

RULE 17.2.1
The three forms of the **present tense** show present actions or conditions as well as various continuing actions or conditions.

EXPRESSING PRESENT TENSE	
Present	I **ride**.
Present Progressive	I **am riding**.
Present Emphatic	I **do ride**.

The main uses of the basic form of the present tense are shown in the chart below.

EXPRESSING PRESENT TENSE	
Present Action	Jake **fishes** in the ocean.
Present Condition	His arm **is aching**.
Regularly Occurring Action	He often **fishes** off Cape May, New Jersey.
Regularly Occurring Condition	This boat **holds** six people.
Constant Action	Many kinds of fish **live** in the ocean.
Constant Condition	Fish **have** scales.

See Practice 17.2A

438 Verb Usage

Historical Present The present tense may also be used to express historical events. This use of the present, called the **historical present tense,** is occasionally used in narration to make past actions or conditions sound more lively.

THE HISTORICAL PRESENT TENSE	
Past Actions Expressed in Historical Present Tense	People gather around a store window to watch the first television.
Past Condition Expressed in Historical Present Tense	People watching the television cannot believe that a picture can come through the air.

The **critical present tense** is most often used to discuss deceased authors and their literary achievements.

THE CRITICAL PRESENT TENSE	
Action Expressed in Critical Present	O. Henry writes many stories with surprise endings.
Condition Expressed in Critical Present	O. Henry is the author of several volumes of short stories.

The **present progressive tense** is used to show a continuing action or condition of a long or short duration.

USES OF THE PRESENT PROGRESSIVE TENSE	
Long Continuing Action	Mark is practicing soccer every afternoon.
Short Continuing Action	He is trying to make the team.
Continuing Condition	He is hoping to make the first team someday.

USES OF THE PRESENT EMPHATIC TENSE	
Emphasizing a Statement	Jane does want to go to the store.
Denying a Contrary Assertion	No, she does not want to walk downtown.
Asking a Question	Does she enjoy shopping for clothes?
Making a Sentence Negative	Jane does not want to stay at the store all day.

See Practice 17.2B

The Correct Use of Tenses

The Correct Use of Tenses

PRACTICE 17.2A → **Identifying the Tense in Present Time**

Read each sentence. Then, write the form of the present-tense verb underlined in each sentence.

EXAMPLE Computers <u>are</u> more popular today than they were ten years ago.

ANSWER *present*

1. The student <u>does prepare</u> well for his presentation.
2. Maya Angelou <u>uses</u> vivid metaphors in her poetry.
3. Some people <u>are accomplishing</u> great things for future generations.
4. Susie <u>shops</u> for school supplies.
5. I <u>am going</u> to summer camp for eight weeks.
6. Surprisingly, my brother <u>does play</u> more than one instrument.
7. The birds <u>wake</u> me every morning with their chirping.
8. The doctors <u>are planning</u> to hold health seminars at their clinic.
9. Two-year-olds <u>are</u> toddlers.
10. My alarm <u>does ring</u> every morning at seven o'clock.

PRACTICE 17.2B → **Supplying Verbs in Present Time**

Read each sentence. Then, rewrite each sentence and the underlined verb, using the tense indicated in parentheses.

EXAMPLE The author <u>writes</u> for hours at a time. (present emphatic)

ANSWER *The author <u>does write</u> for hours at a time.*

11. Sir Arthur Conan Doyle <u>wrote</u> vividly about the workings of his detective's mind. (critical present)
12. Marcia <u>gives</u> Nona a bouquet of flowers. (present progressive)
13. People in the 1700s <u>rode</u> in wagons. (historical present)
14. Fresh cherries and blueberries <u>made</u> the best snacks. (present)
15. The fan <u>waved</u> to the band onstage. (present progressive)
16. Young students on the bus <u>sing</u> songs for the bus driver. (present emphatic)
17. No matter what, I <u>will</u> attend the sporting event on Sunday. (present progressive)
18. Albert Einstein <u>revealed</u> great insights in his writings. (historical present)
19. A top <u>spins</u> on the floor. (present progressive)
20. The bread <u>baked</u> in the oven. (present)

SPEAKING APPLICATION

Take turns with a partner. Tell your point of view on which foods taste best. Use present tense verbs in your description. Your partner should listen for and identify the present tense verbs that you use.

WRITING APPLICATION

Write a few sentences about your favorite author. Use the critical present to describe his or her writing. Use the emphatic present to state your opinion about the author.

Uses of Tense in Past Time

There are seven verb forms that express past actions or conditions.

> The seven forms that express **past tense** show actions and conditions that began at some time in the past.

17.2.2 RULE

FORMS EXPRESSING PAST TENSE	
Past	I danced.
Present Perfect	I have danced.
Past Perfect	I had danced.
Past Progressive	I was dancing.
Present Perfect Progressive	I have been dancing.
Past Perfect Progressive	I had been dancing.
Past Emphatic	I did dance.

The uses of the most common form, the past, are shown below.

USES OF THE PAST TENSE	
Completed Action	Julian worked on his speech.
Completed Condition	He was an interesting speaker.

Notice in the chart above that the time of the action or the condition could be changed from indefinite to definite if such words as *last week* or *yesterday* were added to the sentences.

See Practice 17.2C

Present Perfect The **present perfect tense** always expresses indefinite time. Use it to show actions or conditions continuing from the past to the present.

USES OF THE PRESENT PERFECT TENSE	
Completed Action (Indefinite Time)	We have come to the school dance.
Completed Condition (Indefinite Time)	We have been to the school dances before.
Action Continuing to Present	Our friends have been wanting to go, too.
Condition Continuing to Present	We have been excited all day.

The Correct Use of Tenses

Past Perfect The **past perfect tense** expresses an action that took place before another action.

USES OF THE PAST PERFECT TENSE	
Action Completed Before Another Action	The coaches had analyzed the other team's game before they created their own game plans.
Condition Completed Before Another Condition	They had been careful to recognize when the team became tired.

These charts show the **past progressive** and **emphatic tenses**.

USES OF THE PROGRESSIVE TENSE TO EXPRESS PAST TIME	
Past Progressive	**LONG CONTINUING ACTION** Wei was going to ballet class daily. **SHORT CONTINUING ACTION** She was talking to her teacher about her lessons. **CONTINUOUS CONDITION** She was being honest when she said that she practiced every day.
Present Perfect Progressive	**CONTINUING ACTION** Wei has been dancing since she was five years old.
Past Perfect Progressive	**CONTINUING ACTION INTERRUPTED** She had wanted to take jazz, but she decided that ballet was enough.

USES OF THE PAST EMPHATIC TENSE	
Emphasizing a Statement	The bicycle did work after I oiled the gears.
Denying a Contrary Assertion	Yes, I did check the chain!
Asking a Question	Why did you think I couldn't fix my old bicycle?
Making a Sentence Negative	You did not appreciate my repair skills.

See Practice 17.2D

The Correct Use of Tenses

PRACTICE 17.2C Identifying Tense in Past Time

Read each item. Then, write the verbs that are in the tense indicated in parentheses.

EXAMPLE had scooted, scooted, scouted (past)

ANSWER *scooted, scouted*

1. had enjoyed, had halted, have praised (past perfect)
2. have tried, has worked, did attempt (present perfect)
3. had been finishing, did complete, had been missing (past perfect progressive)
4. did jump, did glide, was swooping (past emphatic)
5. has been leaving, went, disappeared (past)
6. frowned, was weeping, was sighing (past progressive)
7. had decided, had been searching, had been finding (past perfect progressive)
8. hit, kicked, was batting (past)
9. did not understand, comprehended, did care (past emphatic)
10. was skating, did skateboard, was skiing (past progressive)

PRACTICE 17.2D Supplying Verbs in Past Time

Read each sentence. Then, rewrite each sentence and the underlined verb, using the verb tense indicated in parentheses.

EXAMPLE No one <u>used</u> the computer. (past progressive)

ANSWER *No one <u>was using</u> the computer.*

11. A week before, the girl <u>allowed</u> her friend to borrow her textbook. (past perfect progressive)
12. The clown <u>made</u> balloon animals for all of the children. (past progressive)
13. My brother <u>wanted</u> a bicycle for many years. (present perfect progressive)
14. The driver <u>asked</u> for directions before beginning his journey. (past emphatic)
15. Although quite enjoyable, rafting <u>was</u> less fun than hiking. (past perfect progressive)
16. I <u>was thinking</u> about his speech. (past perfect progressive)
17. The treasure hunters <u>made</u> an exciting yet dangerous discovery. (past perfect)
18. The airplane <u>backed</u> onto the runway before taking off. (past progressive)
19. The reference materials <u>show</u> step-by-step instructions. (past)
20. I <u>called</u> John. (present perfect progressive)

SPEAKING APPLICATION

Take turns with a partner. Make up rhyming sentences that use verbs (in some form of the past tense). Your partner should listen for and identify the past-tense verbs in your rhymes.

WRITING APPLICATION

Write a paragraph about something exciting that happened to you when you were a child. Use five different forms of the past tense in your paragraph.

Uses of Tense in Future Time

The **future tense** shows actions or conditions that will happen at a later date.

The future tense expresses actions or conditions that have not yet occurred.

FORMS EXPRESSING FUTURE TENSE	
Future	I will wait.
Future Perfect	I will have waited.
Future Progressive	I will be waiting.
Future Perfect Progressive	I will have been waiting.

USES OF THE FUTURE AND THE FUTURE PERFECT TENSE	
Future	I will go home after school. I will babysit for my little brother.
Future Perfect	I will have babysat for him every day this week. Next week, I will have babysat for him for six months.

Notice in the next chart that the **future progressive** and the **future perfect progressive tenses** express only future actions.

USES OF THE PROGRESSIVE TENSE TO EXPRESS FUTURE TIME	
Future Progressive	Max will be working all weekend.
Future Perfect Progressive	He will have been working at the store for ten weeks by the end of the summer.

The basic forms of the present and the present progressive tense are often used with other words to express future time.

EXAMPLES The play **opens** next weekend.

We **are practicing** our parts.

See Practice 17.2E
See Practice 17.2F

444 Verb Usage

PRACTICE 17.2E Identifying Tense in Future Time

Read each sentence. Then, write the future-tense verb in each sentence and the form of the tense.

EXAMPLE The president will address Congress tonight.

ANSWER *will address* — future

1. A local restaurant will be catering the event.
2. A radio station will sponsor the parade.
3. The shipment you ordered will arrive soon.
4. Surely you will be inviting Tom to the party.
5. Before the concert, we will have distributed the flyers.
6. Next semester, I will have been taking five classes for a full year.
7. The team will be playing its last game on Saturday.
8. My mother will return your call when she arrives home.
9. Kanin will have been giving his speech for at least ten minutes when we get there.
10. The plane will have arrived by evening.

PRACTICE 17.2F Supplying Verbs in Future Time

Read each sentence. Then, rewrite each sentence, filling in the blank with the future-tense form of the verb indicated in parentheses.

EXAMPLE Steven _____ his decision soon. (make, future progressive)

ANSWER *Steven will be making his decision soon.*

11. We _____ different parts of Texas by next month. (tour, future perfect)
12. In another five years, scientists _____ the time capsule. (open, future progressive)
13. She _____ her report. (present, future perfect)
14. Mr. Bishop _____ our class every month for a year starting this morning. (visit, future perfect progressive)
15. Jose _____ you his decision today. (tell, future)
16. I _____ all day. (study, future perfect)
17. She _____ school here for one year next May. (attend, future perfect progressive)
18. The caterers _____ beverages at the meeting. (provide, future)
19. The buses _____ late today because of the rain. (arrive, future progressive)
20. Tammy _____ her lines by this afternoon. (rehearse, future perfect)

SPEAKING APPLICATION

Take turns with a partner. Tell what you hope to be doing in five years. Use future-tense verbs in your sentences. Your partner should listen for and identify the future-tense verbs that you use.

WRITING APPLICATION

Rewrite your corrections for sentences 13, 18, and 19, changing the verbs to include other future-tense verbs. Make sure your sentences still make sense.

Sequence of Tenses

A sentence with more than one verb must be consistent in its time sequence.

> When showing a sequence of events, do not shift tenses unnecessarily.

EXAMPLES   Ursula **will walk** to school, and then she **will take** the bus home.

Dan **has walked** his dogs and **fed** them.

Mom **worked** all day and **cooked** dinner at night.

Sometimes, however, it is necessary to shift tenses, especially when a sentence is complex or compound-complex. The tense of the main verb often determines the tense of the verb in the subordinate clause. Moreover, the form of the participle or infinitive often depends on the tense of the verb in the main clause.

Verbs in Subordinate Clauses It is frequently necessary to look at the tense of the main verb in a sentence before choosing the tense of the verb in the subordinate clause.

> The tense of a verb in a subordinate clause should follow logically from the tense of the main verb.

INCORRECT   I **will understand** that Michael **was** late.

CORRECT   I **understand** that Michael **was** late.

As you study the combinations of tenses in the charts on the next pages, notice that the choice of tenses affects the logical relationship between the events being expressed. Some combinations indicate that the events are **simultaneous**—meaning that they occur at the same time. Other combinations indicate that the events are **sequential**—meaning that one event occurs before or after the other.

The Correct Use of Tenses

SEQUENCE OF EVENTS		
MAIN VERB	**SUBORDINATE VERB**	**MEANING**
	MAIN VERB IN PRESENT TENSE	
I understand…	**PRESENT** that he explores in the woods. **PRESENT PROGRESSIVE** that he is exploring in the woods. **PRESENT EMPHATIC** that he does explore in the woods.	Simultaneous events: All events occur in present time.
I understand…	**PAST** that he explored in the woods. **PRESENT PERFECT** that he has explored in the woods. **PAST PERFECT** that he had explored in the woods. **PAST PROGRESSIVE** that he was exploring in the woods. **PRESENT PERFECT PROGRESSIVE** that he has been exploring in the woods. **PAST PERFECT PROGRESSIVE** that he had been exploring in the woods. **PAST EMPHATIC** that he did explore in the woods.	Sequential events: The exploring comes before the understanding.
I understand…	**FUTURE** that he will explore in the woods. **FUTURE PERFECT** that he will have explored in the woods. **FUTURE PROGRESSIVE** that he will be exploring in the woods. **FUTURE PERFECT PROGRESSIVE** that he will have been exploring in the woods.	Sequential events: The understanding comes before the exploring.

SEQUENCE OF EVENTS		
MAIN VERB	**SUBORDINATE VERB**	**MEANING**
MAIN VERB IN PAST TENSE		
I understood…	**PAST** that he explored in the woods. **PAST PROGRESSIVE** that he was exploring in the woods. **PAST EMPHATIC** that he did explore in the woods.	Simultaneous events: All events take place in the past.
I understood…	**PAST PERFECT** that he had explored in the woods. **PAST PERFECT PROGRESSIVE** that he had been exploring in the woods.	Sequential events: The exploring came before the understanding.
MAIN VERB IN FUTURE TENSE		
I will understand…	**PRESENT** if he explores in the woods. **PRESENT PROGRESSIVE** if he is exploring in the woods. **PRESENT EMPHATIC** if he does explore in the woods.	Simultaneous events: All events take place in future time.
I will understand…	**PAST** if he explored in the woods. **PRESENT PERFECT** if he has explored in the woods. **PRESENT PERFECT PROGRESSIVE** if he has been exploring in the woods. **PAST EMPHATIC** if he did explore in the woods.	Sequential events: The exploring comes before the understanding.

See Practice 17.2G
See Practice 17.2H
See Practice 17.2I
See Practice 17.2J

Verb Usage

The Correct Use of Tenses

Time Sequence With Participles and Infinitives Frequently, the form of a participle or infinitive determines whether the events are simultaneous or sequential. Participles can be present (*watching*), past (*watched*), or perfect (*having won*). Infinitives can be present (*to watch*) or perfect (*to have watched*).

> The form of a participle or an infinitive should logically relate to the verb in the same clause or sentence.

RULE 17.2.6

To show simultaneous events, you will generally need to use the present participle or the present infinitive, whether the main verb is present, past, or future.

Simultaneous Events

IN PRESENT TIME	**Watching** the race, they **cheer**.	
	present / present	
IN PAST TIME	**Watching** the race, they **cheered**.	
	present / past	
IN FUTURE TIME	**Watching** the race, they **will cheer**.	
	present / future	

To show sequential events, use the perfect form of the participle and infinitive, regardless of the tense of the main verb.

Sequential Events

IN PRESENT TIME	**Having watched** the race, they **are cheering**.	
	perfect / present progressive	
	(The race was over *before* they cheered.)	
IN PAST TIME	**Having watched** the race, they **cheered**.	
	perfect / past	
	(The race was over *before* they cheered.)	
SPANNING PAST AND FUTURE TIME	**Having watched** the race, they **will cheer**.	
	perfect / future	
	(They will cheer *after* the race is over.)	

See Practice 17.2K
See Practice 17.2L

The Correct Use of Tenses

PRACTICE 17.2G Identifying the Time Sequence in Sentences With More Than One Verb

Read each sentence. Then, write the verb of the event that happens second in each sentence.

EXAMPLE   After I finished my paper, Jim arrived.

ANSWER   *arrived*

1. I will drive you to school after you eat breakfast.
2. I brushed my teeth and then went to bed.
3. My sister will study medicine, but first she needs to graduate from high school.
4. Phil started jogging after he warmed up.
5. We found the book right where we left it.
6. Maggie slept in the morning and went to work at night.
7. I landed in Portland and arrived two hours later at my hotel.
8. It has been several years since I last saw my grandfather.
9. I walked into the room and found Emily there.
10. As soon as the meeting was over, the committee announced its decision.

PRACTICE 17.2H Recognizing and Correcting Errors in Tense Sequence

Read each sentence. Then, if a sentence has an error in tense sequence, rewrite it to correct the error. If a sentence is correct, write *correct*.

EXAMPLE   Sid is milking the cows now, but finished soon.

ANSWER   *Sid is milking the cows now, but will finish soon.*

11. I was finishing my homework and crawled into bed.
12. When we reached the station, the train had already left.
13. Katherine works on that poem for a week, and it's still not finished.
14. Last summer, we drive to Denver, where we toured the U.S. Mint.
15. Ling made a sandwich and puts it in her lunch box.
16. Every morning, they got up early and ran.
17. She wrote a letter and sends it to her grandmother.
18. The armadillo ran across the yard and hides behind a log.
19. The sun rose and the sky turned pink.
20. Every autumn, the leaves turn brown and fell off the trees.

SPEAKING APPLICATION

Take turns with a partner. Tell about something fun you like to do. Use two verbs in your sentences. Your partner should listen for and identify the sequence of events in your sentences.

WRITING APPLICATION

Use sentences 13, 14, and 15 as models to write your own sentences with incorrect tense sequence. Then, exchange papers with a partner. Your partner should rewrite the sentences, using the correct sequence in tense.

The Correct Use of Tenses

PRACTICE 17.2I **Writing Sentences to Be Consistent When the Main Verbs Are Present Tense**

Read each sentence. Then, rewrite each sentence to change the verb in the subordinate clause to the tense indicated in parentheses.

EXAMPLE I met a boy who hopes for a new skateboard. (present progressive)

ANSWER *I met a boy who is hoping for a new skateboard.*

1. I know that Ken is working. (present emphatic)
2. We think that he painted the entire house. (present perfect)
3. Larry feels that he was working hard enough. (past perfect)
4. He believes the students won. (future)
5. My cousins write that they were traveling in the country. (past perfect progressive)
6. The scientist e-mails that she finished the experiment. (past emphatic)
7. The writer hopes that he will finish the novel soon. (future progressive)
8. The governor says that she has worked hard this year. (present perfect progressive)
9. The actors value that we like the play. (past)
10. Sam believes that Lisa does walk the dogs every day. (present)

PRACTICE 17.2J **Writing Sentences to Be Consistent When the Main Verbs Are Past and Future Tense**

Read each sentence. Then, rewrite each sentence to change the verb in the subordinate clause to the tense indicated in parentheses.

EXAMPLE Noelle felt that the recital was boring. (past perfect)

ANSWER *Noelle felt that the recital had been boring.*

11. Laura e-mailed that she enjoyed the trip. (past progressive)
12. Mr. Ford thought that he had wasted his time. (past perfect progressive)
13. Her mother will wonder if Sue forgets to call home. (past emphatic)
14. The dog will bark if he finds the bone. (past)
15. The dancer hoped that she received the prize. (past perfect)
16. The students will know if they passed the test. (present perfect)
17. Henry's parents will clap if he wins the race. (present progressive)
18. We will be able to tell if Sam built a robot. (present perfect progressive)

SPEAKING APPLICATION

Review the sentences and your answers in Practice 17.2J. Discuss with a partner how changing the tense in the subordinate clause changes the meaning of the sentence.

WRITING APPLICATION

Review the sentences in Practice 17.2I. Rewrite each sentence, keeping the main clause but changing the verb tense in the subordinate clause. In parentheses, identify the new tense.

The Correct Use of Tenses

PRACTICE 17.2K Supplying Participles in Simultaneous Events

Read each sentence. Then, supply a participle to complete the sentence and to show a simultaneous event.

EXAMPLE _____ the story, Ed will laugh.
ANSWER   *Hearing*

1. _____ to the speaker, the audience agrees with her opinions.
2. _____ the truck, the delivery person completes the route.
3. _____ the movie, the students will applaud.
4. _____ the race, the runner collapsed.
5. _____ the house, the workers argued with each other.
6. _____ the cat, the dog barked loudly.
7. _____ the computer, the student will finish the report.
8. _____ the suit, the tailor broke the needle.
9. _____ the flowers, the gardener smiles happily.
10. _____ the trail, the hikers walked briskly.

PRACTICE 17.2L Supplying Participles in Sequential Events

Read each sentence. Then, supply a participle to complete the sentence and to show a sequential event.

EXAMPLE _____ the teacher, Joe is relieved.
ANSWER   *Having met* the teacher, Joe is relieved.

11. _____ the map, they are worrying about being late.
12. _____ the election, the new mayor will work hard.
13. _____ the camera, the photographer took the picture.
14. _____ her dog from the vet, Lisa was taking him to the park.
15. _____ a new house, my parents are busy repainting it.
16. _____ the new song, Mark has been practicing hard.
17. _____ the essay, the student revised it carefully.
18. _____ the meal, the chef did rest for an hour.
19. _____ the test, the teacher had been checking the answers.
20. _____ in the ocean, the children were eating lunch on the sand.

SPEAKING APPLICATION

Take turns with a partner. Say each sentence in Practice 17.2K, providing a new participle to complete each sentence.

WRITING APPLICATION

Review your sentences for Practice 17.2L. Rewrite each sentence, changing the main verb to another tense. In parentheses, identify the new tense.

The Correct Use of Tenses

Modifiers That Help Clarify Tense

The time expressed by a verb can often be clarified by adverbs such as *often, sometimes, always,* or *frequently* and phrases such as *once in a while, within a week, last week,* or *now and then.*

Use modifiers when they can help clarify tense.

17.2.7 RULE

In the examples below, the modifiers that help clarify the tense of the verb are highlighted in orange. Think about how the sentences would read without the modifiers. Modifiers help to make your writing more precise and interesting.

EXAMPLES Richard **plays** computer games **every night**.

He **practices once a day**.

He **practices once in a while**.
(These two sentences have very different meanings.)

Occasionally, he **walks** to the library to read.

He **always stops** to get a drink on the way.

By next year, Richard **will have played** hundreds of different kinds of games.

Richard also **practices** basketball **every day** after school.

Basketball **is now** one of his favorite sports.

Sometimes, he **shoots** foul shots over and over.

He **always gets** many of his shots in the basket.

See Practice 17.2M
See Practice 17.2N

The Correct Use of Tenses

PRACTICE 17.2M ▶ **Identifying Modifiers That Help Clarify Tense**

Read each sentence. Then, write the modifier in each sentence that helps clarify the verb tense.

EXAMPLE   Once again, Claire set a new school record.
ANSWER   *Once again*

1. As always, the paper was delivered on time.
2. Sometimes, wild dogs could be heard howling in the woods.
3. He never loses a tennis match.
4. We sometimes ride the bus to work.
5. Suddenly, a loud clap of thunder rumbled in the sky.
6. He always prepares for his final exams.
7. Yesterday, the kittens were rescued from the tree.
8. Before he left, he opened the front door.
9. I always brush my teeth thoroughly.
10. We will learn the dance by tomorrow.

PRACTICE 17.2N ▶ **Supplying Modifiers to Clarify Meaning**

Read each sentence. Then, fill in the blank with a modifier that will clarify the meaning of each sentence.

EXAMPLE   _____, David waited for his sister.
ANSWER   *Last Friday,*

11. My favorite watch was _____ fixed.
12. We _____ eat breakfast food for dinner.
13. The carpenter sanded each board _____.
14. _____, the deer ran into the woods.
15. Jed _____ orders fish for lunch.
16. _____, I enjoy swimming in the ocean.
17. My sister practices the piano _____.
18. Golf is _____ a very popular sport.
19. I _____ wait my turn to speak.
20. We visited a new museum _____.

SPEAKING APPLICATION

Take turns with a partner. Tell about a trip that you have taken. Use modifiers that help clarify tense in your sentences. Your partner should listen for and identify the modifiers in your sentences.

WRITING APPLICATION

Use your corrections for sentences 13, 16, and 19 as models to write your own sentences. Rewrite the sentences to include different modifiers that clarify the meaning of each sentence.

17.3 The Subjunctive Mood

There are three **moods,** or ways in which a verb can express an action or condition: **indicative, imperative,** and **subjunctive.** The **indicative** mood, which is the most common, is used to make statements (*Karl is helpful.*) and to ask questions (*Is Karl helpful?*). The **imperative** mood is used to give orders or directions (*Be helpful.*).

Grammar Practice
Practice your grammar skills with Writing Coach Online.

Grammar Games
Test your knowledge of grammar in this fast-paced interactive video game.

Using the Subjunctive Mood

There are two important differences between verbs in the **subjunctive** mood and those in the indicative mood. First, in the present tense, third-person singular verbs in the subjunctive mood do not have the usual *-s* or *-es* ending. Second, the subjunctive mood of *be* in the present tense is *be;* in the past tense, it is *were,* regardless of the subject.

INDICATIVE MOOD	SUBJUNCTIVE MOOD
Jaime works with me.	I suggest that he work with me.
Jaime is nice.	He insists that everyone be nice.
He was patient.	If he were not patient, he would not be so successful.

> Use the subjunctive mood (1) in clauses beginning with *if* or *that* to express an idea that is contrary to fact or (2) in clauses beginning with *that* to express a request, a demand, or a proposal.

17.3.1 RULE

Expressing Ideas Contrary to Fact Ideas that are contrary to fact are commonly expressed as wishes, doubts, possibilities, or conditions. Using the subjunctive mood in these situations shows that the idea expressed is not true now and may never be true.

EXAMPLES Dave wishes that the cafeteria **were** less noisy.

He wished that he **were** able to hear his friends.

If she **were** interested, she would have said so.

The Subjunctive Mood 455

> Some *if* clauses do not take a subjunctive verb. If the idea expressed may be true, an indicative form is used.

EXAMPLES   I said that **if** we **won** the game, I'd buy everyone's frozen yogurt.

If I **want** to win, I'll have to practice hard.

Expressing Requests, Demands, and Proposals Verbs that request, demand, or propose are often followed by a *that* clause containing a verb in the subjunctive mood.

REQUEST   I request that the survey results **be** published.

DEMAND   It is required that the survey results **be** published.

PROPOSAL   I proposed that the survey results **be** published.

See Practice 17.3A
See Practice 17.3B

Auxiliary Verbs That Express the Subjunctive Mood

Because certain helping verbs suggest conditions contrary to fact, they can often be used in place of the subjunctive mood.

> *Could, would,* or *should* can be used with a verb to express the subjunctive mood.

The sentences on the left in the chart below have the usual subjunctive form of the verb *be: were.* The sentences on the right have been reworded with *could, would,* and *should.*

THE SUBJUNCTIVE MOOD WITH AUXILIARY VERBS	
WITH FORMS OF *BE*	**WITH *COULD, WOULD,* OR *SHOULD***
If I **were** able to aim, I'd play basketball.	If I **could** aim, I'd play basketball.
If he **were** to leave the party, I'd stay.	If he **would** leave the party, I'd stay.
If you **were** to move, would you miss us?	If you **should** move, would you miss us?

See Practice 17.3C
See Practice 17.3D

456   Verb Usage

The Subjunctive Mood

PRACTICE 17.3A Identifying Mood (Indicative, Imperative, Subjunctive)

With a partner, take turns reading each sentence aloud. Then, identify whether each sentence expresses the *indicative*, *imperative*, or *subjunctive* mood. For each subjunctive mood sentence, discuss whether the verb is used to express doubts, wishes, or possibilities. Then, use the verb in a new sentence in the subjunctive mood.

EXAMPLE   If I were hungry, I would buy something to eat.

ANSWER   *subjunctive; If I were better, I would go to school.*

1. Do you recommend that he visit several places?
2. Harry was here yesterday.
3. If the doctor were to demand it, the patient would obtain several opinions.
4. Be here tonight at 7:00.
5. It is best that you remain calm at all times.
6. If I were still sleepy, I would go to bed.
7. If it were necessary, I would drive the entire trip.
8. Cook eggs for me for breakfast.
9. If I were a doctor, I would like to work for the American Red Cross.
10. She will bring her books to class.

PRACTICE 17.3B Writing the Subjunctive Mood

Read each sentence. Then, rewrite each sentence so that it uses the subjunctive mood to express doubts, wishes, and possibilities. Read your sentences to a partner. Together, discuss if your sentences are correct.

EXAMPLE   Jack closes his eyes.

ANSWER   *If Jack were to close his eyes, he would sleep.*

11. My friend Jose studies in the library.
12. My sister was very tired.
13. The park ranger gives out free maps.
14. The dog is loyal.
15. Our teacher assigns a topic for the story.
16. Sam's new pen pal is interesting.
17. The science laboratory was repainted.
18. The children's museum offers art classes.
19. The new zoo was crowded on Saturday.
20. My vacation is rewarding.

SPEAKING APPLICATION

Take turns with a partner. Say sentences using the subjunctive mood to express doubts, wishes, and possibilities. Your partner should listen for and identify the subjunctive mood that expresses doubts, wishes, and possibilities in your sentences.

WRITING APPLICATION

Use the sentences in Practice 17.3B as a model to write similar sentences. Exchange papers with a partner. Your partner should rewrite your sentences so that they use the subjunctive mood to express doubts, wishes, and possibilities.

The Subjunctive Mood

PRACTICE 17.3C **Supplying Auxiliary Verbs to Express the Subjunctive Mood**

Read each sentence. Then, rewrite each sentence and complete it by supplying an auxiliary verb.

EXAMPLE   If I had the money, I _____ buy the video.
ANSWER   *If I had the money, I would buy the video.*

1. If Dad insisted, they _____ wear their jackets.
2. If you would tell me where the library is, I _____ go.
3. I would take you to school if you _____ stop making me wait.
4. Felicia might be grateful if you _____ wash the car.
5. If Rob _____ see this tree, he'd be really angry.
6. If the baby _____ wake up before we get home, give her a bottle.
7. He would pitch faster if he _____.
8. If I _____ find that dress in pink, I might buy it.
9. If the team _____ practice more, it might win more often.
10. If that rock _____ fall, it might knock down the fence.

PRACTICE 17.3D **Writing Sentences With Auxiliary Verbs**

Read each sentence. Then, rewrite each sentence using auxiliary verbs.

EXAMPLE   If my mother were home, I'd call her.
ANSWER   *If my mother would be home, I'd call her.*

11. If my puppy were to behave, I'd take him to the park.
12. If you were to lose the election, would you run again?
13. If Mona were to agree to cook dinner, I'd help her.
14. If the library were to close, where would we study?
15. If my friends were to visit me, I'd be happy.
16. If Dan were a better artist, he'd be satisfied.
17. If the tickets were to arrive, we'd leave now.
18. If my sister were to get ready, I'd take her sledding.
19. If the doctor were to answer the phone, we'd question her.
20. If the hiker were to reach him, Lou would be relieved.

SPEAKING APPLICATION

Take turns with a partner. Read the sentences you wrote in Practice 17.3D to your partner. Your partner should tell you if your sentences correctly use auxiliary verbs to express the subjunctive mood.

WRITING APPLICATION

With a partner, write sentences that include auxiliary verbs that use the subjunctive mood to express doubts, wishes, and possibilities. Take turns reading the sentences aloud and discussing if the sentences correctly express the subjunctive mood.

Test Warm-Up

The Subjunctive Mood

DIRECTIONS
Read the introduction and the passage that follows. Then, answer the questions to show that you can use and understand the function of the subjunctive mood in reading and writing.

Nell wrote this paragraph about a visit to a famous museum. Read the paragraph and think about the changes you would suggest as a peer editor. When you finish reading, answer the questions that follow.

A Special Museum

(1) I suggested that my older brother visits the National Baseball Hall of Fame and Museum in Cooperstown, New York, with me. (2) If he was not interested in baseball, he would not value the Hall of Fame Gallery. (3) Lining the gallery's oak walls are plaques of the 289 current Hall of Fame members. (4) If our trip were longer, we'd visit the Babe Ruth Room, too. (5) Our visit was memorable. (6) If you were to visit this museum, which exhibits would you see?

---

1 What change, if any, should be made in sentence 1?

  A Change *suggested* to *suggests*

  B Change *visits* to *visited*

  C Change *visits* to *visit*

  D Make no change

2 What is the most effective way to rewrite the ideas in sentence 2?

  F If he were not interested in baseball, he would not value the Hall of Fame Gallery.

  G If he wasn't interested in baseball, he would value the Hall of Fame Gallery.

  H If he should have been interested in baseball, he would have valued the Hall of Fame Gallery.

  J If he could be interested in baseball, he might value the Hall of Fame Gallery.

3 What is the most effective way to rewrite the ideas in sentence 4?

  A If our trip was longer, we would visit the Babe Ruth Room, too.

  B If our trips were longer, we will visit the Babe Ruth Room, too.

  C If our trip could be longer, we'd visit the Babe Ruth Room, too.

  D If our trip might be longer, we will visit the Babe Ruth Room, too.

4 What is the most effective way to rewrite the ideas in sentence 6?

  F If you should visit this museum, which exhibits would you see?

  G If you should visits this museum, which exhibit might you see?

  H If you ever went to this museum, which are the exhibits you would see?

  J If you could be at this museum, which is the exhibit you would see?

17.4 Voice

This section discusses a characteristic of verbs called **voice**.

> **RULE 17.4.1**
> **Voice** or tense is the form of a verb that shows whether the subject is performing the action or is being acted upon.

In English, there are two voices: **active** and **passive.** Only action verbs can indicate voice; linking verbs cannot.

Active and Passive Voice or Tense

If the subject of a verb performs the action, the verb is active; if the subject receives the action, the verb is passive.

Active Voice Any action verb can be used in the active voice. The action verb may be transitive (that is, it may have a direct object) or intransitive (without a direct object).

> **RULE 17.4.2**
> A verb is active if its subject performs the action.

In the examples below, the subject performs the action. In the first example, the verb *telephoned* is transitive; *team* is the direct object, which receives the action. In the second example, the verb *developed* is transitive; *pictures* is the direct object. In the third example, the verb *gathered* is intransitive; it has no direct object. In the last example, the verb *worked* is intransitive and has no direct object.

ACTIVE VOICE

The captain **telephoned** the **team**.
                transitive verb   direct object

Bill **developed** twenty-five **pictures** of the ocean.
    transitive verb   direct object

Telephone messages **gathered** on the desk while she was away.
                      intransitive verb

Bill **worked** quickly.
   intransitive verb

See Practice 17.4A
See Practice 17.4B

Verb Usage

Passive Voice Most action verbs can also be used in the passive voice.

> A verb is passive if its action is performed upon the subject.

RULE 17.4.3

In the following examples, the subjects are the receivers of the action. The first example names the performer, the captain, as the object of the preposition *by* instead of the subject. In the second example, no performer of the action is mentioned.

PASSIVE VOICE

The **team** *was telephoned* by the captain.
    receiver of action   verb

The **messages** *were gathered* into neat piles.
    receiver of action   verb

> A passive verb is always a verb phrase made from a form of *be* plus the past participle of a verb. The tense of the helping verb *be* determines the tense of the passive verb.

RULE 17.4.4

The chart below provides a conjugation in the passive voice of the verb *see* in the three moods.

THE VERB *SEE* IN THE PASSIVE VOICE	
Present Indicative	It is seen.
Past Indicative	It was seen.
Future Indicative	It will be seen.
Present Perfect Indicative	It has been seen.
Past Perfect Indicative	It had been seen.
Future Perfect Indicative	It will have been seen.
Present Progressive Indicative	It is being seen.
Past Progressive Indicative	It was being seen.
Present Imperative	(You) be seen.
Present Subjunctive	(if) it be seen
Past Subjunctive	(if) it were seen

See Practice 17.4C

Using Active and Passive Voice

Writing that uses the active voice tends to be much more lively than writing that uses the passive voice. The active voice is usually more direct and economical. That is because active voice shows someone doing something.

Use the active voice whenever possible.

ACTIVE VOICE — Natasha **requested** help.

PASSIVE VOICE — Help **was requested** by Natasha.

The passive voice has two uses in English.

Use the passive voice when you want to emphasize the receiver of an action rather than the performer of an action.

EXAMPLE — Our team **was awarded** the championship.

Use the passive voice to point out the receiver of an action whenever the performer is not important or not easily identified.

EXAMPLE — The door to the garage **was opened**, and I could see my dad's new car.

The active voice lends more excitement to writing, making it more interesting to readers. In the example below, notice how the sentence you just read has been revised to show someone doing something, rather than something just happening.

EXAMPLE — My dad **opened** the door to the garage, and I could see his new car.
(*Who* opened the door?)

See Practice 17.4D

462 **Verb Usage**

PRACTICE 17.4A Recognizing Active Voice (Active Tense)

Read each sentence. Then, write the active verb in each sentence and use it in a new sentence.

EXAMPLE The doctor warned against eating too much sugar.

ANSWER *warned; Dan warned me not to drink the hot liquid.*

1. The company advertised the new product.
2. I concentrated on the program.
3. She performed publicly for the first time.
4. Several people raced through the airport.
5. I try to eat fruits and vegetables every day.
6. We began our trip this morning.
7. The football players charged the field.
8. My mother saves coupons.
9. The guest speaker explained his theory to the audience.
10. Her best friend lives in Chicago.

PRACTICE 17.4B Using Active Verbs

Read each item. Then, write different sentences, using each item as an active verb.

EXAMPLE shared

ANSWER *I shared my lunch with Will.*

11. bakes
12. assembled
13. reads
14. discovered
15. finished
16. attract
17. slid
18. participate
19. extract
20. blew

SPEAKING APPLICATION

Take turns with a partner. Say sentences in the active voice. Your partner should listen for and identify the active verbs in each of your sentences.

WRITING APPLICATION

Write a paragraph, describing a funny character. Underline all the active verbs in your paragraph.

Voice

PRACTICE 17.4C Forming the Tenses of Passive Verbs

Read each verb. Then, using the subject indicated in parentheses, conjugate each verb in the passive voice for the present indicative, past indicative, future indicative, present perfect indicative, past perfect indicative, and future perfect indicative. Read your conjugated verbs to a partner and discuss if your answers are correct.

EXAMPLE catch (I)

ANSWER *I am caught, I was caught, I will be caught, I have been caught, I had been caught, I will have been caught*

1. find (you)
2. make (it)
3. see (he)
4. like (they)
5. drive (he)
6. give (we)
7. tell (they)
8. answer (it)
9. present (she)
10. close (it)

PRACTICE 17.4D Supplying Verbs in the Active Voice (Active Tense)

Read each sentence. Then, complete each sentence by supplying a verb in the active voice. Read your sentences to a partner and discuss if your sentences are correct.

EXAMPLE Lauren _____ the phone.

ANSWER *answered*

11. The chorus _____ a concert.
12. The new store _____ on Monday.
13. Dad _____ dinner tonight.
14. I _____ the contest entry application today.
15. The children _____ a kite in the wind.
16. The crowd _____ a roar.
17. The principal _____ us for our performance.
18. Did the actor _____ any kind of award?
19. My mother _____ a delicious meal.
20. I _____ at a movie theater this summer.

SPEAKING APPLICATION

Take turns with a partner. Say a sentence with an active verb. Your partner should say a sentence using the same verb but in the passive voice.

WRITING APPLICATION

Show that you understand active and passive tenses by writing four sentences, using active tenses twice and passive tenses twice. Read your sentences to a partner who will tell if the sentence is active tense or passive tense as you speak.

Verb Usage

PRONOUN USAGE

CHAPTER 18

Knowing how to use pronouns correctly will help you clearly present ideas in your writing.

WRITE GUY *Jeff Anderson, M.Ed.*

WHAT DO YOU NOTICE?

Look for pronouns as you zoom in on this sentence from the essay "Making History With Vitamin C" by Penny Le Couteur and Jay Burreson.

MENTOR TEXT

> This small squadron of four ships was under the command of Captain James Lancaster, who carried bottled lemon juice with him on his flagship, the *Dragon*.

Now, ask yourself the following questions:

- Why do the authors use the pronoun *who* rather than *whom*?
- Why do the authors use the pronouns *him* and *his*?

The authors use *who* instead of *whom* because *who* is the subject of the clause that begins with *who carried*. *Whom* is commonly used as the object of a verb or preposition. The pronoun *him* is used because it is the object of the preposition *with*. The pronoun *his* shows that the flagship belongs to Captain James Lancaster.

Grammar for Writers Writers can use pronouns to help guide readers through complicated sentences. Use pronouns in your writing to avoid repeating the same nouns over and over.

I told him, her, and them the whole story.

Wow! You really got personal with all those pronouns.

465

18.1 Case

Nouns and pronouns are the only parts of speech that have **case**.

Case is the form of a noun or a pronoun that shows how it is used in a sentence.

The Three Cases

Nouns and pronouns have three cases, each of which has its own distinctive uses.

The three cases of nouns and pronouns are the **nominative**, the **objective**, and the **possessive**.

CASE	USE IN SENTENCE
Nominative	As the Subject of a Verb, Predicate Nominative, or Nominative Absolute
Objective	As the Direct Object, Indirect Object, Object of a Preposition, Object of a Verbal, or Subject of an Infinitive
Possessive	To Show Ownership

Case in Nouns

The case, or form, of a noun changes only to show possession.

NOMINATIVE   The **ring** had been hidden for years.

(*Ring* is the subject of the verb *had been hidden*.)

OBJECTIVE   We tried to find the **ring**.

(*Ring* is the object of the infinitive *to find*.)

POSSESSIVE   The **ring's** location could not be determined.

(The form changes when *'s* is added to show possession.)

Pronoun Usage

Case in Pronouns

Personal pronouns often have different forms for all three cases. The pronoun that you use depends on its function in a sentence.

NOMINATIVE	OBJECTIVE	POSSESSIVE
I	me	my, mine
you	you	your, yours
he, she, it	him, her, it	his, her, hers, its
we, they	us, them	our, ours
		their, theirs

EXAMPLES I read the book about gardening.

Anne sent the pictures to me.

The book about gardening is mine.

See Practice 18.1A

The Nominative Case in Pronouns

The **nominative case** is used when a personal pronoun acts in one of three ways.

> Use the **nominative case** when a pronoun is the subject of a verb, a predicate nominative, or in a nominative absolute.

18.1.3 RULE

A **nominative absolute** consists of a noun or nominative pronoun followed by a participial phrase. It functions independently from the rest of the sentence.

EXAMPLE We having opened our English books, our teacher had us turn to the sonnet on page 10.

NOMINATIVE PRONOUNS	
As the Subject of a Verb	I will consult the instructions while she fills the prescription.
As a Predicate Nominative	The finalists were she and he.
In a Nominative Absolute	We having finished the brunch, the server cleared the table.

Nominative Pronouns in Compounds

When you use a pronoun in a compound subject or predicate nominative, check the case either by mentally crossing out the other part of the compound or by inverting the sentence.

COMPOUND SUBJECT My counselor and **I** went over college applications.

(**I** went over applications.)

He and his father played baseball.

(**He** played baseball.)

COMPOUND PREDICATE NOMINATIVE The fastest runners were Mark and **he**.

(Mark and **he** were the fastest runners.)

The planners were Kris and **I**.

(Kris and **I** were the planners.)

Nominative Pronouns With Appositives

When an appositive follows a pronoun that is being used as a subject or predicate nominative, the pronoun should stay in the nominative case. To check that you have used the correct case, either mentally cross out the appositive or isolate the subject and verb.

SUBJECT **We** mathematicians use calculators.

(**We** use calculators.)

PREDICATE NOMINATIVE The sponsors were **we** juniors.

(**We** were the sponsors.)

APPOSITIVE AFTER NOUN The team captains, **she** and **I**, ran the soccer practice.

(**She** and **I** ran the soccer practice.)

See Practice 18.1B

Pronoun Usage

PRACTICE 18.1A Identifying Case

Read each sentence. Then, label the underlined pronoun in each sentence *nominative*, *objective*, or *possessive*.

EXAMPLE   Did the waiter give <u>you</u> a menu?
ANSWER   *objective*

1. Gary has sold me <u>his</u> mountain bike.
2. Sondra is signing <u>her</u> name on the application.
3. Do all these muffins have raisins in <u>them</u>?
4. The skateboard in the driveway is <u>yours</u>.
5. The television show that <u>I</u> want to watch has been canceled.
6. The decorator is redoing <u>her</u> bathroom.
7. Basim said that you told <u>him</u> about the meeting tonight.
8. The bird flew around in <u>its</u> cage.
9. Mr. Hamm showed <u>us</u> how to use the copy machine.
10. Paco and <u>he</u> rotate in the lineup.

PRACTICE 18.1B Supplying Pronouns in the Nominative Case

Read each sentence. Then, supply the correct pronoun from the choices in parentheses to complete each sentence.

EXAMPLE   Sally and (he, him) delivered the message.
ANSWER   *he*

11. Fabian and (I, me) assist with many office tasks.
12. The new member of the basketball squad is (he, him).
13. The least likely participants are (them, they).
14. (Her, She) received a cash reward for returning the lost kitten.
15. Frank or (he, him) can give you the directions.
16. Kayla and (us, we) are hosting the event.
17. Gordon and (me, I) went ice-skating last night.
18. (We, Us) freshmen are ordering the jackets.
19. (She, Her) and Matilda are the only ones present.
20. The winners were Laith and (I, me).

SPEAKING APPLICATION

Take turns with a partner. Describe your neighborhood. Use at least one example of a pronoun in each of the three cases. Your partner should listen for and identify your use of pronouns as nominative, objective, and possessive.

WRITING APPLICATION

Write a paragraph about something you did over the last summer vacation. Use at least three nominative pronouns in your paragraph.

The Objective Case

Objective pronouns are used for any kind of object in a sentence as well as for the subject of an infinitive.

RULE 18.1.4

Use the **objective case** for the object of any verb, preposition, or verbal or for the subject of an infinitive.

OBJECTIVE PRONOUNS	
Direct Object	The soccer ball hit her on the arm.
Indirect Object	My friend Myles sent me a book from England.
Object of Preposition	The pilot sat in the cockpit in front of us on the small plane.
Object of Participle	The piranhas swimming around them were very ferocious.
Object of Gerund	Meeting them would be a great honor.
Object of Infinitive	I am obligated to help her work on Saturday.
Subject of Infinitive	The café wanted her to work the early shift.

Objective Pronouns in Compounds

As with the nominative case, errors with objective pronouns most often occur in compounds. To find the correct case, mentally cross out the other part of the compound.

EXAMPLES   The crashing thunder alerted Kris and him.
(Crashing thunder alerted him.)

Ashley wrote Kate and me directions to the party.
(Ashley wrote me directions.)

Note About *Between*: Be sure to use the objective case after the preposition *between*.

INCORRECT   This secret is between you and I.

CORRECT   This secret is between you and me.

See Practice 18.1C

Objective Pronouns With Appositives

Use the objective case when a pronoun that is used as an object or as the subject of an infinitive is followed by an appositive.

EXAMPLES
The art project overwhelmed **us** students.

My mother brought **us** boys sweaters.

The guide warned **us** hikers to be careful.

The Possessive Case

One use for the **possessive case** is before gerunds. A **gerund** is a verbal form ending in *-ing* that is used as a noun.

> Use the **possessive case** before gerunds.

EXAMPLES
Your outlining of the notes was sloppy.

We objected to **her** insinuating that we cheated.

Kate insists on **our** attending the conference.

Common Errors in the Possessive Case

Be sure not to use an apostrophe with a possessive pronoun because possessives already show ownership. Spellings such as *her's, our's, their's,* and *your's* are incorrect.

In addition, be sure not to confuse possessive pronouns and contractions that sound alike. *It's* (with an apostrophe) is the contraction for *it is* or *it has*. *Its* (without the apostrophe) is a possessive pronoun that means "belonging to it." *You're* is a contraction of *you are*; the possessive form of *you* is *your*.

Grammar Game Plan

POSSESSIVE PRONOUNS
The graph had served **its** purpose.

Don't forget **your** essay.

CONTRACTIONS
It's not likely to snow today.

You're the only ones who were late for dinner today.

See Practice 18.1D
See Practice 18.1E
See Practice 18.1F

Case

PRACTICE 18.1C Supplying Pronouns in the Objective Case

Read each sentence. Then, supply an objective pronoun to complete each sentence.

EXAMPLE Quinn taught _____ singers a new song.

ANSWER *us*

1. Lacy borrowed this pen from _____.
2. The discovery was made by Charlie and _____.
3. Give _____ students an opportunity.
4. This discussion is between you and _____.
5. Are these magazines for Keith or _____?
6. I didn't tell _____ the bad news.
7. Will you show this to _____?
8. Give _____ some assistance.
9. Did you hear _____?
10. The waiter asked _____ for our orders.

PRACTICE 18.1D Recognizing Pronouns in the Possessive Case

Read each sentence. Then, write the correct pronoun from the choices in parentheses to complete each sentence.

EXAMPLE (Our, Us) squad lost the competition.

ANSWER *Our*

11. I could be wrong, but isn't this locker (mine, my)?
12. After graduation, the seniors usually store away (they're, their) cap and gown.
13. (You, Your) squeaking brakes need to be repaired.
14. I would like to know which of those houses is (hers, she).
15. Richard asked Joe for (him, his) recipe.
16. The soldiers were given medals for (their, they're) bravery.
17. Nellie claimed that the calculator was (my, mine).
18. Ping was proud to hear them singing (he, his) song.
19. The handlers were elated when (our, ours) dog won the competition.
20. The hurricane left destruction in (it's, its) wake.

SPEAKING APPLICATION

Take turns with a partner. Describe an interesting scene from a book that you have read. Include at least three objective pronouns in your description.

WRITING APPLICATION

Write a paragraph about something fun you plan to do in the next year. Make sure to include three possessive pronouns in your paragraph.

PRACTICE 18.1E Writing Possessive Pronouns Before Gerunds

Read each sentence. Then, rewrite each sentence and include a correct possessive pronoun. Read your sentences to a partner and discuss if your sentences are correct.

EXAMPLE Trey was mad at _____ criticizing of their work.

ANSWER Trey was mad at *his* criticizing of their work.

1. Mr. Hale did not like _____ reporting of the event.
2. The students enjoyed _____ acting in the play.
3. Sam believed _____ following the directions was important.
4. My sister enjoyed _____ practicing the dance steps.
5. We agreed with _____ saying that the movie was funny.
6. Mia was tired by _____ rewriting the report.
7. Our friends disliked _____ quarreling during the trip.
8. Uncle Henry liked _____ watercolor painting.
9. Bob decided to wait two weeks before _____ resigning.
10. Laura remembered _____ losing the watch on the bus.

PRACTICE 18.1F Correcting Common Errors in the Possessive Case

Read each sentence. Then, rewrite each sentence and correct the error.

EXAMPLE Your blocking my view.

ANSWER *You're* blocking my view.

11. Sandra believed her's suggestion is the best.
12. You're essay must be rewritten by Friday.
13. Don brought his' new running shoes to the track.
14. For the injured bird, getting help soon is it's only chance.
15. The backpack that you found is mine's.
16. Remember not to leave you're jacket on the bus.
17. Its likely that the prize-winning science project is ours'.
18. Your making our class trip very unpleasant.
19. You're e-mails were received late this afternoon.
20. The hungry dog carried the food dish in it's mouth.

WRITING APPLICATION

Review Practice 18.1E. For each item, write an additional sentence, using another correct possessive pronoun.

SPEAKING APPLICATION

Take turns with a partner. Use some of the sentences in Practice 18.1E to say similar sentences. Your partner should identify the possessive pronouns and correctly spell them according to how they are used in your sentences.

Case

Test Warm-Up

DIRECTIONS
Read the introduction and the passage that follows. Then, answer the questions to show that you can use and understand the function of pronouns in the objective and possessive case in reading and writing.

Jim wrote this paragraph about volunteering at an animal shelter. Read the paragraph and think about the changes you would suggest as a peer editor. When you finish reading, answer the questions that follow.

Making a Difference

(1) Recently, my friend Erin sent I an e-mail about them volunteering at the local animal shelter. (2) The shelter director, Mrs. Jerome, asked we volunteers to be responsible for walking the dogs in the morning and then bathing them in the afternoon. (3) Our's responsibilities for the shelter dogs were evenly divided between Erin and I. (4) Mrs. Jerome explained the importance of training the dogs to walk on a leash. (5) We followed her advice, and in time, all the dogs learned to obey they're handlers.

---

1 How should sentence 1 be revised?

A Recently, my friend Erin sent them an e-mail about we volunteering at the local animal shelter.

B Erin just e-mailed me about them volunteering at the local animal shelter.

C Erin recently sent I an e-mail about our volunteering at the local animal shelter.

D Recently, my friend Erin sent me an e-mail about our volunteering at the local animal shelter.

2 What change, if any, should be made in sentence 2?

F Change *we* to **me**

G Change *we* to **us**

H Change *them* to **it**

J Make no change

3 How should sentence 3 be revised?

A The responsibilities for the shelter dogs were evenly divided between I and Erin.

B Her's responsibilities for the shelter dogs were evenly divided between Erin and me.

C Our responsibilities for the shelter dogs were evenly divided between Erin and me.

D They're responsibilities for the shelter dogs were evenly divided between Erin and I.

4 What change, if any, should be made in sentence 5?

F Change *they're* to **their**

G Change *they're* to **them**

H Change *her* to **hers**

J Make no change

18.2 Special Problems With Pronouns

Choosing the correct case is not always a matter of choosing the form that "sounds correct," because writing is usually more formal than speech. For example, it would be incorrect to say, "John is smarter than *me*," because the verb is understood in the sentence: "John is smarter than *I [am]*."

Grammar Practice
Practice your grammar skills with Writing Coach Online.

Grammar Games
Test your knowledge of grammar in this fast-paced interactive video game.

Using *Who* and *Whom* Correctly

In order to decide when to use *who* or *whom* and the related forms *whoever* and *whomever*, you need to know how the pronoun is used in a sentence and what case is appropriate.

> ***Who*** is used for the nominative case. ***Whom*** is used for the objective case.

RULE 18.2.1

CASE	PRONOUNS	USE IN SENTENCES
Nominative	who whoever	As the Subject of a Verb or Predicate Nominative
Objective	whom whomever	As the Direct Object, Object of a Verbal, Object of a Preposition, or Subject of an Infinitive
Possessive	whose whosever	To Show Ownership

EXAMPLES I know **who** made that stew.

Kodie snuggled with **whoever** was on the couch.

Bob did not know **whom** the coach chose.

Whose coat is in the kitchen?

The nominative and objective cases are the source of certain problems. Pronoun problems can appear in two kinds of sentences: direct questions and complex sentences.

Special Problems With Pronouns   475

In Direct Questions

Who is the correct form when the pronoun is the subject of a simple question. *Whom* is the correct form when the pronoun is the direct object, object of a verbal, or object of a preposition.

Questions in subject–verb word order always begin with *who*. However, questions in inverted order never correctly begin with *who*. To see if you should use *who* or *whom*, reword the question as a statement in subject–verb word order.

EXAMPLES   **Who** wants a ticket to the new museum?

Whom did you invite tonight?

(You did invite **whom** tonight.)

In Complex Sentences

Follow these steps to see if the case of a pronoun in a subordinate clause is correct. First, find the subordinate clause. If the complex sentence is a question, rearrange it in subject–verb order. Second, if the subordinate clause is inverted, rearrange the words in subject–verb word order. Finally, determine how the pronoun is used in the subordinate clause.

EXAMPLE   **Who**, may I ask, has read the book?

REARRANGED   I may ask **who** has read the book.

USE OF PRONOUN   (subject of the verb *has read*)

EXAMPLE   Is the president the one **whom** they chose?

REARRANGED   They chose **whom.** The president is the one.

USE OF PRONOUN   (object of the verb *chose*)

Note About *Whose*: The word *whose* is a possessive pronoun; the contraction *who's* means "who is" or "who has."

POSSESSIVE PRONOUN   **Whose** pen is this?

CONTRACTION   **Who's** [who has] taken my pen?

See Practice 18.2A

Pronoun Usage

Pronouns in Elliptical Clauses

An **elliptical clause** is one in which some words are omitted but still understood. Errors in pronoun usage can easily be made when an elliptical clause that begins with *than* or *as* is used to make a comparison.

> In **elliptical clauses** beginning with *than* or *as*, use the form of the pronoun that you would use if the clause were fully stated.

18.2.2 RULE

The case of the pronoun is determined by whether the omitted words fall before or after the pronoun. The omitted words in the examples below are shown in brackets.

WORDS OMITTED BEFORE PRONOUN

You told Anna more than **me**.

(You told Anna more than [you told] **me**.)

WORDS OMITTED AFTER PRONOUN

Ben is as persistent as **he**.

(Ben is as persistent as **he** [is].)

Mentally add the missing words. If they come *before* the pronoun, choose the objective case. If they come *after* the pronoun, choose the nominative case.

CHOOSING A PRONOUN IN ELLIPTICAL CLAUSES
1. Consider the choices of pronouns: nominative or objective.
2. Mentally complete the elliptical clause.
3. Base your choice on what you find.

The case of the pronoun can sometimes change the entire meaning of the sentence.

NOMINATIVE PRONOUN

She liked reading more than **I**.

She liked reading more than **I** [did].

OBJECTIVE PRONOUN

She liked reading more than **me**.

She liked reading more than [she liked] **me**.

See Practice 18.2B

Special Problems With Pronouns

Special Problems With Pronouns

PRACTICE 18.2A Choosing *Who* or *Whom* Correctly

Read each sentence. Then, write *who* or *whom* to complete each sentence.

EXAMPLE Jasmine is the one _____ I came to visit.
ANSWER *whom*

1. _____ did the coach select as team captain?
2. Those are the volunteers _____ the mayor will honor.
3. The trip is open to anyone _____ can read a map.
4. To _____ did you give the key?
5. A good educator must be someone _____ enjoys teaching.
6. _____ have you asked to the dance?
7. The prize was given to the person _____ answered the most questions correctly.
8. Jeannette is the person _____ I supported during the campaign.
9. He is the same man _____ I met at the conference.
10. Terry Heath is a student _____ gets lots of praise.

PRACTICE 18.2B Identifying the Correct Pronoun in Elliptical Clauses

Read each sentence. Then, complete each sentence with an appropriate pronoun. If the sentence contains an elliptical clause, write *elliptical* after the pronoun.

EXAMPLE Burke is as loud as _____.
ANSWER *she*

11. Damon plays the drums better than _____ plays.
12. The panel chose Kendra rather than _____.
13. The test results delighted Brian as much as _____ delighted his parents.
14. I do not understand German as well as _____ understands French.
15. That comment impressed Fred as much as _____ impressed Alicia.
16. Leonard decided to ask Zalaima to be his running mate rather than _____.
17. Nathan is as committed to the cause as _____.
18. The Falcons scored as many points as _____ had scored during the playoffs.
19. Corey runs the hurdles faster than _____.
20. Rosa likes her puppy more than _____ brother likes the puppy.

SPEAKING APPLICATION

Take turns with a partner. Ask questions using both *who* and *whom*. Your partner should respond by also using *who* and *whom* correctly in his or her response.

WRITING APPLICATION

Write a true or fictional paragraph describing any type of competition. Use at least two elliptical clauses in your paragraph.

AGREEMENT

Understanding how verbs relate to subjects and how nouns relate to pronouns will help you achieve agreement in your sentences.

WRITE GUY *Jeff Anderson, M.Ed.*

WHAT DO YOU NOTICE?

Look for examples of agreement as you zoom in on this sentence from the play *Antigone* by Socrates, as translated by Dudley Fitts and Robert Fitzgerald.

MENTOR TEXT

> **HAIMON.** The ideal condition would be, I admit, that men should be right by instinct; but since we are all too likely to go astray, the reasonable thing is to learn from those who can teach.

Now, ask yourself the following questions:

- Which noun does the pronoun *we* refer to? How do they agree?
- How do the verbs *are* and *is* agree with their subjects?

The pronoun *we* refers to the noun *men*. Because *men* and *we* are both plural, they agree in number. The verb *are* is plural and agrees with the plural subject, *we*, that precedes it. The verb *is* is singular; it agrees with the singular subject *thing*.

Grammar for Writers Writers are more articulate when they make subjects and verbs and nouns and pronouns agree. Make your writing easier for readers to follow by focusing on agreement.

Your sentences are so agreeable.

That's because I use friendly subjects and verbs.

CHAPTER 19

19.1 Subject–Verb Agreement

For a subject and a verb to agree, both must be singular, or both must be plural. In this section, you will learn how to make sure singular and plural subjects and verbs agree.

Number in Nouns, Pronouns, and Verbs

In grammar, **number** indicates whether a word is singular or plural. Only three parts of speech have different forms that indicate number: nouns, pronouns, and verbs.

RULE 19.1.1

Number shows whether a noun, pronoun, or verb is singular or plural.

Recognizing the number of most nouns is seldom a problem because most form their plurals by adding *-s* or *-es*. Some, such as *mouse* or *ox*, form their plurals irregularly: *mice, oxen*.

Pronouns, however, have different forms to indicate their number. The chart below shows the different forms of personal pronouns in the nominative case, the case that is used for subjects.

PERSONAL PRONOUNS		
SINGULAR	PLURAL	SINGULAR OR PLURAL
I	we	you
he, she, it	they	

The grammatical number of verbs is sometimes difficult to determine. That is because the form of many verbs can be either singular or plural, and they may form plurals in different ways.

SINGULAR He **runs**.

He **has run**.

PLURAL We **run**.

We **have run**.

480 Agreement

Subject–Verb Agreement

Some verb forms can be only singular. The personal pronouns *he*, *she*, and *it* and all singular nouns call for singular verbs in the present and the present perfect tense.

ALWAYS SINGULAR

He **jumps**.

He **has jumped**.

Ben **yells**.

Chris **has yelled**.

She **runs**.

She **has run**.

The verb *be* in the present tense has special forms to agree with singular subjects. The pronoun *I* has its own singular form of *be*; so do *he, she, it,* and singular nouns.

ALWAYS SINGULAR

I **am** starving.

She **is** short.

Ben **is** late.

She **is** waiting.

All singular subjects except *you* share the same past tense verb form of *be*.

ALWAYS SINGULAR

I **was** going to work.

He **was** class president.

Keith **was** late for work.

He **was** getting on the train.

See Practice 19.1A

A verb form will always be singular if it has had an *-s* or *-es* added to it or if it includes the words *has, am, is,* or *was*. The number of any other verb depends on its subject.

The chart on the next page shows verb forms that are always singular and those that can be singular or plural.

VERBS THAT ARE ALWAYS SINGULAR	VERBS THAT CAN BE SINGULAR OR PLURAL
(he, she, Jane) sees	(I, you, we, they) see
(he, she, Jane) has seen	(I, you, we, they) have seen
(I) am	(you, we, they) are
(he, she, Jane) is	(you, we, they) were
(I, he, she, Jane) was	

Singular and Plural Subjects

When making a verb agree with its subject, be sure to identify the subject and determine its number.

RULE 19.1.2

A singular subject must have a singular verb. A plural subject must have a plural verb.

SINGULAR SUBJECT AND VERB	PLURAL SUBJECT AND VERB
The doctor works in South Africa.	These doctors work in South Africa.
She was being secretive about the date of the party.	They were being secretive about the date of the party.
Benji looks through a magazine for ideas about gardening.	Benji and Brice look through a magazine for ideas about gardening.
France is a large country in Europe.	France and Italy are large countries in Europe.
Kira takes biology and anatomy.	Kira and Kim take biology and anatomy.
Bethany is planning a vacation to Australia.	Our cousins are planning a vacation to Australia.
Tiff plays defense on the soccer team.	Tiff and Terry play on the soccer team.
She looks through the plane window.	They look through the plane window.
Benjamin has been studying human anatomy.	We have been studying human anatomy.

See Practice 19.1B

482 Agreement

Subject–Verb Agreement

PRACTICE 19.1A Identifying Number in Nouns, Pronouns, and Verbs

Read each word or group of words. Write whether the word or words are *singular*, *plural*, or *both*.

EXAMPLE   was sleeping
ANSWER   *singular*

1. shuts
2. women
3. adore
4. you
5. they
6. have
7. desk
8. flies above
9. discuss
10. we

PRACTICE 19.1B Identifying Singular and Plural Subjects and Verbs

Read each sentence. Then, write the subject and verb in each sentence and label them *plural* or *singular*.

EXAMPLE   The papers have been ruined in the flood.
ANSWER   subject: *papers*; verb: *have been ruined* — plural

11. The dance starts at seven o'clock tonight.
12. Rick has begun his final art project.
13. New houses have many modern features.
14. This summer, our rosebushes have started to bloom.
15. The old bookshelves from the basement were being sold at our yard sale.
16. My sister often plays with her friends after school.
17. Before the planting season, I clean all the flower pots.
18. Gentle waves slap against the dock.
19. The floor mats in my car are getting worn.
20. The egg has fallen from the carton.

SPEAKING APPLICATION

Take turns with a partner. Tell about what you did this morning before coming to school. Your partner should listen for and name the plural and singular nouns and verbs that you use.

WRITING APPLICATION

For each sentence in Practice 19.1B, change the subject from singular to plural or plural to singular. Make sure that the verb in each sentence agrees with your new subject.

Practice   483

Intervening Phrases and Clauses

When you check for agreement, mentally cross out any words that separate the subject and verb.

A phrase or clause that interrupts a subject and its verb does not affect subject–verb agreement.

In the first example below, the singular subject *discovery* agrees with the singular verb *interests* despite the intervening prepositional phrase *of ancient scrolls*, which contains a plural noun.

EXAMPLES The **discovery** of ancient scrolls **interests** many people.

The **researchers**, whose research is nearly complete, **require** more funding.

Intervening parenthetical expressions—such as those beginning with *as well as, in addition to, in spite of,* or *including*—also have no effect on the agreement of the subject and verb.

EXAMPLES Your **research**, in addition to the data gathered by those working in the lab, **is helping** to cure many diseases.

Christina's **trip**, including visits to Florida and California, **is lasting** six months.

See Practice 19.1C

Relative Pronouns as Subjects

When *who, which,* or *that* acts as a subject of a subordinate clause, its verb will be singular or plural depending on the number of the antecedent.

A relative pronoun may take a singular or plural verb, depending on the number of the pronoun's antecedent.

484 Agreement

EXAMPLES She is the only **one** of the professors **who has** experience teaching American literature.

(The antecedent of *who* is *one*.)

She is the only one of several **professors who have** experience teaching American literature.

(The antecedent of *who* is *professors*.)

Compound Subjects

A **compound subject** has two or more simple subjects, which are usually joined by *or* or *and*. Use the following rules when making compound subjects agree with verbs.

Subjects Joined by *And*

Only one rule applies to compound subjects connected by *and*: The verb is usually plural, whether the parts of the compound subject are all singular, all plural, or mixed.

> **A compound subject joined by *and* is generally plural and must have a plural verb.**

19.1.5 RULE

TWO SINGULAR SUBJECTS A **snowstorm** and an **ice storm hit** the mountain.

TWO PLURAL SUBJECTS **Tulips** and **daisies are** growing in my garden.

A SINGULAR SUBJECT AND A PLURAL SUBJECT A purple **tulip** and many yellow **daisies make** a beautiful arrangement.

There are two exceptions to this rule. The verb is singular if the parts of a compound subject are thought of as one item or if the word *every* or *each* precedes the compound subject.

Subject–Verb Agreement 485

EXAMPLES   **Peanut butter and jelly was** all the child would eat.

Every weather center and emergency network in the United states issues warnings for severe weather.

Singular Subjects Joined by *Or* or *Nor*
When both parts of a compound subject connected by *or* or *nor* are singular, a singular verb is required.

> **RULE 19.1.6**
> **Two or more singular subjects joined by *or* or *nor* must have a singular verb.**

EXAMPLE   A **sandwich** or **salad makes** a great lunch.

Plural Subjects Joined by *Or* or *Nor*
When both parts of a compound subject connected by *or* or *nor* are plural, a plural verb is required.

> **RULE 19.1.7**
> **Two or more plural subjects joined by *or* or *nor* must have a plural verb.**

EXAMPLE   Neither **blizzards** nor **snowstorms cause** as many power outages as ice storms.

Subjects of Mixed Number Joined by *Or* or *Nor*
If one part of a compound subject is singular and the other is plural, the verb agrees with the subject that is closer to it.

> **RULE 19.1.8**
> **If one or more singular subjects are joined to one or more plural subjects by *or* or *nor*, the subject closest to the verb determines agreement.**

EXAMPLES   Neither **Anastasia** nor my **parents are excited**.

Neither my **parents** nor **Anastasia is excited**.   See Practice 19.1D

Agreement

Subject–Verb Agreement

PRACTICE 19.1C Identifying Intervening Phrases and Clauses

Read each sentence. Underline the intervening phrase or clause between the subject and the verb in each sentence.

EXAMPLE The book by Dr. Seuss is well-known by all.

ANSWER The book <u>by Dr. Seuss</u> is well-known by all.

1. A bouquet of red roses was given to Jan.
2. Olivia, the only one of four children, has inherited her mother's eye color.
3. The salespeople, who are working in the shoe department, are at a meeting.
4. The pages of the book, as well as the back and front covers, are in great condition.
5. The lake where trout can be found is being overfished.
6. A house built near the ocean is likely to have beautiful views of the water.
7. The giant trees that tower over the forest floor offer shade to the animals.
8. Three kids from my class were sent acceptance letters from prestigious universities.
9. The storyboards that the student created were helpful in her presentation.
10. The birds, including the fledglings, had to fly south for the winter.

PRACTICE 19.1D Making Verbs Agree With Singular and Compound Subjects

Read each sentence. Then, fill in the blank with the form of a verb that agrees with the singular or compound subject.

EXAMPLE Neither Helen nor Joe _____ going to the meeting.

ANSWER is

11. My mother and father _____ late for the movie.
12. Both fish and ducks _____ in that pond.
13. Broccoli and spinach _____ green vegetables.
14. Either worms or insects _____ the plant crops.
15. Both oil and vinegar _____ used in this salad dressing.
16. Shorts, T-shirts, and sunglasses _____ needed for your vacation.
17. He _____ the hard drive.
18. Neither rain nor snow _____ us from taking this field trip.
19. Blueberries or any other berry _____ good on oatmeal.
20. Writers and illustrators often _____ together to create a book.

SPEAKING APPLICATION

Take turns with a partner. Use sentences with intervening clauses to tell about your best holiday experience. Your partner should identify the intervening clauses in your sentences.

WRITING APPLICATION

Use sentences 14, 16, and 19 as models to write similar sentences. Exchange papers with a partner. Your partner should complete the sentences with the correct form of a verb that agrees with the subject.

Confusing Subjects

Some kinds of subjects have special agreement problems.

Hard-to-Find Subjects and Inverted Sentences

Subjects that appear after verbs are said to be **inverted.** Subject–verb order is usually inverted in questions. To find out whether to use a singular or plural verb, mentally rearrange the sentence into subject–verb order.

RULE 19.1.9 A verb must still agree in number with a subject that comes after it.

EXAMPLE: On the counter **are** two coffee **mugs**.

REARRANGED IN SUBJECT–VERB ORDER: Two coffee **mugs are** on the counter.

The words *there* and *here* often signal an inverted sentence. These words never function as the subject of a sentence.

EXAMPLES: There **are** the family **photos**.

Here **is** the updated **information**.

Note About *There's* and *Here's*: Both of these contractions contain the singular verb *is: there is* and *here is.* They should be used only with singular subjects.

CORRECT: **There's** only one **meeting** scheduled.

Here's a black **suit** to try on.

See Practice 19.1E

Subjects With Linking Verbs

Subjects with linking verbs may also cause agreement problems.

RULE 19.1.10 A linking verb must agree with its subject, regardless of the number of its predicate nominative.

488 Agreement

EXAMPLES **Apples are** my favorite fruit.

One **reason** we expect a snowstorm **is** that the air is freezing.

In the first example, the plural verb *are* agrees with the plural subject *apples*. In the next example, the singular subject *reason* takes the singular verb *is*.

See Practice 19.1F

Collective Nouns
Collective nouns name groups of people or things. Examples include *audience*, *class*, *club*, and *committee*.

> A collective noun takes a singular verb when the group it names acts as a single unit. A collective noun takes a plural verb when the group acts as individuals.

SINGULAR The special **forces embarks** at night.

(The members act as a unit.)

PLURAL The special **forces were going** on separate missions.

See Practice 19.1G

(The members act individually.)

Nouns That Look Like Plurals
Some nouns that end in *-s* are actually singular. For example, nouns that name branches of knowledge, such as *civics*, and those that name illnesses, such as *mumps*, take singular verbs.

> Use singular verbs to agree with nouns that are plural in form but singular in meaning.

SINGULAR **Social studies is** my favorite subject.

When words such as *ethics* and *politics* do not name branches of knowledge but indicate characteristics, their meanings are plural. Similarly, such words as *eyeglasses*, *pants*, and *scissors* generally take plural verbs.

Subject–Verb Agreement 489

PLURAL   Ronnie's **ethics change** all the time.

Indefinite Pronouns

Some indefinite pronouns are always singular, some are always plural, and some may be either singular or plural. Prepositional phrases do not affect subject–verb agreement.

Singular indefinite pronouns take singular verbs. Plural indefinite pronouns take plural verbs.

SINGULAR   *anybody, anyone, anything, each, either, everybody, everyone, everything, neither, nobody, no one, nothing, somebody, someone, something*

PLURAL   *both, few, many, others, several*

SINGULAR   **Everyone** in the concert arena **has left**.

PLURAL   **Many** of the flowers **were planted**.

The pronouns *all, any, more, most, none,* and *some* usually take a singular verb if the antecedent is singular, and a plural verb if it is plural.

SINGULAR   **Some** of the house **was finished** by nightfall.

PLURAL   **Some** of the damaged houses **are** being repaired.

See Practice 19.1H

Titles of Creative Works and Names of Organizations

Plural words in the title of a creative work or in the name of an organization do not affect subject–verb agreement.

A title of a creative work or name of an organization is singular and must have a singular verb.

EXAMPLES **The March of Dimes is** a wonderful charity.
(organization)

Starry Night by Vincent Van Gogh **is** a famous painting.
(creative work)

Amounts and Measurements

Although they appear to be plural, most amounts and measurements actually express single units or ideas.

> **A noun expressing an amount or measurement is usually singular and requires a singular verb.**

 RULE 19.1.16

EXAMPLES **Four hundred million dollars is** the cost to build a new bridge.
(Four hundred million dollars is one sum of money.)

Four miles was our distance from the nearest shopping mall.
(Four miles is a single distance.)

Three quarters of the house **was rebuilt** by the end of the week.
(Three quarters is one part of a house.)

Half of the weeds **were uprooted**.
(Half refers to a number of individual weeds, and not part of an individual garden, so it is plural.)

PRACTICE 19.1E Identifying Subjects and Verbs in Inverted Sentences

Read each sentence. Then, identify the subject and verb in each sentence.

EXAMPLE Here is your assignment.
ANSWER subject: *assignment*; verb: *is*

1. Onto the playground rushed the excited children.
2. How will we ever get back to the road?
3. There are no mistakes in your report.
4. In the cupboard are the fancy dishes.
5. Where did you leave your sneakers?
6. There was the exit from the building.
7. Here are some ideas for your class project.
8. Was the coffee on the counter?
9. May I have another sheet of paper, please?
10. Somewhere between those trees lives the fox.

PRACTICE 19.1F Making Linking Verbs Agree With Subjects

Read each sentence. Then, rewrite each sentence to make the linking verb agree with the subject. If the sentence is correct, write *correct*.

EXAMPLE The house, which has many rooms, are for sale.
ANSWER *The house, which has many rooms, is for sale.*

11. The dogs, which are healthy, is ready for adoption.
12. The window in my bedroom are open.
13. The directions on the invitation is confusing.
14. One problem for the science class is the lack of equipment.
15. Her goal for the year are learning to swim.
16. The factories, which were closed, is now open again.
17. The books that we collected last weekend are in the library.
18. One trail in the park are closed for a week.
19. Those stories is the funniest in the book.
20. The wool sweater on the top shelf are very expensive.

SPEAKING APPLICATION

Take turns with a partner. Say five inverted sentences. Your partner should identify the subject and verb in each of your sentences.

WRITING APPLICATION

Write a paragraph describing your home. Be sure to write some sentences in which the linking verb does not agree with the subject. Exchange papers with a partner. Your partner should correct the subject-verb errors.

Subject-Verb Agreement

PRACTICE 19.1G **Making Verbs Agree With Collective Nouns**

Read each sentence. Then, choose the correct verb that makes the verb agree with the collective noun.

EXAMPLE The gaggle of geese (are being, is being) observed.

ANSWER *is being*

1. The audience (cheer, cheers) the students.
2. The crowd (was, were) quiet during the mayor's speech.
3. The music club (is making, are making) plans for next year.
4. The basketball team (is doing, are doing) different warm-up exercises.
5. The flock (was soaring, were soaring) through the air.
6. The frightened herd (is running, are running) in different directions.
7. Suddenly the angry swam of bees (attack, attacks) the hikers.
8. The jury (has, have) a variety of opinions about the case.
9. The fleet (approach, approaches) the port.
10. The troop (disagree, disagrees) about their leader's suggestion.

PRACTICE 19.1H **Making Verbs Agree With Indefinite Pronouns**

Read each sentence. Then, complete each sentence by supplying a verb that agrees with the subject.

EXAMPLE None of the mice _____ running through the maze.

ANSWER None of the mice *is* running through the maze.

11. Several beaches _____ closed this summer.
12. None of the paint _____ the right color.
13. Somebody in the meeting _____ shouting at the speaker now.
14. Many of the runners _____ too tired to finish the race.
15. Each of the dogs _____ very well behaved around children.
16. Some of the oak tree _____ damaged by lightening.
17. No one in the park _____ picking up the trash.
18. Both books _____ returned by the deadline.
19. Neither of the computer stores _____ the software that I need.
20. None of the artists _____ talking to the art students this morning.

WRITING APPLICATION

Research on the Internet five unusual collective nouns that refer to groups of animals, such as *plague of locusts*. Write a sentence for each collective noun. Make sure that the verbs agree with the collective nouns.

SPEAKING APPLICATION

Take turns with a partner. Use sentences in Practice 19.1H as models to say similar sentences. Your partner should supply a verb that agrees with each of the indefinite pronouns in your sentences.

Subject-Verb Agreement

Test Warm-Up

DIRECTIONS
Read the introduction and the passage that follows. Then, answer the questions to show that you understand how to make verbs agree with confusing subjects in reading and writing.

Jody wrote this paragraph about the eruption of Mount St. Helens. Read the paragraph and think about the changes you would suggest as a peer editor. When you finish reading, answer the questions that follow.

Disaster at Mount St. Helens

(1) Here's some interesting facts about the eruption of Mount St. Helens, a volcano in Washington state, on May 18, 1980. (2) Thirteen hundred feet of the mountain top were blown into the air, and many of the citizens in nearby Yakima was affected. (3) About twelve miles were the actual distance the volcanic debris traveled into the sky that day. (4) Today there're one very exciting way that our class can keeps track of Mount St. Helens all the time—a VolcanoCam! (5) Installed in 1996, this was one of the first web cameras ever pointed at an active volcano.

---

1 What change, if any, should be made in sentence 1?

   A Change *Here's* to **Here was**

   B Change *Here's* to **Here are**

   C Change *Here's* to **There was**

   D Make no change

2 How should sentence 2 be revised?

   F Thirteen hundred feet of the mountain top is blown in the air, and many of the people in Yakima was affected.

   G Thirteen hundred feet of the mountain top was blown into the air, and many of the citizens in nearby Yakima was affected.

   H Thirteen hundred feet of the mountain top were blown into the air, and many of the citizens in nearby Yakima were affected.

   J The mountain's top were blown into the air, and many of the citizens in nearby Yakima were affected.

3 What change, if any, should be made in sentence 3?

   A Change *were* to **was**

   B Change *traveled* to **travels**

   C Change *distance* to **distances**

   D Make no change

4 How should sentence 4 be revised?

   F Today there's one very exciting way that our class keep track of Mount St. Helens all the time—a VolcanoCam!

   G Today there's one very exciting way our class can keeps track of Mount S. Helens all the time—a VolcanoCam!

   H Today there're one very exciting way our class can keep track of Mount St. Helens all the time—a VolcanoCam!

   J Today there's one very exciting way our class can keep track of Mount St. Helens all the time—a VolcanoCam!

19.2 Pronoun–Antecedent Agreement

Like a subject and its verb, a pronoun and its antecedent must agree. An **antecedent** is the word or group of words for which the pronoun stands.

Grammar Practice
Practice your grammar skills with Writing Coach Online.

Grammar Games
Test your knowledge of grammar in this fast-paced interactive video game.

Agreement Between Personal Pronouns and Antecedents

While a subject and verb must agree only in number, a personal pronoun and its antecedent must agree in three ways.

> A personal pronoun must agree with its antecedent in number, person, and gender.

The **number** of a pronoun indicates whether it is singular or plural. **Person** refers to a pronoun's ability to indicate either the person speaking (first person), the person spoken to (second person), or the person, place, or thing spoken about (third person). **Gender** is the characteristic of nouns and pronouns that indicates whether the word is *masculine* (referring to males), *feminine* (referring to females), or *neuter* (referring to neither males nor females).

The only pronouns that indicate gender are third-person singular personal pronouns.

GENDER OF THIRD-PERSON SINGULAR PRONOUNS	
Masculine	he, him, his
Feminine	she, her, hers
Neuter	it, its

In the example below, the pronoun *her* agrees with the antecedent *Lori Smith* in number (both are singular), in person (both are third person), and in gender (both are feminine).

EXAMPLE Lori Smith has opened **her** office to the employees.

Agreement in Number

There are three rules to keep in mind to determine the number of compound antecedents.

Rule 19.2.2 Use a singular personal pronoun when two or more singular antecedents are joined by *or* or *nor*.

EXAMPLES Either Amber **or** Tina will bring **her** copy of the *Mona Lisa* to class.

Neither Sophie **nor** Allie will sleep in **her** new bed.

Rule 19.2.3 Use a plural personal pronoun when two or more antecedents are joined by *and*.

EXAMPLE Brittany **and** I are studying for **our** driver's test.

An exception occurs when a distinction must be made between individual and joint ownership. If individual ownership is intended, use a singular pronoun to refer to a compound antecedent. If joint ownership is intended, use a plural pronoun.

SINGULAR **Adam and Cathy** played **her** piano.

PLURAL **Adam and Cathy** paid for **their** piano.

SINGULAR Neither **Terry nor Todd** let me drive **his** car.

PLURAL Neither **Terry nor Todd** let me drive **their** car.

The third rule applies to compound antecedents whose parts are mixed in number.

Rule 19.2.4 Use a plural personal pronoun if any part of a compound antecedent joined by *or* or *nor* is plural.

496 **Agreement**

Pronoun–Antecedent Agreement

See Practice 19.2A

EXAMPLE If either the **vendor** or the **presenters** arrive, take **them** to the meeting.

Agreement in Person and Gender Avoid shifts in person or gender of pronouns.

> As part of pronoun–antecedent agreement, take care not to shift either person or gender.

RULE 19.2.5

SHIFT IN PERSON **Kevin** is planning to visit California because **you** can see how the Navy Seals train.

CORRECT **Kevin** is planning to visit California because **he** wants to see how the Navy Seals train.

SHIFT IN GENDER The **dog** wagged **its** tail back and forth and barked **his** head off.

CORRECT The **dog** wagged **its** tail back and forth and barked **its** head off.

Generic Masculine Pronouns Traditionally, a masculine pronoun has been used to refer to a singular antecedent whose gender is unknown. Such use is called *generic* because it applies to both masculine and feminine genders. Many writers now prefer to use *his or her, he or she, him or her,* or to rephrase a sentence to eliminate the situation.

> When gender is not specified, either use *his or her* or rewrite the sentence.

RULE 19.2.6

EXAMPLES Each **student** found a useful periodical on which to research **his or her report** on WWII.

Students found useful periodicals on which to research **their reports** on WWII.

See Practice 19.2B

Pronoun–Antecedent Agreement 497

Pronoun–Antecedent Agreement

PRACTICE 19.2A Making Personal Pronouns Agree With Their Antecedents

Read each sentence. Then, for each sentence, choose the personal pronoun in parentheses that agrees with the antecedent.

EXAMPLE Peter and I enjoyed (our, his) trip to New York City.

ANSWER *our*

1. The butterfly is tasting the sap with (her, its) feet.
2. Neither Dee nor Barbara uses (their, her) calculator very often.
3. The manager gets to choose (his, their) office.
4. Joe and Melissa work after school to prove that (he or she, they) can get good grades and earn money.
5. A skunk's odor is (its, their) defense.
6. Maura has washed (her, their) son's hair.
7. Neither Jose nor Laura remembered to bring (their, his or her) swimsuit.
8. Police officers should wear (his or her, their) badges.
9. Neither Mike nor Kyung rode (his, their) bike to practice.
10. Each boy designed (his, their) own robot.

PRACTICE 19.2B Revising for Agreement in Person and Gender

Read each sentence. Then, revise each sentence so that the personal pronoun agrees with the antecedent.

EXAMPLE If you need more information, I will be glad to send them.

ANSWER *If you need more information, I will be glad to send it.*

11. Neither Jenny nor Ashley brought their books to school.
12. I like the kind of movie that leaves you guessing.
13. If Laura doesn't understand the directions, she should ask the teacher to explain it to them.
14. The dog behaved as if she had an injured paw.
15. Manuel writes his assignments in a notebook, a habit that helps you remember them.
16. Each of the salesmen reported their sales figures.
17. One of my neighbors runs to improve the muscle tone in their legs.
18. If a person wants to succeed, you have to be willing to work hard.
19. I am happy for Frank because they won the tournament.
20. The coach expects a lot from us, but you started to appreciate him after a while.

SPEAKING APPLICATION

With a partner, tell about members of your families. Use several different personal pronouns in your sentences. Your partner should name the personal pronouns you use and tell whether they agree with their antecedents.

WRITING APPLICATION

Use sentences 14, 15, and 16 as models to write similar sentences. Then, exchange papers with a partner. Your partner should revise each sentence to make the personal pronoun agree with the antecedent.

Agreement With Indefinite Pronouns

When an indefinite pronoun, such as *each, all,* or *most,* is used with a personal pronoun, the pronouns must agree.

> **Use a plural personal pronoun when the antecedent is a plural indefinite pronoun.**

19.2.7 RULE

EXAMPLES
Many of the students were excited about **their** art lessons.

All the girls forgot to bring **their** uniforms.

When both pronouns are singular, a similar rule applies.

> **Use a singular personal pronoun when the antecedent is a singular indefinite pronoun.**

19.2.8 RULE

In the first example, the personal pronoun *her* agrees in number with the singular indefinite pronoun *one.* The gender (feminine) is determined by the word *actresses.*

EXAMPLES
Only **one** of the actresses practiced **her** lines.

One of the actresses remembered to bring **her** script.

If other words in the sentence do not indicate a gender, you may use *him or her, he or she, his or her* or rephrase the sentence.

EXAMPLES
Each of the athletes wore **his or her** new track uniform.

The **athletes** wore **their** new track uniforms.

For indefinite pronouns that can be either singular or plural, such as *all, any, more, most, none,* and *some,* agreement depends on the antecedent of the indefinite pronoun.

Pronoun–Antecedent Agreement

EXAMPLES **Most** of the fruit had lost **its** appeal.
(The antecedent of *most* is *fruit,* which is singular.)

Most of the shoppers wanted **their** money back.
(The antecedent of *most* is *shoppers,* which is plural.)

Some of the lasagna **was** too hot.
(The antecedent of *some* is *lasagna,* which is singular.)

All of the passports **were** in the suitcase.
(The antecedent of *all* is *passports,* which is plural.)

In some situations, strict grammatical agreement may be illogical. In these situations, either let the meaning of the sentence determine the number of the personal pronoun, or reword the sentence.

ILLOGICAL When **each of the doorbells** rang, I answered **it** as quickly as possible.

MORE LOGICAL When **each of the doorbells** rang, I answered **them** as quickly as possible.

MORE LOGICAL When **all of the doorbells** rang, I answered **them** as quickly as possible.

See Practice 19.2C

Agreement With Reflexive Pronouns

Reflexive pronouns, which end in *-self* or *-selves,* should only refer to a word earlier in the same sentence.

RULE 19.2.9

A reflexive pronoun must agree with an antecedent that is clearly stated.

EXAMPLES **Patricia** made dinner for **herself**.

You should consider **yourself** blessed.

Star **athletes** enjoy making a spectacle of **themselves**.

See Practice 19.2D

500 Agreement

Pronoun–Antecedent Agreement

PRACTICE 19.2C Supplying Indefinite Pronouns

Read each sentence. Then, rewrite each sentence, filling in the blank with an appropriate indefinite pronoun that agrees with the antecedent.

EXAMPLE   Has _____ called for me today?
ANSWER   *Has anyone called for me today?*

1. _____ of my friends plan to enter their essays in the writing contest.
2. _____ of my sisters wants her own room.
3. Only _____ of the horses has its mane brushed.
4. _____ of the books on the shelves need their covers dusted.
5. _____ of the baseball players had his uniform cleaned.
6. _____ of the fish still had a hook in its mouth.
7. _____ of the plants have black spots on their leaves.
8. _____ of the rugs were handmade.
9. _____ of the rooms had curtains covering the windows.
10. _____ of the ducks was black.

PRACTICE 19.2D Supplying Reflexive Pronouns

Read each sentence. Then, write the correct reflexive pronoun that agrees with the antecedent in each sentence.

EXAMPLE   Ladies and gentlemen, please help _____ to some apple cider.
ANSWER   *yourselves*

11. We told _____ that we were improving things.
12. The panel members decided among _____ that they wanted to end the meeting.
13. Jeremy did finish the job by _____.
14. We found _____ wondering what to do after the game.
15. I made _____ a sandwich for lunch.
16. She left the room so that the reporters could talk among _____.
17. The children amused _____ by playing a game.
18. Lance made _____ a race car for the science fair.
19. I told my mom to prepare _____ for good news.
20. The tourists suddenly found _____ in a historic part of town.

SPEAKING APPLICATION

Take turns with a partner. Choose three indefinite pronouns. Your partner should say sentences, using a personal pronoun that agrees with each indefinite pronoun.

WRITING APPLICATION

Use sentences 11, 12, and 15 as models to write similar sentences. Then, exchange papers with a partner. Your partner should rewrite each sentence, using the correct reflexive pronoun that agrees with the antecedent.

Find It/ FIX IT 4 Grammar Game Plan

19.3 Special Problems With Pronoun Agreement

This section will show you how to avoid some common errors that can obscure the meaning of your sentences.

WRITING COACH Online
www.phwritingcoach.com

Grammar Practice
Practice your grammar skills with Writing Coach Online.

Grammar Games
Test your knowledge of grammar in this fast-paced interactive video game.

Vague Pronoun References

One basic rule governs all of the rules for pronoun reference.

RULE 19.3.1
To avoid confusion, a pronoun requires an antecedent that is either stated or clearly understood.

The pronouns *which*, *this*, *that*, and *these* should not be used to refer to a vague or overly general idea.

In the following example, it is impossible to determine exactly what the pronoun *these* stands for because it may refer to three different groups of words.

VAGUE REFERENCE   Emma was hungry, the baby was restless, and the air conditioner was broken. **These** made our trip to the beach unpleasant.

This vague reference can be corrected in two ways. One way is to change the pronoun to an adjective that modifies a specific noun. The second way is to revise the sentence so that the pronoun *these* is eliminated.

CORRECT   Emma was hungry, the baby was restless, and the air conditioner was broken. **These conditions** made our trip to the beach unpleasant.

CORRECT   Emma's hunger, the baby's restlessness, and the air conditioner's breakdown made our trip to the beach unpleasant.

Special Problems With Pronoun Agreement

> **The personal pronouns *it*, *they*, and *you* should always have a clear antecedent.**

19.3.2

In the next example, the pronoun *it* has no clearly stated antecedent.

VAGUE REFERENCE Harold is visiting art museums next month. **It** should be very enlightening.

Again, there are two methods of correction. The first method is to replace the personal pronoun with a specific noun. The second method is to revise the sentence entirely in order to make the whole idea clear.

CORRECT Harold is visiting art museums next month. **The experience** should be very enlightening

CORRECT **Harold's visit** to art museums next month should be very enlightening

In the next examples, the pronoun *they* is used without clear antecedents.

VAGUE REFERENCE I loved tasting the Italian dish, but **they** never explained what ingredients were used.

CORRECT I loved tasting the Italian dish, but **the chef** never explained what ingredients were used.

VAGUE REFERENCE When we arrived at the mall, **they** told us which store was having a sale today.

CORRECT When we arrived at the mall, **the sales associate** told us which store was having a sale today.

RULE 19.3.3

Use *you* only when the reference is truly to the reader or listener.

| VAGUE REFERENCE | **You** couldn't understand a word Steve sang. |
| CORRECT | **We** couldn't understand a word Steve sang. |

| VAGUE REFERENCE | On the team my brother played for, **you** were expected to win all the time. |
| CORRECT | On the team my brother played for, **athletes** were expected to win all the time. |

Note About *It*: In many idiomatic expressions, the personal pronoun *it* has no specific antecedent. In statements such as "It is late," *it* is an idiom that is accepted as standard English.

See Practice 19.3A

Ambiguous Pronoun References

A pronoun is **ambiguous** if it can refer to more than one antecedent.

RULE 19.3.4

A pronoun should never refer to more than one antecedent.

In the following sentence, *he* is confusing because it can refer to either *Jim* or *Wayne*. Revise such a sentence by changing the pronoun to a noun or rephrasing the sentence entirely.

| AMBIGUOUS REFERENCE | Jim told Wayne about the game **he** attended. |
| CORRECT | Jim told Wayne about the game Jim attended. |

(Jim knew about the game.)

RULE 19.3.5

Do not repeat a personal pronoun in a sentence if it can refer to a different antecedent each time.

504 Agreement

AMBIGUOUS REPETITION When Kate asked her mother if **she** could borrow the cellphone, **she** said that **she** needed it.

CLEAR When Kate asked her mother if **she** could borrow the cellphone, **Kate** said that **she** needed it.

CLEAR When Kate asked her mother if **she** could borrow the cellphone, her **mother** said that **she** needed it **herself**.

Notice that in the first sentence above, it is unclear whether *she* is referring to Kate or to her mother. To eliminate the confusion, Kate's name was used in the second sentence. In the third sentence, the reflexive pronoun *herself* helps to clarify the meaning.

Avoiding Distant Pronoun References

A pronoun should be placed close to its antecedent.

> **A personal pronoun should always be close enough to its antecedent to prevent confusion.**

19.3.6 RULE

A distant pronoun reference can be corrected by moving the pronoun closer to its antecedent or by changing the pronoun to a noun. In the example below, *it* is too far from the antecedent *leg*.

DISTANT REFERENCE Blake shifted his weight from his injured leg. Four days ago, he had tripped, scraping himself on the pavement. Now **it** was wrapped with bandages.

CORRECT Blake shifted his weight from his injured leg. Four days ago, he had fallen, scraping himself on the pavement. Now his **leg** was wrapped with bandages.
(*Leg* replaces the pronoun *it*.)

See Practice 19.3B

Special Problems With Pronoun Agreement

PRACTICE 19.3A Correcting Vague Pronouns

Read each sentence. Then, rewrite each sentence to avoid the use of vague pronouns.

EXAMPLE   After the test, they tell you your score.

ANSWER   *After the test, the examiners tell you your score.*

1. They predict that spring will come early this year.
2. Omaya worked in the library and enjoyed it very much.
3. The movie was funny, but they could have made it shorter.
4. To train for a marathon, you must run very often.
5. On the news it mentioned that unemployment has declined.
6. You must speak Spanish to qualify for that job.
7. At the meeting, they spoke about fire safety.
8. In this book, it suggests that the funding was part of a recovery plan.
9. During colonial times, you had to grow your own crops in order to survive.
10. Before each meal, you should wash your hands.

PRACTICE 19.3B Recognizing Ambiguous Pronouns

Read each sentence. Then, rewrite each sentence to avoid the use of ambiguous pronouns.

EXAMPLE   Remove the sandwich from the bag and throw it away.

ANSWER   *Remove the sandwich from the bag and throw the bag away.*

11. Remove the stamps from the envelopes and give them to me.
12. Her mother told Hailey the news as soon as she got home.
13. Uncle Tim read to Zachary until he fell asleep.
14. Please take the towel from the drying rack and fold it.
15. Michelle told Patty that she had to leave by noon.
16. Plant the bush by the new tree and water it.
17. Mother gave Emma a dress that she had made for the dance.
18. After Mrs. Gonzalez talks to Ms. Brewer, ask her to come to my office.
19. Mary talked to Suzanne until she was ready for school.
20. Take the last egg out of the container and recycle it.

SPEAKING APPLICATION

Take turns with a partner. Use sentences from Practice 19.3A as models to say similar sentences that contain vague pronoun references. Your partner should reword each sentence to make it clearer.

WRITING APPLICATION

Use sentences 11, 12, and 15 as models to write similar sentences. Then, exchange papers with a partner. Your partner should rewrite each sentence, correcting the ambiguous pronoun references.

USING MODIFIERS

CHAPTER 20

Knowing how to use adjectives and adverbs correctly will help you make clear comparisons.

WRITE GUY Jeff Anderson, M.Ed.

WHAT DO YOU NOTICE?

Look for modifiers as you zoom in on this sentence from the essay "An American Idea" by Theodore H. White.

MENTOR TEXT

> By the time Jefferson drafted his call, men were in the field fighting for those new-learned freedoms, killing and being killed by English soldiers, the best-trained troops in the world, supplied by the world's greatest navy.

Now, ask yourself the following questions:

- To what are the English soldiers and the navy being compared?
- What are the comparative forms of the modifiers *best* and *greatest*?

The author compares the English soldiers and the navy to all other soldiers and navies by using the adjectives *best* and *greatest*. *Best* and *greatest* are the superlative forms of *good* and *great*; the superlative form compares three or more things. The comparative forms are *better* and *greater*; the comparative form compares two things.

Grammar for Writers Writers use comparisons to add to their descriptions and to state opinions. Be sure to check how many items you are comparing so that you use the correct form of a modifier.

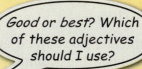

Good or best? Which of these adjectives should I use?

Whichever you think is better!

20.1 Degrees of Comparison

In the English language, there are three degrees, or forms, of most adjectives and adverbs that are used in comparisons.

Recognizing Degrees of Comparison

In order to write effective comparisons, you first need to know the three degrees.

> **RULE 20.1.1**
> The three degrees of comparison are the **positive,** the **comparative,** and the **superlative.**

The following chart shows adjectives and adverbs in each of the three degrees. Notice the three different ways that modifiers are changed to show degree: (1) by adding *-er* or *-est*, (2) by adding *more* or *most*, and (3) by using entirely different words.

DEGREES OF ADJECTIVES		
POSITIVE	COMPARATIVE	SUPERLATIVE
high	higher	highest
eager	more eager	most eager
good	better	best
DEGREES OF ADVERBS		
early	earlier	earliest
eagerly	more eagerly	most eagerly
well	better	best

WRITING COACH Online
www.phwritingcoach.com

Grammar Tutorials
Brush up on your Grammar skills with these animated videos.

Grammar Practice
Practice your grammar skills with Writing Coach Online.

Grammar Games
Test your knowledge of grammar in this fast-paced interactive video game.

See Practice 20.1A

Regular Forms

Adjectives and adverbs can be either **regular** or **irregular,** depending on how their comparative and superlative degrees are formed. The degrees of most adjectives and adverbs are formed regularly. The number of syllables in regular modifiers determines how their degrees are formed.

> **RULE 20.1.2**
> Use *-er* or *more* to form the comparative degree and *-est* or *most* to form the superlative degree of most one- and two-syllable modifiers.

Using Modifiers

EXAMPLES

noisy	noisier	noisiest
healthful	more healthful	most healthful

> All adverbs that end in *-ly* form their comparative and superlative degrees with *more* and *most*.

RULE 20.1.3

EXAMPLES

happily	more happily	most happily
painfully	more painfully	most painfully

> Use *more* and *most* to form the comparative and superlative degrees of all modifiers with three or more syllables.

RULE 20.1.4

EXAMPLES

tolerant	more tolerant	most tolerant
protective	more protective	most protective

Note About Comparisons With *Less* and *Least*: *Less* and *least* can be used to form another version of the comparative and superlative degrees of most modifiers.

EXAMPLES

tolerant	less tolerant	least tolerant
protective	less protective	least protective

See Practice 20.1B

Irregular Forms

The comparative and superlative degrees of a few commonly used adjectives and adverbs are formed in unpredictable ways.

> The irregular comparative and superlative forms of certain adjectives and adverbs must be memorized.

RULE 20.1.5

In the chart on the following page, the form of some irregular modifiers differs only in the positive degree. The modifiers *bad*, *badly*, and *ill*, for example, all have the same comparative and superlative degrees *(worse, worst)*.

IRREGULAR MODIFIERS		
POSITIVE	COMPARATIVE	SUPERLATIVE
bad, badly, ill	worse	worst
far (distance)	farther	farthest
far (extent)	further	furthest
good, well	better	best
late	later	last or latest
little (amount)	less	least
many, much	more	most

RULE 20.1.6

Bad is an adjective. Do not use it to modify an action verb. *Badly* is an adverb. Use it after an action verb but not after a linking verb.

INCORRECT Sam plays soccer **bad**.

CORRECT Sam plays soccer **badly**.

INCORRECT Maya felt **badly** about moving.

CORRECT Maya felt **bad** about moving

Note About *Good* and *Well*: *Good* is always an adjective and cannot be used as an adverb after an action verb. It can, however, be used as a predicate adjective after a linking verb.

INCORRECT Matt plays the guitar **good**.

CORRECT That guitar sounds **good**.

Well is generally an adverb. However, when *well* means "healthy," it is an adjective and can be used after a linking verb.

CORRECT Keisha did **well** on her math test.

CORRECT Keisha should be **well** soon.

See Practice 20.1C
See Practice 20.1D

510 Using Modifiers

Degrees of Comparison

PRACTICE 20.1A Recognizing Positive, Comparative, and Superlative Degrees of Comparison

Read each sentence. Then, identify the degree of comparison of the underlined word or words as *positive, comparative,* or *superlative.*

EXAMPLE The patient's fever is lower this morning.

ANSWER *comparative*

1. Amy is shorter than her older sister.
2. The weather has been perfectly beautiful all weekend.
3. This has been the wettest summer on record.
4. The Turner's house is the oldest one on our street.
5. The waters of Cedar Lake are more calm than the other nearby lakes.
6. The Snipes have the most carefully trimmed shrubs on the block.
7. The teacher greeted each student warmly.
8. Billy just blew the biggest balloon I have ever seen.
9. Lana felt better after she had talked things over with her mother.
10. The fans gave an enthusiastic roar of approval.

PRACTICE 20.1B Forming Regular Comparative and Superlative Degrees of Comparison

Read each sentence. Then, rewrite each sentence with the correct comparative or superlative degree of the modifier indicated in parentheses.

EXAMPLE She is the _____ person on the team. (tall)

ANSWER *She is the tallest person on the team.*

11. My father works _____ than I do. (hard)
12. The novel by Charles Dickens is one of the _____ I've ever read. (impressive)
13. The fussy baby will be _____ after a long nap. (agreeable)
14. The banker is the _____ person in town. (funny)
15. This is the _____ article I've read. (interesting)
16. Is Mark _____ than Rob? (fast)
17. Lori is the _____ person I know. (happy)
18. My dog is _____ than my cat. (lazy)
19. She signed her name _____ than the other members. (carefully)
20. In your opinion, which of the paintings is _____? (attractive)

SPEAKING APPLICATION

Take turns with a partner. Compare the size of objects in your classroom. Use comparative, superlative, and positive degrees of comparisons. Your partner should listen for and identify which degree of comparison you are using in each of your descriptions.

WRITING APPLICATION

Rewrite sentences 11, 15, and 16, changing the modifiers in parentheses. Then, exchange papers with a partner. Your partner should write the correct degree of the modifiers you provided.

Degrees of Comparison

PRACTICE 20.1C Supplying Irregular Comparative and Superlative Forms

Read each modifier. Then, write its irregular comparative and superlative forms.

EXAMPLE good
ANSWER *better, best*

1. bad
2. far (distance)
3. many
4. well
5. far (extent)
6. little (amount)
7. much
8. late
9. ill
10. badly

PRACTICE 20.1D Supplying Irregular Modifiers

Read each sentence. Then, fill in the blank with the form of the modifier indicated in parentheses that best completes each sentence.

EXAMPLE I took medicine, and now I feel _____ today than yesterday. (well)
ANSWER *better*

11. We won't know who received _____ votes until after the recount is made. (many)
12. I ran _____ today than I have ever run before. (far)
13. Even though there had been some rainfall, the crop yield was the _____ that farmers had seen. (bad)
14. The _____ way to keep herbs fresh is to wrap them in paper towels. (good)
15. _____ people came to the festival in the evening than during the afternoon. (many)
16. The _____ amount of dust can make me sneeze. (little)
17. The city council plans to study the problem _____ before taking a vote. (far)
18. Because Dennis had a late start, he crossed the finish line _____. (late)
19. If the weather gets _____, I plan to leave early. (bad)
20. The experiment will probably work better if you apply _____ heat. (little)

SPEAKING APPLICATION

Take turns with a partner. Say sentences with irregular comparative and superlative forms. Your partner should indicate if incorrect comparisons have been used and suggest corrections.

WRITING APPLICATION

Write pairs of sentences using each of the following modifiers correctly: *farthest* and *furthest*, *more* and *most*, *worse* and *worst*, *bad* and *badly*.

Using Modifiers

20.2 Making Clear Comparisons

The comparative and superlative degrees help you make comparisons that are clear and logical.

Writing Coach Online
www.phwritingcoach.com

Grammar Tutorials
Brush up on your Grammar skills with these animated videos.

Grammar Practice
Practice your grammar skills with Writing Coach Online.

Grammar Games
Test your knowledge of grammar in this fast-paced interactive video game.

Using Comparative and Superlative Degrees

One basic rule that has two parts covers the correct use of comparative and superlative forms.

> Use the **comparative degree** to compare two persons, places, or things. Use the **superlative degree** to compare three or more persons, places, or things.

RULE 20.2.1

The context of a sentence should indicate whether two items or more than two items are being compared.

COMPARATIVE   My sailboat is **faster** than Jerry's.

Mom's cooking is **more delicious** than Dad's.

This comedian is **less funny** than the first one.

SUPERLATIVE   My sailboat is the **fastest** on the bay.

Mom's dinners are her **most delicious** meals.

The **least funny** comedian performed first.

In informal writing, the superlative degree is sometimes used just for emphasis, without any specific comparison.

EXAMPLE   Champ has the **silkiest** coat.

Note About Double Comparisons: A double comparison is caused by using both *-er* and *more* or both *-est* and *most* to form a regular modifier or by adding an extra comparison form to an irregular modifier.

See Practice 20.2A
See Practice 20.2B
See Practice 20.2C
See Practice 20.2D

INCORRECT   It's **more** **harder** to swim than to dive.

CORRECT   It's **harder** to swim than to dive.

Making Clear Comparisons   513

PRACTICE 20.2A Recognizing When to Use Comparative and Superlative Degrees

Read each set of items. Then, tell if the comparative or superlative degree would be used to compare the items within each set.

EXAMPLE baseball, hockey, football
ANSWER superlative

1. dogs, cat, turtles
2. the classical tapes, the jazz tapes
3. the fruit, the vegetables, the flowers
4. the children's shoe store, the Italian restaurant, the new bookstore
5. the experienced runner, the beginning swimmer
6. woolen sweaters, silk scarves, leather jackets
7. a long hike, a sprint, a bike ride
8. math class, science lab
9. worn blue jeans, torn T-shirts
10. my aunt's cookbooks, my uncle's photography books, my cousin's novels

PRACTICE 20.2B Identifying Comparative and Superlative Forms

Read each sentence. Then, identify each sentence as using the *comparative* degree or *superlative* degree.

EXAMPLE Driving in the morning is better than driving at night.
ANSWER comparative

11. Sam's new computer is faster than his old one.
12. This novel is more interesting than that one.
13. The most beautiful photograph won first prize in the contest.
14. We decided to eat at the less expensive restaurant.
15. Frank's cartoons are the funniest in the student newspaper.
16. That box with the books is heavier than this one with my sweaters.
17. Jen's instructions are more detailed than Sarah's instructions.
18. The senator's speeches were the longest of the debate.
19. The least talented writer did not enter the contest.
20. My grandmother's bracelet is my most prized possession.

SPEAKING APPLICATION

Take turns with a partner. Choose two sets of items from Practice 20.2A and say sentences using the comparative or superlative degree to compare the items within each set.

WRITING APPLICATION

Review Practice 20.2B. For every sentence that uses the comparative degree, write a similar sentence that contains the superlative degree.

Using Modifiers

Making Clear Comparisons

PRACTICE 20.2C **Supplying the Comparative and Superlative Degrees of Modifiers**

Read each sentence. Then, fill in the blank with the correct form of the underlined modifier.

EXAMPLE   Biographies are good, but autobiographies are _____.

ANSWER   *better*

1. Cole is shy, but Tara is the _____ in the group.
2. All of Mrs. Erezuma's kids are successful, but Edward is the _____.
3. There are many flowers in the garden and even _____ in the greenhouse.
4. Iris is friendly, but of all students, Maddie is the _____.
5. I have little interest in opera and even _____ in jazz.
6. Jerry came later than Vanessa and was the _____ to arrive at the party.
7. We had hiked quite far, but we hadn't much _____ to hike.
8. The new restaurant is fancy, but the old one was _____.
9. Geo is faster than Ivan, but Aaron is the _____ of all.
10. Craig is better at chess than Roberto, but Nancy is the _____.

PRACTICE 20.2D **Revising Sentences to Correct Errors in Modifier Usage**

Read each sentence. Then, rewrite each sentence, correcting any errors in the usage of modifiers to make comparisons. If a sentence contains no errors, write *correct*.

EXAMPLE   The dish he prepares best than any other is roast chicken.

ANSWER   *The dish he prepares better than any other is roast chicken.*

11. Perry swam farthest than Sam.
12. The blizzard was even worst the second day.
13. The less noise in the house keeps Brigitte awake.
14. We caught the more late train before the station closed.
15. I need to develop the hypothesis more further.
16. This statue is the best thing I have ever made in class.
17. Barbie sang more better when her parents were in the audience.
18. Some people need most sleep than others.
19. This car is safer than that one.
20. The movie I saw yesterday was the more uplifting one of all.

SPEAKING APPLICATION

Take turns with a partner. Compare two television shows that you have seen recently. Your partner should listen for and identify the comparisons in your sentences.

WRITING APPLICATION

Write three sentences with errors in modifier usage. Then, exchange papers with a partner. Your partner should correct your sentences.

Making Clear Comparisons

Test Warm-Up

DIRECTIONS
Read the introduction and the passage that follows. Then, answer the questions to show that you can use and understand the function of comparative and superlative degrees in reading and writing.

Sonia wrote this paragraph about looking for a summer job. Read the paragraph and think about the changes you would suggest as a peer editor. When you finish reading, answer the questions that follow.

A Successful Job Hunt

(1) Because my family had moved recently, looking for a job this summer was most difficult than looking for a job last year. (2) I wrote a new resume that was more longer and best organized than the resume I wrote last year. (3) To begin my job search, I checked online employment Web sites, newspaper want ads, and job postings at our school. (4) After comparing all the ads, I found the online ads to be the more detailed and the print ads to be the least detailed. (5) My persistence was rewarded! (6) My summer job at a children's day camp turned out to be the most fun and the better job of all.

---

1 What change, if any, should be made in sentence 1?

A Change *most difficult* to **difficulter**

B Change *most difficult* to **more difficulter**

C Change *most* to **more**

D Make no change

2 What is the most effective way to rewrite the ideas in sentence 2?

F I wrote a new resume that was longer and better organized than the resume I wrote last year.

G I wrote a new resume that was longest and best organized than my last one.

H I wrote a new resume that was longer than the resume I wrote last year.

J I wrote a new resume that was less long and best organized than the one I wrote last year.

3 What change should be made in sentence 4?

A Change *least* to **less**

B Change *more* to **most**

C Change *more* to **better**

D Change *least* to **lesser**

4 The meaning of sentence 6 can be clarified by changing the word ***better*** to —

F worst

G worser

H good

J best

516 Test Warm-Up

Making Clear Comparisons

Using Logical Comparisons

Two common usage problems are the comparison of unrelated items and the comparison of something with itself.

Balanced Comparisons

Be certain that things being compared in a sentence are similar.

> Your sentences should only compare items of a similar kind.

The following unbalanced sentences illogically compare dissimilar things.

UNBALANCED	**Shelly's voice** is stronger than **Ted**.
CORRECT	**Shelly's voice** is stronger than **Ted's**.
UNBALANCED	The **height of the chair** is greater than the **table**.
CORRECT	The **height of the chair** is greater than the **height of the table**.

Note About *Other* and *Else* in Comparisons

Another illogical comparison results when something is inadvertently compared with itself.

> When comparing one of a group with the rest of the group, make sure that your sentence contains the word *other* or the word *else*.

Adding *other* or *else* when comparing one person or thing with a group will make the comparison clear and logical.

ILLOGICAL	Peanuts are more profitable than any crop.
	(Peanuts cannot be more profitable than themselves.)
LOGICAL	Peanuts are more profitable than any **other** crop.

See Practice 20.2E
See Practice 20.2F

Making Clear Comparisons

PRACTICE 20.2E → **Revising to Make Comparisons Balanced and Logical**

Read each sentence. Then, rewrite each sentence, correcting the unbalanced or illogical comparison.

EXAMPLE Was his essay as good as a professional writer?

ANSWER *Was his essay as good as a professional writer's?*

1. The blue boat's motor has more horsepower than the red.
2. Jeb's cat is bigger than Monica.
3. Allison's opinion of this book is even less favorable than Dan.
4. The song of a bluebird is more familiar to me than a robin.
5. Randy's car is in better condition than Arthur.
6. The pitch of a piccolo is higher than a flute.
7. Tom and Vicki's mural is much more colorful than any mural in the gallery.
8. This month's electricity bill is lower than last month.
9. Jerry's essay had better organization than William.
10. Aunt Diane's spaghetti sauce is spicier than any spaghetti sauce.

PRACTICE 20.2F → **Writing Clear Comparisons**

Read each sentence. Then, rewrite each sentence, filling in the blanks to make a comparison that is clear and logical.

EXAMPLE Your report was better than _____ report in the class.

ANSWER *Your report was better than any other report in the class.*

11. The committee's new plan needs more funding than _____ town program.
12. They spent more time talking about their vacations than _____ topic.
13. Cindy's story was longer than _____.
14. Is she a better speaker than _____ on the debate team?
15. The length of Jermaine's arm is greater than _____.
16. Mee Kim's project is more scientific than _____ in the school.
17. The pizza at that restaurant is more delicious than _____ pizza in town.
18. Niall spends more time on the tennis court than _____ in his family.
19. Taller than _____, my brother can be spotted in any crowd.
20. Cara's hamster is smaller than _____.

SPEAKING APPLICATION

Take turns with a partner. Say sentences that have unbalanced or illogical comparisons. Your partner should restate your sentences, using balanced and logical comparisons.

WRITING APPLICATION

Use sentences 11, 13, and 15 as models to write similar sentences. Then, exchange papers with a partner. Your partner should fill in the blanks to make the comparison in each sentence clear and logical.

Avoiding Comparisons With Absolute Modifiers

Some modifiers cannot be used logically to make comparisons because their meanings are *absolute*—that is, their meanings are entirely contained in the positive degree. For example, if a line is *vertical*, another line cannot be *more* vertical. Some other common absolute modifiers are *dead, entirely, fatal, final, identical, infinite, opposite, perfect, right, straight,* and *unique*.

Avoid using absolute modifiers illogically in comparisons.

INCORRECT	That house is **more opposite** ours than any other house on the street.
CORRECT	That house is **opposite** ours on the street.

Often, it is not only the word *more* or *most* that makes an absolute modifier illogical; sometimes it is best to replace the absolute modifier with one that expresses the intended meaning more precisely.

ILLOGICAL	Your facts are **more correct** than my brother's.
CORRECT	Your facts are **more reliable** than my brother's.

Sometimes an absolute modifier may overstate the meaning that you want.

ILLOGICAL	The amount of time I spent playing baseball caused **most fatal** damage to my grades.
CORRECT	The amount of time I spent playing baseball caused the **most severe** damage to my grades.

See Practice 20.2G
See Practice 20.2H

In the preceding example, *most fatal* is illogical because something is either fatal or it is not. However, even *fatal* is an overstatement. *Most severe* better conveys the intended meaning.

Making Clear Comparisons 519

Making Clear Comparisons

PRACTICE 20.2G → **Revising Sentences to Correct Comparisons Using Absolute Modifiers**

Read each sentence. Then, correct each illogical comparison by replacing the absolute modifier with more precise words.

EXAMPLE The new outfit she chose was most perfect.

ANSWER *The new outfit she chose was perfect.*

1. The explanation she gave was most entirely not true.
2. The influenza epidemic of 1918 was more fatal.
3. The test results were most final.
4. The two fingerprints are more identical.
5. The stars seem to be very infinite.
6. The houses across from each other are the most opposite in layout.
7. The birthday gift is more perfect.
8. The committee's vote was more unanimous this time.
9. That line is more straight.
10. My neighbor's flower garden is more dead.

PRACTICE 20.2H → **Revising Overstated Absolute Modifiers**

Read each sentence. Then, rewrite each sentence, revising the overstated absolute modifier.

EXAMPLE The judge's decision is more final.

ANSWER *The judge's decision is absolute.*

11. The plan to build a new bridge is completely dead.
12. The extra use of electricity more overwhelmed the system.
13. If the ending were different, this movie would be more perfect.
14. Regardless of gender, all people should be treated more equally.
15. A dictator's rule is more absolute.
16. In science, gravity is a very universal principle.
17. Didn't Romeo claim that his love for Juliet was extremely eternal?
18. In Greek mythology, humans are more mortal than gods.
19. Buffy's decorating ideas are more perfect than Jane's.
20. Although it was out of water for a few minutes, the fish is somewhat living.

SPEAKING APPLICATION

Take turns with a partner. Say sentences that incorrectly use absolute modifiers. Your partner should restate your sentences correctly.

WRITING APPLICATION

Write three sentences with overstated absolute modifiers. Then, exchange papers with a partner. Your partner should revise the overstated absolute modifiers in your sentences.

MISCELLANEOUS PROBLEMS *in* USAGE

Apply grammar usage rules to add clarity to your writing.

WRITE GUY *Jeff Anderson, M.Ed.*

WHAT DO YOU NOTICE?

Spot the negatives as you zoom in on a sentence from "Sundiata: An Epic of Old Mali: Childhood, The Lion's Awakening" by D. T. Niane, translated by G.D. Pickett.

> **MENTOR TEXT**
>
> It was no use Doua's defending the king's will which reserved the throne for Mari Djata, for the council took no account of Naré Maghan's wish.

Now, ask yourself the following questions:

- Is it correct for two negatives to appear in the same sentence?
- Why would the clause *for the council did not take no account of Naré Maghan's wish* be incorrect?

A sentence can contain two negatives if each negative appears in a separate clause. In this sentence the author uses *no* in two different clauses. The clause *for the council did not take no account of Naré Maghan's wish* would be incorrect because it contains a double negative. Only one negative word is needed to express a negative idea.

Grammar for Writers Writers can use negatives to create emphasis and express strong ideas. Check your negatives carefully to ensure you use them correctly.

I'm trying to stay positive.

Then definitely don't double your negatives!

CHAPTER 21

21.1 Negative Sentences

In English, only one *no* is needed in a sentence to deny or refuse something. You can express a negative idea with words such as *not* or *never* or with contractions such as *can't*, *couldn't*, and *wasn't*. (The ending *-n't* in a contraction is an abbreviation of *not*.)

Grammar Practice
Practice your grammar skills with Writing Coach Online.

Grammar Games
Test your knowledge of grammar in this fast-paced interactive video game.

Recognizing Double Negatives

Using two negative words in a sentence when one is sufficient is called a **double negative.** While double negatives may sometimes be used in informal speech, they should be avoided in formal English speech and writing.

> Do not use **double negatives** in formal writing.

The following chart provides examples of double negatives and two ways each can be corrected.

DOUBLE NEGATIVE	CORRECTIONS
Phil don't like no amusement parks.	Phil doesn't like amusement parks. Phil likes no amusement parks.
He won't even go to no new ones.	He won't even go to any new ones. He will go to no new ones.
He says he won't never like them.	He says he won't ever like them. He says he will never like them.

Sentences that contain more than one clause can correctly contain more than one negative word. Each clause, however, should contain only one negative word.

EXAMPLES Donna **didn't** go to the fair because she **didn't** have any money.

She **wouldn't** tell Ellen her real reason, so she said she **didn't** want to go.

See Practice 21.1A

522 **Miscellaneous Problems in Usage**

Forming Negative Sentences Correctly

There are three common ways to form negative sentences.

Using One Negative Word The most common ways to make a statement negative are to use one **negative word,** such as *never, no,* or *none,* or to add the contraction *-n't* to a helping verb.

> Use only one **negative word** in each clause.

RULE 21.1.2

DOUBLE NEGATIVE	The storm **didn't** damage **nothing**.
PREFERRED	The storm **didn't** damage **anything**.
	The storm damaged **nothing**.

Using *But* in a Negative Sense When *but* means "only," it usually acts as a negative. Do not use it with another negative word.

DOUBLE NEGATIVE	There **wasn't but** one sock left in my drawer.
PREFERRED	There was **but** one sock left in my drawer.
	There was **only** one sock left in my drawer.

Using *Barely, Hardly,* and *Scarcely* Each of these words is negative. If you use one of these words with another negative word, you create a double negative.

> Do not use *barely, hardly,* or *scarcely* with another negative word.

RULE 21.1.3

DOUBLE NEGATIVE	She **hadn't barely** mastered the new language.
PREFERRED	She **had barely** mastered the new language.
DOUBLE NEGATIVE	He **couldn't hardly** see beyond the hill.
PREFERRED	He **could hardly** see beyond the hill.
DOUBLE NEGATIVE	We **couldn't scarcely** believe our eyes.
PREFERRED	We **could scarcely** believe our eyes.

See Practice 21.1B
See Practice 21.1C

Using Negatives to Create Understatement

Sometimes a writer wants to express an idea indirectly, either to minimize the importance of the idea or to draw attention to it. One such technique is called **understatement.**

> **RULE 21.1.4**
>
> Understatement can be achieved by using a negative word and a word with a negative prefix, such as *un-, in-, im-, dis-,* and *under-*.

EXAMPLES Bill did **not underestimate** Norm's speed.

My mom is **hardly inexperienced** at volleyball.

It's **not impossible** that we'll have a good time at the party.

These examples show that the writer is praising the people or things he or she is discussing. In the first example, the writer states that Bill expected Norm's speed. In the second example, the writer states that mom is experienced at volleyball. In the third example, the writer states that the people involved may have a good time at the party.

If you choose to use understatement, be sure to use it carefully so that you do not sound critical when you wish to praise.

EXAMPLES Mary does **not dislike** her new uniform.

Even though it was not the color or style she preferred, she decided it was **not too bad**.

In both examples above, the writer is actually making a negative statement. In the first example, although the writer "does not dislike" her uniform, he or she clearly doesn't like it very much, either. In the second example, the writer seems to think that, although it is not the color or style she prefers, it is all right.

See Practice 21.1D

524 **Miscellaneous Problems in Usage**

Negative Sentences

PRACTICE 21.1A Recognizing Sentences With Double Negatives

Read each sentence. Then, if the sentence contains a double negative, write the double negative. If the sentence is correct, write *correct*.

EXAMPLE Mark hasn't eaten no food today.

ANSWER *hasn't, no*

1. Our car won't not start in cold weather.
2. The singer wouldn't cancel her concert because she couldn't disappoint her fans.
3. My sister announced that she won't never wash our dog.
4. The rain wouldn't stop, so we couldn't go to the beach.
5. The tennis players couldn't compete in no championship this year.
6. Sam wasn't visiting no museums on the trip.
7. We didn't complete the project, because we didn't have time.
8. The council members won't announce no vote on the proposal today.
9. Tina says she won't never go to the park with her sisters.
10. Our visitors didn't call because they didn't have our phone number.

PRACTICE 21.1B Revising Sentences to Avoid Double Negatives

Read each sentence. Then, rewrite each sentence to correct the double negative.

EXAMPLE You shouldn't have told nobody where I was going.

ANSWER *You shouldn't have told anybody where I was going.*

11. We couldn't hardly make our way through the brush.
12. Are you sure you don't have but one day free this week?
13. There wasn't no cloud in the sky.
14. Vanessa didn't have no trouble choosing a topic.
15. The article didn't include no biographical information.
16. I don't have room for but one elective in my schedule.
17. Casey can't never walk away from a stray animal.
18. There wasn't scarcely enough breeze to ruffle a leaf.
19. Ravi didn't go nowhere last night.
20. Stavros hasn't eaten none of his food.

SPEAKING APPLICATION

Take turns with a partner. Say sentences that contain double negatives. Your partner should listen to and correct your sentences.

WRITING APPLICATION

In Practice 21.1A, rewrite the sentences that are incorrect in order to eliminate the double negative. Read your sentences to a partner. Your partner should tell if your sentences are correct.

Negative Sentences

PRACTICE 21.1C Rewriting Sentences to Avoid Double Negatives

Read each sentence. Then, rewrite each sentence to correct the double negative.

EXAMPLE Lauren hadn't but one dress to wear.

ANSWER Lauren *had only* one dress to wear.

1. The shoppers hadn't barely reached the check-out counter in the store.
2. There weren't but two cars available to rent.
3. The new information didn't do nothing to change her mind.
4. The painter can't never work on Saturdays during the summer.
5. They didn't hardly finish the test before the end of class.
6. The hikers won't never reach the end of the trail today.
7. Our friends aren't never ready in time for the movies.
8. The delighted student couldn't scarcely understand the good news.
9. The employees shouldn't have no complaints about the contract.
10. There weren't but three dancers waiting to audition.

PRACTICE 21.1D Recognizing Understatement

Read each sentence. Then, if the sentence expresses understatement, write *understatement* and the words that create the understatement. If the sentence does not express understatement, write *No understatement expressed*.

EXAMPLE Melissa isn't so unentertaining.

ANSWER understatement; *isn't, unentertaining*

11. Simone won't impress Jack.
12. The lead electric guitarist is hardly untalented.
13. The novelist is never uninteresting when she teaches.
14. Mr. Lee isn't wearing a disguise.
15. We did not misunderstand the debaters' statements.
16. The voters weren't unmoved by the election results.
17. I don't like impersonating superheroes.
18. The dog can't understand my commands.
19. Our excited neighbors are not underwhelmed by the good news.
20. It's not unlikely that Ms. Harvey will be mayor.

SPEAKING APPLICATION

Take turns with a partner. Use sentences from Practice 21.1C to say similar sentences with double negatives. Your partner should repeat your sentences, correcting the double negatives.

WRITING APPLICATION

Use Practice 21.1D to write similar sentences, some that contain understatement and some that don't. Exchange papers with a partner. In the sentences that use understatement, your partner should underline the words that express the understatement.

Test Warm-Up

Negative Sentences

DIRECTIONS
Read the introduction and the passage that follows. Then, answer the questions to show that you can use and understand the function of using negatives to create understatement in reading and writing.

Carl wrote this paragraph for an editorial in his school newspaper. Read the paragraph and think about the changes you would suggest as a peer editor. When you finish reading, answer the questions that follow.

Longer School Days

(1) Extending the school day until four o'clock is barely as unwanted as it first sounds. (2) There are many reasons why a longer school day would benefit all students. (3) My fellow students are capable of understanding that a good education is an asset in today's economy. (4) Learning more each school day is an unpopular approach to providing a better education for everyone. (5) It's likely that this will be the solution in the near future.

1 How could sentence 1 be rewritten, yet still create understatement?

A Extending the school day until four o'clock is barely as unimpeachable as it first sounds.

B Extending the school day until four o'clock is hardly as unpleasant as it first sounds.

C Extending the school day until four o'clock is hardly as flattering as it first sounds.

D Extending the school day until four o'clock is scarcely as understandable as it first sounds.

2 What change, if any, should be made in sentence 3 to create understatement?

F Change *are capable* to **are not incapable**

G Change *are capable* to **are not capable**

H Change *are capable* to **are not ever capable**

J Make no change

3 What change should be made in sentence 4 to create understatement?

A Change *providing* to **not providing**

B Insert **Not** before *Learning*

C Change *unpopular* to **popular**

D Insert **scarcely** before *an unpopular*

4 How should sentence 5 be revised to create understatement?

F It's not likely that this will be the solution in the near future.

G It's not unlikely that this will be the solution in the near future.

H It's unlikely that this will be the solution in the near future.

J It's never likely that this will be the solution in the near future.

21.2 Common Usage Problems

(1) a, an The use of the article *a* or *an* is determined by the sound of the word that follows it. *A* is used before consonant sounds, while *an* is used before vowel sounds. Words beginning with *h-*, *o-*, or *u-* may have either a consonant or a vowel sound.

EXAMPLES
a hairstyle (*h* sound)
a one-minute exercise (*w* sound)
a unit (*y* sound)
an honorable person (no *h* sound)
an open door (*o* sound)
an understanding person (*u* sound)

(2) accept, except *Accept,* a verb, means "to receive." *Except,* is usually a preposition meaning "other than."

VERB   She **accepted** the gift generously.
PREPOSITION She gave everyone a gift **except** me.

(3) adapt, adopt *Adapt* means "to change." *Adopt* means "to take as one's own."

EXAMPLES The dog **adapted** to its new home.
People often **adopt** animals from shelters.

(4) affect, effect *Affect* is almost always a verb meaning "to influence." *Effect,* usually a noun, means "a result." Sometimes, *effect* is a verb meaning "to bring about" or "to cause."

VERB The storm **affected** the parade.
NOUN It had the **effect** of reducing the size of the crowd.
VERB The leader **effected** a change in the program.

(5) aggravate *Aggravate* means "to make worse." Avoid using this word to mean "annoy."

INCORRECT The grade I received on the test **aggravated** me.
PREFERRED That grade is **aggravating** my risk of failing.

528 Miscellaneous Problems in Usage

(6) ain't *Ain't,* which was originally a contraction for *am not,* is no longer considered acceptable in standard English. Always use *am not,* and never use *ain't.* The exception is in certain instances of dialogue.

(7) all ready, already *All ready,* which consists of two separate words used as an adjective, means "ready." *Already,* which is an adverb, means "by or before this time" or "even now."

ADJECTIVE	I am **all ready** to go scuba diving.
ADVERB	I have **already** checked my gear.

(8) all right, alright *Alright* is a nonstandard spelling. Make sure you use the two-word form.

INCORRECT	Even though I wasn't well yesterday, I'm feeling **alright** today.
PREFERRED	Even though I wasn't well yesterday, I'm feeling **all right** today.

(9) all together, altogether *All together* means "together as a single group." *Altogether* means "completely" or "in all."

EXAMPLES	Fish in schools travel **all together**.
	They swam in **altogether** fascinating patterns.

(10) among, between Both of these words are prepositions. *Among* shows a connection between three or more items. *Between* generally shows a connection between two items.

EXAMPLES	The debating club argued **among** themselves about which team would face the competition.
	The competition **between** Central and East Side promised to be fierce.

See Practice 21.2A

(11) anxious This adjective implies uneasiness, worry, or fear. Do not use it as a substitute for *eager.*

INCORRECT	The band was **anxious** for the concert to begin.
PREFERRED	The musicians were **anxious** about their performance.

(12) anyone, any one, everyone, every one *Anyone* and *everyone* mean "any person" or "every person." *Any one* means "any single person (or thing)"; *every one* means "every single person (or thing)."

EXAMPLES

Anyone at the school is able to join a club.

Any one of the clubs might be interesting and rewarding to join.

Everyone who is interested in sports can be on a team.

Every one of the players has to practice every day.

(13) anyway, anywhere, everywhere, nowhere, somewhere These adverbs should never end in -s.

INCORRECT I know my homework is hiding **somewheres** in my locker.

PREFERRED I know my homework is hiding **somewhere** in my locker.

(14) as Do not use the conjunction *as* to mean "because" or "since."

INCORRECT Sue didn't make the team **as** she couldn't run fast enough.

PREFERRED Sue didn't make the team **because** she couldn't run fast enough.

(15) as to *As to* is awkward. Replace it with *about*.

INCORRECT The miners had no worries **as to** the amount of iron ore in the mountain.

PREFERRED The miners had no worries **about** the amount of iron ore in the mountain.

(16) at Do not use *at* after *where*. Simply eliminate *at*.

INCORRECT Do you know **where** we are **at**?

PREFERRED Do you know **where** we are?

Miscellaneous Problems in Usage

(17) at, about Avoid using *at* with *about*. Simply eliminate *at* or *about*.

INCORRECT	Phil is going to try to go to bed **at about** 10:00.
PREFERRED	Phil is going to try to go to bed **at** 10:00.

(18) awful, awfully *Awful* is used informally to mean that something is "extremely bad." *Awfully* is used informally to mean "very." Both words are overused and should be replaced with more descriptive words. In standard English speech and writing, *awful* should only be used to mean "inspiring fear or awe in someone."

OVERUSED	That movie was really **awful**.
PREFERRED	That movie was really **terrible**.
OVERUSED	The fighters seemed **awfully** fierce.
PREFERRED	The fighters seemed **very** fierce.
OVERUSED	The howling winds were **awful**.
PREFERRED	The howling winds were **scary**.

(19) awhile, a while *Awhile* is an adverb that means "for a short time." *A while*, which is a noun, means "a period of time." It is usually used after the preposition *for* or *after*.

ADVERB	Lie down **awhile** and rest.
	Angie waited **awhile** to watch the votes being counted.
NOUN	If you can lie still for **a while**, your headache will go away.
	Angie stayed for **a while** to see who would win.

(20) beat, win When you *win*, you "achieve a victory in something." When you *beat* someone or something, you "overcome an opponent."

INCORRECT	Our team **won** all the others in the meet.
PREFERRED	Our team **beat** all the others in the meet.
	Our team wants to **win** the tournament.

See Practice 21.2B

Common Usage Problems

PRACTICE 21.2A Recognizing Usage Problems 1–10

Read each sentence. Then, choose the correct item to complete each sentence.

EXAMPLE Shannon said that she (ain't, isn't) going to watch the game.

ANSWER *isn't*

1. The new tax bill could (affect, effect) all employed workers.
2. The animals (adopted, adapted) to their new surroundings.
3. The press has given (all together, altogether) too much attention to the candidate's family.
4. The coach's pregame speech had a great (effect, affect) on the team's performance.
5. After an hour of instruction, we decided that we were (all ready, already) to take the test.
6. Kevin wouldn't (except, accept) the reward money for finding the lost wallet.
7. I packed both an orange and (a, an) apple.
8. Arturo and I shared the sandwiches (among, between) us.
9. Is it (alright, all right) if I take my dog to the park?
10. The smoke in the building (aggravated, annoyed) my sinus condition.

PRACTICE 21.2B Recognizing Usage Problems 11–20

Read each sentence. Then, choose the correct item to complete each sentence.

EXAMPLE Maggie didn't recognize (anyone, any one) of the teachers.

ANSWER *any one*

11. Once in (awhile, a while) a great thinker comes along to challenge traditional ideas.
12. Mary's ideas (about, as to) a theme for the party sounded exciting.
13. Naomi baked (everyone, every one) of these casseroles.
14. Megan did chores all day long and felt (awfully, extremely) satisfied with her accomplishments.
15. Desmond earned the trophy after (winning, beating) every opponent handily.
16. We will meet you (at about, at) noon.
17. Lucinda was so (eager, anxious) about her first driving lesson that she felt queasy.
18. My brother couldn't go on the ride (as, because) he was not tall enough.
19. (Everyone, Every one) piled into the car.
20. I need to hurry because I have (somewheres, somewhere) important to go.

SPEAKING APPLICATION

Take turns with a partner. Choose the pair of words from either sentence 1 or sentence 8, and tell your partner your choices. Your partner should say two sentences, using both words correctly.

WRITING APPLICATION

Write two sentences that include usage problems. Exchange papers with a partner. Your partner should correct your sentences.

(21) because Do not use *because* after the phrase *the reason*. Say "The reason is that" or reword the sentence.

INCORRECT The **reason** I am sad **is because** our trip to the islands was canceled.

PREFERRED I am sad **because** our trip to the islands was canceled.

(22) being as, being that Avoid using either of these expressions. Use *because* instead.

INCORRECT **Being as** the sky was cloudy, we did not go to the beach.

PREFERRED **Because** the sky was cloudy, we did not go to the beach.

(23) beside, besides *Beside* means "at the side of" or "close to." *Besides* means "in addition to."

EXAMPLES We picnicked **beside** the mountain stream.

No one **besides** ourselves knew we were there.

(24) bring, take *Bring* means "to carry from a distant place to a nearer one." *Take* means "to carry from a near place to a far one."

EXAMPLES Please **bring** me that pile of books.

I'll **take** them back after I've used them.

(25) can, may Use *can* to mean "have the ability to." Use *may* to mean "have permission to" or "to be likely to."

ABILITY Some rain-forest animals **can** climb trees.
PERMISSION Everyone **may** come to my party.
POSSIBILITY There **may** be a chance to save this wildlife habitat.

(26) clipped words Avoid using clipped or shortened words, such as *gym* and *photo* in formal writing.

INFORMAL Where are the **photos** of my family?

FORMAL Where are the **photographs** of my family?

Common Usage Problems

(27) different from, different than *Different from* is preferred in standard English.

INCORRECT	Geometry was **different than** what I expected.
PREFERRED	Geometry was **different from** what I expected.

(28) doesn't, don't Do not use *don't* with third-person singular subjects. Instead, use *doesn't*.

INCORRECT	This machine **don't** work well.
PREFERRED	This machine **doesn't** work well.

(29) done *Done* is the past participle of the verb *do*. It should always take a helping verb.

INCORRECT	Billy **done** his assignment.
PREFERRED	Billy **had done** his assignment.

(30) due to *Due to* means "caused by" and should be used only when the words *caused by* can be logically substituted.

INCORRECT	**Due to** the lack of rainfall, my garden didn't grow.
PREFERRED	My garden's failure was **due to** the lack of rainfall.

See Practice 21.2C

(31) each other, one another These expressions usually are interchangeable. At times, however, *each other* is more logically used in reference to only two and *one another* in reference to more than two.

EXAMPLES	The animals and plants in an ecosystem often benefit **one another**.
	Bees and flowers benefit **each other** when bees pollinate flowers.

(32) farther, further *Farther* refers to distance. *Further* means "additional" or "to a greater degree or extent."

EXAMPLES	Margaret walked much **farther** than Henry.
	Once he yelled at her to stop, she listened no **further**.

Miscellaneous Problems in Usage

(33) fewer, less Use *fewer* with things that can be counted. Use *less* with qualities and quantities that cannot be counted.

EXAMPLES	**fewer** assignments, **less** homework

(34) get, got, gotten These forms of the verb *get* are acceptable in standard English, but a more specific word is preferable.

INCORRECT	**get** thirsty, **got** water, **have gotten** cooler
PREFERRED	**become** thirsty, **drank** water, **have become** cooler

(35) gone, went *Gone* is the past participle of the verb *go* and is used only with a helping verb. *Went* is the past tense of *go* and is never used with a helping verb.

INCORRECT	My brothers **gone** to the store today.
	They really should **have went** yesterday.
PREFERRED	My brothers **went** to the store today.
	They really should **have gone** yesterday.

(36) good, lovely, nice Replace these overused words with a more specific adjective.

WEAK	**good** garden, **lovely** flowers, **nice** color
BETTER	**beautiful** garden, **tall** flowers, **brilliant red** color

(37) in, into *In* refers to position. *Into* suggests motion.

EXAMPLES	My notebook is **in** my backpack.
	I'll put my books **into** my locker.

(38) irregardless Avoid this word in formal speech and writing. Instead, use *regardless*.

(39) just When you use *just* as an adverb to mean "no more than," place it immediately before the word it modifies.

INCORRECT	Bill **just** received one prize at the meet.
PREFERRED	Bill received **just** one prize at the meet.

(40) kind of, sort of Do not use these phrases in formal speech. Instead, use *rather* or *somewhat*.

See Practice 21.2D

Common Usage Problems

Common Usage Problems

PRACTICE 21.2C **Recognizing Usage Problems 21–30**

Read each sentence. Then, choose the correct item to complete each sentence.

EXAMPLE (May, Can) I bring something to the party?

ANSWER *May*

1. The real painting looks quite different (from, than) the reproductions.
2. I (can, may) sleep through any type of noise.
3. I (brought, took) some sandwiches to eat at the game.
4. (Because, Being that) we overslept, Mom drove us to school.
5. Was there anyone (beside, besides) Jerry who saw the lunar eclipse?
6. One reason to eat fruit (is that, is because) fruit is nutritious.
7. Carmelo (doesn't, don't) plan to enter the contest.
8. My camera's special lens helps me take great (photos, photographs).
9. Ms. Lopez said that everyone (done, had done) a great job preparing for the debate.
10. The coach sat (besides, beside) my brother on the bench.

PRACTICE 21.2D **Revising Sentences to Correct Usage Problems 31–40**

Read each sentence. Then, rewrite each sentence, correcting the errors in usage.

EXAMPLE Sara's costume is sort of different from Evelyn's.

ANSWER *Sara's costume is somewhat different from Evelyn's.*

11. We cannot hold the class if less than six students sign up.
12. We had went at least six miles out of our way.
13. Will you travel further tonight?
14. Each of my brothers got a new bike for his birthday.
15. I will buy a new coat irregardless of the cost.
16. The firefighter rushed in the burning building and saved the family pet.
17. The freshly baked bread gave off a good aroma.
18. I just have one thing to say to you: Hello!
19. There was fewer participation in the fishing derby this year.
20. The three friends wrote letters to each other.

SPEAKING APPLICATION

Take turns with a partner. Say sentences with usage problems. Your partner should correct each of your sentences.

WRITING APPLICATION

Take turns with a partner. Use two sentences from Practice 21.2D as models to write similar sentences with usage problems. Exchange papers with a partner. Your partner should correct your sentences.

Common Usage Problems

(41) lay, lie The verb *lay* means "to put or set (something) down." Its principal parts—*lay, laying, laid, laid*—are followed by a direct object. The verb *lie* means "to recline." Its principal parts—*lie, lying, lay, lain*—are not followed by a direct object.

LAY Please **lay** the luggage in the station wagon.

The driver **is laying** the bags next to each other.

The passengers **laid** their carry-on bags next to them.

The luggage will stay where the driver **has laid** it.

LIE After their trip, the passengers just wanted to **lie** down.

They **are lying** on the beach and listening to music.

The child **lay** down across her father's lap.

She hadn't **lain** down all night.

(42) learn, teach *Learn* means "to receive knowledge." *Teach* means "to give knowledge."

EXAMPLES A person has to **learn** many skills to live in the Arctic.

It's best to be **taught** by experienced explorers.

(43) leave, let *Leave* means "to allow to remain." *Let* means "to permit."

INCORRECT **Leave** my little brother go!

PREFERRED **Let** my little brother play!

(44) like, as *Like* is a preposition meaning "similar to" or "such as." It should not be used in place of the conjunction *as*.

INCORRECT We painted **like** we were skilled artists.

PREFERRED We painted **as if** we were skilled artists.

We painted **like** skilled artists.

(45) loose, lose *Loose* is usually an adjective or part of such idioms as *cut loose, turn loose,* or *break loose. Lose* is always a verb and usually means "to miss from one's possession."

EXAMPLES Please don't let your dog **loose** in the neighborhood.

If you don't walk her on a leash, you might **lose** her.

(46) maybe, may be *Maybe* is an adverb meaning "perhaps." *May be* is a helping verb connected to a main verb.

ADVERB	**Maybe** I'll be able to get a good grade on this test.
VERB	I **may be** asking my teacher for some extra help.

(47) of Do not use *of* after a helping verb such as *should*, *would*, *could*, or *must*. Use *have* instead. Do not use *of* after *outside*, *inside*, *off*, and *atop*. Simply eliminate *of*.

INCORRECT	A good sheepdog **would of** protected the sheep.
PREFERRED	A good sheepdog **would have** protected the sheep.

(48) OK, O.K., okay In informal writing, *OK*, *O.K.*, and *okay* are acceptably used to mean "all right." Do not use them in standard English speech or writing, however.

INFORMAL	Sam said today's lunch choice was **okay**.
PREFERRED	Sam said today's lunch choice was **tasty**.

(49) only *Only* should be placed immediately before the word it modifies. Placing it elsewhere can lead to confusion.

EXAMPLES	**Only** Rich wanted to go to the gym.
	(No one else wanted to go.)
	Rich **only** wanted to go to the gym.
	(He didn't want to do anything else.)

(50) ought Do not use *ought* with *have* or *had*.

INCORRECT	We **hadn't ought** to have cut down the trees.
PREFERRED	We **ought not** to have cut down the trees.

See Practice 21.2E

(51) outside of Do not use this expression to mean "besides" or "except."

INCORRECT	Many birds are found nowhere **outside of** tropical rain forests.
PREFERRED	Many birds are found nowhere **except** in tropical rain forests.

Miscellaneous Problems in Usage

(52) plurals that do not end in -s The English plurals of certain nouns from Greek and Latin are formed as they were in their original language. Words such as *criteria, media,* and *phenomena* are plural. Their singular forms are *criterion, medium,* and *phenomenon*.

INCORRECT	Today, the news **media** includes newspapers, television, radio, and the Internet.
PREFERRED	Today, the news **media** include newspapers, television, radio, and the Internet.
	Today, newspapers, television, radio, and the Internet are all part of the news **media**.

(53) precede, proceed *Precede* means "to go before." *Proceed* means "to move or go forward."

EXAMPLES	Jamie **preceded** Mary Beth into the library.
	The two girls then **proceeded** to begin work on their history project.

(54) principal, principle As an adjective, *principal* means "most important" or "chief." As a noun, it means "a person who has controlling authority," as in a school. *Principle* is always a noun that means "a fundamental law."

ADJECTIVE	Evergreens are the **principal** trees on the mountain.
NOUN	Ms. Rodriguez is the **principal** in our school.
NOUN	The student council drew up the **principles** for improved sportsmanship at games.

(55) real *Real* means "authentic." In formal writing, avoid using *real* to mean "very" or "really."

INCORRECT	My dad was **real** disappointed with the new recipe.
PREFERRED	My dad was **deeply** disappointed with the new recipe.

(56) says *Says* should not be used as a substitute for *said*.

INCORRECT	"Why," Ben **says**, "do we have to go home now?"
PREFERRED	"Why," Ben **said**, "do we have to go home now?"

Common Usage Problems

(57) seen *Seen* is a past participle and must be used with a helping verb.

INCORRECT	The judge **seen** a number of contestants.
PREFERRED	The judge **had seen** a number of contestants.

(58) set, sit *Set* means "to put (something) in a certain place." Its principal parts—*set, setting, set, set*—are usually followed by a direct object. *Sit* means "to be seated." Its principal parts—*sit, sitting, sat, sat*—are never followed by a direct object.

SET	Please **set** the flowers on the table.
	Mimi **is setting** the table for dinner.
	I'd like you to **set** the candles on the table.
	I **have set** the timer to ring at 6:30.
SIT	My mom **will sit** at the head of the table.
	We **will be sitting** at the big table tonight.
	Tony **sat** quietly and waited for dinner.
	We **have sat** in the same places at the table for years.

(59) so Avoid using *so* when you mean "so that."

INCORRECT	I use sunglasses **so** I can see in the sunlight.
PREFERRED	I use sunglasses **so that** I can see in the sunlight.

(60) than, then Use *than* in comparisons. Use *then* as an adverb to refer to time.

EXAMPLES	I'm taller **than** my older sister.
	She measured us once; **then**, she measured us again.

(61) that, which, who Use these relative pronouns in the following ways: *that* and *which* refer to things; *who* refers only to people.

EXAMPLES	I saw the humpback whales **that** you described.
	Their mouths, **which** are huge, take in tons of water.
	The marine biologist, **who** studies whales, told us about the whales' feeding behavior.

Miscellaneous Problems in Usage

Common Usage Problems

(62) their, there, they're *Their,* a possessive pronoun, always modifies a noun. *There* can be used either as an expletive at the beginning of a sentence or as an adverb showing place or direction. *They're* is a contraction of *they are.*

PRONOUN	The actors spent a lot of time memorizing **their** parts in the new play.
EXPLETIVE	**There** are so many actors in the play that the rehearsals last a long time.
ADVERB	The table and chairs will be placed over **there** on the stage.
CONTRACTION	**They're** going to be used in several scenes in the play.

(63) them Do not use *them* as a substitute for *those.*

INCORRECT	**Them** sandwiches are delicious.
PREFERRED	**Those** sandwiches are delicious.

(64) to, too, two *To,* begins a prepositional phrase or an infinitive. *Too,* an adverb, modifies adjectives and other adverbs and means "very" or "also." *Two* is a number.

PREPOSITION	**to** the moon, back **to** Earth
INFINITIVE	**to** see the stars, **to** find the constellations
ADVERB	**too** far away, **too** hard to see
NUMBER	**two** space probes, **two** astronauts

(65) when, where Do not use *when* or *where* immediately after a linking verb. Do not use *where* in place of *that.*

INCORRECT	Block parties are **when** you can meet your neighbors.
	In the street is **where** everyone meets.
PREFERRED	Block parties are **occasions** to meet your neighbors.
	In the street is **the place** that everyone meets.

See Practice 21.2F

Common Usage Problems

PRACTICE 21.2E **Recognizing Usage Problems 41–50**

Read each sentence. Then, choose the correct item to complete each sentence.

EXAMPLE Yesterday, I saw a jellyfish (laying, lying) on the beach.

ANSWER *lying*

1. If you don't sew up your pocket, you may (lose, loose) all of your money.
2. Because I had (laid, lay, lain) my drink in the sun, all the ice cubes melted.
3. Who (learned, taught) you that magic trick?
4. He acted (like, as if) he was sleepy.
5. Because bad weather is predicted, there (maybe, may be) very few people at the game.
6. Of all the people in the audience, (Tatum only, only Tatum) knew the answer.
7. As my dog, Spot, and I approached the house, Mom said, "(Let, Leave) the dog outside."
8. The Supreme Court ruled that it is (okay, legal) to delay paying your taxes.
9. Hassan knew that he should (of, have) studied harder for the test.
10. We (ought to have, should have) paid for our own tickets.

PRACTICE 21.2F **Revising Sentences to Correct Usage Problems 51–65**

Read each sentence. Then, rewrite each sentence correcting the usage errors.

EXAMPLE Yesterday, it was to hot to do any work.

ANSWER *Yesterday, it was too hot to do any work.*

11. My parents said that their on there way home.
12. Only three people, outside of my uncle, know where the treasure is buried.
13. The man that wrote the book must be a genius.
14. Please put them candles on the table.
15. Four o'clock is when the club meets.
16. Reliant Stadium is where the Houston Texans play football.
17. I can see them houses across the water.
18. Many people had proceeded us, leaving their footprints in the sand.
19. Luke was real hungry after completing the race.
20. Mary seen the play twice already.

SPEAKING APPLICATION

Reread the sentences in Practice 21.2E and your completed sentences. Discuss with a partner which sentences were hard to complete. Explain why those sentences were challenging.

WRITING APPLICATION

Use sentences 13, 17, 18, and 19 as models to write similar sentences with usage problems. Exchange papers with a partner. Your partner should correct your sentences.

Miscellaneous Problems in Usage

Cumulative Review Chapters 16–21

PRACTICE 1 Combining and Varying Sentences

Read the sentences. Then, rewrite each sentence according to the instructions in parentheses.

1. He studied anatomy and physiology. He learned how to categorize and label the parts of the human body. (Create a compound sentence; use a conjunction.)
2. The class visited Philadelphia. They saw the Liberty Bell. They attended a Philadelphia Phillies baseball game. (Create a complex sentence; include a compound direct object.)
3. The explorers approached the Mississippi River. They discovered a river too high to ford. (Create a complex sentence.)
4. Dinosaur bones are on display at the museum. Other ancient species of animals are also on display. (Create a compound sentence.)
5. The football team practiced on the field. (Invert the subject-verb order.)
6. Brian is my little brother. He is eight years younger than I am. (Create a complex sentence)
7. Elizabeth volunteers at an animal shelter. She also works at a dog grooming shop to help animals. (Create a compound verb; start the sentence with an infinitive.)
8. Elise was worried about making a good impression. The woman interviewing her for the job thought she was great. (Create a compound sentence.)
9. Sandra is captain of the swim team and has swum for years. She won the state title in 2009. (Create a complex sentence)
10. Across the sky flew a flock of geese. (Invert the subject-verb order.)

PRACTICE 2 Revising Pronoun and Verb Usage

Read the sentences. Then, revise each sentence to correct pronoun and verb usage. You may need to reorder, add, or eliminate words.

1. Only someone who likes magic will enjoy their visit to a magic show.
2. Whom, do you think, is the best debater on the debate team?
3. Ben and Adam always asks permission before inviting friends over.
4. Somebody has left their purse on the seat of the city bus.
5. The Math Club, as well as the Chess Club, meet after school on Tuesdays.
6. Not only the students but also their parents has been pleased with the new schedule.
7. Mom left the decision up to him and I.
8. To who did you give the extra ticket?
9. Chris made a shot in the final seconds, and the crowd cheered their approval.
10. He didn't seem to worry much about we kids.

PRACTICE 3 Revising for Correct Use of Active and Passive Voice

Read the sentences. Then, revise each sentence to be in the active voice. You may need to reorder, add, or delete words.

1. Lisa's hair was cut by a well-known stylist.
2. The national anthem is being sung by Jason at the game tomorrow.
3. The track was being swept by the coach before the track meet.
4. The accident was witnessed by Mrs. Thompson's neighbor.
5. The squirrels were being chased by dogs.

Continued on next page ▶

Cumulative Review

Cumulative Review Chapters 16–21

PRACTICE 4 Correcting Errors in Pronoun and Verb Usage

Read the sentences. Then, revise them, correcting all errors in agreement, verb usage, and pronoun usage. If a sentence is already correct, write *correct*.

1. Samantha and her cousins had went to the zoo to see the giant pandas the week before.
2. Neither Lucy nor Cara has choosed their classes for next semester.
3. Miguel learned his brother how to skate.
4. It was her who was asked to gives the speech at the graduation ceremony.
5. After not seeing they for a few days, we realized that her and Maria had moved away.
6. That piece of cake was for me, not him.
7. You didn't tell we that them were here first.
8. I wonder what he could have said to she.
9. "You have to ask you," Dad said, "what would yourself do in his situation?"
10. If any one of your friend needs a ride to dance rehearsal, they can call me.

PRACTICE 5 Using Comparative and Superlative Forms Correctly

Read the sentences. Then, write the appropriate comparative or superlative degree of the modifier in parentheses.

1. Between the two, Juan is the (good) musician.
2. Rome is (far) from Dublin than from London.
3. I think New York is the (exciting) city in the world.
4. She is probably the (cheerful) person I know.
5. Mt. Everest is (high) than Mt. Fuji.

PRACTICE 6 Avoiding Double Negatives

Read the sentences. Then, choose the word in parentheses that makes each sentence negative without forming a double negative.

1. Sadly, I didn't have (any, none) money left to contribute.
2. Michelle won't talk to (nobody, anybody) about the surprise.
3. She hadn't studied, so she (could, couldn't) hardly finish her test in the time allotted.
4. They aren't going (nowhere, anywhere) special for summer vacation this year.
5. Students are permitted to use neither their books (nor, or) their notes during the exam.

PRACTICE 7 Avoiding Usage Problems

Read the sentences. Then, choose the correct expression to complete each sentence.

1. Rachel's birthday (preceded, proceeded) John's by one day.
2. Laura's grandmother wears a hearing aid (so, so that) she can understand the conversation.
3. Steve is more athletic (than, then) his brother.
4. (Lay, Lie) down on the beach blanket.
5. Most first graders can (learn, teach) to read.
6. (Let, Leave) me go see why the dog is barking at the front door.
7. He is likely to (loose, lose) his way.
8. The storm will (affect, effect) their plans.
9. The (principal, principle) was newly hired.
10. Sam was (all ready, already) late to lunch.

CAPITALIZATION

Use capitalization to present ideas clearly to your readers.

WRITE GUY *Jeff Anderson, M.Ed.*

WHAT DO YOU NOTICE?

Focus on capitalization as you zoom in on these sentences from the story "The Monkey's Paw" by W. W. Jacobs.

MENTOR TEXT

> "Sounds like the *Arabian Nights*," said Mrs. White, as she rose and began to set the supper. "Don't you think you might wish for four pairs of hands for me?"

Now, ask yourself the following questions:

- What do these sentences demonstrate about using capitalization with quotations?
- Why are the words *Arabian Nights* and *Mrs. White* capitalized?

These sentences show that the first word in a quotation is always capitalized. When a sentence in a quotation is interrupted and then continued, the first word in the continued portion is not capitalized. However, the second sentence in this quotation is a complete sentence, so the first word needs to be capitalized. *Arabian Nights* is capitalized because it is a proper noun that names the title of a book. *Mrs. White* is capitalized because it is a proper noun that includes a woman's title and her last name.

Grammar for Writers Writers can use capitalization to alert their readers to specific people, places, things, and events in the text as well as to words people say. When you edit your writing, carefully check your capitalization.

Would you listen to me read my lines in the play?

Okay, but be sure to start each sentence with a capital letter!

CHAPTER 22

22.1 Capitalization in Sentences

Just as road signs help to guide people through a town, capital letters help to guide readers through sentences and paragraphs. Capitalization signals the start of a new sentence or points out certain words within a sentence to give readers visual clues that aid in their understanding.

Grammar Practice
Practice your grammar skills with Writing Coach Online.

Grammar Games
Test your knowledge of grammar in this fast-paced interactive video game.

Using Capitals for First Words

Always capitalize the first word in a sentence.

Capitalize the first word in **declarative, interrogative, imperative,** and **exclamatory** sentences.

DECLARATIVE	**S**he went to the game yesterday.
INTERROGATIVE	**H**ow will you ever tell her about it?
IMPERATIVE	**B**e careful when crossing.
EXCLAMATORY	**H**ow could we ever have guessed!

Capitalize the first word in **interjections** and **incomplete questions.**

INTERJECTIONS	**J**ust great!
INCOMPLETE QUESTIONS	**W**ho? **W**hen?

The word *I* is always capitalized, whether it is the first word in a sentence or not.

Always capitalize the pronoun *I*.

EXAMPLE   Alice and **I** went to the dance.

546   Capitalization

Capitalization in Sentences

> **22.1.4 RULE**
> Capitalize the first word after a colon only if the word begins a complete sentence. Do not capitalize the word if it begins a list of words or phrases.

SENTENCE FOLLOWING A COLON She mumbled some words: **S**he was unable to continue speaking.

LIST FOLLOWING A COLON I put all the supplies in the box: **c**ereal, coffee, and bread.

See Practice 22.1A
See Practice 22.1B
See Practice 22.1C

> **22.1.5 RULE**
> Capitalize the first word in each line of traditional poetry, even if the line does not start a new sentence.

EXAMPLE
I think that I shall never see
A poem lovely as a tree. – Joyce Kilmer

Using Capitals With Quotations

There are special rules for using capitalization with **quotations**.

> **22.1.6 RULE**
> Capitalize the first word of a **quotation**. However, do not capitalize the first word of a continuing sentence when a quotation is interrupted by identifying words or when the first word of a quotation is the continuation of a speaker's sentence.

EXAMPLES Jeff said, "**G**olf is my favorite sport."

"**W**hen the train came in," Bob said, "**t**he people on the platform charged forward."

Fred commented that she was "**t**he prettiest girl he ever saw."

See Practice 22.1D

Capitalization in Sentences

PRACTICE 22.1A Capitalizing Words

Read each sentence. Then, write the word or words that should be capitalized in each sentence.

EXAMPLE   i hoped that i would be the first one picked to play on the team.

ANSWER   *I, I*

1. keep your head up while you are dancing.
2. her mother packed Lucy's suitcase for summer camp: shirts, shorts, bathing suit, and sneakers.
3. shall i compare thee to a summer's day? thou art more lovely and more temperate.
4. deb didn't like swimming class because she doesn't like getting her hair wet.
5. are you going to the fair this weekend?
6. she repeated her question loudly: "who needs help completing the registration form?"
7. excellent! now you can join our group!
8. who? who said that?
9. make eye contact with the person you are talking to.
10. we enjoyed the concert very much; it was given by our favorite musician.

PRACTICE 22.1B Using Capital Words in Sentences

Read each item. Then, write a sentence using each item according to the directions in parentheses.

EXAMPLE   we saw (as the first line of poetry)

ANSWER   *We saw a bird in the sky*
Rapidly and gracefully it did fly

11. students (first word in a declarative sentence)
12. firefighters raced to the scene. (after a colon)
13. when (first word in an interrogative sentence)
14. how (first word in an interjection)
15. i (first word in a sentence)
16. a single rose smiled (as the first line of poetry)
17. watch (first word in an imperative sentence)
18. where (in an incomplete question)
19. the fresh vegetables (after a colon)
20. what (first word in an exclamatory sentence)

SPEAKING APPLICATION

Take turns with a partner. Recite a short poem. Your partner should indicate when he or she thinks a word in the poem should be capitalized.

WRITING APPLICATION

Use the items in Practice 22.1B to create additional items. Exchange papers with a partner. Your partner should write sentences for each of your items.

Capitalization in Sentences

PRACTICE 22.1C Using Correct Capitalization in Sentences

Read each sentence. Then, rewrite each sentence, correcting capitalization errors.

EXAMPLE oh no! we're going to be late.

ANSWER *Oh* no! *We're* going to be late.

1. My father and i are planning to visit my cousins.
2. what an incredible sight is the new public park!
3. why now?
4. where is the location of the new high school?
5. We took out the map: it fell apart in our hands.
6. eager fans bought all the tickets for the jazz concert.
7. The playground had new equipment: Slides, swings, and a sandbox.
8. incredible! our team won the tournament.
9. will the highway be closed because of the snowstorm?
10. look out when swimming in the lake.

PRACTICE 22.1D Using Capitals With Quotations

Read each sentence. Then, write the word or words in each sentence that should be capitalized.

EXAMPLE tammy wondered, "is this the proper way to crochet?"

ANSWER *Tammy, Is*

11. abraham Lincoln once said, "a house divided against itself cannot stand."
12. "she has already had her chance," he replied. "it is time for someone else to take a turn."
13. he told me, "you're a fantastic cook!"
14. josie replied, "i will not be attending the conference this week."
15. "just as the weatherman predicted," Cole said, "the hurricane has become a tropical storm."
16. "yvonne always asks questions," said Candace. "she is very inquisitive."
17. simon tells me that he is "always on time."
18. "meanwhile," Shannon said, "we waited patiently for the movie to start."
19. "she left early this morning," Brian said. "i think she was headed for a track meet."
20. the bus driver said, "have a nice day!"

SPEAKING APPLICATION

Take turns with a partner saying sentences with interjections and incomplete questions. Use Practice 22.1C as a model. Your partner should indicate when he or she thinks a word should be capitalized.

WRITING APPLICATION

Write five quotations with a variety of capitalization errors. Exchange papers with a partner. Your partner should rewrite each quotation using capitalization correctly.

Practice 549

Capitalization in Sentences

Test Warm-Up

DIRECTIONS
Read the introduction and the passage that follows. Then, answer the questions to show that you can use and understand the conventions of capitalization in reading and writing.

Leo wrote this paragraph about the reopening of the Statue of Liberty. Read the paragraph and think about the changes you would suggest as a peer editor. When you finish reading, answer the questions that follow.

Our Nation's Crown Jewel

(1) On July 4, 2009, the crown of the statue of liberty reopened for the first time since September 11, 2001. (2) My older sister, Sasha, and I visited this famous national monument for the first time on that eventful day: we were thrilled by our trip. (3) there are now several improvements: Higher handrails, a better public address system, and stricter visitor limits. (4) imagine, tickets for this reopening sold out in just a few hours! (5) Clearly, many people were as excited about the reopening as we were.

---

1 How should sentence 1 be revised?

  A On July 4, 2009, the Crown of the Statue of Liberty reopened for the first time since September 11, 2001.

  B On July 4, 2009, the crown of the Statue of Liberty reopened for the first time since September 11, 2001.

  C On july 4, 2009, the crown of the Statue of Liberty reopened for the first time since september 11, 2001!

  D On July 4, 2009, the crown of the Statue of liberty reopened for the first time since September 11, 2001.

2 What change, if any, should be made in sentence 2?

  F Capitalize *sister*

  G Capitalize *national monument*

  H Capitalize *we*

  J Make no change

3 How should sentence 3 be revised?

  A There are now several improvements: higher handrails, a better public address system, and stricter Visitor limits.

  B There are now several improvements. Higher handrails, a better public address system, and stricter visitor limits.

  C There are now several improvements: higher handrails, a better public address system, and stricter visitor limits.

  D There are not several improvements: Higher handrails, A better publish address system, And stricter visitor limits.

4 What change, if any, should be made in sentence 4?

  F Change *imagine* to **Imagine**

  G Delete the comma after *imagine*

  H Change *tickets* to **Tickets**

  J Make no change

Find It / FIX IT 8 Grammar Game Plan

22.2 Proper Nouns

Capitalization makes important words stand out in your writing, such as the names of people, places, countries, book titles, and other proper names. Sometimes proper names are used as nouns and sometimes as adjectives modifying nouns or pronouns.

WRITING COACH Online
www.phwritingcoach.com

Grammar Practice
Practice your grammar skills with Writing Coach Online.

Grammar Games
Test your knowledge of grammar in this fast-paced interactive video game.

Using Capitals for Proper Nouns

Nouns, as you may remember, are either **common** or **proper.**

Common nouns, such as *sailor, brother, city,* and *ocean,* identify classes of people, places, or things and are not capitalized.

Proper nouns name specific examples of people, places, or things and should be capitalized.

> **Capitalize all proper nouns.**   22.2.1 RULE

EXAMPLES
- **J**effrey   **D**octor **C**allow   **G**overnor **T**ate
- **F**irst **S**treet   **A**rlington **H**ouse   **R**eno
- **A T**ale of **T**wo **C**ities   **USS C**onstitution

Names

Each part of a person's name—the given name, the middle name or initial standing for that name, and the surname—should be capitalized. If a surname begins with *Mc* or *O',* the letter following it is capitalized (McAdams, O'Reilly).

> **Capitalize each part of a person's name even when the full name is not used.**   22.2.2 RULE

EXAMPLES   **J**ohn **B**rown   **E. B. F**rome   **E**mil **C. T**aft

Capitalize the proper names that are given to animals.

EXAMPLES   **S**pot   **F**luffy   **L**assie

Proper Nouns 551

Geographical and Place Names

If a place can be found on a map, it should generally be capitalized.

RULE 22.2.3

Capitalize geographical and place names.

Examples of different kinds of geographical and place names are listed in the following chart.

GEOGRAPHICAL AND PLACE NAMES	
Streets	Madison Avenue, First Street, Green Valley Road
Towns and Cities	Dallas, Oakdale, New York City
Counties, States, and Provinces	Champlain County, Texas, Quebec
Nations and Continents	Austria, Kenya, the United States of America, Asia, Mexico, Europe
Mountains	the Adirondack Mountains, Mount Washington
Valleys and Deserts	the San Fernando Valley, the Mojave Desert, the Gobi
Islands and Peninsulas	Aruba, the Faroe Islands, Cape York Peninsula
Sections of a Country	the Northeast, Siberia, the Great Plains
Scenic Spots	Gateway National Park, Carlsbad Caverns
Rivers and Falls	the Missouri River, Victoria Falls
Lakes and Bays	Lake Cayuga, Gulf of Mexico, the Bay of Biscayne
Seas and Oceans	the Sargasso Sea, the Indian Ocean
Celestial Bodies and Constellations	Mars, the Big Dipper, Venus
Monuments and Memorials	the Tomb of the Unknown Soldier, Kennedy Memorial Library, the Washington Monument
Buildings	Madison Square Garden, Fort Hood, the Astrodome, the White House
School and Meeting Rooms	Room 6, Laboratory 3B, the Red Room, Conference Room C

552 Capitalization

Capitalizing Directions

Words indicating direction are capitalized only when they refer to a section of a country.

EXAMPLES Trevor rode through the **S**outh.

The airport is four miles **e**ast of the city.

Capitalizing Names of Celestial Bodies

Capitalize the names of celestial bodies except *moon* and *sun*.

EXAMPLE The **s**un is ten times larger than **J**upiter.

Capitalizing Buildings and Places

Do not capitalize words such as *theater, hotel, university,* and *park*, unless the word is part of a proper name.

EXAMPLES My son went to Rutgers **U**niversity.

I will drop you off at the **u**niversity.

Events and Times

Capitalize references to historic events, periods, and documents as well as dates and holidays. Use a dictionary to check capitalization.

> **Capitalize the names of specific events and periods in history.**

SPECIAL EVENTS AND TIMES	
Historic Events	the **B**attle of **W**aterloo, **W**orld **W**ar I
Historical Periods	the **M**anchu **D**ynasty, **R**econstruction
Documents	the **B**ill of **R**ights, the **M**agna **C**arta
Days and Months	**M**onday, **J**une 22, the third week in **M**ay
Holidays	**L**abor **D**ay, **M**emorial **D**ay, **V**eterans **D**ay
Religious Holidays	**R**osh **H**ashanah, **C**hristmas, **E**aster
Special Events	the **W**orld **S**eries, the **H**oliday **A**ntiques **S**how

Capitalizing Seasons
Do not capitalize seasons unless the name of the season is being used as a proper noun or a proper adjective.

EXAMPLES   I love to ski in the winter.

I hope to compete in the Winter Olympics.

Capitalize the names of organizations, government bodies, political parties, races, nationalities, languages, and religions.

VARIOUS GROUPS	
Clubs and Organizations	Rotary, Knights of Columbus, the Red Cross, National Organization for Women
Institutions	the Museum of Fine Arts, the Mayo Clinic
Schools	Kennedy High School, University of Texas
Businesses	General Motors, Prentice Hall
Government Bodies	Department of State, Federal Trade Commission, House of Representatives
Political Parties	Republicans, the Democratic party
Nationalities	American, Mexican, Chinese, Israeli, Canadian
Languages	English, Italian, Polish, Swahili
Religions and Religious References	Christianity: God, the Holy Spirit, the Bible Judaism: the Lord, the Prophets, the Torah Islam: Allah, the Prophets, the Qur'an, Mohammed Hinduism: Brahma, the Bhagavad Gita, the Vedas Buddhism: the Buddha, Mahayana, Hinayana

References to Mythological Gods When referring to mythology, do not capitalize the word *god* (the *gods* of Olympus).

Capitalize the names of awards; the names of specific types of air, sea, and spacecraft; and brand names.

EXAMPLES   the Nobel Prize   the Purple Heart

Chewy Treats   Mercury V

See Practice 22.2A
See Practice 22.2B

554   Capitalization

Proper Nouns

PRACTICE 22.2A Identifying Proper Nouns

Read each sentence. Then, write the proper noun or nouns in each sentence.

EXAMPLE The actress Katherine Hepburn has won many acting awards.

ANSWER *Katherine Hepburn*

1. Spending the summer in the Northwest, we stayed in Seattle, Washington.
2. I have never visited the Statue of Liberty, but I have always wanted to.
3. Nadira's mother is from India and her father is from Spain.
4. The Dust Bowl of the 1930's was a severe drought that damaged farmland.
5. My dentist is a member of the American Dental Association.
6. Alpha Centauri is a binary star system in the constellation Centaurus.
7. Joan of Arc fought for France during the Hundred Years' War.
8. The Department of Homeland Security was created in 2002.
9. His favorite brand of pen, SmoothLine, never smudges.
10. The RMS *Titanic* hit an iceberg on April 14, 1912.

PRACTICE 22.2B Capitalizing Proper Nouns

Read each sentence. Then, write the word or words in each sentence that should be capitalized.

EXAMPLE Last memorial day, we visited my grandparents in florida.

ANSWER *Memorial Day, Florida*

11. We always eat at my favorite restaurant, amelia's, on friday nights.
12. Have you ever seen the great wall of china?
13. samuel o'reilly saw a production of *miss saigon* in new york city many years ago.
14. mary and george have lived in the south for as long as i can remember.
15. james k. polk was born in north carolina.
16. i hope the houston astros go to the world series this year.
17. When you go to rome, be sure to see the trevi fountain and the pantheon.
18. Last summer, we went camping and saw the big dipper and orion's belt as we gazed up at the stars.
19. My grandmother's ancestors came from wales and ireland.
20. The kimbell art museum in fort worth, texas, has a collection of paintings by el greco.

SPEAKING APPLICATION

Take turns with a partner. Tell about a foreign country that you would like to visit. Describe what you would see and do there. Your partner should identify the proper nouns that you use.

WRITING APPLICATION

Use sentence 17 as a model to write three similar sentences. Replace the proper nouns in sentence 17 with other proper nouns.

Practice   555

Using Capitals for Proper Adjectives

A **proper adjective** is either an adjective formed from a proper noun or a proper noun used as an adjective.

> Capitalize most **proper adjectives**.

PROPER ADJECTIVES FORMED FROM PROPER NOUNS

Australian boomerang   Shakespearean theater

German Basset hound   Asian settlers

French ambassador   Mexican food

PROPER NOUNS USED AS ADJECTIVES

the Senate floor   the Clinton speeches

Miller festival   a Bible class

the Wang house   New York bagels

Some proper adjectives have become so commonly used that they are no longer capitalized.

EXAMPLES

herculean effort   french fries

pasteurized milk   quixotic hope

venetian blinds   teddy bear

Brand names are often used as proper adjectives.

> Capitalize a **brand name** when it is used as an adjective, but do not capitalize the common noun it modifies.

EXAMPLES

Timo wallets   Switzles fruit bars

Super Cool jeans   Longlasting refrigerator

556   Capitalization

Multiple Proper Adjectives

When you have two or more proper adjectives used together, do not capitalize the associated common nouns.

> **Do not capitalize a common noun modified by two or more proper adjectives.**

RULE 22.2.9

PROPER NOUN	PROPER ADJECTIVES
Missouri River	Arkansas and Missouri rivers
First Street	First, Second, and Third streets
Erie Canal	Erie and Augusta canals
Conservation Act	Conservation and Clean Air acts
Indian Ocean	Indian and Pacific oceans
Passaic County	Passaic and Warren counties
Hawaiian Islands	Hawaiian and Canary islands

Prefixes and Hyphenated Adjectives

Prefixes and hyphenated adjectives cause special problems. Prefixes used with proper adjectives should be capitalized only if they refer to a nationality.

> **Do not capitalize prefixes attached to proper adjectives unless the prefix refers to a nationality. In a hyphenated adjective, capitalize only the proper adjective.**

RULE 22.2.10

EXAMPLES

all-American   Anglo-American

Spanish-speaking   pro-French

American Polish-language newspaper

pre-Romanesque   Sino-Tibetan

pre-Islamic architecture   Indo-Aryan

See Practice 22.2C
See Practice 22.2D

Proper Nouns

PRACTICE 22.2C Capitalizing Proper Adjectives

Read the sentence. Then, write the word or words in each sentence that should be capitalized.

EXAMPLE I have toured a mayan pyramid in mexico.
ANSWER *Mayan, Mexico*

1. The jefferson memorial is forty minutes from my house.
2. The heroine in the movie lives in a georgian manor.
3. The falkland islands are located in the atlantic ocean near argentina.
4. She had a great time in spanish class last year.
5. The american eagle is still a threatened species.
6. President Franklin Delano Roosevelt's dog was a scottish terrier.
7. The cabinet is made of french oak.
8. The malaysian ambassador was last in the receiving line.
9. irish immigrants, who came to america in the nineteenth century, are an important part of the culture.
10. My neighbor's son is a shakespearean actor.

PRACTICE 22.2D Revising Sentences to Correct Capitalization Errors

Read each sentence. Then, rewrite each sentence using the conventions of capitalization.

EXAMPLE harry read an article in the spanish newspaper.
ANSWER *Harry read an article in the Spanish newspaper.*

11. kevin ran all the way to walker avenue.
12. cynthia just finished reading a book by f. scott fitzgerald.
13. bill wanted to install french doors on the porch.
14. father says we will celebrate the fourth of july with aunt melba.
15. montpelier is the capital of vermont.
16. while on vacation, leo bought a swiss watch.
17. bavarian-made cuckoo clocks are designed differently than black forest cuckoo clocks.
18. antoni gaudí was the genius who designed many buildings in barcelona, spain.
19. thompson's gazelle and the african elephant are native to africa.
20. during the civil war, the first shots fired were at fort sumter in south carolina.

SPEAKING APPLICATION

Discuss with a partner the reason why the words *Internet* and the *Web* are capitalized.

WRITING APPLICATION

Write five sentences. In each sentence, include a proper adjective.

22.3 Other Uses of Capitals

Even though the purpose of using capital letters is to make writing clearer, some rules for capitalization can be confusing. For example, it may be difficult to remember which words in a letter you write need to start with a capital, which words in a book title should be capitalized, or when a person's title—such as Senator or Reverend—needs to start with a capital. The rules and examples that follow should clear up the confusion.

Find It / FIX IT

8

Grammar Game Plan

Grammar Practice
Practice your grammar skills with Writing Coach Online.

Grammar Games
Test your knowledge of grammar in this fast-paced interactive video game.

Using Capitals in Letters

Capitalization is required in parts of personal letters and business letters.

> **Capitalize the first word and all nouns in letter salutations and the first word in letter closings.**

22.3.1 RULE

SALUTATIONS	**D**ear **W**illiam,
	Dear **M**adame:
	Dear **M**rs. **L**awrence:
	My dear **U**ncle,
CLOSINGS	**W**ith great respect,
	Yours very truly,
	Forever yours,
	All my best,

Using Capitals for Titles

Capitals are used for titles of people and titles of literary and artistic works. The charts and rules on the following pages will guide you in capitalizing titles correctly.

Other Uses of Capitals 559

RULE 22.3.2 Capitalize a person's title only when it is used with the person's name or when it is used as a proper name by itself.

WITH A PROPER NAME Yesterday, Governor Barth signed the bill.

AS A PROPER NAME I'm glad you can join us, Grandpa.

IN A GENERAL REFERENCE The king rewarded his loyal subjects.

The following chart illustrates the correct form for a variety of titles. Study the chart, paying particular attention to compound titles and titles with prefixes or suffixes.

SOCIAL, BUSINESS, RELIGIOUS, MILITARY, AND GOVERNMENT TITLES	
Commonly Used Titles	Sir, Madam, Miss, Professor, Doctor, Reverend, Bishop, Sister, Father, Rabbi, Corporal, Major, Admiral, Mayor, Governor, Ambassador
Abbreviated Titles	*Before names*: Mr., Mrs., Ms., Dr., Hon. *After names*: Jr., Sr., Ph.D., M.D., D.D.S., Esq.
Compound Titles	Vice President, Secretary of State, Lieutenant Governor, Commander in Chief
Titles With Prefixes or Suffixes	ex-Congressman Randolph, Governor-elect Loughman

Some honorary titles are capitalized. These include First Lady of the United States, Speaker of the House of Representatives, Queen Mother of England, and the Prince of Wales.

Other Uses of Capitals

> **RULE 22.3.3** Capitalize certain honorary titles even when the titles are not followed by a proper name.

EXAMPLE The **p**resident and **F**irst **L**ady visited with the **q**ueen of England.

Occasionally, the titles of other government officials may be capitalized as a sign of respect when referring to a specific person whose name is not given. However, you usually do not capitalize titles when they stand alone.

EXAMPLES We thank you, **G**overnor, for speaking to us this morning.

Only two **s**enators voted against the bill.

> **RULE 22.3.4** Relatives are often referred to by titles. These references should be capitalized when used with or as the person's name.

WITH THE PERSON'S NAME In that summer, **U**ncle **B**ob visited us almost every day.

AS A NAME She said that **G**randmother loved to cook.

> **RULE 22.3.5** Do not capitalize titles showing family relationships when they are preceded by a possessive noun or pronoun.

EXAMPLES his **a**unt   her **m**other   Sam's **u**ncle

RULE 22.3.6 Capitalize the first word and all other key words in the titles of books, periodicals, poems, stories, plays, paintings, and other works of art.

The following chart lists examples to guide you in capitalizing titles and subtitles of various works. Note that the articles (*a, an,* and *the*) are not capitalized unless they are used as the first word of a title or subtitle. Conjunctions and prepositions are also left uncapitalized unless they are the first or last word in a title or subtitle or contain four letters or more. Note also that verbs, no matter how short, are always capitalized.

TITLES OF WORKS	
Books	The Red Badge of Courage, Profiles in Courage, All Through the Night, John Ford: The Man and His Films Heart of Darkness
Periodicals	International Wildlife, Allure, Better Homes and Gardens
Poems	"The Raven" "The Rime of the Ancient Mariner" "Flower in the Crannied Wall"
Stories and Articles	"Editha" "The Fall of the House of Usher" "Here Is New York"
Plays and Musicals	The Tragedy of Macbeth Our Town West Side Story
Paintings	Starry Night Mona Lisa The Artist's Daughter With a Cat
Music	The Unfinished Symphony "Heartbreak Hotel" "This Land Is Your Land"

Other Uses of Capitals

> **Capitalize titles of educational courses when they are language courses or when they are followed by a number or preceded by a proper noun or adjective. Do not capitalize school subjects discussed in a general manner.**

 RULE 22.3.7

WITH CAPITALS
German   Honors Chemistry
Biology 205   Math 3
Economics 100   Russian

WITHOUT CAPITALS
health   psychology
woodworking   history
biology   math

EXAMPLES
This year, I will be taking math, French, Honors Biology, and world history.

Margaret's favorite classes are art history, Italian, and biology.

She does not like physical education and science as much.

After French class, I have to rush across the building to history.

See Practice 22.3A
See Practice 22.3B

Other Uses of Capitals

PRACTICE 22.3A Capitalizing Titles

Read each sentence. Then, write the word or words in each sentence that should be capitalized.

EXAMPLE Here comes doctor Preston.
ANSWER *Doctor*

1. I'm looking for captain Pierce.
2. My aunt linda makes the best lasagna.
3. Karen Aiken, president of winger's department store, presided over the meeting.
4. The article was called "beyond the seas"; it was well written.
5. "Excuse me, mr. secretary, would you answer one question?" asked the reporter.
6. I have a research report due in my honors biology class.
7. My Spanish teacher, senora gonzalez, organized a fiesta for the entire school.
8. The honorable judge Robinson will be presiding.
9. Edgar Allan Poe's poem "annabel lee" may have been written about his wife.
10. It was general Eisenhower who led the allies to victory at Normandy.

PRACTICE 22.3B Using All of the Rules of Capitalization

Read each sentence. Then, rewrite each sentence, using conventions of capitalization.

EXAMPLE i've never seen mr. gutierrez in a suit.
ANSWER *I've never seen Mr. Gutierrez in a suit.*

11. mr. kent asked us to read *the iliad* by homer.
12. I remember dr. laramy was a professor of african history at the university of Texas.
13. The speech was given by ex-mayor rawlins.
14. "oh no!" said gia. "my pen is out of ink!"
15. The sunshine skyway bridge is located in tampa, florida.
16. After a brief halt, major stevens led the troops back to camp.
17. the san diego zoo is home to two giant pandas from china.
18. Nancy attended the ball with mr. edmond sills.
19. The 2004 republican national convention was held in madison square garden.
20. The triassic period ended about 199 million years ago.

SPEAKING APPLICATION

Discuss with a partner the situations when words, such as *general* or *aunt*, are capitalized and when they are not capitalized. What different meaning does the capital indicate?

WRITING APPLICATION

Write a short fictional story about any topic of your choice. Be sure to include dialogue, titles, and proper nouns.

PUNCTUATION

Use punctuation to create sentences that readers can navigate easily.

WRITE GUY *Jeff Anderson, M.Ed.*

WHAT DO YOU NOTICE?

Focus on punctuation as you zoom in on these sentences from *A Connecticut Yankee in King Arthur's Court* by Mark Twain.

MENTOR TEXT

> Presently this thought occurred to me: how heedless I have been! When the boy gets calm, he will wonder why a great magician like me should have begged a boy like him to help me get out of this place; he will put this and that together, and will see that I am a humbug.

Now, ask yourself the following questions:

- What purposes do the colon and the exclamation mark serve in the first sentence?
- How are commas and a semicolon used in the second sentence?

The colon introduces the narrator's thought; the exclamation mark demonstrates strong emotion. In the second sentence, the first comma sets off the subordinate clause *When the boy gets calm*, whereas the second comma is used to place emphasis on the phrase *will see that I am a humbug*. The author uses a semicolon to separate two related ideas.

Grammar for Writers Writers have several punctuation marks available to help them craft a variety of complex sentences. Be sure to use punctuation marks that guide readers through your writing.

"What did the comma say to the semicolon?"

"When did you start wearing that cap on your head?"

CHAPTER 23

23.1 End Marks

End marks tell readers when to pause and for how long. They signal the end or conclusion of a sentence, word, or phrase. There are three end marks: the **period (.)**, the **question mark (?)**, and the **exclamation mark (!)**.

Grammar Practice
Practice your grammar skills with Writing Coach Online.

Grammar Games
Test your knowledge of grammar in this fast-paced interactive video game.

Using Periods

A **period** indicates the end of a declarative or imperative sentence, an indirect question, or an abbreviation. The period is the most common end mark.

> **Use a period to end a declarative sentence, a mild imperative sentence, and an indirect question.**

A **declarative sentence** is a statement of fact, idea, or opinion.

DECLARATIVE SENTENCE   This is a wonderful day.

An **imperative sentence** gives a direction or command. Often, the first word of an imperative sentence is a verb.

MILD IMPERATIVE SENTENCE   Finish sanding the table.

An **indirect question** restates a question in a declarative sentence. It does not give the speaker's exact words.

INDIRECT QUESTION   John asked me whether I could come.

Other Uses of Periods

In addition to signaling the end of a statement, periods can also signal that words have been shortened, or abbreviated.

> **Use a period after most abbreviations and after initials.**

566 **Punctuation**

End Marks

PERIODS IN ABBREVIATIONS	
Titles	Dr., Sr., Mrs., Mr., Gov., Maj., Rev., Prof.
Place Names	Ave., Bldg., Blvd., Mt., Dr., St., Ter., Rd.
Times and Dates	Sun., Dec., sec., min., hr., yr., A.M.
Initials	E. B. White, Robin F. Brancato, R. Brett

Some abbreviations do not end with periods. Metric measurements, state abbreviations used with ZIP Codes, and most standard measurements do not need periods. The abbreviation for inch, *in.*, is the exception.

EXAMPLES mm, cm, kg, L, C, CA, TX, ft, gal

The following chart lists some abbreviations with and without periods.

ABBREVIATIONS WITH AND WITHOUT END MARKS	
approx. = approximately	misc. = miscellaneous
COD = cash on delivery	mph = miles per hour
dept. = department	No. = number
doz. = dozen(s)	p. or pg. = page; pp. = pages
EST = Eastern Standard Time	POW = prisoner of war
FM = frequency modulation	pub. = published, publisher
gov. or govt. = government	pvt. = private
ht. = height	rpm = revolutions per minute
incl. = including	R.S.V.P. = please reply
ital = italics	sp. = spelling
kt. = karat or carat	SRO = standing room only
meas. = measure	vol. = volume
mfg. = manufacturing	wt. = weight

Sentences Ending With Abbreviations When a sentence ends with an abbreviation that uses a period, do not put a second period at the end. If an end mark other than a period is required, add the end mark.

EXAMPLES   Make sure to write Mike Brinks Jr.

Is that Andy Jens Sr.?

See Practice 23.1A

Do not use periods with acronyms, words formed with the first or first few letters of a series of words.

ACRONYMS   NASA (National Aeronautics and Space Administration)

RADAR (Radio Detecting and Range)

Use a period after numbers and letters in outlines.

EXAMPLE
I. Maintaining your pet's health
   A. Diet
      1. For a puppy
      2. For a mature dog
   B. Exercise

Using Question Marks

A **question mark** follows a word, phrase, or sentence that asks a question. A question is often in inverted word order.

Use a question mark to end an interrogative sentence, an incomplete question, or a statement intended as a question.

INTERROGATIVE SENTENCE   Was the project completed yet?

What time are we having company?

INCOMPLETE QUESTION   Small dogs stay with their moms longer. Why?

I'll make you a sandwich. What kind?

Use care, however, in ending statements with question marks. It is better to rephrase the statement as a direct question.

STATEMENT WITH A QUESTION MARK
The night hasn't ended yet**?**

We are having steak for dinner**?**

REVISED INTO A DIRECT QUESTION
Hasn't the night ended yet**?**

Are we having steak for dinner**?**

Use a period instead of a question mark with an **indirect question**—a question that is restated as a declarative sentence.

EXAMPLE
Bella wanted to know when the plane would arrive**.**

She wondered if it would be on time**.**

Using Exclamation Marks

An **exclamation mark** signals an exclamatory sentence, an imperative sentence, or an interjection. It indicates strong emotion and should be used sparingly.

> **Use an exclamation mark to end an exclamatory sentence, a forceful imperative sentence, or an interjection expressing strong emotion.**

RULE 23.1.6

EXCLAMATORY SENTENCE
Look at the huge mountain**!**

FORCEFUL IMPERATIVE SENTENCE
Don't tip the bowl**!**

An interjection can be used with a comma or an exclamation mark. An exclamation mark increases the emphasis.

EXAMPLES
Wow**!** That was a great game**.**

Oh**!** That was a great meal**.**

See Practice 23.1B

WITH A COMMA
Wow**,** that was a great game**.**

End Marks

PRACTICE 23.1A Using Periods Correctly in Sentences

Read each sentence. Then, rewrite each sentence, adding periods where they are needed.

EXAMPLE I asked Dr Blake if he enjoyed reading my paper

ANSWER *I asked Dr. Blake if he enjoyed reading my paper.*

1. Booker T Washington was born in Virginia in 1856
2. Meet me at 8:00 AM by the park bench
3. A A Milne wrote the *Winnie-the-Pooh* series
4. Mail this card to Ms Rachel A Smith on Wood Ave
5. Mt Everest is about 8,848 m tall
6. According to a NASA Web site, Earth rotates on its axis at approx 1,000 mph
7. The experiment requires 3 kg of copper sulfate
8. Saul asked us if we wanted to have Chinese food for dinner
9. The winner of the 100-m race is Grant Tidwell Jr
10. Every Saturday night, that show is SRO

PRACTICE 23.1B Using Question Marks and Exclamation Marks Correctly in Sentences

Read the sentence. Then, write the correct end mark for each item.

EXAMPLE Where are my keys

ANSWER ?

11. How much money is left in the account
12. Where does she keep the tea
13. Don't peek
14. When is the next leap year
15. Quickly, turn on the lights
16. I've won
17. Do we have enough seats for everyone
18. Haven't I seen you somewhere before
19. Happy Birthday
20. Go, Rockets

SPEAKING APPLICATION

Take turns with a partner. Say declarative sentences, imperative sentences, and indirect questions. Your partner should listen for and identify each sentence type.

WRITING APPLICATION

Write two sentences that use question marks and two sentences that use exclamation marks.

23.2 Commas

A **comma** tells the reader to pause briefly before continuing a sentence. Commas may be used to separate elements in a sentence or to set off part of a sentence.

Commas are used more than any other internal punctuation mark. To check for correct comma use, read a sentence aloud and note where a pause helps you to group your ideas. Commas signal to readers that they should take a short breath.

Grammar Game Plan

www.phwritingcoach.com

Grammar Tutorials
Brush up on your Grammar skills with these animated videos.

Grammar Practice
Practice your grammar skills with Writing Coach Online.

Grammar Games
Test your knowledge of grammar in this fast-paced interactive video game.

Using Commas With Compound Sentences

A **compound sentence** consists of two or more main or independent clauses that are joined by a coordinating conjunction, such as *and, but, for, nor, or, so,* or *yet.*

> Use a **comma** before a conjunction to separate two or more independent or main clauses in a **compound sentence**.

Use a comma before a conjunction when there are complete sentences on both sides of the conjunction.

EXAMPLE   Bill is leaving for duty **,** but I won't be able to see him off.
                independent clause   *independent clause*

In some compound sentences, the main or independent clauses are very brief, and the meaning is clear. When this occurs, the comma before the conjunction may be omitted.

EXAMPLES   Bill read carefully but he still didn't understand.

Brent would like to go in July but he doesn't have the time.

In other sentences, conjunctions are used to join compound subjects or verbs, prepositional phrases, or subordinate clauses. Because these sentences have only one independent clause, they do not take a comma before the conjunction.

CONJUNCTIONS WITHOUT COMMAS	
Compound Subject	Ben and Kate met for dinner on the river.
Compound Verb	The family laughed and reminisced while they ate.
Two Prepositional Phrases	My dog flew through the kitchen and out the door.
Two Subordinate Clauses	I enjoy trips only if they are relaxing and if my family comes with me.

A **nominative absolute** is a noun or pronoun followed by a participle or participial phrase that functions independently of the rest of the sentence.

> **RULE 23.2.2**
> Use a comma after a **nominative absolute**.

The following example shows a comma with a nominative absolute.

EXAMPLE Precious memories having been experienced, I decided to record them.

Avoiding Comma Splices

Remember to use both a comma and a coordinating conjunction in a compound sentence. Using only a comma can result in a **run-on sentence** or a **comma splice**. A **comma splice** occurs when two or more complete sentences have been joined with only a comma. Either punctuate separate sentences with an end mark or a semicolon, or find a way to join the sentences. (See Section 23.3 for more information on semicolons.)

> **RULE 23.2.3**
> Avoid comma splices.

INCORRECT The ice formed on the trees, many branches snapped under the weight.

CORRECT The ice formed on the trees. Many branches snapped under the weight.

572 **Punctuation**

Using Commas in a Series

A **series** consists of three or more words, phrases, or subordinate clauses of a similar kind. A series can occur in any part of a sentence.

> Use commas to separate three or more words, phrases, or clauses in a series.

Notice that a comma follows each of the items except the last one in these series. The conjunction *and* or *or* is added after the last comma.

SERIES OF WORDS   The marine life included fish, crabs, coral, and dolphins.

SERIES OF PREPOSITIONAL PHRASES   The map directed them over the mountain, into the cave, and past the waterfall.

SUBORDINATE CLAUSES IN A SERIES   The magazine revealed that the game was perfect, that the players were flawless, that the refreshments were good, and that the fans were excited.

If each item (except for the last one) in a series is followed by a conjunction, do not use commas.

EXAMPLE   I read novels and magazines and newspapers.

A second exception to this rule concerns items such as *salt and pepper*, which are paired so often that they are considered a single item.

EXAMPLES   During the holiday every table was set with a knife and fork, crystal and china, and salt and pepper.

Brett's favorite lunches are peanut butter and jelly, turkey and cheese, and soup and salad.

Commas   573

Using Commas Between Adjectives

Sometimes, two or more adjectives are placed before the noun they describe.

Use commas to separate coordinate adjectives, also called independent modifiers, or adjectives of equal rank.

EXAMPLES   a fabulous, tasty meal

an excellent, lively, fun party

An adjective is equal in rank to another if the word *and* can be inserted between them without changing the meaning of the sentence. Another way to test whether or not adjectives are equal is to reverse their order. If the sentence still sounds correct, they are of equal rank. In the first example, *a tasty, fabulous meal* still makes sense.

If you cannot place the word *and* between adjectives or reverse their order without changing the meaning of the sentence, they are called **cumulative adjectives.**

Do not use a comma between cumulative adjectives.

EXAMPLES   a new car cover
(*a car new cover* does not make sense)

many strange bugs
(*strange many bugs* does not make sense)

Do not use a comma to separate the last adjective in a series from the noun it modifies.

INCORRECT   A big, strong, man lifted the weights.
CORRECT   A big, strong man lifted the weights.

See Practice 23.2A
See Practice 23.2B

574   **Punctuation**

Commas

PRACTICE 23.2A Using Commas Correctly in Sentences

Read each sentence. Then, rewrite each sentence, adding a comma or commas where they are needed.

EXAMPLE   I drove by the house but he wasn't there.

ANSWER   *I drove by the house, but he wasn't there.*

1. The gust of wind blew the stack of papers and they scattered everywhere.
2. Luke mowed the lawn clipped the hedges and watered the garden.
3. Sara must have fallen asleep or she would have called by now.
4. The tired disappointed soccer team walked slowly off the field.
5. The bulb had burned out but it was still hot.
6. My arm had that tingly fuzzy feeling.
7. Its hair blowing away from its face the sheep dog quickly ran down the street.
8. I like Italian Mexican and spicy hot Indian food.
9. We took chairs towels a cooler toys and magazines to the beach.
10. The restaurant offers ham and eggs peanut butter and jelly sandwiches and corned beef hash.

PRACTICE 23.2B Revising to Correct Errors in Comma Use

Read each sentence. Then, rewrite each sentence, adding or deleting commas as necessary.

EXAMPLE   We collected, plastic bags, bits of paper and cans as we helped clean the park.

ANSWER   *We collected plastic bags, bits of paper, and cans as we helped clean the park.*

11. I used my mitt, but left it, at baseball practice.
12. With the play, the concert and the magician this weekend, the auditorium is booked.
13. Cecily skipped, and sang on her way to school.
14. It's quiet in here yet I still can't hear you.
15. Bruce can't find his chemistry book his algebra homework or his three-page, French paper.
16. My cousin drove me to the airport, and gave me a thoughtful going-away present.
17. Her eyes twinkling she gave him the present.
18. Ian ate the last sandwich and then he drank the last of the lemonade.
19. The book cover was torn dirty, and smudged.
20. The dark storm clouds gave way to a golden streak of sunshine.

SPEAKING APPLICATION

Take turns with a partner. Say compound sentences. Your partner should tell where a comma should go if your sentences were written.

WRITING APPLICATION

Write four sentences that use commas incorrectly. Exchange papers with a partner. Your partner should rewrite each sentence, adding or deleting commas as needed.

RULE 23.2.8

Using Commas After Introductory Material

Most material that introduces a sentence should be set off with a comma.

> Use a comma after an introductory word, phrase, or clause.

KINDS OF INTRODUCTORY MATERIAL	
Introductory Words	Yes, we do expect to see them soon. No, there has been no offer. Well, I was definitely surprised by his answer.
Nouns of Direct Address	Marcus, will you go?
Introductory Adverbs	Hurriedly, they gathered up the supplies. Patiently, the teacher explained it to them again.
Participial Phrases	Thinking quickly, she averted a potential medical disaster. Standing next to each other in the line, we introduced ourselves and started to chat.
Prepositional Phrases	In the shade of the palm tree, a family sat on the beach. After the lengthy dance, we were all exhausted.
Infinitive Phrases	To choose the right gift, I consulted her parents and friends. To finish my project on time, I will have to cut some details.
Adverbial Clauses	When he asked for a driving permit, he was sure it would be denied. If you read books, you may be interested in this one.

Commas and Prepositional Phrases Only one comma should be used after two prepositional phrases or a compound participial or infinitive phrase.

EXAMPLES In the back of the cab behind the coat, he found his wallet.

To find their way in the crowd and to avoid confusion, the tourists asked for help.

It is not necessary to set off short prepositional phrases. However, a comma can help avoid confusion.

CONFUSING In the window sun bleached the fabric.

CLEAR In the window, sun bleached the fabric.

Using Commas With Parenthetical Expressions

A **parenthetical expression** is a word or phrase that interrupts the flow of the sentence.

> Use commas to set off parenthetical expressions from the rest of the sentence.

Parenthetical expressions may come in the middle or at the end of a sentence. A parenthetical expression in the middle of a sentence needs two commas—one on each side; it needs only one comma if it appears at the end of a sentence.

KINDS OF PARENTHETICAL EXPRESSIONS	
Nouns of Direct Address	Will you have dinner with us, Meg? I wonder, Mrs. Taft, where Joe is.
Conjunctive Adverbs	Someone had already bought them plates, however. I could, therefore, buy cups.
Common Expressions	I listened to Mara's story as carefully as you did, I think.
Contrasting Expressions	Bea is sixteen, not seventeen. These boxes, not those, are packed.

Commas 577

Using Commas With Nonessential Expressions

To determine when a phrase or clause should be set off with commas, decide whether the phrase or clause is *essential* or *nonessential* to the meaning of the sentence. The terms *restrictive* and *nonrestrictive* may also be used.

An **essential,** or **restrictive, phrase** or **clause** is necessary to the meaning of the sentence. **Nonessential,** or **nonrestrictive, expressions** can be left out without changing the meaning of the sentence. Although the nonessential material may be interesting, the sentence can be read without it and still make sense. Depending on their importance in a sentence, appositives, participial phrases, and adjectival clauses can be either essential or nonessential. Only nonessential expressions should be set off with commas.

NONESSENTIAL APPOSITIVE The project was completed by Jane, the top student in the class.

NONESSENTIAL PARTICIPIAL PHRASE The majestic bridge, built in the 1900s, crosses the largest river in the country.

NONESSENTIAL ADJECTIVAL CLAUSE The river, which overflows in the spring, is popular with rafters in summer.

See Practice 23.2C
See Practice 23.2D
See Practice 23.2E
See Practice 23.2F

Do not use commas to set off essential expressions.

ESSENTIAL APPOSITIVE The part was played by the famous actor Tom Hanks.

ESSENTIAL PARTICIPIAL PHRASE The man carrying the hammer is my brother.

ESSENTIAL ADJECTIVAL CLAUSE The kayaking trip that Bill suggested could change my opinion of kayaking.

Commas

PRACTICE 23.2C Identifying Comma Use

Read each sentence. Then, for each sentence, tell what kind of introductory material is set off with a comma.

EXAMPLE To see the whiteboard, Kevin sat in the front row.

ANSWER *infinitive phrase*

1. Excitedly, the dog scratched at the front door.
2. To find the required book, I had to visit several college libraries.
3. After the destructive flood, we rebuilt our town in a new location.
4. Josh, did you remember to call your grandfather?
5. Before Lauren turned off her computer, she saved her files.
6. Following the detailed instructions, we arrived at the airport before noon.
7. Because our vacation was too short, we didn't feel well rested.
8. On the other side of the fence, the farmer planted the apple orchard.
9. To cook this recipe, we will have to buy more spices.
10. Yes, that is the assignment that we must complete by Friday.

PRACTICE 23.2D Using Commas With Prepositional Phrases

Read each sentence. Then, rewrite each sentence, inserting a comma to set off prepositional phrases.

EXAMPLE On the top shelf Ellen could see the book.

ANSWER *On the top shelf, Ellen could see the book.*

11. Near the book store on the square we found a wonderful restaurant.
12. Between the branches of the oak tree we saw the bird's nest.
13. Next to Sarah's house across from the school a park has a baseball field.
14. To the right of the staircase you will find the classroom.
15. At the edge of the forest deer hid in the tall grass.
16. Across the street flags were clearly visible.
17. Beyond the next town after this one there's a great beach.
18. During the long, hot afternoon all the children rested.
19. Throughout the competition for the trophy the athletes remained friends.
20. With no explanation the runner withdrew from the race.

SPEAKING APPLICATION

Take turns with a partner. Say sentences with different kinds of introductory material. Your partner should write each of your sentences, using a comma to set off the introductory material.

WRITING APPLICATION

Use the sentences in Practice 23.2D as a model to write similar sentences. Exchange papers with a partner. Your partner should insert commas to set off all the prepositional phrases.

Practice

End Marks

PRACTICE 23.2E Placing Commas Correctly in Sentences

Read each sentence. Then, rewrite each sentence, adding a comma where it is needed. Explain whether you used the commas in introductory material, nonrestrictive expressions, contrasting expressions, or other parenthetical expressions.

EXAMPLE Yes we grew zinnias this year.
ANSWER *Yes, we grew zinnias this year.*

1. No my birthday isn't in August.
2. With the mystery finally solved the detective closed the case.
3. Dad I mowed the lawn Tuesday night not Wednesday night.
4. When he's sleepy Martin yawns a lot to stay awake.
5. Really I thought she was very mature.
6. To match the paint color we took a sample to the store.
7. The local Boy Scout group cleaned the statue which commemorates veterans.
8. In a hurry Adelita gathered her things and left the room.
9. We enjoyed reading and studying Homer Dr. Shenk.
10. When the art supplies are getting low let me know.

PRACTICE 23.2F Revising Sentences for Proper Comma Use

Read each sentence. Then, rewrite each sentence, adding or deleting commas as necessary. Discuss with a partner why you added or deleted each comma (include comma placement in introductory material, nonrestrictive expressions, contrasting expressions, and other parenthetical expressions).

EXAMPLE The picture frame, made of wood holds a photograph, of my mother.
ANSWER *The picture frame, made of wood, holds a photograph of my mother.*

11. The ocean my favorite place to swim, was at high tide an hour ago.
12. However the apples bruised, anyway.
13. That animal is an opossum not a raccoon!
14. Annoyingly the clock radio blared on and off as I tried to sleep.
15. On the red carpet, before the awards show the actor gave many interviews.
16. The pilot who was a Navy pilot landed the plane safely.
17. The stamp which was auctioned, on Saturday sold for $18,000!
18. Julia let me know when you want to go home.
19. This book is mine I think.
20. He will not, therefore seek reelection in that state.

SPEAKING APPLICATION

Discuss with a partner the difference between the necessity of a comma in sentence 3 and the necessity of a comma in sentence 4. Tell what the purpose of the comma is in both sentences.

WRITING APPLICATION

Write a fantasy short story. Be sure to use correct punctuation marks, including comma placement in clauses, nonrestrictive phrases, contrasting expressions, introductory material, and parenthetical expressions.

Test Warm-Up

Commas

DIRECTIONS
Read the introduction and the passage that follows. Then, answer the questions to show that you can use and understand the function of placing commas in nonrestrictive phrases, clauses, and contrasting expressions in reading and writing.

Tina wrote this paragraph about NASA's Mars exploration program. Read the paragraph and think about the changes you would suggest as a peer editor. When you finish reading, answer the questions that follow.

Future Mission to Mars

(1) NASA'S exploration of Mars which has taken place in three stages is now focused on landing and exploring the surface of this planet. (2) Currently, scientists are developing the Mars Science Laboratory a critical part of the last stage of this exciting program. (3) Unlike earlier Mars missions the purpose of this laboratory which should land on Mars in the fall of 2011 is to collect and analyze Martian soil and rock samples. (4) Another future Mars mission planned for the second decade of this century is a field laboratory that will use robots to search for signs of past or present Martian life.

---

1 What change, if any, should be made in sentence 1?

  A Insert a semicolon before *which* and after *stages*

  B Insert a semicolon after *stages*

  C Insert a comma before *which* and after *stages*

  D Make no change

2 What change, if any, should be made in sentence 2?

  F Insert a comma after *Laboratory*

  G Insert a comma after *part*

  H Insert a colon after *Laboratory*

  J Make no change

3 What change should be made in sentence 3?

  A Insert a comma after *missions*

  B Insert commas after *laboratory* and *2011*

  C Insert a semicolon after *missions*

  D Insert commas after *missions*, *laboratory*, and *2011*

4 What change, if any, should be made in sentence 4?

  F Insert a semicolon before *planned* and after *century*

  G Insert a comma before *planned* and after *century*

  H Insert a colon after *mission*

  J Make no change

Test Warm-Up 581

Using Commas With Dates, Geographical Names, and Titles

Dates usually have several parts, including months, days, and years. Commas separate these elements for easier reading.

> **When a date is made up of two or more parts, use a comma after each item, except in the case of a month followed by a day.**

EXAMPLES The show took place on January 12, 2001, and the actors arrived January 1, 2001.

The trip began on July 4 and ended three months later.
(no comma needed after the day of the month)

Commas are also used when the month and the day are used as an appositive to rename a day of the week.

EXAMPLES Sunday, March 15, was the day of the picnic.

Mark will arrive on Friday, June 15, and will stay until Monday.

When a date contains only a month and a year, commas are unnecessary.

EXAMPLES I will arrive in April 2012.

Bette will visit Australia in August 2010.

If the parts of a date have already been joined by prepositions, no comma is needed.

EXAMPLE The city bus system ran its second test in May of 1909.

582 Punctuation

Commas

RULE 23.2.11 When a geographical name is made up of two or more parts, use a comma after each item.

EXAMPLES — My brother who works in Miami, Florida, is moving into a new house.

They're going to Toronto, Ontario, Canada, for their vacation.

See Practice 23.2G

RULE 23.2.12 When a name is followed by one or more titles, use a comma after the name and after each title.

EXAMPLE — I see that Bill Johnson, M.D., attended the show.

A similar rule applies with some business abbreviations.

EXAMPLE — Quality Printing, Inc., distributes novels.

Using Commas in Numbers

Commas make large numbers easier to read by grouping them.

RULE 23.2.13 With large numbers of more than three digits, use a comma after every third digit starting from the right.

EXAMPLES — 2,350 cars, 103,200 pennies, 2,500,415 books

RULE 23.2.14 Do not use a comma in ZIP Codes, telephone numbers, page numbers, years, serial numbers, or house numbers.

ZIP CODE	04707	YEAR NUMBER	2011
TELEPHONE NUMBER	(973) 555-0101	SERIAL NUMBER	703-546-791
PAGE NUMBER	Page 1146	HOUSE NUMBER	2435 Frederick Court

See Practice 23.2H

Commas 583

Commas

PRACTICE 23.2G Using Commas With Dates and Geographical Names

Read each sentence. Then, rewrite each sentence to show where to correctly place commas in dates and geographical names.

EXAMPLE Our flight landed in Vancouver British Columbia Canada.

ANSWER *Our flight landed in Vancouver, British Columbia, Canada.*

1. Where were you on March 9 2008?
2. We went to Tucson Arizona in July of 2004.
3. The Carsons will be out of town from Monday February 8 until Saturday February 13.
4. Monterey California and Miami Florida are coastal cities.
5. Our new teacher is from Swansea Wales United Kingdom.
6. Texas became an official part of the United States on December 29 1845.
7. Monday July 17 is my birthday.
8. I'm heading for San Juan Puerto Rico.
9. By Thursday January 2 we will arrive in Kuala Lumpur Malaysia.
10. Heather was born on February 12 2000 in Dallas Texas.

PRACTICE 23.2H Editing Sentences for Proper Comma Usage

Read each sentence. Then, rewrite each sentence, deleting or adding commas where they are needed.

EXAMPLE Next, Monday, April 3 I'll be in Sydney New South Wales Australia.

ANSWER *Next Monday, April 3, I'll be in Sydney, New South Wales, Australia.*

11. Alan R. Wilson Ph.D. has reviewed 1142 cases of allergic reactions to penicillin.
12. My flight has a layover in London England.
13. Exactly 2008 drummers performed at the 2,008 Summer Olympics opening ceremony.
14. Did you vacation in Athens Georgia or Athens Greece?
15. Cole Egan Jr. was born on March 6 1990.
16. Millie lives at 1,452 Main Street in New Seabury Connecticut.
17. Istanbul Turkey has become an international hotspot since June, of 1995.
18. Average Investors Inc. is a new company that opened downtown.
19. I learned about Freetown Sierra Leone in West Africa from the article.
20. Sunday February 1 2009 will be a day long remembered in Pittsburgh Pennsylvania.

SPEAKING APPLICATION

Take turns with a partner. Use sentences 1 and 2 as models to say similar sentences. Your partner should tell which sentence needs a comma in the date.

WRITING APPLICATION

Write four sentences that contain dates, geographical names, and large numbers, but omit all commas. Exchange papers with a partner. Your partner should add commas where necessary.

Using Commas With Addresses and in Letters

Commas are also used in addresses, salutations of friendly letters, and closings of friendly or business letters.

> **Use a comma after each item in an address made up of two or more parts.**

23.2.15

Commas are placed after the name, street, and city. No comma separates the state from the ZIP Code. Instead, insert an extra space between them.

EXAMPLE I received a card from Bill Smith, 125 Mountain Road, Wayne, New Jersey 07470.

Fewer commas are needed when an address is written in a letter or on an envelope.

EXAMPLE
Mrs. Jack Collins
25 Gold Avenue
Miami, FL 32211

> **Use a comma after the salutation in a personal letter and after the closing in all letters.**

23.2.16

See Practice 23.2I

SALUTATIONS	Dear Aunt Jean,	Dear Wanda,
CLOSINGS	Your friend,	Yours forever,

Using Commas in Elliptical Sentences

In **elliptical sentences,** words that are understood are left out. Commas make these sentences easier to read.

> **Use a comma to indicate the words left out of an elliptical sentence.**

23.2.17

EXAMPLE   Michael celebrates his promotion formally; Spencer, casually.

The words *celebrates his promotion* have been omitted from the second clause of the sentence. The comma has been inserted in their place so the meaning is still clear. The sentence could be restated in this way: *Michael celebrates his promotion formally; Spencer celebrates his promotion casually.*

Using Commas With Direct Quotations

Commas are also used to indicate where **direct quotations** begin and end. (See Section 23.4 for more information on punctuating quotations.)

RULE 23.2.18 Use commas to set off a direct quotation from the rest of a sentence.

EXAMPLES   "You came home early," commented Ben's mother.

He said, "The rehearsal ended earlier than planned."

"I hope," Susan's mother said, "my sister doesn't forget her toothbrush."

Using Commas for Clarity

Commas help you group words that belong together.

RULE 23.2.19 Use a comma to prevent a sentence from being misunderstood.

UNCLEAR   Near the highway developers were building an apartment building.

CLEAR   Near the highway, developers were building an apartment building.

586   **Punctuation**

Commas

Misuses of Commas

Because commas appear so frequently in writing, some people are tempted to use them where they are not needed. Before you insert a comma, think about how your ideas relate to one another.

Find It/ FIX IT
7
Grammar Game Plan

MISUSED WITH AN ADJECTIVE AND A NOUN	After work, I enjoy a healthy, nutritious, meal.
CORRECT	After work, I enjoy a healthy, nutritious meal.
MISUSED WITH A COMPOUND SUBJECT	After our meeting, my colleague Bill, and his friend Kurt, were invited to the dinner.
CORRECT	After our meeting, my colleague Bill and his friend Kurt were invited to the dinner.
MISUSED WITH A COMPOUND VERB	He gazed into her eyes, and sang the song he had written.
CORRECT	He gazed into her eyes and sang the song he had written.
MISUSED WITH A COMPOUND OBJECT	She chose a coat with a hood, and a long sash.
CORRECT	She chose a coat with a hood and a long sash.
MISUSED WITH PHRASES	Checking the mail, and looking for a package, Debbie walked past us.
CORRECT	Checking the mail and looking for a package, Debbie walked past us.
MISUSED WITH CLAUSES	She discussed what elements are crucial for a successful meal, and which caterers are most reliable.
CORRECT	She discussed what elements are crucial for a successful meal and which caterers are most reliable.

See Practice 23.2J

Commas

PRACTICE 23.2I Adding Commas to Addresses and Letters

Read each item. Then, add commas where needed.

EXAMPLE Main Street Montclair New Jersey
ANSWER Main Street, Montclair, New Jersey

1. London Ontario Canada
2. Hugs and kisses
   Aunt Susan
3. 16 Maple Street
   Erie PA 16509
4. Dear Mom and Dad
5. Abilene Texas
6. 12 Jones Terrace Suite 1B
7. Greetings my good friend
8. Jill Davis Clover Road Centerport New York
9. Dear Margarita Susannah and Rosa
10. Doug Sargent
    #4 Harrington Road
    Beach Haven CT 04102

PRACTICE 23.2J Revising Sentences With Misused Commas

Read each sentence. Then, if a sentence contains a misused comma or commas, rewrite it. If the sentence is correct, write *correct*.

EXAMPLE When I recall, my visit to Barcelona, Spain I think of all the art.
ANSWER When I recall my visit to Barcelona, Spain, I think of all the art.

11. When Sheila goes hiking she takes her canteen, and compass.
12. Young Dylan looked left and right, and waited for the cars to stop.
13. This Tuesday, July 3, is my friend's party.
14. The teacher, said "Put away your books, and take out your pencils."
15. Melvin Cranford left his house that morning but, he forgot his laptop.
16. Apples, pears, bananas and, oranges are all great examples of healthy foods.
17. The trip started in, Lisbon Portugal, and ended in Madrid, Spain.
18. Before leaving, Anne, and her sister Jean, locked the doors.
19. Sitting on the grass, and drinking lemonade, Lizzy was enjoying the warm day.
20. Jack chose a blue jacket, and a blue tie.

SPEAKING APPLICATION

Discuss with a partner the necessity of placing commas in addresses. Propose an explanation as to why commas aren't used in zip codes.

WRITING APPLICATION

Write ten compound sentences with dates, lists, or multiple adjectives. Be sure to use commas properly.

23.3 Semicolons and Colons

The **semicolon (;)** is used to join related independent clauses. Semicolons can also help you avoid confusion in sentences with other internal punctuation. The **colon (:)** is used to introduce lists of items and in other special situations.

www.phwritingcoach.com

Grammar Tutorials
Brush up on your Grammar skills with these animated videos.

Grammar Practice
Practice your grammar skills with Writing Coach Online.

Grammar Games
Test your knowledge of grammar in this fast-paced interactive video game.

Using Semicolons to Join Independent Clauses

Semicolons establish relationships between two independent clauses that are closely connected in thought and structure. A semicolon can also be used to separate independent clauses or items in a series that already contains a number of commas.

> **Use a semicolon to join related independent clauses that are not already joined by the conjunctions *and*, *but*, *for*, *nor*, *or*, *so*, or *yet*.** — RULE 23.3.1

EXAMPLE   We explored the museum together **;** we were amazed at all the exhibits we found there.

Do not use a semicolon to join two unrelated independent clauses. If the clauses are not related, they should be written as separate sentences with a period or another end mark to separate them.

Note that when a sentence contains three or more related independent clauses, they may still be separated with semicolons.

EXAMPLE   The gate was open **;** the bone was gone **;** the puppy had disappeared.

Semicolons Join Clauses Separated by Conjunctive Adverbs or Transitional Expressions

Conjunctive adverbs are adverbs that are used as conjunctions to join independent clauses. **Transitional expressions** are expressions that connect one independent clause with another one.

> **Use a semicolon to join independent clauses separated by either a conjunctive adverb or a transitional expression.** — RULE 23.3.2

Semicolons and Colons

CONJUNCTIVE ADVERBS	*also, besides, consequently, first, furthermore, however, indeed, instead, moreover, nevertheless, otherwise, second, then, therefore, thus*
TRANSITIONAL EXPRESSIONS	*as a result, at this time, for instance, in fact, on the other hand, that is*

Place a semicolon *before* a conjunctive adverb or a transitional expression, and place a comma *after* a conjunctive adverb or transitional expression. The comma sets off the conjunctive adverb or transitional expression, which introduces the second clause.

EXAMPLE She never lost her cool; in fact, she stayed completely calm.

Because words used as conjunctive adverbs and transitions can also interrupt one continuous sentence, use a semicolon only when there is an independent clause on each side of the conjunctive adverb or transitional expression.

EXAMPLES We arrived yesterday ahead of schedule; therefore, we had time for a meal, a rest, and some sightseeing.

We were very impressed, however, by John's knowledge of leadership skills and his ability to motivate people.

Using Semicolons to Avoid Confusion

Sometimes, semicolons are used to separate items in a series.

Use semicolons to avoid confusion when independent clauses or items in a series already contain commas.

Punctuation

When the items in a series already contain several commas, semicolons can be used to group items that belong together. Semicolons are placed at the end of all but the last complete item in the series.

INDEPENDENT CLAUSES The land, reportedly overflowing with flowers, was a myth; and the disappointed, tired visitors would only find it in storybooks.

ITEMS IN A SERIES On our journey, many people greeted our cousins, who come from Palermo; my uncles, who live in Rome; and our grandparents, the Russos, who live in Venice.

Semicolons appear most commonly in a series that contains either nonessential appositives, participial phrases, or adjectival clauses. Commas should separate the nonessential material from the word or words they modify; semicolons should separate the complete items in the series.

APPOSITIVES I sent invitations to Ms. Watts, my science teacher; Mr. Johnson, my principal; and Mrs. White, the librarian.

PARTICIPIAL PHRASES I acquired a fascination with aquatic life from television, viewing science programs; from scuba diving, learning about oceanography; and from magazines, reading about fish.

ADJECTIVAL CLAUSES The miniature train set that I bought has spare cars, which are brand new; a bridge, which opens and closes; and a tunnel, which has a light.

Using Colons

The **colon (:)** is used to introduce lists of items and in certain special situations.

Rule 23.3.4 Use a colon after an independent clause to introduce a list of items. Use commas to separate three or more items.

Independent clauses that appear before a colon often include the words *the following, as follows, these,* or *those.*

EXAMPLES For my interview, I had to speak with the following people: the president, the manager, and the director.

Rule 23.3.5 Do not use a colon after a verb or a preposition.

INCORRECT William always orders: steak, potatoes, salad, and fruit.

CORRECT William always orders steak, potatoes, salad, and fruit.

Rule 23.3.6 Use a colon to introduce a quotation that is formal or lengthy or a quotation that does not contain a "he said/she said" expression.

EXAMPLE Oliver Wendell Holmes Jr. wrote this about freedom: "It is only through free debate and free exchange of ideas that government remains responsive to the will of the people and peaceful change is effected."

Even if it is lengthy, dialogue or a casual remark should be introduced by a comma. Use the colon if the quotation is formal or has no tagline.

A colon may also be used to introduce a sentence that explains the sentence that precedes it.

> **Use a colon to introduce a sentence that summarizes or explains the sentence before it.**

RULE 23.3.7

EXAMPLE   Her explanation for being late was believable**:** She had gotten stopped by a police officer.

Notice that the complete sentence introduced by the colon starts with a capital letter.

> **Use a colon to introduce a formal appositive that follows an independent clause.**

RULE 23.3.8

EXAMPLE   I had finally decided on a career**:** teaching.

The colon is a stronger punctuation mark than a comma. Using the colon gives more emphasis to the appositive it introduces.

> **Use a colon in a number of special writing situations.**

RULE 23.3.9

SPECIAL SITUATIONS REQUIRING COLONS	
Numerals Giving the Time	5**:**30 A.M. 6**:**15 P.M.
References to Periodicals **(Volume Number: Page Number)**	*People* 74**:**12 *Sports Illustrated* 53**:**15
Biblical References **(Chapter Number: Verse Number)**	2 Timothy 1**:**9
Subtitles for Books and Magazines	*A Field Guide to Lions***:** *African Lands and Wildlife*
Salutations in Business Letters	Dear Mrs. Glenstone**:** Dear Madam**:**
Labels Used to Signal Important Ideas	Warning**:** Private Property

See Practice 23.3A
See Practice 23.3B

Semicolons and Colons

PRACTICE 23.3A Adding Semicolons and Colons to Sentences

Read each sentence. Then, rewrite each sentence, inserting a semicolon or colon where needed.

EXAMPLE I can see your point on the other hand, I can see her point, too.

ANSWER *I can see your point; on the other hand, I can see her point, too.*

1. Sarah always says what she thinks she has a reputation for being honest.
2. There is only one item on the list nuts.
3. Abraham exercised and ate healthy foods therefore, he lived a long, healthy life.
4. Brett likes to take walks in the morning it gives him energy for the rest of the day.
5. I took a trip to see the oldest commissioned warship in the Navy the USS *Constitution*.
6. Nicholas is always doing something he never seems to get tired.
7. Tommy knows what he wants a puppy!
8. He takes a lot of computer courses as a result, he knows how to fix the program.
9. There can be only two outcomes in a football game win or lose.
10. The ship's captain has a very important rule Everyone must wear a life jacket.

PRACTICE 23.3B Using Semicolons and Colons

Read each item. Then, for each item, write a complete sentence, using the item, the punctuation indicated in parentheses, and additional words.

EXAMPLE The class went on two field trips that year (colon)

ANSWER *The class went on two field trips that year: one to the Washington Monument and the other to the Smithsonian Institution.*

11. chicken or fish (colon)
12. The night is so clear (semicolon)
13. Paul's dog knows three tricks (colon)
14. Mary's uncle lives in Rhode Island (colon)
15. He buried the treasure (semicolon)
16. Throughout the day (colon)
17. Jack liked the movie (semicolon)
18. Addie is reading her favorite book (semicolon)
19. The hostess had only one thing to say (colon)
20. consequently (semicolon)

SPEAKING APPLICATION

Discuss with a partner the similarities between your corrections for sentences 2, 7, and 9. Explain how the sentences would be different if commas were used instead.

WRITING APPLICATION

Write a paragraph about a family vacation. Then, combine some sentences with colons and semicolons. Your new sentences must make sense and be grammatically correct.

23.4 Quotation Marks, Underlining, and Italics

Quotation marks (" ") set off direct quotations, dialogue, and certain types of titles. Other titles are <u>underlined</u> or set in *italics*, a slanted type style.

Find It/ FIX IT
6
Grammar Game Plan

Find It/ FIX IT
18
Grammar Game Plan

Writing Coach Online
www.phwritingcoach.com

Grammar Practice
Practice your grammar skills with Writing Coach Online.

Grammar Games
Test your knowledge of grammar in this fast-paced interactive video game.

Using Quotation Marks With Quotations

Quotation marks identify spoken or written words that you are including in your writing. A **direct quotation** represents a person's exact speech or thoughts. An **indirect quotation** reports the general meaning of what a person said or thought.

> A **direct quotation** is enclosed in quotation marks.

RULE 23.4.1

DIRECT QUOTATION | "When I learn to ride," said the boy, "I'll use the bike path every day."

> An **indirect quotation** does not require quotation marks.

RULE 23.4.2

INDIRECT QUOTATION | The boy said that when he learns to ride, he plans to use the bike path every day.

Both types of quotations are acceptable when you write. Direct quotations, however, generally result in a livelier writing style.

Using Direct Quotations With Introductory, Concluding, and Interrupting Expressions

A writer will generally identify a speaker by using words such as *he asked* or *she said* with a quotation. These expressions, called **conversational taglines** or **tags**, can introduce, conclude, or interrupt a quotation.

Quotation Marks, Underlining, and Italics 595

Direct Quotations With Introductory Expressions

Commas help you set off introductory information so that your reader understands who is speaking.

Use a comma after short introductory expressions that precede direct quotations.

EXAMPLE   My sister warned, "If you borrow my cellphone, you'll be responsible for it."

If the introductory conversational tagline is very long or formal in tone, set it off with a colon instead of a comma.

EXAMPLE   At the end of the day, Tom spoke of his plans: "I plan to visit many countries to understand different cultures."

Direct Quotations With Concluding Expressions

Conversational taglines may also act as concluding expressions.

Use a comma, question mark, or exclamation mark after a direct quotation followed by a concluding expression.

EXAMPLE   "If you sign the contract, you'll be responsible for paying the rent," the landlord warned.

Concluding expressions are not complete sentences; therefore, they do not begin with capital letters. Closing quotation marks are always placed outside the punctuation at the end of direct quotations that are followed by concluding expressions. Concluding expressions generally end with a period.

Divided Quotations With Interrupting Expressions

You may use a conversational tagline to interrupt the words of a direct quotation, which is also called a **divided quotation.**

Quotation Marks, Underlining, and Italics

> **RULE 23.4.5** — Use a comma after the part of a quoted sentence followed by an interrupting conversational tagline. Use another comma after the tagline. Do not capitalize the first word of the rest of the sentence. Use quotation marks to enclose the quotation. End punctuation should be inside the last quotation mark.

EXAMPLE "If you sign the contract," the landlord warned, "you'll be responsible for paying the rent."

> **RULE 23.4.6** — Use a comma, question mark, or exclamation mark after a quoted sentence that comes before an interrupting conversational tagline. Use a period after the tagline.

EXAMPLE "You signed the contract," stated the landlord. "You are responsible for paying the rent."

Quotation Marks With Other Punctuation Marks

Quotation marks are used with commas, semicolons, colons, and all of the end marks. However, the location of the quotation marks in relation to the punctuation marks varies.

> **RULE 23.4.7** — Place a comma or a period *inside* the final quotation mark. Place a semicolon or colon *outside* the final quotation mark.

EXAMPLES "Kodie was the best dog," sighed my mom.

EXAMPLES We were recently informed about his "groundbreaking novel"; it was just published.

> **RULE 23.4.8** — Place a question mark or an exclamation mark inside the final quotation mark if the end mark is part of the quotation. Do not use an additional end mark.

EXAMPLE Betty pondered, "How could I fail the test?"

RULE 23.4.9 Place a question mark or exclamation mark outside the final quotation mark if the end mark is part of the entire sentence, not part of the quotation.

EXAMPLE Don't you dare say, "I disagree"!

Using Single Quotation Marks for Quotations Within Quotations

As you have learned, double quotation marks (" ") should enclose the main quotation in a sentence. The rules for using commas and end marks with double quotation marks also apply to **single quotation marks.**

RULE 23.4.10 Use **single quotation marks** (' ') to set off a quotation within a quotation.

EXAMPLES "I remember John quoting Jane, 'If the day was longer we could do more work!' " Bill said.

"The lawyer said, 'Great news!' " Alicia explained.

Punctuating Explanatory Material Within Quotations

Explanatory material within quotations should be placed in brackets. (See Section 23.7 for more information on brackets.)

RULE 23.4.11 Use brackets to enclose an explanation located within a quotation. The brackets show that the explanation is not part of the original quotation.

EXAMPLE The president said, "This treaty is an agreement between two countries [France and Italy]."

See Practice 23.4A
See Practice 23.4B

598 Punctuation

Quotation Marks, Underlining, and Italics

PRACTICE 23.4A Using Quotation Marks

Read each sentence. Then, rewrite each sentence, inserting quotation marks where needed.

EXAMPLE There is something wrong here, he said.

ANSWER *"There is something wrong here," he said.*

1. Leonard asked, Who will be delivering the newspaper in the morning?
2. Throughout the play, the actor repeated the same line: Look into your heart.
3. Who borrowed my magazine? asked Dan.
4. I just heard a great song, remarked Jared.
5. You have to be careful, said his father, about walking the dog in the park.
6. Is that painting by Picasso? asked Susan.
7. Don't be late! Mom warned.
8. Ms. Kane replied, Plato once said, Science is nothing but perception.
9. Is it okay to say, See ya later?
10. The manager explained, The report should give details about the product [cellphones].

PRACTICE 23.4B Revising for the Correct Use of Quotation Marks

Read each sentence. Then, rewrite each sentence correcting the misuse of quotation marks.

EXAMPLE "Beth told me to show up at eight o'clock, said Bill."

ANSWER *"Beth told me to show up at eight o'clock," said Bill.*

11. "Who turned out all the lights"? asked Randy.
12. "I can see the sign, Pat informed us."
13. "Ralph just finished eating lunch, said Luther."
14. "Who, said Marcus, would not appreciate this music?"
15. "The word 'basically' is often overused" and can be unnecessary, said Tina.
16. Melissa asked "for my help," and I said Sure.
17. "Don't go down there", my mother told me, "you'll spoil the surprise."
18. "Ronald said, Not a chance!"
19. "The newest member of our team [Carrie] will play centerfield, said Coach Warren."
20. The story started with: 'Flopsy said to Flor' "I'm sleepy."

SPEAKING APPLICATION

Take turns with a partner. Say some sentences with direct quotes and other sentences with indirect quotes. Your partner should indicate which sentences would need quotation marks if they were written.

WRITING APPLICATION

Write five sentences with misused quotation marks. Exchange papers with a partner. Your partner should correct the misuse of the quotation marks.

Using Quotation Marks for Dialogue

A conversation between two or more people is called a **dialogue.**

When writing a dialogue, begin a new paragraph with each change of speaker.

The sun slowly rose over the edge of the pink-sandy beach, as the waves lapped the shore.

Blake sat on the cool rock and talked with his sister about his plans.

"I'm going north," said Blake. "I think I'll like the weather better; you know I love to ski and snowboard."

"Have you started packing yet?" asked Kate. "Can I have your surfboard?"

"It's all yours," said Blake. "It is fine with me if I never use it again."

For quotations longer than a paragraph, put quotation marks at the beginning of each paragraph and at the end of the final paragraph.

John McPhee wrote an essay about a canoe trip on the St. John River in northern Maine. He introduces his readers to the river in the following way:

"We have been out here four days now and rain has been falling three. The rain appears to be ending. Breaks of blue are opening in the sky. Sunlight is coming through, and a wind is rising.

"I was not prepared for the St. John River, did not anticipate its size. I saw it as a narrow trail flowing north, twisting through balsam and spruce—a small and intimate forest river, something like the Allagash. . . ."

Using Quotation Marks in Titles

Generally, quotation marks are used around the titles of shorter works.

Use quotation marks to enclose the titles of short written works.

 RULE 23.4.14

WRITTEN WORKS THAT USE QUOTATION MARKS	
Title of a Short Story	"The Raven" by Edgar Allan Poe "The Cask of Amontillado" by Edgar Allan Poe
Chapter From a Book	"Playing Pilgrims" in *Little Women* "The Laurence Boy" in *Little Women*
Title of a Short Poem	"The Road Not Taken" by Robert Frost
Essay Title	"Compensation" by Ralph Waldo Emerson
Title of an Article	"Collapse of the Bell Towers" by Barbie Nadeau

Use quotation marks around the titles of episodes in a television or radio series, songs, and parts of a long musical composition.

 RULE 23.4.15

ARTISTIC WORK TITLES THAT USE QUOTATION MARKS	
Episode	"Rendition" from *60 Minutes*
Song Title	"Born in the USA" by Bruce Springsteen
Part of a Long Musical Composition	"Spring" from *The Four Seasons* "E.T. Phone Home" from the *E.T. The Extra-Terrestrial* soundtrack

Use quotation marks around the title of a work that is mentioned as part of a collection.

 RULE 23.4.16

The title *Plato* would normally be underlined or italicized. In the example below, however, the title is placed in quotation marks because it is cited as part of a larger work.

EXAMPLE "Plato" from *Great Books of the Western World*

Using Underlining and Italics in Titles and Other Special Words

Underlining and **italics** help make titles and other special words and names stand out in your writing. Underlining is used only in handwritten or typewritten material. In printed material, italic (slanted) print is generally used instead of underlining.

Underline or italicize the titles of long written works and the titles of publications that are published as a single work.

WRITTEN WORKS THAT ARE UNDERLINED OR ITALICIZED	
Title of a Book	Little Women Oliver Twist
Title of a Newspaper	The Washington Post
Title of a Play	Macbeth Romeo and Juliet
Title of a Long Poem	Paradise Lost
Title of a Magazine	The New Yorker

The portion of a newspaper title that should be italicized or underlined will vary from newspaper to newspaper. *The New York Times* should always be fully capitalized and italicized or underlined. Other papers, however, can be treated in one of two ways: the *Los Angeles Times* or the Los Angeles *Times*. You may want to check the paper's Web site for correct formatting.

Underline or italicize the titles of movies, television and radio series, long works of music, and works of art.

ARTISTIC WORKS THAT ARE UNDERLINED OR ITALICIZED	
Title of a Movie	Gone with the Wind West Side Story
Title of a Television Series	M*A*S*H, I Love Lucy
Title of a Long Work of Music	Rhapsody in Blue
Title of an Album (on any media)	Rubber Soul
Title of a Painting	The Last Supper, Woman
Title of a Sculpture	David, Venus de Milo

Quotation Marks, Underlining, and Italics

> **RULE 23.4.19** Do not underline, italicize, or place in quotation marks the name of the Bible, its books and divisions, or other holy scriptures, such as the Torah and the Qur'an.

EXAMPLE Ben read from Psalms in the Old Testament.

Government documents should also not be underlined or enclosed in quotation marks.

> **RULE 23.4.20** Do not underline, italicize, or place in quotation marks the titles of government charters, alliances, treaties, acts, statutes, speeches, or reports.

EXAMPLE The Taft-Hartley Labor Act was passed in 1947.

> **RULE 23.4.21** Underline or italicize the names of air, sea, and space craft.

EXAMPLE We saw the *Apollo IX* module.

> **RULE 23.4.22** Underline or italicize words, letters, or numbers (figures) used as names for themselves.

EXAMPLES Her *i*'s and her *I*'s look too much like *1*'s.

Avoid sprinkling your speech with *like*.

> **RULE 23.4.23** Underline or italicize foreign words and phrases not yet accepted into English.

See Practice 23.4C
See Practice 23.4D

EXAMPLE "*Buenos noches*," she said, meaning "goodnight" in Spanish.

Using Quotation Marks to Indicate Sarcasm or Irony

Quotation marks are also used to set off words intended as sarcasm or irony. **Sarcasm** and **irony** use words to express the opposite of their literal meaning. Both literary devices are often meant to be humorous, but can also express anger or frustration. Irony often describes situations, whereas sarcasm is speech that expresses mockery or criticism.

Writers may use quotation marks to indicate sarcasm or irony. In the following examples, quotation marks create distance between the author's perspective and the words.

SARCASM   It's so nice of you to buy me a "present" that fits you but not me.

IRONY   The king "won" the war but lost all his wealth.

Words that indicate sarcasm or irony often are not set off by quotation marks. Use quotation marks only to avoid sarcasm or irony being missed or lost altogether, as overuse may dilute their effect.

RULE 23.4.24

Do not overuse **quotation marks.** They should be used only when you want to emphasize sarcasm or irony.

Also, the reader may confuse the words within quotation marks as dialogue, clouding the writer's intent. Instead, make the sarcasm or irony clear by choosing your words carefully or using adjectives like *so-called*, *alleged*, or *supposed* to show the logic of the sentence.

EXAMPLE   Too many people know about Marla's **supposed** surprise party.

See Practice 23.4E
See Practice 23.4F

Quotation Marks, Underlining, and Italics

PRACTICE 23.4C Using Punctuation in Titles and Dialogue

Read each sentence. Then, rewrite each sentence, using correct punctuation where needed. If any words need to be italicized, underline those words.

EXAMPLE   Tanya said Please hurry!

ANSWER   *Tanya said, "Please hurry!"*

1. When does the first train depart? asked Vince.
2. "Tanya replied, In one hour."
3. "It's not exactly the Orient Express, is it? Vince commented."
4. Tanya said, We can read during the ride. I'm bringing To Kill a Mockingbird.
5. I'll bring Newsweek, Vince said.
6. All last month, said John, we read Macbeth in English class.
7. Tonight, Professor McCarthy gives his lecture How Humans Cure the Blues.
8. Ramond's CD More to Come is receiving excellent reviews.
9. "Carly said, My favorite painting is Monet's Water Lilies."
10. Abe replied, "I like classical music, like Debussy's Clair de Lune."

PRACTICE 23.4D Revising Punctuation in Titles and Dialogue

Read each sentence. Then, rewrite the sentence using correct punctuation. If any words need to be italicized, underline those words.

EXAMPLE   Lana said "My favorite book is Jane Eyre."

ANSWER   *Lana said, "My favorite book is Jane Eyre."*

11. I have a copy of van Gogh's painting Sunflowers, said Sam.
12. "I've heard the song Starry, Starry Night is about Vincent Van Gogh, said Monica."
13. My favorite painting is Lucas by Chuck Close said Martha.
14. Have you seen Rodin's sculpture The Thinker? asked Juan.
15. Grant calls his sculpture The Athlete said Nina.
16. I received an A for that sculpture, Grant told us.
17. Have you read The Iliad? asked Ned.
18. Toward the end of the movie Vertigo Karl said, is when the plot starts to twist.
19. Did you see last night's episode of Galaxy Wars? asked Jim.
20. Monica informed us, "The last boat to leave the dock was the Sea Lion."

SPEAKING APPLICATION

Take turns with a partner. Say sentences that contain both dialogue and titles. For each sentence, your partner should indicate which words should be put in quotation marks and/or italicized.

WRITING APPLICATION

Write a short dialogue between two friends discussing a movie. Include incorrect usage of quotation marks, underlining, and italics. Exchange papers with a partner. Your partner should correct the misuse of punctuation marks.

Quotation Marks, Underlining, and Italics

PRACTICE 23.4E Using Quotation Marks, Underlining, and Italics

Read each sentence. Then, rewrite each sentence, adding underlining or quotation marks as needed. If any words need to be italicized, underline those words.

EXAMPLE Since the weather was stormy, I could hardly wait to go outside.

ANSWER *Since the weather was stormy, I could "hardly wait" to go outside.*

1. Joan's painting, Sunset #21, sold quickly.
2. For my birthday, I received a subscription to Popular Science magazine.
3. Considering your sense of direction, I'm glad you don't make maps.
4. What a treat; my dog chewed my sweater.
5. He enjoys the editorials in The Observer.
6. The peaceful protesters shouted at him.
7. I find experimental paintings interesting.
8. René listens to Hearts of Space every Sunday evening on the radio.
9. The history club's trusted treasurer misplaced most of the funds.
10. Arthur Miller's Death of a Salesman opened on Broadway to rave reviews.

PRACTICE 23.4F Using Quotation Marks to Indicate Sarcasm or Irony

Read each sentence. Then, rewrite each sentence using quotation marks to indicate sarcasm or irony.

EXAMPLE Alicia's new pet was a ten-year-old poodle.

ANSWER *Alicia's "new" pet was a ten-year-old poodle.*

11. Josh said he was too sick to pick up the phone and cancel.
12. Who was the genius who unplugged the refrigerator?
13. Mark went to a baseball game to do research for his project.
14. Amanda assured us that she was going to a friend's house to study.
15. The windy conditions predicted were actually a series of tornados.
16. Your work was so good, I had to redo it.
17. It was hard to stay awake during that spectacular performance.
18. They did such a wonderful job fixing my bike that both wheels fell off.
19. Your sweet dog looks like he wants to bite me.
20. Melissa just happened to show up at dinner time.

SPEAKING APPLICATION

Take turns with a partner. Say sentences that require quotation marks, italics, or words that should be underlined. Your partner should listen for and identify the words that should receive special punctuation.

WRITING APPLICATION

Write a story that uses sarcasm or irony in the plot, the setting, or the main character(s). Include two uses of italics in your essay. Be sure to use correct punctuation, including quotation marks to indicate sarcasm or irony.

23.5 Hyphens

The **hyphen** (-) is used to combine words, spell some numbers and words, and show a connection between the syllables of words that are broken at the ends of lines.

Find It/ FIX IT
19
Grammar Game Plan

Grammar Practice
Practice your grammar skills with Writing Coach Online.

Grammar Games
Test your knowledge of grammar in this fast-paced interactive video game.

Using Hyphens in Numbers

Hyphens are used to join compound numbers and fractions.

> Use a hyphen when you spell out two-word numbers from twenty-one through ninety-nine.

⬅ 23.5.1 RULE

EXAMPLES   twenty-two centimeters   seventy-seven feet

> Use a hyphen when you use a fraction as an adjective but not when you use a fraction as a noun.

⬅ 23.5.2 RULE

ADJECTIVE   The recipe calls for one-half cup of flour.

NOUN   Three quarters of the movie is already over.

> Use a hyphen between a number and a word when they are combined as modifiers. Do not use a hyphen if the word in the modifier is possessive.

⬅ 23.5.3 RULE

EXAMPLES   The coach called a 15-minute timeout.

   The editors put 12 months' work into the book.

> If a series of consecutive, hyphenated modifiers ends with the same word, do not repeat the modified word each time. Instead, use a suspended hyphen (also called a dangling hyphen) and the modified word only at the end of the series.

⬅ 23.5.4 RULE

EXAMPLE   The ninth- and tenth-grade students came.

Hyphens   607

Using Hyphens With Prefixes and Suffixes

Hyphens help your reader easily see the parts of a long word.

> **RULE 23.5.5** Use a hyphen after a prefix that is followed by a proper noun or proper adjective.

The following prefixes are often used before proper nouns: *ante-*, *anti-*, *mid-*, *post-*, *pre-*, *pro-*, and *un-*.

EXAMPLES   pre-World War II   mid-May

> **RULE 23.5.6** Use a hyphen in words with the prefixes *all-*, *ex-*, and *self-* and words with the suffix *-elect*.

EXAMPLES   ex-president   president-elect

Many words with common prefixes are no longer hyphenated. Check a dictionary if you are unsure whether to use a hyphen.

Using Hyphens With Compound Words

Hyphens help preserve the units of meaning in compound words.

> **RULE 23.5.7** Use a hyphen to connect two or more words that are used as one compound word, unless your dictionary gives a different spelling.

EXAMPLES   editor-in-chief   re-election
           daughter-in-law   not-for-profit

> **RULE 23.5.8** Use a hyphen to connect a compound modifier that appears before a noun. The exceptions to this rule include adverbs ending in *-ly* and compound proper adjectives or compound proper nouns that are acting as an adjective.

EXAMPLES WITH HYPHENS	EXAMPLES WITHOUT HYPHENS
a well-made pair of boots	widely distributed reports
the bright-eyed student	Native American children
an up-to-date report	a highly unlikely suspect

When compound modifiers follow a noun, they generally do not require the use of hyphens.

EXAMPLE   The boots were **well made.**

However, if a dictionary spells a word with a hyphen, the word must always be hyphenated, even when it follows a noun.

EXAMPLE   The score was **up-to-date.**

Using Hyphens for Clarity

Some words or group of words can be misread if a hyphen is not used.

> **Use a hyphen within a word when a combination of letters might otherwise be confusing.**

RULE 23.5.9

EXAMPLES   re-educate, semi-independent

> **Use a hyphen between words to keep readers from combining them incorrectly.**

RULE 23.5.10

See Practice 23.5A
See Practice 23.5B

INCORRECT   the mail delivery-carrier
CORRECT   the mail-delivery carrier

Hyphens

PRACTICE 23.5A **Using Hyphens Correctly**

Read each sentence. Then, write the words that need hyphenation, adding hyphens where necessary.

EXAMPLE Manuel lived in a high rise building.
ANSWER *high-rise*

1. There is a clear cut reason that a life jacket is worn on a boat.
2. The free throw shot was a last ditch effort to win the game.
3. We bought our skiis at an offseason sale.
4. I had to add three quarters gallon of oil to my car.
5. The film crew took a 15 day hiatus.
6. My mother in law devised a good game plan.
7. The so called expert mishandled restoring the priceless portrait.
8. David told me one third of the school's computers have virusrelated problems.
9. The announcement will be made in mid July.
10. Tracy had a bird's eye view of the outfield.

PRACTICE 23.5B **Revising Sentences With Hyphens**

Read each sentence. Then, rewrite the sentence correcting any error in the use of a hyphen. If the punctuation is correct, write *correct*.

EXAMPLE Can you believe this scarf is hand-made?
ANSWER *Can you believe this scarf is handmade?*

11. You need to make a U turn at the next intersection.
12. I had a short lived-career as a song-writer.
13. If Kyle wins one more time, he is in the semi-final of the tournament.
14. The teacher assigned extra credit homework to any interested student.
15. Richard was twenty six when he bought a dog.
16. This is our best-selling jukebox.
17. Attending the event is a once in a lifetime opportunity.
18. We need an all purpose cleanser for this house-work.
19. The mayor elect will walk in the parade.
20. The sound-effects at the movie theater come from top of the line speakers.

SPEAKING APPLICATION

Take turns with a partner. Use hyphenated words in sentences about your school. Your partner should listen for and identify which words need hyphens.

WRITING APPLICATION

Write a paragraph about what you may be doing seven years in the future. Use at least three hyphenated words not used in Practice 23.5B in your paragraph.

Using Hyphens at the Ends of Lines

Hyphens help you keep the lines in your paragraphs more even, making your work easier to read.

Dividing Words at the End of a Line

Although you should try to avoid dividing a word at the end of a line, if a word must be broken, use a hyphen to show the division.

> **If a word must be divided at the end of a line, always divide it between syllables.**

23.5.11 RULE

EXAMPLE The brave soldiers had been sending let-

ters to their families describing their base.

> **A hyphen used to divide a word should never be placed at the beginning of the second line. It must be placed at the end of the first line.**

23.5.12 RULE

INCORRECT The workers and volunteers made a very de

-tailed plan for the search.

CORRECT The workers and volunteers made a very de-

tailed plan for the search.

Using Hyphens Correctly to Divide Words

One-syllable words cannot be divided.

> **Do not divide one-syllable words even if they seem long or sound like words with two syllables.**

23.5.13 RULE

INCORRECT	ri-dge	ho-use	lod-ge
CORRECT	ridge	house	lodge

Do not divide a word so that a single letter or the letters -ed stand alone.

INCORRECT	a-dept	read-y	e-ject	abash-ed
CORRECT	adept	ready	eject	abashed

Avoid dividing proper nouns and proper adjectives.

INCORRECT	Hea-ther	Is-rael
CORRECT	Heather	Israel

Divide a hyphenated word only after the hyphen.

INCORRECT We are planning a party with my sis-
ter-in-law next week.

CORRECT We are planning a party with my sister-
in-law next week.

Avoid dividing a word so that part of the word is on one page and the remainder is on the next page.

Often, chopping up a word in this way will confuse your readers or cause them to lose their train of thought. If this happens, rewrite the sentence or move the entire word to the next page.

See Practice 23.5C
See Practice 23.5D

612 Punctuation

PRACTICE 23.5C Writing Correctly Divided Words

Read each group of divided words. Then, write the word in each group that is not correctly divided with the correct hyphenation, or write it as one word if it should not be divided.

EXAMPLE   per-son   fol-low   suburb-an
ANSWER   *subur-ban*

1. clo-ak   mys-tery   fol-low
2. embar-rass   fak-ed   em-balm
3. Donn-a   flow-er   mother-in-law
4. rain-y   peti-tion   shut-ter
5. bell-owed   char-acter   pat-ted
6. mar-shall   tap-ped   self-ser-vice
7. can-dle   ap-ple   o-ver
8. clum-sy   Ste-vens   offi-cer
9. comp-lete   mov-able   de-linquent
10. se-vere   no-tion   far-mer

PRACTICE 23.5D Using Hyphens to Divide Words

Read each sentence. If the word at the end of the line has not been correctly hyphenated, then divide the word correctly, or write it as one word.

EXAMPLE   The congressional committee deb-ated all sides of the argument.
ANSWER   *de-bated*

11. My mother and father are celebra-ting their wedding anniversary.
12. Above the treetops, I could see the Olym-pic flag moving in the wind.
13. Aunt Mary offen sends souvenirs fr-om the countries she visits.
14. The name of the student who won is Ann-ette Chima.
15. My brother, sister, cousin, and I had a lov-ely time vacationing in Aruba last summer.
16. My favorite things to do outdoors are runn-ing, cycling, and swimming.
17. I have realized that it is necessary to e-valuate my options before making a decision.
18. The nervous girl looked down self-con-sciously and blushed.
19. Micah's brother is known to borrow man-y of Micah's things.
20. Even though I was on vacation, she call-ed me every day.

SPEAKING APPLICATION

Take turns with a partner. Say ten words not found in Practice 23.5C. Your partner should tell where each word can be divided.

WRITING APPLICATION

Write five sentences that include an incorrectly divided word at the end of a line. Exchange papers with a partner. Your partner should correct your sentences so that they are divided correctly.

Find It/FIX IT 14 Grammar Game Plan

23.6 Apostrophes

The **apostrophe (')** is used to form possessives, contractions, and a few special plurals.

WRITING COACH Online
www.phwritingcoach.com

Grammar Practice
Practice your grammar skills with Writing Coach Online.

Grammar Games
Test your knowledge of grammar in this fast-paced interactive video game.

Using Apostrophes to Form Possessive Nouns

Apostrophes are used with nouns to show ownership or possession.

RULE 23.6.1 **Add an apostrophe and -s to show the possessive case of most singular nouns.**

EXAMPLES   the tie of the man   the man**'**s tie

              the tail of the dog   the dog**'**s tail

Even when a singular noun already ends in *-s,* you can usually add an apostrophe and *-s* to show possession. However, names that end in the *eez* sound get an apostrophe, but no *-s.*

EXAMPLE   The Ganges**'** source is in the Himalayas.

For classical references that end in *-s,* only an apostrophe is used.

EXAMPLES   Moses**'** brother   Zeus**'** thunderbolt

RULE 23.6.2 **Add an apostrophe to show the possessive case of plural nouns ending in -s or -es.**

EXAMPLE   the scent of the foxes   the foxes**'** scent

RULE 23.6.3 **Add an apostrophe and an -s to show the possessive case of plural nouns that do not end in -s or -es.**

614   Punctuation

EXAMPLE   the songs of the choir

the choir's songs

> **Add an apostrophe and -s (or just an apostrophe if the word is a plural ending in -s) to the last word of a compound noun to form the possessive.**

RULE 23.6.4

APOSTROPHES THAT SHOW POSSESSION	
Names of Businesses and Organizations	the All-Sports Company's central office the Navy Officer's Club the Dean of Students' office
Titles of Rulers or Leaders	Catherine the Great's victories Louis XVI's palace the president of the college's decision
Hyphenated Compound Nouns Used to Describe People	my father-in-law's house the secretary-treasurer's notes the nurse-practitioner's manager

> **To form possessives involving time, amounts, or the word *sake*, use an apostrophe and an -s or just an apostrophe if the possessive is plural.**

RULE 23.6.5

APOSTROPHES WITH POSSESSIVES	
Time	a week's vacation four days' vacation an hour's time
Amount	one gallon's worth five cents' worth
Sake	for Benjamin's sake

RULE 23.6.6 — To show joint ownership, make the final noun possessive. To show individual ownership, make each noun possessive.

JOINT OWNERSHIP	I enjoyed Rita and Blane's movie.
INDIVIDUAL OWNERSHIP	Rory's and Beth's shoes are sitting here.

Use the owner's complete name before the apostrophe to form the possessive case.

INCORRECT SINGULAR	Kri's house
CORRECT SINGULAR	Kris's house
INCORRECT PLURAL	three girl's shoes
CORRECT PLURAL	three girls' shoes

Using Apostrophes With Pronouns

Both indefinite and personal pronouns can show possession.

RULE 23.6.7 — Use an apostrophe and -s with indefinite pronouns to show possession.

EXAMPLES
somebody's work boots

each other's addresses

RULE 23.6.8 — Do not use an apostrophe with possessive personal pronouns; their form already shows ownership.

EXAMPLES

her albums	our car	her blue shoes
its windows	their house	whose house

616 Punctuation

Be careful not to confuse the contractions *who's*, *it's*, and *they're* with possessive pronouns. They are contractions for *who is*, *it is* or *it has*, and *they are*. Remember also that *whose*, *its*, and *their* show possession.

PRONOUNS	CONTRACTIONS
Whose homework is this?	*Who's* coming to dinner?
Its tires were all flat.	*It's* going to snow.
Their dinner is ready.	*They're* coming to dinner.

Using Apostrophes to Form Contractions

Contractions are used in informal speech and writing. You can often find contractions in the dialogue of stories and plays; they often create the sound of real speech.

> Use an apostrophe in a **contraction** to show the position of the missing letter or letters.

	COMMON CONTRACTIONS			
Verb + *not*	cannot	can't	are not	aren't
	could not	couldn't	will not	won't
Pronoun + *will*	he will	he'll	I will	I'll
	you will	you'll	we will	we'll
	she will	she'll	they will	they'll
Pronoun + *would*	she would	she'd	I would	I'd
	he would	he'd	we would	we'd
	you would	you'd	they would	they'd
Noun or Pronoun + *be*	you are	you're	I am	I'm
	she is	she's	Jane is	Jane's
	they are	they're	dog is	dog's

Still another type of contraction is found in poetry.

EXAMPLES   e'en *(even)*   o'er *(over)*

Other contractions represent the abbreviated form of *of the* and *the* as they are written in several different languages. These letters are most often combined with surnames.

EXAMPLES   O'Reilly

d'Martino

o'clock

l'Abbé

Using Contractions to Represent Speaking Styles

A final use of contractions is for representing individual speaking styles in dialogue. As noted previously, you will often want to use contractions with verbs in dialogue. You may also want to approximate a regional dialect or a foreign accent, which may include nonstandard pronunciations of words or omitted letters. However, you should avoid overusing contractions in dialogue. Overuse reduces the effectiveness of the apostrophe.

EXAMPLES   "Hey, ol' buddy. How you feelin'?"

"Don' you be foolin' me."

Using Apostrophes to Create Special Plurals

Apostrophes can help avoid confusion with special plurals.

Use an apostrophe and *-s* to create the plural form of a letter, numeral, symbol, or a word that is used as a name for itself.

EXAMPLES   *A*'s and *an*'s cause confusion.

There are three *9*'s in that number.

I don't like to hear *if*'s or *maybe*'s.

Form groups of *3*'s or *4*'s.

You have three *?*'s in a row.

See Practice 23.6A
See Practice 23.6B

618   Punctuation

PRACTICE 23.6A Identifying the Use of Apostrophes

Read each sentence. Then, tell if each apostrophe is used to form a *possessive*, a *contraction*, a *speaking style*, or a *special plural*.

EXAMPLE Who is the party's candidate for mayor this year?

ANSWER *possessive*

1. I watched as the boy's hat blew away in the wind.
2. The man tipped his hat and said, "Good evening, Li'l Lady."
3. The towing company removed the owner's car from where it was illegally parked.
4. He'll be back tomorrow.
5. Queen Victoria's reign was supreme.
6. I received all *A*'s this semester.
7. Snow covered the houses' roofs on my block.
8. The dog's out in the yard.
9. The house address contains two *4*'s.
10. The wind told the naughty children, "Stop your fightin'."

PRACTICE 23.6B Revising to Add Apostrophes

Read each sentence. Then, rewrite each sentence, adding apostrophes as needed.

EXAMPLE Its been hectic, but Ive had fun playing in the school band this year.

ANSWER *It's been hectic, but I've had fun playing in the school band this year.*

11. Didnt he say what time he would arrive at Davids party?
12. Its such a beautiful day; well take a walk around the block.
13. She said the wallet Jim found was hers, but she couldnt describe what was inside it.
14. There are too many *ifs* and *ands* in her essay.
15. The dogs bark was worse than its bite.
16. The suns rays warmed my face.
17. Uncle John just returned from his only nieces recital.
18. We need to pick up Mr. ODonnell at OHare Airport at seven oclock.
19. Jacks car, a vintage model, is his most prized possession.
20. Why cant we stay up a little longer?

SPEAKING APPLICATION

Take turns with a partner. Say sentences with words that indicate possession, contractions, special plurals, or speaking styles. Your partner should identify how each word uses an apostrophe.

WRITING APPLICATION

Write five sentences that correctly use apostrophes to show possession, contractions, or plurals of letters or numbers.

23.7 Parentheses and Brackets

Parentheses enclose explanations or other information that may be omitted from the rest of the sentence without changing its basic meaning or construction. Using parentheses is a stronger, more noticeable way to set off a parenthetical expression than using commas. **Brackets** are used to enclose a word or phrase added by a writer to the words of another.

Grammar Practice
Practice your grammar skills with Writing Coach Online.

Grammar Games
Test your knowledge of grammar in this fast-paced interactive video game.

Parentheses

Parentheses help you group material within a sentence.

RULE 23.7.1 Use parentheses to set off information when the material is not essential or when it consists of one or more sentences.

EXAMPLE: The challenge of climbing the mountain (as they learned from the other teams) was more difficult than they thought.

RULE 23.7.2 Use parentheses to set off numerical explanations such as dates of a person's birth and death and around numbers and letters marking a series.

EXAMPLES: Jim McNash sailed around the world with the help of his friend, John L. Smith (1950–2005).

Go to the store and pick up these items: (1) compass, (2) tent, (3) hiking boots.

Who painted the Sistine Chapel: (a) Michelangelo, (b) DaVinci, or (c) Monet?

Although material enclosed in parentheses is not essential to the meaning of the sentence, a writer indicates that the material is important and calls attention to it by using parentheses.

Parentheses and Brackets

RULE 23.7.3 When a phrase or declarative sentence interrupts another sentence, do not use an initial capital letter or end mark inside the parentheses.

EXAMPLE Bill finally finished his project (we all watched from the beginning) at the end of the fair.

RULE 23.7.4 When a question or exclamation interrupts another sentence, use both an initial capital letter and an end mark inside the parentheses.

EXAMPLE Serena (She is a fantastic runner!) finished first.

RULE 23.7.5 When you place a sentence in parentheses between two other sentences, use both an initial capital letter and an end mark inside the parentheses.

EXAMPLE New York is known for its fabulous museums. (See the Museum of Natural History as an example.) History is interesting to learn about.

RULE 23.7.6 In a sentence that includes parentheses, place any punctuation belonging to the main sentence after the final parenthesis.

EXAMPLE The town council approved the stadium changes (after some debate), and they explained where the new stadium would be built (with some doubts about how the changes will be received).

Special Uses of Parentheses

Parentheses are also used to set off numerical explanations such as dates of a person's birth and death and numbers or letters marking a series.

EXAMPLES Michelangelo (1475–1564) was a famous Italian painter.

Alan's phone number is (909) 963-9644.

Her study abroad will take her to (1) France, (2) Italy, and (3) England.

Brackets

Brackets are used to enclose a word or phrase added by a writer to the words of another writer.

> **RULE 23.7.7**
> Use brackets to enclose words you insert in quotations when quoting someone else.

EXAMPLES Cooper noted: "And with [E.T.'s] success, 'Phone home' is certain to become one of the most often repeated phrases of the year [1982]."

"The results of this vote [75–5] indicate overwhelming support for our new council person," he stated.

The Latin expression *sic* (meaning "thus") is sometimes enclosed in brackets to show that the author of the quoted material has misspelled or mispronounced a word or phrase.

EXAMPLE Michaelson, citing Dorothy's signature line from *The Wizard of Oz,* wrote, "Theirs [sic] no place like home."

See Practice 23.7A
See Practice 23.7B

622 Punctuation

PRACTICE 23.7A Using Parentheses and Brackets Correctly

Read each item. Then, rewrite each sentence, adding the items indicated in parentheses. The items can be placed in parentheses or brackets.

EXAMPLE Your essay is on my desk. (all ten pages of it)

ANSWER *Your essay (all ten pages of it) is on my desk.*

1. He finally answered the phone. (huffing and puffing)
2. The men in question deserve awards. (Jack White, Ted Inge, and Craig Erezuma)
3. "He was a nown celebrity in town." (sic)
4. Some writers don't use word processing programs. (including myself)
5. The statement was made by President Jimmy Carter. (former)
6. Jack bought the tickets. (who is a big football fan)
7. "The school is two miles from the hospital, and three from the police station." (miles)
8. "I'll call you tomorrow." (Friday)
9. I smiled when I saw the expression on his face. (and my heart skipped a beat)
10. She whispered the secret word. (joyful)

PRACTICE 23.7B Revising to Add or Parentheses or Brackets

Read each sentence. Then, rewrite each sentence, adding parentheses or brackets where needed.

EXAMPLE "The prize money $500 was donated."

ANSWER *"The prize money [$500] was donated."*

11. Before it could reach the station, the old train a relic of frontier days broke down.
12. "The mayor Joe Roy attended the ceremony and gave a warm speech."
13. We saw it the ball and ducked.
14. Please read this information I enclosed it as Attachment A.
15. He is a former officer admiral in the Navy.
16. According to the law, the property Holmes Field that borders Crystal Lake belongs to a Native American tribe.
17. "The robber put the monie sic in the bag."
18. This contract promises that we will 1 deliver the refrigerator, 2 install the refrigerator, and 3 take away the old refrigerator.
19. The witness said, "I saw him the defendant coming out of the back door."
20. The movie a box-office hit was made with a shoe-string budget and no catering!

SPEAKING APPLICATION

Discuss with a partner the difference between using parentheses and using brackets. What would the consequence be if they were used interchangeably?

WRITING APPLICATION

Write five sentences. Then, have a partner tell you some additional information to add to each sentence. Rewrite each sentence, including the additional information in brackets or parentheses.

23.8 Ellipses, Dashes, and Slashes

An **ellipsis** (. . .) shows where words have been omitted from a quoted passage. It can also mark a pause or interruption in dialogue. A **dash** (—) shows a strong, sudden break in thought or speech. A **slash** (/) separates numbers in dates and fractions, shows line breaks in quoted poetry, and represents *or*. A slash is also used to separate the parts of a Web address.

Grammar Practice
Practice your grammar skills with Writing Coach Online.

Grammar Games
Test your knowledge of grammar in this fast-paced interactive video game.

Using the Ellipsis

An **ellipsis** is three evenly spaced periods, or ellipsis points, in a row. Always include a space before the first ellipsis point, between ellipsis points, and after the last ellipsis point. (The plural of *ellipsis* is *ellipses*.)

Use an **ellipsis** to show where words have been omitted from a quoted passage.

ELLIPSES IN QUOTATIONS	
The Entire Quotation	"The Black River, which cuts a winding course through southern Missouri's rugged Ozark highlands, lends its name to an area of great natural beauty. Within this expanse are old mines and quarries to explore, fast-running waters to canoe, and wooded trails to ride."—Suzanne Charle
At the Beginning	Suzanne Charle described the Black River area in Missouri as having " . . . old mines and quarries to explore, fast-running waters to canoe, and wooded trails to ride."
In the Middle	Suzanne Charle wrote, "The Black River . . . lends its name to an area of great natural beauty. Within this expanse are old mines and quarries to explore, fast-running waters to canoe, and wooded trails to ride."
At the End	Suzanne Charle wrote, "The Black River, which cuts a winding course through southern Missouri's rugged Ozark highlands, lends its name to an area of great natural beauty . . . "

624 **Punctuation**

> **Use an ellipsis to mark a pause in a dialogue or speech.**

23.8.2 RULE

EXAMPLE   The director shouted, "Ready... and... action!"

Dashes

A **dash** signals a stronger, more sudden interruption in thought or speech than commas or parentheses. A dash may also take the place of certain words before an explanation. Overuse of the dash diminishes its effectiveness. Consider the proper use of the dash in the rule below.

> **Use dashes to indicate an abrupt change of thought, a dramatic interrupting idea, or a summary statement.**

23.8.3 RULE

USING DASHES IN WRITING	
To indicate an abrupt change of thought	The book doesn't provide enough information on the Netherlands—by the way, where did you buy the book?
	I cannot believe how many answers my sister missed—she doesn't even want to talk about it.
To set off interrupting ideas dramatically	The palace was built—you may find this hard to believe—in one year.
	The palace was built—Where did they get the resources?—in one year.
To set off a summary statement	An excellent academic record and great test scores—if you have these, you may be able to get into an Ivy League college.
	To see her name printed in the program—this was her greatest dream.

Ellipses, Dashes, and Slashes

RULE 23.8.4 Use **dashes** to set off a **nonessential appositive** or modifier when it is long, when it is already punctuated, or when you want to be dramatic.

APPOSITIVE   The cause of the damage to the screen and the windows—a strong gust of wind—whipped through the house.

MODIFIER   The sports writer—bored with writing about overpaid athletes—quit the following week.

Dashes may be used to set off one other special type of sentence interrupter—the parenthetical expression.

RULE 23.8.5 Use **dashes** to set off a **parenthetical expression** when it is long, already punctuated, or especially dramatic.

EXAMPLE   Today, we visited an art museum—what a fascinating place—set in a large city.

Slashes

A **slash** is used to separate numbers in dates and fractions, lines of quoted poetry, or options. Slashes are also used to separate parts of a Web address.

RULE 23.8.6 Use slashes to separate the day, month, and year in dates and to separate the numerator and denominator in numerical fractions.

DATES   She listed her employment date as 9/01/09.

Fractions   4/5   2/3   1/2

Ellipses, Dashes, and Slashes

> **RULE 23.8.7** Use slashes to indicate line breaks in up to three lines of quoted poetry in continuous text. Insert a space on each side of the slash.

EXAMPLE I used a quote from William Blake, "Tyger! Tyger! burning bright **/** In the forests of the night," to begin my paper.

> **RULE 23.8.8** Use slashes to separate choices or options and to represent the words *and* and *or*.

EXAMPLES Choose your topping: apples **/** nuts **/** syrup.

Each owner should bring a leash and treats **/** food.

You can type and **/** or hand-write the last page of the essay.

> **RULE 23.8.9** Use slashes to separate parts of a Web address.

EXAMPLES http: **//** www.fafsa.ed.gov **/**
(for financial aid for students)

http: **//** www.whitehouse.gov **/**
(the White House)

http: **//** www.si.edu **/**
(the Smithsonian Institution)

See Practice 23.8A
See Practice 23.8B

Ellipses, Dashes, and Slashes

PRACTICE 23.8A Using Ellipses, Dashes, and Slashes Correctly

Read each sentence. Then, rewrite each sentence, adding dashes to emphasize parenthetical information, slashes, or ellipses where appropriate. Explain the function of the dashes, slashes, and ellipses you added.

EXAMPLE The measurement must be within 1 8 of an inch.

ANSWER The measurement must be within 1/8 of an inch.

1. "I was just wondering" Gia mused.
2. The pandas at the zoo they are so playful are the main attraction.
3. There is one thing actually several things that I need to tell you.
4. Sarah bought a new pet a guinea pig.
5. We only need 3 4 of a yard of that blue material.
6. I listened carefully as the teacher read Lincoln's inaugural address: "Four score and seven years ago."
7. You will need a pen pencil.
8. There was only one thing to do surrender.
9. The movie went on and on.
10. I ended my paper with a quote from a poem by Edgar Allan Poe, "All that we see or seem Is but a dream within a dream."

PRACTICE 23.8B Revising Sentences With Ellipses, Dashes, and Slashes

Read each sentence. Then, use the appropriate punctuation to add or delete the information in parentheses. Be sure to include dashes that emphasize parenthetical information.

EXAMPLE Mr. Lewis is a kind, fair, and knowledgeable teacher. (Delete *kind, fair, and.*)

ANSWER Mr. Lewis is a . . . knowledgeable teacher.

11. Jeff or Jim may return by train. (Add *and.*)
12. The new secretary must be prepared to do a great deal of work. (Add *Lisa.*)
13. The regulation states, "All agencies must document overtime or risk losing federal funds." (Delete *or risk losing federal funds.*)
14. My cousin Jeff is coming to visit. (Add *my favorite relative.*)
15. Many people will attend the Fourth of July festivities. (Add *Independence Day.*)
16. We will invite Susan to our party. (Add *she is the new girl next door.*)
17. Miss Jones is a special guest of my mother. (Add *former college roommate.*)
18. The hungry lion roared. (Delete *roared.*)
19. Grandfather remembers when bread cost a dime. (Add *but that was a long time ago.*)
20. All the presentations were excellent. (Add *speeches.*)

SPEAKING APPLICATION

Take turns with a partner. Say different sentences that would use ellipses, dashes, or slashes if they were written. Your partner should indicate which punctuation each of your sentences needs and why.

WRITING APPLICATION

Use sentences 12, 14, and 16 as models to write similar sentences. Exchange papers with a partner. Your partner should correctly use dashes to emphasize parenthetical information.

Cumulative Review Chapters 22–23

PRACTICE 1 — **Using Periods, Question Marks, and Exclamation Marks**

Read each sentence. Rewrite each sentence, adding question marks, periods, and exclamation marks where needed.

1. What an incredible movie that was
2. Take out the garbage
3. How many classes are you taking this year
4. He asked if I knew anyone who could help out with the production
5. Mark Lucas Sr took the long way home after work
6. Listen when I am talking to you
7. School was canceled today Why
8. How nice it is that we can all get together this weekend
9. Is someone helping you prepare for the big meeting
10. Oh You scared me

PRACTICE 2 — **Using Commas Correctly**

Read each sentence. Rewrite each sentence, adding commas where needed. If a sentence is correct as is, write *correct*.

1. I went to the store but I forgot the list.
2. Sam and Erica met each other at the main gate of the stadium.
3. Losing little time he grabbed his cellphone and dialed 911.
4. The exam included multiple choice short answer and essay questions.
5. The show was a dazzling exciting event.
6. He yelled up the stairs "Mom are you coming down soon?"
7. The party started at 7 not at 8.
8. The Declaration of Independence was signed on July 4 1776.
9. "Her address is 27 Spring Street Lakeville Iowa 35675" Ron said.
10. I thought that happened in May 2003.

PRACTICE 3 — **Using Colons, Semicolons, and Quotation Marks**

Read each sentence. Rewrite each sentence, using colons, semicolons, and quotation marks where needed. If a sentence is correct as is, write *correct*.

1. I am not needed there tonight I am staying at home instead.
2. This radio station plays all kinds of music jazz, pop, country, and R&B.
3. My favorite poem, replied Connie, is Dream Deferred by Langston Hughes.
4. The students told us their favorite subjects Jane English Todd chemistry and Eric history.
5. Will had a great first day of work his new co-workers are really friendly.
6. He didn't need to say anything more I could read his expression from a mile away.
7. Please don't be late, my mother implored. The train leaves at exactly 356.
8. Maria was a little early however, she waited for everyone else to arrive.
9. Caution Falling rock zone ahead.
10. She told me how much she enjoyed my singing.

Continued on next page ▶

Cumulative Review Chapters 22–23

 Using Apostrophes

Read each sentence. Rewrite each sentence, using apostrophes where needed. If a sentence is correct as is, write *correct*.

1. Caras aunt owns two large beauty salons on the south side of town.
2. Frost's poetry is read by many students today.
3. Artemis hunting tools are often depicted alongside the goddess.
4. My mother-in-laws house is always filled with people for the holidays.
5. Susie always adds her two cents to any discussion.
6. Whos in charge here. Its not me.
7. He wouldnt dream of taking his sisters car without her permission.
8. I can't say for certain if he's coming to Chris's holiday party.
9. School starts promptly at 7 oclock every morning.
10. Its not that she doesnt want to be here; its that she hasnt got enough time to attend every meeting.

 **Using Underlining (or Italics), Hyphens, Dashes, Slashes, Parentheses, Brackets, and Ellipses**

Read each sentence. Rewrite each sentence, adding underlining (or italics), hyphens, dashes, slashes, brackets, parentheses, or ellipses. If a sentence is correct as is, write *correct*.

1. This May will be my grandparents' forty fifth wedding anniversary.
2. Arthur's essay describes how "it the Grand Canyon is the most amazing natural treasure in the United States."
3. Amelia's mother she came to the United States when she was a girl told us tales of her journey.
4. Did you ever see the film it's a classic Gone With the Wind?
5. Air Force One is the airplane used by the president.
6. I will see the show on 10 21 2009.
7. The cross country trip unbelievable as it may be only took them one week.
8. This novel is set during Reconstruction 1865–1877.
9. The Pledge of Allegiance is an oath that begins, "I pledge to the flag of the United States of America."
10. Her father a world-renowned author wrote many memorable novels.

PRACTICE 6 **Using Capital Letters Correctly**

Read each sentence. Rewrite each sentence, using capital letters where they are needed.

1. this tuesday i have an important meeting with the board of education.
2. he won the pulitzer prize last year for his article on the republican party, published in *the new york times*.
3. "is your mother english," stephanie asked, "or is she australian?"
4. "the directions say to go south, past interstate 95," Michael read, "and I think we'll drive by springfield."
5. this fall we are going to the pumpkin festival in vermont.

630 Mechanics

RESOURCES FOR Writing COACH

Writing in the Content Areas	R2
Writing for Media	R6
Writing for the Workplace	R12
Creating Note Cards	R12
Writing a Meeting Agenda	R13
Writing Business Letters	R14
Writing Friendly Letters	R15
MLA Style for Listing Sources	R16
Commonly Misspelled Words	R17
English Glossary	R18
Spanish Glossary	R21
Graphic Organizer Handbook	R24
Listening and Speaking Handbook	R28
Index	R32
Index of Authors and Titles	R57
Acknowledgments	R58

WRITING IN THE Content Areas

Writing in the content areas—math, social studies, science, the arts, and various career and technical studies—is an important tool for learning. The following pages give examples of content area writing along with strategies.

FORMS OF MATH WRITING

Written Estimate An estimate, or informed idea, of the size, cost, time, or other measure of a thing, based on given information.

Analysis of a Problem A description of a problem, such as figuring out how long a trip will take, along with an explanation of the mathematical formulas or equations you can use to solve the problem.

Response to an Open-Ended Math Prompt A response to a question or writing assignment involving math, such as a word problem or a question about a graph or a mathematical concept.

Writing in Math

Prewriting

- **Choosing a Topic** If you have a choice of topics, review your textbook and class notes for ideas, and choose one that interests you.
- **Responding to a Prompt** If you are responding to a prompt, read and then reread the instructions, ensuring that you understand all of the requirements of the assignment.

Drafting

- **State Problems Clearly** Be clear, complete, and accurate in your description of the problem you are analyzing or reporting on. Make sure that you have used technical terms, such as *ratio*, *area*, and *factor*, accurately.
- **Explain Your Solution** Tell readers exactly which mathematical rules or formulas you use in your analysis and why they apply. Clearly spell out each step you take in your reasoning.
- **Use Graphics** By presenting quantitative information in a graph, table, or chart, you make it easier for readers to absorb information. Choose the format appropriate to the material, as follows:
  - ✔ **Line Graphs** Use a line graph to show the relationship between two variables, such as time and speed in a problem about a moving object. Clearly label the x- and y-axis with the variable each represents and with the units you are using. Choose units appropriately to make the graph manageable. For example, do not try to represent time in years if you are plotting changes for an entire century; instead, use units of ten years each.
  - ✔ **Other Graphs** Use a pie chart to analyze facts about a group, such as the percentage of students who walk to school, the percentage who drive, and the percentage who take the bus. Use a bar graph to compare two or more things at different times or in different categories. Assign a single color to each thing, and use that color consistently for all the bars representing data about that thing.
  - ✔ **Tables** Use a table to help readers look up specific values quickly, such as the time the sun sets in each month of the year. Label each column and row with terms that clearly identify the data you are presenting, including the units you are using.

Revising

- **Ensure Accuracy** For accuracy, double-check the formulas you use and the calculations you make.
- **Revise for Traits of Good Writing** Ask yourself the following questions: *How well have I applied mathematical ideas? Does my organizational plan help readers follow my reasoning? Is my voice suitable to my audience and purpose? Have I chosen precise words and used mathematical terms accurately? Are my sentences well constructed and varied? Have I made any errors in grammar, usage, mechanics, and spelling?* Use your answers to help you revise and edit your work.

Writing in Science

Prewriting

- **Choosing a Topic** If you have a choice of topics, look through class notes and your textbook, or conduct a "media flip-through," browsing online articles, or watching television news and documentaries to find a science-related topic.

- **Responding to a Prompt** If you are responding to a prompt, read the instructions carefully, analyzing the requirements and parts of the assignment. Identify key direction words in the prompt or assignment, such as *explain* and *predict*.

- **Gathering Details**
  ✔ If your assignment requires you to conduct research, search for credible and current sources. Examples of strong sources may include articles in recent issues of science magazines or recently published books. Confirm key facts in more than one source.
  ✔ If your assignment requires you to conduct an experiment, make sure you follow the guidelines for the experiment accurately. Carefully record the steps you take and the observations you make, and date your notes. Repeat the experiment to confirm results.

Drafting

- **Focus and Elaborate** In your introduction, clearly state your topic. Make sure you tell readers why your topic matters. As you draft, give sufficient details, including background, facts, and examples, to help your readers understand your topic. Summarize your findings and insights in your conclusion.

- **Organize** As you draft, follow a suitable organizational pattern. If you are telling the story of an important scientific breakthrough, consider telling events in chronological order. If you are explaining a natural process, consider discussing causes and the effects that follow from them. If you are defending a solution to a problem, you might give pros and cons, answering each counterargument in turn.

- **Present Data Visually** Consider presenting quantitative information, such as statistics or measurements, in a graph, table, or chart. Choose the format appropriate to the material. (Consult the guidance on visual displays of data under "Use Graphics" on page R2.)

Revising

- **Meet Your Audience's Needs** Identify places in your draft where your audience may need more information, such as additional background, more explanation, or the definition of a technical term. Add the information required.

- **Revise for Traits of Good Writing** Ask yourself the following questions: *How clearly have I presented scientific ideas? Will my organization help a reader see the connections I am making? Is my voice suitable to my audience and purpose? Have I chosen precise words and used technical terms accurately? Are my sentences well constructed and varied? Have I made any errors in grammar, usage, mechanics, and spelling?* Use your answers to revise and edit your work.

FORMS OF SCIENCE WRITING

Lab Report A firsthand report of a scientific experiment, following an appropriate format. A standard lab report includes a statement of the hypothesis, or prediction, that the experiment is designed to test; a list of the materials used; an account of the steps performed; a report of the results observed; and the experimenter's conclusions.

Cause-and-Effect Essay A scientific explanation of the causes and effects involved in natural or technical phenomena, such as solar flares, the digestion of food, or the response of metal to stress.

Technical Procedure Document A step-by-step guide to performing a scientific experiment or performing a technical task involving science. A well-written technical procedure document presents the steps of the procedure in clear order. It breaks steps into substeps and prepares readers by explaining what materials they will need and the time they can expect each step to take.

Response to an Open-Ended Science Prompt A response to a question or writing assignment about science.

Summary of a Science-Related Article A retelling of the main ideas in an article that concerns science or technology, such as an article on a new medical procedure.

Writing in Social Studies

FORMS OF SOCIAL STUDIES WRITING

Social Studies Research Report An informative paper, based on research, about a historical period or event or about a specific place or culture. A well-written research report draws on a variety of sources to develop and support a thoughtful point of view on the topic. It cites those sources accurately, following an accepted format.

Biographical Essay An overview of the life of a historically important person. A well-written biographical essay reports the life of its subject accurately and clearly explains the importance of his or her contributions.

Historical Overview A survey, or general picture, of a historical period or development, such as the struggle for women's right to vote. A successful historical overview presents the "big picture," covering major events and important aspects of the topic without getting lost in details.

Historical Cause-and-Effect Essay An analysis of the causes and effects of a historical event. A well-written historical explanation makes clear connections between events to help readers follow the explanation.

Prewriting

- **Choosing a Topic** If you have a choice of topics, find a suitable topic by looking through class notes and your textbook. Make a quick list of topics in history, politics, or geography that interest you and choose a topic based on your list.

- **Responding to a Prompt** If you are responding to a prompt, read the instructions carefully, analyzing the requirements and parts of the assignment. Identify key direction words in the prompt or assignment, such as *compare*, *describe*, and *argue*.

- **Gathering Details** If your assignment requires you to conduct research, consult a variety of credible sources. For in-depth research, review both primary sources (documents from the time you are investigating) and secondary sources (accounts by those who analyze or report on the information). If you find contradictions, evaluate the likely reasons for the differences.

Drafting

- **Establish a Thesis or Theme** If you are writing a research report or other informative piece, state your main point about your topic in a thesis statement. Include your thesis statement in your introduction. If you are writing a creative piece, such as a historical skit or short story, identify the theme, or main message, you wish to convey.

- **Support Your Thesis or Theme** Organize your work around your main idea.
  - ✔ In a research report, support and develop your thesis with well-chosen, relevant details. First, provide background information your readers will need, and then discuss different subtopics in different sections of the body of your report. Clearly connect each subtopic to your main thesis.
  - ✔ In a creative work, develop your theme through the conflict between characters. For example, a conflict between two brothers during the Civil War over which side to fight on might dramatize the theme of divided loyalties. Organize events to build to a climax, or point of greatest excitement, that clearly conveys your message.

Revising

- **Sharpen Your Focus** Review your draft for sections that do not clearly support your thesis or theme, and consider eliminating them. Revise unnecessary repetition of ideas. Ensure that the sequence of ideas or events will help reader comprehension.

- **Revise for Traits of Good Writing** Ask yourself the following questions: *How clearly have I developed my thesis or my theme? Will my organization help a reader follow my development of my thesis or theme? Is my voice suitable to my audience and purpose? Have I chosen precise and vivid words, accurately using terms from the period or place about which I am writing? Are my sentences well constructed and varied? Have I made any errors in grammar, usage, mechanics, and spelling?* Use your answers to revise and edit your work.

WRITING IN THE Content Areas

Writing About the Arts

Prewriting

Experience the Work Take notes on the subject of each work you will discuss. Consider its mood, or general feeling, and its theme, or insight into life.

- ✔ For visual arts, consider the use of color, light, line (sharp or smooth, smudged or definite), mass (heavy or light), and composition (the arrangement and balance of forms).
- ✔ For music, consider the use of melody, rhythm, harmony, and instrumentation. Also, consider the performers' interpretation of the work.

Drafting

Develop Your Ideas As you draft, support your main ideas, including your insights into or feelings about a work, with relevant details.

Revising

Revise for Traits of Good Writing Ask yourself the following questions: *How clearly do I present my ideas? Will my organization help a reader follow my points? Is my voice suitable to my audience and purpose? Have I chosen precise and vivid words, to describe the works? Are my sentences varied? Have I made any errors in grammar, usage, and mechanics?* Use your answers to revise and edit your work.

Writing in Career and Technical Studies

Prewriting

Choosing a Topic If you have a choice of topics, find a suitable one by looking through class notes and your textbook or by listing your own related projects or experiences.

Drafting

Organize Information As you draft, follow a logical organization. If you are explaining a procedure, list steps in the order that your readers should follow. If they need information about the materials and preparation required, provide that information first. Use formatting (such as headings, numbered steps, and bullet points), graphics (such as diagrams), and transitional words and phrases (such as *first, next,* and *if... then*).

Revising

Revise for Traits of Good Writing Ask yourself the following questions: *Have I given readers all the information they will need? Will my organization help a reader follow my points? Is my voice suitable to my audience and purpose? Have I chosen precise words, using technical terms accurately? Are my sentences well constructed? Have I made errors in grammar, usage, and mechanics?* Use your answers to revise and edit your work.

FORMS OF WRITING ABOUT THE ARTS

Research Report on a Trend or Style in Art An informative paper, based on research, about a specific group of artists or trend in the arts.

Biographical Essay An overview of the life of an artist or performer.

Analysis of a Work A detailed description of a work offering insights into its meaning and importance.

Review of a Performance or Exhibit An evaluation of an artistic performance or exhibit.

FORMS OF CAREER AND TECHNICAL WRITING

Technical Procedure Document A step-by-step guide to performing a specialized task, such as wiring a circuit or providing first aid.

Response to an Open-Ended Practical Studies Prompt A response to a question or writing assignment about a task or concept in a specialized field.

Technical Research Report An informative paper, based on research, about a specific topic in a practical field, such as a report on balanced diet in the field of health.

Analysis of a Career An informative paper explaining the requirements for a particular job, along with the responsibilities, salary, benefits, and job opportunities.

WRITING FOR
Media

New technology has created many new ways to communicate. Today, it is easy to contribute information to the Internet and send a variety of messages to friends far and near. You can also share your ideas through photos, illustrations, video, and sound recordings.

Writing for Media gives you an overview of some ways you can use today's technology to create, share, and find information. **Here are the topics you will find in this section:**

- Blogs
- Social Networking
- Widgets and Feeds
- Multimedia Elements
- Podcasts
- Wikis

Blogs

A **blog** is a common form of online writing. The word *blog* is a contraction of *Web log*. Most blogs include a series of entries known as posts. The posts appear in a single column and are displayed in reverse chronological order. That means that the most recent post is at the top of the page. As you scroll down, you will find earlier posts.

Blogs have become increasingly popular. Researchers estimate that 75,000 new blogs are launched every day. Blog authors are often called bloggers. They can use their personal sites to share ideas, songs, videos, photos, and other media. People who read blogs can often post their responses with a comments feature found in each new post.

Because blogs are designed so that they are easy to update, bloggers can post new messages as often as they like, often daily. For some people blogs become a public journal or diary in which they share their thoughts about daily events.

Types of Blogs

Not all blogs are the same. Many blogs have a single author, but others are group projects. These are some common types of blog:

- **Personal blogs** often have a general focus. Bloggers post their thoughts on any topic they find interesting in their daily lives.
- **Topical blogs** focus on a specific theme, such as movie reviews, political news, class assignments, or health-care opportunities.

WEB SAFETY Using the Internet safely means keeping personal information personal. Never include your address (e-mail or physical), last name, or telephone numbers. Avoid mentioning places you go to often.

Never give out passwords you use to access other Web sites and do not respond to e-mails from people you do not know.

WRITING FOR Media

Anatomy of a Blog

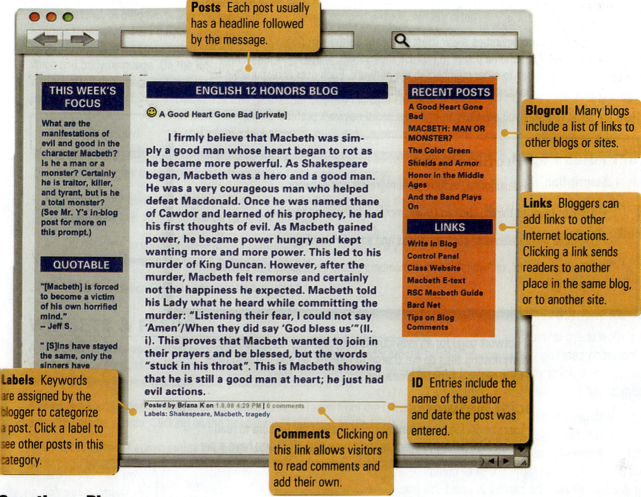

Creating a Blog

Keep these hints and strategies in mind to help you create an interesting and fair blog:

- Focus each blog entry on a single topic.
- Vary the length of your posts. Sometimes, all you need is a line or two to share a quick thought. Other posts will be much longer.
- Choose font colors and styles that can be read easily.
- Many people scan blogs rather than read them closely. You can make your main ideas pop out by using clear or clever headlines and boldfacing key terms.
- Give credit to other people's work and ideas. State the names of people whose ideas you are quoting or add a link to take readers to that person's blog or site.
- If you post comments, try to make them brief and polite.

Social Networking

Social networking means any interaction between members of an online community. People can exchange many different kinds of information, from text and voice messages to video images. Many social network communities allow users to create permanent pages that describe themselves. Users create home pages to express themselves, share ideas about their lives, and post messages to other members in the network. Each user is responsible for adding and updating the content on his or her profile page.

Here are some features you are likely to find on a social network profile:

Features of Profile Pages

- A **biographical description**, including photographs and artwork
- **Lists of favorite things**, such as books, movies, music, and fashions
- **Playable media** elements such as videos and sound recordings
- **Message boards**, or "walls," on which members of the community can exchange messages

Privacy in Social Networks

Social networks allow users to decide how open their profiles will be. Be sure to read introductory information carefully before you register at a new site. Once you have a personal profile page, monitor your privacy settings regularly. Remember that any information you post will be available to anyone in your network.

Users often post messages anonymously or using false names, or pseudonyms. People can also post using someone else's name. Judge all information on the net critically. Do not assume that you know who posted some information simply because you recognize the name of the post author. The rapid speed of communication on the Internet can make it easy to jump to conclusions—be careful to avoid this trap.

> You can create a social network page for an individual or a group, such as a school or special interest club. Many hosting sites do not charge to register, so you can also have fun by creating a page for a pet or a fictional character.

WRITING FOR Media

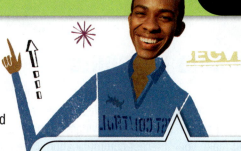

Tips for Sending Effective Messages

Technology makes it easy to share ideas quickly, but writing for the Internet poses some special challenges. The writing style for blogs and social networks is often very conversational. In blog posts and comments, instant messages, and e-mails, writers often express themselves very quickly, using relaxed language, short sentences, and abbreviations. However in a face-to-face conversation, we get a lot of information from a speaker's tone of voice and body language. On the Internet, those clues are missing. As a result, Internet writers often use italics or bracketed labels to indicate emotions. Another alternative is using emoticons—strings of characters that give visual clues to indicate emotion.

:-) **smile** *(happy)*   :-(**frown** *(unhappy)*   ;-) **wink** *(light sarcasm)*

Use these strategies to communicate effectively when using technology:

✔ *Before you click Send,* **reread your message** *to make sure that your tone is clear.*

✔ ***Do not jump to conclusions***—*ask for clarification first. Make sure you really understand what someone is saying before you respond.*

✔ *Use* **abbreviations** *your reader will understand.*

Widgets and Feeds

A **widget** is a small application that performs a specific task. You might find widgets that give weather predictions, offer dictionary definitions or translations, provide entertainment such as games, or present a daily word, photograph, or quotation.

A **feed** is a special kind of widget. It displays headlines taken from the latest content on a specific media source. Clicking on the headline will take you to the full article. Many social network communities and other Web sites allow you to personalize your home page by adding widgets and feeds.

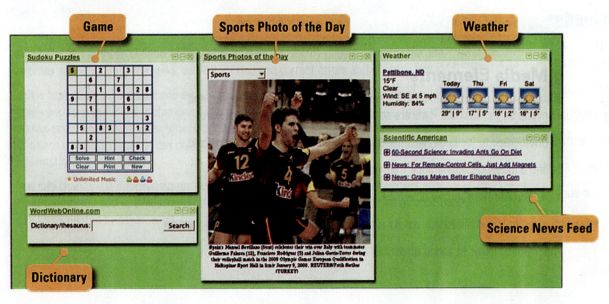

Writing for Media: Widgets and Feeds R9

Multimedia Elements

One of the great advantages of communicating on the Internet is that you are not limited to using text only. When you create a Web profile or blog, you can share your ideas using a wide variety of media. In addition to widgets and feeds (see page R9), these media elements can make your Internet communication more entertaining and useful.

GRAPHICS	
Photographs	You can post photographs taken by digital cameras or scanned as files.
Illustrations	Artwork can be created using computer software. You can also use a scanner to post a digital image of a drawing or sketch.
Charts, Graphs, and Maps	Charts and graphs can make statistical information clear. Use spreadsheet software to create these elements. Use Internet sites to find maps of specific places.

VIDEO	
Live Action	Digital video can be recorded by a camera or recorded from another media source.
Animation	Animated videos can also be created using software.

AUDIO	
Music	Many social network communities make it easy to share your favorite music with people who visit your page.
Voice	Use a microphone to add your own voice to your Web page.

Editing Media Elements

You can use software to customize media elements. Open source software is free and available to anyone on the Internet. Here are some things you can do with software:

- **Crop** a photograph to focus on the subject or brighten an image that is too dark.
- **Transform** a drawing's appearance from flat to three-dimensional.
- **Insert** a "You Are Here" arrow on a map.
- **Edit** a video or sound file to shorten its running time.
- **Add** background music or sound effects to a video.

WRITING FOR Media

Podcasts

A **podcast** is a digital audio or video recording of a program that is made available on the Internet. Users can replay the podcast on a computer, or download it and replay it on a personal audio player. You might think of podcasts as radio or television programs that you create yourself. They can be embedded on a Web site or fed to a Web page through a podcast widget.

Creating an Effective Podcast

To make a podcast, you will need a recording device, such as a microphone or digital video camera, as well as editing software. Open source editing software is widely available and free of charge. Most audio podcasts are converted into the MP3 format. Here are some tips for creating a podcast that is clear and entertaining:

- **Listen to several podcasts by different authors** to get a feeling for the medium.
- **Make a list** of features and styles you like and also those you want to avoid.
- **Test your microphone** to find the best recording distance. Stand close enough to the microphone so that your voice sounds full, but not so close that you create an echo.
- **Create an outline** that shows your estimated timing for each element.
- **Be prepared** before you record. Rehearse, but do not create a script. Podcasts are best when they have a natural, easy flow.
- **Talk directly to your listeners**. Slow down enough so they can understand you.
- Use software to **edit your podcast before publishing it**. You can edit out mistakes or add additional elements.

Wikis

A **wiki** is a collaborative Web site that lets visitors create, add, remove, and edit content. The term comes from the Hawaiian phrase *wikiwiki*, which means "quick." Web users of a wiki are both the readers and the writers of the site. Some wikis are open to contributions from anyone. Others require visitors to register before they can edit the content. All of the text in these collaborative Web sites was written by people who use the site. Articles are constantly changing, as visitors find and correct errors and improve texts.

Wikis have both advantages and disadvantages as sources of information. They are valuable open forums for the exchange of ideas. The unique collaborative writing process allows entries to change over time. However, entries can also be modified incorrectly. Careless or malicious users can delete good content and add inappropriate or inaccurate information. Wikis may be useful for gathering background information, but should not be used as research resources.

You can change the information on a wiki, but be sure your information is correct and clear before you add it. Wikis keep track of all changes, so your work will be recorded and can be evaluated by other users.

Writing for Media: Podcasts and Wikis

WRITING FOR THE Workplace

Writing is something many people do every day at work, school, or home. They write letters and reports, do research, plan meetings, and keep track of information in notes.

Writing for the Workplace shows you some models of the following forms of writing:

- **Note Cards**
- **Meeting Agenda**
- **Business Letter**
- **Friendly Letter**

Creating Note Cards

Whether you are working on a research report or gathering information for another purpose, it is helpful to keep your notes on individual cards or in note files on a computer. You will need to make sure that you note your sources on your cards. You can organize information many different ways, but it is most helpful to keep notes of one kind together.

> The **topic** is the main focus of the notes.

> You can name the **source**, as shown here, or refer to the source by number (e.g., Source 3) if you are using source cards.

Topic: Octopus
Source: PBS Web site Accessed 10/15/2010
http://www.pbs.org/wnet/nature/episodes/the-octopus-show/a-legend-of-the-deep/2014/

- Acrobatic and shy animals
- Can squeeze into very small spaces to hide or catch food
- Talented swimmers
- Can change color
- Live in all kinds of environments

> In the notes section focus on the ideas that are most important to your research. Note that these ideas may not always be the main ideas of the selection you are reading. You do not need to write in full sentences. However, you may want to use bullets to make your notes easier to read.

R12 Writing for the Workplace: Note Cards

Writing a Meeting Agenda

When you have a meeting, it is helpful to use an agenda. An agenda tells what will be discussed in the meeting. It tells who is responsible for which topic. It also provides a guide for the amount of time to be spent on each topic.

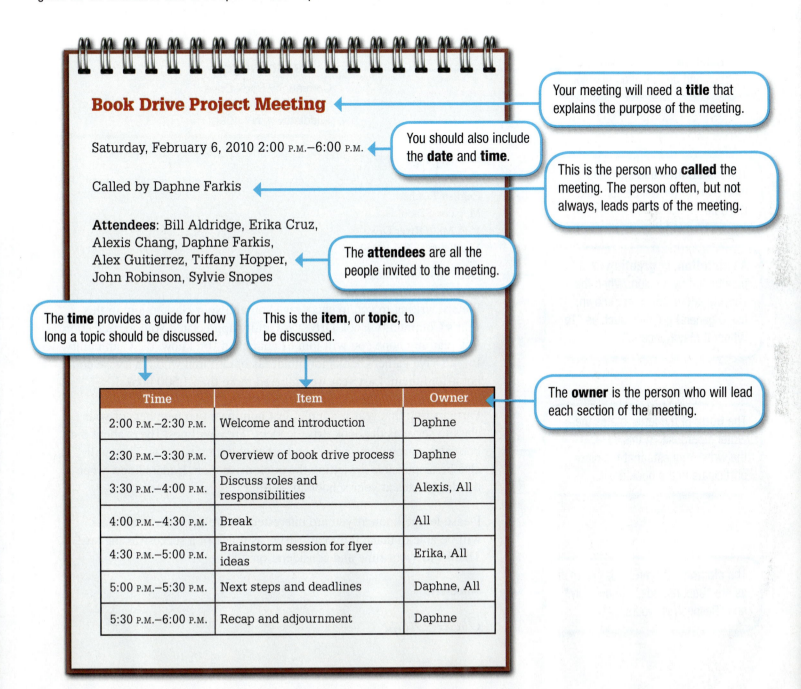

Book Drive Project Meeting ← Your meeting will need a **title** that explains the purpose of the meeting.

Saturday, February 6, 2010 2:00 P.M.–6:00 P.M. ← You should also include the **date** and **time**.

Called by Daphne Farkis ← This is the person who **called** the meeting. The person often, but not always, leads parts of the meeting.

Attendees: Bill Aldridge, Erika Cruz, Alexis Chang, Daphne Farkis, Alex Guitierrez, Tiffany Hopper, John Robinson, Sylvie Snopes ← The **attendees** are all the people invited to the meeting.

The **time** provides a guide for how long a topic should be discussed.

This is the **item**, or **topic**, to be discussed.

Time	Item	Owner
2:00 P.M.–2:30 P.M.	Welcome and introduction	Daphne
2:30 P.M.–3:30 P.M.	Overview of book drive process	Daphne
3:30 P.M.–4:00 P.M.	Discuss roles and responsibilities	Alexis, All
4:00 P.M.–4:30 P.M.	Break	All
4:30 P.M.–5:00 P.M.	Brainstorm session for flyer ideas	Erika, All
5:00 P.M.–5:30 P.M.	Next steps and deadlines	Daphne, All
5:30 P.M.–6:00 P.M.	Recap and adjournment	Daphne

The **owner** is the person who will lead each section of the meeting.

Writing Business Letters

Business letters are often formal in tone and written for a specific business purpose. They generally follow one of several acceptable formats. In block format, all parts of the letter are at the left margin. All business letters, however, have the same parts: heading, inside address, salutation, body, closing, and signature.

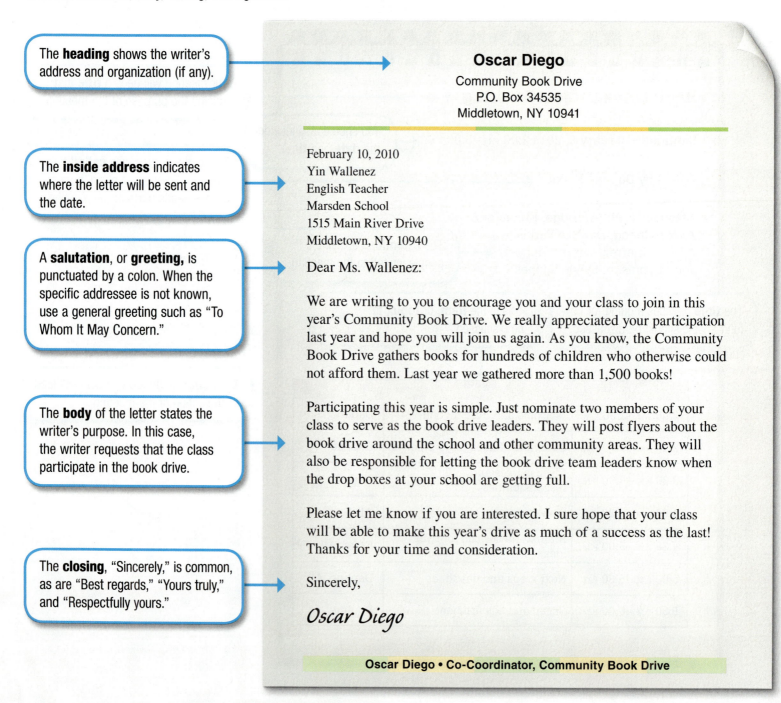

The **heading** shows the writer's address and organization (if any).

Oscar Diego
Community Book Drive
P.O. Box 34535
Middletown, NY 10941

The **inside address** indicates where the letter will be sent and the date.

February 10, 2010
Yin Wallenez
English Teacher
Marsden School
1515 Main River Drive
Middletown, NY 10940

A **salutation**, or **greeting,** is punctuated by a colon. When the specific addressee is not known, use a general greeting such as "To Whom It May Concern."

Dear Ms. Wallenez:

We are writing to you to encourage you and your class to join in this year's Community Book Drive. We really appreciated your participation last year and hope you will join us again. As you know, the Community Book Drive gathers books for hundreds of children who otherwise could not afford them. Last year we gathered more than 1,500 books!

The **body** of the letter states the writer's purpose. In this case, the writer requests that the class participate in the book drive.

Participating this year is simple. Just nominate two members of your class to serve as the book drive leaders. They will post flyers about the book drive around the school and other community areas. They will also be responsible for letting the book drive team leaders know when the drop boxes at your school are getting full.

Please let me know if you are interested. I sure hope that your class will be able to make this year's drive as much of a success as the last! Thanks for your time and consideration.

The **closing**, "Sincerely," is common, as are "Best regards," "Yours truly," and "Respectfully yours."

Sincerely,

Oscar Diego

Oscar Diego • Co-Coordinator, Community Book Drive

Writing Friendly Letters

Friendly letters are less formal than business letters. You can use this form to write to a friend, a family member, or anyone with whom you'd like to communicate in a personal, friendly way. Like business letters, friendly letters have the following parts: heading, inside address, salutation, body, closing, and signature. The purpose of a friendly letter might be:
- to share news and feelings
- to send or answer an invitation
- to express thanks

The **heading** includes the writer's address and the date on which he or she wrote the letter. In some very casual letters, the writer may not include his or her address.

The **body** of the letter is the main section and contains the message of the letter.

Some common **closings** for friendly letters include "Best wishes," "Love," and "Take care."

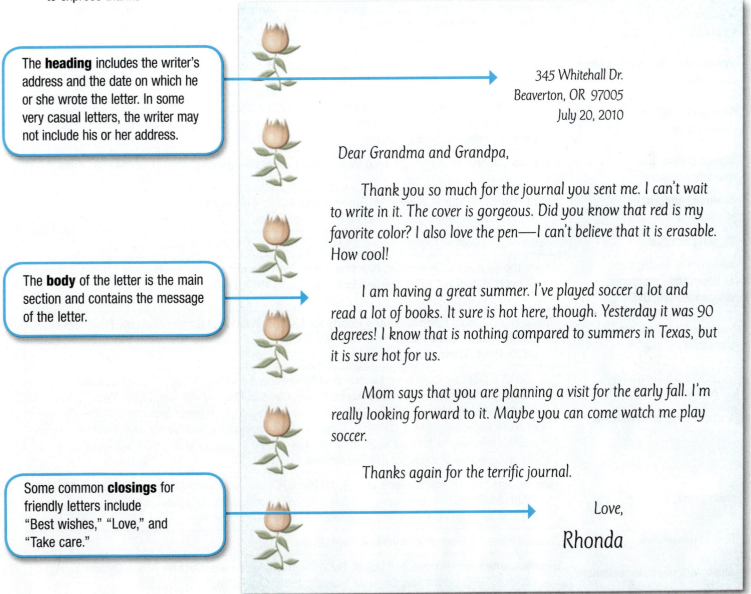

345 Whitehall Dr.
Beaverton, OR 97005
July 20, 2010

Dear Grandma and Grandpa,

Thank you so much for the journal you sent me. I can't wait to write in it. The cover is gorgeous. Did you know that red is my favorite color? I also love the pen—I can't believe that it is erasable. How cool!

I am having a great summer. I've played soccer a lot and read a lot of books. It sure is hot here, though. Yesterday it was 90 degrees! I know that is nothing compared to summers in Texas, but it is sure hot for us.

Mom says that you are planning a visit for the early fall. I'm really looking forward to it. Maybe you can come watch me play soccer.

Thanks again for the terrific journal.

Love,
Rhonda

MLA Style for Listing Sources

Book with one author	London, Jack. *White Fang.* Clayton: Prestwick, 2007. Print.
Book with two or three authors	Veit, Richard, and Christopher Gould. *Writing, Reading, and Research*. 8th ed. Boston: Wadsworth-Cengage Learning, 2009. Print.
Book prepared by an editor	Twain, Mark. *The Complete Essays of Mark Twain.* Ed. Charles Neider. New York: Da Capo, 2000. Print.
Book with more than three authors or editors	Donald, Robert B., et al. *Writing Clear Essays*. 3rd ed. Upper Saddle River: Prentice, 1996. Print.
A single work from an anthology	Poe, Edgar Allan. "The Fall of the House of Usher." *American Literature: A Chronological Approach.* Ed. Edgar H. Schuster, Anthony Tovatt, and Patricia O. Tovatt. New York: McGraw, 1985. 233–247. Print. [Indicate pages for the entire selection.]
Introduction, foreward, preface, or afterward in a book	Vidal, Gore. Introduction. *Abraham Lincoln: Selected Speeches and Writings.* By Abraham Lincoln. New York: Vintage, 1992. xxi–xxvii. Print.
Signed article in a weekly magazine	Walsh, Brian. "Greening This Old House." *Time* 4 May 2009: 45–47. Print. [For a multipage article that does not appear on consecutive pages, write only the first page number on which it appears, followed by a plus sign.]
Signed article in a monthly magazine	Fischman, Josh. "A Better Life with Bionics." *National Geographic* Jan. 2010: 34–53. Print.
Unsigned editorial or story	"Wind Power." Editorial. *New York Times* 9 Jan. 2010: A18. Print. [If the editorial or story is signed, begin with the author's name.]
Signed pamphlet	[Treat the pamphlet as though it were a book.]
Audiovisual media, such as films, slide programs, videocassettes, DVDs	*Where the Red Fern Grows.* Dir. Norman Toker. Perf. James Whitmore, Beverly Garland, and Stewart Peterson. 1974. Sterling Entertainment, 1997. DVD.
Radio or TV broadcast transcript	"Texas High School Football Titans Ready for Clash." *Weekend Edition Sunday.* Host Melissa Block. Guests Mike Pesca and Tom Goldman. Natl. Public Radio. KUHF, Houston, 18 Dec. 2009. Print. Transcript.
A single page on a Web site	U.S. Census Bureau: Customer Liaison and Marketing Services Office. "State Facts for Students: Texas." *U.S. Census Bureau.* U.S. Census Bureau, 15 Oct. 2009. Web. 1 Nov. 2009. [Indicate the date of last update if known or use "n.d." if not known. After the medium of publication, include the date you accessed the information. You do not need the URL unless it is the only way to find the page. If needed, include it in angled brackets at the end, i.e. <http://www.census.gov/schools/facts/texas.html >.]
Newspaper	Yardley, Jim. "Hurricane Sweeps into Rural Texas; Cities Are Spared." *New York Times* 23 Aug. 1999: A1. Print. [For a multipage article that does not appear on consecutive pages, write only the first page number on which it appears, followed by a plus sign.]
Personal interview	Jones, Robert. Personal interview. 4 Sept. 2006.
Audio with multiple publishers	Simms, James, ed. *Romeo and Juliet.* By William Shakespeare. Oxford: Attica Cybernetics; London: BBC Education; London: Harper, 1995. CD-ROM.
Signed article from an encyclopedia	Askeland, Donald R. "Welding." *World Book Encyclopedia.* 1991 ed. Print. [For a well-known reference, you do not need to include the publisher information, only the edition and year, followed by the medium used.]

Commonly Misspelled Words

The list on this page presents words that cause problems for many people. Some of these words are spelled according to set rules, but others follow no specific rules. As you review this list, check to see how many of the words give you trouble in your own writing.

absence	benefit	conscience	excellent	library	prejudice
absolutely	bicycle	conscientious	exercise	license	previous
accidentally	bought	conscious	experience	lightning	probably
accurate	brief	continuous	explanation	likable	procedure
achievement	brilliant	convenience	extension	literature	proceed
affect	bulletin	coolly	extraordinary	mathematics	pronunciation
agreeable	bury	cooperate	familiar	maximum	realize
aisle	buses	correspondence	fascinating	minimum	really
all right	business	courageous	February	misspell	receipt
allowance	cafeteria	courteous	fiery	naturally	receive
analysis	calendar	criticism	financial	necessary	recognize
analyze	campaign	curiosity	foreign	neighbor	recommend
ancient	canceled	deceive	fourth	niece	rehearse
anniversary	candidate	decision	generally	ninety	repetition
answer	capital	defendant	genuine	noticeable	restaurant
anticipate	capitol	definitely	government	occasion	rhythm
anxiety	career	dependent	grammar	occasionally	sandwich
apologize	cashier	description	guidance	occur	schedule
appearance	category	desert	height	occurred	scissors
appreciate	ceiling	dessert	humorous	occurrence	theater
appropriate	certain	dining	immediately	opinion	truly
argument	changeable	disappointed	immigrant	opportunity	usage
athletic	characteristic	distinguish	independence	parallel	valuable
attendance	clothes	effect	independent	particularly	various
awkward	colonel	eighth	individual	personally	vegetable
bargain	column	embarrass	intelligence	persuade	weight
battery	commercial	enthusiastic	judgment	physician	weird
beautiful	commitment	envelope	knowledge	possibility	whale
beginning	condemn	environment	lawyer	precede	yield
believe	congratulate	especially	legible	preferable	

English Glossary

A

accuracy (ak´yər ə sē) *n.* the state of being without error

accurate (ak´yər it) *adj.* without errors; true

adequate (ad´i kwət) *adj.* satisfactory or acceptable; good enough

aesthetic (es thet´ik) *adj.* relating to beauty; artistic; pleasing to the senses

analogy (ə nal´ə jē) *n.* a comparison between two things, often for the purpose of explaining; an extended comparison between two pairs of things, based on the idea that the items in the first pair are related to each other in the same way as the items in the second pair

analysis (ə nal´ə sis) *n.* the process of looking at something closely in order to understand its meaning, structure, or parts

analytical (an´ə lit´ik əl) *adj.* relating to, or using, logical reasoning

anecdote (an´ik dōt´) *n.* a short, interesting, often funny story about something that actually happened

anticipate (an tis´ə pāt´) *v.* to expect or predict; to foresee and then be ready to deal with

appeal (ə pēl´) *v.* to be attractive or interesting; to make a serious request

appreciate (ə prē´shē āt´) *v.* to understand or recognize the value of something; to be grateful for; to fully understand

argue (är´gyü) *v.* to give reasons or evidence to try to prove something in order to persuade others to agree with you; to exchange opposite views, often in an angry way

assertion (ə sʉr´shən) *n.* a strong statement of fact or belief about a subject

audience (ô´dē əns) *n.* the readers of a book or other piece of writing; a group of listeners or viewers

B

ballad (bal´əd) *n.* a song-like poem that tells a story, often of love and adventure

benefits (ben´ə fits) *n.* advantages

C

capable (kā´pə bəl) *adj.* able; having the qualities needed in order to do or achieve a particular thing

chaos (kā´äs´) *n.* a state of complete confusion and disorganization

character (kar´ik tər) *n.* a person (or animal) who plays a part in the action of a story, play, or movie

comparison (kəm par´ə sən) *n.* the act of comparing, examining the differences and similarities between two or more things

conflict (kän´flikt´) *n.* the struggle between people or opposing forces which creates the dramatic action in a play or story

consider (kən sid´ər) *v.* to take into account; to think about with care

context (kän´tekst´) *n.* the part of a sentence which surrounds a word and which can be used to shed light on the word's meaning; the situation in which something occurs which can help that thing to be fully understood; the setting or environment

conversely (kən vʉrs´lē) *adv.* introducing an idea that is the opposite of one which has just been mentioned ("on the other hand")

counter-argument (kount´ər är´gyü mənt) *n.* a reason against the original argument

D

define (dē fīn´) *v.* to explain the meaning of a word or phrase; to fully describe the nature or meaning of something

detective (dē tek´tiv) *n.* a police officer or other person whose job it is to investigate and solve crimes; a person who tries to figure something out

device (di vīs´) *n.* the use of words to gain a particular effect in a piece of writing

dialogue (dī´ə lôg´) *n.* a conversation between two or more people in a book, play, or movie

diction (dik´shən) *n.* a writer's choice of words

distinction (di stink´shən) *n.* the difference between two or more similar things or people; the separation of people or things into different groups; an achievement or honor which sets one person or group apart from others

document (däk´yü mənt) *n.* anything printed or written that gives information; *v.* to support ideas with information from sources

documentation (däk´yü mən tā´shən) *n.* the noting of sources to back up an idea or opinion

E

element (el´ə mənt) *n.* one of several parts that make up a whole

embedded (em bed´əd) *adj.* placed firmly in the middle of something; (of a quotation) placed inside a sentence, not set apart from the rest of the text

essay (es´ā) *n.* a short piece of nonfiction writing on a particular subject

establish (ə stab´lish) *v.* to show or prove with facts and evidence; to set up, start, or create

evidence (ev´ə dəns) *n.* anything that gives proof or shows something to be true

F

figurative (fig´yər ə tiv´) *adj.* (of language) writing that is full of metaphors and images, where the words are very descriptive but not meant to be taken literally

formal (fôr´məl) *adj.* reflecting language that is traditional and correct, not casual

formatting (fôr´mat´ing) *adj.* related to the arrangement of text, images, and graphics on a page

H

headings (hed´ingz) *n.* titles or captions of pages, chapters, or other sections of text

I

imagery (im´ij rē) *n.* descriptive language that paints pictures in the mind or appeals to the senses

impression (im presh´ən) *n.* an idea or feeling about a person or thing that is formed quickly, without a lot of thought

inference (in´fər əns) *n.* a conclusion drawn from available information; the act of drawing this kind of conclusion

information (in´fər mā´shən) *n.* facts about a subject or topic

instructions (in struk´shənz) *n.* steps to be followed to accomplish something

L

literal (lit´ər əl) *adj.* the most basic meaning of a word or words, without metaphor or other figurative language; without any exaggeration or distortion

literary (lit´ər ar´ē) *adj.* of or relating to books or other written material

logical (läj´i kəl) *adj.* based on logic; clear and reasonable

M

meter (mēt´ər) *n.* a poem's rhythmic pattern, made by the number of beats in each line

method (meth´əd) *n.* a particular way of doing something; a systematic plan

mood (müd) *n.* the atmosphere or overall feeling of a piece of writing as created by the author

mysterious (mis tir´ē əs) *adj.* strange; difficult to understand, explain, or identify; (of a person) secretive and deliberately puzzling; (of a place) having a feeling of strangeness and secrecy

O

oppose (ə pōz´) *v.* to go against, disagree

P

poetic (pō et´ik) *adj.* beautiful, expressive, sensitive, or imaginative; like a poem

precise (prē cīs´) *adj.* exact, accurate; careful about details

procedure (prō sē´jər) *n.* the way a task or other work is done

progression (prō gresh´ən) *n.* a natural series of events; a moving forward

purpose (pur´pəs) *n.* the reason something exists, is done, or is created; the aim or goal of an activity or piece of writing

R

reader-friendly (rēd´ər frend´lē) *adj.* easy for an audience to read and understand

realize (rē´ə līz´) *v.* to understand clearly; to become aware of the fact that something is true

relevant (rel´ə vənt) *adj.* closely connected, important, or significant to the matter at hand

repetition (rep´ə tish´ən) *n.* the act of repeating something that has already been said, done, or written

resolution (rez´ə lü´shən) *n.* what happens to resolve the conflict in the plot of a story

rhetorical devices (ri tôr´i kəl di vī´səz) *n.* strategies and techniques, for example metaphor and hyperbole, used by writers to draw in or persuade readers

rhyme (rīme) *n.* the repetition of the same sounds at the ends of words, especially in poetry

rhythm (rith´əm) *n.* the pattern of stressed and unstressed syllables in spoken or written language, particularly in poetry

S

sense (sens) *n.* one of the five abilities of sight, touch, taste, hearing, smell; the ability to make good judgments (common sense); the meaning intended or conveyed; a feeling that something is so; *v.* to become aware of something

sensory (sen´sər ē) *adj.* relating to the senses

setting (set´ing) *n.* the time and place of the action in a story or other piece of writing

sonnet (sän´it) *n.* a poem of fourteen lines, often with a set pattern of rhymes

standard (stan´dərd) *adj.* used as a basis for comparison

stanza (stan´zə) *n.* a group of lines of poetry, usually with a similar length and pattern, separated from other lines by spaces

strategy (strat´ə jē) *n.* in a piece of writing, a literary tactic or method (such as flashback or foreshadowing) used by the writer to achieve a certain goal or affect

structural (struk´chər əl) *adj.* having to do with the form an object takes or the way an object appears

style (stīl) *n.* a way of doing something; a way of writing, composing, or painting, etc. special to a period in history, a group of artists, or a particular person

summarize (sum´ə rīz´) *v.* to briefly state the main points or main ideas

suspect (sə spekt´) *v.* to believe that something is probably true, without any proof

suspense (sə spens´) *n.* a feeling of anxiety and uncertainty about what will happen in a story or other piece of writing

symbol (sim´bəl) *n.* anything that stands for or represents something else

T

technique (tek nēk´) *n.* a method of doing an activity or carrying out a task, often involving skill

theme (thēm) *n.* a central message, concern, or purpose in a literary work

thesis (thē´sis) *n.* an idea or theory that is stated and then discussed in a logical way

tone (tōn) *n.* a writer's attitude toward his or her subject

topic (täp´ik) *n.* a subject that is written about or discussed

transition (tran zish´ən) *n.* the change from one part, place, or idea to another

U

urge (ŭrj) *v.* to try to persuade someone to do something

Spanish Glossary

A

accuracy / exactitud *s.* el estado de no tener errores

accurate / correcto *adj.* sin errores; verdadero

adequate / adecuado *adj.* satisfactorio o aceptable; suficiente

aesthetic / estético *adj.* perteneciente a la belleza, artístico; agradable a los sentidos

analogy / analogía *v.* examinar algo detenidamente para entender su significado o estructura

analysis / análisis *s.* los lectores de un libro u otra obra escrita; un grupo de oyentes o espectadores

analytical / analítico *adj.* relativo a o utilizando el razonamiento lógico

anecdote / anécdota *s.* un cuento breve, interesante y muchas veces cómico sobre algo que realmente ocurrió

anticipate / anticipar *v.* esperar o predecir; prever y estar preparado para tratar con algo

appeal / atraer, pedir *v.* ser atractivo o interesante; solicitar algo seriamente

appreciate / apreciar *v.* entender o reconocer el valor de algo; agradecer; comprender completamente

argue / discutir *v.* dar razones o pruebas para intentar probar algo con el fin de persuadir a otros; intercambiar puntos de vista opuestos, muchas veces de una manera agresiva

assertion / aseveración *s.* una declaración fuerte de un hecho o creencia sobre un tema

audience / audiencia, público *s.* los lectores de un libro u otra obra escrita; un grupo de oyentes o espectadores

B

ballad / balada *s.* una canción poética que cuenta una historia, muchas veces del amor y la aventura

benefits / beneficios *s.* ventajas

C

capable / capaz *adj.* hábil; que posee las cualidades necesarias para hacer algo o lograr algo particular

chaos / caos *s.* un estado de confusión total y desorden

character / personaje *s.* un individuo (humano o animal) que tiene un papel en la acción de un cuento, una obra de teatro o una película

comparison / comparación *s.* el acto de comparar, examinar las diferencias y semejanzas entre dos más cosas

conflict / conflicto *s.* la lucha entre personas o fuerzas opuestas que crea la acción dramática en una obra de teatro o un cuento

consider / considerar *v.* tomar en cuenta; meditar sobre algo

context / contexto *s.* la parte de una oración que rodea una palabra y que se puede usar para determinar el significado de la palabra; la situación en la que algo ocurre que puede facilitar la comprensión de la cosa; el escenario o entorno

conversely / en cambio *adv.* expresión que se utiliza para plantear una idea opuesta a la idea mencionada antes ("por otra parte")

counter-argument / contraargumento *s.* una razón contra el argumento original

D

define / definir *v.* explicar el significado de una palabra o expresión; describir completamente la naturaleza o significado de algo

detective / detective *s.* un policía u otra persona cuyo trabajo es investigar y resolver crímenes; una persona que trata de comprender algo

device / técnica (literaria) *s.* el uso de palabras para tener un efecto específico en una obra escrita

dialogue / diálogo *s.* una conversación entre dos personajes o más en un libro, obra de teatro o película

diction / dicción *s.* la selección de palabras de un escritor

distinction / distinción *s.* la diferencia entre dos o más cosas o personas similares; la separación de personas o cosas entre diferentes grupos; un logro u honor que marca las diferencias entre personas o grupos

document / documento *s.* cualquier cosa impresa o escrita que aporta información; *v.* apoyar ideas con información de fuentes

documentation / documentación *s.* la anotación de fuentes para apoyar una idea u opinión

E

element / **elemento** *s.* una de varias partes que forman una totalidad

embedded / **colocado** *adj.* metido firmemente en medio de algo; (de una cita) insertada dentro de una oración, no separada del resto del texto

essay / **ensayo** *s.* una obra de escritura breve de no ficción sobre un tema particular

establish / **establecer** *v.* demostrar o probar con hechos y evidencia; arma, empezar o crear

evidence / **pruebas** *s.* cualquier cosa que demuestre o indique que algo es cierto

F

figurative / **figurado** *adj.* (de lenguaje) escritura que está repleta de metáforas e imágenes, donde las palabras son muy descriptivas pero su significado no debe ser interpretado literalmente

formatting / **formateo** *s.* la colocación de texto, imágenes y gráficos en una página

formal / **formal** *adj.* que refleja el lenguaje tradicional y correcto, no informal

H

headings / **encabezamientos** *s.* los títulos o subtítulos de las páginas, capítulos u otras secciones de texto

I

imagery / **imaginario** *s.* lenguaje descriptivo que crea dibujos en la mente o atrae los sentidos

impression / **impresión** *s.* una idea o sentimiento que se forma rápidamente sobre una persona o cosa sin mucho pensamiento

inference / **inferencia** *s.* una conclusión sacada de la información disponible; el acto de llegar a este tipo de conclusón

information / **información** *s.* datos o hechos sobre un tema

instructions / **instrucciones** *s.* los pasos que hay que seguir para realizar algo

L

literal / **literal** *adj.* el significado más básico de una palabra o palabras, sin metáfora u otro lenguaje figurado; sin exageración o distorsión

literary / **literario** *adj.* perteneciente o relativo a los libros u otros materiales escritos

logical / **lógico** *adj.* claro y razonable; basado en la lógica

M

meter / **métrica** *s.* el patrón rítmico de un poema, marcado por el tiempo y ritmo de cada verso

method / **método** *s.* una manera particular de hacer algo; un plan sistemático

mood / **ambiente, tono** *s.* el ambiente o sentimiento general de una obra escrita creado por el autor

mysterious / **misterioso** *adj.* extraño, difícil de entender, explicar o identificar; (de una persona) reservado y enigmático a propósito; (de un lugar) que tiene un ambiente extraño y secreto

O

oppose / **oponer** *v.* estar en contra de; no estar de acuerdo

P

poetic / **poético** *adj.* bonito, expresivo, sensible, o imaginativo; como un poema

precise / **preciso** *adj.* exacto, correcto, cuidadoso de los detalles

procedure / **procedimiento** *s.* la manera en la que se hace una tarea o un trabajo

progression / **progresión** *s.* una serie natural de eventos; un movimiento hacia adelante

purpose / **propósito** *s.* la razón de que algo existe, es hecho, o es creado; el objetivo o meta de una actividad u obra escrita

R

reader-friendly / **fácil de leer** *adj.* no complicado, fácil de entender y leer

realize / **darse cuenta de** *v.* comprender claramente; enterarse del hecho de que algo es verdadero

relevant / relevante *adj.* conectado estrechamente, importante o significativo al asunto en cuestión

repetition / repetición *s.* el acto de repetir algo ya dicho, hecho o escrito

resolution / resolución *s.* lo que ocurre para resolver el conflicto en el argumento de una historia

rhetorical devices / técnicas retóricas *s.* estrategias y técnicas (por ejemplo, metáfora e hipérbole) utilizadas por los escritores para atraer o persuadir a los lectores

rhyme / rima *s.* la repetición de los mismos sonidos al final de las palabras, especialmente en la poesía

rhythm / ritmo *s.* el patrón de sílabas tónicas y átonas en el lenguaje oral y escrito, especialmente en la poesía

S

sense / sentido *s.* una de las cinco habilidades de visión, tacto, gusto, audición y olfato; la capacidad de utilizar el buen juicio (sentido común); el significado deseado o expresado; un sentido que algo es así; **sentir** *v.* enterarse de algo

sensory / sensorial *adj.* perteneciente o relativo a los cinco sentidos

setting / escenario *s.* el lugar y el momento de la acción en un cuento u otra obra escrita

sonnet / soneto *s.* un poema de catorce versos, muchas veces con un patrón determinado de rima

standard / estándar *adj.* usado como base de comparación

stanza / estrofa *s.* un grupo de líneas de poesía, normalmente con un patrón y extensión similar, separado por espacios de otras líneas

strategy / estrategia *s.* en un texto, una táctica o método literario (como el *flashback* o el presagio) empleado por el autor para lograr un objetivo o efecto específico

structural / estructural *adj.* relativo a la forma que toma un objeto o la manera en la que parece un objeto

style / estilo *s.* una manera de hacer algo; una forma de escribir, componer, o pintar, etc.; especial a un período de la historia, un grupo de artistas o una persona específica

summarize / resumir *v.* exponer de una manera breve los puntos o ideas principales

suspect / sospechar *v.* creer que algo es probablemente cierto, sin prueba alguna

suspense / suspenso *s.* una sensación de ansiedad e incertidumbre sobre lo que va a pasar en una historia u otra obra escrita

symbol / símbolo *s.* algo que representa o significa otra cosa

T

technique / técnica *s.* una manera de hacer una actividad o llevar a cabo una tarea, muchas veces con destrezas específicas

theme / tema *s.* una idea, asunto, o propósito principal de una obra literaria

thesis / tesis *s.* una idea o teoría que se expone y que se discute de una manera lógica

tone / tono *s.* la actitud del autor hacia su tema o materia

topic / tema *s.* una idea de la cual se escribe y que se discute

transition / transición *s.* el cambio entre partes, lugares y conceptos

U

urge / instar *v.* intentar persuadir a alguien que haga algo

Graphic Organizer Handbook

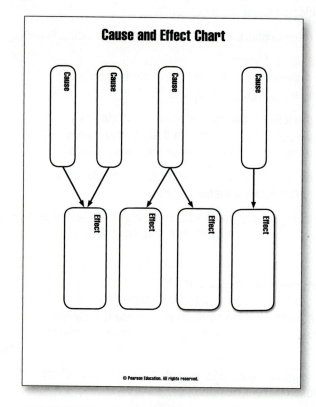

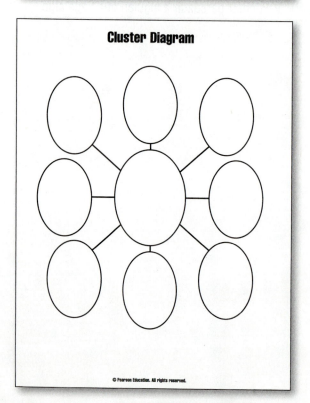

R24 Graphic Organizer Handbook

Writing Coach Online

Resource Go online for printable versions of these graphic organizers.

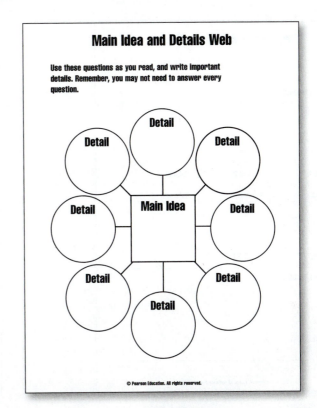

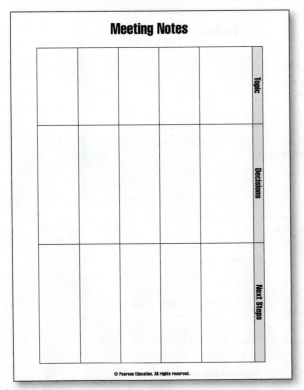

Graphic Organizer Handbook R25

Graphic Organizer Handbook continued

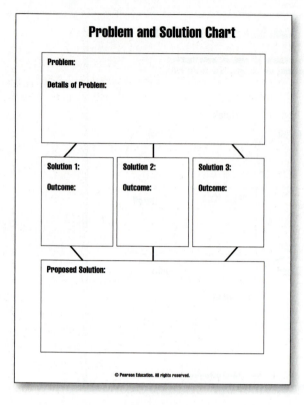
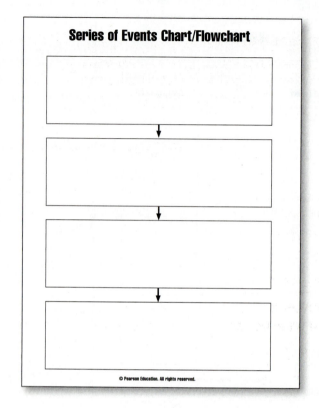
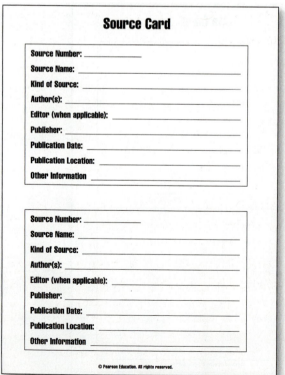

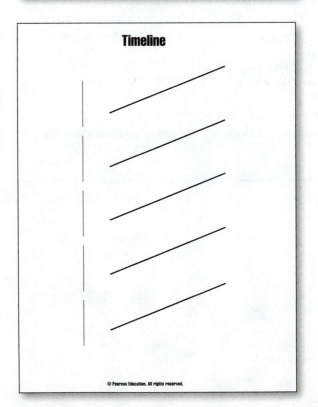
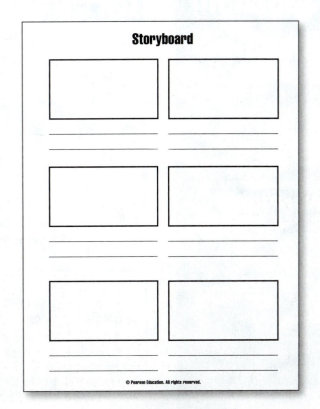
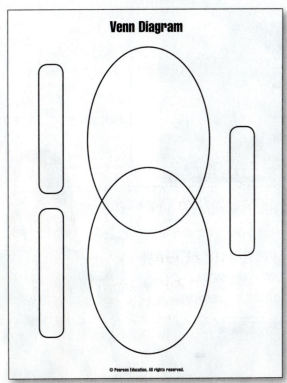

Graphic Organizer Handbook R27

Listening and Speaking Handbook

Communication travels between people in many forms. You receive information by listening to others, and you convey information through speaking. The more developed these skills are, the more you will be able to communicate your ideas, as well as to comprehend the ideas of others.

If you improve your listening skills, it will become easier to focus your attention on classroom discussions and to identify important information more accurately. If you develop good speaking skills, you will be better prepared to contribute effectively in group discussions, to give formal presentations with more confidence, and to communicate your feelings and ideas to others more easily.

This handbook will help you increase your ability in these two key areas of communication.

Listening

Different situations call for different types of listening. Learn more about the four main types of listening—critical, empathic, appreciative, and reflective—in the chart below.

Types of Listening		
Type	**How to Listen**	**Situations**
Critical	Listen for facts and supporting details to understand and evaluate the speaker's message.	Informative or persuasive speeches, class discussions, announcements
Empathic	Imagine yourself in the other person's position, and try to understand what he or she is thinking.	Conversations with friends or family
Appreciative	Identify and analyze aesthetic or artistic elements, such as character development, rhyme, imagery, and descriptive language.	Oral presentations of a poem, dramatic performances
Reflective	Ask questions to get information, and use the speaker's responses to form new questions.	Class or group discussions

Using Different Types of Questions

A speaker's ideas may not always be clear to you. You may need to ask questions to clarify your understanding. If you understand the different types of questions, you will be able to get the information you need.

- An **open-ended question** does not lead to a single, specific response. Use this question to open up a discussion: "What did you think of the piano recital?"

- A **closed question** leads to a specific response and must be answered with a yes or no: "Did you play a piece by Chopin at your recital?"

- A **factual question** is aimed at getting a particular piece of information and must be answered with facts: "How many years have you been playing the piano?"

Participating in a Group Discussion

In a group discussion, you openly discuss ideas and topics in an informal setting. The group discussions in which you participate will involve, for the most part, your classmates and focus on the subjects you are studying. To get the most out of a group discussion, you need to participate in it.

Use group discussions to express and to listen to ideas in an informal setting.

Communicate Effectively Think about the points you want to make, the order in which you want to make them, the words you will use to express them, and the examples that will support these points before you speak.

Ask Questions Asking questions can help you improve your comprehension of another speaker's ideas. It may also call attention to possible errors in another speaker's points.

Make Relevant Contributions Stay focused on the topic being discussed. Relate comments to your own experience and knowledge, and clearly connect them to the topic. It is important to listen to the points others make so you can build off their ideas. Work to share the connections you see. For example, say whether you agree or disagree, or tell the goup how your ideas connect.

Speaking

Giving a presentation or speech before an audience is generally recognized as public speaking. Effective speakers are well prepared and deliver speeches smoothly and with confidence.

Recognizing Different Kinds of Speeches

There are four main kinds of speeches: informative speeches, persuasive speeches, entertaining speeches, and extemporaneous speeches.

Consider the purpose and audience of your speech before deciding what kind of speech you will give.

- Give an **informative speech** to explain an idea, a process, an object, or an event.
- Give a **persuasive speech** to get your listeners to agree with your position or to take some action. Use formal English when speaking.
- Give an **entertaining speech** to offer your listeners something to enjoy or to amuse them. Use both informal and formal language.
- Give an **extemporaneous speech** when an impromptu occasion arises. It is an informal speech because you do not have a prepared manuscript.

Preparing and Presenting a Speech

If you are asked to deliver a speech, begin by choosing a topic that you like or know well. Then, prepare your speech for your audience.

To prepare your speech, research your topic. Make an outline, and use numbered note cards.

Gather Information Use the library and other resources to gather reliable information and to find examples to support your ideas.

Organizing Information Organize your information by writing an outline of main ideas and major details. Then, when you deliver your speech, write the main ideas, major details, quotations, and facts on note cards.

When presenting your speech, use rhetorical forms of language and verbal and nonverbal strategies.

Use Rhetorical Language Repeat key words and phrases to identify your key points. Use active verbs and colorful adjectives to keep your speech interesting. Use parallel phrases to insert a sense of rhythm.

Use Verbal and Nonverbal Strategies Vary the pitch and tone of your voice, and the rate at which you speak. Speak loudly and emphasize key words or phrases. Avoid consistently reading your speech from you notes. Work to maintain eye contact with the audience. As you speak, connect with the audience by using gestures and facial expressions to emphasize key points.

Evaluating a Speech

Evaluating a speech gives you the chance to judge another speaker's skills. It also gives you the opportunity to review and improve your own methods for preparing and presenting a speech.

When you evaluate a speech, you help the speaker and yourself to learn from experience. Listed below are some questions you might ask yourself while evaluating another person's speech or one of your own speeches.

- Did the speaker introduce the topic clearly, develop it well, and conclude it effectively?
- Did the speaker support each main idea with appropriate details?
- Did the speaker approach the platform confidently and establish eye contact with the audience?
- Did the speaker's facial expressions, gestures, and movements appropriately reinforce the words spoken?
- Did the speaker vary the pitch of his or her voice and the rate of his or her speaking?
- Did the speaker enunciate all words clearly?

Listening Critically to a Speech

Hearing happens naturally as sounds reach your ears. Listening, or critical listening, requires that you understand and interpret these sounds.

Critical listening requires preparation, active involvement, and self-evaluation from the listener.

Learning the Listening Process Listening is interactive; the more you involve yourself in the listening process, the more you will understand.

Focus Your Attention Focus your attention on the speaker and block out all distractions—people, noises, and objects. Find out more about the subject that will be discussed beforehand.

Interpret the Information To interpret a speaker's message successfully, you need to identify and understand important information. You might consider listening for repeated words or phrases, pausing momentarily to memorize and/or write key statements, watching non-verbal signals, and combining this new information with what you already know.

Respond to the Speaker's Message Respond to the information you have heard by identifying the larger message of the speech, its most useful points, and your position on the topic.

Index

Note: Page numbers in **boldface** refer to pages where terms are defined; *italicized* page numbers refer to writing applications.

A

Abbreviations, R9, 560, 566–568, 583
ABCD (Attack, Brainstorm, Choose, Detect)
    analytical essays, *168–169*
    argumentative essays, *194–195*
    informational research reports, *254–255*
    interpretative responses, *220–221*
    narrative nonfiction essays, *88–89*
    poetry/description, *142–143*
    procedural text, *268–269*
    short stories, *116–117*
Absolute modifiers, 519, *520*
Abstract ideals, write about, *126*
Abstract nouns, 295, *297*
Acronyms, 567, 568
Action
    call to, 172, 183
    focused/well-paced, 24, 77, 104–105, 108, *115, 117*
    rising/falling, 74, 102
Action verbs, 308–310, *311*
    complements and, 347
    transitive/intransitive, 312
    voice and, 460–461
Active voice or tense, 188–189, 460, 462, *463–464*
Addresses, 585
Adjectival clauses, 376–377, *379, 386*
    commas and, 279, 283
    fragmented, 409
    relative adverbs and, 383–384, *386*
    relative pronouns and, 301, 383, *386*
    restrictive/nonrestrictive, 377, 578, 591
    words introducing, 389–390

Adjectival phrases, 356–357, *359*
Adjectives, 315–316, *319*
    adverbial clauses modifying, 384
    adverbial phrases modifying, 358, *359*
    adverbs modifying, 321, 322–323, *324*
    adverbs versus, 323
    articles as, 316, *319*
    commas with, 574, 587
    compound, 317, *320*, 351
    coordinate and cumulative, 574
    degrees, 508
    fractions as, 607
    gerund phrases with, 369
    indefinite pronouns as, 306
    infinitives as, 370
    noun clauses as, 388–389
    nouns as, 316, 318, *319*
    participles as, 318, 364–365
    possessive, 317, 318
    predicate, 347, 350–351, 405
    prefixes and hyphenated, 557
    pronouns as, 317–318, 320
    proper, 214, 317, 320, 556–557, 558, 608, 612
    relative pronouns as, 383
    review, 332–333, 334
    verbs as, 318, 320
    See also Modifiers
Adverbial clauses, 384–385, *391*
    commas after introductory, 274, 576
    dangling, 413, *414*
    elliptical, 387, *391*
    fragmented, 409
    words introducing, 389–390
Adverbial phrases, 358, *359*
    infinitive phrases with, 371
    participles with, 365
    starting sentences with, 405
Adverbs, 315, 321, *324*
    adjectives versus, 323
    adverbial clauses modifying, 384
    adverbial phrases modifying, 358, *359*

    adverbs modifying other, 321, 322, 324
    clarifying tense with, 453
    commas after introductory, 576
    conjunctive, 328, 329–330, 331, 577, 589–590
    degrees, 508
    gerund phrases with, 369
    infinitive phrases with, 371
    infinitives as, 370
    noun clauses as, 388–389
    nouns as, 322
    participles with, 365
    as parts of verbs, 322
    prepositions versus, 326, *327*
    relative, 376, 383–384, *386*
    review, 333, *334*
    starting sentences with, 405
    See also Modifiers
Advertisements, 19, 24, *139*, 173
Advice columns, *166–167*
Aesthetic effects, analysis of
    interpretative responses, 198, *221, 255*
    response-to-literature essays, *207, 212, 213*
Affixes, 147, 199
Agenda, meeting, R13, R24
Agreement. *See* Pronoun-antecedent agreement; Subject-verb agreement
Allegory, 55
Alliteration, 54, 129, *141, 157*
Ambiguous pronouns, 504–505, *506*
Amounts and measurements, 491, 567, 615
Analysis, complex/in-depth
    compare-and-contrast essays, 146
    expository essays, 17
    informational research reports, 224, 239
    interpretative responses, 198, *221, 255*
    response-to-literature essays, 200, 203, 208–209, *211,* 212

staged dialogue, *217*
Analytical essays, 15, 146
　characteristics, 146
　forms of, 147
　mentor model, 148–149
　use writing skills of
　　for interpretative responses, 198, *221*, 255
　　for response-to-literature essays, *207*, 209
　　for TV talk show scripts, 165
　writing, to a prompt, *168–169*
Antecedents, pronoun, 289, 298, 299, *302***, 495.** *See also* Pronoun-antecedent agreement
Anthologies, *253*
APA (American Psychological Association), 236
Apostrophes, 614, *619*
　in contractions, 617–618
　with possessive nouns, 286, 614–616
　with pronouns, 286, 471, 616–617
　in special plurals, 618
Appeals, range of appropriate, *181, 195, 221*
　research process critique, *269*
　response-to-literature essays, *204, 207, 211, 213, 215*
Appositive phrases, 356, 360–362, *363***, 401**
Appositives, 360–362, *363*
　colon introducing formal, 593
　combining sentences with, 362, *363*
　commas and, 279, 283
　compound, 362
　gerunds as, 368
　infinitives as, 370
　nominative pronouns with, 468
　noun clauses as, 388–389
　objective pronouns with, 471
　restrictive/nonrestrictive, 360, 578, 591, 626

Argumentative essays, 18, 172, 173, *194–195*
Arguments, persuasive, 177, 180, 181–182, 186, 189. *See also* Counter-arguments
Articles (grammar), 281, 316, *319*
Articles (text). *See* Magazine articles; Newspaper articles
Artistic effects. *See* Aesthetic effects, analysis of
Artistic works, titles of. *See* Titles
Assonance, 54, 129
Attention, focused, R31
Audience
　address issues/needs of
　　analytical essays, 157–158, 160, *161*, 166–167
　　nonfiction narratives, 78–*81*, 106–109
　　poetry/description, 132–135
　　research writing, 242–244
　　response-to-literature essays, 210–213
　　workplace writing, *267, 269*
　address questions/objections/concerns of, 184–186, 187
　identify appropriate/intended, 32
　　analytical essays, 146–147, 164
　　argumentative essays, 174, 180, 182, 190, *195*
　　informational research reports, 238
　　nonfiction narratives, 67, 84, 93, 112
　　poetry/description, 121, 138
　　research writing, 248, *251*
　　response-to-literature essays, 216
　　workplace writing, 257-258
　influence attitudes/actions of, 183, 186–187, *195, 249*
　target specific, *114–115, 139, 140–141*
　See also Reader interest

Audiences, consider multiple
　argumentative essays, 173, 179, *191*
　expository writing, 17, 153
　fiction narratives, 12, 101
　interpretative responses, 205
　nonfiction narratives, 12, 73
　persuasive writing, 19
　poetry/description, 15, 127
　research writing, 21, 231
　responses to literature, 20
　workplace writing, 23
Audio elements, 86–*87*
Authorities, quote, 240
Autobiographical essays, 9
Autobiographical narratives
　characteristics, 66
　mentor/student models, 68–71
　Spiral Review, *143*
　writing applications, *85–87*
　writing process, 72–84
Auxiliary verbs. *See* Helping verbs

B

Background reading, 100
Ballads, 13, 121
Basic tenses, 424–425, *426***, 435,** *437*
Beginning of draft. *See* Introductions, effective
Bias, 232–233
Bibliographies, annotated, 21, 244
Big Questions, Connect to the
　Do you understand a subject well enough to write about it?, 223, 248
　How do we best convey feeling through words on a page?, 119, 138
　What can fiction do better than non-fiction?, 91, 112
　What is the point? How will you determine whether you made it successfully?, 171, 190
　What should we put in and leave out to be accurate and honest?, 65, 84

Index continued

What should we tell and what should we describe to make this information clear?, 145, 164
What should you write about to make others interested in a text?, 197, 216
Biographical description, R8
Biographical narratives, 9, 67
Biographical profiles, 225
Block format (letter), modified and, R14
Block organization, 156–157
Bloggers, R7
Blogs, R7, 9
    comments/entries, 7, 20, 24, 67, 199
    creating interesting/fair, R7
    effective messages for, R8
Body of drafts/writing, 35, 53
    argumentative essays, 182–183
    autobiographical narratives, 76–77, 80
    business letters, R14
    compare-and-contrast essays, 156–157, 160
    expository writing, 15
    informational research reports, 238–239, 244
    mystery stories, 104–105, 108
    op-ed pieces, 186
    response-to-literature essays, 208–209, 212
Boldfacing, R7
Book citations, 236
Book titles, 559, 562, 593, 602
Brackets, 598, 620, 622, *623*
Brainstorm, 6
    compare-and-contrast essays, 164
    to find a topic, 32
    interpretative responses, 216
    persuasive writing, 178, 190
    poetry/description, 126
    research writing, 225, 230, *251*
    workplace writing, 261, *266–267*

See also ABCD (Attack, Brainstorm, Choose, Detect)
Brand names, 554, 556

C

Capitalization, 545, *548*, 550
    autobiographical narratives, 82, *83*
    compare-and-contrast essays, *163*
    fictional-interview scripts, *253*
    fragments, 407
    inside parentheses, 621
    in letters, 559
    proper adjectives, 556–557, *558*
    proper nouns, 280, 296, 551–554, *555*, *558*
    response-to-literature essays, 214–*215*
    run-ons, 410
    sentences, 546–547, *548–549*
    sonnets/free-verse poems, 136–*137*
    titles, 280, 559–563, *564*
    unnecessary/missing, 280
Cases, 466
    choosing correct, 475–477, *478*
    nominative, 467–468, *469*
    in nouns, 466
    objective, 470–471, *472*, 474
    possessive, 471, *472–473*, 474
    in pronouns, 467, *469*
Cause-and-effect chart, R24
Cause-and-effect essays, 15, 147
Celestial bodies, names of, 553
Change, describe effects of, 72
Characteristics of genres, 8. *See also specific genre*
Characterization, 66
Characters
    analysis of, 198, 204
    interesting/believable
        autobiographical narratives, 68–69, 70–71, *143*
        fiction narratives, 11

    mystery stories, 92, 99, 102–105, *117*
    nonfiction narratives, 9
    radio play scripts, *114–115*
    results of actions of, 108
    staged dialogue between, 217
Charts, 241. *See also* Graphic organizers; Graphic/visual elements, relevant
Citations, 236–237, 246, 275. *See also* Sources
Claims, 240
Clarification, ask for, R9
Class yearbooks, *85*
Classification essays, 16, 147
Clauses, 355, 375
    commas with, 83, 110–111, 274, 285, 576, 578, 581, 587
    elliptical, 387, *391*, 413, *414*, 477, 478
    independent/subordinate, 49, 82–83
    main, 393, 409
    negative words in, 523–524
    parallel/nonparallel, 415–417
    relative pronouns and adverbs in, 383–384, *386*
    restrictive/nonrestrictive, 377, 378, *381*, 382, 578, 591
    restrictive/nonrestrictive relative, 110–111
    subject-verb agreement and, 484, *487*
    subjunctive mood in, 455–456
    See also Adjectival clauses; Adverbial clauses; Independent clauses; Noun clauses; Relative clauses; Subordinate clauses
Climax of events, 74, 102, 104–105
Closed questions, R29
Closing. *See* Conclusions of drafts/writing, effective
Clues, 104
Cluster diagram, R24
Coherence, 156, 208, 238

Collaborative writing, 6–7, R11, 37, 52. *See also* Partner Talk; Work with partner
Collective nouns, 295, *297*, *489*, *493*
College applications, 23
Colons, 589, 592, *594*
    capitalization after, 547, *548*
    quotations with, 592, 596–597
    special situations, 593
Comma splices, 288, 410, *411*, 572
Commas, 571, 581
    adding to sentences, *584*, *588*
    in addresses and letters, 585
    with adjectival clauses, 377
    between adjectives, 574
    after introductory material, 274, 576–577, 596
    for clarity, 586
    with compound sentences, 285, 571–572
    with conjunctive adverb or transitional expressions, 330, 590
    correcting run-ons with, 410
    with dates and geographical names, 582–583
    in elliptical sentences, 585–586
    with interjections, 569
    joining independent clauses, 392, 400
    misuses, 587, *588*
    with nonrestrictive expressions, 360, 365–366, 578
    in numbers, 583
    with parenthetical expressions, 577, 621
    prepositional phrases and, 576–577
    quotations with, 586, 592, 596–597
    relative clauses and, 110–*111*
    in series or list, 573, 574, 592
    special situations, *584*
    using correctly/revising errors, 82–83, 274, 279, 283, 285, *575*, *579–580*

Common nouns, 296, *297*, 551
    capitalizing, 551
    proper adjectives with, 556–557, *558*
Communicate effectively, R30
Community cooperation, foster, 7
Comparative degree, 508, *511*
    irregular forms, 509–510, *512*
    regular forms, 508–509, *511*
    using, 513, *514–515*, 516
Compare-and-contrast essays, 15, 20, 146
    characteristics, 146
    student model, 150–151
    writing process, 152–164
Comparing writings
    analytical essays, 145, 148, 166
    fiction narratives, 95, 114
    nonfiction narratives, 68, 86
    persuasive writing, 174, 192
    poetry/description, 122, 140
    responses to literature, 200
    scripts, 218, *253*
    workplace writing, 266
Comparison, degrees of, 508–510, *511–512*
    absolute modifiers and, 519, *520*
    irregular forms, 509–510, *512*
    logical, 517, *518*
    regular forms, 508–509, *511*
    using comparative and superlative, 513, *514–515*, 516
Comparison essays, 199
Comparisons
    develop points of, 152, 154, 156, 160, 163, 165, 166–167
    double, 513, *515*
    making clear (using degrees), 513, *515*, 517, *518*, 519, *520*
    nonparallel, 417, *420*, 422
Complements, 347
    appositive phrases and, 361
    infinitive phrases with, 371

    participles with, 365
    simple sentences with, 392
    starting sentence with, 405
    types, 347–351, *353*
    See also Direct objects; Indirect objects; Predicate nominatives
Complete predicates, 336, *338*
Complete subjects, 336, *338*
Complex sentences, 392, 393, *394*
    in autobiographical narratives, 82
    creating, 401, *403*
    pronouns in, 475–476
Compositions, composing, 53. *See also* Body of drafts/writing; Conclusions of drafts/writing, effective; Introductions, effective
Compound adjectives, 291, 317, *320*
Compound antecedents, 496–497
Compound appositives, 362
Compound nouns, 295, *297*, 615
Compound objects, 49
    combining sentences with, 400, *402*
    commas with, 587
    direct, 348
    indirect, 349
Compound predicate adjectives, 351
Compound predicate nominatives, 351, 468, 470
Compound predicates, 279
Compound sentences, 49, 392, 571
    autobiographical narratives, 82
    commas with, 571–572
    creating, 400, *403*
Compound subjects, 49, 341, *342*, 485
    combining sentences with, 400, *402*
    commas with, 285, 571–572, 587
    nominative pronouns in, 468
    simple sentence with, 392
    verb agreement with, 485–486, *487*
Compound titles, 560

Index continued

Compound verbs, 49, 341, *342*
   combining sentences with, 400, *402*
   commas with, 285, 571–572, 587
   simple sentence with, 392
Compound words, hyphens with, 291, 295, 317, 608–609
Compound-complex sentences, 82, 392, 393, *394*
Compromiser, 6
Computer graphics. *See* Graphic/visual elements, relevant
Concepts, identify new. *See* Vocabulary words
Concluding expressions, quotations with, 595–596
Conclusions, don't jump to, R8
Conclusions of drafts/writing, effective, 35, 53
   analytical essays, 149, *169*
   argumentative essays, 182–183
   autobiographical narratives, 76–77, 80
   business letters, R14
   compare-and-contrast essays, 146, 151, 156–157
   expository writing, 15
   informational research reports, 238–239, 244
   mystery stories, 104–105, 108
   op-ed pieces, 175, 186
   problem-solution essays, *195*
   response-to-literature essays, 208–209, 212
Concrete nouns, 295, *297*
Conflict, well-developed
   autobiographical narratives, 66, 68, 71, 74, *75*, 76–78, 80, *143*
   compare-and-contrast essays, 160
   fiction narratives, 11
   mystery stories, 92, 102–109, *117*
   narrative nonfiction essays, 89, *117*
   nonfiction narratives, 9
   radio play scripts, *114–115*

Conjugation, 430, 435–436, *437*
Conjunctions, 325, 328, *331*
   correcting run-ons with, 410
   joining compound subject/verb, 341
   joining objects, 356
   nonparallel, 416
   review, 333, *334*
   types, 328–330, *331*
   See also Coordinating conjunctions; Subordinating conjunctions
Conjunctive adverbs, 328, *331*, 589
   common, 329–330
   punctuation with, 330, 577, 589–590
Consonance, 54, 129
Consult with others, 126, 164, 190, 217, 225. *See also* Partner Talk
Context, 89, 146, 157, 182
Contractions, 617
   apostrophe in, 617–618
   of *not*, 522
   possessive pronouns vs., 471, 476, 617
Contrasting expressions, commas in, 577, *580*, 581
Contrasts. *See also* Compare-and-contrast essays
Contrasts, develop points of
   advice columns, 166–*167*
   compare-and-contrast essays, 152, 154, 156, 160, 163
   TV talk show scripts, *165*
Contributions, make relevant, R30
Conventions, use, 27, 59
   autobiographical narratives, 82–*83*
   compare-and-contrast essays, 162–163
   informational research reports, 224, 246–247
   letters to the editor, *193*
   mystery stories, 110–111
   op-ed pieces, 188–189

   response-to-literature essays, 214–215
   sonnets/free-verse poems, 136–137
   as writing trait, 27, 28, 59, 63
   See also Rubrics; *specific convention, i.e.,* Spelling, correct
Conversational taglines, 595, 596–597
Cooperative writing, 6
Coordinate adjective, 574
Coordinating conjunctions, 328, *331*
   combining sentences with, 400, *403*
   commas with, 288, 571–573
   faulty coordination of, 418–419
Coordination, faulty, 282, 418–419, *421*, 422
Correlative conjunctions, 328, *331*, 416
Counter-arguments
   argumentative essays, 172, 182, 195
   op-ed pieces, 177, 180–181, 183, 186
   persuasive essays, *221*
Credentials, provide, 166
Critical present tense, 439
Critical reviews, 20, 199
Cumulative adjective, 574
Cumulative reviews, *395–396, 543–544, 629–630*

D

Dangling hyphens, 607
Dangling modifier, 412–413, *414*
Dashes, 624, 625–626, *628*
Data
   collect/organize, 234, *251*
   compile, 232, *265, 269*
   relative value of specific
     in analytical essays, *169*
     in argumentative essays, 172, *195*
     in compare-and-contrast essays, *155*, 157, 160
     in op-ed pieces, 181, 183
     in persuasive essays, *221*

Databases, electronic, 232
Dates, 233, 567, 582, 626
Debates, identify major, 232, 233, *251,* **265**
Declarative sentences, 398, *399*
    capitalizing, 546
    in parentheses, 621
    punctuating, 566
    subjects in, 343–344, *346*
Definite articles, 316, *319*
Definition essays, 14
Degrees of comparison. *See* Comparison, degrees of
Delivery, adjust. *See* Presentations, adjust
Demands, expressing, 455–456
Demonstrative pronouns, 300–301, *305,* **317–318**
Denouement, 105
Describe, genre to, 8
Description, clear, 126, 131, 172, 207. *See also* Poetry and description
Descriptive essays, 14, 121
Descriptive essays, *140–141*
Descriptive writing, 13, 14
Details
    descriptive. *See* Description, clear
    gathering, R25, 34, 75, 103, 181, 207
    sensory
        fiction narratives, 92, 95, 98–99, 103, 105, 107, *114-115, 117*
        nonfiction narratives, 66, 68, *75,* 76-77, 80, *89, 117, 143*
        poetry/description, 13, 120, 125, 128, 131, 134, 141, *169*
    specific
        expository writing, 146
        fiction narratives, 92, 94, 103, 105-106, 108, *115*
        nonfiction narratives, 66, 70-71, 76, *87*
        persuasive writing, 193
        poetry/description, 138, 141
        research writing, *252*
        responses to literature, 206, *218-219*
    supporting. *See* Evidence
    supporting-text
        well-chosen relevant, 146, 154, *155,* 160, 195
Diagrams, 241. *See also* Cluster diagram; Graphic organizers; Graphic/visual elements, relevant; Multimedia resources; Venn diagram
Dialogue, 600
    contractions in, 617–618
    to enhance plot, 92, 97, 104, 107
    punctuating, 600, 605, 625
    realistic/believable
        autobiographical narratives, 68, 75–77
        fiction narratives, 11
        mystery stories, 99, 103
        nonfiction narratives, 9
        radio play scripts, 115
        scripts, 24
    staged, between characters, 217
Diary entries, 10, 67
Diction, 122, 187
Dictionary, use
    to check definition, 67, 93, 121, 147, 173, 199, 225, 257
    to clarify similar words, 135, 273
    for correct spelling, 136, 137, 277
    for correct use of hyphens, 291
    for pronunciation, 67
Differences. *See* Contrasts
Digital idea file, 4
Direct address, nouns of, 296, 576–577
Direct objects, 347–348, *352*
    adjectival phrases modifying, 357, *359*
    appositive phrases and, 361
    compound, 348
    fragments with, 408
    gerund phrases with, 369
    gerunds as, 368
    indirect and, 349
    infinitive phrases with, 371
    infinitives as, 370
    noun clauses as, 388–390
    object complements and, 350
    objective pronouns as, 470
    relative pronouns as, 383
Direct quotations, 278, 586, 595–597
Directions, 553, *555*
Discussion, participate in, R30
    in collaborative writing, 6
    expository writing, 145, 150, 152, 165
    fiction narratives, 113
    interpretative responses, 204
    poetry/description, 126, 139
    research writing, *249*
    in writing process, 33, 37, 52
    See also Partner Talk; *Try It!*
Divided quotations, 596–597
Dividing words, 611–612, *613*
Documentaries, 24, 225
Documentation. *See* Citations; Sources
Documented essays, 21
Double comparisons, 513, *515*
Double negatives, 522, 523, *525–526*
Doubt, expressing, 162, 455
Draft, planning first. *See* Prewriting/planning first drafts
Drafting, 30, 35
    advice columns, 167
    argumentative essays, 182–183
    autobiographical narratives, 76–77
    business letters, 263
    compare-and-contrast essays, 156–157
    descriptive essays, *141*
    fictional-interview scripts, *252*
    informational research reports, 238–241

Index continued

instructions, set of, 259
memos, 261
mystery stories, 104–105
project plans, *267*
public service announcement, *193*
radio play scripts, *115*
radio shows, *87*
response-to-literature essays, 208–209
scripts, *219*
sonnets/free-verse poems, 130–131

E

Editing drafts, 30, 42–45
advice columns, *167*
autobiographical narratives, 82–83
business letters, 263
checklist, 42
compare-and-contrast essays, 162–163
descriptive essays, *141*
fictional-interview scripts, *253*
informational research reports, 246–247
instructions, set of, 259
memos, 261
mystery stories, 110–111
op-ed pieces, 188–189
podcasts, R11
project plans, *267*
public service announcement, *193*
radio play scripts, *115*
radio shows, *87*
response-to-literature essays, 214–215
scripts, *219*
sonnets/free-verse poems, 136–*137*
using multimedia elements, R10

Editorials, 18, 173
Educational courses, titles of, 563
Electronic resources, 232
Elements, interesting/believable, 11. See also specific element
Ellipses, 624–625, *628*

Elliptical clauses
adverbial, 387, *391*
dangling, 413, *414*
pronouns in, 477, *478*

Elliptical sentences, 339, 585–586
E-mails, business, 22, 257
Emoticons, R8
Emotions, expressing, 218–219. See also Feelings, expressing
Emphatic tenses, 425, *426*
past, 441–442
present, 438–439

Encyclopedia. See Print resources

End marks, 566–569, *570*
correcting run-ons with, 410
inside parentheses, 621
quotation marks with, 596–598
in sentences, 398, *399*

Ending. See Conclusions of drafts/writing, effective

Entertain, genre to, 8
Entertaining speeches, R30
Equipment, 25
Errors. See Grammatical errors, guide to major; Mistakes, identify possible

Essential phrases or clauses. See Restrictive phrases/clauses

Evaluate drafts. See Revising drafts
Evaluation. See Analysis, complex/in-depth; Rubrics

Event names, 553
Events
response to current, 172
sequence/pace of
fiction narratives, 11, 111, *115*
flowchart for, R26
nonfiction narratives, 74, 77, 83, *89*
See also Action
single important, 83, 111

Evidence, supporting-text
collect/organize

fictional-interview scripts, *252*
informational research reports, 224, 227, 229, 234, 238–240, 247
research reports (workplace writing), 265
distinctions about the value of, 146, *155*, 157, 160, 163
documentation of. See Sources
effective/credible
interpretative responses, 20, 198, *221*, 255
response-to-literature essays, 203, 215
logical/precise/relevant
argumentative essays, 172, *195*
letters to the editor, *192–193*
op-ed pieces, 174, 177, 180, *181*, 182–183, 186, 189
persuasive essays, *221*
well-chosen relevant
analytical essays, *169*
compare-and-contrast essays, 146, 154, *155*, 157–158
problem-solution essays, *195*
response-to-literature essays, 201–202, 206, *207*, 208–209, 212

Examples, relevant
analytical essays, 146
classification essays, 16
compare-and-contrast essays, 152
documentation of, 240
informational research reports, 238
interpretative responses, 198
response-to-literature essays, 206–207

Exclamation marks, 566, 569, *570*
with quotation marks, 596–598
sentences with, 398, *399*

Exclamatory sentences, 398, *399*
capitalizing, 546
in parentheses, 621
punctuating, 569
subjects/verbs in, 345, *346*

Experiment journals, 21, 225

Expert opinion, 181, 224, 232, 240
Explanatory material, punctuating, 598, 620
Exposition, 15
Expository essays, 15–17
Expository text, 145, 197
Expository writing, 15–17
Express, to, 2. *See also* Feelings, expressing; Ideas, expressing; Opinions, expressing
Extemporaneous speeches, R30
Eyewitness accounts, 10

F

Facilitator, 6
Facts
    check for correct, 42
    distinguishing, from opinions, 233
    ideas contrary to, 455–456
    relative value of specific
        in analytical essays, *155,* 157, 160, 163, *169*
        in persuasive writing, 172, 183, *195, 221*
    supporting
        in analytical essays, 146, 148, 155
        documentation of, 240
        in persuasive writing, 181–182
        in research writing, 224, 234, 238
Factual questions, R29
Family titles, 296, 561
Fantasy stories, 11, 93
Feedback, 37
    family, 81, 241, 245
    listener/viewer, 165, 191, 217, *249*
    peer, 6
        fiction narratives, 109, 115
        multimedia projects, 25
        nonfiction narratives, 81, 87
        persuasive writing, 187
        poetry/description, 141
        research writing, 241

        responses to literature, *217,* 219
        workplace writing, 259, 267
    teacher
        expository writing, 161
        poetry/description, 135
        research writing, 241, 245
        responses to literature, 213
        workplace writing, 259, 263
Feeds (widget), R9
Fiction narratives, 11–12, 13, 91. *See also* Short stories
Fictional-interview scripts, *250–253*
Fiction/nonfiction, choose/determine if, 12. *See also* Genres
Figurative language, use/improve, 55
    autobiographical narratives, 80
    descriptive essays, *141*
    mystery stories, 107, *109*
    narrative nonfiction essays, *89*
    op-ed pieces, *187*
    poetry/description, 13, 120, 129
    sonnets/free-verse poems, 122, 125, 131, 134, 135, 137
Figures. *See* Graphic/visual elements, relevant
Film/play script, *114–115*
Film teaser, *113*
First person, 299, 300, 495
Five Ws Chart, R24
Focus
    compare-and-contrast essays, 156
    informational research reports, 238
    interpretative responses, 208
Focused attention, R31
Font colors, R7
Foreign words and phrases, 603
Form of genres, select correct, 8, 20, 23. *See also* specific genre
Format/formatting techniques
    correct/standard

        research writing, 224, 226, 228, 236–237, 244, 246, 247
        workplace writing, R14
    user-friendly, 22, 257–261, 263, *267, 269*
Forms (graphic). *See* Graphic/visual elements, relevant
Forms (workplace), 22
Forums, online, *253*
Fractions, 607, 626
Fragments, *253,* **292,** 339–340, *342,* 407–409, *411*
Free writing, 4
Free-verse poems, 13, 121
    characteristics, 120, 130, 131
    mentor/student models, 123, 125
    writing process, 126–138
Fused sentences, 287, 410, *411*
Future perfect progressive tense, 425, 444
Future perfect tense, 424, 444
Future progressive tense, 425, 444
Future tense, 424
    sequence of events in, 448–449
    uses, 438, 444, *445*
Future time, tenses expressing, 444, *445*

G

Gender, 289, 495, 497, *498,* 499
Generic masculine pronouns, 497
Genres, 8
    address issues of
        autobiographical narratives, 78–*81*
        compare-and-contrast essays, 158, 160, *161*
        informational research reports, 242, 244
        mystery stories, 106–109
        op-ed pieces, 184–186, *187*

Index continued

response-to-literature essays, 210–213
sonnets/free-verse poems, 132–135
select correct, to convey intended meaning, 8
  exposition/other, 17, 19
  fiction/nonfiction, 12
  interpretative responses, 20
  poetry/description, 14
ways to publish different, 47

Geographical names, 552, *555*, **583**
Gerund fragments, 408
Gerund phrases, 356, 369, *372–373*
Gerunds, 368, *372–373*
  adverbial clauses modifying, 384
  cases, *473*
  nonparallel, 416
  objective pronouns and, 470
  possessive pronouns and, 369, 471
  use of, in poetry, 136, *137*
  verbs or participles versus, 368
Global awareness, increase, 7
Glossary, use
  to check definition, 67, 93, 121, 147, 173, 199, 225, 257
  English, R18–R20
  Spanish, R21–R23
Government bodies, names of, 554
Government titles, 560–561, 603
Grammar, correct, 42
  expository writing, 146, 162–163
  fiction narratives, 110–111, *115*
  nonfiction narratives, 82–*83*
  persuasive writing, 188–*189*
  poetry/description, 136–*137*, *141*
  research writing, 246, *247*
  responses to literature, 214–*215*, *219*
  workplace writing, 257
Grammar textbooks, consult, 274, 280, 284, 289
Grammar-check feature, 43, 286–288

Grammatical errors, guide to major, 272–292
  capitalization, 280
  documentation, 275
  pronouns, 276, 289
  punctuation, 274, 278–279, 283, 285–286, 288, 291
  quotations, 290
  sentences, 282, 287, 292
  spelling, 277
  verb tenses, 284
  word use, 273, 281
Graphic novels, 24
Graphic organizers, R24–R27
  to narrow topic, 33
    autobiographical narratives, *73*
    compare-and-contrast essays, *153*
    informational research reports, *231*
    mystery stories, *101*
    op-ed pieces, *179*
    response-to-literature essays, *205*
    sonnets/free-verse poems, *127*
  to structure writing, 34
    compare-and-contrast essays, 154
    ideas/details (poem), 128
    op-ed pieces, 180
    plot events (autobiography), 74
    response, 206
    storyline (mystery stories), 102
Graphic/visual elements, relevant, 54, 269
  descriptive essays, *141*
  documentation of, 241
  fictional-interview scripts, *251*
  infomercial scripts, *249*
  informational research reports, 224, 228–229, 233, 238–239, 241, 244
  poetry/description, 129, *139*
  public service announcement, 191
  radio play scripts, *115*
  workplace writing, 267
  See also Multimedia elements
Graphs, 241. *See also* Graphic/visual elements, relevant; Multimedia resources

Greeting, letter/e-mail. *See also* Salutations, letter
Group names, 554, *555*

H

Haiku, 14, 121
Headings, 234, 257
Headlines, blog, R7
Health reports, 225
Helping verbs, 313
  conjugation with, 435
  passive voice and, 461
  subjunctive mood and, 456, *458*
Historical fiction, 11, 93
Historical present tense, 439
Historical reports, 225
Homophones, 277
Hyperbole, 55, 77
Hyphenated words
  apostrophes with, 615
  capitalizing, 557
  dividing, 612
  See also Compound words, hyphens with
Hyphenation setting, auto-, 291
Hyphens, 607, *610*, *613*
  for clarity, 609
  with compound words, 295, 317, 608–609
  to divide words, 611–612
  at ends of lines, 611
  in numbers, 607
  with prefixes and suffixes, 608
  suspended, 607
  unnecessary/missing, 291

I

Idea, develop controlling
  compare-and-contrast essays, 146

op-ed pieces, 180
poetry/description, 120
sonnets/free-verse poems, 128, 131–132, 137
See also Main idea/points; Theses, clearly stated

Ideas
building on one another, 83, 111, 130, 154–155
contrary to fact, 455–456
expressing
　analytical essays, 145
　autobiographical narratives, 65
　persuasive writing, 171
　poetry/description, 13
　research writing, 223
　response-to-literature essays, 197, 202
　short stories, 91, 119
how to find, 3, 33
how to keep track of, 4, 7
logical progression of
　fictional-interview scripts, *252*
　informational research reports, 224, 227, 238–239, *243*, 244, 247
　interpretative responses, 208–209, 212
　research reports (workplace writing), *265*
relative value of specific
　in analytical essays, 169
　in compare-and-contrast essays, *155*, 157, 160, 163
　in persuasive writing, 172, 181, 183, *195*, *221*
structure, in persuasive way, 180, 182–183, *193*
structure, in sustained way
　autobiographical narratives, 74
　mystery stories, 102
　response-to-literature essays, 206
　sonnets/free-verse poems, 128, 130, 137
supporting. *See* Evidence,

supporting-text
　using another writer's, 235
as writing trait, 26–28, 56, 63
See also Rubrics

Idioms, 504
Illustrations. *See* Graphic/visual elements, relevant
Imagery, use, 125, 132, *141*
Images, 13, 125, *139, 140–141*
Imperative mood, 455, *457*, **461**
Imperative sentences, 398, *399*
　capitalizing, 546
　punctuating, 566, 569
　subjects/verbs in, 345, *346*
Impression, create, 122
Indefinite articles, 316, *319*
Indefinite pronouns, 306, *307*
　as adjectives, 317–318
　antecedent agreement with, 289, 499–500, *501*
　apostrophes with, 616
　verb agreement with, 490, *493*
Independent clauses, 375–376, *379–380*
　adjectival clauses and, 376–377
　autobiographical narratives, 82–83
　colon after, 592
　commas separating, 571
　faulty coordination between, 418–419
　joining, 392, 400, 589–591
　nonparallel, 416
　in types of sentences, 392–393
Independent modifiers, 574
Indicative mood, 455, 456, *457*, **461**
Indirect objects, 347, 349, *353*
　adjectival phrases modifying, 357, *359*
　appositive phrases and, 361
　compound, 349
　gerund phrases with, 369
　gerunds as, 368
　infinitive phrases with, 371

noun clauses as, 388–389
objective pronouns as, 470
Indirect questions, 566, 569
Indirect quotations, 278, 595
Inferences, valid, 146, 148, 155, 198
Infinitive fragments, 408
Infinitive phrases, 356, 371, *374*
　commas after introductory, 576
　dangling, 413, *414*
　nonparallel, 416
　starting sentence with, 405
Infinitives, 370–371, *373–374*
　adverbial clauses modifying, 384
　objective pronouns and, 470
　prepositional phrases versus, 370
　time sequence with, 449
　use of, in poetry, 136
　without *to*, 371
Infomercial scripts, *249*
Inform, to, 2. *See also* Expository writing
Information
　add/delete. *See* Presentations, adjust; Revising drafts
　cite all researched. *See* Sources
　consider whole range of, 172, 179, *181*, 183, *195*, *221*
　evaluate relevance/quality/sufficiency of, *181*, 183, *195*, 207, *252*
　evaluate/synthesize collected, 227, 233, *234*, 238–239, *264*, *269*
　organize accurate, R11, 22, R30, 257–263, *267*, *269*
　paraphrase research, *234*, 235
Informational research reports, 224
　characteristics, 224
　student model, 226–229
　writing, to a prompt, *254–255*
　writing applications, *249–253*
　writing process, 230–248
Informative speeches, R30
Initials, 566–567
Insights, provide new, 72

Index continued

Instructions, 23, 257, 258–259
Intensifier, 321
Intensive pronouns, 299–300, *302*
Interjections, 325, 330, *331*
   capitalizing, 546
   punctuating, 274, 569
   review, 333, *334*
Internet
   browsing, using key words, 230, 232
   for collaborative writing, 7
   magazines/newspapers, 147
   for research, 164, 178, 216
   See also Blogs; E-mails, business; Podcasts; Web sites; Wikis
Internet articles, 17
Interpretation of primary source, 233
Interpretative responses, 198
   apply analytical essay skills to, 167, 198, *207*, 209, *221*, 255
   characteristics, 198
   forms of, 199
   speeches, R31
   writing, to a prompt, *220–221*
Interrogative pronouns, 306, *307*, 317–318
Interrogative sentences, 398, *399*
   capitalizing, 546
   in parentheses, 621
   punctuating, 568–569
   subjects in, 344, *346*
   See also Questions
Interrupting expressions, quotations with, 595–597
Interviews
   fictional, script of, *250–253*
   to find topic, **33**, 72, 100
   See also Expert opinion
Intransitive verbs, 312, 314
Introductions, effective, 35, 53
   analytical essays, 148, *169*
   argumentative essays, 182–183
   autobiographical narratives, 76–77, 80

   compare-and-contrast essays, 146, 151, *155*, 156–158, 160
   expository writing, 15
   informational research reports, 238–239, 244
   mystery stories, 104–105, 108
   op-ed pieces, 172, 186
   problem-solution essays, *195*
   response-to-literature essays, 200, 208–209, 212
Introductory phrases, 246
Introductory words/expressions
   capitalizing, 546–547, *548–549*
   commas after, 576–577, *579*
   here, there, 343, *346*
   in noun clauses, 388–390, *391*
   quotations with, 595–596
   varying, 405, *406*
Irony, 55, 215, 604, *606*
Irregular modifiers, 508, 509–510, *512*
Irregular verbs, 429–432, *434*
Issues
   clear description of, 189
   focus on single, 172, 178
   identify major, 230, 232, *233*, *251*, *265*
Italics, 595, 602–603, *605–606*

J

Job applications, 23
Journals
   experiment, 21
   idea, 4
   online. *See* Blogs
   personal, 10
   readers', 7
   writing for, 7

K

Key words/phrases/points, 156, 230, 281
Keyboarding tips, 52
KWL chart, R25

L

Lab reports, 21
Language
   informal, 167
   monitor spoken, *115*, 167, 219, 263
   patterns of natural speech in, 120, 134
   precise, 13
   rhetorical (speeches), R30
   vivid/persuasive, 172, 175, 182
Languages, names of, 554, *555*
Lead, strong. *See* Beginning of draft
Leader, 6
Learning log, 4
Legends. *See* Myths and legends
Length of essays, R7, 154, 156, 169. *See also* Presentations, adjust; Sentences, length of
Letters
   to author, 20, 199
   business, R14, 22, 257
      capitalization in, 559
      model for, 262
      punctuation in, 585, 593
   to editor, 19, 173, *192*
   friendly, R15, 22, 559, 585
Letters of alphabet
   apostrophe for plural, 618
   in outlines, 568
   in parentheses, 621, 622
   underlining/italicizing, 603
Library for research, 164, 178, 216, 232
Linking verbs, 308–310, *311*
   complements and, 347
   intransitive, 312
   subjects with, 488–489
List of items, 547, 592. *See also* Series
Listeners, 6, R11
Listening, types of, R28
Listening and speaking activities
   advice columns, 167
   class yearbooks, *85*

film teaser storyboard, 113
infomercial scripts, 249
multimedia advertisements, 139
public service announcement, 191
research reports (workplace writing), *265*
staged dialogue, 217
TV talk show scripts, 165
See also Partner Talk; *Try It!*

Listening and Speaking Handbook, R28–R31

Listening process, R11, R31

Literary strategies/devices, range of, 54–55
autobiographical narratives, 66, 75, 76–77, 80, *143*
fiction narratives, 11
mystery stories, 92, *103*, 104–105, *117*
narrative nonfiction essays, *89, 117*
nonfiction narratives, 9

Literary texts, 65, 91, 119

Literary works, titles of. *See* Titles

Logic. *See* Arguments, persuasive; Evidence, supporting-text; Ideas, logical progression of; Reasoning, logical

Lost items/memories as mystery, 100

Lyric poems, 121

M

Magazine articles, 17, 147. *See also* Print resources

Magazine citations, 236

Magazines, 562, 593, 602

Main clauses, 285, 393, 409. *See also* Independent clauses

Main idea/points
explain significance of, 208
identify explicit/implicit, *140–141,* 150
state, for paragraph, 239, 244, 258
web diagram on, R25

See also Themes; Theses, clearly stated; Topic sentences, clear

Maps, 241. *See also* Graphic/visual elements, relevant; Multimedia resources

Meaning
clarify, of similar words, 273
convey intended, 277. *See also* Genres; Rhetorical devices/techniques; Transition words/phrases; Word choices, precise
determining. *See* Context; Dictionary, use; Glossary, use
subtlety of, 80, *81, 109, 161, 187*

Measurements and amounts, 491, 567, 615

Mechanics, correct, 42
expository writing, 162–163
fiction narratives, 110–*111*, 115
nonfiction narratives, 82–*83*
persuasive writing, 188–*189*
poetry/description, 136–*137*, 141
research writing, 246, *247*
responses to literature, 214–*215*, 219

Media
watching, for ideas, 7
writing for, R6–R11, 24
advice columns, 166–*167*
to connect globally, 7
descriptive essays, *140–141*
fictional-interview scripts, *250–253*
letters to the editor, 192–*193*
multimedia projects, 25
project plans, *266–267*
radio play scripts, *114–115*
radio shows, 86–*87*
scripts, *218–219*

Memoirs, 10, 67

Memos, 22, 257, 260

Mentor Texts
analytical essays, 148–149
autobiographical narratives, 68–69, 83

mystery stories, 94–97, 110–111
op-ed pieces, 174–175, 188–189
response-to-literature essays, 200–201, 214
scan
for apostrophe use, 286
for comma use, 279, 283
for complex ideas, 282
for consistent tenses, 284
for integration of quotations, 290
sonnets/free-verse poems, 122–123, 136

Message, convey/respond to, 25, R31

Message boards, R8

Metaphors, 55, 123, 129

Meter, 54, 120, 129, 134

Middle of drafts. *See* Body of drafts/writing

Mind Map, 32

Misplaced modifiers, 412, *414*

Mistakes, identify possible
apostrophe use, 286
comma splices, 288
faulty parallelism/coordination, 282
pronoun-antecedent non-agreement, 289
spelling errors, 277
vague pronouns, 276
verb tenses, 284
words with similar meaning/spelling, 273

MLA (Modern Language Association), R16, 228, 234, 236–237, 246, 275

Modifiers, 315, 507
absolute, 519, *520*
comparisons using, 513, *515*, 517, *518*, 519, *520*
degrees of comparison, 508–510, *511–512*
independent, 574
misplaced/dangling, 412–413, *414*
punctuating, 574, 607–609, 626
that clarify tense, 453, *454*
See also Adjectives; Adverbs

Index continued

Mood
    convey, 66, 125, *141*
    define/develop, 92, 98, 102–105, 107, *117*
    indicative/subjunctive, 455–456, *457–458*, 459, 461
    set/create
        autobiographical narratives, 74, *75*, 77
        poetry/description, 13
        scripts, 24, 86–*87*, 114–115
        sonnets/free-verse poems, 122

Movies. *See* Multimedia resources

Multimedia elements, R8, R10, *165.* *See also* Graphic/visual elements, relevant

Multimedia presentations
    descriptive essays, *141*
    film teaser (mystery stories), 113
    infomercial scripts, *249*
    informational research reports, 248
    poetic advertisements, *139*
    project plans, *266*
    public service announcement, *191*
    radio shows, 86–*87*
    research reports, *264*
    TV talk show scripts, *165*

Multimedia projects, 25

Multimedia resources, 232. *See also* Graphic/visual elements, relevant

Music titles, 562, 601

Music/musical effects, 122, *139, 141, 249*

Mystery, solving, 108

Mystery stories, 11
    characteristics, 92
    mentor/student models, 94–99
    writing applications, 113–115
    writing process, 100–112

Mythological god names, 554

Myths and legends, 12, 93

N

Names

    capitalizing, 551–554, *555*, 556
    punctuating, 567, 583, 615
    titles with, 560–561
    underlining/italicizing, 602–603
    verb agreement with, 490–491

Narrative essays, 67

Narrative nonfiction. *See* Nonfiction narratives

Negative sentences, 522–524, *525–526,* 527

Negative word, using one, 523

Neuter pronouns, 495

Newspaper articles, 17, 147. *See also* Print resources

Newspaper titles, 602

Nominative absolute, 467, 572

Nominative case, 466
    elliptical clauses and, 477
    nouns in, 466
    pronouns in, 467–468, *469*
    who and *whom* in, 475–476, *478*

Nonfiction narrative essays, *88–89, 117*

Nonfiction narratives, 9
    characteristics, 66
    forms of, 9–10, 67
    writing, to a prompt, 255

Nonrestrictive (nonessential) phrases or clauses
    adjectival, 377
    appositive, 360
    participial, 365–366, *367*
    punctuating, 110, 283, 578, *580,* 581, 591, 620, 626
    relative, 378, *381,* 382

Notebook, idea, 4

Notecards/notetaking, use, R12
    to keep track of details, 70, *155*
    to keep track of sources, R26, *234,* 235, 240, 275
    for meetings, R25
    for partner's responses, 176
    to record research findings, *251*

Noun clauses, 387–390, *391*

complex sentences with, 393
fragmented, 409
introductory words in, 388–390, *391*
nonparallel, 416

Noun fragments, 408

Nouns, 294
    as adjectives, 316, 318, *319*
    adjectives modifying, 315, 317–318, 323
    as adverbs, 322
    apostrophes and possessive, 286
    case in, 466
    collective, 295, *297,* 489, *493*
    commas with, 587
    compound, 295, *297,* 615
    contractions with, 617
    of direct address, 296, 576–577
    fractions as, 607
    gerunds as, 368–369
    infinitives as, 370
    nonparallel, 416
    number in, 480–481, 482, *483*
    plural, not ending in -s, 539
    possessive, 614–616
    review, 332
    starting sentence with, 405
    that look like plurals, 489–490
    types, 295–296, *297*
    See also Common nouns; Proper nouns

Number
    in nouns, pronouns, and verbs, 480–481, *483*
    pronoun-antecedent agreement in, 289, 495, 496–497, 498, 499–500
    subjects of mixed, 486
    subject-verb agreement in, 482, *483*

Numbers
    apostrophes with, 618
    colons with, 593
    commas with, 583
    hyphens in, 607
    in outlines, 568
    in parentheses, 620, 622

slashes between, 626
underlining or italicizing, 603

O

Object
compound, 400, *402*, 587
of a verb, 312
See also Direct objects; Indirect objects

Object complements, 347, 350, *353*, **361**

Object of the preposition, 325, 326
appositive phrases and, 361
direct object as, 348
gerund as, 368
indirect object as, 349
infinitive as, 370
noun clause as, 388–389
objective pronoun as, 470
in prepositional phrases, 356, *359*
relative pronoun as, 383
as simple subject, 337

Objections, writer's, 192–193. *See also* Counter-arguments

Objective case, 466
elliptical clauses and, 477
nouns in, 466
pronouns in, 467, 470–471, *472*, 474
who and *whom* in, 475–476, *478*

Observations, personal
compare-and-contrast essays, 152, 155
to find ideas for writing, 3
response-to-literature essays, 207

Online writing. *See* Blogs; E-mails, business; Internet; Social networking, online; Web sites, authors'

Op-ed (opposite-editorial) pieces, 18, 172
characteristics, 172
mentor/student models, 174–177
writing, to a prompt, *195*
writing applications, *191*
writing process, 178–190

Open-ended questions, R29. *See also* Research questions/plan

Opening. *See* Beginning of draft; Sentences

Opinions
expressing, 98, 124, 150, 176
identify support for, 261
objective/subjective, 233, *250*

Options, slashes separating, 626–627

Oral presentations, 248, *267*. *See also* Speeches, giving/evaluating

Organization (writing trait), 26, 27, 28, 57, 63. *See also* Rubrics

Organization names, 490–491, 554, 555, 615

Organizational strategy
autobiographical narratives, 76–77
compare-and-contrast essays, 156–157
fictional-interview scripts, *252*
to include graphics. *See* Graphic/visual elements, relevant
informational research reports, 238–239
mystery stories, 104–105
response-to-literature essays, 208–209
sonnets/free-verse poems, 130
See also Steps in a process (order of)

Organizing structure
analytical essays, 148, *169*
argumentative essays, 172, *195*
compare-and-contrast essays, 146, 154, 157–158, 160
op-ed pieces, 180, 182–183
persuasive essays, *221*
problem-solution essays, *195*
response-to-literature essays, 208–209, 212, 215

Outline for Success
argumentative essays, 182
autobiographical narratives, 76
compare-and-contrast essays, 156
informational research reports, 238

mystery stories, 104
response-to-literature essays, 208

Outlines, R11, R26, 568

Oxymoron, 55

P

Packaging, 24, *139, 249*

Paired items, commas and, 573

Paradox, 55

Paragraphs, writing strong, 48, 50–52

Parallelism, 282, 415–417, *420, 422*

Paraphrase, *234*, **235,** 246, *251*, 265

Parentheses, 620–622, *623*

Parenthetical citations, 226, 237, 246

Parenthetical expressions
punctuating, 577, *580*, 621, 626
subject-verb agreement and, 484

Participial fragments, 407–408

Participial phrases, 356, 365–366, *367*
combining sentences with, 366, *367*
commas after introductory, 279, 283, 576
dangling, 413, *414*
nonparallel, 416
noun fragments with, 408
restrictive/nonrestrictive, 365–366, *367*, 578, 591
starting sentences with, 405

Participles
as adjectives, **318, 364,** 365
adverbial clauses modifying, 384
present/past, 364, 427, *428*, 429–432, *433–434*
pronoun as object of, 470
time sequence with, 449, 452
use of, in poetry, 136, *137*
verbs or gerunds versus, 365, 368

Partner Talk
collaborative writing, 7
effective composition, 52, 55, 57, 59
expository writing, 17, 150, 162, 167
fiction narratives, 98, 110, 115

Index continued

interpretative responses, 20, 202, 214, 219
multimedia projects, 25
nonfiction narratives, 70, 82, 87
persuasive writing, 19, 176, 188, 193
poetry/description, 13, 15, 124, 136, 141
research writing, 21, 235, 237, 241, 246, *251, 253*
workplace writing, 23, 259, 261, 263, 267
writing process, 37, 41, 47
See also Collaborative writing; Listening and speaking activities; Work with partner

Parts of speech, 293, 332–333, *334*. *See also* specific part of speech

Passive voice or tense, 188–*189*, 460, 461, 462, *463–464*

Past emphatic tense, 425, 441–442

Past form of verbs, 427, *428*, 429–432, *433–434*

Past participles, 364, 427, *428*
of irregular verbs, 429–432, *434*
of regular verbs, 429, *433*

Past perfect progressive tense, 425, 441–442

Past perfect tense, 424, 441–442

Past progressive tense, 425, 441–442

Past tense, 424
sequence of events in, 448–449
uses, 438, 441–442, *443*

Past time, tenses expressing, 441–442, *443*

Perfect tenses, 424–425

Periodicals, 562, 593, 602

Periods, 566–568, *570*
to correct comma splices, 288
in indirect question, 569
quotations marks with, 596–597
sentences with, 398, *399*

Person

agreement in, 289, 497, *498*
personal pronoun, 299, 300, 495

Personal blogs, R6

Personal fulfillment, 2

Personal narratives. *See* Autobiographical narratives

Personal pronouns, 299, *302*
ambiguous, 504–505
antecedent agreement with, 495–497, 498, 499–500
antecedents of, 299
apostrophes with, 616–617
cases, 467
contractions with, 617
distant references to, 505
gender, 495, 497
number, 480–481, 495
person, 299, 495
vague references to, 503–504

Personification, 55, 122, 129

Persons, describe interesting, 126

Perspective. *See* Points of view

Persuade, genre to, 8

Persuasive essays, 18, 173, *221*. *See also* Argumentative essays

Persuasive speeches, 18, R30, 173

Persuasive texts, 19, 171

Persuasive writing, 2, 18, 19, 192–193

Photographs, 241. *See also* Graphic/visual elements, relevant; Multimedia resources

Phrases, 355, 356
adjectival, 356–357, *359*
appositive, 360–362, *363*, 401
clarifying tense with, 453
combining sentences with, 401, *402*
commas with, 274, 576, 587
faulty coordination with, 419
foreign, underlining/italicizing, 603
fragmented, 407–408
gerund, 356, 369, *372–373*
parallel/nonparallel, 415–417

in parentheses, 621
restrictive/nonrestrictive, 578
simple sentences with, 392
starting sentences with, 405, *406*
subject-verb agreement and, 484, *487*
verb, 313, *314*
verbal, 364–366, *367*, 368–371
See also Adverbial phrases; Infinitive phrases; Participial phrases; Prepositional phrases

Place, describe, *140–141*

Place names, 552–553, *555*, 567

Plagiarism, 55, 235

Planning. *See* Organizational strategy; Prewriting/planning first drafts

Plays, titles of, 562, 602

Plot
enhanced, 66, *75*, 77, 92, 104–105, 108. *See also* Stories/storylines
response to a, 198

Plot events, develop, 74, 76, *89*. *See also* Action

Plot map, 34, 74, 89

Plurals
apostrophes with, 614–615, 618
not ending in -*s*, 480, 539
nouns that look like, 489–490
See also Number

Podcasts, R11, 217. *See also* Multimedia resources

Poems, effective, 13–14, 120

Poetic advertisements, *139*

Poetic forms, 121, 129, 131, 134, 143, 169

Poetic techniques
poetry/description, *143, 169*
sonnets/free-verse poems, 126, 129, 131, 133, 134–135, 137

Poetry
capitalizing lines of, 547, *548*
contractions in, 617
and description, 13, 120

forms of, 13–14, 121
   mentor/student models, 122–125
   writing, to a prompt, *142–143*
   writing applications, *139–141*
slashes in, 626–627
titles of, 562, 601–602

Poet's Toolbox, 129

Point-by-point format, 156–157

Points of view
   clearly stated, 224, 240, 247, *265*
   consider other, 182–183. See also Counter-arguments
   distinctive, *139*, 141, *165, 191, 249*
   genre to convey, 8
   images to show, *266*
   inferred, 226
   opposite, *192–193*
   reveal/restate, 228

Political parties, 554

Portfolio, manage, 7, 84, 112, 138, 216, 248

Position
   clearly state, 171, 180, 182, 189
   restating, 182, 186, 192

Positive degree, 508, 509–510, *511*

Possessive adjectives, 317, 318

Possessive case, 466
   apostrophes with, 286, 614–616
   hyphens and, 607
   nouns in, 466
   pronouns in, 467, 471, 472–473, 474
   who and *whom* in, 475–476, *478*

Possessive pronouns
   as adjectives, 317–318
   apostrophes with, 616–617
   contractions vs., 471, 476, 617
   gerunds and, 369

Possibilities, expressing, 162, 455

Practice, 25. See also Rehearse

Predicate adjectives, 347, 350–351, 405

Predicate nominatives, 347, 350–351

adjectival phrases modifying, 357, *359*
appositive phrases and, 361
compound, 351, 468, 470
gerunds as, 368
infinitives as, 370
nominative pronouns as, 467–468
noun clauses as, 388–389

Predicates, complete/simple, 336–337, *338*. See also Verbs

Prefixes
   hyphens with, 608
   interpretative responses, 199
   negative, 524
   proper adjectives with, 557
   titles with, 560
   word meaning and, 147

Prepositional fragments, 407–408

Prepositional phrases, 325, *327,* **356**
   adjectival, 356–357, *359*
   adverbial, 358, *359*
   combining sentences with, *363*, 401
   commas and, 571–573, 576–577, *579*
   gerund phrases with, 369
   infinitives versus, 370
   recognizing, *359*
   starting sentences with, 405

Prepositions, 325–326, *327*
   adverbs versus, 326, *327*
   colons after, 592
   in prepositional phrases, 356, *359*
   review, 333, *334*
   See also Object of the preposition

Present emphatic tense, 425, 438–439

Present form of verbs, 427, *428,* **429–432,** *433–434*

Present participles, 364, 427, *428*
   of irregular verbs, 429–432, *434*
   of regular verbs, 429, *433*

Present perfect progressive tense, 425, 441–442

Present perfect tense, 364, 424, 441

Present progressive tense, 425, 438–439, 444

Present tense, 424, 438–439, *440, 451*
   expressing future time with, 444
   sequence of events in, 447, 449

Present time, tenses expressing, 438–439, 440

Presentations, adjust, 165, 191. See also Multimedia presentations; Oral presentations

Presenting writing. See Publishing/ Presenting and Reflecting

Prewriting/planning first drafts, 30, 32–34
   advice columns, *167*
   autobiographical narratives, 72–75
   business letters, 263
   compare-and-contrast essays, 152–155
   descriptive essays, *141*
   fictional-interview scripts, *251*
   informational research reports, 230–237
   instructions, set of, 259
   memos, 261
   mystery stories, 100–103
   op-ed pieces, 178–181
   project plans, *267*
   public service announcement, *193*
   radio play scripts, *115*
   radio shows, *87*
   response-to-literature essays, 204–207
   scripts, *219*
   sonnets/free-verse poems, 126–129

Primary sources, 233

Principle parts
   in conjugation, 435
   of irregular verbs, 429–432, *434*
   of regular verbs, 427, *428*, 429, *433*

Print resources, 232

Privacy in social networks, R8

Problem in plot structure, 74, 77. See also Conflict, well-developed

Index continued

Problem-solution chart, R26
Problem-solution essays, 16, 147, *195*
Procedural writing, 23, 257–259, *268–269*
Pro-con chart, 34
Pro-con essays, 16, 147
Product packaging, 24, *139, 249*
Progressive tenses, 424, 425, *426*
   conjugation, 436, *437*
   future, 444
   past, 441–442
   present, 438–439, 444
Project plans, 23, 257, *266*, 267
Pronoun-antecedent agreement, 479
   indefinite pronouns and, 499–500, *501*
   personal pronouns and, 495–497, *498*
   problems with, 276, 289, 502–505, *506*
   reflexive pronouns and, 500, *501*
Pronouns, 294, 298, 465
   as adjectives, 317–318, *320*
   adjectives modifying, 315–316, 323
   ambiguous, 504–505, *506*
   antecedents, 298, 302
   apostrophes and possessive, 286
   apostrophes with, 616–617
   cases, 466, 467–468, *469*, 470–471, *472–473*, 474
   distant references to, 505
   errors in using, *253*
   fragments with, 407
   number, 480–481, *483*
   problems with, 276, 475–477, *478*
   reflexive, 299–300, *302*, 500, *501*
   review, 332, 334
   types, 299–301, *302–305*, 306, *307*
   vague references to, 276, 502–504, *506*
   See also Demonstrative pronouns; Indefinite pronouns; Personal pronouns; Possessive pronouns; Reciprocal pronouns; Relative pronouns

Proofreading marks, 43
Propaganda, 19, 173
Proper adjectives, 317, *320*, 556
   capitalizing, 214, 556–557, *558*
   dividing, 612
   prefixes with, 608
Proper nouns, 296, 297, 551
   as adjectives, 317, 556
   capitalizing, 214, 551–554, *555, 558*
   dividing, 612
   identifying, *555*
   prefixes with, 608
   spell-check errors, 277
Proposals, expressing, 455–456
Prose poems, 14, 121
Public service announcement, *191*
Publication date, recent, 233
Publishing/presenting and reflecting, 30, 46–47
   advice columns, *167*
   autobiographical narratives, 84
   business letters, 263
   class yearbooks, 85
   compare-and-contrast essays, 164
   descriptive essays, *141*
   fictional-interview scripts, *253*
   informational research reports, 248
   instructions, set of, 259
   memos, 261
   mystery stories, 112
   op-ed pieces, 190
   project plans, *267*
   public service announcement, *193*
   radio play scripts, *115*
   radio shows, *87*
   response-to-literature essays, 216
   scripts, *219*
   sonnets/free-verse poems, 138
Punctuation, 565
   to combine sentences, 400, *403*
   correct, 82–83, 162, 247, 257
   of fragments, 407

   identify missing, *253*, 287
   inside parentheses, 621
   quotation marks with other, 597–598
   of run-ons, 287, 410
   of sentences, 398, *399*
   See also specific type
Purpose
   address issues of
     analytical essays, 157–160, *161*
     argumentative essays, 174, 184–186, *187*
     fiction narratives, 106–109
     nonfiction narratives, 78–*81*, 86–*87*
     poetry/description, 132–135
     research writing, 242, 244
     response-to-literature essays, 210–213
   convey clear (workplace writing), 257, 259, *269*
     determine appropriate, 32
     analytical essays, 146, 150
     argumentative essays, 173, 180, 182
     fiction narratives, 93, *115*
     multimedia projects, 25
     nonfiction narratives, 67
     poetry/description, 121, *140–141*
     scripts, 24
     workplace writing, 258
   genre and, 8
   organize/present ideas to suit, 106
Purposes, consider multiple
   autobiographical narratives, 73
   compare-and-contrast essays, 153
   informational research reports, 231
   mystery stories, 101
   op-ed pieces, 179
   response-to-literature essays, 205
   sonnets/free-verse poems, 127

Q

Question marks, 566, 568–569, *570*
   quotation marks with, 596–598
   sentences with, 398, *399*

Questions
  anticipate reader's, 259–263
  ask follow up
    advice columns, 167
    group discussion, R29
    op-ed pieces, 178
    radio play scripts, 115
    scripts, 219
    sonnets/free-verse poems, 136
  direct object in, 348
  incomplete, 546, 568
  indirect, punctuating, 566, 569
  pronouns in, 475–476
  revising statement into, 569
  types of, R29
  See also Interrogative sentences; Research questions/plan

Quotation marks, 595, *599,* **605–606**
  for dialogue, 600
  for direct and divided quotations, 234–235, 278, 595–597
  to indicate sarcasm/irony, 214–215, 604, *606*
  introductory material and, 246
  with other punctuation, 278, 597–598
  single, 598
  for titles, 214, 601, 603

Quotations
  brackets in, 598, 622
  capitalizing, 547, *549*
  colons introducing, 592
  commas with, 586
  direct, 234–235, 240, *251, 265,* 278, 586, 595–597
  divided, 596–597
  effective embedded/integrated
    interpretative responses, 20, 198, *255*
    response-to-literature essays, 203, 206–207, 209
  ellipses in, 624
  indirect, 278, 595
  with introductory phrases, 246, 290
  with other expressions, 595–597
  quotation marks with, 595
  within quotations, 598
  supporting, 181–182, *234,* 238, 246

R

Race or nationality, 554
RADaR (Replace, Add, Delete, Reorder), 38–41. *See also* Revising drafts
Radio shows, 86
Reach out to connect with others, 2
Read
  asking five Ws questions, R24
  to find ideas for writing, 3
  to find topic, 100
  to search literature, 126
Read aloud, 36, 135, 165, *252–253*
Read carefully
  to identify direct/indirect quotations, 278
  to identify missing words, 281
  to locate comma splices, 288
  to locate spelling errors, 277
  to locate vague pronouns, 276
  for pronoun-antecedent non-agreement, 289
  to use words correctly, 273
Reader interest
  engage/capture
    autobiographical narratives, 76, 80
    compare-and-contrast essays, 156
    informational research reports, 238–239
    mystery stories, 106, 108
    op-ed pieces, 182
    radio play scripts, *115*
    response-to-literature essays, 208, 215
    sonnets/free-verse poems, 131
  sustain, 105, *115,* 215
  See also Audience
Realistic fiction, 11, 93
Reasoning, logical, 146, 148, 155, 172, 181

Reciprocal pronouns, 300, *303,* **304**
Records, electronic, 25
Red herring, 104
Reference guides. *See* Dictionary, use; Glossary, use; Thesaurus, use
Reference list. *See* Works Cited list
Reflecting, 7, 25, 72, 175. *See also* Publishing/Presenting and Reflecting
Reflective essays, 10, 67
Reflexive pronouns, 299–300, *302,* **500, 501**
Regular modifiers, 508–509, *511*
Regular verbs, 429, *433*
Rehearse
  public service announcement, 191
  infomercial scripts, *249*
  multimedia projects, 25
  podcasts, R11
  problem-solution newscasts, 165
  staged dialogue, 217
Relative adverbs, 376, 383–384, *386*
Relative clauses, restrictive/nonrestrictive, 110–*111,* **378, 381, 382**
Relative pronouns, 301, *305*
  in clauses, 376, 383, *386*
  as subjects, 484–485
Relative value. *See* Data; Facts; Ideas
Religious references, 554, *555,* **593, 603**
Repetition, 55, 129
Reports. *See* Health reports; Historical reports; Lab reports; Statistical analysis reports
Requests, expressing, 455–456
Reread, R9, *89*
Research process, critique, 237, 264, 269
Research questions/plan
  ask/develop open-ended, 223, *265*

Index continued

clarify/critique/modify/refocus, *233*, 237, 255, *264*
formulate/make
  compare-and-contrast essays, 164
  fictional-interview scripts, *250–251, 252*
  informational research reports, 224, 230, *231*, 232–233
  op-ed pieces, 190
  research reports (workplace writing), *264–265*
  response-to-literature essays, 216

Research reports, 21, *233,* **264**
Research writing, 21, 224, 225
Resolution, well-developed
  autobiographical narratives, 66, 69, 71, 74, *75*, 76–77, 80
  fiction narratives, 11
  mystery stories, 92, 97, 102, *103*, 104–105, 108–109, *117, 143*
  narrative nonfiction essays, *89, 117*
  nonfiction narratives, 9

Resource materials, use, 34
Resources, review, 33, 232. *See also* Sources

Responses, analyze/share
  compare-and-contrast essays, 150
  letters to the editor, *192–193*
  mystery stories, 98
  op-ed pieces, 176
  response-to-literature essays, 202
  See also Partner Talk; Student Models

Responses to literature, 20, 197, 255. *See also* Interpretative responses

Response-to-literature essays
  characteristics, 198
  mentor/student models, 200–203
  writing applications, *217–219*
  writing process, 204–216

Restating problem/thesis/position
  argumentative essays, 182
  compare-and-contrast essays, 156–157, 160

informational research reports, 238–239, 244
op-ed pieces, 186
response-to-literature essays, 208, 212
See also Paraphrase

Restrictive phrases/clauses
  adjectival, 377
  appositive, 360
  commas with, 110, 578
  participial, 365–366, *367*
  relative, 378, *381*, 382

Résumés, 23
Review notes, 275
Reviews, 19
  critical, 20, 199
  opinion, 173
  responses to literature, 204

Revising drafts, 30, 36–41
  advice columns, *167*
  apostrophe use, 286
  autobiographical narratives, 78–81
  business letters, 263
  capitalization, 280
  comma splices, 288
  comma use, 274, 279, 283, 285
  compare-and-contrast essays, 158–161
  descriptive essays, *141*
  faulty parallelism/coordination, 282
  fictional-interview scripts, *252*
  fused/run-on sentences, 287
  informational research reports, 242–245
  instructions, set of, 259
  integration of quotations, 290
  memos, 261
  missing words, 281
  mystery stories, 106–109
  project plans, *267*
  public service announcement, 193
  quotation marks, 278
  radio play scripts, 115
  radio shows, 87

response-to-literature essays, 210–213
scripts, 219
sentence fragments, 292
sonnets/free-verse poems, 132–135
unclear sentences, 281
unnecessary/missing hyphens, 291
vague pronouns, 276

Rhetorical devices/techniques, 54–55
  analytical essays, 149, *169*
  autobiographical narratives, 77
  compare-and-contrast essays, 146, 151, 157, 159
  expository writing, 15
  interpretative responses, *221, 255*
  mystery stories, 105
  narrative nonfiction essays, *89*
  problem-solution essays, *195*
  response-to-literature essays, 209

Rhetorical language, R30
Rhyme, 13, 54, 125, 129
Rhyme scheme, 120, 122, 134
Rhythm, 13, 125, 131, 157
Root words, 147, 199
Rubrics, 28–29
  autobiographical narratives, 83
  compare-and-contrast essays, 163
  how to use, 28–29
  informational research reports, 247
  mystery stories, 111
  op-ed pieces, 189
  response-to-literature essays, 215
  revising using, 37
  sonnets/free-verse poems, 137
  using, with others, 29

Run-ons, *253,* **287, 407, 410, 411, 572**

S

Salutations, letter, R14
Sarcasm, 215, 604, *606*
Scanning
  apostrophe use, 286

capitalization, 280
comma use, 274, 279, 283
compound sentences, 285
consistent verb tenses, 284
integration of quotations, 290
presentation of complex ideas, 282
run-ons, 287
sentence fragments, 292

Scene, set the. *See* Settings

Science fiction, 12, 93

Screenplays, 24

Scripts, 24, 114
fictional-interview, *250–253*
film, *115*
infomercial, *249*
radio play, *114–115*
radio shows, *86–87*
TV talk show, *165*
writing process, 218, *219*

Seacraft names, 554, 603

Search engines. *See* Internet

Seasons, names of, 554

Second person, 299, 300, 495

Secondary sources, 233

Semicolons, 589, *594*
to correct comma splices, 288
to correct run-ons, 410
to join independent clauses, 392, 400, 589–591
parentheses and, 621
quotation marks with, 597
to separate series, 590–591

Seminars. *See* Multimedia resources

Senses, appealing to. *See* Details, sensory

Sentence fluency (writing trait), 27, 28, 58, 63. *See also* Rubrics

Sentence structures, 392–393, *394*
effective, 66, 92, 172, 198, 224
variety of, 52, *245*
analytical essays, *169*
autobiographical narratives, *81*, 82, *83*
compare-and-contrast essays, 146, *155*, 157, 159

expository writing, 15
problem-solution essays, *195*
response-to-literature essays, *213*

Sentences, 48, 335, 397
adverbial clauses in, 385
adverbs in, 321
appositive phrases in, 361
basic parts of, 335
complements, 347–351, *353*
hard-to-find subjects, 343–345, *346*
subjects and predicates, 336–337, *338*
beginning with *here* or *there*, 343, *346*
capitalizing, 546–547, *548–549, 558, 564*
colons introducing, 593
combining, 49, 400–401, 402–403
with adjectival clauses, 377
with appositives/appositive phrases, 362, 363
with participial phrases, 366
with prepositional phrases, 363
with compound subject/verb, 341
effective supporting, 51
elliptical, 339, 585–586
ending with abbreviations, 567–568
faulty coordination in, 282, 418–419, *421*, 422
faulty parallelism in, 282, 415–417, *420*, 422
fragmented, 253, 292, 339–340, *342*, 407–409, 411
functions, 398, *399*
fused, 287, 410, *411*
identify unclear, 281
inverted. *See* Word order, inverted
length of, 52, *213*, 245, *252*
locating subjects/verbs in, 340, *342*
negative, 522–524, *525–526*, 527
opening, engaging, 52, *252*
autobiographical narratives, 76–77, 80
compare-and-contrast essays, 157, 160

mystery stories, 108
in parentheses, 621
pronoun usage in, 475–476, *478*
run-on, 253, 287, 407, 410, *411*, 572
simple, 392, *394*
tense sequence in, 446–449, *450*
types of, 82
varying, 245, 404–405, *406*
word order. *See* Word order, inverted
writing strong, 49
See also Complex sentences; Compound sentences; Declarative sentences; Exclamatory sentences; Imperative sentences; Interrogative sentences

Sequential events, expressing, 284, 446–449, *450*
Series
commas in, 573, 574, 592
fragmented, 407, 409
hyphens in, 607
nonparallel items in, 416–417, *420*, 422
numbers/letters marking, 620, 622
semicolons in, 589–591

Settings
analysis of, 198, 204
create particular, 92, 94, 102
interesting/believable, 11, 24, 74, 103–104, 108

Share writing, 2, 37, *85***, 113**

Short stories
characteristics, 92
formatting titles of, 562
forms of, 93
titles, 601
writing, to a prompt, *116–117*

Sights. *See* Details, sensory

Signature, letter, R14

Similarities. *See* Comparisons

Simile, 55, 129

Index R51

Index continued

Simple predicates, 337, *338*
Simple sentences, 392, *394*
Simple subjects, 337, 338, 342
Simultaneous events, expressing, 446–449, *450, 452*
Single quotation marks, 598
Situations, open-ended. *See* Ideas
Skim texts, 126, 152
Slashes, 624, 626–627, *628*
Slogans, *139*
Smells. *See* Details, sensory
Social networking, online, 7, R8
Solutions, identify/develop, 166–167
Song-like structure. *See also* Music/musical effects
Songs, *139*
Sonnets, 14, 121
   characteristics, 120, 130, 131
   mentor/student models, 122, 124
   writing process, 126–138
Sort of subjects, 16
Sound devices, effective use of, 54
   descriptive essays, *141*
   mystery stories, 104
   poetry/description, 120, 129, *169*
   sonnets/free-verse poems, 122, 125, 131, 134, *139*
Sounds. *See* Details, sensory; Music/musical effects
Source cards, R26, 234–235, 240
Sources
   accurately cite, *234, 236, 252–253, 265*
   distinguish between types of, 233, 237
   documentation of
      research writing, 224, 228–229, 236–237, 240, 244, 246, *247,* 251
      workplace writing, *265*
   evaluate, 232–233, 247, *251,* 255
   explore range of relevant, *233*

   find authoritative/objective, 232, *251, 265, 269*
   identify/credit, R7, 235, 246
   incomplete/missing, 275
   list possible, 254
   multiple, keeping track of, 181–182, 234, 238, *251*
   review, 33, 178
   types of, distinguishing, 232–233
   See also Works Cited list
Spacecraft names, 554, 603
Speakers, identify, *252*
Speaker's message, respond to, R31
Speaking. *See also* Discussion, participate in; Listening and speaking activities
Special events/times, names of, 553
Speech
   patterns of natural, 120, 134
   pause in, 625
   See also Dialogue
Speeches, giving/evaluating, 18, R31, 173
Spell-check feature
   duplicate vs. missing words, 281
   inappropriate substitutes, 43
   similar spellings, 277
   similar words, 273
Spelling, correct
   editing process, 42
   expository writing, 146, 162–163
   fiction narratives, 110–*111,* 115
   homophones, 277
   nonfiction narratives, 82–*83*
   persuasive writing, 188–*189*
   poetry/description, 136–*137, 141*
   research writing, 246, *247,* 253
   responses to literature, 214–*215, 219*
   similar words, 273
   workplace writing, 257
Spelling errors (word list), common, R17
Spiral Review
   autobiographical narratives, *143*

   narrative nonfiction essays, *117*
   nonfiction narratives, *255*
   persuasive essays, *221*
   poetry/description, *169*
   problem-solution essays, *195*
   research process, critique, *269*
   responses to literature, *255*
Stage dialogue, 217
Stage directions, *218–219, 250*
Stanzas, 120, 134
Statements, 174. *See also* Quotations
Statements with question mark, 568–569
Statistical analysis reports, 21
Statistics, supporting, 182, 240
Steps in a process (order of), R27, 258, 267, *269*
Stories/storylines
   elements of, 70, 75
   engaging
      autobiographical narratives, 66, 71, *75,* 76, 80, *143*
      mystery stories, 92, 99, 102, 104–105, 108–109, *117*
      narrative nonfiction essays, *89*
      radio play scripts, *114–115*
      See also Plot, enhanced
   loose ends of, 108
   See also Short stories
Storyboards, R27, 24, 113
Stranger, mysterious, 100
Stringy sentences, 418–419
Structural elements/devices, 13, 54, 120, 129, 134
Structure. *See* Organizational strategy; Organizing structure; Sentence structures
Student Models, 40–41
   autobiographical narratives, 70–71, 75, 78–79, 82
   compare-and-contrast essays, 150–151, 155, 158–159, 161–163

informational research reports, 226–229, 237, 240, 242–243, 245–247
mystery stories, 98–99, 103, 106–107, 109
op-ed pieces, 176–177, 181, 184–185, 187
response-to-literature essays, 202–203, 207, 210–211, 213, 215
sonnets/free-verse poems, 124–125, 132–133, 135, 137
workplace writing, 258, 260, 262

Style, convey clear, *109,* **161,** *187, 213,* **259**

Style manuals, use, **R16, 224, 228, 236–237,** *241, 246, 247, 269,* **275**

Stylistic devices
analyze author's use of, 198, *207,* 209
interpretative responses, 198, 201, *255*
podcasts, R11

Subject complements, 350–351, *353,* **354**

Subjective resources. *See* Bias

Subjects, 336
adjectival phrases modifying, 357, *359*
appositive phrases and, 361
complete, 336, *338*
confusing, 488–491, *492*
fragments with, 408
gerunds as, 368
hard-to-find, 343–345, *346*
in independent clauses, 393
of infinitive, 470
infinitive phrases with, 371
infinitives as, 370
lack of, 292
with linking verbs, 488–489
locating, 340, *342*
nominative pronouns as, 467–468
noun clauses as, 388–389
relative pronouns as, 383, 484–485
simple, 337, *338, 342*
in simple sentences, 392

singular/plural, 482, *483,* 484–485, *487*
understood, 387
of the verb, 308
voice and, 460–461
See also Compound subjects

Subject-verb agreement, 479, 494
compound subjects and, 485–486, *487*
confusing subjects and, 488–491, *492–493*
errors in, *253*
in number, **480–481,** *483*
singular/plural subjects and, 482, *483,* 484–485, *487*

Subject-verb order. *See* Word order, inverted

Subjunctive mood
about, 455–456, *457–458,* 459, 461
in compare-and-contrast essays, 162–163

Subordinate clauses, 375–376, *379–380*
in autobiographical narratives, 82
combining sentences with, 401
commas with, 571–573
conjunctions in, 329
faulty coordination with, 419
fragmented, 292, 407, 409
logical verb tenses in, 284
pronouns in, 476
relative pronouns/adverbs in, **383–384**
in strong sentences, 49
in types of sentences, 392–393
verb tense in, 446–448, *451*
See also Adjectival clauses; Adverbial clauses; Noun clauses

Subordinating conjunctions, 328–329, *331*
clauses beginning with, 384–385, *391*
combining sentences with, 401, *403*

Subtitled phase, *266*

Suffixes, 137, 147, 199, 560, 608

Summaries, in-depth, 198, 209, *211,* **212,** *221,* **255**

Summarize
expository writing, 15
fictional-interview scripts, *251*
informational research reports, *234,* 235, 246
partner's thoughts aloud, 150
research reports, *265*
workplace writing, 261

Superlative degree, 508, *511*
irregular forms, 509–510, *512*
regular forms, 508–509, *511*
using, 513, *514–515,* 516

Support. *See* Evidence, supporting-text

Supporting sentences, effective, 51

Surprise, describe a, 72

Suspended hyphens, 607

Suspense, create/build
autobiographical narratives, 75, 77
fiction narratives, 11
mystery stories, 92, 97–98, 102–105, 108
nonfiction narratives, 9

Symbolism, 55, 126

Symbols, 129, 618

Synthesize. *See* Information

T

Tables, 241. *See also* Graphic organizers; Graphic/visual elements, relevant; Multimedia resources

Tags, conversational, 595, 596–597

Talk directly, R11

Tall tales, 12, 93

Tastes. *See* Details, sensory

Teaser, *113*

Tech Tips
auto-capitalization errors, 280
auto-hyphenation errors, 291
grammar-check gaps, 286–288
problems when cutting/pasting

Index continued

citations, 275
commas, 274, 279, 283
compound sentences, 285
integration of quotations, 290
missing punctuation marks, 278
missing words, 281
pronoun-antecedent agreement, 289
sentence fragments, 292
sentence structure, 282
vague pronouns after restructuring, 276
spell-check errors, 273, 277

Technology, using, 7, 39, 43, 52

Tenses. *See* Verb tenses

Tension, emphasize, 107

Terms, define, *269*

Text as primary source, 233

Text books. *See* Grammar textbooks, consult; Print resources

Text evidence. *See* Evidence, supporting-text

Text features. *See* Graphic/visual elements, relevant

Text support. *See* Evidence, supporting-text

Themes
clear, 11, 66, 74, 120, 123, 128, 132, 134
explicit/implicit, 24, 86–*87*, *114–115, 131, 165, 218–219*

Thesaurus, use, 135, *161, 273*

Thesaurus tool (word processor), 39

Theses/thesis statements
clearly stated
compare-and-contrast essays, 150, 151, 154, *155,* 156, 158, 160
informational research reports, 229, 247
op-ed pieces, 174, 177
problem-solution essays, *195*
response-to-literature essays, 203
on ideas to be compared/contrasted, 146

on main idea and how supported
analytical essays, 15, *169*
compare-and-contrast essays, 146
informational research reports, 238–239
interpretative responses, 20, 198, *221*
research writing, 224, 226, 244
response-to-literature essays, 200, 206, 208–209, 212
workplace writing, *265*
on point of view/position
argumentative essays, 172
fictional-interview scripts, *252*
letters to the editor, 193
op-ed pieces, 174, 180, 182–183, 186, *195*
persuasive essays, *221*
See also Restating problem/thesis/position

Third person, 299, 300, 495

Time
capitalizing references to, 553
punctuating references to, 567, 593, 615
tense sequence through, 446–449, *450*
tenses for expressing, 438–439, *440,* 441–442, *443,* 444, *445*

Timed writing
analytical essays, *169*
narrative nonfiction essays, *89*
persuasive essays, *221*
podcasts, R11
procedural text, *269*

Timeline (diagram), R27

Timetable for completing work, 232, *233,* 237

Title slide, *266*

Titles
capitalizing, 214, 559–563, *564*
of people, 560, 567, 583, 615
of works
capitalizing, 280

identify, in responses to literature, 208–209
punctuating, 593, 601–603, *605*
verb agreement with, 490–491

Tone, create
advice columns, 166–*167*
autobiographical narratives, 66, *75,* 77
business letters, 262
compare-and-contrast essays, 161
fictional-interview scripts, 250
media scripts, 86–*87, 115*
mystery stories, 92, 94, 104–105
op-ed pieces, 187
scripts, 24

Topic
clearly stated, 120, 141
complex, multifaceted, 269
determine appropriate, 32
advice columns, 167
autobiographical narratives, 72
compare-and-contrast essays, 152
informational research reports, 230
mystery stories, 100
narrative nonfiction essays, *89*
op-ed pieces, 178
radio shows, 86–87
research reports, *264*
response-to-literature essays, 204
sonnets/free-verse poems, 126, 127
focus on single, R7
narrow, **33–34**
autobiographical narratives, *73*
compare-and-contrast essays, *153*
informational research reports, 231
mystery stories, *101*
op-ed pieces, 179
response-to-literature essays, 205
sonnets/free-verse poems, *127*
See also Views, representing of range of

Topic sentences, clear, 50, 239

Topical blogs, R7

Touch. *See* Details, sensory

Trade books. *See* Print resources

Transition words/phrases
   advice columns, 167
   analytical essays, *169*
   autobiographical narratives, 80, 83
   compare-and-contrast essays, 146, 156–157, 159–160, *161*
   expository writing, 15
   interpretative responses, *221*
   mystery stories, 111
   narrative nonfiction essays, *89*
   problem-solution essays, *195*
   response-to-literature essays, 212
   sonnets/free-verse poems, *135*
   workplace writing, *269*

Transitional expressions, 589–590

Transitive verbs, 312, *314*, 347

Travel essays, 14

Travel guides, *140*

Trend analyses, 225

TV talk show scripts, *165*

U

Underlining, 595, 602–603, *605–606*

Understatement, 524, 527

Understood words, 345, 383, 387, 390

V

Value, analyze relative. *See* Data; Facts; Ideas

Venn diagram, R27

Verb fragments, 408

Verb moods, 162–163

Verb phrases, 313, *314*

Verb tenses, 424–425, *426*
   active/passive, 460–462, 463–464
   complex, 188–*189*
   conjugating, 430, 435–436, *437*
   in future time, 438, 444, *445*
   modifiers clarifying, 453, *454*
   for participles, 364
   in passive voice, 461, *464*
   in past time, 438, 441–442, *443*
   in present time, 438–439, *440*, 451
   revising for consistent, 284
   sequence of, 446–449, *450*

Verbal phrases, 364–366, *367*, **368–371**. *See also* Gerund phrases; Infinitive phrases; Participial phrases

Verbal/nonverbal strategies, R30

Verbals, **136**, 137, **364**, **368**, **369, 370–371**. *See also* Gerunds; Infinitives; Participles

Verbs, 308, 423
   action, 308–310, *311*
   active/passive voice, 460–462, *463–464*
   as adjectives, 318, *320*
   adverbial clauses modifying, 384
   adverbial phrases modifying, 358, *359*
   adverbs as parts of, 322
   adverbs modifying, 321, 323, *324*
   colons after, 592
   complements of, 347
   contractions with, 617
   in independent clause, 393
   irregular, 429–432, *434*
   lack of, 292
   linking, 308, 309–310, *311*
   locating, 340, 342, *346*
   mood, 455–456, *458*, 461
   number, 480–481, *483*
   participles or gerunds versus, 365, 368
   preceding infinitives without *to*, 371
   in predicates, 336–337
   principle parts, 427, *428*
   regular, 429, *433*
   review, 332–333, *334*
   in simple sentence, 392
   subjects after, 343–345, 488–489, *492*
   transitive/intransitive, 312, *313*
   understood, 387
   verbals and, 364
   See also Compound verbs; Helping verbs; Subject-verb agreement

Video games, 24

Video recordings, *115*, 219, 249

Views, representing of range of, 172, 174, 179, *181*, 183, *195*, *221*. *See also* Points of view

Visual elements. *See* Graphic/visual elements, relevant

Vocabulary words
   academic, 88, 116, 142, 168, 194, 220, 254, 268
   analytical essays, 147
   fiction narratives, 93
   interpretative responses, 199
   narrative nonfiction, 67
   persuasive writing, 173
   poetry/description, 121
   research writing, 225
   workplace writing, 257

Voice
   active/passive, **460–462**, 463–464
   as writing trait, **26**, 27, 28, 57, 63
      authentic/engaging, 83, 111, 163
      natural/authoritative/persuasive, 189
      unique, 137
   See also Rubrics

W

Web addresses, 627

Web authoring tools, use, *139*

Web page, post on, *140*, 167

Web safety, R6

Web site development, 85

Web sites
   authoritative/reliable, 232
   authors', 20, 199
   citations of, 236
   forum, *253*
   media, 24
   See also Blogs

Who?, What?, When?, Where?, and Why? chart, R24

Widget, R9

Index continued

Wikis, R11
Wishes, expressing, 162, 455
Word arrangement, 129
Word Bank. *See* Vocabulary words
Word choice (writing trait), 27, 28, 58, 63
    business letters, 263
    compare-and-contrast essays, 161
    fictional-interview scripts, *252*
    research writing, *245*
    response-to-literature essays, 213
    sonnets/free-verse poems, 122, 132, 133, 134, *135*
    See also Rubrics
Word meaning. *See* Vocabulary words
Word order, inverted
    direct objects in, 348, *352*
    in direct questions, 476
    subjects in, 343–345, *346*
    subject-verb agreement in, 488–489, *492*
    varying sentences using, 405, *406*
    who, whom and, 476
Word processing programs
    do own proofreading along with, 273, 276, 280, 286–288
    tools/features, 39, 43, 291. *See also* Grammar-check feature; Spell-check feature; Tech Tips
Words
    identify missing, 281, 292
    identify new. *See* Vocabulary words
Work with partner
    analytical essays, 147
    fiction narratives, 93
    interpretative responses, 199
    nonfiction narratives, 67, 85
    persuasive writing, 173
    poetry/description, 121
    research writing, 225
    using rubric, 29
    See also Collaborative writing; Partner Talk
Workplace writing, R12–R15, **22–23**
    characteristics, 257
    forms of, 22–23, 257
    student models, 258, 260, 262
    writing, to a prompt, *268–269*
    writing applications, *264–267*
    writing process, 259, 261, 263
Works Cited list, 226, 228, 236–237, 244. *See also* Sources
Write legibly
    autobiographical narratives, 84
    op-ed pieces, 190
    sonnets/free-verse poems, 138
Writing
    analyze/judge. *See* Mentor Texts; Rubrics; Student Models
    how to start (environment, materials, time), 5
    ideas for, 3–4
    as open-ended process
        analytical essays, *169*
        autobiographical narratives, 77
        compare-and-contrast essays, 157
        interpretative responses, *221*
        mystery stories, 105, 109
        narrative nonfiction essays, *89*
        sonnets/free-verse poems, 135
        workplace writing, 269
    to a prompt (on-demand), 17
        analytical essays, *168–169*
        argumentative essays, *194–195*
        informational research reports, *254–255*
        interpretative responses, *220–221*
        narrative nonfiction essays, *88–89*
        poetry/description, *142–143*
        short stories, *116–117*
    reasons for/ways of, 2–3
    types of. *See* Genres
Writing for Assessment
    analytical essays, *168–169*
    argumentative essays, *194–195*
    narrative nonfiction essays, *88–89*
    procedural text, *268–269*
Writing process, 30–31. *See also* Drafting; Editing drafts; Planning; Publishing/Presenting and Reflecting; Revising drafts; Rubrics
Writing traits, 26–28, 56–59
Written works, titles of. *See* Titles

Index of Authors and Titles

A
"Acquainted with the Night," 122, 136

B
Book Drive Project Meeting, R13
Bradshaw, Ryan, 150–151, 155, 158–159, 161, 162–163
"Building of the Great Brooklyn Bridge, The," 226–229, 237, 240, 242–243, 245–247
Business Letter, 262

C
"Cafeteria, The," 125

D
Diego, Oscar, R14
Dunham, Jaymie, 202–203, 207, 210–211, 213, 215

E
Esch, Mary, 148–149

F
Frost, Robert, 122, 136

G
"Good Things in Small Packages," 202–203, 207, 210–211, 213, 215
Gutierrez, Jorge, 226

H
"Horror in 'The Monkey's Paw,'" 200–201, 214
"How to Take a Phone Message," 258
Hunt, Kalim, 70–71, 75, 78–79, 81, 82

J
Jackson, Terrence, 258

L
Larimer, Mary, 94–97, 110–111
"Little More Life in Our School, A," 176–177, 181, 184–185, 187
"Local BMX Riders Need Our Support," 174–175, 188–189

M
McElroy, Shari, 174–175, 188–189
McKee, Jack, 98–99, 103, 106–107
"Memo," 260
Mueller, Lisel, 123
"Mystery of the Golden Locket, The," 94–97, 110–111

O
Orr, Tamra, 200–201, 214

P
"Paradise," 124, 132–133, 135, 137
"Playing Video Games and Board Games: Different Ways To Have Fun," 150–151, 155, 158–159, 161, 162–163

R
"Rough Night, A," 98–99, 103, 106–107, 109

S
Schmich, Mary, 68–69, 83
Soto, Luis, 176–177, 181, 184–185, 187

T
"Team Player," 70–71, 75, 78–79, 81, 82
"Technology Book Drives Reviewer Wild," 40–41
"Things," 123
Trevino, Tiffany, 124, 125, 132–133, 135, 137
"Trip to Beautiful, The," 68–69, 83

W
"Where Have Ladybugs Gone?," 148–149

Y
Yang, Rhonda, R15

Acknowledgments

Grateful acknowledgment is made to the following for copyrighted material:

Elizabeth Barnett, Literary Executor for Estate of Edna St. Vincent Millay

"Conscientious Objector" by Edna St. Vincent Millay from *Collected Poems.* Copyright © 1934, 1962 by Edna St. Vincent Millay and Norma Millay Ellis. Used with permission of Elizabeth Barnett, The Millay Society.

Chicago Sun Times

"Where Have the Ladybugs Gone?" by Mary Esch from *Chicago Sun-Times 9/5/2009.* Copyright © 2009 Chicago Sun-Times. Used by permission.

Chicago Tribune

"The Trip to Beautiful—For a mother and daughter, an adventure in France is a gift of hope" by Mary Schmich from *Chicago Tribune, Magazine Section, 6/21/2009 Issue, Page 10.* All rights reserved. Used by permission of Chicago Tribune and protected by the Copyright Laws of United States. The printing, copying, redistribution, or retransmission of the material without express written permission is prohibited.

Henry Holt and Company, Inc.

"Acquainted with the Night" by Robert Frost from *The Poetry of Robert Frost,* edited by Edward Connery Lathem. Copyright © 1969 by Henry Holt and Company. Copyright © 1936 by Robert Frost, copyright © 1964 by Lesley Frost Ballantine. Used by arrangement Henry Holt and Company.

Louisiana State University Press

"Things" by Lisel Mueller from *Alive Together: New and Selected Poems.* Copyright © 1996 by Lisel Mueller. Used by permission.

National Council of Teachers of English (NCTE)

"Mistakes are a fact of Life: A National Comparative Study" by Andrea A. Lunsford and Karen J. Lunsford translated from *bcs.bedfordstmartins.com/lunsford/PDF/Lunsford_article_Mistakes.pdf.* Copyright © NCTE. Used by permission of National Council of Teachers of English (NCTE).

Note: Every effort has been made to locate the copyright owner of material reproduced in this component. Omissions brought to our attention will be corrected in subsequent editions.

Image Credits

Illustrations
    Martin Haake

All interior photos provided by Jupiter Images. Except

    64: © Jules Frazier/age fotostock; 90: © MOODBOARD/age fotostock; 118: © George Doyle/age fotostock; 144: © AMERICAN SPIRIT/age fotostock; 170: © Ned Frisk/age fotostock; 196: © Creatas Images/age fotostock; 222: © Image Source/age fotostock; 250: Courtesy of The Library of Congress; 256: © Javier Larrea/age fotostock.